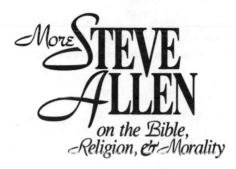

MORE STEVE ALLEN
on the Bible,
Religion, & Morality

Books by Steve Allen

BOP FABLES (1955)
FOURTEEN FOR TONIGHT (1955)
THE FUNNY MEN (1956)
WRY ON THE ROCKS (1956)
THE GIRLS ON THE TENTH FLOOR (1958)
THE QUESTION MAN (1959)
MARK IT AND STRIKE IT (1960)
NOT ALL YOUR LAUGHTER, NOT ALL YOUR TEARS (1962)
LETTER TO A CONSERVATIVE (1965)
THE GROUND IS OUR TABLE (1966)
BIGGER THAN A BREADBOX (1967)
A FLASH OF SWALLOWS (1969)
THE WAKE (1972)
PRINCESS SNIP-SNIP AND THE PUPPYKITTENS (1973)
CURSES! (1973)
WHAT TO SAY WHEN IT RAINS (1974)
SCHMOCK!-SCHMOCK! (1975)
MEETING OF MINDS, VOL. I (1978)
CHOPPED-UP CHINESE (1978)
RIPOFF: THE CORRUPTION THAT PLAGUES AMERICA (1979)
MEETING OF MINDS, VOL. II (1979)
EXPLAINING CHINA (1980)
FUNNY PEOPLE (1981)
THE TALK SHOW MURDERS (1982)
BELOVED SON: A STORY OF THE JESUS CULTS (1982)
MORE FUNNY PEOPLE (1982)
HOW TO MAKE A SPEECH (1986)
HOW TO BE FUNNY (1986)
MURDER ON THE GLITTER BOX (1989)
THE PASSIONATE NONSMOKERS' BILL OF RIGHTS (1989)
DUMBTH: AND 81 WAYS TO MAKE AMERICANS SMARTER (1989)
MEETING OF MINDS, VOL. III (1989)
MEETING OF MINDS, VOL. IV (1989)
THE PUBLIC HATING (1990)
MURDER IN MANHATTAN (1990)
STEVE ALLEN ON THE BIBLE, RELIGION, AND MORALITY, BOOK ONE (1990)
MURDER IN VEGAS (1991)
HI-HO, STEVERINO: MY ADVENTURES IN THE
    WONDERFUL WACKY WORLD OF TV (1992)
HOW TO BE FUNNY (re-release, 1992)
THE MURDER GAME (1993)

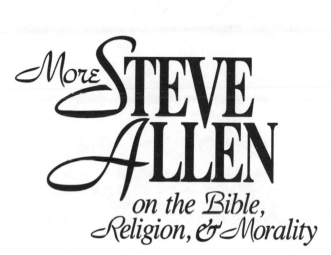

More STEVE ALLEN

on the Bible, Religion, & Morality

PROMETHEUS BOOKS · BUFFALO, NEW YORK

Published 1993 by Prometheus Books

97 96 95 94 93   5 4 3 2

Library of Congress Cataloging-in-Publication Data

Allen, Steve, 1921–
    More Steve Allen on the Bible, religion, and morality. Book II / by Steve Allen.
        p.   cm.
    Companion vol. to: Steve Allen on the Bible, religion & morality.
    Includes bibliographical references.
    ISBN 0-87975-736-1
    1. Bible—Criticism, interpretation, etc. I. Allen, Steve, 1921–
Steve Allen on the Bible, religion & morality. II. Title.
BS511.2.A43   1993
220.6—dc20   92-41364
                                                                    CIP

Printed in the United States of America on acid-free paper.

Dedication

To Dan, Julie, Stephanie, Christopher, Michael, Bradley, Bobby, Andrew, and Ryan, my dear grandchildren.

Contents

CONTENTS

CONTENTS

CONTENTS

Acknowledgments

I express my thanks first to my secretary, Cristina Gutierrez, who has had the no doubt sometimes tiresome job of transcribing the dictated text of the present volume, and then to Karen Hicks who at the second stage supervised the editing and organization of the manuscript.

I am indebted, too, to Mark Hall for his good services as supervising editor and to publisher Paul Kurtz for having considered my analysis of sacred Scripture worthwhile in the first place.

Introduction

Some readers of this book will be familiar with the volume that preceded it titled *Steve Allen on the Bible, Religion, & Morality.* For those who have not read the earlier report, perhaps I should briefly explain that the two volumes resulted from some twenty years of concentrated reading of the Bible, in addition to a good deal of commentary on Scripture. The latter represented almost every conceivable point of view, since it is a poor method of education to consult only materials harmonious with one's biases rather than challenging to them.

On the point of bias, the reader should know that I was born and educated in the Catholic faith and remained a loyal son of the church until, at the moment of my second marriage, I incurred automatic excommunication.

The original title of this and the prior study was "The Mystery Of The Bible" because I had not been studying Scripture in an analytical way for very long before I realized that it is profoundly mysterious. One clue to this, of course, is the fact that there has never been any such thing as one Christian church; rather the last 2,000 years have seen thousands of variations on the Christian theme.

As the reader will discover, my survey of the Old and New Testaments has forced me to revise certain particulars of the faith I held as a young man. Even then, of course, I was not so blind to intellectual currents that contradicted my own that I had not been faced with the by-now-classic difficult questions.

But it occurred to me quite early that there was little point in questioning specifics of my faith since I had the strong impression not only that it was the One True Religion but that, by logical necessity, it had to be true in its totality. To consider the possibility that the faith was erroneous in certain particulars was to lead to the conclusion that it might therefore be wrong in almost any. This being unthinkable, doubts were put to rest for many years by some such inept process of thought.

It was when my rational mind could no longer ignore such doubts and questions that I began the present study, the first volume of which was published by Prometheus Books in 1989.

The Purpose of the Present Study. This book seeks neither to attack nor praise the Bible but to simply attempt to determine the truth about it, so far as the professional scholarship of others makes that possible. It would, of course, be naive in the extreme to assume that one could handily attain an ideal that has defied the most painstaking and conscientious efforts of generations of scholars, many of them devout Jews and Christians, over long centuries. But the achievement of truth is certainly not an either-or matter. There is no such thing as one, large, all-encompassing truth. In reality there is an infinite number of small, specific truths.

As regards the Bible, it is now clear that it is impossible for us ever to arrive at total knowledge concerning it. The various witnesses are long dead and the identity of most of them has never been determined. The original documents no longer exist, and even the most sophisticated inves-tigators cannot—after the passage of so many centuries—know enough about the general social conditions of the times in which the many separate portions of Scripture were written to analyze biblical writings properly. This is obviously no reason to argue for a sense of passive futility and resignation.

Fortunately there are now small armies of scholars devoting their attention to scriptural study so that almost daily the march toward fuller, more responsible knowledge progresses, albeit with continuing controversy. The absurd argument that there is something suspect about impartial, analytical Bible study itself is best answered by pointing to the thorough work being done by great numbers of the devout within Christianity and Judaism.

True believers are usually not totally unaware that there are honest differences of opinion about the interpretation of Bible passages. And many millions of Christians have at least a passing knowledge of certain portions of Scripture that are true stumbling blocks to the faith of intelligent adults. But even those who are aware of these difficulties often imagine that over 99 percent of the Bible presents no such problems at all. Such an opinion, however common, bears no relation to reality. The truth is very much the opposite; there are difficulties on almost every page. There is not a book of Scripture that, even among believers, has not been the subject of controversy, much less sometimes devastating critical analysis by those outside the Jewish and Christian folds.

To make the same point by way of analogy, let readers ask the question: Does the U.S. Constitution deserve our respect? Obviously it does, inasmuch as our freedoms largely depend on it. It is one of the most sublime documents in human history—a dazzling achievement judged by any standard. But let us now suppose that a particular group of Americans becomes so enamored of the Constitution that they promulgate a new doctrine to the effect that its true author was not any of the esteemed gentlemen known to have set its words to paper but, in the most literal sense, God himself.

To those who would quote irrefutable evidence that the various contributors to the Constitution were actually seen at their desks composing various portions of it, the new True Believers would, we may confidently assume, respond, "Of course. But it matters not whose hand sets words to paper. We refer to something more basic and essential, the inspiration that motivated the mere scribes. On that basis, we assert, the author of the U.S. Constitution is God himself."

Among the negative results of such an unfortunate debate, in which reason was once again opposed by absurdity, would be that those who accepted the belief in the divine authorship of the Constitution would, were their faith ever to waver, have a greatly weakened respect for the document itself.

Precisely such a process has taken place as regards the long list of separate works now collectively known as the Bible. That mere humans were the agents responsible for affixing words to parchment has never been in question. The argument is between those who defend the Bible on such reasonable grounds as it deserves and those who defend it in toto with an unswerving faith that simply turns a blind eye to the enormous mountain of evidence that calls that literal faith into question.

Reading the Bible analytically is a far more difficult task than might at first be assumed. The volume of data offered is enormous. The Old Testament consists of approximately 900,000 words and some 900 chapters. The New Testament adds another 252 chapters to the arithmetic. A careful reading of only three chapters per day, with time for attendant reflection and study, means well over a year would be required to read through the book.

Another factor that adds to the difficulty is the endless lists of individuals, families, tribes, cities, and nations that appear, especially in the Old Testament. It is obviously impossible to keep such a mass of details organized in one's memory. The student would do well, therefore, to acquire two Bibles so that he can underline and make marginal notes and comments and also use them to compare passages side by side. A good modern concordance, as well as a dictionary or encyclopedia of scriptural terms, is also helpful.

As in the case of Book One, I beg the patience of scholars, to whom many of the questions raised here will already be familiar and hardly resolved to the satisfaction of all. Their inclusion is justified because the average reader will have done little or no critical thinking about the Scriptures.

Tone of the Present Study. In referring to the results of responsible scientific research in the fields of astronomy, geology, and paleontology, I am afraid I have not limited myself solely to the largely emotionless, circumspect tone of civilized discourse that characterizes scholarly philosophical argument. Although there is much to say for this objective distancing since the use of pejorative terms tends to short-circuit the transmission of factual or philosophical information, nevertheless, as I shall repeatedly point out, this book is not written by a scholar, nor intended for an audience of academics, few of whom, if any, require the author's personal instruction.

Earnest truth-seekers would be poorly advised to perceive me as an expert in the field, whether the many individual points I make fall pleasantly or harshly on their ears. What I fervently hope, however, is that to the extent that readers' minds are at least open to the fair-minded consideration of a number of views I share, they will put my own book aside and repair to the work of true authorities.

Since my own expertise is clearly not scriptural, I have therefore included a great many references to the works of well-qualified scholars. It is important to note that these works have been divided between those who defend the Bible and those who either attack it outright—as did Paine and Ingersoll—or raise serious and troublesome questions about portions of it. It is dismaying to observe how common it is, in both the religious and rationalist camps, for men to study little or nothing that does not harmonize with that mixture of prejudice and knowledge they have already arranged comfortably within their minds. As education such a system leaves a great deal to be desired.

The objection will also no doubt be made that at certain points in my arguments I have "spoken disrespectfully" of Scripture. But for this to stand as criticism, it must follow that the objector believes that under no circumstances may the Bible be referred to in such terms. The rational response is that the debate is meaningful only as regards specifics. Since I cannot see how it can be argued that one should speak in tones of reverence and awe about the alleged divine instruction—in Psalms—to grab the defenseless bodies of innocent infants and dash their brains out against the nearest rocks or walls, I naturally reserve the right to make appropriate decisions.

INTRODUCTION

As regards those portions of Scripture that constitute powerful poetry, moral exhortation, or a valid historical narrative, one would naturally speak or write with respect. The same can certainly not be required as regards those passages that are obscene, that incite to atrocious crimes, or that urge the killing of millions of people. Oddly enough, when I began the present study I was quite prepared, largely on the basis of half a century of social conditioning, to address the ancient writings in either an emotionally neutral or complimentary tone. It was only after I had encountered those portions of Scripture that any morally sensitive person must describe as shameful that I realized a variety of modes of address was required.

One of the strangest aspects of both popular and scholarly writing on the Bible is the clear aura of fearfulness that surrounds it. Scholars who would not have the slightest reluctance, on the basis of their professional expertise, in making certain sorts of analytical observations about Shakespeare, Chaucer, or any other important literary source; who would feel perfectly at liberty to theorize about Oriental or other extraneous religious literature; who would speak freely on a long list of political or social questions, even those considered controversial, suddenly become mealy mouthed and wary when the combination of their own reason and scholarship forces them at last to make an observation about the Bible that is at variance with one traditional view or another.

This is dreadful. Except for those who live in societies characterized by political despotism, in which case fear is a perfectly reasonable response to very real dangers, scholars and laymen in Western nations ought to be able to think, speak, and write freely about the traditional documents of any religion whatever. Thankfully, there is no union of church and state in the United States.

If the Bible becomes the object of responsible, disciplined study, it is the Bible that should be on trial, not the well-intentioned scholars and students who undertake to examine it. If a clear, hard fact emerges inescapably from one's study of the scriptural record one should state that fact in plain language and feel free to indulge in hypothetical speculation about it. Unfortunately, the common practice is to wrap each critical observation in layers of compliments whose most notable quality is often their immediate irrelevance.

As an example of the trepidation with which some scholars state their findings, note the following sentence from Gerald Larue's *Old Testament Life and Literature:*

> Although it is clear that the Bible reports events with a high degree of accuracy, it cannot be assumed that all biblical history is accurate.

INTRODUCTION

As can be seen, the wording of the statement suggests that the Bible *generally* reports events "with a high degree of accuracy." It does nothing of the sort. That the Bible has its virtues, its value, its claims to distinction is clear enough. But there is also a very great deal in it that is neither edifying nor factual.

The Bible has been interpreted to justify such evil practices as, for example, slavery, the slaughter of prisoners of war, the sadistic murders of women believed to be witches, capital punishment for hundreds of offenses, polygamy, and cruelty to animals. It has been used to encourage belief in the grossest superstition and to discourage the free teaching of scientific truths. We must never forget that both good and evil flow from the Bible. It is therefore not above criticism. It is the individual who believes that it is unassailable who should be on the defensive in a moderately rational society, rather than the earnest seeker after truth whose personal integrity forces him or her to speak honestly about the Scriptures.

That the Catholic church is still uncomfortable with the idea of casting the strongest possible light on the pages of Scripture except to an audience of scholars was clarified as recently as 1964. With the personal approval of Pope Paul VI, the church published in the Vatican paper *II Osservatore Romano* an important instruction on "The Historical Truth of the Gospels." While not totally forbidding the introduction of new theories on Scripture—which would have been absurd—the commission said that such opinions, if "already solidly demonstrated," might be expounded "if necessary, with caution and *keeping in mind the nature of the audience*." (IA) This means, in part, that whatever scholars might say to each other is one thing but that they ought to be cautious about permitting the unsophisticated faithful to know what the light of the best scholarship has discovered about the Bible.

Part of the problem is that an *opinion* gradually comes to seem part of the self. That mysterious well, the ego—from which much of our energy springs—has a remarkable capacity for self-defense. We daily add opinions, guesses, assumptions, errors, as well as factually supported knowledge to our inner being so that in time it seems to us that whoever attacks our opinions is, in fact, attacking us personally. I take it as a mark of the more civilized individual that he is able to perceive the distinction between his *views* on the one hand and *himself* on the other.

It is axiomatic that one ought to approach every complex question with as open a mind as possible. This is often as difficult to do as it is easy to say, but despite the difficulty, the attempt is obligatory if one is to educate one's self and communicate rationally with others. It is troublesome enough to be open-minded on political questions; concerning theological disputes, the difficulty is compounded. All the more reason, however, to make the attempt.

The writer of a second volume of a book on any subject whatever—or even a second edition of an already published work—has one fortunate advantage in that he can incorporate into the later rendering whatever he might have learned from critical commentary on the initial work. In that connection, two critics of my first volume on the Bible, religion, and morality observed that I seemed to place undue emphasis on the astonishingly bloodthirsty nature of a very large proportion of the Old Testament or Jewish Bible. I feel that I should explain, therefore, that such repetition was not inadvertent but quite conscious.

First of all the Bible itself provides literally hundreds of instances of the most sadistically gory accounts, each rendered as factual history and still accepted as such by millions of believers. Second, I know from personal experience that one-time exposure to a surprising assertion—even the most sensible and true—is simply incapable of penetrating the armored consciousness of the average believer. My own incredibly insensitive perception of the Scriptures, which persisted for decades, establishes this, at least to my own satisfaction. It was only when I finally undertook to read the Bible through from beginning to end that I perceived that its depiction of the Lord God—whom I had always viewed as the very embodiment of perfection—was actually that of a monstrous, vengeful tyrant, far exceeding in bloodthirstiness and insane savagery the depredations of Hitler, Stalin, Pol Pot, Attila the Hun, or any other mass murderer of ancient or modern history. We cannot have it both ways—either God is indeed such a viciously depraved monster or he is not. But if he is not, then not just a few scriptural passages but a very large portion of the Bible is wrong and on a question of the most fundamental importance.

An unbiased student of the question can easily grasp this simple message upon nothing more than exposure to it. But the vast majority of those who undertake scriptural studies are not unbiased at all. Most are people who have been taught from the cradle that the Bible is perfect. For this reason the most dedicated, ablest Bible scholars—even those within the church—are treated with cruel contempt by their intellectual and quite probably moral inferiors in the fundamentalist, literalist camp.

That some of my observations were misinterpreted certainly did not come as a surprise; two humans can scarcely exchange three sentences without a misunderstanding. Such a minor breakdown occurred in my favorite review of volume one, that by Father William O'Malley in the April 13, 1991, issue of the Jesuit intellectual periodical *America:* "It is too simple to claim Jesus was not the son of God when clearly that was the only reason he was assassinated."

I have no personal knowledge of whether Jesus was the son of God in a way that the rest of us are not. What I did attempt to demonstrate was that if indeed he is, then that belief would appear to be inconsistent with certain portions of the New Testament, as presently available to us. The same is true, of course, as regards the even more important dogma that the man called Jesus was, in fact, Almighty God himself in human disguise. That, too, may indeed be the case, for all that I am competent to prove the contrary. But again, if it is, then certain elements of Scripture must represent either poor writing or editing since they are clearly inconsistent with the belief that Jesus was God.

Secondly, Father O'Malley, in pointing to my not having supplied commentary on Wisdom, the Song of Solomon, Romans, Galatians, Ephesians, and Philippians, seemed to assume that such omissions were a delinquency from the fair-mindedness that he perceived I was striving for. In reality the operative factor was simply a shortage of page space, a problem for which the present second volume is at least a partial solution. Even so, should I write twenty such books there would still be numerous important questions not touched on, much less satisfactorily resolved.

It has also been suggested that in applying rational left-brain analysis to Scripture I did not properly attend to, as O'Malley puts it, "right-brain symbols, fables, myths and folk tales." Not very many centuries ago the good father and I could have literally been consigned to the flames for suggesting that portions of Scripture are indeed symbols, myths, fables, and folk tales. It is gratifying, in this connection, to note the many instances in which precisely this concession is now made by Christian scholars of the most impeccable credentials. One of the reasons I undertook an exercise in scriptural analysis in the first place was my disappointment at learning that nearly 99 percent of the world's Christians are almost totally unfamiliar with the ground covered by a few hundred years of Bible study. The scholars devoted to this work were guided by no motivation more malign than that of intellectual honesty and respect for evidence. Without such attitudes, the best sort of human development is not even possible.

A Few Technical Matters

Feminist Concerns in Referring to God. I must beg the indulgence of staunchly feminist readers concerning references to the Almighty Creator of the universe as a *he*. This is merely a convenience. Since God is invariably defined as pure spirit, it logically follows that "he" is incorporeal and therefore cannot have any identity that could be remotely described by the masculine gender pronoun.

Alphabetical Form. I have chosen to present the topics in this volume in alphabetical form, from A to Z. It is offered as a collection of short essays containing my reflections on the Bible, religion, and morality. It is in no way intended as an exhaustive, scholarly study, but as statements of ideas and issues that have intrigued me and I hope will intrigue you as well.

A Note About Abbreviations. Wherever I have added italics for emphasis in a Bible verse or other quotation, the letters *IA* in parentheses will appear at the end of the passage.

Cross References. Capitalized words refer to topics that are treated in separate essays.

A

ABORTION. For centuries the Catholic church, among other Christian groups, held that there were literally no circumstances in which abortion could be justified. By way of sharp contrast, many Catholic and Protestant spokesmen now concede that abortion is permissible if medical advisors consider it necessary to preserve the life and health of the mother. But it is not clear, given the original Christian position, why such a concession should be granted. Even the strict anti-abortion laws that as of 1990–1991 were being passed in certain American states included exceptions in addition to the health-of-the-mother factor, such as pregnancies resulting from incest or rape and cases where the expected child was known to be grossly deformed. But if abortion is nothing more or less than a simple act of murder then on what moral grounds can it be permissible to kill all those thousands of infants whose deaths Christians are now willing to endorse?

In the case of a pregnancy resulting, say, from incest between a young woman and her father, it is the father who is morally at fault, and perhaps in rare cases his daughter as well. But under no conceivable circumstances could the child be held blameworthy. And in the case of fetuses that are seriously ill or tragically monstrous there, too, the children who we are now told may be "murdered" could not possibly have done anything whatever to deserve the imposition of the death penalty.

It therefore does not ravage reason to argue that the original position of the church was sound and that the relevant concessions never ought to have been granted. Indeed there are individual Christians who so regard the matter.

This brings us inescapably to the question why, in a certain number of cases—which in fact number thousands per year—the churches are now willing to permit what they consider the actual commission of murder.

One possible answer is that if such exceptions were not part of the anti-abortion case, anti-abortion laws would not have the slightest chance of being passed, at least in the United States of America.

ALCOHOLISM. For unknown numbers of centuries, both the families of alcoholics and the unfortunate drinkers themselves have prayed to be released from their addiction. One never seems to hear of such prayers being answered, but we do know of countless cases in which they were not. Alcoholics Anonymous finally changed all that by constructing a program of practical measures—including, primarily, mutual encouragement—to address the problem. Even so admirable an approach does not always succeed, but it is clearly far preferable to prayer alone in achieving practical results. Part of the Alcoholics Anonymous program gives credit to religion in that it incorporates references to God. There is nothing inherently wrong with this, particularly if the overall program works and the drinkers already have a firm belief in the existence of a Deity, but it is still the case that when the appeal was to God alone the common result was failure.

In modern times, adherents of the Catholic church, who for a variety of cultural reasons had a greater incidence of alcoholism than did the members of Protestant groups, added the concept of The Pledge. The alcoholic would make a solemn promise, with the prayerful assistance of a priest, not to drink liquor ever again, or at least not for a specified period of time. I know from the sad experience of members of my mother's family that in no instance did The Pledge resolve the problem for more than a few days at a time.

ALTRUISM. Although I have been a Christian for much of my life, I concede that never did I seriously consider giving away all that I had, despite the absolutely clear-cut instructions of Jesus, who—we must constantly remind ourselves—is considered to be God Almighty. What kind of Christian was I that I would never even passingly entertain the idea of obeying a direct commandment from the supreme creator of the universe? In my defense, I can say only that, except for a number of my fellow Christians so small as perhaps not to occupy totally all the seats of a Greyhound bus, the other hundreds of millions who salute the banner of Christ have never had any more interest than I in that particular commandment.

2

But now let us address the degree of wisdom in the advice itself.

When I was young and poor, there was little enough to have gotten rid of, but in later years, after I had become financially secure, let us consider, just briefly, what would have resulted from such a divestiture. It would have taken no more than a busy weekend to dispose of the million or two dollars at hand. The great bulk of it would go to those doing charitable and compassionate work in the world—a hundred thousand here, fifty thousand there, perhaps dispensing a few hundred-dollar bills to the impoverished walking the streets of our slums.

At the end of such a process I would have to inhabit a slum myself since I would no longer be a homeowner or be able to afford the rent of even a modest apartment. But more significantly, I would never again be able to send out charitable contributions of the sort that I have willingly made for the past four decades. This points to no particular virtue on my part since I had more money than I needed to live, eat, be clothed, and attend to the needs of my family, but I have been able to assist hundreds of worthy groups and individuals. All such generosity, however modest, would cease—after the one brief flurry of charitable contribution—were I to listen to the advice of Jesus. And that, of course, does not even take into consideration the wishes of my family, who might energetically object to any such saintly decision on my part.

But perhaps it will be argued that there is nothing so very bad about accumulating riches and possessions, as long as in doing so we have not become gluttons or debauchees and do not commit such absurd crimes as did Imelda Marcos of the Philippines, for example, who, instead of donating a sizable amount of money to the poor of her impoverished country, purchased for herself hundreds of pairs of expensive shoes, even though she could wear only one pair at a time.

Granted, such excesses may not be statistically significant, but what is so bad about being rich? Cannot one be enormously wealthy and a good Christian at the same time?

If we accept every word of the New Testament as the true and literal word of God, the answer is exceedingly simple—*no,* one cannot. Jesus said, "But woe unto you that are rich, for you have received your consolation." He did not qualify this admonition in any way, nor did he say "woe to you who are rich, for you may be tempted to misuse your wealth or live a life of selfishness." Jesus, assuming we may trust the testimony of Luke's Gospel, was very precise in his remarks on this point.

To make his views on the question even more clear-cut, Jesus used the illustration of a person consigned to hell for no other reason than that he had been wealthy. Lest there should be the slightest misinterpretation, Jesus next referred to another believer enjoying the eternal bliss of heaven only because he was poor when alive.

There is Jesus' even more famous observation that it is more difficult for a rich man to get into heaven than for a camel—or rope in some translations—to pass through the eye of a needle (Matt. 19:24). As even children know, it is impossible for so large an object to pass through a space so small as the eye of a needle. What this inescapably means—unless we are to abandon all considerations of logic and the meaning of words—is that it is impossible for the wealthy to get to heaven. Presumably, then, they will all end up in hell. What all of this says about the current rapturous embrace between capitalists and Christians, though chiefly in the American context, I leave for the ablest representatives of those persuasions to decide.

In Jesus' defense, it may be argued that in his time there was not the slightest hope of doing anything about the problem of poverty. To be born poor was to die poor. Therefore, he may have been charitably concerned to bring at least a degree of spiritual comfort to the downtrodden majority of the human race by holding out the hope of a better life after the present one.

But if such a defense is reasonable, we must recognize that economic conditions have changed greatly during the past two thousand years. In the modern age it is possible to do a great deal indeed to alleviate poverty, both in individual cases and in the statistical general. For example, the rich—whom, according to the Gospel of Luke, Jesus, like prophets of the Old Testament, apparently despised—can by judicious investment and management create jobs that at least help alleviate certain aspects of the poor's misery.

There is an ancient literary convention in various parts of the scriptural record in which the writer opposes an *A* to a *B* to speak theoretically rather than simply asserting *A,* as is the more normal mode of communication. On the subject of hunger, for example, Jesus might have said—as Luke alleges that he did—"Blessed are you that hunger, for you shall be filled." That assurance inspires hope. But adhering to the ancient A-B formula, Jesus proceeded to say something that inspires no hope at all and, in fact, gives cause for concern on the part of millions (or at least it would if men were in the habit of thinking through almost any important social question). He says, "Woe unto you who are full, for you shall hunger." In the present context, he is then addressing almost half of the human race, the great majority of which are in industrialized nations such as our own. If the reader could afford to purchase this book, presumably he is also able to pay for his next meal. Why, therefore, should Jesus threaten him with a semi-curse that has thundered down the corridors of time for over twenty centuries? (See also CHARITY, POVERTY.)

ANGELS. Those who believe in the existence of angels are united in affirming that such creatures come in two forms—the good and the bad. If angels indeed inhabit our world, it seems reasonable to assume that these two groups exist in approximately equal numbers. But, guided by the admonition of Jesus that "BY THEIR FRUITS shall you know them," a most bizarre thing happens when we analyze the evidence for the existence of both heavenly and hellish spiritual creatures. What we find is not that their acts have been approximately equal, but that the game has been easily won by the forces of perdition.

We need only look about us each day to see that even the popular media are alive with reports of devilish visitations, the frightening haunting of houses, the demonic possession of certain humans, or the strange and evil apparitions referred to in even such lighthearted and comic films as *Ghostbusters*. If the news media are to be trusted, it would appear that demons have had the field to themselves, since there have been almost no allegations of appearances by benign spirits. Why this should be, in a universe created and supervised by a God tenderly concerned for the welfare of His creatures, is a perplexing question. Recent films such as *Ghost Dad* and the box-office hit *Ghost* may have started to turn the tide in this regard.

As a child I was taught that not only I, but every human who had ever lived, had a personal angel, an invisible guardian providing protection against moral or physical dangers. Unfortunately, I have never encountered evidence consistent with this comforting belief.

In the summer of 1988, in San Clemente, California, a toddler who had been briefly left alone in a car with the motor running playfully shifted the vehicle into drive. The car lurched forward into a group of campers, one of whom—a two-year-old boy—it decapitated. The dead child's mother, also injured, became hysterical. Pointing to the mother of the child in the car, she shouted, "She murdered him, she killed him!"

Since we are often numbed with the statistics of large-scale DISAS-TER—hundreds killed here, thousands wiped out elsewhere—we sometimes react in a more human way at hearing of specific tragedies such as this.

It is not clear how such deeply disturbing stories—of which there are millions—can be accommodated with the belief in guardian angels. (See also GHOSTS.)

ANIMAL RIGHTS. Those who have a compassionate concern for the well-being of animals must inevitably construct their case on a basis of secular rather than religious concerns. Once that foundation is established, then religious add-ons may be introduced, but the original rationale for a serious consideration of what are sometimes referred to as animal rights cannot sensibly be rooted in the traditional theistic view of the physical universe for the simple reason that *in that universe there is not the slightest evidence of any overarching concern for its animal creatures.*

All of these—from the smallest single-celled living organisms to the fullest and latest flower of the massive evolutionary tree—live in the most dangerous of circumstances, at all moments succumbing painfully to the perils that jeopardize their existence, their lives being daily snuffed out by the billions. Vast armies of creatures scarcely survive the moment of their conception. Others are destroyed shortly after by the hostility of their immediate surroundings. Additional swarms are eaten alive by other also-doomed creatures motivated by nothing more malign than their own naturally programmed hunger. Did an overactive conscious mind do the programming? The question is of fundamental importance.

Man, of course, is not an exception to the functioning food-chain process since he, too, must eat to live and, like other creatures, subsists entirely on a diet of once-living material.

Certainly nothing in such a review of the relevant facts would justify a human resort to the same instinctive bloody slaughter by which life on planet earth perpetuates itself. We are quite right in being horrified to witness cruelty to animals. But again, unless we are prepared to argue the absurdity that man is superior to God, it is futile to search the heavens, as it were, for an explanation of the total absence of justice and compassion that characterizes the fate of all living creatures.

A search of religious Scripture for a solution to this question is pointless. There are, of course, references to animals, but they have no relevance to the question under consideration. The famous *his eye is on the sparrow* by no means resolves but only further deepens the mystery since it is evident that all actual sparrows die in painful and miserable circumstances. Nor can it be said of sparrows or of any other animals of the world what is often said of the human animal: although their lives may involve long years of poverty, suffering, disease, war, and other trials, they are at least assured the possibility—although never the certainty—of a better existence on some future unphysical plane.

APOCRYPHA, THE. It will be instructive to consider the very concept of the Apocrypha. That human beings are prone to lie in various kinds of situations is clear enough. An individual will lie to avoid detection or embarrassment; he may lie out of malice; or he may tell what he regards as a perfectly justified lie, although in such situations the pejorative word itself is not used, at least by the teller. The reader unfamiliar with the history of religious literature may at first find it difficult to believe that an entire book of lies could be prepared, and lies dealing with religious subject matter at that. A religious man is, at least by self-definition, one concerned with his relationship with a Deity and with the resultant improvements in his own behavior that presumably follow the sense of loyalty to a God or gods and their code. Speculation whether large-scale religious lies are possible was once unnecessary because the churches themselves absolutely assured us that such shameful impostures have never taken place. They now concede that certain religious scriptures are false and not in any sense inspired by God. Moreover, churches have excluded them from the canon of Scriptures that are considered divine and authentic.

It may come as a shock to learn that official representatives of the Christian churches, acting in formal authority, have deliberately perpetrated brazen frauds that, if committed in any other field, would have had them not only arrested and jailed but also hooted out of their professions in dishonor. The key word in the preceding sentence is *shock*. Truths that come into abrasive contact with cherished, long-held, and comforting assumptions are literally unable to triumph in a moment as—on a rational plane—they should. The common response to such painful discoveries is not gratitude at the enlightenment they bring but rather a surge of negative emotions—fear, anger, and foreboding. At some subconscious level the information is perceived as a personal attack.

This is never so true as in the area of religion. In science, those holding views contrary to scientific assertions may differ either in a dignified manner or heatedly, but with rare exceptions opponents are unlikely to urge that their adversaries be consigned to flames or to make it illegal to promulgate divergent opinions. But in religion, where speculation outweighs factual knowledge, feelings are more likely to be rigid, even violent, in expression.

Almost no religious believer is able to accept calmly the information that the welfare of his own church has in some instances been promoted by illegal, immoral, even atrocious means. Nevertheless, every religious believer ought to make the most earnest possible effort to accommodate himself to such a realization simply because it is based on incontrovertible truth. The ultimate acceptance of such information by no means leads inevitably either to the abandonment of one's faith, to agnosticism, to atheism, to nihilism, or to any other given philosophical alternative. It may, in fact, have nothing but the most beneficial effects in that it will separate the lies, frauds, and errors from whatever may be good, sound, and enlightening in a faith.

Consider some cases of such a crime perpetrated by churchmen. The Decretals of Isidore were for long centuries cherished and honored in the Christian church. The Decretals were a collection of documents—papal letters, councilory decrees allegedly dating from the time of the Apostles to the eighth century—that supported significant positions of doctrine and custom, thus apparently authenticating Catholic claims. In the fifteenth century, however, the courageous Cardinal Nicholas of Cusa subjected the documents to careful scrutiny. His research, involving nothing more remarkable than the application of reason, led Cardinal Nicholas to doubt the authenticity of the documents. Once his skepticism had been announced, others joined him in his research and, shortly, in his conclusions.

Far from bestowing upon the good cardinal the combined gratitude and honor that his pious scholarship deserved, his church subjected him to hostile criticism while simultaneously attempting to obscure the realities that had emerged. Rome resorted to its traditional method of placing the relevant works of Catholic—not atheistic—scholarship on the Index of forbidden reading matter. Even more shamefully, scholars who defended the reliability of the Decretals were specially rewarded: one was even made a cardinal. Truth—most fortunately—while it does not always win out, does so at least frequently. In this case the scholarly world eventually agreed that the early churchmen had resorted to forgery in their zeal for their faith. (See also AUTHENTICITY OF THE BIBLE; VERSIONS OF THE BIBLE.)

Enoch. Another such instance of PIOUS FRAUD is the Book of Enoch, which consists of certain alleged prophecies that, although actually circulated during the last two centuries B.C., are nevertheless attributed to the much earlier Enoch, Noah, and Methuselah. No version in either the original Aramaic or Hebrew remains, but the work has been preserved in the form of a few brief fragments and an Ethiopian translation of the entire book based on a now lost Greek copy. The book predicts the coming of a godly kingdom, with Jerusalem triumphant and a Resurrection and Last Judgment of, oddly enough, not all mankind but merely the sons of Israel. The general state of affairs in the happy time, it is said, will involve eating, drinking, and the begetting of children, in which respect it would seem in no way different from life as we presently know it. Those who have left the True Faith will be cast into *Gehenna*. Although Christians frequently translate this word to mean the Christian *hell,* which in the most literal of senses is a sort of enormous blast furnace, the earlier Hebrew form was *Ge Hinnom,* which meant a specific garbage dump outside Jerusalem where not only refuse but the bodies of criminals were discarded. The virtuous who have been resurrected will, strangely, not live forever; they will only live long enough to beget a thousand children each. While such a fate could obviously be extremely pleasurable for men, it is not explained what would be so attractive about it to women, for whom the procreative process is considerably more troublesome, not to mention the widespread POLYGAMY involved.

Gospel of St. Thomas. Another instance of what is a pious fraud, even according to Protestant and Catholic scholarship, has now been available to American readers for some years. It is the so-called *Gospel of St. Thomas,* found in leather-bound papyrus form in 1946 in a grave about sixty miles from the city of Luxor, Egypt. The book is apparently a collection of what are represented as 114 direct quotations from Jesus, but written in the third or fourth century and derived from an earlier Greek manuscript produced during the first half of the second century. A certain percentage of the quotations are precisely as rendered in the Gospels; others, although bearing an obvious relationship to the Gospel versions, vary somewhat. A third category consists of sayings attributed to Jesus but unknown in modern times, before the 1946 discovery.

2 Maccabees. Another deplorable instance of what the reader will by now perceive as the too common willingness to lie for one's faith is found in Maccabees. Consider, by way of example, the story related in chapters six and seven of 2 Maccabees concerning the murder of seven brothers executed before their mother's eyes. It is important to know, first of all, that no Catholics, Protestants, or Jews consider 2 Maccabees to be divinely inspired. It is not, in other words, part of the Bible by any standard, although it is obviously of considerable historical and literary interest, dealing as it does with the fierce resistance of a group of pious Jews against their Seleucid overlords. The author, as unknown to us as are almost all other writers of ancient documents, at least deserves credit for his honesty in revealing that it is his intention merely to popularize an earlier, more scholarly work consisting of five books actually or allegedly composed by a Jason of Cyrene.

As for the tragic story of the martyred mother and sons, it is noteworthy that the Maccabean author provides *no information about their names,* a fact that at the very least casts doubt on the authenticity of the account. Some such event may well have occurred, but it is at this stage of the story's development that fraud is introduced. Father Bruce Metzger, in his excellent *An Introduction to the Apocrypha* (Oxford), provides details:

> In the calendar of martyrs current in the Syrian Church, preserved in a manuscript dating from A.D. 411, we find the name of the mother given as Shamuni. In the following centuries, the Greek Menaea, or ritual books of the Eastern Orthodox Church, duly record on August 1st the names of all the sons and that of the mother, namely, Abion, Antonius,

Gourias, Eleazar, Eusebonas, Alim, Marcellus; their mother is here called Solomonis. Furthermore, the scene of their martyrdom was transferred from Jerusalem to Antioch, where a basilica, or large church, was erected in their honor. In one of his sermons on the festival of the Maccabean martyrs, Augustine comments on the irony that the church should have been erected in the city which bore the name of the persecutor [Antiochus]. It goes without saying that interest came to be shown in their remains. At first it was supposed that their bones were preserved in the basilica at Antioch. According to one legend, these sacred relics were removed in the sixth century from Antioch to Constantinople, and from there to Rome in the Church of St. Peter ad Vincula, with whose festival their commemoration coincides. Later in the Middle Ages a rivalry over the relics developed between Rome and Cologne, for in the latter city a convent, dedicated to the holy Maccabees, boasted that it possessed their heads, preserved in golden vases.

It is important to note the process whereby falsehood is piled upon falsehood. That at some stage of such an extrapolation the voices of honest, principled objectors were raised is nowhere indicated. It seems reasonable to assume, however, that such may have happened. If so, we can note only that the honest churchmen were out-shouted and out-voted. The liars prevailed, as they often have in the writing of both secular and religious history.

The Apocalypse of Adam. For centuries a totally dishonest method of writing and rewriting religious documents was common. There is no way of knowing now how many pseudepigraphic works circulated in antiquity among both Jews and Christians, but scholars agree that such writings were numerous. One such, unknown until it was described by Doresse in 1958, is the *Apocalypse of Adam,* a Gnostic revelation predicting a future salvation disclosed to Adam. Since there was no such person as Adam, we may be certain that whoever wrote the Gnostic Apocalypse could not have been the first human. But despite the basic falsity of its creation and presentation to Gnostic readers, it is nevertheless a fully religious and spiritual work. Given that the entire document from beginning to end is a lie, it is interesting that its message "the hidden gnosis [knowledge] of Adam which he gave to Seth" is described as having been delivered by angelic beings from the place where it had long been hidden, "on a high mountain *upon a rock of truth.*" (IA)

To modern Christian scholars, the most interesting portion of the book is the following speculation about the origin of the Illuminator of Gnosis, who is expected to "redeem their souls from the day of death."

10

The Third Kingdom says of him
That he came from a virgin womb.
He was cast out of his city, he and his mother;
He was brought to a desert place.
He was nourished there.
He received glory and power.
And thus he came to the water.

1 Esdras. Catholic scholars, not Protestant, are embarrassed by the official position taken by the Council of Trent, which in 1546 pronounced anathema upon those who refused to accept as sacred and hence canonical in its entirety the traditional Latin Vulgate Bible. Proving themselves at least capable of that intelligence often suggested by inconsistency, the fifty-three prelates specifically denied blessed status to three books: the Prayer of Manasseh and 1 and 2 Esdras. Since the church here spoke authoritatively on "a matter of faith and morals," thereafter it was of course not possible for even the most painstaking and intelligent scholarship to affect the judgment. The church is therefore, to this day, the object of scholarly derision for the glaring error of Trent.

For those who wish to know more about the subject, I recommend the aforementioned *An Introduction to the Apocrypha,* based on the Revised Standard Version. Concerning 1 Esdras, Metzger says:

It is, except for one portion, merely a divergent account of events which are related in several canonical books of the Old Testament (Ezra and Nehemiah). . . . *What the relation is between I Esdras and the canonical narratives has perplexed scholars of many generations.* There are three possible solutions: Ezra-Nehemiah may have been derived from I Esdras; or I Esdras may be a modification of Ezra-Nehemiah; or both forms may derive from a common original. Of these possibilities, it appears that the last solves the greatest number of problems . . . as *regards the historical sequence of events as recorded in I Esdras, the list of repetitions, errors, and inconsistencies in the book is a long one . . .*

The date of the composition of I Esdras . . . is difficult to determine. Josephus' use in compiling his own history provides a limit of time in one direction. The majority of scholars find reason to think that it was written sometime during the previous two centuries, that is, sometime after about 150 B.C. (IA)

As an example of error and inconsistency, Metzger notes:

It will be observed that the author records three different occasions when Jewish exiles returned to Jerusalem—one in 538 B.C. or soon after, headed by Sheshbazzar; one in 520 B.C., headed by Zerubbabel; one in 397 B.C., headed by Ezra. *Curiously enough, each caravan is said to bring back the long-lost sacred vessels which Nebuchadnezzar had plundered from the temple.* (IA)

One of the more interesting commentaries on the ethics and morality of the period described in 1 Esdras concerns Ezra's shock at learning that many inhabitants of Jerusalem, including priests and other Jewish officials, had married non-Israelites. So heatedly does Ezra criticize the practice that a great number—perhaps all—agree to divorce their alien wives. The prophet is so proud of this obedience to his command that he compiles a list of priests and laymen who not only turned their backs on their wives but also abandoned the innocent children born to them. So much for the sanctity of family in those biblical times! There is, of course, no way of knowing how many Jews of the period were glad to get rid of their wives and therefore cooperated with Ezra as a guiltless way of obtaining divorce. Comments Metzger:

The author of 1 Esdras leaves much to be desired from a historical point of view. *Not only does he contradict other sources, but he is involved in internal inconsistencies.* In view of these *serious deficiencies* the most charitable verdict . . . is that the writer aimed more at inculcating a moral lesson than at recounting an accurate chronicle of events. (IA)

It is interesting how often writers of religious literature have sought to provide moral instruction by creating immoral lies.

Scholars agree that the most interesting portion of 1 Esdras is the story of the Three Guardsmen, which describes an imaginary competition of wits for the entertainment of the Persian King Darius. Three young men connected with the royal household agree to give their views of the strongest thing in the world. When the king rises the following morning, he discovers three pieces of paper on which the separate guesses are inscribed. The first suggests that the king himself is the strongest, another that women are strongest since even the strongest men often do their bidding, and the last that truth is the strongest thing in the world. The third statement is naturally the most acceptable. The account includes the much-quoted sentence: "Truth abideth, and is strong forever; she liveth and conquereth forevermore." Although those who excluded 1 Esdras from the canon of the Bible had perfectly sensible ground for doing so, Cyprian, Augustine, and other early church fathers apparently thought that the book had some validity and worth.

Esther. Also called *The Rest of the Chapters of the Book of Esther which are Found Neither in the Hebrew nor in the Chaldee.* As the title itself makes clear, this book is a bewildering and largely chaotic record that renders its attribution to divine inspiration obviously absurd. Jabez T. Sunderland, in his informative *The Origin and Character of the Bible* (first published 1893; last printing, 1953), comments:

> All scholars agree that the book of Esther is not history but fiction. This group of brief apocryphal writings consist of certain additions which some unknown author has seen fit to make to the original book. Naturally the additions are as fictional as the book itself; nor do they add much, if anything, to its literary value. . . . Esther has been much criticized by certain writers because it does not contain anywhere the name of God. The author of these additions . . . seeks to remove that defect by adding a section in which there is plentiful use made of the divine name. All the craft and hate and cruelty of the original book are left, and indeed more still are added; but since references to God are often brought in, the religious character of the book is supposed to be much improved.

Scholarship since Sunderland's time has to some extent clarified the confusion about the book but has in no way enhanced its reputation as honest religious literature. Explains Metzger:

> Sometime in the second or first century before Christ a certain Lysimachus (11.1) translated the Hebrew text of the Book of Esther in the Old Testament to Greek. At six different places in the Greek narrative he or someone else added substantial episodes not in the Hebrew totaling 107 verses.
> The elaborated form of the book subsequently passed from Greek into an old Latin version. Later, when Jerome, who had been commissioned by Pope Damasus at the close of the 4th Century to prepare a standard Latin version of the Bible, came to the Book of Esther, he translated the Hebrew form of the book as it stands. Then, having gathered together the several additions found in Latin copies, he added them at the close of his rendering of the Hebrew, attaching notes to indicate where each addition belonged . . . but in the course of the subsequent transmission of Jerome's Vulgate . . . careless scribes would frequently omit these explanatory notes, resulting in a meaningless amalgam of separate portions.
> The final confusing step came in the Middle Ages when Stephen Langton, Archbishop of Canterbury . . . numbered the chapters of the canonical and the apocryphal consecutively, as though all of the latter

material formed a direct continuation. Luther's Bible . . . follows this absurd chapter numeration.

It is fair to speculate about the possible motives of Lysimachus or whoever else added portions to what was already regarded as sacred Scripture. Comments Metzger:

At the same time it must be recognized that the work of the Greek continuator . . . is far from being entirely commendable. The literary style of the additions tends to be wordy, not to say bombastic. More serious are the discrepancies and contradictions which have been introduced. . . . Most serious of all is the increase of anti-Semitism and the answering hostility against the Gentiles which are to be found in the additions.

Tobit. Another apocryphal work is the Book of Tobit, which appears to be based on the teachings of the Pharisees about the time of Herod and the birth of Jesus. Significantly, there is no suggestion of messianic expectation in it. Tobit is, in fact, free of the bellicose air of superiority typical of Old Testament writing. Its story concerns a captive Jew named Tobit, a pious and virtuous man who goes blind. He dispatches his son Tobias to Nebia to recover a modest amount of silver Tobit had earlier left with a fellow Israelite. In search of a traveling companion, Tobias meets a helpful fellow who offers to guide him on his way. The strange benefactor, we are told, is the ANGEL Raphael. Upon reaching their destination, the two men lodge with Raguel, a relative of Tobit and Tobias. To this point the story has—if one accepts the fact of the traveling companion being an angel in disguise—a certain reasonableness to it.

The Persian origin of the tale becomes clearer, however, with its next development, which concerns Raguel's daughter Sarah who has been pledged in marriage to no less than seven husbands, none of whom has actually consummated the arrangement. The reason for this strange turn of events, it is said, is that each bridegroom has, on his wedding night, been strangled to death by an evil spirit named Asmodaeus.

Scholars of Persian mythology believe this is Aeshma Daeva, one of the evil spirits or devils attendant upon the angry god Angra Mainyu. As professional authors or habitual readers will no doubt have perceived, the stage is now set for a contest between young Tobias and the demon. The angel Raphael, still unidentified by Tobias, advises him to apply for the hand of the lovely Sarah, which he does.

The contest between Tobias and the evil spirit is resolved in a very strange way—but then it is difficult to imagine what other than a strange method might be used to resolve the situation. Tobias's solution is to trouble the demon by smoke from the heart and liver of a fish caught in the River Tigris. If this ancient story—absurd as history but entertaining as literature—had not been excluded from the canon, we would probably today have some fundamentalist Louisiana Christian telling us that the smoke-and-fish story reveals the origin of Cajun cooking.

The tale concludes happily as Tobias recovers the silver for his father, returns with his bride to Nineveh, and is even able to restore his blind father's sight by applying the gall of the magical fish to the old man's eyes. Tobias generously offers his traveling companion half the money for his services, at which point Raphael reveals his identity.

Tobit, on his deathbed, utters a prophecy concerning the future fate of Israel, which refers to the rebuilding of the temple by Herod and conversion of all nations to Judaism.

Herod did, in fact, rebuild the temple when governing Palestine under the authority of Augustus Caesar. No Jew today, however, foresees the conversion of all peoples to the Jewish faith. Scholars feel that the Book of Tobit was written at or after the time of the temple's reconstruction and did not in any sense embody true prophecy.

In *The Bible: Word of God in Words of Men,* Jean Levie, S.J., comments:

> For the past 50 years a number of Catholic exegetes have been wondering whether Tobias and Jonas may not also be essentially didactic works rather than history properly so called . . . in support of this view it has been pointed out that in the case of Tobias there are grave historical difficulties in several details of the story, that there are certain connections with the Assyrian work *The Wisdom of Ahikar,* that the style is clearly moralizing and didactic and finally, that the sequence of events is artificial, contrived and out of the ordinary.

Voltaire himself could have written nothing more devastating to every-word-from-God's-mouth fundamentalism.

Assumption of Moses. In this book, written around 8 or 9 A.D.—the time of Christ—the author attributes to Moses a prophecy of the fate of Israel that refers to the sufferings of the people after Herod's death. The disseminaters of false prophecy were generally not content with simply fabricating stories; they often told a double-level sort of lie by referring to events of their day in the future tense, as if the words had been written earlier.

ARGUMENT

ARGUMENT. Whether formal or informal, argument is always a somewhat tedious process. Questions of fact are difficult enough; differences and nuances of opinion are even more troublesome. Part of the difficulty of the endless dialogue on religious questions grows out of the fact that to at least one sort of religious mind, there is generally no proposition too preposterous to "prove," at least to the satisfaction of the proposer.

To be specific, I will here introduce a deliberately nonsensical assertion and then proceed to "prove" it. The proof will not, of course, be of the scientific sort, but it will be consistent with a certain kind of theological argumentation that has persisted down through the centuries.

Let our true believer assert, for example, something patently absurd: that God is a hockey puck. Now the reader and I are both perfectly aware that God is nothing of the sort. But let us see how we fare in a debate on this simple point.

BELIEVER: God is a hockey puck.

SKEPTIC: That is the worst nonsense I've ever heard.

BELIEVER: I doubt that very much. We do, after all, live in a day when we are constantly exposed to nonsense of all sorts.

SKEPTIC: Well, we can agree on that much at least. But I don't see how you can possibly say that God is a hockey puck.

BELIEVER: My dear fellow, I *have* just said it, and with the greatest of ease.

SKEPTIC: Oh, the saying of it is easy enough, but I don't see how you can *prove* it.

BELIEVER: Of course you don't, with your limited human intelligence.

SKEPTIC: Are you suggesting that your own intelligence is superhuman?

BELIEVER: If unaided, no. But I have been granted, by the grace of God, the honor of personal communion with the Lord, and he has assured me that what I say is true.

But let us stop arguing about arguing, my friend, and get to the heart of the matter. I shall now demonstrate to you, with no great difficulty, that God in several senses is precisely a hockey puck.

SKEPTIC: Name one.

16

BELIEVER: I shall do far more than that. First of all, let us consider the properties of a hockey puck. The most evident is its blackness. Now what we, with our limited powers of perception and analysis, call *black* is really something that absorbs all light. That is certainly one quality of God. He not only creates all things but also possesses them all, takes them all unto himself, draws them back to the point of origin, as it were.

And is there not always mystery associated with blackness? And what can be said to be more mysterious than both the idea and the reality of God? Of course, it is in the very blackness of the puck that it is distinguished from its surroundings. The manufacturers of hockey pucks did not make an idle or random choice. No other color would stand out so clearly from the whiteness of the ice it moves across. And is not God the Ultimate Other when compared to all things natural, including the human? Does not God stand in stark contrast to the things of this world as the black puck stands in contrast to its frigid and pristine context?

SKEPTIC: But it is absurd to—

BELIEVER: Please, permit me to continue setting out my arguments. Consider now the relationship of the hockey players—individual men, representing all mankind—to the puck. What do they do ceaselessly? Ignore it? Pretend to be oblivious to it? Disdain it? No, they pursue it with the utmost abandon, sometimes to the point of seeming madness. They are drawn to it as fragments of iron are drawn to a magnet. They literally have no purpose on the ice except to pursue that puck. As for the thousands of observers and the millions more now capable of witnessing such spectacles through the medium of television, their eyes, too, follow the puck. It is the center of attention, the only true object of interest. The men, despite their individual strength, speed, or finesse, are not rewarded for the ease with which they skate or the handsomeness of the figure they cut in their uniforms. They are judged only for the effectiveness of their relationship to the hockey puck.

Consider next the material of which the puck is made. It is on the one hand quite hard but yet is made of rubber, which is the epitome of softness and resiliency. Are not these extremes also divine attributes? Is not God firm and unyielding and yet able to manifest a certain resilience of mercy and compassionate intervention in human affairs?

SKEPTIC: That's creative, my friend, but I still cannot accept it because—

BELIEVER: I'm not surprised that you can't. How could you, conditioned as you are to see things only in rational or coldly scientific terms?

ARGUMENT

SKEPTIC: But it doesn't take a scientist or a rationalist to see that a hockey puck is nothing but a little, round—

BELIEVER: Ah, roundness. Circularity. And what could be a better illustration of the essence of God? One never hears of the perfect square, or the perfect triangle, only the perfect circle. The circle is the only line form that endlessly returns to its point of origin. We gradually perceive that life has neither beginning nor end but only existence, only *is-ness*. Of what else can this be said but the Almighty God?

SKEPTIC: But this is madness, to believe that one little thing—

BELIEVER: A thing? A thing indeed. And does not the very definition of divinity instruct us that all things must have a cause? And what can be their ultimate cause except God?

   If you, my friend, were to make a watch, would not the artifact somehow represent you in a way that it could be said to represent no other individual, simply because you conceived, fashioned, and created it in all its parts?

   Well, given that God made all things, and that a hockey puck is a thing, it follows that God made the hockey puck out of his boundless creativity, which is to say, out of himself. So it is inescapable that the hockey puck is God and God is the hockey puck.

And so goes the bizarre method of argumentation, which would not be considered convincing if applied to any other area of human activity but the religious or mystical. Another instance—among thousands that might be cited—is the following from an article "Authority and Scripture: I" by H. H. Rowley (*Christian Century,* March 1, 1961):

What is needed . . . is some objective test to *show* whether the authority of God is behind the Bible or not. And there are tests which can satisfy reason. Some may be briefly indicated here. (IA)

Mr. Rowley speaks clearly enough to this point. Therefore, we lean forward attentively, sincerely eager to accept the instruction we have just been promised concerning certain objective tests of the validity of Scripture—"tests which can satisfy reason." Note what is actually delivered:

In the days of Moses the Israelites were in bondage in Egypt. Moses came to promise them deliverance in the name of Yahweh, whose very name was new to them as the name of their God. In the vital hour, when the hosts of Pharaoh had pursued the Israelites and caught up with them, the faith of Moses did not waver; he promised his people deliverance; neither he nor they had means to achieve it. It came through natural events, which were not under the control of Moses. His prior faith did not effect the deliverance; no fortuitous deliverance could effect his prior faith. He and the people believed that his faith was divinely inspired and the deliverance divinely achieved, and no other hypothesis could explain both.

Rowley has offered not so much as a syllable consistent with the concept of even one test—let alone *tests*—that could satisfy reason. I proceed on the assumption that Mr. Rowley is guilty of no conscious intent to deceive, that he is in fact morally blameless in this instance. What seems to be operative is a certain manner of thought that is simply inconsistent with the logical, the scientific, the disinterestedly analytical, even the bare commonsensical. Such a method of argumentation would not be countenanced for a moment in such disciplines as physics, mathematics, history, or medicine, though it is by no means an absolute stranger to the more metaphysical realms of philosophy. But in the field of religion, it is not only encountered, but it also seems at times to be dominant. (See also BELIEFS AND MYTHS.)

ATONEMENT. The enormous difficulty facing the Christian church, should future Bible research or theological reasoning force it to fundamentally revise its dogma, is almost impossible to exaggerate. In the past the churches have from time to time simply thrown overboard both BELIEFS and practices that had become cumbersome and indefensible. But while a ship may throw over certain appurtenances, it can hardly discard its rudder, hull, and main support timbers and still remain a ship.

The Atonement is in both Catholic and Protestant theology a doctrine that is susceptible only to literal—as opposed to allegorical or poetic—interpretation. It is clearly stated that for the purpose of man's salvation God came down from heaven and assumed the form of one particular man: Jesus Christ.

Second, it is asserted that Christ did indeed redeem the world.

Third, the church teaches (according to Father Cuthbert, O.F.M., in *God and the Supernatural: A Catholic Statement of the Christian Faith,* an article written by four distinguished Catholic theologians and published by the Catholic firm of Sheed and Ward):

There can be no redemption from sin, and consequently no attainment to the supernatural life, except through Christ and by the grace of His redemptive work. No sin can be forgiven except it be forgiven in and through Him. . . . Christ is our salvation; not merely in the relative sense in which we speak of ordinary men being the salvation of their erring brothers, but in the absolute sense of one who is the very principal and source of our redemption, and apart from whom there can in truth be no salvation.

But if we assume that the Roman church is correct in such a pronouncement, it inescapably follows that Luther, Calvin, and other pessimists were right in their assumption that the great majority of the human race is predestined for hell. Only a modest percentage of the world's population—after two thousand years of effort—is enrolled in the Christian faith. Furthermore, no knowledgeable Christian has ever suggested that all members of the church were guaranteed salvation merely by the fact of their affiliation. They are assured of nothing more than the *availability of the means to achieve salvation.*

I am not the first to draw out the inevitable logical extension of the dogma of the Atonement, with its horrifying implications. A Catholic response to such questions—although it is by no means as admirably clear as is the assertion of the basic dogma itself—weasels away from the simple and inescapable meaning of the dogma by suggesting that God, "in his infinite wisdom and mercy," might make it possible for those who, because of invincible ignorance, are rather—but why finish? Such a pitiful argument is never tacked on the bulletin board, so to speak, side by side with the original dogma. It is kept in the back of a drawer and produced only when its service is required, on the probably quite reasonable grounds that such troublesome questions will occur to few among those who seek conversion.

Again, if discoveries by Bible scholars were to compel a revision of this essential Christian dogma, it is impossible now to predict how churches might be effected. They could not possibly continue in their present philosophical structure—that is clear—but precisely what alternative forms might emerge cannot now be foretold.

In time, some theologian would probably argue that God had now granted a new revelation, substantially supplanting that which had served for the preceding two thousand years. In the lifetime of Christ God had vouchsafed a then-new dispensation to replace the Old Law that had served his specially loved people for many centuries before that time. Just such an argument, in fact, is now made by both Muslims and Bahais, although neither maintains that Judaism's and Christianity's adherents are doomed to hell.

Though the argument may, in terms of our present combination of knowledge and bias, seem absurd, it is, as historians well know, typical of theological argumentation in which the alternative common to science— that of saying, "I realize I was utterly mistaken in my prior assumption. Evidence forces a revision as follows . . ."—is apparently unthinkable. Churches almost never apologize and concede important error. In such refusal they reveal where their hearts really lie as regards the ideal of truth. Churches never employ reason to develop or discover a faith that is logically and morally consistent. Typically they start with a body of opinion and then later—sometimes quite tardily—employ reason in defense of positions already held. As both devout theologians and atheists understand clearly enough, the kingdoms of faith and reason are two quite separate domains, although there is a certain overlapping area between them. (See also RITUAL.)

AUTHENTICITY OF THE BIBLE. It has always been difficult to evaluate the reliability and accuracy of those ancient religious documents that are not obviously fully mythological because early religious literature from all parts of the world (including the Eastern Mediterranean areas) has always represented a blend of fantasy and fact. Unfortunately the factual component has often been minor, consisting merely of references to actual tribes, communities, mountains, rivers, and other physical locations. Such references do not establish the authenticity of the reports in which they appear, in the same sense that references to Chicago or London in a purely fictional narrative are not evidence that such accounts represent history or indeed truth of any sort.

Nor does use of the names of actual individuals establish truth. Despite the fact that Parson Weems quoted young George Washington as saying "I cannot tell a lie," the first president of the United States never made any such statement. The Reverend Weems devised the story out of nothing more than his imagination as a way of offering sound enough moral instruction to young readers. As we have seen, Weems's dishonesty has much precedent. The solons of the Christian and Jewish religions, in separately deciding which long-revered religious documents deserved to be included in the Bible, were obliged by the essential nature of their task to deny the seal of authenticity to a great many holy books that earlier generations of Jews and Christians had assumed were perfectly genuine. When we say that they were not authentic, it inevitably follows that the original authors and subsequent editors of such documents had engaged in the deliberate creation and subsequent promulgation of deceitful assertions.

Every professional theologian of whatever persuasion is perfectly in

21

agreement with what I am outlining here, despite the fact that such ideas are almost never purposefully suggested to the armies of the faithful. In fact, religious teachers hope that such lines of speculation will never occur to believers in the first place. And to the great majority of the faithful, no doubt, such troubling considerations do not often come to mind. But if such concepts as truth and reality have any value at all, then such questions are of the most fundamental importance to religion. Nevertheless, some church voices in effect say, "Oh, is it not better to leave the simple faithful alone with their simple faiths?"

No, it is not better at all. Perhaps it might be if humankind knew only one form of religion, but unfortunately there are thousands of such forms. Since they embody a great many mutually exclusive beliefs, it inescapably follows that among the assorted categories of religious belief on our planet there is a very great amount of ERROR mixed in with whatever truth and moral edification may be encountered. Ideas have consequences, and totally erroneous ideas are likely to have destructive consequences. Leaving the ignorant alone in their often-pathetic philosophical assumptions can, therefore, never be more than a matter of social convenience. It certainly cannot be justified on the level of serious dialogue, scholarship, or dedication to God's truth.

But to perceive the debate over the authenticity of Scripture as a man-or-God question is to suffer a fundamental misunderstanding. All informed parties agree that both the Old and New Testaments were written by fallible men. The only question at issue is, Did God personally and directly *inspire* those men in their writing?

It is not enough to suggest that they were inspired in the same way that Shakespeare or Dante were said to be: that is, in a loose, poetic manner whereby a creative person is so seized by an idea that he is, in a sense, in its power. This has nothing whatever to do with the question of direct divine inspiration.

The question that must be faced, then, is: As the increasing sophistication of scholarship makes less likely the possibility that either all or any significant portion of the Bible was truly and directly inspired by God, what sort of criteria would it be reasonable to apply to a document that was actually conceived by a Deity? Robert G. Ingersoll answers as follows:

> It should be a book that no man—or number of men—could produce.
> It should contain the perfection of philosophy.
> It should perfectly accord with every fact in nature.
> There should be no mistakes in astronomy, geology, or as to any subject or science.

Its morality should be the highest, the purest.

Its laws and regulations for the control of conduct should be just, wise, perfect, and perfectly adapted to the accomplishment of the ends desired.

It should contain nothing calculated to make men cruel, revengeful, vindictive, or infamous.

It should be filled with intelligence, justice, purity, honesty, mercy, and the spirit of liberty.

It should be opposed to strife and war, to slavery and lust, to ignorance, credulity and superstition.

It should develop the brain and civilize the heart.

It should satisfy the heart and brain of the best and wisest.

It should be true.

Its most fervent or devout contemporary defenders could not possibly argue that the Bible conforms to Ingersoll's eminently reasonable description of a divinely inspired work. (See also APOCRYPHA, THE; ERROR; PIOUS FRAUD.)

B

BELIEFS AND MYTHS. It is probably impossible to exaggerate the power of societal pressure on the individual so far as the personal formation of a constellation of beliefs is concerned. As Barrows Dunham observes in *Heroes and Heretics: A Social History of Dissent* (Alfred A. Knopf):

> One of the things a man has to do in life is to discover, so far as he can, the grounds for believing what he is asked to believe. Reason, of course, bids him believe all those assertions, and only those assertions, that seem likely to be true. Yet, so soon as he tries faithfully to follow reason, he grows aware of other grounds, or at least of pressures, which derive from the organized society around him. That is to say, he finds himself enticed or driven to beliefs he would not otherwise have held.

Man has long been subjected to outside pressure to believe blindly in the Scriptures. Freethinkers down through the ages have been reviled, persecuted, and even murdered for questioning the reality of stories in the Holy Book.

Nevertheless, in many instances in the Bible, that which purports to be an explanation of observable physical or social reality is no such thing but rather a theoretical rationalization of that reality—a myth. The unknown authors of the first chapter of Genesis, for example, observed—as may the reader himself—that man is, in some clearly discernible sense, higher than all other animals of the earth. He, for example, is more intelligent, can perform thousands of acts of which no animal is capable, and feels not the slightest guilt at using for food any animal he pleases. The authors of Genesis dealt with this in the following manner (Gen. 1:28).

And God blessed them, and God said unto them, Be fruitful and multiply, and replenish the earth, and subdue it: and have dominion over the fish of the sea, and over the fowl of the air, and over every living thing that moveth upon the earth. (IA)

It can be seen from this illustration that it is absurd to suppose that the fact of such dominion somehow authenticates the verse itself.

Explains R. A. MacKenzie, S.J., in *Faith and History in the Old Testament* (University of Minnesota Press):

There undoubtedly are myths contained in the Old Testament . . . narratives invented to explain the ultimate reasons of things, and to express the myth-maker's faith in a particular divine activity. (IA)

It is not necessary to repeat here the dictionary definition of the word *myth*. There is no serious obscurity about it. But it is important to focus on one aspect of mythology: it deals with stories that are imaginary, that do not directly reflect any physical reality whatsoever. Myths may be said to point to moral truths, to have poetic beauty, to be instructive in one way or another. But a myth is, by definition, not history. It does not relate what actually happened. Therefore, when we realize that there are myths in the Bible we are simultaneously accepting that the Scriptures contain narrative material that is simply not factual reporting. It relates to things that never happened. An unprejudiced twelve-year-old reading the Scriptures will have no difficulty in grasping this simple point. The wonder is that there are at least a few presumably learned scholars who are made uncomfortable by it.

This is not to say that myth in all its forms cannot possibly have any realistic components. One can, after all, create a myth about George Washington, Henry VIII, Julius Caesar, or any other actual personage. Moreover, one may locate the scene of the myth in an actual geographical setting. But if it is a myth, it is simply an imaginary story, which may or may not relate to actual beings. Significantly, most of the world's mythology concerns purely imaginary personages.

Philosophical idealism—which argues that what seems to be apparent, concrete knowledge actually exists in the mind rather than in physical reality—has always seemed essentially nonsensical to me. Whether this should be attributed to the modest degree of my own intelligence, or to the inherent absurdity of such arguments might be reasonably debated.

But let us propose a simple experiment. If a pedestrian perceives—and therefore believes—that a brick wall is directly in front of him, he will, naturally, not walk into it at high speed. However, direct a blind man on the same path and offer him no protective instructions. When he finally bumps painfully into that wall, breaks his dark glasses, and skins his knees, he is unlikely to be convinced by arguments that his physical suffering was caused only by his mind's belief that the wall actually existed.

The Creation. One example of myth in the Bible is, of course, the story of creation. When I interpret the biblical tale as myth, I am mindful of that physical history that each individual lives out, starting from the initial moment of his existence as a simple protoplasmic, amoebalike creature, through the stages of his prebirth development in which at times he bears more resemblance to a fish, frog, or rabbit than anything commonly perceived as human. But from the day of his birth he launches upon an extended period during which it is impossible for him—either physically or psychologically—to experience the emotion of shame. Freud was probably correct in asserting that the idea of Paradise is itself nothing but the collective fantasy of the guiltless childhood of the individual.

Circumcision. Another biblical myth, which has, in fact, led to a now longstanding custom, concerns the ritual of circumcision. In general, scholarly scriptural commentary is often a good deal more clear than Scripture itself. Some commentary, however, may include hazy details that, because of their very vagueness, are difficult either to grasp or to oppose. In a creative but not particularly enlightening commentary on Genesis by the late Chief Rabbi J. Hertz, there is the statement that "circumcision guarantees the survival of Israel's mission." Circumcision does nothing of the kind. It is merely a custom so ancient that no one now has the slightest idea how it started. There is serious debate among medical authorities—both Jewish and gentile—whether the benefits of circumcision, granting that there are any at all, outweigh the risks of the procedure.

Since I happen to be biased in favor of the world's Jews, I personally hope that they survive both as individuals and as a people, but I cannot see how it can be responsibly claimed that a certain amount of skin from the end of the penis will, if removed, account for the survival of Israel's mission or, if retained, its total collapse.

Aged Women Giving Birth. T. W. Doane in *Bible Myths and Their Parallels in Other Religions* (Truth Seeker) comments on the apparently unique Israelite literary tradition depicting old and long-barren women giving birth:

> As illustrations we may mention [the] case of Samson, and that of Joseph being born of Rachel. . . .Isaac was born of a woman [Sarah] who had been barren many years. . . . Samuel . . . was also born of a woman

[Hannah] who had been barren many years. . . . John the Baptist was also a miraculously conceived infant. . . . His mother Elizabeth bore him in her old age. . . . Mary, the mother of Jesus, was born of a woman [Anna] who was "old and stricken in years" and who had been barren all her life.

As Doane observes, such stories typically feature an angel that was said to have appeared to each old woman telling her of her good fortune. That the average seventy-five- or eighty-year-old woman would hardly consider it good fortune to be told she was pregnant is apparently never considered. In any event, once we grant that an all-powerful Deity is able to perform any miracle he might wish, it becomes no more remarkable that he might choose to enact a specific miracle on several separate occasions.

The Flood. Doane discusses another biblical myth, that of the great flood, or the Deluge. Says Doane:

About 725 B.C. the Israelites were conquered by Salmanassar, King of Assyria, and many of them were carried away captives. Their place was supplied by Assyrian colonists from Babylon, Persia and other places. This fact is of the greatest importance and should not be forgotten, as we find that the first of the three writers of the Pentateuch . . . wrote about this time, and the Israelites heard, from the colonists from Babylon, Persia and other places—for the first time—many of the legends which this writer *wove into the fabulous history which he wrote, especially the accounts of the Creation and the Deluge.* (IA)

One reason we may be quite sure that the story of the ark is mythical is that among the land creatures that have inhabited the earth are mammoths, mastodons, and dinosaurs. Though these beasts are known to have died off before man appeared, the arithmetic given in the Bible would require us to believe they existed in Noah's time.

Of course, when we refer to dinosaurs, we are not considering simply one specific sort of animal. The word applies to a group of reptiles of many different types: Brontosaurus, Diplodocus, Ornithischia, Saurischia, Thecodontia, Tyrannosaurus rex.

The idea that pairs—or seven—of such enormous creatures were housed in a handmade boat is ludicrous. I addressed even more absurdities about the story in Volume 1 of my study (see NOAH).

The Tribulations of Job. Are present-day fundamentalists aware that they have been abandoned by the very best Christian and Jewish scholars concerning the historical accuracy of the Book of Job? Comments Jean Levie, S.J., in *The Bible: Word of God in Words of Men:*

Does the Book of Job relate a genuine dialogue between Job and his friends, or is this dialogue more probably a philosophical and religious essay on the problem of evil, composed by the author under the form of a dialogue? *The second hypothesis seems to be adopted today by the majority of exegetes, whether higher critics or Catholics, and it is far and away the more convincing.* (IA)

Levie grasps the obvious: that we have no way of knowing whether such an individual as Job ever existed or whether, if he did, he ever suffered the dreadful trials referred to in the story about him. In any event, explains Levie, on what was either a historical or merely a mythical foundation the inspired author wrote a didactic dialogue with a view of casting some light on the problem of evil. The historical debate on the authenticity of the Bible, therefore, has now moved forward—thank God— to the point where the argument seems to be essentially whether fables and other old tales, morally edifying or not, can be said to be instances of divine inspiration. If motivated by a combination of common sense, fair-mindedness, and standards of scientific analysis, the reader will have little difficulty in settling the question for himself.

Again I have addressed the story of JOB more completely in Volume 1.

The Bible as Revelation. Concerning the meaning of the word *revelation* Thomas Paine, among other scholars, has made a point to which believers should at the very least give thoughtful attention:

Revelation is a communication of something which the person to whom that thing is revealed did not know before. For if I have done a thing, or seen it done, it needs no revelation to tell me I have done it, or seen it, nor to enable me to tell it, or to write it.

Revelation, therefore, cannot be applied to anything done upon earth of which man himself is the actor or the witness; and consequently all the historical and anecdotal part of the Bible—which is almost the whole of it—is not within the meaning and compass of the word *revelation,* and, therefore, is not a word of God.

Believers will naturally reject Paine's conclusion but his philosophical observation is worthy of attention. Paine turns to a specific to clarify his point additionally:

When Samson ran off with the gate-posts of Gaza, if he ever did so (and whether he did or not is nothing to us), or when he visited his Delilah, or caught his foxes, or did anything else, what has revelation to do with these things? If they were facts, he could tell them himself, or his secretary—if he kept one—could write them, if they were worth either telling or writing. And even if they were fictions, revelation could not make them true; and whether true or not, we are neither the better nor the wiser for knowing them. When we contemplate the immensity of that Being who directs and governs the incomprehensible whole, of which the utmost ken of human sight can discover but a part, we ought to feel shame at calling such paltry stories the word of God.

Tree of Life. Reference to the Tree of Life is found in Genesis.

2:9. And out of the ground made the Lord God to grow every tree that is pleasant to the sight, and good for food; the tree of life also in the midst of the garden, and the tree of knowledge of good and evil.

3:22. And the Lord God said, "Behold, the man is become as one of us, to know good and evil: and now, lest he put forth his hand, and take also of the tree of life, and eat, and live for ever.

A number of religious scholars have now clarified that the concept of such a tree did by no means originate with the author of that portion of the Bible. The much earlier Babylonian document *Gilgamesh* relates that its hero searched for the "Plant of Life." As delicately as his orthodoxy requires, Father Auzou says of this earlier reference, "obviously one thinks of Genesis 2:9; 3:22." The Tree of Life, therefore, is undoubtedly an ancient myth, incorporated into Genesis by that Scripture's unknown authors.

BY THEIR FRUITS YE SHALL KNOW THEM. Of all the judgments that have been applied to organized religion, none is more devastating than the admonition of Jesus that we ought to judge things by their fruits. He does not say that results are the only criteria to be employed in coming to a reasonable decision about people, things, and institutions, but the essence of his advice is so wise that it has never been contested. When we apply this eminently sensible suggestion to the record of religion, however, the results are deeply troubling, whatever the questioner's own bias might be. (See also RELIGION.)

Good Works. Millions of Christians personally believe and preach that living a good, charitable life—doing good works—is of literally no avail in regard to salvation.

Whether they are correct in that belief is, of course, simply one more aspect of the religious debate that will presumably continue throughout all time, as it already has for thousands of years. But whatever the authenticity of the belief, Christians must never forget that the non-Christian majority of the human race judges the followers of Christ by precisely that standard that so many Christians explicitly reject. It is indeed not by their professed faith but by their works, by their behavior in everyday life, that Christians are judged. To the extent that they daily commit every sin known to history, to the extent that in our own time and place Christians are spiteful toward blacks, Jews, fellow Christians, non-Christians, women, homosexuals, scientists, humanists (secular or religious), atheists, agnostics, or anyone else, the world quite properly not only judges them but also often renders harsh judgment indeed. The ancients' sarcastic joke, "Observe the Christians, how they love one another," usually applied in the context of some intramural Christian atrocity, represents an ongoing scandal to the faith concerning which fundamentalists, among others, would do well to give the most careful possible attention.

Miracles. John 14:12 quotes Jesus as saying, "Verily, Verily, I say unto you, He that believeth in me, the works that I do he shall do also, and *greater works than these shall he do;* because I go unto my Father." (IA)

The problem here, obviously enough, is that there is no evidence that, of the hundreds of millions of those who have followed and endeavored to live under the guidance of the precepts of Jesus, any have ever been able to work the wonders he did, much less surpass them, as Jesus is said to have predicted.

Peace. As a child I was taught to refer to Jesus as the Prince of Peace. Everyone loves peace. Even pugnacious individuals want peace most of the time and would, I suppose, be happy if no one ever contested their right to dominate so that a practical peace—defined as the absence of hostilities—resulted. The New Testament provides much evidence that Jesus himself was essentially a peaceful person. In this, of course, as in so much else in the Bible, the waters are somewhat muddied because incidents are related that show that if Jesus was peaceful most of the time, he certainly was not so at all times.

But we are not judging Jesus in this instance. This time his hundreds of millions of followers for the last two thousand years are on the weighing scales. Have those followers behaved in a peaceful manner? The truth is that a good many of his admirers have done precisely the opposite. Nations that marched most proudly under the Christian banner have been the most militarily aggressive in history. Perhaps they have been equaled in some instances, but they have never been surpassed in the endless commission of organized atrocities and brutalities. We ought not to dismiss such shattering truths with only a moment's reflection and a sad concessionary nod of the head, for we are not talking about one offense here only in the abstract sense. In reality, we are talking about countless millions of individual beatings, stabbings, maimings, shootings, burnings, stranglings, and rapings. We are talking about a seemingly unlimited number of deaths, of massive destruction of property, including priceless and irreplaceable treasures of art and culture.

At nearly the end of the twentieth century, the world is quite properly gravely concerned over the militant fanaticism of the Islamic religion. Our nightly radio and television newscasts are filled with atrocities and murders committed proudly by devout followers of Mohammed who subsequently experience neither shame nor regret. Such realities would indeed be horrifying in any era, but they are even more disturbing in this age when the scientific theory and technology required for the construction of monstrous weapons—chemical and nuclear—are falling into an ever larger number of hands.

But on what philosophical ground can a Christian properly stand from which to hurl criticisms at today's Moslem fanatics and revolutionaries, given that the Christian record of organized violence is so bloodstained that nothing short of universal amnesia or the nuclear destruction of humanity could ever expunge it from the record?

Tolerance. The enemies of religion wish to hear of and preach only its evils and bitter fruits. The adherents of religion are equally one-sided: they wish to hear only of the institution's benefits and blessings. The wiser person will be interested in the *truth* about religion, which will encompass some information that is flattering and other that is shameful. All intelligent atheists acknowledge that religion has produced a great deal of good for both societies and individuals. But the devout must be honest enough to recognize, and not deceitfully hide, the appalling amount of evil and viciousness for which both religion generally, and the Bible specifically, have been responsible. (See also CRIME, BIBLICAL IMPETUS TO; CRUSADES, THE; FANATICISM; SAINTLINESS; VIRTUES, THE.)

C

CALF OF GOLD. The characters of the Old Testament include a larger number of fools, knaves, murderers, and other criminals than one encounters in any other known work of literature. One of the stupidest people—if the story of the Calf of Gold is to be credited—is Aaron. Consider: Here is a man who has had a close communication with God Almighty, as direct and intimate as the reader's contact with wife, sibling, or close friend. The Lord has worked incredible wonders for Aaron, personally. Any reader granted such an honor would certainly achieve that impressive degree of spiritual confidence and sanctity that leads to saintliness. But observe what happens in the peculiar story told in Exodus, chapter 32.

While Moses was up on the hillside for forty days, the people became restless, for reasons not made clear. A number of followers approached Aaron and said:

> "Up, make us gods, which shall go before us; for as for this Moses, the man that brought us up out of the land of Egypt, we wot not what is become of him." (Exod. 32:1)

If there ever were such a personage in reality as Aaron, and if he had an I.Q. markedly higher than that of a broccoli plant, he would have responded by saying, "You are out of your minds, ye of little faith. Do you not remember what wonders Moses and the Lord God have worked? Have you already forgotten the miracles, the special favors that God has showed you, and in such recent times? Have you not heard the seventy tell of seeing God face-to-face on the mountain? I forbid you to even talk of idolatry." No doubt an author more gifted could create a more eloquent response, but the meaning would be much the same. Instead, according to the Old Testament, Aaron gives not a moment's thought to the incredible experiences he has had, to his face-to-face encounters with the true God of the universe, but at once says—translating into modern terms— "Okay, you've got a point. I'll tell you what. Take off the earrings that your wives, sons, and daughters are wearing and bring them to me."

Now really.

The people bring their earrings to Aaron; he melts the metal down, then fashions it into the shape of a calf with "a graving tool." How he performed this remarkable technological feat while wandering with his people in the desert, presumably with a few personal belongings, is not explained. We have not previously been told of his prowess as a goldsmith or artisan of any kind.

Not only does Aaron create such an idol, but he at once constructs an altar for it and officiates at the performance of religious services to it! It is therefore quite understandable that when Moses finally does come down off the mountainside, having for some hours carried what must have been two enormously heavy stone tablets—and that in precarious footing—and weak and emaciated from forty days without food and water (a clear impossibility in itself), he becomes so infuriated at seeing what Aaron and his people have done that in a fit of pique he smashes not Aaron's nose but the Ten Commandments on the ground!

This act of Moses must surely be one of the stupidest, most incredible insults ever given to God. Exodus clearly stipulates—beyond the slightest opportunity for alternative interpretation—that the finger of God directly, personally wrote the Ten Commandments on these two tablets. Not that Moses himself did the writing, having been somehow inspired by a spiritual visitation; not that Moses found the engraved tablets under a bush and simply surmised that God might have left them there, but that God himself wrote out the Ten Commandments in the specific literal sense that your neighborhood printer would print words on a pasteboard. Can the reader imagine with what trepidation he would even physically approach such tablets?

So another dunce of the Old Testament, Moses, in a fit of annoyance, smashes something God had personally just given to him. If, as the Bible claims, a poor innocent lamb deserves to be painfully slaughtered for having unwittingly wandered near the foot of that mountain, then what would be a fitting punishment for Moses for having committed such an incredible theological and cultural crime? Of course by now the reader will have perhaps joined me in being unable to believe a word of the whole preposterous account.

If one—out of the innocent, virtuous habit of faith—keeps trying to reconstruct a literalist belief in such accounts, one is frustrated at almost every turn. In the next part of the story we are told that Moses "took the calf which they had made, and burned it in the fire, and ground it into powder, and strewed it upon the water, and made the children of Israel drink of it" (Exod. 32:20). The following questions occur:

1. How could Moses lift the metal calf?

2. How did he personally know anything about subjecting metals to fires hot enough to melt them?

3. In that technologically primitive age, what tools or machines did he employ to grind cooled gold metal to powder?

4. Since they were in the desert, upon what body of water did he scatter the powder?

5. Did the metal fragments not sink, as metal always does in water?

6. What could possibly be meant by the statement that he made the children of Israel drink the water?

(See also GIFTS TO GOD; RELIGIOUS THEORIES, DEVIANT; RITUAL.)

CHARITY. A number of philosophers have argued—or agreed—that the morality of a society ought to lead it to produce the greatest happiness of the greatest number. But there has never been unanimous agreement on what happiness is, or what specific human acts are likely to produce it. Such questions involve matters of opinion; since no two humans are identical, it is therefore inevitable that they will have widely varying views on many subjects. This variety, however, is not totally chaotic; there is always some rough statistical order to it. We might determine that 97 percent of a given population describe certain acts of charity as virtuous, 47 percent describe spanking and other forms of physical abuse of children as evil, and so forth.

The wish to produce the greatest good for the greatest possible number of citizens is part of the philosophical justification for the various forms of what is called the Welfare State. Since conservatives are often politically powerful enough to promulgate their views effectively, the welfare state has been subjected to a great deal of criticism in recent years. This is not because the critics have anything against public welfare itself. They recognize that to deprive the poor of the security of *all* strands of the safety net woven by progressives over the last century would make a violent revolution not only inevitable but also imminent. What conservatives object to is paying for such benefits for others who, unlike themselves, are very poor and likely not only to remain so their entire lives but also to endure intense suffering if they were to wait for practical assistance from the charitable impulses of the well-to-do.

Those obviously insufficient charitable impulses, after having thousands of years to solve the larger problems of poverty, hunger, disease, and illiteracy *and having been found utterly unequal to the task,* have led to the adoption of welfare measures. (See also MORALITY; POVERTY.)

Churches and the Poor. Creatures of a hypothetical rational planet who could observe the behavior of earthlings from an impartial distance would no doubt judge as profoundly foolish those societies in which the suffering, struggling 95 percent of a population seemed willing to submit to the dominance of a selfish and pampered wealthy class that has only cruel contempt or blind indifference to their luckless subjects, and almost never a good-hearted and charitable concern.

The church boasts of its martyrs, though it does not always give them full-fledged support while they are alive. But it is a fair if disturbing question to ask why, after long centuries of opportunity to convert and propagandize the minds of millions of Latin Americans, the church has nevertheless done such a poor job of encouraging dedication to living by the light of philosophical ideals acknowledged even by ancient pagan philosophies. It has not succeeded in inculcating respect for even those ideals that are considered specifically Christian. The Scriptures ring with repeated denunciations of the selfish rich, and this was true long before the New Testament came into existence. Why, then, have the princes of the church so often served the interests of the rich and left the poor to the loving attention of those few orders of priests and nuns who morally distinguish themselves by their loving concern?

The pro-rich bias of some churchmen would be a moral outrage if the poor numbered only 5 percent of a given population. When they number 95 percent, as they do in some countries, we are addressing more than an outrage: it is massive moral idiocy.

Secular humanism, at its best, can enlist the minds of men and women by its inherent reasonableness. Whether it can enlist their hearts is still an open question. But the church has had access to both hearts and minds for two thousand years and yet has obviously failed to inculcate a decent social conscience in the great majority of its adherents, whether Catholics or Protestants.

It has clearly failed to create a widely accepted social ethic in Latin America.

It has failed to inculcate such a conscience in that not inconsiderable portion of Catholicism dominated by the Mafia in both Europe and the United States.

It has failed to instill a moral conscience in more than a minority of Christians forced to address racial injustice in this country in the nineteenth and twentieth centuries.

There are reasons for all this, of course, and some of them can no doubt be interpreted as excuses. The Scriptures themselves have little or nothing to say in condemnation of the vile institution of slavery. But the American Catholic branch of Christendom was hideously embarrassed at what it learned in the 1960s when Martin Luther King, Jr., and other campaigners for social justice for blacks marched through predominantly Catholic neighborhoods, with courageous priests and nuns heading such parades.

Were they welcomed, applauded, cheered by their fellow Christians?

No. They were attacked, assaulted with sticks, bottles, stones. They were spat upon and addressed in foul and insulting language.

Obviously the church had made some sort of monstrous mistake in so seriously neglecting to apply the gospel of Jesus to the practical realities of Christians living in twentieth-century America.

There have always been heroic exceptions—may God bless them and their tribe increase—but it is painfully embarrassing that they are only exceptions.

The same uncharitable sentiments have colored the behavior of Christians toward Jews for two thousand years. That entire chapter of Christian history is in fact one long, almost-unrelieved tragedy.

There are in the American context, thank God, sensible and humane countercurrents to all such ugliness. Some of the virtuous work has been done by Christians, partly because the Christian conscience had been publicly shamed, often by non-Christians, into a more virtuous mode of conduct.

I have suggested in this connection, in one of my recent books, that the secular humanists have actually done modern Christians a very great service in forcing them to practice what they preached, forcing them to be just and humane to Jews, to blacks, to the poor when, for centuries, they had often behaved quite otherwise.

I was a personal friend of the late John Cogley, one-time editor of the Catholic periodical *Commonweal,* later religion editor of the *New York Times.* Mr. Cogley was a heroic gentleman who, parenthetically, shortly before the end of his life made the conscious decision to leave the church, although he remained a Christian.

I have never forgotten John's telling me one evening that as a young Catholic and follower of the heroic Dorothy Day, he sometimes, at the end of a long working period doing what little he could for the poor of New York City, would just sit in his car, alone, and weep at the massive proportions of the difficulties he faced and at the pathetic sufferings of the impoverished.

In this connection, I think of the shock I felt when, in my twenties, I first heard the term *bleeding hearts* applied, with a sneer, to those who, like John Cogley, actually wished to do something practical for the poor. Such a term, still used as an expression of contempt, reveals far more about those who utter it than it does about the targets of their invective.

Conservatives of the world, can you not see that we need *more,* not fewer bleeding hearts?

The church is honored and glorified by those who participate in the never-ending campaign for social justice.

The church is *dis*honored by those who make heroes of such bums as the late Senator Joseph McCarthy.

I use such a term freely. I'm not running for office, and I have no time at present to communicate with all those whom I am honored to call friends so I have no motive for enlarging their circle. It is no proper defense of Mr. McCarthy to say he was an anticommunist. Hitler was an anticommunist! Ninety-eight percent of the American people have always been anticommunist, to their great credit. But if anything ever muddled the mind of the Catholic church over the past century it has been anti-communism. Under that banner there was never any shortage of church-men to bless Franco's, Mussolini's, and Hitler's bombers and tanks, nor at present is there any lack of Christian churchmen to take the side of the Latin American dictators and murderous oligarchs, who so guiltlessly kill priests, nuns, and the poor.

One generally wants to know what a man is against; but we must also ask what he is for. Are there or are there not Christian principles that clearly address such questions?

If there are—let Christians act upon them.

If there are not—let us hasten to derive them.

Just as the banner of anticommunism is not enough to establish either political or personal virtue, so the banner of Christianity itself is insufficient to that task. The great majority of the German people who enthusiastically welcomed Hitler and demanded that he take control of their nation were Christians. Damned poor Christians, true, but Protestants and Catholics nevertheless. (See also ALTRUISM; CONSERVATIVISM.)

CHRONICLES, THE FIRST BOOK OF THE. The Jews of ancient times who wrote and rewrote this section of the Bible did not call it Chronicles. The title is a Christian mistake made by Jerome who, for reasons unknown to us, did not accept the Hebrew title "Book of the Words [Events] of the Days" but changed it to "Chronicle of the Entire Divine Mystery."

Whatever it is, it is certainly not, by even the most traditional Christian evaluation, a chronicle of the *entire* Divine Mystery.

Second, the division of Chronicles into two distinct books was unknown to its original authors.

The reader must now grasp that the defense offered for certain portions of Scripture—that they are to be interpreted in an allegorical, figurative, or mythical sense—cannot be offered for Chronicles. From the beginning it has been—and still is—presented as straightforward history.

Chronicles places heavy emphasis on the foundation of the Israelite monarchy. The periods dominated by David and Solomon are seen as the acme of Israel's achievement. Oddly, however, during the time in which the two Chronicles books were written there was no longer a monarchy among the Israelites. Unfortunately, there is now no way that even the most competent scholars can discern the reasons for the chronicler's emphasis on the time of Israel's past glory.

Some Christians have suggested that there is reference to the Messiah in the Chronicles account, a looking forward to the time when there will again be a king of Israel. It seems much more probable that, as Celine Mangan puts it in *Old Testament Message* (Michael Glazier, Inc.), ". . . the Chronicler's interest was not so much in the monarchy as such but in the plan of God for his people, in which David played his own particular role." Mangan points out that the two Chronicles "are among the least-read books of the Bible." Even scholars and specialists have given them relatively scant attention over the centuries, partly because they are, as Mangan says, "a rather dull retelling" of material already touched on in SAMUEL and KINGS. Could Almighty God inspire dull prose?

Chapter 10. In October of 1989, Chicago police apprehended a vicious killer who had murdered three young brothers of one local family. The crime itself was sadistic, and the community united to demand quick and severe punishment for the offender, largely because his motive was simply that he had a grudge against Robert Carter, the young men's father. Carter, it seems, had consulted an alleged psychic/astrologer and, for reasons that remained unclear, the killer held this stupidity against him.

The reaction of citizens to this despicable crime was typical of any community on earth, but—as scholars of Scripture may have already perceived —I have here related a parable, not a factual story. It is found in this chapter and, according to the unknown authors, the murderer was God himself.

Even by this early point we have seen that the Bible cites dozens, scores, hundreds of instances in which a clearly criminal act is not only defended, which is morally outrageous enough, but—even worse—is also attributed to God.

We do not have the slightest trouble morally judging precisely such offenses when they are committed by men. The combination of a moral sense and our gift of reason tell us, in the instant, that we are considering a dreadful and inexcusable deed. Then, why do many defend such violent acts when they are encountered in the pages of Scripture? There can be only one answer. We become, in a sense, accomplices to such crimes simply because we have already taken a *the-Bible-can-do-no-wrong* position. Fortunately all we have to do to stop being guilty of such moral idiocy is abandon that position.

Chapter 12. This section primarily lists names of old warriors, battles, descriptions of military units, explanations of which troops were armed with bows, which could use both the right and left hand in hurling stones, in shooting arrows, and so forth. In the entire forty-verse chapter, there is not a single word that could possibly be interpreted as uplifting, morally instructive, or indeed religious in any sense. Whether the book is even historically reliable is very doubtful, but there is certainly nothing of spiritual interest in it. How then can it possibly be argued that it is the Word of God, presumably sent from the throne of the Almighty for the moral enlightenment of the sons and daughters of earth?

Out-and-out nonsense is encountered in verse 14 in which, in reference to the sons of Gad who were captains of the army, we are told: "He who was least was equal to a hundred and the greatest to a thousand." Let us imagine the mightiest soldier of all time, armed with one or more of the weapons of primitive days—perhaps a sword, a spear, or a bow and arrow. Does the reader actually believe that such a warrior could defeat one hundred enemy fighting men? And the assertion that the best of the group was equal to *one thousand* enemy warriors is so absurd as not to require analytical comment.

Verse 23 begins numbering the divisions equipped for war under the command of David. Their total would make them one of the largest armies in the history of military action: 340,823 strong.

Given such an enormous number of men in arms, one recalls Napoleon's observation that an army travels on its stomach. In all ages and locations, humans have wished to eat something at approximately eight-hour intervals—a morning meal, something at midday, and a third repast in the evening. If we therefore multiply the 340,823 by three, this gives us the figure of 1,022,469. That number, in turn, we also multiply by three, since verse 39 has told us that this vast army ate and drank for that number of days—that's 3,067,407 meals!

We need not even discuss what is nevertheless an enormously important factor for all individuals and groups: the disposal of human waste. Such commonsense considerations obviously put such stories under deep suspicion.

Chapter 13. Let the reader imagine what his instantaneous reaction would be if any of his prized material objects were suddenly to appear in danger of falling to the ground. Whether the object is the flag of his country, the communion wafer served at a Catholic mass, or any other precious object, every sensible and devout person would immediately, instinctively put out his hand to steady the relic or artifact that was in danger. The otherwise unknown man named Ussa, therefore, committed no moral offense whatever in responding in just this way when the sacred ark was in danger of falling to the ground.

In verse 9 we are told that the reason for the ark's precariousness was that "the oxen stumbled." It is not explained whether one beast stumbled or several did simultaneously, although the latter sounds like rather unlikely choreography. In any event, Ussa, reacting as automatically as his eyelids would blink to shield his eyes from the invasion of a bright light, lifts his hand only to be helpful and respectful.

If this were a true story, and if the Divine Creator of the universe were actually a participant in it, the most he might reasonably do is say, in effect, "My son, while I respect your instinctive reaction—and indeed I programmed you for it—I must nevertheless remind you that it is written that no one is permitted to touch the ark." But we are told nothing so moral or sensible. It is actually alleged that the reaction of a perfect God was violent anger, an anger so extreme that he struck Ussa dead on the spot. Is capital punishment assumed by today's Christian or Jewish theologians to be a reasonable penalty for such an act committed out of admirable intentions? Of course it is not, and so, in one more case, we must refuse to believe such a preposterous story because it is an insult to God.

But it is instructive to think for a moment about the order that the ark must never be touched. How, then, could objects be placed inside of it or removed from it? How could it be cleaned, dusted, washed? How could it be repaired when, as centuries passed, it began to decay?

In thinking about this particular puzzlement, recall the millions of true atrocities—committed daily unto the present moment—that are of the most shocking seriousness: the endless slaughters of innocents, the rape and other physical abuse of little children, the beheadings, the tortures, the massive thefts. Has the Lord punished any of these with his personally delivered capital punishment? Strangely, no. Most such crimes go undetected and therefore unpunished, and among those that are detected the guilty are often able to evade punishment. God certainly has it in his power to mete out justice in the very sort of cases that, it is said, cry to him for vengeance. How absurd, then, to hold that on the one hand he has ignored billions of such seriously immoral acts and yet, on the other, moved purposefully and swiftly to blast poor Ussa to death a moment after his entirely accidental transgression.

Chapter 14. This chapter is equally devoid of spiritual content. David, it is said, perceived that the Lord had confirmed him king over Israel. According to verse 3, he celebrates this intelligence by taking more wives, by whom he has thirteen children, all of whom are named. In the present day, when a Christian, Jew—or, for that matter, pagan or atheist—does any such thing, he is roundly criticized as a sinner and said to be a disgusting slave to lust. But David, we are instructed, began to spend less time in either the worship of God or the business of administration and more time enjoying the pleasures of the bed with his wives, whose number we do not know.

The rest of the chapter merely builds on the monotonous detail with which the Scriptures must certainly have bored even the most meticulous historians of the ancient Israelites.

> 10. And David enquired of God, saying, "Shall I go up against the Philistines? and wilt thou deliver them into mine hand?" And the Lord said unto him, "Go up; for I will deliver them into thine hand."

David, we are told, duly slaughtered more Philistines. Eventually even the most sympathetic reader wonders how the ancient history of the Jews can be one of such suffering, travail, and subjection, since they seem to win a resounding victory in almost every military engagement. It is small wonder, of course, that they would enjoy such an almost-unbroken string of triumphs since they had the secret weapon of Almighty God to direct against one luckless enemy after another. Still, it is strange that the ancient Jews could win so many victories and yet spend so much time in subjection and suffering. (See also JEWS AND JUDAISM.)

Chapter 15. In all twenty-nine verses of this section there is no more religious instruction or intelligence than in the preceding chapters of Chronicles. Most of the verses consist of names of totally obscure Israelites concerning whose deeds, marriages, and begettings even today's Jews must have little serious concern. The only interesting verse in the chapter is the last:

> 29. And it came to pass, as the ark of the covenant of the Lord came to the city of David, that Michal the daughter of Saul looking

out at a window saw king David dancing and playing: and she despised him in her heart.

Chapter 16. In this next section, wherein one might expect to hear more about Michal and the reasons for her hatred of David, one instead encounters tedious descriptions of religious ceremonies.

We do learn something more intriguing for a change, however, from verse 26:

For *all the gods of the people are idols:* but the Lord made the heavens. (IA)

Inasmuch as today's Jews are a people of striking intelligence, perception, and social sensitivity, one wonders at the incredible denseness of their ancestors—if, that is, one can credit the Old Testament accounts in which again and again the people know that the Lord addresses them directly, gives them military victories, performs stunningly dramatic miracles for them, and yet in which they repeatedly forget the true Deity and turn to the worship of lifeless, powerless statues. There is no way one can now know the Israelites of several thousand years ago, but I know many Jews living today and because of familiarity with their virtue I consider a good deal of the material in the Old Testament an insult to the intelligence of so superior an ethnic group.

Chapter 16 introduces more theological confusion. After promising the land of Canaan to the Israelites, the Lord "suffered no man to do them wrong" (v. 21). But this cannot be, for in the same Scriptures we are told of countless instances in which wrong has indeed been done to the followers of Moses, much of it at the instigation of God himself.

A refreshingly sweet phrase appears in verse 29, in which the people are advised to worship the Lord "in the beauty of holiness." While we perceive holiness as a form of beauty, and all—no doubt—lament the pitiful scarcity of it in an evil world, the Scriptures never long remain on such a high plane of discourse. Only a moment later we are told that the Lord's "mercy endureth forever" (v. 34). If it does, what are we to make of the countless stories that offer no evidence of merciful treatment at the hands of the Lord, but only the clearest possible account of the psychotic savagery with which, at least according to the Bible's largely unknown authors, he has dealt with his children?

Chapter 16, like so many other chapters of the Jewish Scriptures, refers to *burnt offerings:*

40. To offer burnt offerings unto the Lord upon the altar of the burnt offering continually morning and evening, and to do according to all that is written in the Law of the Lord, which he commanded Israel.

I had been reading about burnt offerings for several weeks before it suddenly occurred to me that there was something inherently stupid about the practice of placing perfectly good food—grain, oil, meat, milk—upon an altar and destroying it by fire in the belief that the food was in some sense "offered" to God. Let us attempt to reason our way around and about the practice and see if we can bring it into sharper focus.

A true God, by definition, requires nothing whatever material from man. What he does require—again by the nature of definition—is man's adherence to moral principles. It is reasonable to assume that an all-virtuous Deity will be very concerned that man should do good and avoid sinful evil, love others, not be cruel, visit the sick, bury the dead, make crutches for the lame, provide homes for orphans, and do all manner of charitable works, which is to say that he should love God and his neighbor as himself. But to suggest that it is far more important that man destroy good foodstuffs by burning them rather than give them to the poor is, in my view, to utter an absurdity.

Within the context of Catholic theology there is one sense—and one only—in which the "offering" of material goods can have any intelligible meaning at all and that is in the context of selfless *sacrifice*. If the religious believer very much wishes to possess or use some object, then it can at least be argued that he merits some credit for deliberately denying himself the pleasure such possession or use would provide. If a man wishes, for example, to buy himself a handsome coat, it is understandable that he would be praised for denying himself the pleasure of acquiring and wearing the garment. He would deserve even more moral credit for giving the coat to a poor man who had none. But to argue that the coat ought to be placed on an altar and burned when there are people shivering in the world from cold is to state not only nonsense, but harmful, destructive nonsense at that. When there are so many in the world—often close to us—who are hungry, it is safe to say that history has seen enough of the destruction of food for religious purposes.

Fortunately, such destruction seldom takes place in today's world. I'm not aware of any responsible Jew, no matter how orthodox and devout, who today believes that the proper thing to do with food is to destroy it, except perhaps in symbolic fragments. But if common sense prevails in resolving this question in our own time, why must we be tolerant of the Jews described in the Old Testament who are said to perform what we now perceive as an absurd and wasteful act?

This is not to argue that the ritual of adoration has no place in religious practice. If we assume that there is a God and if, secondly, humans wish to express their veneration for that God by concrete acts, it is perfectly reasonable that they sing hymns or psalms, march in processions, light candles or incense, shoot off firecrackers, strike their breasts, kiss the ground, or engage in any other acts that dramatically express their submission to the will of God and true affection for him.

Members of one religion may view as comical or pointless certain such practices engaged in by others, but such practices can be justified in general. But—I repeat—there can be no respectable case for the deliberate, wasteful destruction of food.

Nor is it in any sense edifying that innocent animals are painfully slaughtered for purely ritualistic purposes. Over the centuries the suspicion has occurred to some students of the matter that the priesthood of various faiths has encouraged the bringing of tangible offerings to temples because the priests intended to eat the food themselves when the faithful had retired from the premises. But this attributes more intelligence to the practice than it deserves. It attributes hypocrisy and chicanery to the priesthood whereas the fault here is not dishonesty but the stupidity of loyalty to dumb custom. (See also GIFTS TO GOD; RITUAL.)

Chapters 17–19. This section recounts more strikingly repetitive conversations between David and God in which simple enough points are repeated for the hundredth time. We are told that David killed 22,000 Syrians and that Abishai killed 18,000 Edomites. No one expresses shame at such slaughters.

In Chapter 19 we are told that David "slew of the Syrians seven thousand men which fought in chariots, and thirty thousand footmen" (v. 18). What seems to have occasioned this savagery is told in the strange story in the early verses of the chapter concerning messengers sent from David to Hanun of the children of Ammon.

4. Wherefore Hanun took David's servants, and shaved them, and cut off their garments in the midst hard by their buttocks, and sent them away.
5. Then there went certain, and told David how the men were served. And he sent to meet them: for the men were greatly ashamed. And the king said, "Tarry at Jericho until your beards be grown, and then return."

Considering the atrocious way in which the Israelites constantly treated those who displeased them, it would not seem to have been a remarkably severe punishment that a few of David's servants simply had their beards shaved and their clothes cut in such a way that they were greatly ashamed. But again we see that trying to make sense of a good many Old Testament stories is a frustrating and certainly not edifying experience.

Chapter 20. All the chapters of this section of Chronicles detail endless mass slaughters. War itself is the greatest atrocity, as has been observed, so it is only natural that in the heat of battle, hideous moral offenses will occur not only occasionally but also daily and endlessly. But there has always been a clear mark of distinction between honorable military men angered by attacks upon themselves on the one hand, and those who *after* the cessation of hostilities continue to treat their captives, and even innocent civilians, in a violently sadistic way.

David, we must remember, is not simply one more leader of the Israelites but is counted among the greatest, most noble, and most dedicated to God's service. How then did such an admirable representative of this people treat his captives in the city of Rab'bah?

> 3. And he brought out the people that were in it, and *cut them with saws, and with harrows of iron, and with axes.* . . . (1A)

From what high moral ground do today's Christians and Jews criticize television for its paltry representations of individual crimes when the greatest heroes of the Old Testament—which many Jews and Christians consider the literal word of God—were involved with endless mass-horror stories such as this?

As I dictate these reflections, the supreme religious ruler of Iran, the Ayatollah Khomeini, is quite properly subject to a worldwide torrent of criticism for his outrageous order that author Salman Rushdie be murdered because he has written a book critical of the religion of Islam. Even many members of the faith were aghast at the Ayatollah's combined ruthlessness and foolishness in this instance. He has not bloodied his own hands but merely ordered that one individual be struck down for having committed what he considers blasphemy. If all this criticism is justified—and God knows it is—then why must we continue to regard as heroic leaders such as David when he ordered large numbers of captives, some of them civilians including innocent women and children, not only to be killed but also to be put to death in the most horrible of ways? (See also WAR.)

Chapter 21. This chapter opens with another inherently nonsensical tale in which we are told that *Satan* provoked David to take a census of Israel. Do today's Christian and Jews object, on moral or any other grounds, when they either serve as census-takers or give personal information to those who perform this social duty? Of course not. Why then are we to believe, on the basis of this absurd passage, that in commissioning the taking of a census of the people of Israel David committed an offense so grave that it is said to have been personally inspired by Satan? Yet we read:

> 7. And God was displeased with this thing; therefore he smote Israel.
> 8. And David said unto God, "I have sinned greatly, because I have done this thing: but now, I beseech thee, do away the iniquity of thy servant; for I have done very foolishly."

The story of the census and its aftermath is clearly typical of myth and not of history. After the offense, David and the Lord engage in a totally unintelligible conversation, considering that David's "cruel offense" has merely been to instruct his servants to take a count of his people. But if this makes little sense, we are nevertheless told that it made sense to God, who offers David his choice of three hideous punishments:

> 12. Either three years' famine; or three months to be destroyed before thy foes, while that the sword of thine enemies overtaketh thee; or else three days the sword of the Lord even the pestilence, in the land, and the angel of the Lord destroying throughout all the coasts of Israel. . . .

Oddly enough, according to the somewhat disorganized account in this chapter, David never actually gets around to making a choice. Therefore, the Lord takes matters into his own hands:

> 14. So the Lord sent pestilence upon Israel: and *there fell of Israel seventy thousand men.* (IA)

I suggest that the reader go back and study the preceding sentence. After reading endless stories of nonsense and atrocity, it is likely that one's sensibilities will have become dulled. In the present day there is great fear in the various nations because of the numbers of people who have died of AIDS over a period of several years. If the present reactions are justified, then what would be an appropriate emotional and moral response to God's quick, intentional killing of 70,000 men—no women, apparently— simply because the Israelite king had taken a census?

First of all, there is nothing whatever wrong in commissioning a census. But even if there were, it was David who ordered it. If there really is a God, and if from time to time he considers it necessary to punish individual offenders, then it would be reasonable, in this context, for him to have raised his hand against David himself. The killing of an enormous army of innocent bystanders is merely one more atrocity like those perpetrated by Attila the Hun, Joseph Stalin, Adolf Hitler, or Pol Pot.

Further on, we find an even more absurd message. The Deity was apparently not satisfied with the deaths of seventy thousand innocent Israelites.

> 15. And God sent an angel unto Jerusalem to destroy it: and as he was destroying, the Lord beheld, and *he repented him of the evil,* and said to the angel that destroyed, "It is enough, stay now thine hand." And the angel of the Lord stood by the threshingfloor of Ornan the Jebusite. (IA)

This passage is as insulting to an all-wise, all-loving Deity as anything ever written. Religious believers sometimes refer to atheists as those who "hate God." Such charges are unfounded. It is logically preposterous to assert that an atheist hates God; one can not possibly hate something that one personally believes does not exist. It is possible to argue, however, that the unknown authors of such horrendous passages of Scripture as these quoted had a great contempt for God. In instance after instance they attribute to him emotions and behavior that would be considered reprehensible in any human. God is described as constantly flying into violent fits of fury so extreme that he slaughters innocent human beings by the tens of thousands, as if they were insects. Then, we are told that in the midst of such slaughter and destruction God, like a remorseful alcoholic, suddenly realizes the evil and enormity of what he has done and repents. This part of the Scriptures, therefore, *clearly teaches that God can do evil.*

Now it is reasonable to use the word *repent* only in association with the concept of sin. But an all-good Deity—by definition—is incapable of sin. If a living entity is capable of sin, one may be quite certain that that entity is not the Supreme Creator of the universe. So no matter what standard is employed to analyze these passages, one comes face-to-face with the realization that either they are largely raving nonsense, or they are profoundly insulting to every decent believer's concept of a Supreme God. Therefore, if we are to retain our faith in God, we are absolutely bound, by both standards of common sense and MORALITY, contemptuously to reject this story, among many others so rejected in Scripture. (See also EVIL, THE PROBLEM OF.)

Chapter 22. Here we find more of the same silliness, except for a specially interesting verse that makes of the Lord God a hypocrite more despicable than any human ever guilty of that lamentable failing. King David has constructed an altar to the Almighty but not completed the building, apparently because God considers him unworthy. On what grounds?

> 8. "But the word of the Lord came to me saying, 'Thou hast shed blood abundantly, and hast made great wars: thou shalt not build an house unto my name, because thou hast shed much blood upon the earth in my sight.' "

This comes from the very God who for centuries has been not only encouraging the shedding of blood by the Jews but also shedding it himself in countless direct and unmistakable ways. He has specifically *commanded* David to slaughter the peoples of other tribes and nations by the thousands, and now one is expected to believe that all of this bloodshed has made *David* unworthy. The authors of these peculiar passages cannot have it both ways. They cannot on the one hand tell us that the Lord has ordered widespread slaughter, and then on the other ask us to believe that God blames David for having done nothing more than follow his own supreme orders. (See also BELIEFS AND MYTHS; CRIMES, BIBLICAL IMPETUS TO.)

CHRONICLES, THE SECOND BOOK OF THE. More nonsense and error is found as the Chronicles of history continue into a second book.

Chapter 9. There is an absolute falsehood in this chapter, where we read:

> 22. And king Solomon passed all the kings of the earth in riches and wisdom.
> 23. And all the kings of the earth sought the presence of Solomon, to hear his wisdom, that God had put in his heart.

The unknown author of these words had very close to no knowledge whatever about "all the kings of the earth." He thought that the earth was much smaller than we know it to be and knew nothing of distant continents, races, peoples, and their rulers. And it is combined error and impossibility for all the kings of earth to seek an audience with Solomon, of whom almost none of them had ever heard.

Chapter 10. Yet another error is introduced in the first verse of this chapter, which states that *all* Israel traveled to the city of Shechem to make Rehoboam king. There is no way of knowing how many Israelites made that particular journey, but we may be quite certain that nearby lands were not left denuded of human inhabitants in that connection.

Chapter 13. The military arithmetic provided in the first few verses of this chapter is nonsense. The Judean king Abijah, it is said, entered battle with an army of 400,000 mighty warriors. Jeroboam joined the battle against him with 800,000 picked troops. No living historian believes anything of the sort, nor should he.

In the ensuing confrontation, we are told, God personally defeats Jeroboam and all Israel!

> 17. And Abijah and his people slew them with a great slaughter: so there fell down slain of Israel *five hundred thousand chosen men.* (IA)

Chosen people indeed.

Chapter 14. Here additional nonsensical military arithmetic is encountered:

> 9. Zerah, the Ethiopian came up against them with an *army of a million and three hundred chariots.* . . . (IA)

Asa, the son of Abijah, had only an army of about half that size, but he easily resolves his problem by praying to God. The result:

> 12. Then the Lord struck down the Ethiopians before Asa and Judah so that the Ethiopians fled.

So God himself wiped out over a million blacks.

I am not aware that today's advocates of Black Studies programs—to which I take no exception—have concentrated their professional intentions on the story, which fundamentalist Christians still insist is a perfectly reliable historical record of one of the most incredible defeats in military annals.

Asa's forces might have considered themselves remarkably fortunate at that point, but additional absurdity is suggested in the following verse.

> 13. Asa, and the people with him, chased them as far as Gerar, and there fell so many of the Ethiopians that *none were left alive.* . . . (IA)

In other words, because of a prayer, plus a bit of energy expended in hot pursuit, *over one million Ethiopians were killed!* Can there at present be a fundamentalist, no matter how devout or fanatical, who seriously defends the accuracy of such accounts?

CHURCH AND STATE RELATIONS. Anyone with even a casual acquaintance with history will be aware that the traditional close connection of church and state down through the centuries brought relatively few benefits but numerous horrors and atrocities.

It is sadly true, as Amnesty International and other courageous organizations have pointed out, that we still have organized torture in our modern day. Almost all of it is perpetrated by the authority of states or by men convinced that they are acting in the best interest of states. Let the confessors of Christendom tell us, in unambiguous terms and without in any way violating the secrecy of the confessional, whether any of their flock who perpetrate such moral monstrosities ever actually mention them when they seek the comfort of the sacrament of penance.

But dreadful as the present situation is, the instantaneous global communication made possible by modern scientific technology has at least given us the power to shame the torturers publicly, to bring up such awkward subject matter at meetings of the United Nations, to appeal to the moral judgment of the human race, shaky as that may be. Nothing of the sort was possible during long centuries of European history because *the church, the highest societal authority of all, was not separated from the state— as is the American ideal—but firmly united with it.*

Certain modern Christians—Reconstructionists—who apparently have given up on the American system of law and justice, seek a return to the system in which the law of Christian nations is either dictated or strongly influenced by the views of churchmen.

Unfortunately, although it is painful for American Christians and Jews to admit, simple justice requires the inescapable concession that practically every component of the American political philosophy of which we rightly boast was achieved in spite of, not in conformity with, the Old Testament. One is perfectly free to argue that the essentials of the American political philosophy are harmful or foolish, but one may not simultaneously defend them and the combined moral instructions of the Old Testament. The two are logically mutually exclusive.

We in this country strongly disapprove of the idea of the union of church and state. We in the United States are free to be members of any church or members of no church. Therefore we would feel it just as incorrect for a government to be, for example, officially Catholic or Protestant as it would be for another government to be officially atheistic. Matters of religious belief are not the proper concern of governments.

While Americans tend to view the separation of church and state as the norm in the context of world history it is, in fact, very much the exception. Perhaps the union of church and state was a necessity in centuries long past when civil authority was generally unstable or unpopular and therefore required priestly endorsement to legitimatize it. As for the Jewish experience, it is difficult to see how social cohesiveness could have been maintained in the face of frequent adversity without appeal to scriptural authority. It does not matter whether God was truly the author of The Law or whether Moses and other early leaders simply told a pious lie to that effect, using as justification that men would be more likely to live by a moral code if they believed it had the support of divine authority.

To what extent is it necessary for informed Jews around the world today to believe in the divine inspiration of the ancient lawgivers? Many religious Jews would assert that faith in Judaism's traditional forms is required to maintain Jewish social cohesiveness. But to determine whether this is in fact the case, we should study instances in which individual Jews do not hold to the literal, simplistic faith of past ages but are nevertheless undeviating in their ethnic loyalties and support of the nation of Israel.

Let us arbitrarily assume that a statistical study of the question would show that 15 percent of today's Jews—whether or not they publicly voice such reservations—nevertheless take a generally agnostic position in regard to the traditional verities. If the millions who comprise that 15 percent are just as loyal to Jewish interests as their peers, then it will have been demonstrated that adherence to the age-old interpretations of Scripture is no longer necessary to Jewish survival.

The number of Jews converted to Christianity over the centuries has relevance to the question in that some of them say: "In becoming a Christian I did not become any less a Jew."

The New Testament makes things no more clear as regards the subject of church and state relations. Matthew, Mark, and Luke, far from stating a simple point as one would expect from either the Son of God or God himself, all relate a story that is—like many other passages of Scripture—so ambiguous as to have confounded Christian scholars over the centuries. Matthew 22:21, Mark 12:17, and Luke 20:25 all attribute to Jesus the quote:

> Render unto Caesar the things which are Caesar's and unto God the things which are God's.

If it was a relatively easy matter to determine precisely what are the things of Caesar and the things of God, this passage would have presented no difficulties in this regard over the centuries. Protestant clergyman and historian Paul Hutchinson stated the problem correctly and succinctly when he attested that this Scripture "settled nothing, for who is to say what is Caesar's and what is God's?" In other words, the statement is meaningless. This is not only a very reasonable concession but quite a startling one, given that most Christians believe that Jesus was God. In this context, Hutchinson is saying that a statement attributed to the very source of perfection and wisdom has little, if any, practical use.

Nor does the story offer any advice on what to *do* when things generally taken to be of God come into direct conflict with things commonly assumed to apply to Caesar, which is to say to civil government. Indeed, we are left none the wiser by the story. Ergo: If Jesus is God then the story must be false. (See also PIOUS FRAUD; ROMANS.)

COMMUNICATION. On the one hand we have the Bible, and on the other we have millions of commentaries about thousands of aspects of Scripture. The combined study and controversy about such phenomena will never end so long as human life persists, because what appears to be the simple process of communication itself is, in reality, puzzlingly complex.

The reader's acquisition of verbal information is not the unitary act he might have imagined but involves at least a four-stage process. For purposes of illustration, consider a simple physical reality: a yellow beach ball lying on a green pool table. That is the first stage of concrete reality. The second stage is our *perception* of that reality. The third stage involves our transmission of a verbal description of the reality, and the fourth stage is the hearer's reception of our message.

Even such simple raw material leaves more than enough room for error, but when we realize that the actual incidents, events, and experiences of our lives are vastly more complex than the simple case given, we begin to appreciate the inescapable difficulty of human communication. Even in the minority of instances in which the receiver correctly "understands" the message—which is to say knows the meanings of the separate words involved and does, in fact, perceive the general drift of the transmission— it is rare that any appreciable number of resonant implications of that message become apparent to him.

In the light of such considerations the enormous superiority of writing over speaking as a method of communicating complex messages becomes clear. A spoken message transmitted through a chain of, say, ten points, will be altered at each individual point. But it need not be so if the message has been written. Consequently, it is important to recognize that for centuries before any of the stories of the Old Testament were written down, they were handed down from generation to generation as part of an oral tradition. The reader is perfectly aware that if he attempts to relate on Tuesday an amusing story that he has heard on Monday, he will add certain details, which may be improvements, and will—usually unwittingly—neglect to include certain factors of the story as he heard it. Such changes take place not only as a result of conscious intentions but also at least as often because of the million-and-one unconscious components of our intellectual selves, including the pathetic weakness of the human memory.

Consequently we are indebted to the ancient Babylonians and others who independently developed the art of writing. To this day it is reasonably certain that in some far corner of the earth an archeologist's spade is bringing to light a long-lost scroll, papyrus, cuneiform tablet, or other document, the finding of which assures us of the reception of a message as it existed at some specific past point. If all history was still oral, no such happy discoveries could be made.

Another truth known to scholars but perceived by few others concerns words and their meanings. As children we acquire the impression that words have simple meanings and that we either intuitively know these, or, if the word is new to us, need only look it up in the dictionary. The truth is more complex. Most words have multiple meanings, and those are often fuzzy around the edges. Consider some of the simplest possible examples, common nouns such as *tree, bread, wood,* or *stone.* If there were only one sort of tree in the world, and if it emerged in an instant fully grown, we might then say that the word *tree* had a clear-cut meaning; however, there are countless thousands of kinds of trees.

Stone, bread, wood, and other such words also point not to specific objects but to classifications and categories of objects. My recognition of this occurred earlier than most, perhaps because of my lifelong involvement in the field of humor, much of which grows out of the ambiguity rather than the clarity of words. Therefore, when this simple realization affects our view of the enormously compressed library of separate volumes that is the Bible, and we consider how scholars have wrestled for long centuries with numerous passages of Scripture—many with meanings still elusive even after almost two thousand years of concentrated analysis—perhaps we can begin to give up the absurd notion that all one has to do to work through the difficult problems of life is read the Holy Book.

CONSERVATISM. The majority of those who interpret the Bible literally describe themselves, politically, as conservative. Many of them are properly so called. Middle-of-the-roaders and liberals may also be Christians or Jews but are more likely to be guided by the preponderant scholarly opinion on scriptural questions.

Given this background, it is instructive to consider the conservative mind-set generally. (See also LIBERALISM.)

Unlike Christianity, Marxism, or capitalism, which are definable philosophies characterized by certain beliefs, conservatism is not a philosophy: it is merely an attitude of mind. This is not necessarily a criticism, any more than it would be a criticism of a horse to point out that it is not an elephant. Conservatism, defined purely as such, is devoid of inherent philosophical content, but there are conservatives in every philosophical movement. There are communist conservatives, Jewish conservatives, Protestant conservatives, and other conservatives defined by their race, tribe, ethnic grouping, or nationality. Conservatives are simply those who wish either to maintain a status quo, if it largely pleases them, or to revert to an earlier state of opinion and practice if conditions in their immediate context disturb them. It is pointless to argue about the "essence" of conservatism since it is merely a matter of feeling; intelligent critical dialogue can take place only on specific issues.

It is unfair, however, to accuse conservatives of wishing to return to past beliefs and practices in toto. George Will, William F. Buckley, and Dan Quayle would certainly not argue that our society ought to return to, say, the practice of burning witches, pulling out the fingernails of heretics, or denying freedom of the press to our philosophical opponents. These esteemed gentlemen are actually quite liberal on some specifically defined questions, considering them in the long historical view.

Conservatives frequently delude themselves that they stand on bedrock principle in their opposition to government meddling in affairs that ought more properly be left in private hands. But so far as one may judge them from their actions, they apparently hold to no such belief. This, of course, leads to the question why they sincerely *believe* they respect the principle. The answer to the apparent mystery is simple enough. Conservatives want the government to take a hands-off position on a long list of particulars. For example, they want little or no government "meddling" in the marketplace, even if the motive for, and indeed the direct result of, such interference is the protection of the public health or aid to the poverty-stricken. But on certain other matters of profound public concern, conservatives not only are prepared to permit government to play a role, but they also demand that it do so as energetically and immediately as possible. They clearly want government involvement in the abortion controversy, for example. They also want government to establish the practice of prayers in public schools, to strengthen federal police and espionage agencies, to invade the privacy of political opponents, and to encourage the use of capital punishment. So much for the pure theory of strictly limited government.

No one denies that conservatives distrust change and novelty, even if the resulting new situation might be described as a decided improvement by all disinterested parties. Conservatives will still very likely resist change, simply because of its newness. It is difficult enough to keep track of things as they stand in this troublesome world, so any significant change is almost invariably viewed at the least as a bother, and at the greater extreme as a threat. This understandable human propensity for stasis fuels the engines of conservatism in all societies; they are not stoked by any inherent wisdom in ancient institutions and practices, some of which may be sound, and others not. Of course, the more important the subject matter—religion being a perfect example—the more vocal and sometimes violent the resistance to evolutionary change.

Some people profess to be puzzled by the venomous animosities that are stirred up by those religious controversies in which one participant in the exchange is considered guilty of heresy. Strangely, true believers are more cruel and spiteful to heretics than they are to pagans, even though the heretic may share 95 percent of the relevant religious assumptions while the unbeliever shares practically none. The explanation is that the individual now perceived as heretic was once a member of the same family, philosophically speaking, and is therefore viewed as a traitor to the true, righteous cause. A lifelong atheist, agnostic, or infidel, on the other hand, may be regarded simply as hopelessly misguided, or in the grip of invincible ignorance.

According to the testimony of the Christian Scriptures, Jesus taught that the proper response to anger is love, that the wealthy ought to sell all their belongings and share the proceeds with the poor, and that charity is the greatest of all the virtues. Sadly, few Christians behave as if they have even heard such edifying moral advice. If an atheist is pugnacious toward us, we Christians are more than prepared to respond in kind; but we have historically reserved our special fury for our fellow Christians, always taking care to leave a remainder of spite for the Jews. This historical and psychological background must be grasped by anyone undertaking to participate, even as a casual student, in any area of human controversy and certainly in the religious.

That great gentleman Cardinal Newman expressed the important idea that, far from being generally troubled by a lack of logic, men are actually frighteningly, relentlessly logical. Paraphrasing Newman, Pierre Charles, S.J., in his brilliant exposé of the notorious czarist, anti-Semitic forgery, *The Learned Elders of the Protocols of Zion,* says:

CONSERVATISM

> The disagreements which separate [men] are not at all derived from short-comings in reason. They have their origin in an inner zone much deeper than that in which judgments are formed, in what Newman calls "assumptions," that is, orientations at once confused and imperative: there man engages himself as a whole, with his desires and passions, his fears and furies, even his dreams and his resentments. Starting off from these orientations, logic works its way though everything, caring but rarely to adapt itself to reality, but making everything it meets serve the conclusions imposed in advance.

Newman and Charles are right in this. But applied reason can nevertheless be effective against a million-and-one forms of human error if it is used not as an isolated tool to support arguments for or against any proposition—in the way that lawyers and debaters use it—but rather within the context of *an enveloping, passionate determination to unearth and support truth.* This, of course, is not the method of lawyers but of scientists.

We would do well to remain ever mindful of Newman's warning, however. In a modest attempt to reason with American rightists *(Letter To A Conservative,* Doubleday & Company, Inc., 1965), I noted that to me political conservatives—particularly the more dedicated among them—actually seemed to be a different kind of people from liberals or political middle-of-the-roaders. They have something in common with communists, Nazis, and fascists, not similarities of specific political beliefs but rather resemblances of spirit, attitude, or approach to problems. We often consciously become conservatives—or for that matter affiliates of any other political camp—for reasons that are emotional and psychological and have nothing directly to do with economics or politics.

But does not such an ideal as respect for truth run the risk of cutting across lines of loyalty to nation, church, political party, employer, school? Yes—and there is some sad irony in the fact that it does. But if from time to time we feel obliged to place ourselves in opposition to the truth—as in war, for example—then, let us do so knowingly. This is, obviously, an exercise in relative morality, which all absolutists profess to abhor, though they practice it daily. If we are to commit such offenses against the divine ideal of truth then it should be done in an attitude of sad, even tragic cynicism rather than in the sort of mindless, fanatical certitude that, ever so willing to be convinced of the rightness of a cause, will so casually proceed from lies and distortions to cruel invective, infringements upon freedom, violence, and finally, to mass murder. How many hundreds of millions more will have to be slaughtered before this simple lesson is grasped?

Conservatives versus Reactionaries. It is difficult to determine what percentage of the American population consists of true conservatives. That the group constitutes a minority is clear enough, but precise statistics are hard to come by. The problem is further complicated because the majority of those who label themselves conservatives are, in reality, more properly described as reactionaries.

Since the word *reactionary* is an extension of the simpler verb *react*, it is easy to understand that this group, generally speaking, is responding—either fearfully or angrily—to proposals and programs advanced by middle-of-the-roaders or liberal, progressive forces. It will help to bring American reactionaries into sharper focus if, rather than trying to agree on precise definitions, we concentrate on actual opinions of most American rightists. A typical, modern American reactionary has, since the arbitrary date of 1950, held all or most of the following views:

1. The *internal* communist menace is inexpressibly dangerous, far worse than the external threat. The communists, in fact, may take over the entire nation at any moment or—at the latest—by 1995. The popularity of this particular opinion has greatly diminished since the Marxist collapse in Eastern Europe. The fear it expressed was never sensible and was characterized chiefly by its absurdity. It nevertheless rang clear and loud almost daily through rightist newspapers and periodicals during the last several decades. No apology has ever been proffered by those conservative and reactionary leaders who on this point for so long, so seriously, and so dangerously misled the American people.

2. The United Nations is communist-dominated, and we ought to get out of it.

3. We had better keep an eye on the Jews. We can never grant the Jews full equality, because, after all, they are the ones who killed Jesus.

4. The mental health movement is either a communist or Jewish plot—or probably both. Psychiatry is brainwashing.

5. Fluoridation of water is another communist or Jewish plot and a diabolical scheme to poison loyal Americans.

6. We must not only retain the death penalty, but also make prison sentences ever stiffer, else criminals will rule the streets and turn our cities into jungles.

7. The Negro was quite happy with his lot until the communists fomented the so-called "civil rights" trouble. The real problem with the Negro is his intellectual and moral inferiority to Anglo-Saxons and other Americans of northern European background.

8. President Eisenhower, Milton Eisenhower, John Foster Dulles, Dean Acheson, Chief Justice Warren, and other leading Americans of the 1950s and 1960s may have been communist agents, or not far from it. Warren should have been either hanged or impeached.

9. You cannot trust most intellectuals. They are generally fuzzy-minded *eggheads* or *pinkos*—if not worse.

10. There are too many Social Security programs, welfare benefits, and other devices for coddling the poor, most of whom are poor because they're too stupid or lazy to get out and make a living. The so-called War on Poverty was a harebrained scheme dreamed up by liberal bleeding hearts and do-gooders.

11. We ought to do away with the income tax altogether, or else change it drastically so that the industrious man won't be penalized by having to support shiftless members of minority groups.

12. Unions and the laboring classes generally have gotten much too powerful. Therefore, we should pass right-to-work laws so that a man can get a job in a unionized plant if he wants to, without having to join the union that forces helpless employers to provide "decent" working conditions and wages.

13. Foreign aid is *Operation Rathole*. It has not made foreign nations stronger, it has only made America weaker.

14. The biggest single group aiding the communist conspiracy in the United States is the Protestant clergy.

15. You can't even trust the Vatican any more because at best it's become left-liberal. Though Catholic priests were once all firmly anticommunist, now a certain percentage of the Roman clergy are either actual communists or communist sympathizers.

16. We do not have nearly enough nuclear weapons, and we should not hesitate for one moment to use the ones we do have if the enemy threatens us. If this brings about the end of civilization—so what? Nobody lives forever and the Bible *does* tell us the last days are close at hand.

17. Lee Harvey Oswald was not just a deranged Marxist acting on his own. The assassination of President Kennedy was a communist plot because Kennedy—secretly a communist himself—was falling behind in his assignment to deliver our nation into enemy hands.

18. Narcotic addicts are the scum of the earth and it is only another example of liberal mollycoddling to try to rehabilitate them. They should be thrown into jail, and for a long time. That's the only way to straighten them out. That many of them now suffer from AIDS is an example of God's rightful punishment of sinners.

19. It doesn't matter whether schools are substandard in some communities or not. Federal aid to education is not only unnecessary but is also actually a Machiavellian scheme on the part of Washington to get control of the minds of American youth.

20. This country is *not* a democracy. It is a republic and don't forget it. The idea of one-man-one-vote is mistaken and un-American.

21. The American peace movement has always consisted of 90 percent dupes led by 10 percent communists.

22. We could have easily defeated communism all over the world, including in Korea and Vietnam, if Presidents Roosevelt, Truman, Eisenhower, Kennedy, Johnson, and Nixon hadn't agreed on a no-win policy.

23. The move toward registration of firearms is another plot by the commies, pinkos, socialists, and liberals in Washington. If firearms are registered, when the communists take over the nation they'll know right where to go to pick up and shoot patriots. Every patriot should keep a hidden supply of firearms and explosives to protect himself against the day of reckoning.

24. Abortion, even of fetuses resulting from rape or incest, is murder. All murderers should be jailed or executed, and that's all there is to it.

25. The liberals are up to their old tricks in trying to increase federal funding to combat AIDS, another example of their tendency to coddle homosexuals. When God wants to stop the AIDS epidemic, he will. In the meantime AIDS is God's punishment of homosexuals for having willingly chosen a sinful life-style.

The list could be lengthened, but these twenty-five examples suffice to give the tone of reactionary thinking over the last few decades without exaggeration or distortion. Many of the phrases in the list are direct quotations from various organs of the far-right press. It is small wonder that high-minded conservative intellectuals have used such words as *lunacy, madness,* and *irresponsibility* to describe such political programs.

The reactionary is often identifiable by the alarming ferocity and hostility with which he writes, speaks, and acts. Interestingly enough, reactionaries themselves rarely deny this particular accusation. They respond by saying that in extreme circumstances extreme emotions are well justified.

The *methods* that characterize the far rightist also separate him from the true conservatives, most of whom would never dream of stooping to physical assaults, threatening phone calls, psychotic anonymous letters, and bullying tactics at meetings—actions that have served to draw so much attention to the far right over the years.

One last point must be pondered in this connection—almost all reactionaries are Bible-believing Christians. (See also FANATICISM; LIBERALISM; MORALITY.)

CONTRADICTIONS, BIBLICAL. One of the foundation stones of my study has been the self-evident fact that there is literally nothing perfect in human experience. The very abstract idea of perfection, in my view, properly applies only to God. If we move from the theoretical to the practical and consider the most dazzling instances of human achievement, it is immediately apparent that even the most striking examples of excellence cannot be spoken of as totally without fault.

It follows that the Bible, despite its assorted virtues, not only is not, but cannot be, an absolutely perfect collection of documents.

Unfortunately, some defenders of Scripture conduct themselves as if the ancient books were without fault. They do little actual honor to the Bible in defending it from so weak a position. By refusing to concede any imperfection whatever in the scriptural record as it is presently available to us, they render rational, fair-minded dialogue on the matter almost impossible. It is as if the question at issue concerns something so simple as, say, stains on a garment.

Let us assume that two individuals both view a garment believed to be a relic with profound religious significance and attempt to engage in meaningful discourse about the matter. Let us also assume, for purposes of illustration, that one of the individuals involved is literally unable to *see* certain stains, despite the fact that they are obvious not only to the other person but also to all disinterested passersby.

To the fundamentalist observer, the many hundreds of contradictions and discrepancies in the pages of Scripture are equally unseen.

The word *contradiction* in the context of this work does *not* refer to the common understanding of the word's meaning—that is, the countermanding of orders such as when a parent snaps "Don't contradict me" to a child who presents a differing version of facts or suggests a revision of plans. Rather, *contradiction* here means two separate, conflicting statements about the same matter, at least one of which must be incorrect. If, for example, I assert that President Bush never wears anything but dark-blue suits and someone else asserts that he personally has seen Bush wear a gray suit on various occasions, it is obvious that both statements cannot be true. It is theoretically possible that both are untrue, but no more than one can be correct.

Now, although the faithful would naturally prefer that the Scriptures be internally consistent, every Christian and Jewish theologian is perfectly aware that they are not. Even if they were consistent, that fact in itself would establish nothing; the reader himself may at this moment create a totally false story that is nevertheless consistent within the boundaries of its own terms. Therefore, when someone flatly asserts "Every word of the Bible is true," the rest of us must realize that such a statement is inconsistent with the truth that there are numerous contradictions in the Scriptures as obvious and inescapable as the Bush blue-suit/gray-suit example given above. It is interesting that even a small child has no difficulty in perceiving such inconsistencies when they concern matters with which he is familiar; yet some learned churchmen have difficulty grasping them when they concern matters biblical.

What follows are just a few instances of biblical contradictions, with italics added to stress the discrepancies.

1. Man was made *before* the beasts and *after* the beasts.

Gen. 1:25–26. And God made the beast of the earth after his kind, and cattle after their kind, and every thing that creepeth upon the earth after his kind: and God saw that it was good. And God said, "Let us make man in our image, after our likeness. . . ."

Gen. 2:18–20. And the Lord God said, "It is not good that the man should be alone; I will make him an help meet for him." And out of the ground the Lord God formed every beast of the field, and every fowl of the air; and brought them unto Adam . . . .

2. Adam was to die on the *day he ate of the tree of knowledge,* but he *lived to the age of 930.*

Gen. 2:17. But of the tree of knowledge of good and evil, thou shalt not eat of it: for in the day that thou eateth thereof thou shalt surely die.

Gen. 3:6; 5:5. And when the woman saw that the tree was good for food . . . she took of the fruit thereof, and did eat, and gave also unto her husband with her; and he did eat. . . . And all the days that Adam lived were nine hundred and thirty years: and he died.

3. Noah was ordered to take *two* of each beast in the ark, but also *seven.*

Gen. 6:19. And of every living thing of all flesh, two of every sort shalt thou bring into the ark, to keep them alive with thee; they shall be male and female.

Gen. 7:2, 8.9. Of every clean beast thou shalt take to thee by sevens, the male and his female: and of beasts that are not clean by two, the male and his female. . . . Of clean beasts and of beasts that are not clean, and

61

of fowl . . . There went in two and two unto Noah into the ark, the male and the female, as God had commanded Noah.

4. God promises Abraham and his children *everything,* and gives them *nothing.*

Gen. 17:8. And I will give unto thee, and to thy seed after thee, the land wherein thou art a stranger, all the land of Canaan, for an everlasting possession;

Heb. 8–13. By faith Abraham, when he was called to go out into a place which he should after receive for inheritance, obeyed: and he went out . . . also Sara herself received strength to conceive seed and was delivered of a child. . . . Therefore sprang there . . . so many as the stars in the sky in multitude. . . . These all died in faith, not having received the promises, but having seen them afar off. . . .

5. Aaron died on *Mount Hor,* and he also died in *Mosera.*

Num. 33:39. And Aaron was an hundred and twenty and three years old when he died in mount Hor.

Deut. 10:6. And the children of Israel took their journey from Beeroth of the children of Jaakan to Mosera: there Aaron died, and there he was buried;

6. The Lord commanded followers *not* to kill and *to* kill.

Exod. 20:13. Thou shalt not kill.

Exod. 32:27. Thus saith the Lord God of Israel, "Put every man his sword by his side, and go in and out from gate to gate throughout the camp, and slay every man his brother, and every man his companion, and every man his neighbor."

Other examples:

1 Chron. 21:1. And *Satan* stood up against Israel and provoked David to number Israel.	2 Sam. 24:1. And again the anger of the *Lord* was kindled against Israel, and he moved David against them to say, Go, number Israel and Judah.
Acts 13:34. And as concerning that he raised him up from the dead, now no more to return to corruption, he said on this wise, "I will give you the sure *mercies of David.*"	1 Chron. 20:3. And he brought out the people that were in it, and cut them with saws, and with harrows of iron, and with axes. *Even so dealt David* with all the cities of the children of Ammon.
2 Sam. 6:23. Therefore Michal the daughter of Saul *had no children* unto the day of her death.	2 Sam. 21:8. . . . and the *five sons* of Michal the daughter of Saul, whom she brought up for Adriel . . .
Acts 10:36. The word which God sent unto the children of Israel, preaching *peace* by Jesus Christ.	Matt. 10:34. Think not that I am come to send peace on earth: I came *not to send peace,* but a sword.
Luke 14:26. If any man come to me, and *hate not* his father, and mother, and wife, and children, and brethren, and sisters, yea, and his own life also, *he cannot be my disciple.*	1 John 3:15. Whosoever *hateth his brother is a murderer:* and ye know that no murderer hath eternal life abiding in him.
Matt. 5:17. *Think not that I am come to destroy the law,* or the prophets: I am not come to destroy, but to fulfil.	2 Eph. 2:15. Having *abolished* in his flesh the enmity, *even the law of commandments . . .*

If Peter's reference to Joel's prophecy in Acts is compared with the actual prophecy found in JOEL 2:28–32, contradictions are encountered immediately. Peter, for example, quotes Joel as having said, "and it shall come to pass *in the last days,*" whereas in the Old Testament the equivalent phrase is rendered "and it shall come to pass afterward." Many possible explanations can account for this discrepancy.

One is that Peter's memory was faulty and that he was having about the same degree of success remembering a specific prophecy that the average scholar might have if attempting to call to mind relevant text while speaking extemporaneously about it. Peter was indeed far from being a scholar, although it might be alleged that, in this instance, his memory received the benefit of divine inspiration. But this can hardly be the case if, as we have seen, his quotation of the relevant portion of Joel is faulty.

Another possible explanation is that the text of Joel is in error; however, the devout cannot accept this alternative either, since it means that the Bible is by no means error-free.

Another possibility is that Peter himself is not responsible for the discrepancies, but that those who translated the texts into today's languages and who authorized the translations as divinely inspired are to blame for them.

Any unbiased scholar who carefully studies the two texts side-by-side can not avoid concluding that, if accurately quoted, Peter was guilty of doctrinal error in this instance, despite whatever other triumphs, virtues, or accomplishments he might have had. He is, of course, revered by Catholics as the first pope, the one to whom Catholics believe Christ gave the keys to his kingdom on earth. It is unassailable dogmatic theology that a pope can utter no error when he addresses the faithful on a matter of either morality or belief; yet here, in one of Peter's first and most profoundly important official pronouncements, he does appear to be in error.

Additional examples are unnecessary; a single pair of mutually contradictory statements would have sufficed to establish the point. But it is necessary to emphasize, for the benefit of those impressed by quantity, that the instances given comprise a very small percentage of the total available. A number of rationalist studies may be consulted for further edification, including *The Bible Handbook for Free-Thinkers and Inquiring Christians,* edited by G. W. Foote and W. P. Ball (Pioneer Press, London).

Add to these specific examples of biblical discrepancies the historical contradiction of the Bible's significance. Christian martyrs over the centuries have derived comfort from the Bible while being consumed by flames. Unfortunately, this inspiring picture is clouded by the fact that their persecutors and murderers were often every bit as dependent upon the Bible as were their victims.

The fundamentalist stance, when confronted with these incongruities, is that they are only *apparent,* not real. Their case is constructed according to a now time-honored formula.

In the first step of the argument, it is said that an all-good God cannot possibly be guilty of the negative behavior attributed to him, an argument that is perfectly reasonable once the premise of a morally pure Deity is accepted. The difficulty comes, of course, in the attempt to explain away the other, opposite assertions so common in Scripture. At this point the defender's argument becomes embarrassing, absurd, illogical, or dishonest.

In a particular instance, the author, who is arguing for the unchanging nature of God, says, "These are absolute and unconditional affirmations which Scripture everywhere teaches." The gentleman has absolutely no justification for using the word *everywhere* since it obviously does not accord with the numerous portions of Scripture that state in the plainest possible language that God *has* changed his mind.

Part of the difficulty here stems from a belief common to almost all forms of religion—that God knows all things. At first glance this simple affirmation of omniscience seems inevitable because of the prior belief that God is all-powerful. Clearly, if he could *not* foresee the future then we could not possibly continue to argue that he is, in fact, possessed of *all* power. But there need be no what-might-have-been speculation on this narrow point since, as we know, almost all religions are consistent in arguing that God can do all things and knows all things. But as soon as we believe that God can know the future, in the same simple way that his human creatures can know a good deal of the past, there is no avoiding the awareness that it is totally impossible for him to be surprised by anything whatever. After all, surprise can result only from lack of knowledge.

If I tell you that tomorrow morning at 9 o'clock I'm going to hand you a $100 bill, and if you have known me long enough to be aware that my word is my bond, then you would never say that you were surprised by your good fortune when it finally occurred. What would surprise you in such a context would be my failure to deliver on my promise. But surprises—the occurrence of unexpected events—force us, quite reasonably, to change our minds. If we think that a given river cannot possibly rise, we will take no precautions against its doing so. However, if we are surprised by subsequent events and the river does overflow its banks, then we revise our thinking on the matter. We change our minds.

These few steps in reasoning are so elementary that they may occur to anyone or, at the very least, be easily grasped when explained.

Through all of this the reader ought constantly to keep in mind that what is at issue is not the nature or competence of God but the inaccuracy of certain scriptural references to him. (See also BELIEFS AND MYTHS; EDUCATIVE PROCESS, THE; ERROR; PIOUS FRAUD; VERSIONS OF THE BIBLE.)

CORPORAL PUNISHMENT. Let us briefly consider that most appealing of creatures, the human infant. For a combination of evolutionary, genetic, and socially conditioned reasons, normal adults almost invariably smile at even the casual contemplation of a very young child. Complimentary comparisons involving words such as *angel, dolls, puppies,* and *kittens* come to mind, and everywhere the same adjectives are used: *cute, adorable, beautiful, sweet, precious.* It does not particularly matter to what race the infant belongs—black children, Orientals, Native Americans, Caucasian—all babies are considered appealing.

Having agreed upon what is so self-evident, let us now envision a scene that is disturbing because we know it is all too often a reality: an adult savagely assaults a helpless infant, either beating him or her mercilessly with fists or a club, or else attacking with a knife, gun, or even more gruesome weapon. Is there any crime more revolting to the moral sense, any offense so horrifying that even the mere abstract consideration of it causes the facial muscles to wince and the very soul to shudder?

Now, perhaps for the first time the reader will perceive the sadistic horror of the endless Old Testament accounts that not only described such depraved crimes, which would be distressing enough, but—far worse—also recount them with not the slightest sense of shame or outrage but rather as moral acts justified because they are said to have been literally commanded by God!

We need waste no time wondering whether such an accusation against the Deity could be justified. Of course it cannot. If God exists and if he is by definition the essence and embodiment of all virtue, then we may be quite certain that he does not order the commission of atrocities that in another breath he absolutely forbids. The proper object of our contempt, it therefore follows, is not the Deity but either the fools who attributed such viciousness to him in their allegedly holy writings or the members of ancient tribes who apparently did indeed commit such crimes without feeling the slightest guilt as a result.

Although decent Christian and Jewish parents deliberately avoid physically assaulting their children, many still engage in the form of corporal punishment referred to as *spanking.* The verb *spank* has always seemed to have a rather playful sound that tends to obscure its true meaning. To spank is to beat. One may spank or beat lightly or violently but the basic act is the same. It usually involves hitting a quite small child. If certain sensitive, loving, and religious parents deliberately choose not to subject their sons and daughters to corporal punishment, it could hardly be because of their reliance upon Scripture. In Proverbs chapter 23 we read:

13. Withhold not correction from the child: for if thou beatest him with the rod, he shall not die.

14. Thou *shalt beat him with the rod, and shalt deliver his soul from hell.* (IA)

Never mind that the verse's basic assertion is so groundless as to merit the adjective *stupid* legitimately. My point here is simply that the Bible not only does not forbid the beating of children, but it also absolutely commands it. Repeated present-day studies have shown a direct correlation between the amount of physical abuse to which children are subjected and their own sadistically cruel behavior as adults. This pattern can be seen in the childhood histories of thousands of murderers. Obviously, the degree of violence is important. Most parents have given their offspring an occasional swat, but that is not at all what the unknown author of this passage of Scripture recommends. Nevertheless, the many modern parents who do not beat their infants at all provide another example of the generally civilizing influence of those modernist, humanist philosophies that have had such beneficial effects during the past few centuries. (See also LEVITICUS.)

CRIMES, BIBLICAL IMPETUS TO. Thomas Paine said of the sordidness and bloodthirstiness of a large part of the Old Testament:

Whenever we read the obscene stories, the voluptuous debaucheries, the cruel and tortuous executions, the unrelenting vindictiveness with which more than half the Bible is filled it would be more consistent that we called it the word of a demon than the word of God.

No Christian or Jewish theologian in the world would dream of denying that the Bible has been directly responsible for a dismayingly long series of individual crimes and large social disruptions over a period of many centuries. Naturally no one alleges that the Bible bears full responsibility in such cases, since a book lying on a table or library shelf cannot cause harm—or good— by itself; the destructive action is subsequently performed by humans who are exposed to the ideas in the book, whatever the volume might be. When we say that the Bible is responsible for individual crimes and atrocities, we refer to the fact that human beings in great numbers have committed various serious offenses while believing that their conduct was not only justified but also absolutely required by the Bible. No intelligent person denies this. However, the fact needs to be brought to the attention of those who are not well informed about the historical record or even the events of their own times.

67

Let the reader put the following question to any religious believer: What would you think of a man who instructed his followers to attack a particular village, to kill not just its able-bodied male defenders but to slaughter, without mercy, every aged person, woman, cripple, child; every blind or retarded individual; every babe in arms, after which the village, dead bodies and all, is to be put to the torch?

The answer would be immediate: Whoever issues such orders is either deranged or a sadistic murderer.

Then direct to the same believers the question: But what will you say when you are told that the leader who again and again issued precisely such orders is—at least according to the Old Testament—the Lord God himself?

Now the answers show more variety. An unknown number of individuals has responded by simply abandoning their former faith. Others have considered the question and have retained their firm faith in God but abandoned their unquestioning trust in the Old Testament.

Not only did the allegedly religious literature of the ancient Jews attribute such revolting behavior to Yahweh, their God, but the civilizations with which they came into contact also seemed to have an equally savage and primitive conception of the Deity. King Mesa of Moab, who lived in the ninth century B.C. boasts that he captured the city of Ataroth and "killed all the people in the city, a sight pleasing to Kamosh" (his god), and also slaughtered all the inhabitants of Nebo, who numbered seven thousand, as a result of his having dedicated the community to Kamosh. The Assyrian rulers, as well, not only committed atrocities but apparently as a guilt-relieving device also attributed their despicable acts to nothing more than having followed the commandments of God, as they perceived him.

Can Christian and Jewish scholars who are aware of these facts draw the obvious conclusion that it is either nonsense or blasphemy to credit atrocities to the personal commands of God? Some cannot because if they did they could no longer maintain that the Bible was divinely inspired. They resort, therefore, to devices of argumentation that are not only unconvincing but are also, sad to say, devious. Even the distinguished Catholic theologian Jean Levie, for example, "explains" the unexplainable by saying, "It is a type of 'literary form' to attribute such acts to Yahweh."

Even if we assume that there is such a literary form, one must say that the form is tantamount to the common promulgation of lies—lies said to be sanctioned by God himself, given his habit of rewarding some of his worshippers. Where this leaves the concept of divine inspiration is a fair question. People who have already accepted the view that the Old

Testament God is the worst murderer who ever lived will not be troubled at also having to attribute to him the reputation of Father of Lies.

Certainly the least edifying and indeed the most morally objectionable argument in all of Father Levie's otherwise generally reasonable and well-ordered case is found in *The Bible, Word of God in Words of Men:*

> The religious idea which inspired the interdict was, in principle, a just one. Israel's duty to remain faithful to Yahweh and to his covenant demanded that the nation should abstain from all idolatrous worship, that the people should avoid all danger of religious contamination. (p. 235)

Incredible! All of the Old Testament slaughters, more savage by far than even the most depraved atrocities committed by rightist and leftist political fanatics in our own century, are somehow not so bad after all because the rationale behind all the stabbing, the chopping off of heads, the strangling, the beating, the burning, the raping is that it was at least an effective way of preventing the "religious contamination" of the slaughterers!

Nature itself provides quite enough bloodletting to satisfy the most sadistic tastes. Thousands of species of animals sustain themselves by eating less powerful creatures, usually alive. Such natural disasters as forest fires, lightning storms, floods, earthquakes, hurricanes, tornadoes, avalanches, famines, plagues, epidemics, and droughts result in more than enough human suffering, not to mention the concomitant death of millions of animal creatures.

In the context of this massive, endless process of slaughter, which goes on night and day in every corner of the planet, man is certainly not required to add to such an enormous ocean of suffering by a conscious act of will. Whenever, therefore, I encounter published or preached rationalizations or alleged justifications for killing, whether of great numbers or of lone individuals, I am not disposed to admire the preacher, publisher, or justifier.

Of course, some will agree with my argument but make the one qualification that our sympathy need not apply to those victims who have themselves committed vicious and violent crimes. But even if the validity of such an exception is granted, the concession has no relevance to the great majority of mass atrocities referred to in the Old Testament. In many cases the victims were guilty of nothing other than defending their homes against military attack.

Whether God did in fact promise the land of Canaan (subsequently Palestine) to the invading Israelite tribes thousands of years ago there is now no way of ascertaining. One can only observe that the overwhelming majority of the world's peoples and scholars do not perceive the thesis as legitimate in the slightest. Even if we grant the point for purposes of argument, the news would still have fallen very strangely upon the ears of those whose homelands were invaded. The pre-Hebrew inhabitants of that land that is called holy—although it has seen far more unholiness than its opposite—were in all likelihood neither better nor worse than humankind generally, or the Israelites. If their conduct left a great deal to be desired, then the question might profitably be taken up with the Divine One who, it is alleged, created them. That he had it within his power to create hundreds of thousands of more peaceable species is clear either from the evidence of the definition of godliness itself or from the testimony of our senses that reveals the existence of such species all about us.

Any unbiased student who encounters the annals of a primitive society in which it is stated that ruler after ruler was knifed to death, frequently by a member of his own family or tribe; in which it is related that the tribe customarily not only slaughtered its enemies to the last man but also sought out innocent women, children, and babes in arms and hacked them to pieces as well; in which it is revealed that prisoners of war were commonly tortured, terrorized, and murdered could not possibly avoid concluding that the tribe in question consisted very largely of bloody savages.

It would be totally irrelevant that in addition to their being depraved murderers, rare individual members of such a group might have certain claims to distinction or virtue. In any of history's courts of law it is certainly not counted as intelligible defense that a murderer is also a competent craftsman, a priest, a musician, a poet, or a political officeholder. The decisive moral factor is always the crime itself. Certain instances may have mitigating circumstances. If, for example, a killer is incited to fury by long-continued abuse or to irrational anger by sexual jealousy, judges or jury members might take such factors into account in passing sentence. But the fact that the killers were members of particular professions, races, or religions would be properly perceived as having no relevance whatsoever, except perhaps to classify them as hypocrites.

It cannot possibly be interpreted as a criticism of today's Jews to assert that their remote ancestors—like everyone else's—were bloodthirsty brutes. However, what is totally unacceptable, by any reasonable standard of judgment, is that such ancient societies of mass murderers should be regarded by modern man as worthy of the highest moral respect.

Such esteem would be understandable, perhaps, if it were asserted that those deserving of veneration were a small remnant distinguished for their piety and spirituality, but this is by no means the case made for the Old

Testament by its Christian, Jewish, and Muslim apologists. The murders and mass slaughters are not alleged to have been perpetrated by a psychopathic minority, nor by an unruly majority acting against the peaceable, gentle admonitions of their would-be leaders. It is precisely the leaders themselves, the great kings and chieftains, who authorized the abominable atrocities not excelled for viciousness by any crimes of Nazis, Stalinists, or other tyrant mobs of the present century.

It would be erroneous to assume that the hundreds of instances of bloodthirstiness and savagery in the Old Testament suggest that the pre-Christian Jews and Israelites were in any sense unique in their degree of bellicosity. They were merely of average human viciousness, although how this can be consistent with the hypothesis of superiority growing from divine election is not readily clear.

The ancient Hebrews seem neither more nor less violent than their contemporaries. But the Christians—whose religion is based on the essential ideals of love-for-enemies, turning the other cheek, meekness, humility, and the like—have proved to equal the savagery of the ancient Hebrews. Writing of just one period of European history, that of the Wars of Religion, Egon Friedell, in his wide-ranging *A Cultural History of the Modern Age* (Knopf) observes:

> If Christianity and war are in any case an irresolvable contradiction, the most grotesque climax of this fearful paradox, which has defiled the whole history of Christianity, was attained in the deceitfulness, cruelty, and insolence towards all laws of God and man, such as was never surpassed by Tartars and Turks, Huns and Hottentots. For in these it is only a blind passion for destruction, but in the Christian of the Counter-Reformation Age it is a complex system built on a basis of high intellectual refinement and a perfected technique of villainy. For three generations the most highly developed and civilized countries of Europe vied with each other in inhumanity and wallowed in a merciless passion for vengeance, a tricky viciousness, and every devilish instinct that the Savior had taken up his cross to destroy.
>
> . . . Everywhere—in Spain, Italy, France, England, Scotland—we come upon masterpieces of callous villainy at the head of public affairs, unfeeling mass-murderers, having the ferocity of primitive man, but having also an icy calculating power, and thus deeper far in vileness than he. . . . The split in the Church had, on the whole, produced only negative results; it had merely shaken the faith in the authority of the divine canons, while as yet only a few enlightened minds saw glimmerings of a new *ethic, founded on secular considerations of reason and fitness,* which might take the place of the medieval.

> It is only with the Religious Peace of Augsburg, in 1555, which is quite unworthy of its title, that religious fanaticism let loose its destructive forces in full blast in both camps. (IA)

Any list of social atrocities for which the Bible is in part responsible must certainly include the destruction of the magnificent library at Alexandria by Christian zealots in A.D. 389. Since the Bible was considered morally correct, it therefore followed that any texts—however ancient, however revered—that contradicted it had to be wrong. It seemed self-evident to those watchdogs of dogma that anything wrong deserved to be destroyed or extinguished. As a result of such narrow-minded intellectual depravity, mankind—including everyone alive today and everyone who ever will live in the future—was deprived of untold thousands of important documents in their original texts.

Indeed it is likely that biblical texts themselves were among those destroyed since the vandals involved made no pretense of inventorying the works available and then specifically destroying only those that they found objectionable.

The Bible itself makes clear that formal affiliation with a religion is no guarantor whatever of moral behavior. Authors of Scripture inveigh against the sinfulness of the faithful on page after page. The chief criticism of those of other tribes—and consequently other religions—is that they have not recognized Yahweh as the true God. But it would be both illogical and unfair to argue that religious belief *causes* criminal or immoral behavior: to prove the case in one direction or another we would have to turn back the universal clock to a given period of time and permit the members of a control test-group to live in the second instance without religious affiliation if they had had it in the first, or vice versa. Perhaps a sample thousand criminals would have behaved in an even worse fashion if they had not been Catholics, Baptists, Mormons, or whatever. Although the argument has been made that religious affiliation may in fact cause rather than prevent antisocial behavior, it is unconvincing.

The Bible is clearly responsible in large measure for an instance of social disruption. The puzzling nationwide movement first attracted attention in the 1960s and then grew to much larger proportions in the next decade as thousands of young people converted to new religions of a generally bizarre sort. The right-wing Unification Church, the Children of God, Hare Krishna, and dozens of other sects are clearly part of the phenomenon. This trend (discussed in my book *Beloved Son: A Story of the Jesus Cults,* Bobbs-Merrill), though hardly unprecedented in the history of religion, is viewed as disturbing by most observers. The most striking common factor within the movement is the apparently *instantaneous* nature of the conversion experience. Reports of such cases all describe instances in which a young person who might previously have been a Catholic, Protestant, Jew, or atheist suddenly—in one morning or afternoon—decides to attach himself to a new social entity. Conversions—the moving from one philosophical camp to another—have probably been a part of human experience for its entire course, but generally an individual's conversion extends over a considerable period of time. Gentle or heavy social pressures might be involved, but conversions are usually accompanied by a long period of study, reflection, and weighing the decision. Only when the initiate is confident of the rightness of his decision is the commitment to the new philosophy made. This traditional process bears practically no resemblance to the conversion to cult groups. Indeed, the instantaneousness of the latter process resembles that of hypnosis far more than the normal, slow combination of philosophical study and mind-changing.

Practically all the new sects have one factor in common; specific aspects of their beliefs and practice are quite properly described as bizarre. Words such as *strange, weird, crazy, mysterious* occur again and again in the reports of family members, friends, and associates of those who join the new groups. They even emerge in reports by relatively impartial observers.

Brainwashing, too, is common, although it is generally employed by relatives of those who undergo the sudden conversions. It seems strange that so many different spiritual leaders—real or alleged—should simultaneously discover techniques that no professional psychologist seems able to employ or indeed even knows much about in an authoritative sense.

The precedent of the brainwashing of political prisoners in recent wars provides an analogy of doubtful validity. Such changes of mind that occurred in the statistically few cases of prisoners who renounced their former views and joined the enemy's camp resulted from a sometimes years-long combination of sensory deprivation, physical abuse, terrorization, and unremitting political indoctrination. It is therefore difficult to see what this sort of precedent has to do with instances in which the conversion seems to take place in just a few minutes or hours and in which there is no physical abuse, no terrorization, or any of the common forms of intimidation.

Some parents, understandably shocked and saddened by the experience of having sons and daughters turn away from them, point to the use of drugs as a possible explanatory agent, but the more one explores this possibility the less valid the theory seems. Sadly, millions of young Americans now use drugs of various sorts but, statistically, very few of these cases result in religious conversion.

The entire cult phenomenon might be more meaningfully examined in the larger context of the peculiar sort of social manias that have swept over large populations from time to time over the centuries. Some years ago an important book called *Popular Delusions and the Madness of Crowds* dealt with just such phenomena. To consider the facts of such cases, of course, is not the same as explaining them, but it might nevertheless be instructive to study the many earlier instances in which large numbers of people have suddenly fallen victim to the same delusion or mania.

Perhaps the puzzle is really a matter of untangling not just one, but numerous explanatory factors that only in the aggregate will explain the mystery. Humans may possess a genetically inherent tendency to commit their loyalty fervently to some social entity greater than themselves, originally a biological mutation that encouraged the herding or tribal instinct. Some may express this as patriotism; others, as religious fanaticism; a third group may feel almost maniacal admiration for a popular entertainer.

The power of words may defend almost any proposition, even the most depraved and absurd. This is not to say that every proposition can be argued irrefutably, but merely that some sort of defense can be erected for even the shabbiest of cases. We see this demonstrated, for example, in our courts of law where there is no Mafia murderer so obviously guilty, no criminal so clearly the perpetrator of a heinous atrocity that there will not be a defense attorney who will employ the combined arts of logic, rhetoric, and debate to defend the wretch.

Defenses have been constructed for every conceivable sort of position in the policies of politics and religion. Indeed we even boast of the freedom that permits the continuance of such debate, as well we might, granting the brief and fragmentary history of freedom in human experience. This places the individual under a fearful and burdensome obligation: to struggle, every day of this life, toward the dim light of truth at the end of the dark and lush forest of error.

Even the most sincerely devout Christians today totally ignore a plainly worded admonition from Jesus that if an individual's right hand "offends" him he ought literally to cut it off (Matt. 5:30). There is no available evidence, after almost two thousand years of the sincere practice of Christianity, that any believer has followed this specific advice.

Even on its own merits the order has internal problems. It is not totally clear how a person's hand can offend him. Hands do not have wills of their own, nor, for that matter, does any other part of the human body, though it sometimes seems that the genitals make certain demands that are not in harmony with the general thrust of an individual's will. In any event, there are no recorded instances of Christian hand-amputation. There have been a few mental cases, over the centuries who, apparently having despaired of controlling their behavior by more conventional means, have surgically removed their own penises, only to discover that thereafter their sexual desires, since they do not originate in the male member, are as troubling and unruly as ever. It is perhaps instructive to know that the only devout believers in the present world who heartily endorse hand-chopping are Muslims, who are interested only in removing the hands of others and would be guilty of no behavior so self-destructive as that said to be recommended by the good Lord in this instance.

Yet another crime for which the New Testament, if not the Old, has been responsible has been the shameful and frequently atrocious persecution of the Jews over the centuries. Nazi Germany's "solution to the Jewish problem" was one of the supreme atrocities in history, although it merely repeated a form of persecution that had flourished for centuries under Christian auspices. One declines to call it the worst crime in history only because the record of human progress has been so spattered by the blood of large-scale massacres that it is not possible to say which of the tragic crimes has been the most shocking. But no philosophical view, no matter how negative and harmful, cannot be defended in some way. Even the sickening record of the Holocaust might be defended by a Nazi as follows:

> First of all there are authorities who believe that the figure of six million deaths is a gross exaggeration. This is a figure provided by the Jews themselves, who it can hardly be argued are disinterested or unbiased. That a certain number of deaths occurred no one will seriously deny. After all, in the larger context of World War II some forty million were killed, a very considerable portion of them, be it remembered, Germans.
>
> Secondly, much anti-German propaganda has carried the implication that the executed Jews were innocents guilty of no crimes whatsoever. If the figure of those executed were six million, who could possibly suggest that among so many people no criminals were included? But the fact is that a good many of the Jews were guilty of crimes against the German state and the German people.
>
> Thirdly, it must be remembered that in the 1930s Germany suffered in the grip of fearful financial and social depression. The Germans had been defeated and betrayed in World War I and had by no means fully recovered. The experiment of the Republic had proved only the weakness of those who believed they could solve the problems of the German people by such ineffectual liberal means. Meanwhile, however, the Jews in the main were not suffering the same deprivation. Many, because of their well-known gifts for the management of financial affairs, were well-to-

> do merchants, bankers, capitalists, money lenders, shopkeepers, doctors, lawyers, and other professionals. How can it possibly be argued that the Jews should live as a privileged caste when ordinary Germans suffered? This was an intolerable state of affairs, particularly when some of it had been achieved by trickery and dishonest business practices.

Enough. This sickening and deceitful argument does not justify the death of a single European Jew, but it again proves the point: practically any position at all can be defended. Consequently, defenders of one version of the faith or another ought not to be unduly impressed by the simple *existence* of a philosophical bulwark for their positions. (See also ARGUMENT.)

Of the hundreds of millions of Christians living at present, many assume that the uglier pages of history represent unfortunate mistakes of the past that have little to do with the present world, Christian or otherwise. Would that it were so. Much of the unrest today, especially in the Third World, is the miserable legacy of the period of imperialism and colonialism. We are now paying a terrible price for the crimes committed by the European powers of a few centuries ago; few seem to recall that they were Christian powers.

Not many Americans need to be told that a large part of the tension between blacks and whites in our country flowed directly out of the long and disgraceful period of slavery, which was, of course, a subchapter of the history of imperialism. Here again the chief perpetuators of slavery were white Christians, even the most knowledgeable of whom easily assuaged their guilt by referring to how casually the Scriptures tolerate slavery, one of the worst crimes in the human record.

These thoughts came to mind a few years ago when I happened to see two motion pictures of excellent quality: *Mississippi Burning* and *Dangerous Liaisons*. The former, as the reader may know, is a horrifying drama based on events that occurred during the 1960s in the state of Mississippi, but it could easily have taken place in many other parts of the South. To judge by the current wave of right-wing fanaticism made painfully evident by the resurgence of white racist hate groups such as the Klan, it could easily happen again. Only a few days before the dictating of these paragraphs the white citizens of Metairie, Louisiana, elected to office a Republican well known for his longstanding involvement not only with the Klan but with Nazi philosophy. Again, almost every one of these professional haters considers himself a Christian.

The other film—somewhat slow-moving but well-photographed and directed—exposes the immorality and depravity of the eighteenth-century

French nobility. It is painful to reflect that that society, too, was a Christian one, of the Catholic order.

Considering how poorly we have been educated on such matters, it is easy enough for Americans to assume that the Jeffersonian wall of separation between church and state, which is one of the noblest aspects of the intellectual and moral inheritance bequeathed to us by the founding fathers, has always been heartily endorsed by the American people. Unfortunately, this has not been the case. From the very first there were those who perceived, rightly enough, that such political and moral wisdom by no means flowed out of Christian influence but resulted purely from the eighteenth-century humanist mind-set loosely referred to as *The Enlightenment.*

Catholics were wiser than their Protestant cousins in regard to the separation of powers, although Catholic cooperation was somewhat like the communists' relationship with American freedoms. The latter are totally sincere when they defend the American ideals of free speech, free press, and free assembly for the obvious reason that such guarantees work to their benefit within our borders. At the same time, communists would not dream of endorsing the full-throated expression of precisely these same freedoms in any nation in which Marxists have assumed totalitarian powers. American Catholics were also sympathetic to the philosophy of our founding fathers, while at the same time they averted their gaze from the spectacle of the church's repressive political authority in the Catholic nations of Europe.

There is no doubt that American society at present—the early 1990s— is psychologically sicker and more depraved than it has ever been. The unbearable present situation additionally empowers assorted alternatives to it by imbuing them with a quite understandable anything-would-be-better-than-this feeling.

One of the alternatives presently being considered is that of making the United States a formally Christian society. This is by no means merely an extremist fringe proposal that can safely be ignored, if only because of its source. What might be described as the more centrist Moral Majority constituency heartily endorses such an idea, but it has more respectable conservative intellectual endorsement, as indicated by an article by Russell Kirk in the Winter, 1989, issue of *This World,* an intellectual journal of religious opinion.

Kirk recalls that earlier T. S. Eliot had proposed that modern society would be far less depraved and disturbed than it is if it became Christianized. Kirk, Eliot, et al. are right about this if we consider the question in ideal terms, since it would be difficult to imagine a more troubled society than that in which we presently live. But before deciding on a purely or largely Christian alternative, however defined, we ought to look back through history and carefully examine the results of supreme Christian authority. Most of them were neither pretty nor edifying. Something always seems to have gone wrong as the word was transmitted from the cloistered writing tables of Christian scholars to the streets. The working details that actually emerged were different from the message sent.

It is clear that there have been frequent examples of immorality and depravity among the clergy. In Europe cardinals and bishops lived in palaces and on other luxurious estates, sometimes conducting themselves more like conniving princes than saints. By virtue of their example, they did far more for the cause of religious skepticism than they ever did for religious faith. The early Voltairean critics were frequently correct when they referred to corrupt, cynical churchmen.

While the churches will understandably be inclined to suggest that they drew upon nothing but internal Christian resources in the fortunate process of moral uplift that has occurred during the past two or three hundred years, they seem to have been shamed into the more edifying behavior that all now applaud.

Who were the shamers? They were largely rationalist and humanist critics who—though it may come as news to relatively uninformed believers—were also passionately concerned with moral and ethical questions. Whether there is a God or not, the advantages of virtuous behavior and the grave dangers of evil behavior are of the greatest possible importance to all human societies. So the critics of organized religion performed a heroic public service by revealing religion's often-scandalous aspects.

The churches did not gradually outlaw the enormous machinery of legal- and church-sanctioned torture. Instead, the gradually emerging secular social philosophies shamed Europe into reforming itself so that the torture-and-dungeon aspects of civil "justice" in Europe's Christian nations in time gave way to the vastly superior modern model of which the American legal system, despite its imperfections, is representative. Some Christians, to their eternal credit, had the moral sensitivity and personal courage to take part in this great process of moral uplift, but they had to fight elements within their own congregations to do so. (See also CHURCH AND STATE RELATIONS.)

It would be a serious mistake to consider the few examples given here as simply several instances in which the Bible bears responsibility for social evil. They are rather large categories within which countless millions of separate cases of suffering were caused in the lives of individual men, women, and children because they happened to live in societies dominated by adherents of the Old and New Testaments. Has the Bible produced good or evil? Every intelligent and unprejudiced person knows it has produced both. The problem is that some still imagine that the Bible has been productive only of good. (See also BY THEIR FRUITS YE SHALL KNOW THEM; CRUSADES, THE; EVIL, THE PROBLEM OF; PIOUS FRAUD; RELIGIOUS THEORIES, DEVIANT; REVENGE.)

CRUSADES, THE. The films of Cecil B. DeMille and other Hollywood filmmakers of the 1930s taught many of us what little we know of the Christian Crusades. What was at issue in the Crusades was nothing more than the resolve of Christian Europe to wrest control of the Holy Land from uncivilized Arabs, followers of the prophet Mohammed.

That degree of distortion of truth is not only occasionally encountered but actually characterizes versions of history written by sources with a biased point of view. Since almost all history involves such prejudice and distortion, the wise student will therefore consult a good many sources in trying to arrive at a reasonable assessment of one ancient drama or another. The first Crusade, in the middle of the fifth century, was about war—not war between Christians and infidels but war between competing groups of Christians.

The resulting savage European destruction in Constantinople was primarily a matter of an assault on Christian property and the indiscriminate slaughter of devout Orthodox Christians. Even poorly educated schoolchildren at least have a hazy familiarity with the Dark Ages. While light glimmered here and there, the darkness nevertheless predominated during a period that was—painful as it may be for some to concede—thoroughly Christian. (See also CRIME, BIBLICAL IMPETUS TO; FANATICISM; IRRATIONALISM.)

CURSING. Before discussing the subject of cursing, it would be helpful to explain some of the relevant terms.

Cursing is the expression of a wish that misfortune, evil, doom, calamity, or utter destruction befall another person. It also refers to the act of reciting a formula or charm intended to cause such misfortune to another.

Swearing is committing one's self to a vow or promise with an appeal to some superhuman being. When swearing involves the heartfelt wish to inflict evil, it becomes a curse.

Spells are words or phrases supposed to have the magical power to put others into a state of enchantment, either good or evil.

Incantations are chantings of words said to have magical power.

CURSING

The Evil Eye is rooted in the superstitious belief that some people can cause harm just by looking. This strange and remarkably inane belief has existed for thousands of years in many parts of the world and, incredibly, still has followers in southern Europe and the Middle East. Believers may try to counteract the effects of the evil eye by reciting magic words, pointing with a prong of coral, or wearing charms or crosses,

Charms are trinkets or amulets worn on chains or bracelets for supposed magical effect. In addition, any action that is thought to have magical power (such as the chanting or recitation of a verse or formula of magic) is called a charm.

Hex is a term that originated in the United States and means casting an evil eye or putting a curse on.

Voodoo is one of the religious beliefs of certain African natives. The word means Spirit or God. As practiced in the West Indies and a few areas of the United States, voodoo includes the pursuit of magic and contains some elements borrowed from the Catholic religion. Its devotees believe that spirits of the dead live in a world of ghosts but can visit the world of the living to bless or curse people. If one makes a wax image and sticks pins into it, one is practicing voodoo to injure one's enemy.

Witchcraft is the practice of magical acts by witches (generally women) or people supposed to have supernatural power. Although most self-described witches today claim to be "good" witches, or those who invoke only helpful magic, witchcraft is generally perceived as applying to evil powers. This power is believed to have been given or sold by devils, and a witch may call upon spirits or demons to rise up and hurt her enemies. Sometimes a witch is said to lay a curse by using parings of the victim's fingernails, a lock of hair, or a piece of clothing. In times long gone, people used to destroy their nail parings and hair clippings in order to keep from being cursed. In a period of religious fanaticism in early American history, women thought to be witches were killed, as the Bible directs. The Salem Witch Hunt is now considered a time of religious persecution since many of those so murdered were innocent victims.

At first it might seem that so destructive a custom as cursing has no proper connection with a book on religion and morality, which are assumed to be largely matters of worship of the Deity, compassion for one's fellow creatures, and respect for the time-honored virtues. Cursing and religion, alas, have been closely connected down through history, for while religion has sought to encourage positive, uplifting behavior, the very reason for its emphasis on virtue is the common existence of evil. There would be no need for a commandment such as *Thou shalt not kill* were it not that men have been freely slaughtering each other for millions of years. Cursing is essentially a substitute for direct physical aggression and is now—at long last—condemned by Christians as a sin.

If the curser desires that bodily harm should befall his opponent he is already seriously guilty morally. But the fear of either direct retaliation or punishment under the law may keep him from physically attacking the hated one. The curser substitutes *words* for physical weapons. Because he feels that his own unaided anger is unlikely to bring about the physical suffering he desires to inflict, he invokes the aid of a third party, the Deity, or other supernatural force.

Cursing involves ancient ethical and moral questions as is suggested by the first commandment, which forbids the taking of the Lord's name in vain (Exod. 20:7). It is applied not only to oaths and personal vows but also to the custom of cursing.

The Talmud provides evidence of the importance the ancient Jews attached to prohibiting the use of the Lord's name for purposes other than spiritual worship or respect. Interestingly, the ancient prohibitions on cursing stemmed from the belief that it is not merely disrespectful but that it represented a thoughtless use of an authentic power.

Though it is easy for us to smile at what we regard as dimwitted superstition, we should realize that even today solemn invocations, particularly those in which reference is made to God, seem to carry considerable social power.

The curse was common in ancient times, as indicated by the many biblical references to the practice. One of the most familiar passages is found in Matthew chapter 26.

> 73. And after a while, came unto him they that stood by, and said to Peter, "Surely thou also art one of them; for thy speech betrayeth thee."
> 74. Then began he to curse and to swear, saying, "I know not the man." And immediately the cock crew.

If a mere human utters a curse we can assume that it will cause no literal harm whatever except perhaps to those gullible enough to believe that it carries weight, in which case they will actually be harming themselves by the absurdity of their belief. But when we are told, as is clearly asserted in chapter 28 of the Book of Deuteronomy, that no less a personage than God has hurled curses at his human creatures, that is quite another matter.

God, we are told here (v. 15), addresses himself to the question how he shall punish those of his children who do not obey "all his commandments and his statutes." The remaining fifty odd verses of the chapter are devoted to a list of horrible threats. Every single aspect of the lives of those Jews alive at the time was to be cursed: their cities, their farm fields, their storage rooms; the fruit of their trees, their cattle, their sheep were to be struck with pestilence, consumptions, fever, and inflammations. They were to be attacked by swords, mildew, drought, and by birds that would eat the carcasses of their bodies; they were to be struck with assorted skin infections, blindness, insanity; their wives were to be unfaithful; their children were to be sold into slavery, and so forth.

Other than the total absurdity of attributing such vile nonsense to God, there is also the embarrassing fact that not even the Scriptures—and certainly no secular source of historical information—suggests that any such dire fates were actually suffered. It must be borne in mind that 100 percent of the human population would be subject to this curse, since not one of mankind has been perfect enough to keep all of the Lord's commandments and statutes all of the time.

And this was not an isolated incident of the Lord issuing curses. Note the following:

> Gen. 8:21: . . . and the Lord said in his heart, "I will not again curse the ground any more for man's sake; for the imagination of man's heart is evil from his youth; neither will I again smite any more every living thing, as I have done."

> Gen. 12:1, 3: Now the Lord said to Abram . . . "And I will bless them that bless thee, and curse him that curseth thee: . . ."

> Num. 5:11, 21–22: And the Lord spake unto Moses, saying, ". . . the priest shall say unto the woman, 'The Lord make thee a curse and an oath among thy people, when the Lord doth make thy thigh to rot, and thy belly to swell; And this water that causeth the curse shall go into thy bowels, to make thy belly to swell, and thy thigh to rot: . . .' "

Although the New Testament generally condemns cursing and advocates turning the other cheek, as when Jesus exhorts his followers to "love your enemies and pray for those who curse you" (Matt. 5:44), several direct references to cursing are found there as well, including Jesus Christ's invoking a curse in Matthew 21:

> 18. Now in the morning as he returned in the city, he hungered.
> 19. And when he saw a fig tree in the way, he came to it, and found nothing thereon, but leaves only, and said unto it, "Let no fruit grow on thee henceforward for ever." And presently the fig tree withered away.

The biblical record itself clarifies that the incident occurred at the wrong time of year for fig trees to bear fruit; a mindless tree could not be blamed for doing what was inherent to its nature—as created by God.

Centuries later, the Catholic and Eastern churches employed ritual cursing as a means of excommunicating the unfaithful. Sir Thomas Malory referred to excommunication when he wrote in *Le Morte d'Arthur,* "I shall curse you with Bell, and Book and Candle."

Pope Clement VI in the fourteenth century rendered a real curse of excommunication:

> Let him be damned in his going out and coming in. The Lord strike him with madness and blindness and mental insanity. May the heavens empty upon him thunderbolts and the wrath of the Omnipotent burn itself unto him in the present and future world. May the Universe light against him and the earth open to swallow him up!

S. M. Shirley of Littlerock, California, sent the following curse to me in the form of a pamphlet that reproduced an ancient curse of excommunication apparently employed by the Catholic church. While the curse is too lengthy to reproduce in full, the following excerpts give an indication of its vigor and heat:

> We excommunicate and anathematize him from the threshold of the Holy Church of God Almighty.
> We sequester him, that he may be tormented.
> May the Father, who creates man, curse him!
> May the Son, who suffered for us, curse him!
> May the Holy Ghost, who is poured out in baptism, curse him!
> May the Holy Cross, from which Christ for our salvation, triumphing over His enemies, ascended, curse him!
> May the Holy Mary, ever Virgin and the Mother of God, curse him!
> May all the Angels, Principalities and Powers, and all Heavenly Armies curse him!
> May the glorious band of the Patriarchs and Prophets curse him!
> May all the Saints, from the beginning of the world to everlasting ages who are found to be beloved of God, damn him!

So much for Christian love. (See also IRRATIONALISM; MAGIC IN THE BIBLE.)

D

DESCENT FROM ONE ANCESTOR. The assertion that any large social entity—an ethnic tribe, a nationality, a race—can be said to have descended from one man arouses a certain dissatisfaction. Before any such claim could be accepted, the mathematics of generation would have to be examined. The reader is *one,* an individual. His parents numbered *two.* Of grandparents he had *four* and of great-grandparents, *eight.* Counting back through just a few generations, the reader's ancestors number 16; 32; 64; 128; 256; 512; 1,024; 2,048; 4,096; 8,192. If we assume that a new generation emerges approximately every twenty-five years, our computation spans only a very brief period—less than four hundred years.

Now common sense will tell us that if one travels that far back along the branches of his physical descent, there is something absurd about singling out and asserting that one is, in any unique or even detectable sense, the descendant of a particular male ancestor, to the exclusion of the thousands of others, male and female. The fact is that one is equally the descendant of all such ancestors.

Even in the modern age when systems of record-keeping are readily available, few know the identity—much less the personal history—of an ancestor just a few short generations removed. Total or general ignorance of one's distant ancestry is the rule and certain knowledge so very much the exception that one is entitled to be extremely skeptical about reports of ancient descent.

Nevertheless, the biblical scribes considered it important to claim to know something of the ancestry of individuals and tribes. Since there was a perceived need for such information, it is reasonable to assume that it was simply created, either out of whole cloth or very largely so, with perhaps an admixture of rumor, oral tradition, and guesswork.

Another complication in tracing lines of descent is that every infant born in the world is by no means, in fact, the child of his mother's husband. Societies totally untroubled by sexual promiscuity have been extremely rare and perhaps nonexistent. One such mistake or happenstance in a line of genealogy covering several centuries can render the pronounced lineage erroneous.

DISASTERS. In 1737 approximately 300,000 inhabitants of the area of Bengal died from the ravages of a typhoon.

In August of 1784 an unexpected drop in temperatures froze the maize and bean crops in a large part of the Spanish Catholic colony of Mexico causing the starvation death of another 300,000 people.

In *Darkest Hours,* Jay Robert Nash lists the following natural disasters that have occurred in the present century:

Estimated Deaths

3.7 million—flood, Yellow River, China, 1931
655,000—earthquake, Tangshan, China, 1976
500,000—cyclone, tidal wave, Bangladesh, 1970
200,000—floods, China, 1939
180,000—earthquake, landslides, Gansu, China, 1923
160,000—earthquake, Messina, Sicily, 1908
143,000—earthquake, fire, Tokyo, Japan, 1923
100,000—floods, Canton, China, 1915
100,000—earthquake, Gansu, China, 1927
100,000—flood, Canton, China, 1915
66,794—earthquake, Yungay, Peru, 1970
50,000—tidal wave, Italy, 1908
50,000—earthquake, Chile, 1939
50,000—earthquake, Turkey, 1939
40,000—cyclone, Bengal, India, 1942
30,000—earthquake, Avezzano, Italy, 1915
25,000—earthquakes, northeast Iran, 1978
24,047—cyclone, E. Pakistan, 1965
12,200—earthquake, Guatemala, 1902
12,000—earthquake, Iran, 1968
10,000—cyclone, tidal wave, Hong Kong, 1902
10,000—earthquake, Managua, Nicaragua, 1972
10,000—floods, India, 1979.

DISASTERS

An update of this list would include the following:

    150,000—cyclone, Bangladesh, 1991
    25,000—earthquake, Armenia, 1988
    23,000—volcano, Columbia, 1985
    15,000—cyclone, Bangladesh, 1985.

In addition to natural disasters, WARS have taken their tolls of lives. The Vietnam war cost 58,000 American lives, a million South Vietnamese lives, and an estimated 500,000-1,000,000 North Vietnamese. The war between Iran and Iraq claimed 175,000 lives between the years 1980–1983 alone. No accurate count has been given of how many lives were lost as a result of the events preceding, during, and following the Gulf War.

Yearly DISEASE kills untold numbers on our planet earth. Over one million people died from famine in Africa in 1984 alone, and another million continue to die from malaria each year on that continent. In the United States, heart disease claims 950,000 lives each year; cancer, 500,000. Statistics as of the time of this writing show 100,777 deaths worldwide from AIDS-related causes.

No living Christian or Jewish theologian imagines that these monumental disasters, and the hundreds of others that might be cited and that in the aggregate have caused the painful death of countless millions, have anything whatever to do with Divine Providence. Atheists and agnostics have for centuries considered such tragedies merely massive accidents, no more caused by a conscious will—either divine or human—than is the chance collision of meteorites with larger bodies light years away from earth. The churches have also gradually, albeit grudgingly, given up their former insistence on the prevalence of divine wrath in human experience. Their wise concession, however, puts them at odds with the Old Testament.

The ancient view that God actually causes such catastrophes poses myriad difficulties and hard questions. For example, why does every human creature have a vermiform appendix, a suborgan that serves no purpose and frequently causes sickness and death? It used to cause even more deaths until modern medical science learned how to deal with it. So why in the world would God create Adam, just a few thousand years ago, with such an organ?

It is far more reasonable to assume that he did *not* so create him. We now know that the appendix is something *vestigial,* a suborgan for which, in ages past, there was a use. It would have to have had a use, would it not, if it were created by the source of all intelligence?

In regard to animals, Genesis clearly states God created them in one day. But why, *before* Adam sinned, did God create such creatures as man-eating sharks and assorted poisonous creatures?

In this connection, I recall an early moment of doubt when my FAITH was shaken and revised, though not abandoned. Many years ago *Time* magazine featured an account of a shipwreck that occurred as a result of enemy attack during World War II.

Large numbers of American servicemen were thrown into the water. Most quickly drowned, but hundreds swam about or clung to wreckage for long, agonizing hours, *during all of which time they were subjected to the bloody assaults of schools of man-eating sharks* that happened to be in the area.

Men aboard a vessel who tried to save the poor souls in the water took photographs of the resulting slaughter. Very few were saved, even though they could be heard praying and pleading for God's help. Those on board the ship fired rifles at the frenzied sharks and killed a few. But a far greater number of men could be seen with their hands, arms, and legs ripped off, drifting on the red froth of a bloodied sea. One photograph clearly showed a young man, his face contorted in fear, with a large portion of his left shoulder missing.

Reading that report and giving long thought to it weakened my faith. These men, the majority of them Christians, prayed desperately for God's help and yet were granted none of it; they died a hideous tormented death that only came after long hours of the most pathetic terror.

This unhappy story has its counterpart in the millions of instances over the years in which various violent land animals have brought about similar bloody destruction.

Many decent people have put aside the simple faith of their childhood upon contemplation of such tragic spectacles that occur daily by the thousands. Such reality is depressing enough. To assert that every such occurrence represents the conscious will of a malicious, vengeful God is to view the world as an ongoing nightmare. (See also DISEASE; EVIL, THE PROBLEM OF; MIRACLES.)

DISEASE. One of the numerous Old Testament errors that still handicaps reason and medical practice in the modern world concerns the Israelite view that an individual fell ill because either he or a family member had sinned. It is simple enough now to recognize that such an opinion was groundless. How, then, did it come to be accepted? The reason is that in some cases sickness *does* result from immoral activity. People pay physical penalties for alcoholism, for example, and obesity may be said to result from the sin of gluttony. Venereal diseases generally result from such illicit sexual practices as adultery, although they will sometimes be transmitted through the morally blameless act of intercourse within marriage. These few examples do not cover so much as even one percent of the tragic physical afflictions from which man suffers: starvation, malaria, heart disease, cancer, and tuberculosis, to name only a few.

Nevertheless, the view that diseases are consciously directed punishments from the hand of God made something of a comeback in the 1980s, but only in the context of one disease, AIDS, which many fundamentalist Christians immediately assumed was God's expression of his displeasure with HOMOSEXUALITY. One wit at the time commented that if AIDS is proof that God loathes homosexuals, it might also be the case that he has an equal contempt for American Legionnaires, since the first outbreak of what has come to be called Legionnaires' disease occurred during a legion convention.

But if for purposes of discussion we entertain the notion that God decided to address the problem of homosexuality by introducing one more tragic affliction to an already seriously troubled world, then we are faced with the undeniable fact that the ruler of the universe has been remarkably imprecise in pointing his hideous weapon at properly designated targets: AIDS also kills people who are not homosexuals, including great numbers of innocent infants. Opinions, of course, affect conduct. Ronald Reagan was in the White House—whether he remembers it or not—when AIDS became a matter of public concern. If he had any sympathy for the afflicted, it was overwhelmed for a very long time by the loud chorus from the conservative camp stressing "God's wrath" as the explanation of the epidemic.

So long as Christianity held to the absurd view that sickness was the result of God's vindictive fury, it was not surprising that so little was done to make intelligent war on disease. Pasteur, Lister, Florence Nightingale, and other modern medical pioneers, not the churches, deserve credit for the sanitary improvements that have wiped out certain diseases altogether and greatly diminished the tragic effects of others. It is intriguing to speculate where mankind might stand today if the farsighted scientific innovators of the last five hundred years had not had to overcome intense Christian opposition in disseminating the results of their studies.

So radically has public opinion reversed itself on such matters that today those Christians who adhere to the once-common belief that diseases are divine punishments and that the proper method of cure is fervent prayer are looked upon by the rest of the faithful as either dangerously fanatical or at best sadly deluded.

Much of what we regard as bodily disease or decay involves the health and normal function of organisms whose survival is often inimical to our personal interests. We do not call it disease or decay when a wolf catches a squirrel and eats it, an act certainly programmed into the canine's nature. We do not consider it disease or decay when a tiger makes a meal of a rabbit, or a lion dines on a deer. Much the same process is at work when humans or other animals are eaten, in the same natural chain of events, by organisms *smaller* than themselves. In the jungle instances the process may take a few seconds or minutes; in the case of the smaller-to-larger attacks, the destruction of the host may take months or years. In either case the essential nature of the act is the same.

Among the numerous physical tragedies obviously caused by an indifferent NATURE rather than a malignant Deity are the birth defects that sometimes result from German measles. Women who happen to be pregnant at the time they contract this disease are likely to give birth to pathetically deformed infants. It would be absurd to suggest that the unfortunate women so afflicted have somehow been so evil as to be struck with this dread curse. Fortunately, very few Christians or Jews presently alive would argue that if a woman has suffered from German measles her tragic misfortune has resulted from a deliberate, conscious decision on God's part. Even many otherwise fanatical Christians are now aware that such diseases are caused by minute life forms—germs, bacteria, viruses.

The modern understanding is all to the good, but *it is in flat contradiction with biblical understanding.* Obviously both cannot be valid. For every Christian or Jew of the present day who prefers the biblical tradition on the point, there are at least 999 who will choose to be guided by common sense. The honest Christian or Jew is reasonably entitled to say, "In the last analysis I simply do not know, do not understand, how a God I still insist is all-loving can possibly tolerate the painful slaughter of innocent babies and the countless millions of other such unwarranted tragedies. I cling to my firm FAITH. I am still convinced that there *is* a God and that he loves all his creatures. But I concede that there is *no* way to reconcile this belief with the painful realities all about us. So be it. I rest secure in my faith and only pray that God, in his infinite wisdom, may one day vouchsafe the answer for which our hearts hunger."

This rationally acceptable, philosophically dignified—even touching—attitude would certainly be far preferable to thinking that the ways of God are not those of man, that God has a purpose for everything, however tragic, if we could only perceive it, and so forth. (See also DISASTERS; EVIL, THE PROBLEM OF; MEDICINE; MIRACLES; NATURE.)

DIVINE RIGHT OF KINGS. A Bible-oriented belief that mankind has finally cast aside is the view that rulers of a country—even the most barbarous—are authorized by heaven. Both theologians and laymen long held that ruling powers derived their legitimate power, in the most literal sense possible, from God. Even if tyrannical, these rulers were nevertheless to be obeyed because of their divine sanction. This belief was dominant in many cultures for an unknown number of centuries. From the modern vantage point, we perceive at once that the belief was utterly erroneous. Very few modern Christians think that Joseph Stalin, for example, ought to have been obeyed. Anyone who were to argue so today would perhaps be investigated by some congressional committee specializing in the study of un-American activities. As Charles Bradlaugh has observed:

> It can scarcely be necessary to argue to the citizens of the United States of America that the origin of their liberties was in the *rejection* of faith in the divine right of George III. (IA)

But just as humankind today is united in rejecting the idea, so it was unthinkable to question it in ages past. The idea dominated social custom for so long because of its utility.

The masses have ever been unruly, dangerous, and undependable. Tyrants and benevolent despots of earlier ages had to rule with a firm hand since, if their authority was not visibly displayed, it would soon be questioned and, if questioned, ultimately challenged. But even men who had little respect for particular rulers had much respect for their gods. Thus, nation after nation combined human with divine authority. Divine right also gave social MORALITY the appearance of timelessness, a cohesiveness and order independent of the strength and wisdom of a particular ruler, whether king or priest. Human rulers die, but ships of state continue on their course. (See also CHURCH AND STATE RELATIONS.)

DIVORCE. Man is notoriously inconsistent: any two people are prone to disagree, but even one individual will disagree with himself over a period of time. A perfect God will not be troubled by such human weakness. Nevertheless, the devout believer may be perplexed at the veritable mountains of inconsistency and contradiction in all portions of the Bible. The discrepancies continue when divorce is at issue.

In Deuteronomy chapter 24, we read:

1. When a man hath taken a wife, and married her, and it come to pass that she find no favour in his eyes, because he hath found some uncleanness in her: then let him write her a bill of divorcement, and give it in her hand, and send her out of his house.
2. And when she is departed out of his house, she may go and be another man's wife.

In Ezra chapter 10, we find another reason why Old Testament peoples practiced divorce:

2. . . . We have trespassed against our God, and have taken strange wives of the people of the land: yet now there is hope in Israel concerning this thing.
3. Now therefore let us make a covenant with our God to *put away all the wives, and such as are born of them,* according to the counsel of my lord, and of those that tremble at the commandment of our God; and let it be done according to the law. (IA)

God himself, we are told here, ordered the abandonment not only of the wives, but of the innocent children of the union as well. That seems clear-cut enough until we read chapter 5 of Matthew's Gospel in which the scribe quotes Jesus:

32. But I say unto you, "That whosoever shall put away his wife, *saving for the cause of fornication,* causeth her to commit adultery: and whosoever shall marry her that is divorced committeth adultery. (IA)

This happens to be in perfect agreement with Jewish tradition and, in fact, with what millions of decent citizens in the present day consider a reasonable approach to the painful question of divorce, but, again, it represents a CONTRADICTION within the supposedly divinely inspired Scripture. Our courts of law, too, will grant a man or woman a divorce on grounds of adultery committed by the other party. The Catholic church, nevertheless, simply disregards this passage of the New Testament. It has every freedom to do so, but if it does, it is no longer, on logical grounds, entitled to insist that every word of the New Testament is inspired by God.

A few centuries ago the Protestant churches generally agreed with the Catholic view that divorce was wrong, period, and could never be countenanced. But, as we have seen, RELIGIONS too undergo a process of evolution in their beliefs, and gradually the once-rigid no-divorce-under-any-circumstances rule began to be modified. This was partly a matter of simple common sense, since it is absurd to argue that if one finds oneself married to a moral monster, one must nevertheless put up with the attendant horrifying experiences.

Another reason for the gradual erosion of the original strictness was that more and more individuals—many of them decent, law-abiding Christians—found themselves inadvertently trapped in loveless marriages. Human nature being what it is, some persons so caught later developed sincere love relationships with individuals other than those to whom they were married.

Life on planet earth would be simpler if all moral questions had sharply defined boundaries. Unfortunately, our social reality is much more complex. Some kinds of marital problems are clearly better resolved if the two participants undergo a formal, legal separation, foregoing the question whether a second marriage to another party is permitted. In any case, there is nothing happy about any divorce, even those that are clearly necessary, and this is never so clear as when children have been born to the couple in question. Indeed children sometimes suffer more from the separation of their parents than the adults themselves. Those who argue against divorce on the grounds that it tends to weaken the stability of individual families, and therefore, if they are statistically common, disturbs the societies in which they occur are indeed speaking the truth.

No knowledgeable person has ever denied anything so obvious. The larger question is: For Christians, is divorce ever permitted? Protestant clergymen of half a century ago would certainly be shocked that so many of their brothers of the cloth not only are at present countenancing divorce among their parishioners but are also divorcing their wives themselves. If the present continuing debate within the Catholic fold—whether priests should be permitted to marry—ends in favor of matrimony, a popular question in the future might be, "Why are so many Catholic priests now getting divorced?" (See also MORALITY; POLYGAMY.)

DREAMS. The capacity for dreaming was one starting place for the development of religious theory. If dreams are often striking, amusing, creative, horrifying, erotically stimulating, fascinating, and puzzling to modern man —with all his knowledge—we may be certain that they made an even more profound impression in primitive times. We know from controlled experimentation that an individual who is deprived of that portion of sleep during which dreams occur becomes psychotic. It follows that dreaming is a necessary psychological/physiological function. As an aspect of brain function, there is nothing necessarily religious or mystical about it. Nevertheless, those who are familiar with RELIGION or superstition but know nothing of the science of psychology will naturally attribute enormous practical significance to dreams.

The several accounts of dreams that appear in the Scriptures as reported, are nothing like the dreams with which we all are familiar. Events in the typical dream take place with near-total disregard for the laws of physics. The protagonist or other characters are not restrained by gravity, they pass through apparently impenetrable walls or other structures, and they travel in an instant from one place to another.

Secondly, just as dream content is not affected by physical laws, it seems not to be affected by any law whatever. Social and moral restraints; limitations imposed by ignorance of language; inhibitions resulting from want of money, water, food, clothing, or other material requirements— all of these have no relevance to the ability of dream-characters to act. It is extremely likely that the seemingly wondrous abilities characteristic of dream activity would be associated with already held religious ideas, however vague, and not at all likely that the dreamer would make no such connections in the subsequent wakened state.

Since the dreamer is aware that he does not *will* the contents of his dreams, it could easily occur to him that they were introduced into his mind by an outside spiritual agency, whether benign or malign. (See also FREE WILL; PSYCHOLOGY AND RELIGION; REVELATION, THE [OF ST. JOHN THE DIVINE].)

E

ECCLESIASTES. This most interesting volume of the Old Testament has a tone that differs markedly from the other Hebrew books. The unknown author was obviously highly intelligent, sophisticated, and blasé. His writing style is in striking contrast to the strident, vengeful, military, and revolutionary tone of much Old Testament rhetoric. Ecclesiastes seems somehow Socratic, Indian, or Chinese in its sense of the necessity to hold one's self apart from the turmoil and travail of life. Perhaps the book is more appealing to modern man because it is the most markedly rational in the Old Testament, having nothing fanatical or visionary about it. It can, moreover, be interpreted as a strikingly irreligious book—if not antireligious—in that it vibrates with a cynicism that Christians feel is incompatible with their essential doctrine of hope.

Observes Archibald Robertson in *The Bible and Its Background* (Watts):

> The opinions of Ecclesiastes are those of the more cultured section of the Jewish aristocracy. The book is, in fact, an unusually frank rationalization of their class privileges. Open Hellenizers they could hardly be: the Maccabean Revolution had forced them to conform outwardly to Judaism. They held to it loosely, treating it as the established cult of their country but not as an article of export, still less as an instrument of social justice. Those who shared this outlook became known as Sadducees—a name of uncertain origin—perhaps connected with the Zadokites, the old high priestly family of Jerusalem.

Jean Levie, S.J., too, gives Ecclesiastes high marks in the context of literature, if not Christianity:

The inspired text does not necessarily indicate the best or the ideal solution of a problem, even when it praises a given solution. The "wisdom" of Ecclesiasticus is sometimes of a very high order, but for the most part it represents a practical wisdom, a combination of common sense and shrewdness, but *very inferior to the Christian ideal of the New Testament.* The author intended it to do no more. His intention determines the scope of his assertions. (IA)

Chapter 1. In the first chapter of Ecclesiastes the author describes the earth as motionless. He is mistaken.

Chapter 3. Here we find a quite cryptic verse:

15. That which hath been is now; and that which is to be hath already been; and God requireth that which is past.

Reviewer F. G. H., in the February 1968 edition of *Old Testament Abstracts* (Catholic Biblical Association), in commenting on a study by R. E. Salter, states about this verse:

A survey of interpretations of Ecclesiastes 3:15 reveals that *no satisfactory explanation of this text has ever appeared.* The kind of exegesis exhibited by commentators reminds us of the *midrashin* where a text is isolated and interpreted in complete disregard for context. (IA)

Chapter 7. In all ages men have assumed that *past* times were better than those *present,* but in verse 10 of this chapter we read:

Say not thou, "What is the cause that the former days were better than these? for thou dost not enquire wisely concerning this."

EDUCATIVE PROCESS, THE. The churches distinguished themselves only very late in the dramatic process of popular education. True, during centuries of darkness in Europe the lamp of learning was kept burning, however fitfully, in certain monasteries, but at no time was it the policy of any church to educate their own believers, much less humankind. Clearly the ability to read and write provided power, and power, it was felt, was best left in the hands of those most naturally able to wield it. The last thing either church or state wanted was a truly informed populace.

If the religious reader continues this historic bias and considers both the Democratic and Republican movements of recent centuries modernist and hence dangerous, then of course he declares himself an enemy of George Washington, James Madison, Thomas Jefferson, Benjamin Franklin,

Thomas Paine, and the other courageous social philosophers who created our great country.

But even though the need for formal education for the masses has at last been recognized, the process is still far from perfect. Flight from REASON is at present increasingly more apparent, as I have noted in *Dumbth: And 81 Ways to Make Americans Smarter* (Prometheus Books, 1989).

One factor that contributes to the inability-to-reason problem is that the educative process must start when the individual is very young. Everything imparted to him will be expressed in simplistic and consequently, to some extent, misleading terms. Characters from history are painted as either grandly heroic or totally despicable. Complex and cataclysmic events are perceived through the thick lens of national, ethnic, or religious bias. The process of distortion scarcely applies to mathematics or to science properly perceived, but it is generally prevalent in music and the other arts. In all of these, basic material details must be grasped before more profound levels of complexity can be reached.

However, the messages transmitted to children in the study of history and religion are often *not in accord with the facts.*

Perhaps no great harm befalls those fortunate enough to continue their education through to the university level. But millions never proceed beyond the basic grades, or those of high school. Thus, a large percentage of us, though chronologically adult, have minds not greatly different from those of ten-year-old children, so far as matters of historical, political, philosophical, and religious importance are concerned.

The present educative process often imparts instruction in a harsh or domineering manner. Millions of young souls have been trained to react unsympathetically to the conventional academic subjects because of the rudeness or sadism of certain teachers. The young, when they make their errors in reasoning, must be corrected in a pleasant and affectionate manner.

We in the Western world can certainly take a cue from such Eastern countries as China. There the young women conduct kindergarten and early-grade classes with a warm, cheerful attitude and provide instruction in social cooperation in addition to the conventional subjects. As purely physical creatures we may be driven to certain forms of competitive behavior, for example, in acquiring food and other necessities for our loved ones. Very young children still retain their natural egotistical behavior and are dominated by the concept of me and mine. They require some moral training so that individuals will mature knowing that it is necessary for them to share the world's blessings. No one should try selfishly to increase his own portion so as to deprive others of their fair share.

It will be helpful, then, to perceive any training in reason as requiring a moral imperative. Just as a sharing, cooperative person is more morally admirable than a selfish, grasping individual, one who reasons honestly is superior to one who employs logical powers for selfish or devious ends.

Most of us think of education incorrectly. The word itself does not come properly into focus. We know readily enough what it means in a general sense, and we grasp the obvious, which is that the process is a matter of acquiring knowledge. But when we think of the *procedure,* what comes to mind is a series of vague images of school buildings, books, teachers, classrooms, tests, data. All of these have their relevance, but we should pass through them to the heart of the matter. The central item in the process of education is the individual human being. To you, the most important player in the ongoing drama of education is yourself.

If you are eminently self-satisfied with your present state, then the process of education has ended for you, if indeed it ever properly began. But no one should be fully satisfied with his intellectual estate. The importance, the excitement of education, is that—beyond any question— it will change you. It will not change you in slight and inconsequential ways, for as Norman Cousins has put it, "Education represents a flying leap from the tenth to the twentieth century." Education is the process by means of which the startling discoveries of the greatest scholars, philosophers, and scientists are made available to you. It is a rare individual who, when he turns on a light that instantly converts a black room to one in which all objects are clearly visible, pauses for even a fleeting moment to feel gratitude to Volta, Edison, and the other pioneers in the field of electricity. Just so, it is a rare individual who, upon learning a fact, or being introduced to an idea, ever gives the slightest thought to the thousands of scholars who devoted lifetimes to unearthing such information and developing such ideas.

But the great mysterious mountain of accumulated data is there nevertheless, and we are all privileged to march toward it, through whatever mists and over whatever obstructions, and to make its substance our own. For it is all, in a sense at least, free for the taking. The scholars of the world do not copyright their dazzling discoveries and dole them out only to the highest bidders. They publish, they share, they freely dispense their knowledge to the world. Would not a man be counted a great fool who passed through a field strewn with gold and diamonds but never paused to pick them up and convert them to his benefit and to that of the world? Would we not be equally foolish if, passing through a world in which dearly bought information lies about us at every hand, we disdained it and instead directed our concentration to the most inconsequential, trivial, and indeed harmful or superstitious things?

Nevertheless, we seem to close our minds to education and enlightenment in one area especially: that of religion. And it is precisely here that we need to do much rethinking. (See also CHURCH AND STATE RELATIONS; MORALITY.)

ERROR. One of the numerous oddities that gradually emerges when one enters the fascinating territory of Bible analysis is the common faulty thinking of those who assert that not only is the Bible totally without error but that there is not even the remote possibility that it could incorporate any mistakes. The assertion itself is simple enough. The problem comes from the fact that those who advance it often themselves argue to the contrary when they are attempting to explain away one of the Bible's many so called "HARD SAYINGS."

What is at fault in such instances, the defenders suggest, is not the Bible itself—whatever that phrase might mean—but *translations* of it. Says the Catholic scholar J. E. Doherty, C.S.S.R., in *The Dead Sea Scrolls and the Bible*:

> The King James Version, most popular of all Protestant Bibles in this country, has had to be revised twice to correct inaccuracies. The last time, in 1952, scholars corrected *more than five thousand errors,* though most of them were minor. (IA)

The argument that biblical errors result from *translation* carries little weight. Those who put forth this defense seem to forget that all we have of the Scriptures is translations. No original texts of any portion of Scripture still exist.

The editors of the excellent Dartmouth Bible are intellectually honest in acknowledging difficulties.

> If the manuscripts of the Old and the New Testament books had been transmitted intact from the time when they were first officially approved, many present-day problems concerning them would not exist. This is not, however, the case. *Few believe that the texts now accepted as authoritative are identical with the original manuscripts.* In this respect Jews and Christians are not in the favored position of Mohammedans. For when the Caliph Othman authorized a text of the Koran, within only fifteen years after the prophet's death and when only few copies had as yet been made, he set out to destroy those differing from it. In the case of the Bible, however, *numerous variations exist among the known early manuscripts.* (IA)

One should naturally be grateful for a scriptural text of even partial reliability, but how such a reality can be reconciled with the traditional, fundamentalist every-word-the-word-of-God position is nowhere explained.

If we assume that a Deity—on hundreds of separate occasions over several centuries—would inspire individuals to quote his divine admonitions in written word, it is quite unreasonable to assume further that he thereafter paid no attention as errors and contradictions were introduced and perpetuated. Men are so careless and forgetful, but it is surely an insult to the Almighty to suggest that he could initiate the most important of all human communication and then absentmindedly fail to see it through the ages.

Early Christian documents were reportedly inscribed on papyrus, which is short-lived. The Scriptures are therefore available to us today only because unknown armies of scribes copied them repeatedly over long centuries.

In referring to the numerous errors that these processes have inevitably created, scholars use such delicate phrases as *textual difficulties* and *apparent contradictions,* but it must be understood that "difficulties of translation" *revolve around the fact that there are repeated errors in the Scriptures being translated.* Every biblical scholar is aware of this fact, but their failure to share this information with the average believer has at last created the very climate of opinion that now troubles these same academics: They are now condemned as heretics, traitors, and anti-Christs by thousands of ignoramuses in their own folds.

Another point that rarely becomes apparent at the outset of Bible study is the common use of qualifying phrases such as *some scholars feel, it may be the case, it is possible,* or *the author may have intended.* There is nothing inherently wrong with the use of these qualifiers; indeed their use is both wise and virtuous in debate about unclear issues. However, such devices are also used by those whose views are characterized by the most dogmatic certainty. They repeat their assumptions not as possibilities but as bedrock facts, but if they are indeed truths as certain as any ever uttered, then it makes no sense to defend them by qualifiers.

If the reader is largely unbiased on the question, he may wonder how otherwise relatively intelligent people could accept anything so patently preposterous as the literal interpretation of the Holy Bible. Such believers inevitably fall into the trap of error simply because they are already committed to the proposition that if they read something in the Bible it absolutely must be true. Consequently, when, for instance, they read Isaiah 45:7—"I form light and create darkness. I burn prosperity and create disaster; I, the Lord, do all these things"—they simply accept the assertion. Similarly, they accept the numerous other instances, chiefly in the Old Testament, that plainly state, for example, that it is God who is responsible for natural disasters and the incredible pain and destruction they cause.

Millions of wiser though still-devout religious believers have no difficulty with the contradictions that trouble literalists. They do believe that God's word is findable in the Scriptures, but they are aware of imprecise translation, honest error, dishonest error, and other perfectly understandable causes of the thousands of inaccuracies that have crept into the Scriptures during the perhaps three-thousand-year process of their creation, copying, printing, and rendering into hundreds of languages. Catholics, Protestants, and Jews in good standing have written a good deal of extremely helpful Bible commentary and analysis concerning such questions. Most of the relevant controversy comes, as we have seen, from the error of assuming that it is a literal impossibility for there to be any sort of error in the Bible.

Oddly enough, literalists are not even consistent in holding to their fundamental belief; they exhaust a considerable amount of their energies attacking as error-laden certain editions of the Scriptures, while reserving to themselves the right to determine, however inadequate their scholarly credentials, the one version that achieves absolute perfection in its correctness.

One of the reasons for the confusion which characterizes the human predicament is that truth is unitary; whereas error may take an infinite variety of forms. To state this in simpler terms: To the question "What is the sum of two and two?" the answer *four* is obviously the correct one. Therefore every other number to the theoretical infinity is a wrong answer. So are such answers as *egg-salad sandwich* or *your sister*. This being the case, error will always have truth outnumbered.

One of the most redeeming aspects of Christian social witness is that individual Christians have had such respect for the ideals of truth and honesty that they were forced to address their more fanatical brethren concerning certain passages of Scripture. A century ago the English Bishop J. G. Richardson observed of the Old Testament:

> It was no longer honest or even safe to deny that this noble literature, rich in all the elements of moral or spiritual grandeur . . . was *sometimes mistaken in its science, was sometimes inaccurate in its history, and sometimes only relative and accommodatory in its morality. It assumed theories of the physical world which science had abandoned and could never resume. It contained passages of narrative which devout and temperate men pronounced discredited, both by external and internal*

evidence. It praised, or justified, or approved, or condoned, or tolerated conduct which the teaching of Christ and the conscience of Christians alike condemned. (IA)

Thousands of such testimonies by devout and responsible believers could be introduced, and many are quoted in the present work. But when will the churches at large begin to share with their theologically naive adherents the news of these gracious and fair-minded concessions?

Something more than magnanimity is involved when churchmen make such concessions. They would deserve great credit for doing so had they personally introduced such ideas into the debate. Unfortunately this has not been the case. The types of errors possible and, more importantly, observable in Scripture have been enumerated by a number of scholars as part of the process of formal criticism. Only when it finally becomes apparent that it is no longer morally responsible to deny that such errors have occurred do churchmen feel at liberty to refer publicly to such truths. Almost never will the casual reader learn of the long and sometimes painful process that preceded such concessions.

For years Christians who often do not seem to understand what critics or doubters are talking about have advanced some of the more asinine defenses of the absolute truth of the Bible. How many times, for example, have we heard believers say, "How dare you pit your weak human intelligence against that of God?"

All such a question establishes is that the speaker totally misunderstands his opponent's position. Obviously only a madman, convinced of the existence and all-pervading wisdom of God, deliberately places himself in opposition to him. That has nothing whatever to do with doubts expressed by humanists, atheists, agnostics, or free-thinkers of any stripe. What such critics are saying is that, having given the Scriptures long and careful study, they cannot see how such a bizarre melange of contradictions, horror stories, fables, legends, distorted action-dramas, and instances of shameful morality can have been written by a God who, by definition, is the embodiment of truth itself. (See also CONTRADICTIONS, BIBLICAL; MORALITY.)

If one is to make even a casual attempt at thinking rationally about the physical universe, it is crucially important to perceive that when we say that early ideas about the world around us were erroneous, we are understating the case to a striking degree. Not only was there just a certain modest amount of error in our original conceptions, but they were also almost *totally* wrong.

Early man, for example, believed the earth to be flat. He was mistaken.

101

He believed the earth to be stationary. Again he was wrong.

Very early humans conceived the idea that the earth was the center of the universe. The belief was groundless.

The authors of Genesis believed that the stars were bright points fixed in a more-or-less solid hemisphere. They were in error.

An ancient belief held that heavenly bodies had been placed in their positions for purposes of human convenience or betterment—another error.

The Old Testament authors—among other men of their times, and of earlier places and times as well—believed that falling stars, comets, and eclipses were deliberate, direct instances of divine intervention, almost invariably intended to indicate godly displeasure. The belief is not only false, but it is also ludicrous.

Daniel Boorstin, in his stimulating *The Discoverers: A History of Man's Search to Know His World and Himself,* observes that "a great obstacle to discovering the shape of the earth, the continents and the oceans was not ignorance but the illusion of knowledge." The creative, poetic imaginations of the unknown authors and revisers of the early chapters of Genesis postulated absurd views about the physical universe, but they were not the only people of the pre-Christian era to do so. Everyone else did too. Even the greatest scientists and philosophers of ancient times— chiefly the Greeks—held a great many erroneous opinions.

It is most unfair to use hindsight to hold this against them since it would be inevitable that man in such early times would believe things we now know to be preposterous. What was striking about the thought of these early geniuses was the degree of *validity* in what they believed. Human beings are prone to error, partly because the evidence their senses can provide is limited. Only a very rare individual will stop thinking when he runs out of evidence. When we reach that point we typically venture into the unknown and allow our imagination to work.

The great harm in this process, which leads to the deification of error and the restrictions on freedom to oppose it even speculatively, comes from the partly accidental, partly inevitable congruence of (1) the mixture of error and belief of a scientific nature, common in all ages, and (2) a religious philosophy that considers itself not the product of human speculation but of divine revelation. Once these two come together, then the large admixture of error is given every bit as much authority as the usually minute portion of truth.

One of the beauties of historian Boorstin's study is that it provides a wealth of information not only about the scientific truths established by brilliant and courageous individuals over long centuries but also about the vast sea of error, nonsense, and superstition in which occasional islands of fact were only rarely encountered.

Boorstin's book provides numerous examples of the sort of error all too typical of religious theorizing down through the ages, error that is appealing and would be beguiling even to the intellectually elect were it not so patently spurious. In all ancient religions, and in some in our own day, error tends to have a poetic, creative, imaginative component. The Manichaean followers of the pre-Christ Persian philosopher Manes believed a strangely beautiful assortment of things about the relationship among the sun, the moon, and human souls. All religious believers of the present day are now perfectly prepared to concede that such views were totally erroneous.

For a long time rationalist critics have pointed out that certain New Testament authors have also written erroneously in their references to passages of the Jewish Scriptures. On this point, Father Jean Levie comments:

> The apostles quote the sacred books under the names of the writers who were then *considered* to be their authors. All the Psalms are quoted as David's, the Sapiential books as Solomon's, the Pentateuch as composed by Moses, etc. We are not entitled to conclude from this that this attribution is taught to us by the Holy Spirit. When St. Jude in his epistle (vv. 1:14–15) quotes the apocryphal book of Enoch as though Enoch were its author, his intention is to condemn the heretics of his time, by using this passage, *not to teach us that the book is itself authentic.* (IA)

Father Levie is, of course, correct in conceding that the church is not entitled to conclude from such errors that the errors themselves are "taught to us by the Holy Spirit." But, neither is he entitled to confidently assert his knowledge as to what the authors—inspired or not—personally intended to convey. As a great scholar he is as free as anyone else to speculate about such intentions, but the evidence permits him to do no more. In fact, whether Saint Jude wished or did not wish to teach us that the book of Enoch is authentic is of no central relevance. What is of enormous significance is that Jude (1) *believed* the book to be authentic and (2) that he was *in error* in this belief. It is clearly the case that in yet one more instance the Bible transmits error.

Error Due to Memory. Those who have given even casual attention to the process of memory will be aware that the ability to recall any experience precisely is far more limited than is commonly assumed. Those who are frequently interviewed and subsequently quoted are often troubled— though not necessarily surprised—by the inability of even the best journalists to report exactly what is said to them. The gist is usually there, but even the most accurate reports almost always have errors.

ERROR

In 1985, the president of the National Academy of Education, Dr. Robert Glazer, in writing a foreword to a national report on reading, said that some twenty years of meticulous research "have produced an array of information which is unparalleled in the comprehension of language." Dr. Glazer's observations came to my attention through E. D. Hirsch, Jr.'s *Cultural Literacy—What Every American Needs to Know*, in which Hirsch makes an observation of obvious and crucial relevance to serious scholars of Scripture:

> The best introduction to the new research is a psychological insight that goes back some thirty years to George Miller's path-breaking work on short-term memory, which is a special function of our minds that lasts just a matter of milliseconds. It is distinguished from long-term memory (what most of us think of as memory), which lasts from a few seconds to a lifetime. Miller noticed that our capacity for remembering briefly presented disconnected items is severely limited. The mind cannot reliably hold in short-term memory more than about four to seven separate items, whether numbers, letters, points on the body, degrees of loudness, degrees of warmth, and so on. Miller's observation holds true for discrete items in every domain of experience, not just those presented in language.

In other words, it has now been clearly established what those concerned with the matter of being quoted have long known: If we make a speech—or even a much shorter statement—in front of, let's say, ten witnesses, *there is not the slightest chance that all ten will subsequently issue the same report.* What is common is ten separate accounts in which even quotations of the same material will vary, sometimes widely.

Since this is now the undisputed case, it follows that we can no longer have the traditional degree of confidence about the accuracy of the thousands of quotations given in Scripture. There is, of course, the one theoretical possibility that God would have gone to the trouble to intervene miraculously at all moments of quotation-recollection so as to render them error-free. Unfortunately, when we inspect the actual written record we become immediately aware that the hypothesis of miraculous divine involvement is ruled out because of the frequent instances in which portions of Scripture are mutually contradictory, including instances in which direct quotation is claimed.

The ancient debate concerning the question whether the Bible can contain any error is—so far as the best scholarship is concerned—over. It has been firmly settled that not only can the Bible contain error, but that it also contains a good deal of it.

What about historical error? The same is true. Observes Father Levie:

> Religious respect for the Bible had habituated many minds readily enough to attribute a more definite, more certain historical value to the data provided by it [the Bible] than to the records of history or of archaeology. Traditional biblical chronology, fixing creation in 4004 B.C., was still regarded by many as beyond doubt.

The scholars who were immediately prepared to abandon such literalist nonsense were familiar with Akkadian and Sumerian historical records, which disclosed to modern man the existence of advanced civilizations flourishing well before the fourth millennium B.C. (See also AUTHENTICITY OF THE BIBLE; PIOUS FRAUD; VERSIONS OF THE BIBLE.)

EUTHANASIA. It would seem that no one could responsibly argue that there are absolutely no circumstances in which an individual may choose death. To refute such an argument it is necessary only to refer to categories of cases in which to choose to die is not only considered permissible but literally heroic. Every war produces a few cases in which fighting men have willingly sacrificed their own lives to preserve those of others in their immediate vicinity. Who has not heard, for example, of those brave enough to fling their bodies over a hand grenade that would, if detonated uncovered, kill or maim several victims? In such instances, there is no question that the heroic individual is bringing about his own death. It is no respectable contrary argument that the means of his death is an exploding weapon rather than his own hand, since the natural instinct to preserve one's life will control the operative decision in probably 99 percent of such cases.

This argument does not include seemingly similar instances in which men *risk* their lives to save others and, in the attempt, unwillingly suffer death themselves. This conduct too is heroic, but the risk-takers clearly do not want—or even expect—to die, whereas the fighting man who flings himself on a grenade knowingly chooses death.

In wartime SUICIDE would also be a noble, selfless act in a prisoner-of-war situation. Down through history many captured men have been threatened with the most hideously barbarous torture if they did not reveal certain intelligence of military use to their captors. An individual, in such a predicament, who doubted his ability to withstand the pains of sadistic torture and feared that for relief from his sufferings he might reveal to the enemy information that could endanger his fellow soldiers or civilians, might consider it wise to end his life rather than risk those of others.

Such cases in themselves establish that it is not only permissible but sometimes even admirable to sacrifice one's life for the benefit of others. This is what happens when an aged or terminally ill individual, realizing that continued medical treatment may totally dissipate a family's savings, elects to die with dignity rather than subject his loved ones to additional years of the financial burden caused by treatment that cannot possibly cure his disease but can only extend a once full but now painful and unproductive life.

The overwhelming pain suffered by their ailing relative is, of course, a relevant factor in those cases where a loved one or doctor might wish to assist another in the choice to commit suicide. More and more patients in the last stages of a painful and certainly fatal illness are choosing self-inflicted deaths, especially now that dramatic advances in medical science are producing a much larger population of very old people.

Despite such situations, churchmen are still almost unanimous in arguing that there is never the slightest justification for choosing to die before the moment of extinction caused by the ravages of cruel nature. An increasing number of followers, however, simply ignores the church's advice on this question. Joseph Lewis, in his *The Ten Commandments,* refers to a story in the August 8, 1940, issue of the *New York Times* reporting the case of a mother who committed suicide after killing her hopelessly invalid son. She left the following message:

> This is done in the name of mercy. Every night my son got on his knees and begged me not to leave him alone. He was so terrified that it was horrible. I, his mother, could not permit this. *The law should relieve such helpless sufferers. The burden should not be on me.* (IA)

Another horrible incident occurred in the late 1940s. A staff announcer at the CBS radio headquarters in Hollywood named Tom Hanlon once told me about the worst moment of his life. Not long before, while he was on duty one night, he heard a muffled explosion from somewhere else in the building. Hurrying downstairs to see what had happened, Tom suddenly heard the sound of a man screaming. The poor fellow was an electrician who had been working on some highly dangerous equipment in which power switches were enclosed in large metal boxes full of oil. The duty was considered so hazardous that safety precautions and procedures were carefully spelled out, one of which, Hanlon told me, involved the workman's slapping the equipment with a glove so that, if a shock was received or a spark released, it would affect only the glove and not the man's hand.

Something went wrong in this instance. The power unit blew up, and the workman's entire body was instantly covered with boiling hot oil. Hanlon rushed into the workroom where the accident had occurred and found the unfortunate victim writhing and rolling about on the ground like a bug on a griddle, in a way that almost froze Hanlon's blood. When he realized that his cries had at last attracted attention, the man looked at Hanlon and began shouting, "Kill me, kill me! For Christ's sake get a gun and kill me quick!"

Hanlon ran to the telephone and summoned help. Some twenty minutes later medical personnel administered a pain-killing injection to the victim, who later died.

Let the reader place himself into this all-too-real drama and imagine that he had ready access to a weapon. Would it have been a morally justifiable act to grant the poor sufferer's request? Most people, including many decent Christians and Jews, would say yes. *The churches say no.* (See also SITUATIONAL ETHICS.)

EVIL, THE PROBLEM OF. The Western mind, that often has a tendency to try to be scientific about philosophical questions, finds its desire for clarity and certainty frequently frustrated when the questions being considered deal largely with abstract rather than concrete concepts. A definition of evil, for example, probably seems simple enough to a ten-year-old, but it has proved notoriously difficult for professional philosophers. The latter have no difficulty speculating at length about the matter, and a good deal of what they have had to say is creative, reasonable, or stimulative. However, for both the naive and the informed the thing-in-itself continues to be elusive.

There are two large categories of experiences that we commonly describe as evil. One concerns what may, in its purely physical attributes, represent nothing more than the perfectly natural functioning of the laws of physics. Despite the primitive superstitious belief, which persists into modern times, that natural calamities such as storms or earthquakes are caused quite directly by God as a punishment for human sins, there is, in fact, not a fragment of evidence that such is the case. Indeed if it were true that typhoons, floods, lightning bolts, wide-ranging fires, plagues, and other natural disasters *are* chastisements of a furiously vengeful Deity, the God in question—if judged by the same standard applied to everything else, that is, by his actions, his fruits—would not be a proper object of love and adoration but a spiritual entity quite properly deserving of intense moral loathing and contempt. Our poor planet would not be the simple way station suspended between either the mental concept or physical realities of heaven and hell but rather a sort of hell itself in which every hour of every day enormous hordes of human beings, both sinful and decent enough, would be devoured by wild animals, crushed beneath falling buildings, dashed to death at the base of tall structures, or otherwise brutalized by a savage God.

Unless we perceive the daily, hour-by-hour, minute-by-minute element of this widespread human suffering when considering the larger question, we might foolishly assume that we were talking only about extremely rare events—of which the flood that Noah is said to have survived was one rare example—that because of their very rarity could not be said to be typical of human experience.

But the problem we are considering, that of the apparent murderous vengefulness of God, does not exist at all in reality. It is a problem in thought that exists only in the minds of those who argue that all human and animal suffering caused by purely natural events is consciously ordained by that God.

But if God does not by his personal, free will decide to hurl such blows at his luckless creatures, we are still left with a separate and puzzling question: Why does God *permit* natural, physical debilitating events—which, of course, includes attacks by microorganisms, germs, bacteria, viruses, and by more visible creatures as well as assaults from natural phenomena—when it would be no trouble whatever (God being all-powerful) to prevent such suffering?

Suggesting that some of those who suffer have brought their tragic fates on themselves by the great evil they have done is not a proper answer. Such a response cannot possibly apply to the fates of those who are not evil, either because they are too young to have reached what theologians call the age of reason, or because, as adults, they have lived not sinful but decent lives. Some spokesmen for the churches continue to sputter over this dilemma without clarifying it. Usually they merely obscure the basic, simple question rather than resolve it. Better, wiser theologians humbly concede their inability to provide a relevant answer and say, as does, for example, Walter C. Kaiser, Jr., in his *Hard Sayings of the Old Testament,* "It is at this point that we begin to invade the realms of divine mystery."

When we call something a mystery, we are conceding that on the question at issue we are ignorant. Nevertheless, most theologians continue to assert that God is all-good and all-loving but admit that they cannot prove the assertion and that their continued assumption that the Deity is compassionately concerned about not only every human but also animal creatures is only a matter of faith and not knowledge. The literalist fundamentalists of the various forms of belief generally continue to insist—in defiance of reason itself—that (1) God does love all his creatures and (2) he nevertheless continues to subject millions of them daily to hideous pain and death because he has consciously decided to do so. The wiser and more appealing believers simply bow their heads in humility and comfort themselves by pulling the garment of their faith more securely about their shoulders.

Evil human acts constitute another category of evil. The behavior of animals must obviously be excluded from such a condemnation, given that science and religion—not to mention common sense—agree that animals are incapable of evil. That creatures by the millions do wreak bloody destruction is self-evident. The depredations of man-eating sharks, for example, cause the most agonizing suffering for other living creatures, including humans, but the shark itself is morally blameless unless we are prepared to argue that the simple act of eating to sustain one's physical self is sinful. To blame an animal for any destruction it may cause would be as stupid as blaming fire for the pain it causes.

Only humans are capable of evil, but in so saying we have only narrowed the field of inquiry and inadequately encompassed the subject. We are now addressing the larger philosophical puzzle with which the law in all nations daily concerns itself. Even in the tiny minority of cases where it is possible for witnesses, offenders, or victims to state precisely what has happened in the commission of a crime, the law will concern itself with far more than "the facts."

We may know, for example, that a man entered a certain room, that there was a revolver on a table, that an occupant of the room was shot, and that we have identified his assailant. But if that assailant was either temporarily or permanently insane he is unlikely to stand trial and will be ordered to undergo psychiatric treatment, usually under conditions of confinement. Or perhaps the victim was preparing to physically assault his visitor and the weapon was fired in self-defense. So society is likely to decide that, although there was a killing, it was perfectly justified. In both cases described, therefore, it could be reasonably argued that no evil has been committed.

Evil in humans is oftentimes disguised. Some years ago a young soldier just back from Vietnam was a guest on one of my television programs. He had escaped from a Vietcong prison camp, and his story was fascinating.

He was a likable fellow from a small town, an average, middle-class American. After the program was over our production group invited him to join us for dinner at a nearby restaurant, where we continued our cordial conversation about the Vietnam War. At one point the young soldier expressed the fear that our ultimate problem in that part of the world was not the National Liberation Front but mainland China.

"What do you think we ought to do about that problem?" I asked.

"I think," he said, speaking calmly, as if he were discussing football strategy, "we ought to drop the bomb on them."

"You mean attack China with nuclear weapons?"

"Yes," the young man said.

"Do you mean wipe *all* of them out?" I asked incredulously.

"That's what I mean," he said. "I know it would be a hard thing to do, but the way I look at it, if we don't do just that then we're only gonna have to fight them right here at home in a few years."

Re-read the young man's remarks. Here was the boy next door saying quite dispassionately that *it was morally permissible to kill 700 million mostly civilian and innocent people—the majority not even sympathetic to communism—because of his dislike of the bluster and presumed threat of the Chinese Communist leadership.*

Remember too that the American military has never recognized any danger of a Chinese attack on American shores.

The young man's pathetic ignorance remained invisible to him because it was disguised as patriotism. Yet, somehow, the moral evil here is so enormous that one is at a loss to know how to even think of it. We have no trouble dealing with the moral darkness present in one man armed with a gun. Such crimes are personal; we grasp them. We disapprove of them and attempt to apprehend the criminals and punish or reform them.

This other evil looms so great that one tends to respond to it not with argument, not with analytical criticism, but by merely shaking one's head and fearing for the future of ourselves and our children. This evil is not confined merely to the identifiable neurotics and psychotics who people our prisons and political hate groups of the right and left. This stain rots the soul of a nation, particularly one whose leaders attempt to justify it.

When Lester Maddox, for example, passed out ax handles to his admirers, he exhibited that sickness of spirit that leads to the systematic denial of justice, to the formalized endorsement of brute violence, to the torture chamber, the firing squad, and the concentration camp. (See also TORTURE.)

The Biblical Approach. One of the fundamental faults of the biblical approach to evil is that it perceives the distinction between good and bad, between virtue and wickedness in terms so simplistic that they are unrealistic, even within the context of theology. That there are certain rare individuals apparently almost totally committed to evil or at least frequently behaving in an immoral, illegal, or otherwise destructive manner is clear enough. It is equally clear that a small number of men and women lead lives distinguished by innocence and decency. But alas for scriptural simplicity, these two groups together make up a very small fraction of one percent of the human race.

Imagine that each of us is assigned the task of simply writing down the names of wicked and righteous individuals in two separate lists. We may take our names not only from the contemporary scene but also from all history. Certainly no one can imagine that there would be any sort of order or cohesion—indeed, any statistically measurable patterns—in the aggregate of such personal evaluations. Muslims, for example, would tend to include rather a notable percentage of their religious opponents on their bad-people lists, while Jews, Christians, and others would do the equivalent within the context of their conditioned prejudices. Catholics would list some of their saints on the side of virtue, perhaps to be told by the Vatican later that some of those named had never existed. Upon comparing their lists with those of their Protestant friends and neighbors, the Catholics would find that from the Protestant point of view some of these very same heroes of the Catholic pantheon might be perceived as fanatics, bigots, persecutors, or psychotics.

In our own limited social circles, each of us knows that a given individual will be judged in complimentary fashion by one observer and pejoratively by another.

Further, many who would have to be perceived as wicked and ruthless on purely moral or religious grounds may nevertheless be idolized by the masses in their capacities as motion picture actors, popular singers, presidents, political philosophers, authors, military leaders, or artists. Contemplating excruciating, eternal torture by fire for unidentified billions of humans classified only as *the wicked* is simple unless one is asked to make a series of *specific* evaluations. Then the matter assumes startlingly variant proportions.

Consider the case of the singer Elvis Presley. Neither Mr. Presley nor any of those who were close to him would have ever argued that he was a candidate for sainthood. If, for example, the Catholic church is correct in its theology, then we must conclude that when he died in 1977 Mr. Presley—soul and body—was ushered straight to the infernal regions, there to scream and writhe in agony for all time. A high proportion of his hundreds of millions of admirers will, however, at the very least, debate the matter of the after-death treatment of the "wicked" Presley.

Fundamental error in the Old Testament approach to evil is revealed in its frequent attribution of moral fault to *entire peoples*. That this is

111

a common delusion in times of war is certainly no defense for its wisdom. During the two World Wars, all Germans were stereotyped and characterized in a foolishly unitary way, as if an entire people could share *any* qualities of character, good or bad.

Both world wars saw the Germans uniformly described as vicious, fanatical, and daily given to atrocious behavior, among other equally unsavory judgments. It required the passing of many years after the armistice before these attitudes were revised and ultimately abandoned. Now even many victims who suffered most at the hands of the Germans and Japanese can distinguish between those who were "good," and those who were "evil." Even this simplistic either-or categorization is very much an improvement over the former alternative of labeling groups wholesale.

The authors of the Scriptures, however, endlessly assert that the Chaldeans *as such* were evil, that the Egyptians, the Assyrians, the Amorites, and scores of other tribes against whom the Israelites warred were all evil individuals. Such absurd beliefs can not possibly represent reality.

The Bible plainly says that physical evils come from God. In LAMENTATIONS chapter 3, we read:

> 38. Out of the mouth of the most High proceedeth not evil and good?
> 39. Wherefore doth a living man complain, a man for the punishment of his sins?

We see here not only error, but two combined instances of it. The verse not only attributes evil to God but also states that such sufferings are not merely the accidents of nature that most people believe them to be but also occur because of the sinfulness of particular human beings.

An all-powerful being would have the power to punish a sinner, by any means he might choose to employ. However, the Scriptures not only attribute to God a horrible vengefulness but also suggest that God is incredibly stupid. It would be stupid if an individual, intent on punishing a sinner or group of them, expended his destructive energy not only on those who it might be said deserved such punishment but also on enormous numbers of innocent people who simply had the bad luck to be in the physical proximity of evildoers. To argue that God works in this way is to put him precisely on the same moral plane as those modern terrorists who, to kill a particular individual or small group, will place a bomb on an airplane in the full knowledge that in addition to the five or six intended victims all the other occupants, in whom the terrorists have no particular interest, will be killed.

Let us say that 20 percent of a given population is so sinful that they deserve some sort of punishment. What sense does it make to kill not only them but also all the other inhabitants of their community?

This point is so simple that a five-year-old child could grasp it even in abstract terms. For those of us who cannot accept that God is, in fact, guilty of such outrageous crimes, it follows that scriptural quotations stating precisely that must be in error. (See also CRIME, BIBLICAL IMPETUS TO; ERROR; WAR.)

Change and Its Effect on Evil. Philosophers have long pondered the question why there must be change or what, given its inevitability, is its basis. That basis seems inherent in the structure of the atom, the basic building-block of all matter. An atom is an incredibly tiny universe with its own equivalents of whirling planets. Motion itself is change. In recognizing that a given object does not forever remain at one point in space, we acknowledge the necessary existence of change; it is the endless process of movement that leads to the idea of impermanence.

Nothing material lasts forever, even though matter is not destroyed but is endlessly recycled. It is impossible even to envision a permanent, unchanging object or universe. On this point there is little, if any, room for argument. Casual philosophers of almost all schools of thought experience no difficulty in agreeing with what has just been stated. The most violent sorts of disagreement, however, are encountered as soon as we relate the idea of endless change to the million-and-one daily points of contact between the animal world and the totally mindless aspects of the physical universe.

It is of little importance if stones are perceived to crack and erode, to change. But when the cracking and eroding relate to living tissue, a sobering assortment of philosophical questions present themselves. The endless disorder characteristic of the material world works uncountable tragedies upon billions of individual living creatures, large and small, animal and human.

A bolt of lightning striking a tree in the forest that, let us say, has never been seen by human eyes, is obviously not taken into account in considering the large puzzle of existence itself. But when that same searing bolt strikes a loved one, the very blind injustice of the act is deeply troubling to us, especially if we believe that there is a God who is the very essence of compassion. In such dramas we are brought face-to-face with the uncomfortable recognition that the supposed compassion of our utterly compassionate God has, in this context, not been extended. It is not only violent acts of nonliving *nature* that cause suffering but also contacts with other animals, including those of our own species. (See NATURE.)

While this large, tragic realization is depressing to the believer and unbeliever alike, it presents a philosophical problem only for the believer.

Science simply perceives and measures what is fact and, as such, is not inherently concerned with the philosophical questions surrounding that fact.

Nor is there merely one large question that puzzles believers. Millions of believers are, for example, firmly committed to the idea of benevolent, watchful, spiritual creatures called guardian ANGELS; yet no member of the faithful so firmly believes in the protection of such creatures that he would willingly toss his own beloved child into a swimming pool occupied by several ravenous man-eating sharks on the assumption that the child's personal angel will pluck it to safety. If the powers of angels are limited, as they obviously must be according to the definition of such creatures, certainly the same cannot be said of God Almighty. But again, there are apparently no believers with faith so firm or trust in the Deity so strong that they would permit their children to swim in such frothing and angry waters.

In addition to the destruction of living animal tissue that humans wreak in satisfying their appetites, there is a far more serious universe of disorder and pain caused by an element of which no animal is even capable: simple vindictiveness. The only evil animal on the planet earth is modern *Homo sapiens*. As with other animal species, some humans are tame, lovable, housebroken, indeed exhibit the most endearing characteristics. But millions of others are capable of such crimes as wars, assaults, rapes, stranglings, maimings, knifings, electrocutions, hangings, gassings, beheadings, shootings, and tortures.

Although the horrors of several wars should have purged our species of evils that originate in the human motivation to greed and power—or else in deranged personalities—this does not seem to have happened. Those who were once tormented now torment others, as in Africa and the Middle East. Nations that fought the evils of fascism now aid dictators to murder their own people, as for example the United States and the former USSR, who long conducted a vicious cold war that kept Americans and Russians relatively safe but that killed millions in "client" states.

Perhaps the greatest and most disturbing changes that human flesh is heir to are aging and death from purely natural causes. From the time a child is capable of understanding that a beloved pet has died and will play no more, he or she begins to understand that death will come one day. Each person works out for himself what happens afterward: whether our bodies rot and join the elements or are resurrected to go to heaven or hell.

Most people are able to live their lives without becoming suicidally depressed if they believe the former; some are able to devote themselves to perfecting or understanding the world, or to raising offspring who will leave the world a better place. (See also BY THEIR FRUITS YE SHALL KNOW THEM; CRUSADES, THE; FREE WILL; MORALITY; SITUATIONAL ETHICS.)

EZRA. The earnest believer in God and in the validity of the Scriptures, who admirably seeks information that can help facilitate his personal salvation, would do well to forego studying the Book of Ezra and instead look to more edifying portions of Scripture for moral uplift.

Chapter 1. The compilers of the Old Testament were occasionally guilty of simple carelessness. The first three verses of this book are a good example, in that they are almost identical to the last two verses of CHRONICLES, excepting that the Chronicles section terminates in the middle of a sentence, the meaning of which cannot be determined without reference to Ezra.

2 CHRONICLES 36	EZRA 1
22. Now in the first year of Cyrus king of Persia, that the word of the Lord spoken by the mouth of Jeremiah might be accomplished, the Lord stirred up the spirit of Cyrus king of Persia, that he made a proclamation throughout all his kingdom, and put it also in writing, saying,	1. Now in the first year of Cyrus king of Persia, that the word of the Lord spoken by the mouth of Jeremiah might be accomplished, the Lord stirred up the spirit of Cyrus king of Persia, that he made a proclamation throughout all his kingdom, and put it also in writing, saying,
23. Thus saith Cyrus king of Persia, "All the kingdoms of the earth hath the Lord God of heaven given me; and he hath charged me to build him an house in Jerusalem, which is in Judah, Who is there among you of all his people? The Lord he is God be with him, and let him go up."	2. Thus saith Cyrus king of Persia, "The Lord God of heaven hath given me all the kingdoms of the earth; and he hath charged me to build him an house at Jerusalem, which is in Judah. 3. "Who is there among you of all his people? his God be with him, and let him go up to Jerusalem, which is in Judah, and build the house of the Lord God of Israel, (he is the God,) which is in Jerusalem."

Scholars of the Old Testament commonly observe that the preceding sections of Chronicles and Ezra contain a falsehood in the statement of the Persian king Cyrus that he had been given "all the kingdoms of the earth." The counterargument might be advanced, however, that the unknown author simply quoted Cyrus and was therefore not responsible for the ruler's own error.

Chapter 2. Either this chapter is in error, or the seventh chapter of the Book of Nehemiah is mistaken, since each purports to give a list of those who returned from Babylonian captivity. Since the two lists are mutually contradictory, they cannot both be correct. Both can be wrong, and it is highly probable that they are.

Chapter 3. Here we find a description of what was done when all had "gathered themselves together as one man to Jerusalem." So overjoyed were the participants and observers of the building project that they both cheered and wept so loudly that "the noise was heard afar off."

Chapter 4. This chapter relates what happened when "the adversaries of Judah and Benjamin" heard about the project and offered to participate in it. Being rebuffed, they began to hamper the building work.

> 5. And hired counsellors against them, to frustrate their purpose, all the days of Cyrus king of Persia, even until the reign of Darius king of Persia.

Under subsequent rulers the campaign of obstruction continued. Eventually King Artaxerxes issued an edict commanding that the building be stopped.

> 24. Then ceased the work of the house of God which is at Jerusalem. So it ceased unto the second year of the reign of Darius king of Persia.

Chapter 6. Now we are told that King Darius instructed that a search be made of the royal records and in due course a copy of the earlier decree of King Cyrus was located. Darius, therefore, said that the work on the temple could once again be resumed.

> 15. And this house was finished on the third day of the month Adar, which was in the sixth year of the reign of Darius the king.

Chapter 7. In Chapter 7 we at last find reference to the man named Ezra. Since he is written about in the third person, it is unlikely that he wrote the portions of Scripture commonly attributed to him. Further, King Artaxerxes, we are told, gave Ezra, the priest and scribe, a letter of instruction, the full details of which need not concern us here, except that in verse 25 the king instructs Ezra to set up judges of all his people and then proceeds to define the duties of these same judges:

26. And whosoever will not do the law of thy God, and the law of the king, let judgment be executed speedily upon him, whether it be unto death, or to banishment, or to confiscation of goods, or to imprisonment.

Those Christians of the modern day who recommend that our nation be converted to a purely biblical mode of life presumably cannot find anything to object to in the recommendation of this verse. But it would be interesting to see the reactions of twentieth-century Americans, among others, at being told that because they are unable to accept the teachings of the modern self-chosen representatives of the Almighty, some of them are to be put to death, others banished from their native country, others punished by the confiscation of their material possessions, and still others thrown into prison. Such proceedings could never be conducted without subverting every known principle of American justice and social morality. (See also JUSTICE.)

The last subject with which Ezra concerned himself—at least so far as this scant record of his life reveals—was the matter of the thousands of Jews who had taken unto themselves "strange wives"—women not of their tribe or faith. Although this would not be counted a grave sin in the present day, even by many religious Jews, it was considered an abomination in the time of Ezra. Accordingly, a revival was preached and large numbers of the faithful rid themselves of their wives. This tragic enough drama was made even more so because the fathers, who now perceived themselves as especially holy and religious, also abandoned the children they had sired of the wives who were now being divorced.

Readers of the Scriptures are told nothing of the subsequent fate of the great numbers of women and abandoned children, although we can surmise their fate. We now know what sort of suffering generally befalls women who are discarded—the more so if they have sons and daughters.

Naturally not a word in Ezra suggests that the faithful who rid themselves of their wives thereafter contributed anything to the support of their children. Modern day conservative Christians vociferously criticize divorced fathers who do not contribute to the sustenance of their children. If we were to return to a purely biblical morality, these Christians would no longer have a basis in moral theology from which to mount such criticisms. (See also DIVORCE; ERROR; MORALITY; WOMEN'S LIBERATION.)

F

FAITH. For Christians, the three greatest virtues are said to be faith, HOPE, and CHARITY. It is typical of the wisdom of Jesus that he held the last virtue superior. Without feeling at least a minimum degree of compassionate concern for our fellow creatures, and manifesting that concern by concrete acts of material assistance, humans would be far sorrier creatures than they observably are. The superiority of charity lies also in its practical value as a survival mechanism, in the direct sense that those who receive the charitable attentions of others are literally enabled to survive. (See VIRTUES, THE.)

Although my proposed topic is faith, beginning with the subject of charity enables drawing a sharp distinction between it and the two other widely praised virtues or ideals. The distinction is that charity is always productive of some degree of good whereas the same cannot be said of faith and hope.

Faith, considered purely in the abstract, is devoid of content. The word *faith* is, in some respects, like the word *food.* Food is merely a convenient term used to refer to that classification of biological substances that may be safely ingested by living creatures. No one ever walks into a grocery store and says, "I'd like to buy two pounds of food, please." One buys meat, corn, wheat, tomatoes, and thousands of other specific material substances that living bodies require for fuel.

Faith, then, is merely an overall abstract term that functions more as a verb than a noun. We *have faith* in something, but whether that faith is sensible and wise or foolish and destructive depends entirely on its object. Millions of Germans had absolute faith in Hitler. Millions of Russians had faith in Stalin. Millions of Chinese had faith in Mao. Billions have had faith in imaginary gods. The ongoing act of having faith in something cannot possibly be construed as being always good, much less as being properly revered virtue. The object of faith determines whether a specific instance of faith is reasonable.

One might respond that references to Hitler, Stalin, and Mao refer to political faith; that faith in such a context will always be a shaky proposition but that the same cannot be said of religious faith. Any such argument would be sadly mistaken. Adherents of any one religion usually insist that the faith of their rivals is seriously misguided except as it applies to specifics the separate forms might share. We do not refer here only to minor and thus unimportant differences among religions. Many such contradictions have been viewed as serious enough by those concerned to lead to centuries of mass slaughters, wars, pillage, rape, the desecration of temples, and the infliction of the most hideous tortures upon those who survive the initial military confrontations. (See also RELIGION; RELIGIOUS THEORIES, DEVIANT.)

The religious believer considers it the height of presumption to doubt that certain alleged spiritual experiences did in fact take place. He argues: How can one far removed in time and space satisfy even his own mind about such questions, much less that of anyone else? This same religious believer may understand the integrity of the skeptical approach if he consults his own responses to unusual religious phenomena reported by *churches other than his own*. For example, a Mormon is every bit as convinced of the reality of Joseph Smith's visions and heavenly visitations as the Catholic is convinced of the reality of those phenomena attributed to the saints. But no Catholic, or for that matter other non-Mormon Christian, places the slightest confidence in Smith's claims.

There is not just one religion but thousands. It is hardly surprising that atheists and agnostics are essentially united in viewing all of them as misguided, though not necessarily in every particular. What is noteworthy is that the overwhelming majority of religious believers also hold that most of the world's religions—that is, those other than their own—are largely nonsense.

So, it is meaningless to praise faith in the absence of specific content, just as it is meaningless to praise, say, courage before one knows to what end courage is put. A rapist who breaks into a home at night, risking being shot or arrested if discovered in the commission of his awful act, is undoubtedly courageous. But would anyone dream of praising such courage?

Still, faith is a natural tendency since the great majority of humans profess belief in something, whether religious, political, or philosophical. Where then does faith come from? Most believers will quickly answer that it comes from God. Such an answer produces more confusion than clarity: we have already agreed on the absurdity of assuming that God endorses every one of the thousand-and-one religions of the world, many of whose dogmas are mutually exclusive.

Given the puzzling nature of the universe itself and the natural human inclination to "make sense" of things, we understandably tend to impose solutions in advance of adequate evidence. Science, too, works in a somewhat similar way, except that its creative ideas are at first not treated as conclusions but merely working hypotheses that are entertained only as long as they are not contradicted by evidential facts. (See also ARGUMENT.)

Faith always refers to hope and never to knowledge. Imagine an individual in a television production studio where cameras, microphones, and recording equipment are in the on-mode just at the moment when he has a visitation from God—who, we will assume, actually exists. Assume further that seven technicians witness the event. Let us also say that the man is a skeptic, perhaps a physicist of impeccable intellectual and scholarly credentials. So God suddenly appears, in such a setting, without having had to walk through a door to gain admittance. The skeptic, being aware of the long-documented existence of such phenomena as hysterical visions, hallucinations, hypnosis, mental derangements, and deliberate deceit by magicians and alleged seers, at first refuses to accept the evidence of his senses. However, the audio and video recording equipment is providing incontrovertible proof that what the gentleman thinks he is seeing and hearing is actually taking place. Within a few minutes the man has satisfied himself that the available evidence is reliable and leads to only one conclusion: that the mysterious visitor is indeed a creature of superhuman powers, clearly not limited by the known physical laws of the universe.

Given this acceptance, let us now assume that the skeptic converses with God and clarifies questions that have resisted the efforts of history's ablest philosophers. From that moment the ancient question whether there is in fact a real God is settled to the full satisfaction of our physicist and all the others who have witnessed his astonishing experience. No longer would any of them dream of making a statement so foolish as "I *believe* in God." They now *know* that there is a God.

The purpose of this little story is to demonstrate that all the religious believers of the world, who constitute by far the great majority of the human race, do not have such knowledge at all. What they do have is fervent hope, a hope they express by an act of faith. This is perfectly true whether there is a God or not in fact.

We must also understand that the only entity that could not possibly have faith is God himself. If knowledge obliterates faith and a supreme

God is by definition the holder of all possible knowledge, it would be impossible for him to have faith in anything. Faith, then, is built upon ignorance and hope.

Hope is a term that is intelligible only as it relates to the future. No one says, "I very much hope that I went to Chicago last Wednesday" since, in the absence of amnesia, one *knows* whether or not one performed a given act in the past. Nor does anyone express a hope about something he is already aware is occurring in the present.

Faith, too, may refer to the future. It is expressed in statements such as "I have faith that I will recover from this illness," or "I have faith that the Lord will save me." Even though the speaker refers to his present condition, *it is always in the context of some hoped for or urgently needed future outcome that he speaks.* (See also FUTURE, THE.)

A particularly puzzling aspect of the story of early Christianity is that both Mark and Matthew make frequent references to the disciples' lack of faith. That the faith of even the most devout may occasionally waver is perfectly understandable to all those who know even a little about the staggering injustice of life itself and the consequent widespread suffering of the innocent and faithful. Religious believers of the present day can only have faith concerning many aspects of religious philosophy because their accumulation of firm knowledge is no more than slight. But if the accounts attributed to Matthew, Mark, Luke, and John are even substantially accurate, then the Apostles and other witnesses in Jesus' retinue had a great deal of concrete knowledge concerning him. They saw him, heard him, touched him. They dined with him. They were healed by him, raised from the dead by him. They saw him walk on water. As a mental exercise, place yourself into the New Testament drama; if anyone had had such an enormous amount of evidentiary experience could he later doubt what he had seen and heard?

Certain aspects of the historical tradition about Jesus could only be addressed on grounds of faith rather than knowledge. Even after spending three full years with the great leader, one would not necessarily be absolutely certain whether he was, in fact, God in human form. Nor could one even be sure that he was, if not himself God, at least the only direct son of God, in a sense distinct from the way in which all of us may be said to be sons of God, if God did indeed create the universe. The Gospels never tell us whether it was on these two questions that the actual sympathetic witnesses to the ministry of Jesus experienced a wavering of the faith. Like so many of the Bible's puzzles and mysteries, this one apparently cannot be resolved by even the most profoundly insightful speculation or an appeal to archaeological or historical evidence, since there is so little of that available.

Weakening the Faith of Others. The question of weakening the faith of others occurs quite naturally to anyone who subjects traditional theological views—of any sort—to an impartial critical analysis. Voltaire, albeit facetiously, argued that the faith of simple people ought perhaps not to be disturbed because otherwise how would we prevent our servants from stealing our silverware? Mark Twain, though an agnostic and no friend of organized religion, nevertheless felt a degree of guilt at the fact that his wife's religious faith had been undermined as an effect of his own philosophy.

When churches seek to discourage fair-minded appraisal of their teachings, we should understand that they do not decry the weakening of faith in general but *merely the weakening of their own specific position.* In fact, churches are not only perfectly prepared to see faith in general weakened but also devote a large part of their creative energies toward that very end. For two thousand years Christians have made it almost their primary business to weaken the faith of those affiliated with what were considered pagan religions. Nor have Christians ever had anything but an earnest desire to weaken the faith of the world's millions of Jews. Such attitudes are not unique to Christians; members of all sects are pleased when the faith of others is weakened, at least insofar as the suddenly theologically bereft might flock to the sectarian's own fortress of faith.

Let us assert that faith does indeed change one's life, but it doesn't seem to matter a great deal where one's faith lies. Some peoples' lives have taken on purpose, dedication, courage, and satisfaction through faith in Protestantism, Catholicism, Judaism, communism, socialism, Nazism, Buddhism, vegetarianism, pacifism, or atheism. (See also VIRTUES, THE.)

FANATICISM. To praise a person simply because he believes in some religious philosophy is as absurd as praising him because he daily ingests food. It can be perfectly reasonable to confer praise for specific spiritual beliefs or dietary regimens but certainly not in the abstract, in the absence of concrete particulars. One who ingests three collar buttons a day and washes them down with a bottle of ink would not be praised by any rational nutritionist. On the other hand, if he eschews harmful or fattening foods and eats wisely, then he deserves to be complimented. Just so, our complimentary observations should be reserved for those situations in which religious opinions, customs, and acts are reasonable and socially productive.

It is meaningless—even dangerous—to praise others simply because of their degree of commitment or sincerity. Hitler, Mao, and Stalin were three of the most fervently committed and sincere individuals in history, but the very energy of their convictions led them to destructive acts and policies that cost the lives of scores of millions. Any reasonable society would far prefer a decent law-abiding atheist or agnostic to a fanatical religious believer convinced of one sort of patent nonsense or another.

If all that were involved with political and religious fanaticism was adherence to absurd or bizarre opinions, that would be unfortunate enough. But as the bloodstained pages of history demonstrate, the delusionary is rarely content with holding to his True Belief. His own firm convictions make him perceive those who do not share his views as The Enemy, to be opposed by any and all means. The means themselves—no matter how deceitful, violent, criminal, or depraved—seem justified in the mind of the deluded simply because the end sought—the triumph of the True Belief— is perceived as virtuous to the highest degree. (See also CRUSADES, THE; EVIL, THE PROBLEM OF.)

The American founding fathers, having recent enough evidence of the savagery of much of European history, sought to erect institutional and legal devices that would make it difficult for fanatics to seize power. Freedom is one thing that the fanatic absolutely cannot countenance. If he could, a fanatic would put an end to many or all of our freedoms, insisting only on his own. If he lacks the power to commit such crimes on a broad scale, he commits them individually.

The fanatic is an intellectual rule breaker who will readily manipulate both evidence and logic. If one is permitted to write the rules of the game, one can "prove" anything. Consider, for example, the absurd assertion that the world began not some six thousand years ago as many fundamentalist Christians believe, not billions of years ago as modern science tells us, but last Wednesday morning. A debate on the question might be conducted as follows:

FANATIC: The world began last Wednesday morning.

NONBELIEVER: Do you mean that as a statement of literal fact? That the entire physical universe as we know it did not exist in any sense until last Wednesday morning?

FANATIC: That is precisely what I mean.

NONBELIEVER: How can you believe anything so preposterous?

123

FANATICISM

FANATIC: Oh, I do not *believe,* I *know.*

NONBELIEVER: How do you know?

FANATIC: Because God personally has communicated the information to me.

NONBELIEVER: Ah, but how do you account for massive physical evidence to the contrary?

FANATIC: Very simply. I know what sort of things you're talking about: the fact that there are coins stamped 1914, books that seem to have been published in 1822, rocks that geologists assert are hundreds of millions of years old. The answer is simply that God, in his infinite wisdom, would hardly have erected a universe in which everything appears to be brand new.

NONBELIEVER: I don't know what you're talking about.

FANATIC: Of course you don't. You have not been enlightened by God's grace. Are you arrogant enough to pit your puny human mind against that of the Almighty? Don't you think that he has the power to create a universe only a few days old and yet give it the appearance of age, as a concession to the weakness of our minds?

It is obvious that no combination of science and logic, no exercise of pure reason, will be able to permeate such invulnerable fanaticism.

The impartial observer can readily see that the fanatic's position and his method of defending it are nonsensical. However, there may be no way to convince the fanatic of what is so obvious to others. (See also ARGUMENT; REASON.)

Consequently, the ancient debate about the validity of the reports of religious experiences will presumably never be concluded satisfactorily. Even if such a thing were possible—if, for example, within a fifty-year time frame a thousand of the world's most gifted intellects, equally divided on the two general sides of the question, could convene for the sole purpose of exploring assorted questions and possibilities—all that would happen is that the new consensus, whatever its dimensions, would evaporate as the debaters and scholars themselves died and their papers were blown away by the winds of time. A new generation would then come along, to be followed by a succession of others down through the ages, each starting with a relatively blank slate, the name of which is ignorance.

The ancient questions will never be universally resolved because the two general sides are by no means in a black-and-white, either-or relationship. Religious believers share a widespread agreement that a great deal of religious belief is not only nonsense but also dangerous. The believers do not so describe their own religious opinions, but they hold a good many of the views of other believers in intellectual contempt, which is often disguised purely for reasons of social convenience.

Consider, for example, the three great religious figures: Moses, Jesus, and Mohammed. The followers of each insist that their founder had the most direct personal contact with God and, in the case of many Christians, was in fact himself God. Not only atheists and agnostics question such belief. Those believers—especially the more intelligent and reasonable among them—who owe loyalty to one of the three great prophets entertain serious reservations about the other two camps.

Individual Jews, Christians, and Muslims find it troubling that their founder is flatly opposed by two other widely influential teachers. But more, it is disquieting and puzzling to Christians of the present moment to observe that the followers of Mohammed constitute the fastest-growing group on earth. If Jesus is God and by definition possessed of all power, then how can he permit the remarkable energy and growth of a rival and false religion, while many Christian churches are losing members and religious vocations are dwindling? (See also IRRATIONALISM; JEWS AND JUDAISM; RELIGIOUS THEORIES, DEVIANT.)

FIRMAMENT. There is no such thing as a firmament in the sense that the word is used in the first chapter of Genesis:

> 6. And God said, "Let there be a firmament in the midst of the waters, and let it divide the waters from the waters."
> 7. And God made the firmament, and divided the waters which were under the firmament from the waters which were above the firmament; and it was so.
> 8. And God called the firmament Heaven. . . .

Christians, among others, have a variety of answers to the simple question: What, or where, is heaven? When debating the issue, absolutely no present-day Christian or Jew makes reference to "the firmament," nor to any sort of vaguely defined space between the lowest and highest clouds. The inescapable conclusion, therefore, is that on yet one more point—and one of major importance—the Bible is in error.

FIRMAMENT

Primitive man believed there was an actual physical arch over the earth because he could perceive the earth—and what little of the surrounding universe he could see with the naked eye—only through the evidence of his senses. He lacked the sophistication to know, as we do today, that the senses are severely limited and consequently sometimes lead us to erroneous conclusions.

For eons the senses assured man that the earth was flat; only science demonstrated that it is spherical in shape. *Firmament* is simply a word to describe what appears to be an enormous dome to anyone who stands on the surface of the earth and looks upward and outward. In terms of the limited knowledge available in past ages, it would have seemed evident, even to highly intelligent observers, that the sun, moon, and stars were fixed into the surface of this dome, even though they were observed to move. Ancient man was unable to guess how close the higher clouds were to the surface of the dome-firmament itself, although he must have frequently observed, particularly in mountainous territories, that certain clouds neared the surface of the earth. Because primitive man observed that rain fell from above, he understandably assumed that somehow there were waters above the firmament, and that downpours would pass through certain "floodgates" from time-to-time. That water did not rain down continuously was attributed to the apparent solidity of the firmament-dome, which is, of course, why the word *firm-ament* was used.

We now know that there is no such thing and that therefore no such "division of waters" occurred. Since there are no such things, it is naturally meaningless to state that God made them.

The reader who has followed these observations will perceive that it is also misleading to say that God called the firmament by a particular name in a particular language. Even if we momentarily entertain the assumption that it was to God's interest to attach names to things, he would hardly have given such a completely misleading name as *heaven* to the planets and stars—which could not, in any event, be inhabited. God would have applied the term solely to the spiritual realm as it is described elsewhere in the Scriptures: the mysterious area of his residence and the ultimate gathering place for the elect. (See also BELIEFS AND MYTHS; ERRORS; SCIENCE AND RELIGION.)

FREEDOM. Given the enormous importance that has been attached to both the concept and the reality of freedom in recent centuries, it is remarkable that there are so few references to it in the Scriptures. We are told of the occasional captivity of portions of the Hebrew population, and since we know that no slave ever consciously chooses such an unhappy estate we can assume that these particular Jews wanted their freedom.

But the idea that freedom is a general good—a *right*—that ought to be accorded to everyone is quite a modern and still debated assumption.

What *is* freedom? Definitions tend to be unsatisfactory in that they often reword what we already know about the word being defined. Some men so venerate the idea of freedom that they become like those who worship gods that have never existed. Such people imagine that there is something called absolute freedom which both exists and is good. But there is no such thing, either in reality or in imagination. Not even 'God has absolute freedom, since an all-virtuous power by definition has no freedom to commit evil.

Natural laws make absolute freedom impossible. If all natural laws were suddenly canceled out by some cosmic magic, the universe would change. We do not know how it would change, or whether it would vanish. It is an impenetrable mystery.

So, man's freedom has physical, natural restrictions. He has no freedom to defy the law of gravity. When he is stabbed, he has no freedom not to bleed. When he is denied food, he has no freedom to elect to live without sustenance. If his head is held under water, he has no freedom to breathe. In all of these respects, he is the same as the lesser animals.

It is sometimes said that freedom is essentially a human condition because only man can freely choose among different possibilities. However, if one sets two dishes of food before a hungry animal, the animal will choose to eat one or the other first, thereby exercising his freedom in this regard. Even an animal within the cage has certain freedoms: freedom to walk, now to this side, now to that; freedom to lie, stand, or sleep; freedom to eat or not to eat; and so forth. An animal may be released from a cage and is therefore free; once freed from his prison he is still to a degree *un*-free. For example, a freed lion must still keep within a certain jungle area, near a certain waterhole, within the confines of the domain roamed by other members of his pride. Thus we distinguish what is essential: that *freedom is not an either-or matter but one of degree and relativity.*

The popular opinion that has always countenanced the idea that animals are free is superior to the speculations of those Christian philosophers who assert that freedom arises out of the SOUL of man and that therefore animals are not free merely because they have no souls. What arises out of the soul of man instead is *limitation of freedom*. On that day in evolutionary development when *Homo sapiens* became Adam—in other words, the day when his *soul* was created—man's freedom began to be limited. The biblical tradition clearly states, for example, that Adam promptly lost his freedom to eat the fruit of a particular tree. From that moment to this the passing of time has brought endless limitations upon human freedom.

Like physical health, freedom may sometimes be appreciated only in its absence. Traditionalists contend that genuine freedom does not allow the individual to become a slave to error and passion. To contradict this view, one must first concede that the difference of opinion is largely about the meanings of the words involved. All would agree that it is an evil thing to become the slave of error and passion, but wherever and whenever this happens it is as a result of *the exercise* of freedom; where it does not happen it is the *inhibition* of freedom that is responsible. Such inhibition may be caused by either an internal force—the conscience—or external power exercised by another individual, by society, or by the state.

We now know that each of us is partly free and partly manipulated by the puppet strings attached to his unseen spirit, his conscious self. Most of the body runs itself. The heart, other organs, and cells are not commonly operated by conscious control, and we are only now beginning to get the first glimmerings of what goes on in the human mind. Our freedom is limited by our anxieties, fears, and inhibitions. In some of us freedom is further restricted by our formal codes of behavior. Each man is evidently destined to discover the hard way that he is a prisoner of the past, both his own and that of his civilization. But this knowledge need not plunge him into pessimism because it by no means disproves FREE WILL. Though we are indeed the prisoners of our own heredity and environment, we still may take encouragement from the knowledge that it is always possible to escape from a prison.

The difficulty in arriving at common agreement when discussing such an abstraction as *freedom* is that every individual has his own definition of the word. Even those who realize that the matter of definition breaks down into a series of separate questions—freedom *from* what? free to *do* what?—will place the acts to which freedom entitles them in varying hierarchies. The businessman, for example, may think that freedom *means* free, capitalist enterprise.

Others may see freedom chiefly in religious or political terms. About sixty-five million Americans, so far as one can determine, have no real interest in religion but are still prepared to defend to the death the *idea* of freedom of religion, just as there are those who rarely, if ever, bother to vote and yet are ready to go to war in defense of their freedom to do so.

If ever a commonly spoken word was misunderstood by many who use it daily, that word is *freedom*. The meaning of *freedom* is infinitely relative, with as many definitions as applications.

A totally free world would be a madhouse. I would have freedom to take your house, your food, and your wife, unless you happened to be present and desired to frustrate my wishes. The myriad laws of God and man—however necessary—are restrictions upon our freedom. Do we appear to bridle at these restrictions? Rarely. We engrave them on stone and burn incense before them, though we are prone to *act* as though they were mostly intended for others. Moreover we add to the number of limits with each passing day. In the United States, the freest country on earth, the average citizen's solution to any social, economic, or political situation of which he disapproves is, "There ought to be a law!"

Laws are heavy stones that men carry upon their backs, after having placed them there themselves. If we did not derive pleasure from committing adultery, there would be no need for a law that says *Thou shalt not commit adultery*. If men did not derive enjoyment from driving their automobiles at ninety miles an hour, there would be no need for laws such as *Thou should not drive faster than sixty-five miles per hour*.

In modern society laws are so numerous that one citizen could not hope to familiarize himself with them all in his lifetime. They vary from city to city and county to county; what is a crime in one area is perfectly legal in the next. The laws of the county, state, and federal governments blanket the local laws of communities. Interestingly enough, though the cry of states' rights goes up when the national law is imposed upon a state, that same state would not countenance a call for county rights or city rights from a rebellious community within its borders.

Clearly it is possible to have either too little or too much freedom. But no one has ever been wise enough to point to a particular moment and say, "Halt! As of this day we have the perfect number of laws. One more legal stipulation and we will have taken the first step toward tyranny."

When engrossed in such considerations, we begin to hear the distant siren song of anarchy. The vision is indeed tempting. Great freedom would undeniably abound if virtue were the mode of society. It would obviously be marvelous, after all, if we did not have to be forever looking over our shoulders for traffic police, tax collectors, customs inspectors, bureaucratic functionaries, and all the other animal trainers now required to keep peace in the cages we inhabit.

Freedom is neither good nor bad in itself. Goodness and badness enter into the equation according to *what one does with one's freedom*. If some people really ordered their actions and disposed of their possessions and persons as they thought fit, they would offend almost all society greatly. So long as a nudist, for example, satisfies his inclinations in the privacy of his own premises, most people would take no issue with him. But should

129

he think it fit to walk unclad into my house in the presence of my family, I, like many individuals, would take any measures necessary to limit his freedom.

A sadist may be able to find a few masochists who approve of his functioning in a perfectly free way, but the majority will nonetheless continue to believe him misguided. One could accumulate an infinite list of such examples. Give communists perfect freedom—and power—and they inevitably limit the freedom of noncommunists. Fascists with perfect freedom respond similarly.

Therefore, it is impossible to deal with questions of this sort scientifically because they are essentially questions of MORALITY, which directly concerns not facts but opinions. Although it may be comforting to believe that there exists an absolute and universal moral law, it is clear that humankind has never been able to arrive at anything resembling a consensus as to what it is.

Even though it is an abstract idea, freedom sometimes seems to have material properties in that the freedom of one can oftentimes be increased only by decreasing the freedom of another. Under laissez-faire capitalism the powerful industrialist had great freedom but his employees had very little. They had freedom to take a particular job or, if they were unhappy about it and willing to risk hunger and eviction, to quit; but in many cases they did not have the freedom to better their working conditions in their job or to secure more money for performing it. The factory owner had the power to fire his workers without notice, to reduce their salaries, and to compel them to work twelve or fourteen hours a day. In these circumstances the freedom of the employer had to be diminished if that of the employee was to be enlarged. Parenthetically, in the context of that particular controversy, conservatives have usually sided with the rich employers, not the poor laborers.

This process also occurs in times of war or other national danger. The freedom of the total population is guaranteed by immediate restrictions upon the freedom of those who are drafted for military service. Even in the freest of nations, men in uniform live under the strictest sort of totalitarian—not democratic—rule, earn small incomes, and in almost all particulars live under precisely that sort of system that free men are supposed to abhor deeply. One cannot resist the fascinating conclusion that, given an inspiring cause and competent, considerate leadership, men will usually submit cheerfully to this sort of totalitarian existence. The legions of Caesar, Napoleon, Hitler, Stalin, Mao Tse-tung, Peron, Castro, and Saddam Hussein were not all unwillingly recruited.

Freedom requires of the individual certain things that are not demanded of him when he simply receives orders and responds like an automaton. A free man must constantly make important decisions, some of which can be made only through internal suffering and doubt. This is an obligation to which not all of us are equally receptive. Sometimes, in this sense, freedom is rather like a maiden caught between two grimly determined suitors. In other words, she is apt to be trampled to death in the fight between those who are sworn to defend her.

One reason freedom may be difficult to defend is that it is not only an abstraction but a negative one, and not even as recognizable a thing as are the virtues. What *has* definite existence of the sort that is understandable to even the least enlightened is encroaching legislation or other restrictions upon liberty or the use of private property.

It is sometimes said that freedom is the only thing you cannot have unless you are willing to give it to others. This is not necessarily so. When considering the question of freedom, it is most instructive to examine cases where it has been denied, such as we see in the institution of SLAVERY. Today almost all churchmen oppose slavery, but not very far back in our history these very same forces opposed its abolition, *citing the Bible as their justification.* The moral force of the churches was not brought to bear on the condemnation of slavery until the 1870s, by which time the custom had been abolished throughout most civilized nations due to *secular, liberal, humanitarian* pressures.

In this connection, given my Christian background, it grieves me that the forces of organized religion have a shamefully blemished record in the whole history of the battle for human freedom. Advocates of a predominant faith frequently intimidate and persecute those among their fellow citizens who harbor philosophical convictions at odds with those of the majority. What is involved is tyranny and cruelty; he who is not sworn to oppose them is not entitled to consider himself a true advocate of human liberty.

The meaning of freedom as outlined in the American Constitution, or even in present-day U.S. political oratory, does not correspond to the meaning the word is given throughout the so-called free world. Naive Americans sometimes assume, for example, that the popular freedom flowing from the idea of separation of church and state is a widely acknowledged boon. Such is not the case. Even where such separation has been achieved it does not always follow that ecclesiastical authorities admit its wisdom. American conservatives have never been totally at ease with the Jeffersonian ideal though for a very long time they concealed their displeasure, given that the majority of Americans were very proud of state-church separation. However, the conservative and/or reactionary revival of recent decades has emboldened the American Right, so that at present one encounters frequent flagrant condemnations of the wall of separation and ever more strident calls for much closer connection between government and, if not religion in the broad sense, at least the Christian subdivision of it.

Americans err in supposing that the entire "free world" shares the American attitude toward the ideal. Some of our ideological allies believe it contrary to reason that error and truth should have equal rights. Now it may be legitimately argued that the American founding fathers were mistaken and that freedom of religious and political expression as we know it is philosophically insupportable. *One may not logically defend both this proposition and its opposite.* The principles of separation of church and state and of freedom of religion are inseparable. It is not difficult to understand why such principles have usually been postulated by political philosophers of a nondogmatic, humanistic, or agnostic frame of mind. (See also CHURCH AND STATE RELATIONS; CRUSADES, THE.)

One of the most alarming things about our present situation is the common readiness to deny the rights of free speech to those holding views considered anathema. Two centuries ago when Voltaire said, "I wholly disagree with what you say, but I will defend to the death your right to say it," he defied every government on earth. In that day, a good way to draw to oneself the notice of the public executioner was to advocate— or attempt—the free expression of opinion. Though Voltaire was not the first to assert the right of free expression, he still deserves our praise for having done so at a time when authority was hostile to the idea.

Eventually the American Bill of Rights guaranteed the right of every U.S. citizen to free speech, and since then the bill has protected it against the pressures emerging from changing times and conditions. The American tradition of tolerance is one of the chief strengths of our democracy. Americans usually seem to sense that if they are given the opportunity to hear all sides of a question they can be counted upon to render a fair and wise verdict. However, the traditional American respect for tolerance and rights of free speech seems weaker today than it was in earlier periods of our history.

Forces within our society are attempting to deny freedom to certain individuals. Does a freedom disappear when it is denied? No. Because society denies me the legal right to commit murder it might be assumed that I do not have the freedom to murder. This is not actually the case. I am, in fact, physically free to murder anyone I can, although if I do so I run extreme risks myself. In other circumstances, however, society both denies a freedom and makes it physically impossible for the individual to activate it. History shows us the long, arduous battle fought before blacks and women overcame entrenched conservative opposition and were allowed to exercise their free right to vote.

Just as there are some among us who are denied freedoms by others, there are also some who deny *themselves* the full exercise of their political prerogatives. Freedom is precious—there is less of it in the world than we suppose—yet there are millions of Americans who rarely, if ever, go to the polls, rarely interest themselves in basic questions that affect their own lives; rarely give thought to the heroic sacrifices that our forefathers made in battle and death to bequeath to us that freedom.

Individualism. Let us consider a group—found in the conservative camp—that does concern itself with freedom, albeit from a selfish point of view: the individualists, organized or not.

The individualist faces the dilemma of how to maintain his identity and freedom in an increasingly complex society. Unless he plans to live the life of a hermit or monk, the individualist must deal with the reality of our ever-increasing socialization. Wishing the world were in this respect different is much like wishing that the laws of nature were different. A great deal of traditional morality applies to man only in his social aspect. The good is considered socially acceptable in nearly all societies, and there are few communities that do not forbid killing, stealing, fraud, or violence within the social unit. Therefore, formal morality itself is in one sense anti-individualistic. (See also MORALITY.)

The word *individualism* expresses an appealing idea but there is a grave danger that it—like all words expressing exalted concepts—may be used to disguise evil. This can occur if the individualist begins to see his individualism as one pole of an either-or structure; some individualists make precisely this mistake. If individualism is truly an ideal to them, then they ought to honor the ideal generally, or at the very least be sensitive enough to recognize its various manifestations.

Conscientious Objectors. During the two world wars the United States treated conscientious objectors with harsh restrictions on freedom. Some individuals were subjected to forced labor, cruel exposure to cold, beatings, attempted terrorization by weapons, hazing by mobs of servicemen, and thumb-digging into objectors' eyes. Norman Thomas, in *The Conscientious Objector in America,* gives a disturbing account of how actual cages were used on two pacifists in Alcatraz prison in the year 1920. The cages were deliberately constructed so that the occupants could neither stand nor sit but were forced to remain in a crouched position. The two prisoners were accorded this treatment—yes, in America—long after the Armistice had been signed simply because they refused to obey orders. This is common knowledge among scholars, but were the skies rent at the time by the outraged protests of conservative, Bible-believing defenders of freedom? No. Almost the only organizations that have an excellent record in opposing restrictions on freedom—*regardless of the identity of the victim*—are the American Civil Liberties Union, the Catholic Council on Civil Liberties, and Amnesty International. (See also TORTURE; WOMEN'S LIBERATION.)

FREE WILL. The whole of Scripture, so far as its references to morality are concerned, is based on the assumption that the human will is absolutely free. It is extremely rare to hear anything of mitigating circumstances or the kind of considerations that now quite properly concern courts of law and compassionate confessors. Let us, then, consider whether the many authors of Scripture were correct in their assumptions about free will.

A while back, speaking at Radford University in Virginia, I mentioned that I would be discussing free will. To my surprise, the woman to whom I was speaking—a person with higher-than-average intelligence—had literally no idea what the term meant. She thought it had something to do with the freedom guaranteed by the American Constitution and political tradition. Perhaps, therefore, before speculating about the concept we should spend a few moments clarifying what we are talking about.

First, we are referring to the things we humans *do*. Human activity takes an almost infinite variety of forms. A child would be able to make only a short list of human activities: running, walking, playing, eating, sleeping, going to school, getting dressed, riding a bicycle. But an adult of even moderate intelligence would be aware that humans are capable of not just a few dozen acts but of hundreds of thousands of them.

The variety of human abilities becomes clearer if we look in the Yellow Pages, where we find reference to a multitude of activities. To say that humans are capable of a large number of actions does not mean that every member of the species is so versatile, but each of us as individuals is still remarkably multifaceted. So the question that concerns us is, of all those acts that humans can perform, how many are the result of simple, conscious decision?

The most extreme form of statement that volition is free would be to say that the will—the deciding machinery of the brain—is in charge of every single act we perform. But is this the case? Do you personally, consciously decide to do everything you do? The answer is no, it is impossible.

But with this response, we agree that the conduct of human affairs is not entirely in control of the will. The will cannot possibly govern all of our actions and responses. For example, it cannot be accountable for what we do during that third or more of our lives when we are asleep, or when we are unconscious for any other reason. Even those things that humans do while fully conscious cannot all be said to be totally in our control.

Do we decide to be hungry? Do we decide to perspire when the temperature rises? Do we decide to shiver when we are cold? Do we decide to increase our pulse rate and pump a powerful hormone from our adrenal glands when we are frightened? Do we consciously decide to which members of the human race we will be sexually attracted and to which we will not? Do we decide to be tall or short, to have brown hair, blue eyes? Do we decide to be born? Are we permitted to say anything of our racial, ethnic context or the place or time of our birth?

We do not decide to feel sleepy. Nor, when we have been deprived of sleep can we simply decide to remain awake. When someone slaps us in the face we obviously do not consciously arrange to be angry. The anger is as spontaneous as ducking to avoid a blow or closing the eyes to exposure to very bright light. No, for these and innumerable similar examples we perceive that we personally have nothing conscious to do with a great deal of what we are and do; a certain percentage of what human bodies do is automatic.

For over 99 percent of their time on earth humans had not the slightest accurate information about what goes on under their skins. Even now they don't have much understanding of what goes on inside their brains. When Freud and the other early scientists and philosophers of the mind first began to make a few modest discoveries and advance a few theoretical ideas, they were met with the same kind of skepticism and hostility that has greeted innovators in almost all disciplines down through the ages. Only in very recent years, in the process of studying the cell, have we learned about genes, the means by which factors inherited from a combining male and female determine a good deal about the physical and intellectual characteristics of the offspring of their union. Yet, if a couple has fifteen children, no two of them will be identical. From this we become aware that pure chance—accident—is also operative in determining what we are and at least some of what we do. The will is not totally free.

Determinism versus Free Will. An extreme position holds that the will is not free at all, that literally everything we do is determined—which is to say, *caused*—by prior factors of birth or our experience. This is the pure deterministic argument. Although it sounds absurd to most who first consider it, when we make the attempt either to refute determinism or to approach the general question in an unbiased way, we find that individual bits of evidence often *support* the case for determinism.

So what makes us what we are? What makes us behave as we do?

Determinists believe one factor is genetics. It's fascinating that long before we knew anything scientific about the cell and the nucleus of the cell (the genes, chromosomes, DNA, etc.), long before we had accumulated such knowledge we were still aware, from the breeding of animals, plants, and humans, that certain physical and mental traits were in some mysterious fashion passed along the generations. A parent and offspring may both be musical, or both pugnacious, or both tall, or grossly fat. We are able to breed certain horses for speed, others for strength.

Consider identical twins who have been raised apart. In a sense such people are freaks of nature for, while very strictly speaking they cannot possibly be precisely identical, they are nevertheless strikingly similar. In physical terms, each half of such a pair has inherited the same combination of genes from their parents. They may both, for example, have blond hair, brown eyes, a tendency to tallness and thinness, a genial disposition, an ability to easily manipulate mathematical symbols, and a tendency to asthmatic allergies. All of this exists solely because of genetic inheritance.

So far no one becoming familiar with such information will have any reason either to doubt or to marvel at it. But the "Twilight Zone" aspect of the lives of identical twins is they often exhibit remarkable similarities in their behavior *even when they have been raised apart and in quite different environments.* When such twins are separated shortly after birth, by adoption for example, similarity of environment is ruled out, but later comparisons are invariably astonishing.

A typical case would involve two men both married to women who have the same first name. Both not only own dogs, but their dogs, too, have been given the same name, and it's not some statistically commonplace name such as Rover, Sport, or King. Sometimes the men have taken up the same trade or profession: both, for example, may be firemen, dentists, or history teachers. Moreover, they may have the same tastes and preferences as regards commercial products: both may prefer particular brands of beer, toothpaste, and automobiles. If they smoke, they may exhibit the same mannerisms while inhaling or holding the cigarette.

Parenthetically, such an oddity occurred in my own family. It did not involve identical twins but rather my mother and her first child who had been born out of wedlock years before my time. The boy had been given away to adoptive parents when he was four years old and had no recollection of my mother at all. My mother was a heavy smoker who had not begun to smoke until many years after she had last seen her first child. Nevertheless, years after my mother's death, the gentleman—then in his sixties—and I met. He bore a remarkable physical resemblance to my mother. In fact, he looked like my mother with a man's haircut. He also smoked precisely as my mother had, not only holding the cigarette in the same way but also inhaling on it—as she did—so deeply that the intake of breath could be heard across the room. He also had the same nicotine stains on his second and third fingers, and the same sound to his smoker's cough.

The work of scores of scientific investigators finally gave us an explanation of how specifically, in physical nature, such remarkable happenings take place. (It's interesting that such answers, while they clear up some mystery, seem invariably to create new mystery.) Nevertheless, no one now argues that it is purely a matter of blind, uncaused chance, the special dictate of God, or the result of a sin on the part of an ancestor that contributes to who we are and how we exert such freedom of the will as we may have.

In 1989 another scientific finding came to support the genetic theory when it was discovered that shyness was inheritable. This is one of the most fascinating facts ever unearthed. We have long known that physical traits such as color of eyes, length of limbs, type of body size, and the thousand-and-one other attributes of the flesh are a matter of biological inheritance working through the DNA. But what was *not* known previously, and what some will probably deny even after hearing of the discovery, is that it is biology that is the dominant influence on some factors that directly affect our *behavior*. Earlier studies of criminals, particularly of those who might be described as of the *bad seed* sort, are consistent with this theory. Just as some people are born naturally shy, some are born with pleasant, law-abiding dispositions; others seem from infancy to be naturally aggressive and dominating, as well as more readily prone to anger. All of this, plus similar findings that may emerge in the future, has the inevitable result of greatly limiting the freedom of the will.

But genetics—it is commonly agreed—does not account for everything that we are and everything that we do. Environment too exerts its influences. Churches in particular expound the belief that either the individual himself or those who created the conditions of his early upbringing bear the responsibility for both virtues and vices. There is no doubt that human beings—and other animal creatures as well—act as they do on the basis of both genetic and environmental experiences. Given what we know about the mother and father of Charles Manson, we would certainly not expect him to grow up as a model of virtue. In fact, we can create all the Charles Mansons we want by subjecting children to the same sort of monstrous influences during their early years. Indeed our prisons are now overflowing with millions of such individuals, partly because the American home has fallen very short of an even remotely ideal state.

There are also, as we know, social influences outside the narrow confines of the family that have a destructive influence on growing children. Some certain *societal cultures* even accept a high degree of criminal behavior as normal. Not every Sicilian is a criminal, but the culture of Sicily engenders a degree of criminality and tolerance of criminality much greater than the degree of tolerance of criminality shown by, say, Swedes, Englishmen, or Japanese.

The same is true in somewhat different regards of the fascinating culture of the Gypsies. You and I, given our general background, think that theft is a terrible thing and that those who steal ought to be arrested, tried, convicted, and jailed, especially if stealing represents a habituated pattern of behavior. The Gypsies do not agree with us.

Because of my Irish-American cultural background I am aware that the Irish tolerate a degree of drinking, physical brawling, and violence that more refined elements of society would find shocking. The reputation of the Irish as fighters led the English to recruit large numbers of them into the British armed forces, where they often distinguished themselves. When the same ferocity is turned to revolutionary ends, however, it is described as barbarous terrorism.

We are also aware that people often behave worse in groups than as individuals. This fact has its military usefulness, but over the course of recorded history and for unknown long ages before history was inscribed, the earth ran red with the blood of millions who suffered mob or other group violence.

Thus, the list of factors that affect and influence behavior and/or exercise of free will is quite a long one indeed. Included on that list would be the various phobias. Some people have an uncontrollable fear of heights. Others have a deep fear of certain insects or animals. Others are deathly afraid of being enclosed in certain relatively small spaces such as closets, elevators, or small rooms. Phobic individuals frequently decide—*will*—to, let us say, enter an elevator because it is either the only, or most convenient, way to get from the ground to the fifty-eighth floor of a building. But despite their willingness, despite their most fervent intentions, despite the fact that it will be greatly to their advantage to get up to that fifty-eighth floor quickly, claustrophobics are nevertheless unable to enter the elevator.

Millions of people wish to give up cigarette smoking, alcohol or other narcotics, or certain forms of sexual behavior, or perhaps sexual behavior altogether. Millions of these individuals have no problem at all knowing what is right and wrong in such contexts. And millions of them want very much to do what might be described as *the right thing*. They sincerely desire to give up their compulsive-obsessive addictions or behavior patterns. But, at least at certain times and certain places, they are not able to behave as their will tells them to. *Something about such individuals is more powerful than their will.*

The determinists have no trouble with any of this; it is tucked into their argument. But those of us who are not determinists find it uncomfortable to face such realities.

Another area of human psychological reality that is problematic for those who believe that the will is free, at least to some extent, is that of unconscious motivation. This means simply that we often act in either partial or total ignorance of the true reasons for our conduct. And when we are asked to state the reasons we behaved as we did, we cite reasons that in reality have nothing whatever to do with our actions.

This is well documented by experiments with hypnosis. In a typical instance, an individual is hypnotized and then told that within a specified amount of time after he has been awakened he will perform some specific act, let us say moving a small flower pot from a window ledge to a nearby table. In reality there is no reason for moving the pot except that the hypnotist has instructed the subject to do so. The hypnotist also informs the subject, while he is still in the hypnotic state, that he will have no conscious memory of having received the relevant instruction. A few minutes after the individual is awakened, perhaps while he converses with others in the room, he suddenly rises, walks to the window ledge, lifts up the flower pot, and positions it on the nearby table as instructed. This may take place while his attention is focused on the conversation or on the conduct of some other business.

"By the way, Tom," someone says, "I noticed you just moved that flower pot. Why did you do that?" Everyone else in the room is perfectly aware that Tom moved the pot only because he had been instructed to do so under hypnosis. If Tom were perfectly honest in his answer he would say something like, "To tell the truth, I haven't the slightest idea why I moved that pot, although I have the nagging feeling that I was somehow supposed to do so."

Such an answer is never forthcoming. What does happen is the process called rationalization. In other words, Tom gives us a lot of what we would immediately recognize as pure bull. He says things such as, "Well, it occurred to me that it's getting a little chilly out these days and I suddenly thought that the flower, because of its general delicacy, really ought not to be so close to that cold pane of glass so I thought it would be nice if I—" You can write the rest of Tom's dialogue yourself. Sometimes the subjects are quite creative and imaginative in giving reasons for their acts, but their "reasons" have no actual relevance.

FREE WILL

*   *   *

Another aspect of human consciousness that appears strangely independent of the will—though not totally so—is that kind of thinking characterized as creativity. Certain creative acts involve totally new factors, but more often what is operative is seeing the old with fresh eyes or combining two or more already commonplace elements into a new and theretofore unexpected whole. Because of the nature of my professional work, I have had many experiences that bear this out.

One of them involved "inventing" the electric typewriter back in 1943. I put the verb in quotation marks because, although there were then no electric typewriters available on the marketplace—or at least none that had ever come to my attention—I nevertheless assume that others had conceived the same idea and perhaps had carried it forward to the level of engineering development. In my own case all that was involved was the creative thought, which was stimulated by two factors.

I was at that moment sitting at an even then old-fashioned typewriter, the keys of which had to be struck very forcefully to raise the entire heavy carriage. The use of such equipment was a rather tiring process, particularly if carried on for several hours a day. The unit I was using was on a small table next to a wall, and as I paused for a moment in thought I looked down and noticed an electrical outlet next to my ankle. "I wish," I said to myself, "that I could run a cord from this typewriter and plug it into that power source."

That is, quite literally, all it takes to invent a new device. All the rest of the work is developmental and not necessarily creative at all. The important factor, in terms of this and the thousands of other instances of creative thinking that have occurred to me for over half a century, is that they all appear to have been done by the unconscious rather than the conscious mind. The ideas invariably come instantaneously. In the case described, I had spent at least several seconds thinking of how troublesome it was to use that particular typewriter, although the great majority of creative insights lack even this limited conscious component.

Dreams are on a separate plane of creativity. While dreaming we are no longer bound by physical laws, no longer limited to acting in time and space as they exist in the real world, no longer exercising any form of free will.

From time to time I write jokes in my sleep and sometimes songs. Oddly enough, my most successful song, "This Could Be the Start of Something Big," was written in a dream. Thank goodness it occurred just before awakening one morning, since we remember most clearly the dreams

140

we experience at those moments. I jotted down the first few lines of the lyric, which enabled me later to recall the music consciously, and the job was done. In many other instances, I am perfectly aware that I am creating an attractive melody in a dream, but I am unable to recall its structure hours later, when I awaken.

Bertrand Russell, when wrestling with a particularly knotty problem— which in his case might involve mathematical, political, or philosophical concepts—would cram himself with as much material on the subject as possible and then retire for a good night's sleep. The solution to the problem, he discovered, was often present in his mind, sometimes quite fully developed, when he awakened in the morning. One thing that seems to happen in the act of sleeping is that we get out of our own way, so to speak, and let one portion of the mind roam wherever it will, without being inhibited by our will, conscience, or other ego-affecting faculties.

Creativity, then, is an activity perhaps most productively engaged in *without* the exercise of free will.

Even if we try to isolate bits of evidence suggesting that we do have free will, that we are able to decide some things, we find that it is difficult to be clear-cut about its presence. It is easy enough to say, for example, that I brought six ties with me on a certain trip and that I did consciously choose to wear the green one today and not any of the others. But the determinists argue that my freedom in making such a choice was an illusion and that an unknown number of factors of my past experience and present condition were operative—most of them below the level of consciousness— to lead me to select the green tie.

Perhaps, they might argue, the green one was selected because a certain cultural bias suggests that its color was more harmonious with the trousers, jacket, and shirt I was wearing when I stood at the closet and began to look at my collection of neckties. I might have chosen, let us say, a pair of brown slacks rather than a navy blue pair because inasmuch as the weather had turned colder the brown slacks, being made of wool, would better protect me against the physical discomfort caused by low temperature. Determinists would argue that a great many other factors could have influenced my decision without my being consciously aware of them. Perhaps I had always admired my father's taste in neckties so that without realizing why I was doing so I selected the sort of tie he might have worn on the same occasion.

Despite all such combined knowledge and theory, however, most of us reject the purely deterministic argument. Something in us tells us that our will is at least partially free. Our entire system of law is based on the belief that individuals are responsible for their actions. It does not matter particularly—at least on one level—whether that responsibility is total or only partial. The law is not much interested in excuses. It is concerned—and in being concerned it expresses the popular will—that those who harm others must be apprehended, tried, convicted, and punished.

We sometimes hear the phrase *government of laws and not of men.* There is no question that we do need laws; all societies have them. We have also seen that individual prosecutors and judges have been corrupt, stupid, vengeful, biased, prejudiced, and prone to error. They are guilty of such faults not because they are prosecutors and judges but because they are human beings, and humans—as many other animals would no doubt insist if they had the words—are a notoriously untrustworthy bunch. It is precisely this understanding that makes us want to put our trust in formal, written laws so that we need only refer to the published record to know how to deal with a convicted criminal. But we cannot settle happily into the practice of that ideal either, simply because, as the common saying puts it, circumstances alter cases.

Let us suppose that two men rob separate grocery stores, each stealing $100. The offense, in both cases, is exactly the same. A government of laws that specifies a particular punishment—say five years in prison—for such an offense will deal with both the same way.

However, such a sentence might be fair to one criminal and atrociously unfair to the other. Let us suppose that Criminal A is a sadistic thug who robs grocery stores at gunpoint as a matter of common practice, whereas Criminal B, who has never before committed an illegal act, was driven to such desperation in this instance only because he had no money with which to feed a sick wife and hungry children.

It would obviously be moral nonsense to punish both men in exactly the same way. So, as a practical solution we must have a government of both laws and men. All this relates, too, to the debate over the freedom of the will. (See also FREEDOM; SITUATIONAL ETHICS.)

The question of free will cannot be neatly resolved once and for all. It is one of those knotty but all-important dilemmas with which both philosophers and the rest of us ought to reasonably concern ourselves. The purpose of these observations is merely to introduce you to the debate. You are free to continue it on your own, though you will find little clarification from Scripture. (See also HOMOSEXUALITY; PSYCHOLOGY AND RELIGION; REASON; WILL TO BELIEVE.)

FUTURE, THE. Everyone knows what the word *future* means. Fundamentalist commentators, however, say that the Bible contains solutions to literally all of our problems. The world's scientists and philosophers now unanimously agree that even the short-term future for humans presents us with challenges and problems that will make some of our present difficulties seem modest by comparison. It is perfectly natural, then, that the religious believer, or even the unbiased student of the question, would consult the Scriptures for instruction about the future.

Does the Bible refer to the future? Indeed it does, but it makes reference only to what are called the LAST DAYS. Some may object that the Bible is a guide only in regard to moral questions, not to problems of economics, science, foreign policy, the application of military resources, or the continuing befouling of our planet. Such objections evaporate in light of the fact that all of our social problems now, and the even-greater difficulties to come, have moral and ethical dimensions.

For example, sexual function among humans obviously involves moral questions. Sex itself is not inherently a problem; it just happens to be the physical means by which new creatures come to exist. A century ago there were only one billion humans. *Today we are fast approaching the five-billion level.* Few people outside the scientific community have perceived that the growth in population is like the increase in speed that enables an enormous jet airplane to be lifted into the air. It is not simply a matter of steady progression along a runway but rather one of ever-increasing pace. The five billion figure for human population, sobering as it is, is merely a convenient measurement. Barring some cataclysmic disaster, the actual population will increase ever faster and faster beyond that point.

To this frightening prospect, link the fact that we cannot provide adequate food and water for the human population now. Certain long-overdue remedial measures exist that at least offer temporary help, but it is generally recognized that they are merely delaying the almost-inevitable disaster, not permanently averting it.

The only nation that seems to have gotten the dimensions of this enormous difficulty into at least fairly sharp focus is China. But not even the propaganda campaigns and sometimes stringent measures adopted by the Chinese Marxists have fully resolved the problem. In various parts of the earth, even now, an extended drought or a disease suffered by a specific basic food plant—such as what caused the tragic Irish potato famine in the last century—can plunge large land masses and their populations into the misery and suffering of hunger and starvation, and the consequent dangerous social unrest to which such situations give rise.

In the light of such global difficulties it is destructive nonsense to avoid material remedies and rational thinking, saying only that "God will take care of his own." It is obvious that *for the entire record of human history*

God has not taken care of hundreds of millions of his creatures when they stood in danger. There may have been a few cases in which miraculous intervention did occur, but not even the most devout believer would dream of suggesting that such instances constitute more than an almost invisible portion of one percent. (See also MIRACLES.)

Clearly, then, God is not going to solve this and other problems for us; we are going to have to solve them ourselves. That in turn requires a wholesale revision in the theological thinking of Catholics and any others who, despite the current calamity, continue to assert that birth control per se is contrary to the will of God. It is, first of all, notoriously difficult to know what the will of God is. Happily, nonbelievers and believers alike generally agree that God—assuming he exists—may be pleased by an increase in moral behavior and a decrease in immorality. (See also MORALITY.)

The Genesis commandment to *multiply* is sometimes pointed to in connection with overpopulation. It was very reasonable of God, at the point of time when—we are told—he had only two people on earth, to urge them to multiply, although they would no doubt have done so had he never mentioned the matter. But nowhere is it written, in any sacred Scripture of the world, that God has said "go forth and multiply yourself to the point of widespread starvation, misery, poverty, and social chaos." The gods—real or imagined—have been accused of a number of failings over the ages, but stupidity was never one of them.

To those of us who prefer a generally republican/democratic form of government to its various totalitarian alternatives, it is of interest that the Bible also has had nothing constructive to say about such political questions, and what it has had to say has generally been in favor of authoritarian rule.

Both democratic and fascistic governments agree on the importance of education, although philosophical bias will naturally determine its content. Now evidence indicates that it is not even possible to educate people if they are seriously distracted by the burdens of life. Clearly, our present situation—and its gradual worsening yet to come—is a grave threat indeed not only to our political ideals but also to the institutions based on them. People will tolerate only a certain degree of social chaos. Beyond that point they not only easily fall victim to a charming or impassioned dictator, but they also actually plead with him to seize power. The moral and ethical factors for this scenario find a strikingly impractical guide in the sacred scriptures.

The Bible does have moral advice or encouragement to which we can refer. The commandment to love our fellow creatures, for example, is excellent counsel indeed, though it seems to have been pitifully neglected over the centuries. During the conservative resurgence of the late 1960s and 1970s that led into the early years of the Reagan presidency (a time when organized Christian influence was strong), Christian moral leadership resulted not in increased concern for the poor and their needs, but precisely in the opposite: a cold-hearted, contemptuous rejection of the poor, side-by-side with unprecedented emphasis on the acquisition of wealth by both honest and dishonest means and a depressing degree of greedy accumulation of material possessions. In stark contrast to the quite discreet displays of wealth by the rich of the early part of the century, the wealthy of the seventies engaged in a tasteless public flaunting of luxury before the hollow eyes of the poor. Atheists, agnostics, secular humanists, or other free-thinkers were not guilty of such offenses. It was by and large the conservative Christian community. Needless to say, it would be unjust to accuse all American Christians of such moral vulgarity. Some of the most insightful criticism of such behavior came from other Christians, many of whom made admirable, sometimes even heroic efforts to help the poor, the homeless, and the suffering of all kinds. (See also ALTRUISM; BY THEIR FRUITS YE SHALL KNOW THEM; CHARITY.)

As we rush toward the future with ever-accelerating speed, those who presently see the world through the colored spectacles of Jewishness or Christianness might ponder for a moment the wise saying that travel is broadening. It teaches us, in essence, that we are not after all the center of the universe but simply individual players in a vast drama with an enormous cast. Rather than wanting to discourage reading of the Scriptures, my hope is that they will be much more widely—and analytically—studied, and in the larger context, that we will familiarize ourselves with the Scriptures, beliefs, myths, legends, and opinions of those other believers who do not see things as we do. We may be certain that those strangers are not wrong about everything. (See also EDUCATIVE PROCESS, THE; PROPHECY AND PREDICTION; SOUL, THE.)

G

GHOSTS. I personally have no knowledge whether in reality there are such creatures as ghosts, although it would greatly surprise me to learn that there are. If the countless testimonies one hears from people who are apparently convinced they have had an encounter with a ghostly apparition are true, then one of the most striking characteristics of such spirits is that they lead a remarkably pointless existence. We define a ghost here as the spirit of a human being that once led a normal, physical existence but is no longer connected to the material body by which it was once identified.

Although the appearance of disembodied spirits has been reported by affiliates of hundreds of forms of religious belief, there are very few faiths, if any, that have had the foresight to incorporate an explanation of earthbound ghosts into their overall philosophy or dogma. Christianity, for example, has long taught quite clearly that at the moment of physical death the spirits of human beings go either to heaven, hell, or—as some believe—purgatory. Our religious instructors are not in the habit of adding, "Oh, and by the way, if your surviving spirit happens *not* to go to one of these three classic destinations, it might just end up wandering around Cleveland for a few hundred years," which would return us to the point of pointlessness.

Assuming that there are free-floating spirits, it would at least be reasonable for there to be some edifying purpose to their occasional encounters with human beings. For example, a ghost might choose to say something like, "Do not be startled, my friend; I intend you no harm. Rather I appear before you to assure you not only that there is life after physical death but also that mankind must now repent, return to the Lord, and prepare for his imminent coming." Aside from the question whether such a message is sound and reliable or totally out of touch with any sort of reality, it is at least coherent and consistent with much that religious people already believe.

Oddly enough, such communications are almost never reported. The actual or alleged messages received all suffer from a depressing vagueness, a disappointing insubstantiality. But if the ghosts themselves are notorious for their poor powers of communication, the humans who claim to encounter the ghosts are not much better. Perhaps in the future such meetings will be more instructive if the still-human participants in such dramas take the following line:

HUMAN: Oh, you startled me.

GHOST: Forgive me, it was not my intention.

HUMAN: Precisely what is your intention?

GHOST: What?

HUMAN: Well, surely you must have had some reason for scaring the wits out of me. And you must also have had some reason for selecting me in particular to communicate with.

GHOST: No, not really.

HUMAN: Well, then, may I put a few questions to you? You see, as a human gifted by God with at least some degree of intelligence, it is only natural that I would attempt to make sense out of our exchange.

GHOST: I suppose that would be all right.

HUMAN: First of all, what are you doing here in South Bend, Indiana? I've always been clearly taught by the church that you should be in heaven, hell, or purgatory.

GHOST: A fair question indeed. Unfortunately I haven't the slightest idea how to answer it.

HUMAN: You mean you yourself don't know why you are here at this place and this time?

GHOST: I'm afraid that's the size of it.

GHOSTS

HUMAN: A very strange state of affairs, if you don't mind my saying so. Well, let me see if I can somehow grasp your essential function as a ghost. I mean, living human beings generally do have some specific function. Painters paint, writers write, football coaches coach football— that sort of thing. What do *you* do?

GHOST: Not a great deal actually. I engage in a certain amount of moaning.

HUMAN: Yes, I've heard that ghosts are often heard to moan. But why?

GHOST: Again I'm sorry to disappoint you, but I haven't the slightest idea.

HUMAN: Well, if you cannot enlighten me, perhaps I can enlighten you. In living human beings, moaning generally communicates the emotion of unhappiness or depression. Does that ring any sort of bell?

GHOST: I'm afraid not.

HUMAN: At least according to literary lore, ghosts are often heard to rattle chains. Have you personally ever rattled a chain?

GHOST: Not a one. I'd be happy to rattle them if I had any, but—

HUMAN: I understand. Well, we sometimes hear stories that ghosts are encountered in places where dreadful crimes have taken place.

GHOST: Aren't they all?

HUMAN: Aren't what all?

GHOST: Aren't all crimes dreadful?

HUMAN: That's the first sensible thing I've heard you say. Congratulations.

GHOST: Thank you kindly.

HUMAN: So, in your own case, has there been any such connection?

GHOST: Not that I can recall. And I think I would recall such an experience, don't you?

HUMAN: Indeed. Well, I have to be running along.

GHOST: Oh, really?

HUMAN: Yes. We living creatures, you see, have a great many obligations, tasks we're required to attend to.

GHOST: I wish I could say the same for us ghosts.

Although the tone of the above exchange is facetious, the living human character has, by virtue of his reasonableness, at least raised perfectly fair questions.

Reports of such ghostly encounters are invariably met with a great deal of skepticism. In some cases the reporters are simply assumed to be lying. If the general decency and reliability of the individual involved rules this out, then the next skeptical response is that the individual has been deluded and that the incident, which may have seemed very real, was nevertheless something like a dream but experienced in a state of wakefulness. Perhaps anyone who believes he is actually communicating with a disembodied spirit should remember to say, "I'm afraid that few people, if any, will believe me when I tell them about this experience; and yet, wouldn't you agree that if ghosts do indeed exist then mankind ought commonly to acknowledge that fact?"

Given the spirit's presumed acceptance of this premise, the human participant should then say, "It would be enormously helpful—not only to me but also to the entire human race—if you could arrange to visit me again in the presence of witnesses. I would be more than happy to make a definite appointment for such an encounter and can personally assure you that I will convene a group of observers having different philosophical views on relevant questions."

If I were a ghost I should be almost tearfully grateful to hear such a proposal. If the ghost should subsequently return—perhaps by walking through the locked doors of a closed room—and sit down for a time in the presence of, say, not only a few priests, rabbis, and ministers but also a number of scientific skeptics, as well as such well-trusted keepers of the public record as Ted Koppel, Bill Moyers, or George Will, the occasion would be of historic importance. (See also ANGELS.)

GIDEON, the son of Joash from the tribe of Manasseh, was one of Israel's judges. He is said to have been called by God to save Israel.

The Gideon Society that has placed millions of copies of Scripture across the nation in hotel and motel rooms not otherwise known for the spirituality of many of the acts performed in them seems to be an organization of decent, God-fearing fellows who took the name of a heroic figure noted for his personal sanctity. This is not the case.

Considering the thousands of names available in the Scriptures, it seems unfortunate that these American Christians would deliberately choose to identify themselves with a notorious fanatic and murderer, as demonstrated by Gideon's exploits in JUDGES 6, 7, and 8. Consider: He leads the Israelites in a general slaughter of a tribe called the Midianites. When two of their princes—Oreb and Zeeb—are captured, not only are they beheaded, but their bloody heads are presented to Gideon personally. There is no suggestion that Gideon is in the least shocked by this gift.

GIFTS TO GOD. A hypothesis has occurred to me that may explain the inherently absurd but nevertheless long-common practice of presenting material gifts to God. We know that one practical result of such a custom was that priests—of all religions—have generally been reasonably well-clothed and fed. This would seem to be a beneficial and rational side-effect of the practice, but for an explanation of its origin we should look to the beginnings of religion itself, insofar as our general ignorance about early times permits such speculation.

It seems reasonable to assume that the early gods, in addition to representing certain forces of nature, were also stylized versions of powerful kings in history. Even though almost all the historic glamour of royalty has vanished with the winds of history, we can readily imagine how truly godlike kings on their thrones in their palaces must have seemed to simple people of ages past. We can today observe how the appearance of someone great— an American president, a popular figure of the entertainment or athletic world, a religious personage—can affect crowds—even though that person may in reality be an unglamorous and unprepossessing figure. Hearts quicken, backs straighten, music plays. There is an undeniable thrill that ripples through the audience. If this is so in our relatively blasé and jaded culture, we may be assured that the effect was even more dramatic in ancient times.

Next, consider the custom whereby tribal chieftains or other leaders had the semi-divine right to dispose of property. Their first concern, naturally, would be to acquire such material means as were necessary for their own survival and power. Therefore, peasants and workmen were commonly required to present their powerful ruler of a nearby hilltop with the fruits of their labors, their vineyards, fields, and flocks. (See also DIVINE RIGHT OF KINGS.)

Nothing more than a combination of these two factors over a long span of time led to the presentation of material gifts to God. No matter what rationale is given for it, the custom is absurd in its essence, for the Creator and possessor of all things natural can certainly acquire nothing additional of a material nature. Also, God by definition is of the spiritual realm and therefore would have no need for anything physical. It might have made sense to present a gift to such a divine personage as Jesus, since, having a human body, he could eat the gift, drink it, wear it, or spend it, though *the Gospels refer to no such instances of adoration.* One cannot in any intelligible sense give such gifts to a spirit.

The countless millions of such presented objects over the centuries were either used by priests or simply burned and hence wasted. The Catholic tradition includes the concept of sacrifice, interpreted as giving up something that one very much wants but willingly relinquishes as a gesture of subservience and affection for God. But it by no means logically follows that such presentation must involve the physical destruction of the valued object. If as a farmer I contribute ten bushels of corn to God, I would think God remarkably stupid if he actually preferred that I burn that corn rather than distribute it to the poor and hungry.

There is, however, a third sense in which—granting the existence of God—one can meaningfully offer up something to him: one can offer things that are not physical, but are rather one's own abilities or talents. A poet, for example, might dedicate his poetic gift to God. So might a painter, sculptor, carpenter, executive, merchant, or salesman. The last three seem never to have made such a presentation to the Lord, but the possibility nevertheless is as available to them as to anyone else. The businessman will, of course, frequently make a material sacrifice—not to God but to a particular church—in the form of a tithe or other financial offering, although rarely to such an extent as to seriously weaken himself in the marketplace. The idea that the same combination of selflessness and love ought to be addressed to his customers and competitors would be regarded as heresy, despite its evident beauty and virtue. (See also CHRONICLES, THE FIRST BOOK OF THE; RITUAL.)

GLOSSOLALIA, or Speaking in Tongues. If, as appears to be the case, little or no actual meaning is conveyed in such instances of babbling in incomprehensible sequences of syllables, what may be happening is a simple reversion to the first language of all humanity, the experimental play with vocal sounds that is our maximal speech ability during the first year or two of our lives.

The natural cries, gurgles, coos, and babbles to which humans give voice before their partly undeveloped brains are capable of perceiving verbal meanings seem to be carried forward in certain basic elements of adult speech. The two most interesting entities to human infants are those enormous figures who hold them, feed them, and sustain their lives—mother and father. The infant's code for these, in many languages, involves the use of words that are almost automatically formed by the simple act of opening the mouth and making the *ah* sound—mama and papa. For example, it is a simple matter to see the connection between *mama* and *papa* and the Latin *mater* and *pater,* or the Eastern Mediterranean word *abba.*

Since all living creatures die if deprived of water, some word such as *wawa*—clearly related to words such as *water, wasser,* or *agua*—is also one of the first to be developed.

Then, too, once the developing infant perceives that he has the power to make vocal noises of his own, he seems to delight in the basic ability itself so that at an early stage it is quite enough for him or her to simply exercise the vocal equipment and not at all necessary to attach meaning to every sound.

If this hypothesis is valid, it would account for the otherwise strangely pleasurable aspect of speaking in syllables that are meaningless even to the speakers themselves, much less to those who hear them. The sudden uninhibited freedom to revert to a pleasurable pattern from our early past is sensed as playful, free, primitive, innocent. It is something of a chore, after all, for the brains of growing children and adults constantly to have to be connecting sequences of sounds to utter even fairly coherent verbal messages. In the glossolalian mode we are relieved of this tiresome burden and once again free to use our mouths in the unselfconscious, uninhibited way we did during the first phase of our intellectual development.

Despite references in biblical texts (most notably Acts 2:4), which might or might not be relevant, it is not clear, on grounds of common sense or logic, why the psychological phenomena referred to as *speaking in tongues* is properly associated with religion.

It would not take the addition of any particularly complicated factors to make such behavior religious. Obviously if it were possible to interpret remarks made in strange tongues, and if upon translation it were to be found that the message was a prayer, a revelation of moral wisdom, or the long-sought answer to a perplexing philosophical question, then glossolalia would be properly described as religious. But in the absence of such factors there would appear to be no more reason to attach the qualitative adjective *religious* to such phenomena than there would be to call religious other frenzied activity such as dancing to the point of exhaustion, foaming at the mouth, or hitting oneself on the head with a stick.

Even if it were to be determined that speaking in tongues is a fact for which psychological science has no ready explanation, it still would not follow that science's ignorance makes it logically inescapable that the behavior involved was miraculous or religious in any other sense.

On one occasion, in the context of a religious meeting, I witnessed a man begin to speak what were to me—and presumably everyone else in the room—a totally incomprehensible series of syllables. The probability that the man was speaking gibberish is very high, although we cannot, in the absence of further investigation—at this late date an impossibility—rule out that he might have spoken in some obscure or long-dead language. But clearly, if he were speaking in an ancient dialect, no one present had the slightest hint as to the meaning of the words. Nor did he. It would seem a very peculiar source of spiritual communication if it were characterized by a total absence of reception of the message. Therefore, to propose that such psychological manifestations are an argument in favor of the Deity generally, or Christianity specifically, is more likely to encourage skepticism and unbelief than it is to inspire religious devotion. In some churches that practice glossolalia the gibberish message is immediately "interpreted" into English by the same person or a different person, who is, of course, free to attach whatever alleged "meaning" he wishes.

Because the factors of such an equation are potentially so numerous that we can't even identify them all, it may be impossible to determine whether there is anything more than babbled nonsense in such phenomena. Among the possibilities is that a minor percentage of such instances are either miraculous or at least intelligibly rooted in some meaningful communicative religious experience, but that the majority of such instances are based on self-delusion and mass hysteria.

The greatest problem with glossolalia—at least insofar as the Christian assertion that it is literally inspired by God is concerned—is that it is such a dumb thing to attribute to an all-wise, all-knowing Deity.

Let us assume that there is indeed a God. Let us assume further that God exercises his inherent power, on certain rare occasions, to intervene in human events. Would it not then be reasonable to assume that the forms such interventions take would be consistent with the conception and/or reality of that God?

Most religious believers have no difficulty believing that God has acted to save the life of a drowning person, to restore a sufferer to good health, to inspire a leader with a socially constructive thought, to found a religion, and so forth. But the belief that it is to both God's and man's interest to suddenly begin babbling what is usually total gibberish—or reportedly in some cases an ancient or obscure language—defies the very common sense that religious believers tell us, in another breath, comes to us from God.

Let us view the problem from another perspective. Let us assume now that either there is no God or that if there is some mighty central source of power it permits far too many children to burn screaming in panic in tenement fires, far too many devout believers to be eaten by sharks, far too many worshippers to be crushed in earthquakes inside shattered cathedrals to preserve its reputation as gentle and loving overseer of human events. In other words, let us regard with as much disinterest as possible various phenomena generally ascribed to divine causes: cures for illnesses, dramatic rescues of individuals from death, victory in battlefield confrontations, and so forth. All such acts or experiences are clearly to the good. Lives are saved, families are reunited, health restored, hope for the future strengthened. All such experiences replace tears, pain, and anguish with smiles of joy and gratitude.

But now let us consider babbling incoherently. By what possible criteria could the making of unintelligible sounds be said to be properly placed in the same category as the aforementioned productive actions? The answer is by no criteria whatsoever.

Practitioners of some Oriental religions claim to have the power of levitation, the ability actually to defy the law of gravity by the exercise of FREE WILL. I do not believe any such claims and will not, unless I am witness to the performance of such acts, but these feats fall within the category of what is called the miraculous; if it were to occur within the context of exhortations to virtue it would bear a very great weight indeed among both the already convinced and the theretofore skeptical. Mouthing incomprehensible syllables makes no such favorable impression. If any relative or friend of mine were suddenly to behave in such a manner in my presence, my reaction would be acute embarrassment. And if I should come out of a religious seizure to be told that *I* had been speaking in a "strange" tongue I should be hideously embarrassed for myself.

Would it not be far more reasonable to assume that a God believed to be the possessor of all possible wisdom and science would—if he saw fit—personally inspire believers with an unusual and dramatic power of speech, enable them to speak words of enlightenment and inspiration rather than a series of meaningless syllables?

GRACE. The Bible makes scores of references to grace. Alas for clarity, the word is used in a variety of ways to convey a variety of meanings. The one almost never conveyed is that which the word takes in common speech: *she moved across the stage with incredible grace,* or *a graceful tree stood alone in the field. Grace,* in its biblical use, appears to be an extraordinary blessing or special favor of God.

References to grace are common in the New Testament. It appears in approximately 150 instances, mostly in writings by Paul or in other books attributed to him through long-defended error. Oddly, the concept is rarely encountered in Jewish scripture.

In endeavoring to grasp more adequately such elusive subject matter, it would be helpful to know how grace affects the lives of those fortunate enough to receive it. Here the picture is muddled. No scholarly study— not even by the most devout and well-qualified analytical believers—has investigated the possibility of a cause-and-effect relationship between (1) the bestowal of grace and (2) the subsequent virtuous lives of the lucky recipients. It seems reasonable to assume that after the bestowal of grace human conduct would be improved, but apparently no relevant statistical evidence has been accumulated. (See also BY THEIR FRUITS YE SHALL KNOW THEM.)

The concept denoted by the word *grace* brings us face-to-face with one more mystery of the sort with which almost all forms of religion abound. Grace at first thought seems an idea not only simple but appealing. In addition to the divine love with which almost all faiths assure us we are constantly blessed, God, according to the theory, dispatches to a minority of the human inhabitants of one of his millions of galaxies a special, distinct form of affectionate blessing.

There would be no analytical problem with this, once the idea of a loving God is accepted. But on a slightly more complex level, difficulties of the most serious sort immediately present themselves. The human race is seriously deluded if it thinks it has some *right* to expect grace in the same uncomplicated sense in which it does have a right to expect divine love; only a certain small percentage of even the most highly devout believers are said to be the recipients of God's grace.

Since God is considered to be the very epitome, the source, the ideal representation of all wisdom, we must immediately discard the notion that the dispensing of grace is done on a capricious or totally random basis. If that were the case it would be absurd to speak of God's absolutely perfect wisdom and intelligence. And yet, when we try to get the concept and/or reality of grace into a clearer focus, we are forced to acknowledge that there is no "sense" to the distribution of it.

It would be sensible, by way of contrast, if those who had already shown themselves worthy of such special favors were the ones chosen as the objects of grace. Those whose faith was firm, whose conduct was exemplary, whose love for God and their fellow creatures was glowingly evident would, in a more rational universe, obviously deserve a separate sort of divine concern, while those who led sinful, scandalous, and selfish lives could hardly expect such specialized, compassionate attention. Unfortunately for such reasonable expectations, the concept of JUSTICE appears totally unconnected to the dispensation of grace.

As the point is stated by Walter C. Kaisar, Jr., in *Hard Sayings of the Old Testament:* "his grace had nothing to do with natural rights or works."

Additional confusion is added to the equation by the belief common to Catholics, Eastern Orthodox, and some Protestants that grace is conferred through the sacraments. The statement seems to imply that those who have availed themselves of the sacraments will, simply by virtue of that fact, receive grace. But if this were so, then it would be fair to speak of the apparent arbitrariness of the dispensing of such a divine blessing. Theologians themselves have clearly failed to communicate the assertion that either (1) everyone who receives the sacraments therefore also receives grace, or (2) only *some* of those who receive the sacraments are lucky enough to have the additional benefit of grace conferred on them.

Christian believers are, of course, not careless enough to argue that the only means of receiving grace is through the sacraments, since any such assumption would amount to saying that God's grace never existed until the Christian church was organized—quite some time after the death of Jesus—and declared that certain religious rituals were to be considered sacraments. Since such an argument is not advanced, it therefore follows that we will find occasional references to grace in the older Scriptures.

Whatever the origin of the belief in grace, it cannot be exclusively attributed to either the Jewish or Christian religions since Hindus and Buddhists, too, refer to such divine favoritism.

Perhaps the sweetest, most appealing, and uplifting elements of religion may be attributed not, as commonly thought, to the grace of God but rather to the warm hearts of the very best believers. These last should, in any event, always be honored because while there is still respectable debate about that most crucial aspect of divine grace—its reality—there can be no doubt about the value of those humans who are morally graceful. In a world so dominated, so threatened by evil, the essential goodness of such men and women shines like Shakespeare's candle.

There might be material, genetic factors behind the human capacity for unusual goodness and personal decency. This question calls to mind a thousand-and-one others, one of which concerns the still-unknown extent to which environmental factors determine our characters and therefore, very largely, our moral fates. It is highly probable that both nature and nurture are involved, but we do not know which is dominant.

Long before Freud it was believed that as the twig is bent so would the tree grow. Today we assume that it is literally impossible for an individual raised by a mother and father incapable of fulfilling such parental roles to become a responsible, decent adult. This still leaves open the question of what might be termed a gift for morality. Clearly, there are gifts, physically locatable in genetic material, that account for certain individuals' dazzling superiority in music, mathematics, painting, sculpture, and the other arts and disciplines in which genius manifests itself. Indeed, freakishly high intelligence itself, quite aside from questions of its application, is clearly a matter of genetics, even if—as is obviously the case—that gift must flower within an environmental context.

It does not follow that all we have to do to produce a larger number of saints is to encourage physical union between morally charming men and women, any more than we can guarantee a generation of superb violinists by breeding for such a trait. We can, as every farmer or stock breeder is aware, encourage the replication of purely physical abilities—strength, speed, or size, for example. This is just as true among human animals as it is among the lesser creatures.

But might there be an actual gene for decency, for loving kindness, for exceptional sensitivity to the needs of others, for that overpowering emotional sense of love for all humankind to which there have been occasional references in the works of certain mystics and saints? If there is such a genetic endowment, there still would remain the purely scientific question of *how* it produces its effects. The answer might ultimately be found in the field of brain chemistry, the mysterious "Twilight Zone" of knowledge concerning which elusive and tantalizing discoveries are continually being made. There is no longer any debate whether there are physical reflections of those states of mind we call moods or emotions. Specific brain chemicals have been identified and related to fear, anger, joy, and erotic appetite. During the 1960s, scholarly literature about the effects of lysergic acid diethylamide (LSD) on the human mind and/or brain began to appear. (It has since been revealed that the chief source of funding for such studies, which took place at major universities, was the Central Intelligence Agency (CIA). The CIA was interested in knowing whether LSD could be used as a peace drug or a truth serum. Since it was obvious that it could be employed as an offensive weapon by being introduced into the water supply of any given community, it was therefore reasonable to wonder what sort of defense might be mounted against such a ploy.

Among the experimental work done at the time was a study funded by the CIA to determine the effects of the drug on individuals already recognized as creative. Painters, philosophers, composers, musicians, theologians, dramatists, and others were studied in this connection. I was one of them.

A significant percentage of those who had issued reports, either formally or casually, about their own responses to the drug had a reaction similar to mine: a quite clear and strong feeling of willingness to embrace not only all humankind but nature as well. One part of my brain was experiencing such emotions, while another more analytical part was studying my own responses. I recalled thinking that anyone who could maintain such an emotional state would be entitled to consider himself a saint. Large numbers of people have reported much the same thing, in varying degrees of intensity. Is it possible that grace has a chemical, hormonal, or genetic connection? (See also FREE WILL; SAINTLINESS; VIRTUES, THE.)

H

HAPPINESS. Mortimer Adler observes in his *Ten Philosophical Mistakes* that the word *happiness* is commonly identified with a purely psychological state to which we give the name *contentment,* the experience that results from having gotten what we want. But there is a higher-minded meaning, Adler says, which is, "the moral quality of a whole life well lived." No doubt all would concur that there is a tragic shortage of both kinds of happiness in the world, but both definitions are imperfect and thus require further consideration.

In the former instance, it is by no means inevitable that the experience of getting what we want—or even what we need—will produce a state of utter contentment or happiness.

Creatures of earth do not live on only one continuum. Change and complexity are basic to our lives. Consider an example of an individual (1) wanting something very much and (2) being fortunate enough to secure it. Let us suppose that a man is on such a busy schedule that he does not have time to stop work for his midday meal. The inevitable result is that as evening draws near, his hunger is extreme and his anticipatory sensitivity to the taste, aroma, and ingestion of food is exquisite. Eventually our subject dines on a sumptuous meal, and he thoroughly enjoys every morsel. Are we now entitled to say that because of his sense of physical contentment he is a happy man?

Hardly. Despite the physically enjoyable nature of eating a delicious meal, that individual may still face such realities as financial straits, death or illness of a loved one, recent damage to his automobile, the theft of valuable property from his home, or any number of situations that range from the annoying and inconvenient to the profoundly tragic and painful.

HAPPINESS

The mere experience of physical satisfaction, therefore, whether the desired object be a cold glass of water on a hot day, a rich and satisfying meal when hungry, or a profoundly desired sexual consummation—absolutely none of these will, in and of themselves, produce happiness. They may be perfectly respectable and reasonable ends, but the conscious sense of being happy involves a process vastly more complex.

The sense of being happy seems to occur only within a limited time frame. An individual may be hospitalized for depression and yet, upon hearing an unexpected play on words or being told a very funny joke, may laugh heartily. During the—say—twenty-seven seconds that he is laughing, he is actually happy. In this case, the state is achieved not by satisfying a longing or need, but more as a result of sudden felicitous surprise. Stubbing one's toe while strolling through a meadow and thereby finding a gold coin in the grass; or turning a corner and in the instant coming upon a view of an incredibly beautiful sunrise when just a moment earlier one had not been at all conscious of longing for such a wondrous sight are other examples of time-limited happiness caused by an unexpected event.

The reverse of this scenario occurs in the case of a person who is so fortunate as to have his every desire quickly satisfied. Not only are his elemental needs—water, food, sleep, sexual expression—appropriately gratified, but even his wants, being harmless to others, are attended to. By our definition, this man would certainly be happy. But this is not necessarily so. Consider, for example, a person rich in compassion and general sensitivity, financially and socially secure but who is, nevertheless, frequently depressed at contemplation of the evident sufferings of the majority of the human race, who daily experience poverty, hunger, squalor, sickness, ignorance, war, natural disasters, and assorted other tribulations.

There is also the case where a person's limited period of happiness actually results in *unhappiness*. The grossly fat individual who snatches brief moments of gratification by gorging himself experiences actual pleasure while consuming—say—two quarts of ice cream at one sitting, but after such bouts of excess he is once again tormented by guilt and by the sorrowful spectacle of his physical self in the nearest mirror. The same can be said of the alcoholic and the narcotics addict. True pleasure, contentment, even moments of ecstasy may be achieved by the momentary satisfaction of desires and/or needs, but the saner world nevertheless considers the addict's method of achieving satiation and contentment a remarkably stupid one, rather than a path to happiness.

The other definition of happiness implies that only those on their deathbeds can be happy. Otherwise, how can one speak of "a whole life"?

And what of the satisfaction that comes from a life well lived? Would not the superior individual who lives such a life still weep inwardly at awareness of that vast portion of misery that surrounds him?

Perhaps precisely such speculations led the American founding fathers, who drafted the Bill of Rights, to refer not to the *achievement* but only the *pursuit* of happiness.

HARD SAYINGS. For some two thousand years Christian scholars have wrestled with the difficulties posed by those passages of Scripture commonly referred to as *hard sayings*. These are rarely verses that are so peculiarly worded that there is little certainty about their clear meaning, if they have one. The classic hard sayings are also not usually of the sort to which a dozen analysts may offer as many interpretations. What they *are* are passages the meaning of which is clear, and of which the best possible wording has long been commonly accepted. The reason they are "hard" is that they flatly contradict either common sense, the general thrust of the rest of the Jewish and Christian Scriptures, or the commonly accepted view of God. To illustrate a point, suppose we were to read, "And the Lord said, 'Because I have given your children to you as your property, inasmuch as you have physically created them, you may properly demand of them not only hard physical labor without compensation but also such sexual favors as your natural appetites might from time to time demand.' "

It is perfectly apparent that the most devout Jew or Christian on earth, happening upon such a passage, would react with horror and immediately conclude that since such morally revolting advice cannot possibly have come from God, the alleged quotation was therefore created by a human—a remarkably perverted one at that. We would be witnessing, then, an admirable instance of the combination of moral revulsion and common sense quickly working through a not especially difficult problem. (See also CONTRADICTIONS, BIBLICAL; ERROR; PIOUS FRAUD.)

There are many equally revolting or nonsensical portions of Scripture, though the moral would be the same whether there were thousands of such examples or merely a single one. But since we have just seen how easily and properly such problems may be resolved, the question arises why this simple process seems rarely to be resorted to by believers. The answer, of course, is that they have had programmed into their internal computers, so to speak, one factor that by itself is guaranteed to disrupt the common reasoning processes that would otherwise make short work of such difficulties.

We refer to the a priori assumption that every word of the Bible is the inspired word of God. But it is possible to reason logically enough even if the validity of this common assumption is granted. The reasoning goes as follows: (1) if every word of the Bible is divinely inspired, and (2) if in certain passages the moral advice given is evil, criminal, and depraved, then the conclusion is absolutely inevitable that God numbers among his other remarkable attributes evil, criminality, and depravity.

With such reasoning there is no difficulty in accepting even the most asinine or destructive biblical admonition. Of course only mentally disturbed individuals could possibly worship a god who was the epitome of evil—which means that we are forced to rethink the matter. For our second pass at the problem let us assume (1) God is perfect and (2) when we encounter instances in which he is alleged to be recommending highly imperfect conduct, we accept that we have been had—that the disgusting advice is of human and not divine origin.

All of this may be reasoned through with little trouble by all but those who are convinced that every word of the Bible is God's personal truth.

So sometimes highly intelligent scholars try to explain the unexplainable and to soften the hard sayings with qualifications of time and space that might have created the mind-set for the morally revolting or factually erroneous passages in question. The arguments put forth are reminiscent of the work of those resourceful lawyers assigned to defend Mafia leaders, drug sellers, corrupt corporate executives, murderers, or the other moral scum that so trouble modern society. It is a rare and strong-minded juror who will not find himself affected by clever legal arguments on behalf of even the most vile criminals.

Indeed there may well be circumstances in which a juror who might personally wish to impose the death penalty on an obviously guilty defendant might be moved to modify his harsh judgment by taking into account the defendant's troubled early family situation or the poverty of his culture. The gift of argumentation, then, may be turned, sometimes quite brilliantly, to either good or evil purposes.

Just so, those who defend outrageously vindictive or otherwise erroneous passages of Scripture often exhibit clever arguments in defense of their cause. We must not, nevertheless, permit ourselves to become beguiled by the suasion of such apologists. Whether we personally love God or have honest intellectual difficulty accepting his existence, those who respect the ancient ideals of truth, justice, and moral decency can use those ideals as guides through the thicket of scriptural analysis. (See also ARGUMENT.)

The most talented apologists for Scripture have never been able to convince the world jury of the total rightness of their case because the very bedrock of their case is myth. Although myth can contain factual components, as, say, an imaginary character who is said to have lived and died in Athens, the reality factor—in this case the city of Athens—establishes nothing about the historical reliability of the myth.

Consider that period of human experience with which Genesis deals. It is perfectly possible to construct a moving, convincing argument that although it is absurd to assume that an actual individual named Adam lived and did what he is said to have done in Genesis, there is a sense in which what was said of Adam is true of all humanity: that is, that mankind has a natural tendency for disobedience, arrogance, pride, and so forth.

Even an atheist could construct such an argument as an intellectual exercise. But all this reasoning is beside the point by which the Christian philosophy is said to be justified. If an actual individual named Adam did not have an actual wife named Eve who was created out of his rib bone, and if these two did not live in a neighborhood named Eden and did not eat the forbidden fruit, then Christian philosophers must set about the task of building an entirely new base on which to support their intellectual structure. (See also AUTHENTICITY OF THE BIBLE; ERROR.)

HISTORICAL RELEVANCE OF THE BIBLE. It is sometimes alleged, as a defense of the Bible's general cultural importance—which the Book indeed has—that it is a reliable and valuable source of historical information. But what would the reader think of a book on American history about which the most complimentary thing that might be said was that it was perhaps 25 percent accurate as regards certain factual details?

It is commonly assumed, by those aware of the frequency of scriptural errors-in-fact, that such overall unreliability constitutes the chief hindrance to the Bible's being perceived as historical record. An even worse failing is the *deliberate distortion of perspective* of which all the Old Testament authors were guilty, most particularly when referring to tribes and nations other than their own.

It is a rare historian who will not be misled by the realities of his own life experiences, culture, and philosophical commitments when assembling a collection of facts to form a historical report. Although children assume that history books written by residents of their own countries are accurate reports of significant events, every informed person knows that a description of, say, World War I written by a French scholar of the highest credentials will differ significantly from one written by an equally responsible German historian. Two reports on a given Christian controversy will differ greatly if the author of one is a Protestant and the other a Catholic. This would be the case even if there were no conscious enmity or philosophical opposition between or among the various camps. In the case of the writers of practically every section of the Bible, disagreement—frequently of a violent and warlike nature—was often not only evident but dominant.

The modern age enabled the achievement of relatively disinterested scholarship that primarily respects the ideal of truth. Still, even now, with the best of intentions, such unbiased analysis is not always achieved. But such a cast of mind was totally foreign during the twelve-hundred-year period when both the Old and New Testaments were actually written. The modern, Western, secular, and to some extent American social and political ideals of toleration for freedom of expression of all points of view, separation of church and state, civil rights and liberties, and the like, would have seemed in biblical times the most despicable forms of social, political, and religious heresy. In those periods, certain tribes and peoples were viewed as being evil by nature, while the Israelite group was seen as not only being in the right, but also being guaranteed as such by the personal election of no less than the Deity. (See also CHURCH AND STATE RELATIONS; RELIGIOUS THEORIES, DEVIANT; TRUTH; TOLERANCE.)

Such bias could not produce a record remarkable for its fair-mindedness, factual accuracy, or dispassionate respect for truth. While it is true that the Old Testament authors were also often critical of the moral failings of individuals within their own camps, in perceiving other tribes as "The Enemy," they were no more reliable as historians than the Nazi propagandists of the 1930s and 1940s were about the Jews of Europe. The argument that biblical historians were nevertheless divinely preserved from error—while not a convincing defense—at least has the grace of recognizing that error would have been inevitable without divine aid.

Conversely, that the Jewish-Christian Scriptures include references to actual places, events, or personages of the past is not the slightest proof of divine inspiration. Within a general tissue of lies or a work of fiction, a modern writer may refer to London, Paris, Berlin, or Bayonne, New Jersey, and mention as many actual human beings, mountains, rivers, oceans, buildings, and hamburger stands as he wishes without adding so much as a jot of truth to his overall account.

Just so, nothing whatever is established if certain elements of a two-thousand-year-old Bible story embody references to persons and places that history has established as authentic.

The proverbial disinterested observer from another universe would certainly find it strange that a book that gives an enormous volume of allegedly historical details and that is said to be God-inspired is in fact far less accurate than almost any other history book ever written. No other authors—nor their readers or admirers—would dream of making a claim of divine inspiration.

Although it was a long time in coming, the best-informed Christian and Jewish scholars now concede, as Father Jean Levie puts it:

> ... there may be *fictional historical forms* whose sole aim, in the mind of the inspired writer, is to supply moral or didactic teaching and *not to provide an account of real events in the past.* . . . It is therefore possible today to discover that a book, interpreted in the past as strictly historical, was in reality a kind of moral fable, . . . an edifying lesson, . . . *an imaginary tale situated in the past, but not a historical narrative.* (IA)

Where were such modern critics when earlier generations of heretics, rationalists, Protestants, dissenting Catholic scholars, and other thoughtful souls needed them? And how much longer will we have to wait before the point is communicated to the great mass of the faithful, to whom even now it will come as a shock?

Levie writes in such a reasonable fashion and is obviously such an admirable individual himself that one hesitates to contradict him, but he is less than convincing when he compares such "fictional historical forms" as the Bible with novels like those of Sir Walter Scott. The latter are *admittedly* fictionalized biographies of actual personages and narratives of events that in the main took place. This may well be the case with the Scriptures, but we were a damned long time in arriving at the point where Christian and Jewish scholarship could make such concessions.

Generations of rationalists and others have suggested precisely this, but one shudders to recall the torrent of abuse to which they were subjected for what now counts, in the long sweep of history, as nothing more than agreeing with the distinguished Father Levie and many other modern scholars within the church. Rationalists, of course, will find it impossible to see how the former idea of the Bible as the direct, personal truth of God can possibly be accommodated with what even the best Christian and Jewish scholars now concede: that it often does not contain valid historical narrative.

There is something in a sense unfair about criticizing ancient practitioners of any art or science on the grounds that they did not play their individual games by rules devised thousands of years later. The historical method of analytical criticism was developed only in the last century; it would be unrealistic to expect any Old or New Testament authors to manifest the rationality and relative lack of bias of the best of modern historians. To say as much, however, still requires recognition of the fact that they did *not* do so, which in turn means that it is absurd to imply that they *have* done so.

HISTORICAL RELEVANCE OF THE BIBLE

Wilhelm Dilthey, in *The 18th Century and the Historical World,* notes that the writing of valid history must *begin* with a criticism of sources. Dilthey, among other scholars, has explained that the emerging science of the construction of reliable history both led to and was greatly aided by a concomitant interest in the historical component of the Scriptures:

> In this respect the great philology of the sixteenth and seventeenth centuries rendered a valuable service to historiography. It undertook to reconstruct a lost world out of the decayed remnants of its literature, and in the process, criticism and interpretation developed into an art and a conscious method. The religious struggles and confrontations which filled these two centuries brought further assistance.

Another important factor to an even partially adequate understanding of the earliest historical records of the Israelites is that there is a definite pattern to the development of the histories of all peoples. The present and recent past may be known with reasonable certainty, but as we measure a backward path through the centuries we make a steady retreat from the ground of factual knowledge. At last we totally lose our way in the dim region where there is no longer the slightest demonstrable fact at all but only tantalizing wisps of oral tradition, myth, legend, fantasy, rumor, or dream. Since this has been so with all the separate peoples of earth, it would be strange—indeed, impossible—that it should not also be the case with the ancient Hebrews.

Historians tend to stand polarized in the debate about the historical value of the Scriptures. The truth, of course, lies between the two. A book by a modern historian may be said to be very largely reliable in its accuracy, but the Bible is a poor source indeed for factual information.

The writers of Scripture were mistaken in many of their beliefs. Any public figure today, for example, who seriously preached that wars, floods, tornadoes, street riots, and such were in the literal sense purposely caused by God Almighty to chastise a sinful people, would run the risk of being accused of mental instability. At the very least, the leaders of dominant religious sects would advise him that he was seriously in error. Nonetheless, he would certainly be able to boast that—insane or not, erroneous or not— his view coincided with that of the authors of the Old Testament; whereas it is modern popes, rabbis, and ministers who are the heretics within the context of traditional scriptural understanding. (See also AUTHENTICITY OF THE BIBLE; CHRONICLES, THE FIRST BOOK OF THE; JUDGES; VERSIONS OF THE BIBLE.)

HOMOSEXUALITY. Ask a cross-section of fundamentalist Christians to list major sins in even an approximate order of severity, and no doubt homosexuality will appear high on the list. Fundamentalism is a crucial factor in that attitude, given that nonfundamentalist Christians, while they overwhelmingly disapprove of homosexual behavior, nevertheless have some degree of understanding that being homosexual is not a matter of choice.

While certain individuals are clearly more likely than others to murder, those who murder make the actual decision to commit the crime. Most other moral and/or legal offenses require conscious decisions on the part of the transgressor. Not everyone has an equally sensitive conscience nor an equal thirst for virtue and justice, but the will does indeed participate at moments of decision. The same will, however—controlled intention— has no connection to the practice of homosexual behavior by millions of humans. (See also FREE WILL.)

In an age when millions of dollars fund the work of scientific researchers concerned with natural phenomena that do not always appear to be of major importance, we hear very little about research into the question of what factors lead an individual to prefer his or her own gender for sexual gratification or as a recipient of true romantic love.

The question of whether performing a homosexual act is right or wrong does not concern me here. Such acts may be grievously wrong in certain circumstances, but they would still be wrong regardless of the genders involved. For example, to commit the act of rape is clearly wrong. Adultery is thought to be wrong by the moral and legal codes of almost all societies, and the sexual violation of children is never justified. But only homosexual behavior, purely in and of itself, is considered essentially wrong and has been generally so regarded for centuries by the great majority of the human race.

But again, we do not, at the age of sexual maturity, either toss a coin or *decide* by any other means to become homosexual. All the fundamentalist nonsense about homosexuality being a moral sin—in the same category as bank robbery, murder, or any such offense that one may choose or refuse to commit by an exercise of the will—obscures the relevant reality: *We simply do not yet know what causes the development of one's main sexual pattern.*

Some, primarily those of the Freudian school, assume that the causative factors are purely environmental. The other extreme postulates the "they're-born-that-way" argument. But, in neither case does the individual, in early childhood, puberty, or adulthood, have the remotest opportunity to make a choice in the matter.

A purely biological context, of course, requires that the two partners must be sexual opposites for the creation of a new human being. But this argument has certain difficulties: almost all sexual activity takes place in either the mindless or quite conscious pursuit of pleasure and not for reasons of procreation. We may be quite certain that of all the millions of human sexual consummations taking place on earth in a given twenty-four-hour period, only a very small minority of the actors in such dramas are playing their roles purely because they wish to produce a new life. It is no counter-argument that the majority of those sexual partners who are married *do* eventually wish to have children, since those same people may wish to savor the delights of sexual consummation five thousand times in their lifetimes, while over the same span of years they may elect to have only two or three children.

Clearly, then, much study remains to be done on this difficult question.

In the television series "Star Trek" one creature, Spock, was fully rational. Knowing only this much we would not have to be told that he was not an inhabitant of planet earth. If we, like Spock, were completely reasonable we would be able to accept any news, however unpleasant or painful. In reality, however, we have great difficulty grasping any information that is contrary to our perception of our situation.

This is dramatized in those tragic scenes, now all too common on our television newscasts, where a mother learns of the unexpected death, by accident or murder, of one of her children. In many such sad cases, the first word uttered is an anguished "No!"—an immediate, automatic attempt to deny the tragic reality.

Even in less dramatic contexts it causes us extreme discomfort to acknowledge and internalize any information that stands in contradiction to what we want to believe. An illustrative instance would be the reaction of millions of Ronald Reagan supporters to assorted bits of information that gradually established his remarkable ineptness. Even many who were in the neutral or Democratic camp took quite a long time to get Reagan in focus. He was, after all, our president—and for two terms at that— but even though literally hundreds of instances in published material flatly opposed the image of the genial, alert Great Communicator, it took a full decade for the American public to develop a more realistic picture of him.

It was simply too painful for his admirers to see that he was inadequately educated, poorly informed about both history and modern world events, thoroughly dominated by his driven wife, given to dependence on professional astrologers, and possessed of nothing more than the smiling geniality of the average salesman or radio announcer—announcing being his actual original profession.

A top executive of a major oil company had been invited to the White

House with a group of other business leaders in order to assure themselves that this particular president would be sensitive to the interests of the corporate sector. When, a few days later, a friend asked the industry leader what he thought of the new president, the executive said, "Well, he seems very nice but—my God, he is dumb." The speaker was himself a Republican.

Admirers of President John Kennedy gradually perceived that the entire Camelot image was an illusion and that Kennedy's sexual conduct—even while in the White House—was compulsive and addictive to such a degree that his close advisors considered it scandalous. This information was not conveyed to the public in a single shocking revelation. Rather it became part of the public record, in separate increments, over the course of several years. Such information, because it was inharmonious with the image of John Kennedy as a resolute, principled, high-minded young American leader, tended to be doubted or ignored. So it is with the fact that the Bible is absolutely clear and consistent in condemning homosexuality.

In the simplest possible terms: *if the Bible is right, then homosexuality is wrong.*

This essentially either-or case leads to a painful dilemma for the millions of homosexuals who are either Jews or Christians. Obviously that majority of the world's homosexual population who have no interest in the Judeo-Christian Scriptures have no such problem.

However, with a few exceptions, humankind generally—including the enormous masses outside the Christian or Jewish folds—also take a negative view of homosexuality, a point that the reader may confirm by consulting other sources and authorities.

I am certainly not about to resolve this issue since that is something that has not been accomplished by anyone and, in fact, can not be. It is all to the good, however, that a frank and open dialogue on the dilemma of homosexuality—and, for that matter, sexuality in general—has been initiated.

Some, of course, are made extremely uncomfortable by the fact of the debate itself. Many people are so uneasy about sex that they would, if they had the power, either discourage or forbid all public discussions of it, except perhaps among concerned theologians or medical authorities. And we do well to remember that this is by no means only a Jewish or Christian failing. Gandhi, the great Indian leader, regarded sex as did the the Catholic Church of a century ago: that sexual function was inherently a necessary evil, the only possible justification of which was the continuance of the human species. He was, consequently, thoroughly opposed to any form of birth control, despite India's socially destructive overpopulation dilemma.

HOMOSEXUALITY

A general uneasiness has characterized the human approach to sex over recorded time. While on the one hand it is (1) required for the creation of new human beings and (2) provides a degree of pleasure that exceeds any other, it is nevertheless dangerously anarchic. Even among those who are not out-and-out hedonists or rakes, there are instances of loss of control that often have tragic consequences. This is, of course, partly because either a conscious God or an unconscious nature has programmed humans—and particularly males—to respond almost like robots to certain sensory cues from members of the opposite sex. There is a sense in which there are "computer chips" in most male human brains that seek out and respond to not merely random objects in the environment—roller skates, typewriters, orchids, blueberry pies, and so forth—but portions of the female anatomy and/or depictions thereof. Vast modern industries are built on this male reaction.

Since it is a biological given that the majority of human males derive instantaneous pleasure from just the sight of a beautiful woman, it was inevitable that lucrative markets would spring up for photographs, magazines, motion picture films, and videotapes that market this particular commodity. The use of sex in the advertising industry is so well-known that it requires no particular comment. Even companies noted for their executives' personal political conservatism are no exception to this. For example, the Coors family, who brews Coors beer, is famous in conservative circles as a financial supporter of right-wing organizations and campaigns. The wealthy have a right to support their chosen political associates. But despite Coors's prominence in the conservative camp, their television commercials are famous—some would say infamous—for showing young ladies with beautiful bodies wearing extremely skimpy bathing suits and disporting themselves in seductive poses.

The Time-Life publishing empire, generally perceived as a middle-of-the-road bastion of the status quo, derives considerable profit from its annual *Sports Illustrated* swimsuit issue. No one has ever suggested that the millions of young male readers who purchase such magazines have any interest whatever in the swimming attire exhibited, given that no one would be interested in buying such a magazine if the bathing apparel shown was not exhibited on long-legged and full-breasted young women.

The anarchic nature of even the most common sexual impulse constitutes a social danger. Oddly enough, Scripture is a thoroughly inconsistent guide in regard to sexuality generally. The Bible says absolutely nothing critical, for example, about the numerous woman who were the bed partners of such still-revered Old Testament leaders as Solomon and David, and it relates certain sexual stories that are clearly scandalous and immoral, by any sensible standard, without a word of criticism of such behavior. The point is not that the Old Testament is opposed to sexual virtue, but rather that the Jewish and Christian testaments differ in defining it.

But to return again to the question of homosexuality—even those who generally feel no guilt about their homosexual behavior pattern, if they are Christian, inevitably feel extreme discomfort when they consult scriptural references to their estate.

Given the overall complexity of the ongoing debate on the issue one can hardly hope to do justice to it in such a short commentary as this. I was recently criticized, in this connection, for suggesting that one branch of the Christian conservative movement formally and repeatedly recommends the imposition of death for homosexuals, but a Christian Reconstructionist (who also happens to be a personal friend), journalist and speaker John Lofton, has recently sent me a copy of the first issue of a newsletter called *The Lofton Letter* in which he once again frankly states the following:

> Yes, the Old Testament laws are still God's laws which are binding on believer and unbeliever alike and, yes, the Old Testament law does prescribe the death penalty for homosexuals, among others.

Mr. Lofton is absolutely correct in reporting on the Old Testament view of homosexuality. He and his cohorts do indeed wish to make the United States of America a formally Christian nation, one in which there will be little difference, if any, between the laws and commandments of the Bible and those of the civil community.

In addition to prescribing the death penalty for homosexuals the Christian Reconstructionists also insist that adulterers be killed and that the same treatment be accorded to habitually troublesome teenagers.

To most people such perfectly serious proposals seem so astonishing that the mind simply tends to reject them. Lofton's segment of the Christian far right is, of course, talking about the actual physical extinction of— to use a very round number—perhaps fifty million Americans. Nor are such conservatives the least bit apologetic about their plans. Generally speaking, they feel that our nation has become so corrupt and depraved that the time for traditional moral education and nothing more is long past. The Christian Reconstructionists are perfectly aware that among those they would like to see shot, gassed, electrocuted, or hanged are a considerable number of their fellow Christians and a certain percentage of political conservatives as well.

Regardless of where right and wrong are situated in this vast context, it is difficult to see how homosexual Christians, and those sympathetic to them, can possibly justify their assertion of rights in a formally Christian or Jewish context, given the inescapable fact of biblical condemnations of homosexual conduct.

Paul's Views as Expressed in Romans Chapter 2. Although the Scriptures are consistent in condemning homosexuality, one of the strongest attacks is Paul's, in his letter to the Romans. Again, simply leaving the question of rightness and wrongness aside, Paul himself is in error in explaining what is behind attraction to one's own sex. Before considering his argument, it is important to reflect that, at least as of the moment of this writing (early 1992), the best-informed scientific authorities have been unable to resolve the painfully knotty problem. It increasingly appears, however, that genetic factors are among the constellation of causative agents. Since Paul can have known nothing of matters genetic, he must naturally look elsewhere and, in fact, mistakenly attributes the homosexual behavior pattern to a lack of faith in the specific form of religion that Paul personally prefers.

Such doubters, he suggests, tend either toward atheism or a far more absurd belief that likenesses of men, "or of birds or of four-legged animals or of snakes" literally possess divine power. In verses 24–27 of chapter 2, Paul reasons as follows:

> 24. *Therefore,* God handed them over to impurity through the lusts of their hearts for the mutual degradation of their bodies.
> 25. They exchanged the truth of God for a lie and revered and worshipped the creature rather than the creator who is blessed forever. Amen.
> 26. *Therefore: God handed them over to degrading passions.* Their females exchanged natural relations for unnatural,
> 27. And the males likewise gave up natural relations with females and burned with lust for one another. Males did shameful things with males and thus received on their own persons the due penalty for their perversity. (IA)

It does not require the slightest bias in favor of homosexuality to recognize the groundless nature of this argument. Since no Christian has ever argued that Paul was correct in his every utterance it is not necessary to attack an assertion that has yet to be made. Paul was a truly great man—a powerful writer, an eloquent, charismatic speaker, possessed of remarkable courage and perseverance. He certainly left his mark on history. But the fact that he was only human and therefore less than perfect would inevitably have led him into certain instances of faulty argumentation.

Paul makes a far more serious error, however, which could even be perceived as blasphemous, when he continues:

> 28. And since they did not see fit to acknowledge God, *God handed them over to their undiscerning mind to do what is improper.* (IA)

Paul did not say that because of their inability to believe in the one supreme and indeed only God, combined with their idolatry, God simply turned his back on them, as a result of which they fell into sinful ways. Or that the Devil entered the picture and enticed them into sin. This, I repeat, is clearly what he does *not* say. On the contrary, he states the theological absurdity that God himself led them into their perverse ways.

Another odd component of Paul's case here is that he does not say, as innumerable other Christian and Jewish spokesmen have suggested, that turning one's back on the true God generally tends to lead people into sexual excess. Paul suggests, on the other hand, not that the all-too-common offense of adultery, premarital sexual intercourse, compulsive Don Juanism, or onanism may follow in part from lack of belief in the one true God, but only that *one* form of sexual behavior engaged in by homosexuals and lesbians.

We do not require further evidence to perceive the weakness of Paul's case. The millions of homosexuals who are, in fact, believers in the Catholic, Jewish, and Protestant persuasions attest that in this one instance Paul's views make no serious contribution to the ongoing dialogue about homosexuality.

Of course, the reference to Christian and Jewish homosexuals does not apply solely to the laity. Only in recent years have we discovered that the percentage of gay rabbis, ministers, and priests is much larger than had been previously assumed. Parenthetically, the problem—if the word will not seem too controversial—is more serious among the Christian than the Jewish clergy.

Another fascinating aspect of the modern phase of the debate on this issue—and one that seems not to have been commented on in the public record—is that a certain number of homosexuals are politically conservative. They are, in other words, members of the very camp that is home to their most vitriolic and murderous critics.

It seems never to have occurred to Paul, and rarely to modern homophobes, that our sexual preferences are determined by causes still not well established during our very early years. My original reason for making this assumption was based on an experience I had at the age of five. My mother had sent me from Chicago to live, for what turned out to be several months, with her married sister Nora, a resident of Los Angeles. The streets of the Western city were beautiful in those days, the climate balmy, and the area's natural attractions striking.

One afternoon as I was playing alone in the neighborhood I happened to meet a cheerful, dark-complexioned child who appeared slightly younger than myself. We struck up a casual conversation as we walked along a nearby alley. After a few moments the little boy stepped over to a fence, opened the front of his short pants, and began to urinate. I looked away, with a feeling of slight embarrassment, but attached no particular importance to the moment. When a moment later he had completed relieving himself, however, the child quite calmly asked whether I wanted to engage in oral sex. My immediate sense of shock and revulsion was so automatic and powerful that I still recall the incident with striking clarity, but I hasten to explain that I am unlikely to have had the same emotional reaction if my new companion had been a little girl.

I would have been shocked, no doubt—even perhaps made uneasy—but I am honest enough to concede that I might also have felt a strong temptation to explore the possibility that had been offered had my companion been a girl. So what was behind my reaction had nothing whatever to do with being a good, virtuous, spiritual little fellow who would have been shocked by any invitation to sexual activity. It was purely the fact that the conversation was about homosexual activity, which elicited my automatic revulsion. It would be absurd to attach either credit or blame to my reaction, since it was only that—a physical response as inevitable as ducking a blow or blinking in excess light. *Choice,* the word invariably used by conservative Christian critics, was not part of the picture at all.

It is possible to forgive Paul for his mistake since he lived two thousand years ago. On the other hand, right-wing gay-bashers of the present day have no such excuse, at least as regards the narrow issue of homosexual motivation. If, however, those in the present day who argue that homosexual behavior in and of itself is no more criminal or immoral than heterosexual behavior are correct, then it inescapably follows that on the same point the Bible is wrong. (See also CONSERVATISM; DISEASE; MORALITY.)

HOPE. Thomas Hart, one of the most gifted sculptors of the modern age, has suggested that great art must, among other things, give hope for the future. The word *hope* itself must have come into our assorted languages simply because there are things we want that we do not presently have. Hope applies only to the future. Even when it seems to apply to the past— as in such statements as "I hope I remembered to turn off the gas this morning" or "I hope I didn't leave my car unlocked last night"—the thrust of these messages is clearly toward future consequences.

Hope concerns the things we desire because we perceive them as good. No one would say, "I hope I'm struck by lightning," or "I hope my children become ill." Although hope is referred to as one of the supreme virtues, it may retain its glowing reputation only in the abstract, for when we examine specific instances of hope we at once perceive that some are reasonable and productive while others are pointless. In one of my professional fields— songwriting—many people with little or no talent invest lifetimes of hope for success in a notoriously competitive field, sometimes wasting a good deal of money in the process and dooming themselves to endless frustration and disappointment. There are all too many situations in this difficult world where a particular drama cannot possibly have a happy ending for all concerned, or, to quote the title of a song I once wrote on this theme: "In Every Horserace Ever Run, Most of the Horses Lose."

Ideally, then, hope should not persist in total disregard of the attendant realities. To be effective it should be *rooted* in those realities. Obviously, in frequent instances the investment of hope in an extremely unlikely outcome does no great harm. Buying a two-dollar lottery ticket, for example, even though the statistical odds of success may be literally a million to one, elicits a certain kind of crazy hope that one will win. Even though most of us would never enjoy such a moment of success were we to buy a lottery ticket every day of our lives, it could still be argued that the money so wasted was not needed for true essentials. The world is not much worse off for such luckless little adventures; indeed the sense of hope the tickets give to the purchaser is sometimes worth the cost.

When philosophers and theologians think of hope, they are clearly not thinking of lotteries or other trivial spheres of action. In the famous scriptural reference to faith, hope, and charity, why is it stated that the last is the greatest? We shall never know precisely what was in the mind of the speaker. But if we address the question personally, we can see that charity refers to practical, concrete particulars whereas faith and hope refer only to our desires. Charity, in fact, is so practical that it is difficult even to think of it in the abstract. We may be quite confident that we will never hear such a statement as "Mr. Jones is a remarkably compassionate man although he has never performed a single charitable act in his life."

No, we refer to someone as charitable because of a series of individual instances of giving. We give money, food, clothing, time, labor. We may even give love where it is a much-needed commodity. Charity, then, is a matter of brass tacks whereas hope is a matter of desires and dreams. Faith is always a substitute for knowledge for if we are quite certain of something it would be a logical absurdity to say that we have faith that it is so. Children may be taught things in totally random sequence, but a thinking adult first hopes and then, on the basis of those hopes, develops faith. The connection between the two virtues, alas, has no inherently wise basis. One may, for example, fervently hope that a God exists and then, on the basis of that hope, proceed to have faith that God is a large pumpkin. This is not to suggest that the historically important question whether God does or does not exist has any necessary connection with the faith and hope of humans. On some level there is a reality—whether that be the existence or nonexistence of God—but it is precisely because we cannot be certain about that narrow question that we must content ourselves with faith and hope. (See also VIRTUES, THE.)

Hope is a matter of wanting the future to be better than the present and is usually applied to specific concerns. We never seem to encounter instances of people hoping simply that either God or blind chance will make this world a better place. When we encounter hope in a context of reality, it always has a distinct content. Cancer victims hope that a cure for their disease will be found. Investors hope that the stock market will not collapse and wipe out their life savings. Residents of lowland areas hope that the heavy rains will not lead to a flood that destroys their homes. In such contexts hope can have a reasonable and energizing effect if it leads us to address our material circumstances in such a way as to bring about the desired end. Obviously this does not mean that even the most vigorous campaigns by large numbers of people will always produce the desired results. But such crusades greatly increase the likelihood of relatively happy resolutions and, in some instances, turn out to be successful.

When we speak of *the future,* we mean in the larger sense: (1) the future of human life on earth, either our own or that of our species, or (2) some sort of life after death. The latter sort of future by no means refers to a time yet to come except for us as individuals. From the first days of human life on earth humans have died. If, then, there is anything that may be referred to as our future home, it has been furnished and densely occupied since early times.

But what if there is no God? What should we then be forced to conclude about our individual fates after the moment of physical death? Many believers feel that if it could be demonstrated that there is either no God at all, or at least one not anything like the one they have traditionally believed in, there would then be no hope for the future. There is no purely logical reason why some sort of spiritual life could not continue whether there is a God or not. Perhaps it's not likely for spirituality to continue, but there is no reason that it could not possibly be the case. It would clearly be a remarkably strange state of affairs but then it is difficult to imagine anything stranger than what we already know about life. The only reason we do not perceive the strangeness and awe-inspiring wonder of even the most commonplace things is that, as the old saying goes, familiarity breeds contempt, or at least insensitivity.

To the hypothesis that an incorporeal life may persist after the mechanical failure of the body even if there is no God, the question may be raised: What would be the point? The same question may be raised about the grand drama of life as it has traditionally been perceived. If there is anything that is striking about life as we know it, it is its apparent pointlessness. It is no intelligible answer to this question to refer to those aspects of life that are sweet and lovely—the smiles of infants, the scent of flowers, the glory of sunsets, the lacy grace of waterfalls, the beauty of saints—since these are only a part of life and a minor part at that. Was there really a *point,* a *necessity* for creating a vast universe in which every hour of every day is characterized by the most hideous suffering for millions of creatures sensitively equipped to feel pain? The question as to pointedness or pointlessness of life has never been satisfactorily dealt with so perhaps it is wise to set it aside as irrelevant to our analytical discourse on the narrow subject of hope.

But what if it could be established not only that there is no God but that physical death is also simply the end? What then of hope? There are still scores of years of time for hope for billions of currently living individuals as well as those continually being born. While some humans die a few moments after conception and others die at every other moment on the theoretical time span of human life, the majority are granted better luck. For all those individual futures, then, and for the practical good it can achieve when it serves as a source of energy leading to social action, hope has a perfectly reasonable place in human experience. (See also FUTURE, THE; SOUL, THE.)

I

IRRATIONALISM. It has never been denied that religion, even in its most depraved and superstitious forms, accomplishes a certain amount of good. Even atheists commend the material ministrations of self-sacrificing religious nurses, doctors, teachers, ambulance drivers, and others. But it is equally undenied that the practice of religion also results in harm. This connected pair of truths are of great importance; they must be grasped simultaneously.

If asked to list specific instances of the harm done by religion most people—even the devout—will refer to classic outrages and atrocities known to every student of history. A smaller number will recall scandalous behavior of individual believers. Not nearly as many will perceive one of the most destructive of all the results of religion, which is less recognizable because it occurs not in the streets or other physical theaters but in the mind. I refer to the early, unremitting, irrational habit of accepting a church's opinion, whether or not it is supported by evidence. Even if all views accepted on this basis were wise, it would still be dangerously destructive to the precious capacity for reason that distinguishes man from other living creatures. Unfortunately, in reality it leads not only to the acceptance but also to the subsequent fierce defense of opinions that even the majority of believers describe as absurd, though they are able to perceive illustrations chiefly in religions with which they personally are not affiliated.

One of the most disturbing aspects of irrationalism—as the experience of Salman Rushdie demonstrates—is the readiness of its practitioners to resort to vigilante methods to attack those perceived as the opposition, which usually means those who have dared to criticize.

Reaction to biblical criticism is another notable example. In the very

178

essence of both popular and, to a certain extent, scholarly approaches to the Bible there is a fundamentally irrational element. All other literature is evaluated on its merits. In the case of the Bible, however, churches have for centuries urged that we must first accept it as divinely inspired and then, to the extent that we might have a degree of rational curiosity about its contents, our evaluative studies must consist of a defense of the original proposition. This is irrational. If the Bible is indeed of divine origin, then its merits ought to be so self-evident that an impartial and fair-minded analysis will serve only to confirm rather than undermine belief in them. (See also FANATICISM; REASON; RELIGION; RELIGIOUS THEORIES, DEVIANT.)

J

JAMES, THE EPISTLE OF. It is not clear, first of all, that anyone named James actually wrote the epistle. Many Christian scholars believe that it is not now possible to determine the identity of the author. Even if authorship by someone named James could be established, we would still not know whether that person was (1) James, the son of Zebedee, who was called to discipleship with his brother John while fishing with their father; (2) James, the son of Alphaeus, another member of the Twelve; (3) James, the brother of the Lord; or (4) some other James altogether.

It has been commonly assumed that Jesus' half-brother, who was the leader of the church in Jerusalem, was the author. If this is the case, however, the document would have to have been produced before the year 62. Tradition holds that this James was stoned to death in that year because he represented a pacifist approach to Rome whereas the Zealots wished to take a strong stand against the Roman Empire.

The existence of an actual brother would also establish that, contrary to Catholic teaching, Mary was not a virgin throughout her life. By making such a statement one is, of course, simply dealing in a logical and literal way with the available references. There is a scholarly reference to the point in *The Interpreter's Dictionary of the Bible:*

> The relationship between James and Jesus has been much discussed. . . . NT and early Christian writers refer to James as a "brother" of Jesus, and the natural interpretation of the language of the period is the literal one, that James was a son of Joseph and Mary, younger than Jesus. *Though this view was rejected by most of the ancient church, it is probably correct.*

The difficulties with the epistle itself start immediately, since verse 1 clearly specifies that the author is writing "to the twelve tribes which are scattered abroad." In response to this the New American Standard Bible, in the Walk-Thru Reference Edition, says:

> Traditionally the phrase, the twelve tribes, was used to indicate the entirety of the Jewish nation. But since the entire Jewish nation, no matter how widely it may have been scattered in the Diaspora, could not have its entire existence outside Palestine, it seems best to understand the subscription symbolically.

In truth, nobody knows whom the unknown author had in mind, although he was presumably writing to Jews who had been converted to Christianity.

Regardless of who the book was written by or to, if one approaches it purely in terms of its content, one is gratified to discover that by and large it is one of the most reasonable, appealing, and morally instructive portions of the entire Bible.

Even atheists and agnostics can perceive the goodness and wisdom in the statement in chapter 1:

> 27. Pure religion and undefiled before God and the Father is this, To visit the fatherless and widows in their affliction, and to keep himself unspotted from the world.

Religion so perceived is an admirable combination of compassion and morality, and of both there is always a shortage. An indication of the unknown author's general reasonableness and common sense is encountered again in the first chapter, where James clearly states:

> 13. Let no man say when he is tempted, I am tempted of God: for God cannot be tempted with evil, neither tempteth he any man:
> 14. But every man is tempted, when he is drawn away of his own lust, and enticed.

Like Hebrews, the epistle is more a sermon than a letter. Its spirit is like that of the synoptic Gospels; its protests against social injustice and its doctrine of salvation by works ring with heroic concern. It appeals to moderns because of its admirable social-mindedness. Its author, whoever he was, was a good-hearted man.

Despite its evident virtue and wisdom, the book of James was for quite a long time *not* accepted as properly part of the New Testament! It was almost rejected from the canon because of its anti-Paulism and was criticized by Luther for the same reason. Eusebius, an early church father, refers to it as among "the disputed writings."

Although not unanimous, the general scholarly consensus now is that the letter was written during the period between A.D. 125 and 150. Origen made the letter widely known in Alexandria and very gradually it became accepted in the East. It was not until the fifth century that the authenticity of James was accepted in such Syrian communities as Antioch and Edessa.

When the author of James says "Faith without works is dead" (2:26), it is inescapable that he is directly contradicting Paul. Christian apologists, however, obviously uncomfortable with such clear-cut disagreements, deny this one, explaining that what James means when he uses the word *faith* is empty professions of belief—giving mere lip service to the particulars of faith. A sensible response to such a defense is that James does not say this. It is interesting that, according to Matthew 7, Jesus sided with James rather than Paul on this narrow point when he said:

> 21. Not every one that sayeth unto me, Lord, Lord, shall enter into the kingdom of heaven; but he that doeth the will of my Father which is in heaven.

Paul, of course, did not carry the point as far as do some of his Protestant followers. It is obvious, in any event, that empty observance of ritual or churchly formalities isn't worth a damn so far as either achieving personal salvation or helping one's fellow creatures is concerned. Christians should easily recognize the moral soundness and simple common sense of doing good works, which is to say being of practical help to suffering men, women, and children. Fortunately millions of them do—Mother Teresa being an illustrative example—but the rich conservatives of the Christian world never list James as among their favorite portions of Scripture for reasons that are obvious. (See also ALTRUISM; BY THEIR FRUITS YE SHALL KNOW THEM; CHARITY.)

JEWS AND JUDAISM. According to *The Interpreter's Dictionary of the Bible:*

> The usage of the term *Jew* was very fluid even in biblical times. It does not refer exclusively to members of the tribe of Judah. While it is freely

used to indicate national origin, this usage begins only after the southern kingdom of Judah had survived the northern kingdom of Israel in the 7th century B.C. Soon, however, one was called a Jew, regardless of nationality, if he adhered to Judaism. . . .

Today the term is even more fluid. There are Jews both by religion and by birth, by religion but not by birth, and by birth but not by religion.

Jewish Subjection and Anti-Semitism. Since biblical times the Jewish people have been called the Chosen People and yet their history is filled with subjugation and persecution. The tribe of Judah came into contact with two quite separate classifications of rival powers. One consisted of small tribes such as the Philistines, the Amorites, and the like, with whom Israel seemed to be almost constantly at war. That they won victories over these small populations and city-states is entirely probable. They obviously could not hope for equal success against superpowers like Egypt, Rome, Syria, Greece, Persia, or Assyria. These latter entities dominated the Jews from time to time.

Early Christian persecution of Jews resulted from the perception that it was the Jews who killed Jesus. But the historical record itself is open to other interpretations. In 1974 one of French legal history's most peculiar trials pitted a conservative Catholic lawyer and legal historian, Jacques Isorini, against an equally conservative priest, Father Georges de Nantes.

Isorini had in 1967 published a book titled *The True Trial of Jesus* that argued that the Jews were quite absolved of any personal responsibility for the execution of Jesus for the reasons that they had not been at all aware that he was divine, that only the local Roman authority—Pontius Pilate—had the legal power to impose death sentences, and that in any event the Romans wanted Jesus dead because they regarded him as a politically subversive troublemaker who might stir the Jews to yet another attempt to throw off the yoke of Roman authority. The argument is one that many Bible scholars—chiefly Christian—find intellectually respectable, but anti-Semitic Father de Nantes, who had called Pope Paul VI a heretic and consequently been forbidden to preach or celebrate Mass, charged that Isorini was a forger who had "opted for the Jews against their victim." He went on to say that "to absolve the Jews of their crime, even in the cause of a better ecumenical understanding, is to contradict all that constitutes Catholic dogma."

In their decision, the three-judge panel observed that Vatican Council II had already absolved the Jews of guilt by historic proclamation in 1965. Understandably enough, the judges ruled in favor of Isorini, but one would be deluded in assuming that the larger issue itself has been resolved. In light of such dangerous nonsense, however—caused entirely by the Bible—it is understandable that the Jews would not exactly knock each other down organizing public expressions of thanks to the Vatican for its modern lurch in the direction of civilization.

Christian churches still do not seem totally at ease with Jews. Some individual Christians do reach out lovingly and with great understanding to their Jewish brothers and sisters, but they are only a sadly small minority. The churches conduct certain rituals as repentance for sin. What are we to think of a religious philosophy that for two thousand years, far from preaching against the vicious depravity of anti-Semitism, actually encouraged it and in many instances actively led assorted personal attacks, mob onslaughts, pogroms, and officially sanctioned denials of human rights? (See CRIMES, BIBLICAL IMPETUS TO.)

Even now, after progressive reformers have turned the bright spotlight of public secular morality into such dark corners, not every wretch has been shamed enough to either correct or at least disguise his hostility. When does the worldwide campaign of atonement for two thousand years of one of the most vicious sins imaginable get under way?

There seems to be a difference between Christian negativity toward Jews and that toward blacks. Many of the blacks my peers held in contempt were themselves Christians but that accounted for not a thing among their fellow Catholics, Methodists, or Baptists. Their skin color counted for everything. In most social respects, Negroes were held to be literally inferior. In many respects the conditions of their lives, in fact, contrived to make them inferior in education, in income, in housing, and in social prestige.

But the Jews, despised for historical reasons, were often acknowledged as superior to their critics. Because of the remarkable intellectual achievements of Jews in modern times, we tend to think that they must always have been able to boast such gifts as they presently display. While such an error is almost inevitable, it is still an error. Words such as *superior* and *inferior,* of course, are relative terms. The Jews, at the nadir of their social and intellectual development, were clearly still superior to certain primitive tribes, although in ancient times their achievements were not nearly as remarkable as those of the Greeks. To this day Greek accomplishments in philosophy and the arts are respected, although they were not the only people of biblical times to leave behind a remarkable record in architecture and pictorial art. Greek thinkers such as Socrates, Plato, and Aristotle are still revered.

Throughout the centuries, Jews have disagreed among themselves about their Bible. For example, the Sadducees, the highly conservative minority who were dominant during the lifetime of Jesus, considered only the first five books of the Bible as sacred and specifically rejected *all* the others! So much for the view that there is only one true Bible, from which all other versions are heretical deviations.

Regardless, any critical examination of the Old Testament today will inevitably be perceived, by at least a certain number of Jewish readers, as a criticism of Judaism itself. Even the most reasonable questioning of ideas held sacred is seen by some as an attack upon themselves. That the critic may have no such intention will be considered irrelevant. Indeed, for Jews the Bible has a kind of importance it cannot possibly have for Christians. Except for that statistically invisible percentage of Christians whose forebears lived in the Holy Land two thousand years ago, Christians perceive the early documents of their faith as having only religious relevance. To an Irish Christian, for example, any assault upon Christianity is seen as anti-Christian, but certainly not as anti-Irish. For the Jew, however, the books of the Law, the Prophets, the Writings are historical documents of a racial, tribal, or nationalistic nature. Indeed the very factor that has drawn criticism over many centuries—that the pre-Christian portions of the Bible are largely a record of a single nation—is seen by Jews as a reason for pride.

Another reason for the uniqueness of the Jewish response to criticism of the Scriptures is that even modern, educated Jews who no longer hold to the simplistic literalism that characterized the belief of their grandparents are often reluctant to articulate their faith's erosion. In a sense, doing so makes them feel somewhat traitorous to their people and their culture. The Jews, after all, have survived for at least four thousand years, through most of which they generally adhered to the religious construct outlined in the Old Testament. The ancient code, however irrelevant parts of it may be considered at the present stage of human development; the ancient history, despite the many now-recognized imperfections and inaccuracies; and the ancient image of the physical universe, now known to be both naive and scientifically groundless—all of these nevertheless played important roles in the cultural and physical survival of a great people. Even if such traditions did not perform their own function, the non-Jewish world—Christian and otherwise—would nevertheless have forced a philosophical dependence upon them simply by the mindless cruelty it frequently visited upon a people seen as The Other. (See also ORIGINS OF MONOTHEISTIC RELIGIOUS PRACTICES.)

JOEL. The book of Joel is the second of twelve short prophetic books that conclude the Old Testament. It has only three chapters.

Chapter One begins with a description of a plague of locusts that Joel sees as a certain sign of the Lord's wrath and the *imminent Judgment Day*. On the factor of imminence, Joel, and therefore the Bible, was in error. Verse 5 is of moderate interest in that it laments the loss of grape-vines—and the resultant wine—as a result of the plague:

> 5. Awake, ye drunkards, and weep; and howl, all ye drinkers of wine, because of the new wine; for it is cut off from your mouth.

This verse is hardly to be cited by those millions of fundamentalist and other Christians who vehemently oppose the consumption of alcohol on moral grounds. The verse clearly implies that at least this prophet of Jesus saw nothing evil about the imbibing of fermented grape juice, though he was opposed to intoxication.

Chapter Two. The second chapter of Joel begins with a theme quite common in the Scriptures:

> 1. Blow ye the trumpet in Zion, and sound an alarm in my holy mountain: let all the inhabitants of the land tremble: for the day of the Lord cometh, for it is nigh at hand;

The day of the Lord, particularly in the Old Testament, is endlessly described as approaching; it has never arrived. When reading this passage of Scripture, one inevitably thinks of a thousand-and-one instances over long centuries in which self-appointed prophets of doom have proclaimed with total confidence that the LAST DAYS would officially commence on a certain specified date and, in some cases, at a precise hour. Obviously in every such instance the prophets were deluded.

That men frequently lie to themselves and then act on the basis of such falsehoods is all too painfully obvious. The tragic part of such dramas is that they often succeed in deluding thousands of others as well, who then proceed to make public fools of themselves by closing down their businesses, walking away from their homes, and standing upon some mountaintop or other public place until at last, with shame, disappointment —or sometimes perhaps relief—they resume their accustomed tasks, unfortunately rarely any the wiser.

One verse in Joel's second chapter is puzzling:

24. And the floors shall be full of wheat, and the fats shall overflow with wine and oil.

The words *fats* in this verse makes the message partly incomprehensible. If the English word *vats* were used, there would be no such problem. Apparently some translators have come to the same conclusion since certain versions—The New King James Version, The New World Translation, The Living Bible, to name a few—have replaced *fats* with such words as *vats, vat presses, or presses.*

Chapter Three. Peace-loving Jews and Christians are fond of quoting the biblical passage about beating swords into ploughshares and spears into pruninghooks, but here we read the opposite:

9. Proclaim ye this among the Gentiles; Prepare war, wake up the mighty men, let all the men of war draw near; let them come up:

10. Beat your *ploughshares into swords, and your pruninghooks into spears:* let the weak say, "I am strong." (IA)

A little later in the same chapter we find another prediction that has never been borne out, despite the fact that we are told that all of the Bible's prophecies are perfectly dependable.

17. So shall ye know that I am the Lord your God dwelling in Zion, my holy mountain: then shall Jerusalem be holy, and there shall be no strangers pass through her any more.

(See also MICAH; PROPHECY AND PREDICTION.)

JONAH. One quick reading of the story of Jonah leads immediately to the conclusion that the account could not possibly be true. Catholic scholar John L. McKenzie came to the same conclusion in this account from his excellent *Dictionary of the Bible:*

There are convincing reasons why *the book cannot be historical.* There is little doubt that the author has adopted Jonah of II Kings 14:25 as his hero; but the name was chosen apparently almost at random. The book knows nothing of Nineveh, which is only a vague memory at best. It is altogether impossible that Nineveh, the ruins of which have been explored, could have been a city of "three day's journey" by which the author clearly means a city which it takes three days to walk through (3:4). A city of 120,000 infants implies a total population of over a million, far too large for Nineveh. . . . It is not merely the fish which is wonderful in the story, but the entire story is motivated by wonders from beginning to end: the storm, the fish, the gourds, and the greatest wonder of all, the instantaneous conversion of Nineveh. A search therefore after the species of fish which swallowed and regurgitated Jonah or for parallels to this wonder is idle; the fish is the creation of the author. The literary type of the book is *didactic fiction or parable.* (IA)

No one has the slightest idea who wrote the book of Jonah, although for centuries the churches insisted that if it had Jonah's name at the head it must therefore have been written by him. Even if we grant that the Jonah mentioned in 2 Kings existed, he must have lived around 780 B.C. At that time, however, Nineveh was not "that great city," the capital of the Assyrian empire. It was, in fact, no longer great in any sense.

The editors of the Dartmouth Bible, being mostly professors of theology and Bible history, are naturally concerned to speak as respectfully as they can of any and every portion of Scripture. They unwisely overstate their case as regards Jonah, however; when quoting Carl Cornill (*The Prophets of Israel*) they say, "This apparently trivial book is *one of the deepest and grandest ever written"* (IA).

Both Cornill and the editors are mistaken. The book appears to be trivial because it is. If it is indeed one of the deepest and grandest ever written, it would be difficult to think of an observation more insulting to the rest of the Bible. Jonah is neither deep nor grand. When the instructionary elements are abstracted from the legendary story line we find (1) the suggestion that God's word is not for one tribe alone but for the human race, something so obvious it requires no special instruction to perceive; (2) the readiness of the pagans to acknowledge Israel's God— absurd because God was never exclusively Israel's; and (3) the saving of the heathen sailing crew, which supposedly evidences God's mercy to non-Hebrews as well as Hebrews—not enlightening since even many ancient Hebrews supposed God's mercy extended to the entire human race.

We should at least be grateful that the Dartmouth editors unequivocally describe the story of the whale as an allegory.

Chapter 1. Several questions are immediately raised by Jonah's story. The first grows out of his flight to escape the Almighty's attention (1:3). If the unknown author believed it reasonable that a man could escape God by going to a particular community—Tarshish or any other—he was obviously seriously, or even stupidly, mistaken.

Another question that comes to mind while reading this account is why Jonah is traditionally perceived as of heroic stature. Perhaps in past ages it was considered heroic for Jonah to say,

12. "Take me up, and cast me forth into the sea; so shall the sea be calm unto you: for I know that for my sake this great tempest is upon you."

Does anyone today believe that the stormy seas are created by God's personal anger? It would certainly have been heroic for Jonah to ask to be thrown off the ship if that action would have saved others. However, we see by the second part of verse 12 that his reasoning was *not* that the loss of the amount of his body's weight would lighten the load and thus save the boat from sinking. He was instead indulging in the rankest egocentrism: assuming fault for the storm. It is difficult to attribute heroism to someone so misguided.

But throw Jonah into the sea they do. And his fate has him immediately swallowed by a whale. Current knowledge of biological science makes it clear that the unknown author of Jonah knew nothing of the eating habits of whales: they consume a multitude of small sea creatures rather than a few large ones. It is also a well-documented fact that the only kind of whale with a throat capacious enough to accommodate the passage of a man is a sperm whale, a type never found in the Mediterranean area.

The next thing we must conclude, if we accept this story as truth, is that God is a plagiarist. Godfrey Higgins observes in his *Anacalypsis:*

The story of Jonah swallowed up by a whale is nothing but part of the fiction of Hercules, described in the *Heracleid* or *Labors of Hercules,* of whom the same story was told, and who was swallowed up at this very same place, Joppa, and for the same period of time, three days. Lycophron says that Hercules was three nights in the belly of a fish.

Chapter 2. Verses 2–9 of this chapter consist of the prayer the unknown author would have us believe Jonah spoke while he was inside the fish. It is absurd to believe a word of it, or even to accept it as an effective literary device. If we assume for a moment that it is physically possible for an enormous fish to swallow a man whole and alive, it is not difficult to imagine that before breathing his last the man might cry out in terror and panic, calling upon God for aid as we know millions have done. But his cry of distress and anguish would certainly not take the form of a poem.

In any event, the story would have us believe that the prayer is effective:

10. And the Lord spake unto the fish, and it vomited out Jonah upon the dry land.

It is no intelligent response to criticism of this irrational conclusion to ask, "Are you suggesting that God does not have the power to perform such miracles?" Such questions hardly require answers, but nonetheless, "No, no such suggestion is intended." Once we posit the existence of a God with literally unlimited powers, it follows that he can do anything, provided it does not involve a logical contradiction in terms. The classic instance of such a contradiction is represented by the question, "Can God make a stone so large and heavy that he cannot lift it?"—obviously he can't.

In terms of the miracle of Jonah's alleged experience, not only could an unlimited Deity keep a man in the stomach of a whale for any given period of time, he could also somehow contrive to keep a man in the belly of a mouse for the same period. But the real point here is, A God defined as the embodiment of all wisdom can hardly be said to perform an act of such glaring inanity as is encountered in the story of Jonah.

It can only be concluded then that the story of Jonah is precisely what Father McKenzie, among numerous other scholars, suggested—a story, and a rousing good adventure story at that. The hideous image of a human being swallowed by a whale must have occurred to thousands over long centuries once they saw the massiveness of such wondrous creatures. The esteemed biblical authors at least had the excuse of profound ignorance about science or nature. But what can one say about men of the present day, who have access to an incredible treasure of scientific information but who nevertheless turn their backs on such an intellectual resource and insist on believing as fact obviously preposterous stories concocted thousands of years ago? These sincere fundamentalists and literalists—those who insist that such nonsensical stories as Jonah are as true as the accounts rendered on the front page of tomorrow's *New York Times*—do the greatest possible disservice to the Bible since they make it impossible for intelligent people to respect much of it.

Chapter 3. Another absurd element of the story emerges, when not only the people of Nineveh repent as a result of Jonah's preaching, but the king himself also takes steps to secure escape from the Lord's wrath for his city:

> 6. . . . he stepped down from his throne and laid aside his royal robes and put on sackcloth and sat in ashes.
> 7. And the king and his nobles sent this message throughout the city, "Let no one, not even the animals, eat anything at all, nor even drink any water.
> 8. "Everyone must wear sackcloth and cry mightily to God. . . ."

We need not detain ourselves in asking why God considered the wearing of one particular kind of cloth or sitting in filthy ashes praiseworthy. There is something to say for rejecting luxury and wearing simple garments, but to wear the cloth from which sacks are made and to sit in ashes would surely strike an unprejudiced visitor from another galaxy as bizarre and unproductive behavior. If an individual wishes to humble himself and manifest repentance for sinful acts, it would be more reasonable for him to give his luxurious garments to the poor and render aid to the sick, impoverished, imprisoned, or the lonely. This would both improve the state of the world and, if there is a God, merit favor in his eyes. To engage in empty symbolism is to behave less admirably and less rationally. And to further suggest, as is stated here, that such behavior should apply to dogs, cats, sheep, goats, and cattle is to indulge in beliefs so ridiculous that it is small wonder that such details are now never preached to those whose conversion to either Judaism or Christianity is being sought. Neither Jews nor Christians now wear sackcloth and ashes.

Chapter 4. The least attractive element of the fable is the reaction of Jonah after Nineveh is suddenly converted and thus spared God's punishment:

> 1. But it displeased Jonah exceedingly, and he was very angry.

The man had predicted that in forty days the city would be overthrown because of its wickedness. Let the reader imagine his own tearful joy if many thousands of sinners suddenly repented because of his missionary efforts. Jonah feels no such admirable emotion; he is not in the least gratified that the pagans of Nineveh have repented. *He had counted on their murderous destruction,* and now he is so angry that such massive suffering is not to come that he literally asks God to take his life (v. 3)!

So he goes out of the city to the east and erects himself a booth in which he can sit and watch what will happen to the city (v. 5). This is ludicrous enough, but now read what happens:

> 6. And the Lord God prepared a gourd, and made it to come over Jonah, that it might be a shadow over his head, to deliver him from his grief. So Jonah was exceedingly glad of the gourd.
> 7. But God prepared a worm when the morning rose the next day, and it smote the gourd that it withered.

Gourd is one more of the Bible's many errors—a mistaken translation of the Hebrew word *kikayon.* The mistake is at least understandable in that even Jewish scholars today are not sure what the word *kikayon* meant in ancient times. It can only be said that it was probably some broad-leafed growth such as a castor-oil plant. In any event, it is not clear why additional shade was required for Jonah when it has already been stated that a booth was providing shade.

Yet one more nonsensical element of the story is the suggestion that the purpose of the shade was "to deliver him from his grief."

Shade has no such power.

No modern editor would accept such a poorly thought-out story, and yet we are asked to accept that such inept literature is the very word of God.

There is no way of knowing whether the death of the plant by the worm's attack was more-or-less instantaneous—which is to say miraculous—or whether it took the normal span of time to wither and fade, but God next causes a strong east wind to blow so that the sun beats down on Jonah. Again, we are not told why he could not have avoided the sun by sitting under his booth. In any event, he once more attests that he wants to die.

Perhaps the strangest element of this thoroughly nonsensical tale is that God assumes that Jonah "hast had pity on the gourd" (v. 10) even though there has been not the slightest evidence of pity in Jonah's actions. To the contrary, it is expressly stated that Jonah's dominant emotion was anger.

Verse 11 seems to point to the interpretation of the book of Jonah as an allegorical criticism of the narrowness of one sort of Jewish thought that perceived Yahweh as a purely national Deity. That men were ever so ignorant as to believe that any God could exist for the benefit of only one tribe is difficult to believe, but the evidence of ancient literary history would seem to establish the point. If the unknown author of Jonah was criticizing such a shortsighted view, therefore, he was at least attacking an easy and deserving target.

The story need not have created awkwardness for Christians except for the fact that in Matthew *Jesus refers to Jonah's spending "three days and three nights in the whale's belly"* (12:40) (IA). Since we know that the story is preposterous fiction, Christians can no longer maintain, as they long did, that Jesus' reference to the incident serves to authenticate it. The argument is absurd structurally, quite apart from its content. If Jesus were to refer to the story of *Goldilocks and the Three Bears* that would do nothing whatever to make the original story historically true. Some churchmen have consequently been embarrassed by the reference since it apparently involves an error on the part of Jesus, who believes a story that we now know is nonsense. If Jesus was aware that the story of Jonah was mythical or allegorical, why did he not say so and thereby remove yet one more question from the minds of his believers? It is also possible that Jesus personally never made any such reference and that the suggestion that he did is simply an error on the part of the various writers who contributed to Matthew's gospel in the form in which it presently exists. (See also ERROR.)

JUDE, THE EPISTLE OF. With this book of the New Testament we are yet again confronted by mystery. First of all, the church has no true idea who Jude was. He is identified in the first sentence of this short document as "Jude, the servant of Jesus Christ, and brother of James." This would seem to make him one of the Twelve Apostles, but this interpretation is justified only by Luke. *In the Matthew and Mark listings of the disciples we find the name Thaddeus but no Jude.* It is conceivable that these are two separate names for the same individual but, if so, no one knows why two names are used. Comments John L. McKenzie in his *Dictionary of the Bible:*

> Most modern scholars believe that Jude of the Twelve and Jude the kinsman of the Lord are two distinct individuals, and it is to Jude the kinsman of the Lord that the Epistle is traditionally attributed.

This seems clear-cut enough, but McKenzie adds:

> Several reasons are induced by critics *against* this attribution. In 17 it seems that the Apostles are dead. If this is a general statement Jude must certainly be put in the post-apostolic age. (IA)

Support for those who doubt that anyone named either Jude or Thaddeus actually wrote the text is acknowledged by Father McKenzie who says,

> It is also pointed out that the Greek of Jude is very good for a Palestinian Jew, and it is; here as elsewhere the traditional origin can be maintained only by supposing that an amanuensis had a very large part in the composition of the epistle.
>
> The letter does not appear to be addressed to Jewish Christians; there is no specifically Jewish interest. Indeed it is addressed to no particular group; this does not strengthen the traditional attribution.

It is naturally not surprising that the churches also have no way of dating the original authorship of the document. It is merely arbitrarily assumed to be of late in the first century.

Along with 2 Peter, the epistle of Jude has been rejected by certain Eastern churches on the quite sensible grounds that it quotes books known to be apocryphal. It has, however, been accepted in the Western church since the fourth century. Whether rightly canonical or not, it is of little interest. (See also APOCRYPHA, THE.)

Nor is it a source of enlightenment. The author—whoever he was—rails angrily against "certain men" who "crept in unawares." They are described as ungodly, lascivious, filthy dreamers; mockers who walk after their own ungodly lusts. Apparently sexual excess has been a problem for both societies and religious organizations through all time. In discrediting "filthy dreamers," however, Jude diverges from traditional moral theology that very sensibly teaches that we are not responsible for our dreams since we neither will them nor have control over them. The book might be considered of some intelligible value if the dreamers of filthy dreams were identified. The spokesman for any organization in the world may rightly warn his followers to be aware of false teachers, but unless the teachers or their lessons are identified the warning is close to meaningless.

JUDGES. As usual, experts disagree on who wrote this book. Although some attribute it to Samuel, many accept the opinion of the German biblical expert Martin Noth who calls the author of the books of Deuteronomy, Joshua, Judges, Samuel, and Kings the Deuteronomist and suggests that he may have compiled these books from earlier sources but wrote them down only after the fall of Jerusalem, which occurred in 586 B.C.

The title *Judges* itself is misleading, an erroneous translation from the Hebrew *shofet,* which means a kind of military ruler or leader, someone who preserves the Israelites from defeat. The office is not hereditary but rather bestowed by Yahweh. Although the book of Judges does contain accounts of warfare, it has as its main and more interesting theme the cultural struggle between the advanced agricultural society of the Canaanites with its worship of fertility deities, the *baalim,* and the more primitive, newly settled nomads who had come out of the desert with their concept of a single Deity. As the Hebrews settled and intermarried, some began to accept the POLYTHEISM of the Canaanites. The "judges"—Deborah, Barak, Gideon, Abimelech, Jephthah, and Samson—figure most prominently as the leaders who adhered unswervingly to Yahweh.

Chapter 1. One of the more distressing aspects of even the best Bible scholarship is the tendency to disguise hopeless contradictions by revising reality. We perceive this manipulation of fact in the opening words of Judges:

> 1. Now after the death of Joshua it came to pass that the children of Israel asked the Lord, saying, "Who shall go up for us against the Canaanites first, to fight against them?"

This does not seem like a problem unless we have already read the book of Joshua, where we find the claim that before the leader died the Israelites had *destroyed every Canaanite* and taken undisputed mastery of the Promised Land. Although several Christian scholars have sought to make these two accounts agree, the fact is they cannot be reconciled. They are mutually contradictory and therefore either one or both must be in error.

Recent archaeological studies now support the version rendered in Judges. William Neil, in his fair-minded and reliable *Harper's Bible Commentary,* says of the Judges version:

> It is indeed a vastly different picture that is given here. Far from being a dramatic saga of a conquering host, the impression given by Judges is of a piecemeal infiltration of the tribes, of individual settlements, of intermarriage with the natives, and of a long process, *lasting perhaps a couple of centuries,* during which Israel grew from being an ill-armed nomadic invasion into being the strongest united element in the country. (IA)

So what are we to say of the Joshuan report of a whirlwind conquest of Canaan? The account is fiction based on a few elements of historical reality. It is comparable to one of those modern films that gives the impression that John Wayne or Gregory Peck was personally largely responsible for winning World War II.

Let us assume for a moment that the book of Joshua is, so to speak, a short-story version of a novel and that one author composed both accounts. The Joshua version is a fictional rendition based on the oral traditions of, say, the Ephraim tribe (of which Joshua was a member and who would therefore want to put forth their leader as a person capable of almost superhuman exploits), and the Judges account, a more historical rendering adopted by a more realistic faction. Does this remove the problem? No, it does not. We know that varying accounts are indeed given of historical events in our own time. Take, for instance, the volumes of literature that have been published recounting conflicting versions of the assassination of John F. Kennedy or the death of Marilyn Monroe. We could accept these accounts because they presented information by comparison of discrepancies. No such qualifications are placed in these two books. Instead we have certain Christians and Jews who insist that every word of the Old Testament is true and inspired by God and that, moreover, everyone in the modern world must be governed by those who so believe.

In any event, the Israelites are said to have killed precisely ten thousand men. The Canaanite leader Adonibezek flees but the children of God

> 6. . . . pursued after him, and caught him, and cut off his thumbs and his great toes.

What possible moral edification can be derived from this bloodthirsty passage and the hundreds like it with which the Old Testament abounds? Any ethical person—Christian or not—would call savage a military force who so mutilated the captured enemy. Perhaps if the Old Testament had not been taken as God's word down through the centuries, we would not today in so many parts of the world be reading horrific accounts of torture and mayhem, often justified by references to the Scriptures.

In verse 7 we read that Adonibezek accepts this punishment as just since he apparently had done the same to seventy other kings in the past. We can only conclude that the Israelites felt they were observing the eye-for-an-eye method of justice stipulated by Old Testament law. Let us thank God that most states and churches no longer accept this primitive method of criminal punishment.

The rest of chapter 1 contains such other "morally edifying" stories as further military attacks, atrocities, and uninteresting and pointless personal stories.

Chapter 2. This chapter also wastes the time of the intelligent reader sincerely seeking ethical enlightenment. One is told the same endless story—that no matter how often the Israelites receive personal instruction and help from God, they constantly "go a-whoring" after other gods, naturally kindling the anger of the Lord, which translates into threats, insults, criticisms, and calamities.

The chapter begins with a verse that resonates with an ancient magic incantation of now-obscure place names of Canaan/Israel:

> 1. And the angel of the Lord came up from Gilgal to Bochim, and said, I made you to go up out of Egypt, and have brought you unto the land which I sware unto your fathers; and I said, "I will never break my covenant with you."

If a prophet of the present day were to write "and an angel came up from Chicago to Denver," intelligent believers would be inclined to respond, "Why not simply report that an angel appeared in Denver? How does claiming your angel started his journey in Chicago add sense to your story? Indeed, since angels are assumed to live in heaven, wouldn't he have come from there?"

Before examining the next verses, let the reader consider what his reaction would be if he heard that a band of Catholic vandals had broken into, desecrated, and destroyed every Protestant church in his community. Or that Protestants had committed the same crime in Catholic churches and cathedrals. Or that Christians had been guilty of vandalizing Jewish temples. Who would not be shocked? Yet not only are we asked to condone precisely such behavior in the Old Testament, but we are also asked to believe that such crimes were committed *at the specific instructions of Yahweh.* Once again we can see a perverse justification for the long centuries of religious intolerance and bloody persecution.

> 2. And ye shall make no league with the inhabitants of this land; ye shall throw down their altars: but ye have not obeyed my voice: why have ye done this?
>
> 3. Wherefore I also said, "I will not drive them out from before you; but they shall be as thorns in your sides, and their gods shall be a snare unto you."
>
> 4. And it came to pass, when the angel of the Lord spake these words unto all the children of Israel, that the people lifted up their voice, and wept.

The perceptive reader will already have noted that verse 4 asserts that the angel addressed his words not solely to a select few, but "unto all the children of Israel." He must have spoken in a thunderingly loud voice to have been heard by such a vast audience. (See also CRIMES, BIBLICAL IMPETUS TO.)

Verses 16–19 clearly announce the theme of the book of Judges:

> 16. Nevertheless the Lord raised up judges, which delivered them out of the hand of those that spoiled them.
>
> 17. And yet they would not hearken unto their judges, but they went a whoring after other gods, and bowed themselves unto them: they turned quickly out of the way which their fathers walked in, obeying the commandments of the Lord; but they did not so.
>
> 18. And when the Lord raised them up judges, then the Lord was with the judge, and delivered them out of the hands of their enemies

all the days of the judge: for it repented the Lord because of their groanings by reason of them that oppressed them and vexed them.

Those people who today live by the theory "Sin like hell on Saturday night and repent in church on Sunday, and all will be forgiven" could reasonably cite the Israelites as their role models. Here we have a tribe of people who, even though rescued by their God time and time again, continue to return to the worship of idols. Their angry Lord seems never to follow through on his threats of abandonment but continues to save them from their own folly. Would that he were so generous to pagans who worshiped other gods because it was part of their culture, and not because they consciously chose to do something their Supreme Ruler had explicitly forbidden.

Chapter 3. When I was younger and heard criticisms of the Bible, I would be puzzled—and occasionally moderately angered—at assertions that the God depicted in the Old Testament was warlike, bloodthirsty, and vengeful. My reactions arose out of ignorance. I now do not see how any fair-minded person can possibly read the Old Testament analytically without coming to the same conclusion. Note, for example, the following story:

15. But when the children of Israel cried unto the Lord, the Lord raised them up a deliverer, Ehud the son of Gera, a Benjamite, a man left-handed: and by him the children of Israel sent a present unto Eglon the king of Moab.

16. But Ehud made him a dagger which had two edges, of a cubit length; and he did gird it under his raiment upon his right thigh.

17. And he brought the present unto Eglon king of Moab: and Eglon was a very fat man.

18. And when he had made an end to offer the present, he sent away the people that bare the present.

19. But he himself turned again from the quarries that were by Gilgal, and said, "I have a secret errand unto thee, O king": who said, "Keep silence." And all that stood by him went out from him.

20. And Ehud came unto him; and he was sitting in a summer parlour, which he had for himself alone. And Ehud said, "I have a message from God unto thee." And he arose out of his seat.

21. And Ehud put forth his left hand, and took the dagger from his right thigh, and thrust it into his belly:

22. And the haft also went in after the blade; and the fat closed upon the blade, so that he could not draw the dagger out of his belly; and the dirt came out.

23. Then Ehud went forth through the porch, and shut the doors of the parlour upon him, and locked them.

This is not a pretty story for innocent children—or sensitive people of any age—to read, what with a dagger being buried into a fat belly and blood and feces pouring from the gaping wound. If one believes the story, it will immediately be concluded that Ehud was a vicious, deceiving assassin. But how can this be when he was "a deliverer" raised up by none other than God himself?

Does the murderer Ehud now retire in disgrace? No, we see in verse 27 that he travels to the mountain of Ephraim where he blows a trumpet so that the children of Israel gather around him. Then—for reasons that remain unclear—the Israelites agree to follow this scoundrel into battle against the Moabites:

> 29. And they slew of Moab at that time about ten thousand men, all lusty, and all men of valour; and there escaped not a man.

By this point we are no longer surprised to read of more bloodshed and genocide.

Chapter 3 ends with reference to the judge who followed Ehud, citing an example of his qualifications that are as unedifying as they are unbelievable.

> 31. And after him was Shamgar the son of Anath, which slew of the Philistines six hundred men with an ox goad: and he also delivered Israel.

Has the reader ever heard of a modern-day infantryman, even one provided with a machine gun or automatic rifle, who has claimed that in one engagement—or even an entire tour of duty—he personally killed six hundred of the enemy? Movies such as *Rambo* and *Die Hard*—which were never touted as anything but action fiction—were criticized for stretching believability in the abilities of one man to destroy so many single-handedly, even with modern means of destruction available to him. Yet we are asked to believe far wilder claims simply because they appear in a book of which every word is supposedly inspired by God himself.

Chapter 4. American suffragist Elizabeth Cady Stanton wrote about the cruelties inflicted upon the non-Hebrew tribes of God in her excellent *The Woman's Bible*.

> Though he made all the tribes, we hope, to the best of his ability, yet he hated all—the sacred fabulist tells us—but the tribe of Israel, and even they were objects of his vengeance half the time.

This chapter of Judges brings us additional examples of that hatred. Notice the revolting story of the Israeli defeat of Canaanite troops led by General Sisera. Beginning in verse 16 we find that the Israelites surprise Sisera's army and that "there was not a man left," except for General Sisera, who deserts his army and flees, a deed punishable by court martial today. Sisera then goes to the tent of Jael, the wife of Heber the Kenite, who apparently had a mutual-assistance agreement with Sisera's tribe. Jael takes him in, hides him under a blanket, gives him milk to quench his thirst, and promises to stand guard at the door while he sleeps.

But it is instructive to observe what happens next:

> 21. Then Jael Heber's wife took a nail of the tent, and took an hammer in her hand, and went softly unto him, and smote the nail into his temples, and fastened it into the ground: for he was fast asleep and weary. So he died.

Far from feeling the slightest shame or revulsion at the bloody murder she has perpetrated, Jael proudly flaunts her act, meeting the Israelite leader Barak and taking him into her tent to "show you the man whom you are seeking." The Scriptures make it inescapably clear that the author of these passages intended to present the deed not only as grandly heroic but—worse—as also consistent with the will of God:

> 23. So God subdued on that day Jabin the king of Canaan before the children of Israel.

Chapter 5. If the Old Testament is to be considered as a moral guide— as the churches for centuries have insisted—then the question raised by a contributor to *The Woman's Bible* concerning the position of Deborah is a fair one:

> The woman who most attracts our attention in the Book of Judges is Deborah, priestess, prophetess, poetess, and judge. What woman is there in modern or in ancient history who equals in loftiness of position, in public esteem and honorable distinction this gifted and heroic Jewish creation? The writer who compiled the story of her gifts and deeds must have had women before him who inspired him with such a wonderful personality. How could Christianity teach and preach that women should be silent in church when already among the Jews equal honor was shown to women?

Even the Jews have apparently forgotten the honor the Lord accorded Deborah. Although Reform Judaism has softened their sanctions against women, the Orthodox sect still insists that women sit separate from men in the synagogue, that only boys study the Torah, and only men be rabbis and cantors.

The long poem that comprises this chapter is called the Song of Deborah. Among other things, it praises Jael for the bloody murder she committed in chapter 4.

Walter Harrelson, in *From Fertility Cult to Worship,* observes that this oft-quoted chapter "shows great influence of Canaanite religion as well as the influence of Canaanite literary motifs." It is certainly unusual among the Jews to find women playing two important roles usually reserved to men: the prophet and charismatic leader, and the female who kills an important enemy.

Chapter 6. Here we find the Israelites falling victim to the Midianites. Their agricultural plots, donkeys, and flocks of sheep and oxen are destroyed by the camel-riding nomads from the Arabian desert. Apparently the Midianites do to the Hebrews what the Hebrews had done to the Canaanites.

Historians and archeologists point out that indeed over a millennium or two various nomadic groups tried to live in Palestine, thus corroborating the accuracy of the first six verses of this chapter. The reasons this land was coveted by so many were twofold: (1) the Fertile Crescent is the only portion of the vast stretch of Asia, from the Mediterranean to the Zagros Mountains in Iran, that is naturally fertile; and (2) the area lay on the main trade route between Egypt and the hinterland of Asia, thereby assuring wealth for the controlling parties. This information, of course, leads us naturally to the conclusion that the constant warfare depicted in the Old Testament had not so much a religious context (as the Hebrews claimed) as an economic one.

Be that as it may, the prophet GIDEON is selected to fight the Midianites. The process of selection makes an interesting story. First we see "an angel of the Lord" who sits under an oak tree and engages in conversation with Gideon, assuring him that he is a "mighty man of valour" and that God is on his side (v. 11, 12). But in verse 14, we suddenly find that it is *not* the angel of the Lord but the Lord himself with whom Gideon speaks. Now God—by definition—can certainly become a third party to any conversation that might interest him, but if that is the case here, what was the purpose of sending an angel in the first place? It appears that the writer or reviser of these passages was careless, attributing divine instructions in one instance to a mere angel and in the other to the Lord of the universe.

201

Incredibly, even seeing an angel and speaking directly to his Creator doesn't seem to convince Gideon. He asks for a sign to prove it is indeed God himself who has addressed him (v. 17). God is not displeased with his doubt, but rather sends Gideon away to "bring forth my present and set it before thee," promising to wait for him to complete the task. So Gideon gets a young goat and some unleavened cakes and places them on a rock as instructed.

But when he returns, we find not the Lord God but, again, the *angel* of the Lord, who puts forth his staff and touches the meat and cakes. Immediately fire springs from the rock and consumes the offering, convincing Gideon that he has indeed been face-to-face with a powerful being, whoever it is. Now it is the Lord who speaks again. Thus assured, Gideon attends to the instruction he's been given, which is to destroy a religious altar of the regional god, Baal, a desecration that understandably leads to animosity between the worshippers of Baal and those of Yahweh.

The chapter ends with yet one more incident that seems to argue for the astonishing denseness of the Old Testament leaders and prophets who have to be shown miracle after miracle before they can properly receive a message. As Gideon prepares his men for battle, he asks God for proof that he will help them win the foray:

> 37. "Behold, I will put a fleece of wool in the floor; and if the dew be on the fleece only, and it be dry upon all the earth beside, then shall I know that thou wilt save Israel by mine hand, as thou hast said.
>
> 38. And it was so: for he rose up early on the morrow, and thrust the fleece together, and wringed the dew out of the fleece, a bowl full of water.

Not only did God grant Gideon's request but he also supplied so much dew in the miracle that there should have been no possibility of doubt. But note Gideon's response:

> 39. And Gideon said unto God, "Let not thine anger be hot against me, and I will speak but this once: let me prove, I pray thee, but this once with the fleece, let it now be dry only upon the fleece, and upon all the ground let there be dew.
>
> 40. And God did so that night: for it was dry upon the fleece only, and there was dew on the ground.

Chapter 7. Any reader who has had the experience of military service will notice that the Old Testament accounts of battles rarely seem to include

202

details of actual military planning. Nonsense is once again encountered in chapter 7 when the question arises whether there are too many people in Gideon's military force. Even the least warlike reader should find it odd that a commander would seek to decrease his forces; not only does Gideon do so, but apparently not feeling himself intelligent enough to tell a certain percentage of his followers to stay behind, he also once again has to have the Lord step in to assist in the decision-making process. This supposed great leader of the Israelites shows an astounding lack of confidence that surrounds his every action. The average child, if asked to finish such a story, would have little trouble in suggesting that the Lord might instruct only the strongest men to take part in the battle, or the fleetest of foot, or the most practiced archers. But such is the wisdom the authors of Judges attribute to the all-powerful, all-wise God:

> 5. So he brought down the people unto the water: and the Lord said unto Gideon, "Every one that lappeth of the water with his tongue, as a dog lappeth, him shalt thou set by himself; likewise every one that boweth down upon his knees to drink."

By this absurd method exactly three hundred fighting men were chosen. All the others were sent home. The casual reader will perhaps next wonder about the size of the fighting force against which the chosen three hundred are to be arrayed. The information is provided in verse 12:

> 12. And the Midianites and the Amalekites and all the children of the east lay along in the valley *like grasshoppers for multitude; and their camels were without number, as the sand by the sea side for multitude.* (IA)

So—three hundred water-lapping soldiers arrayed against thirty thousand opponents. The solution to the military problem is said to have come to Gideon in a dream; if it is questionable, it is at least ingenious:

> 16. And he divided the three hundred men into three companies, and he *put a trumpet in every man's hand, with empty pitchers, and lamps within the pitchers.*

Several questions immediately spring to mind when contemplating this verse: (1) Whence did Gideon suddenly produce three hundred trumpets, something that would be difficult even in today's well-stocked urban areas? (2) Were the pitchers wide-mouthed in order to allow the lamps (candles) enough oxygen to stay lit, or are we perhaps dealing with a miraculous suspension of the normal laws of physics here? (3) How did the men propose to fight with swords while their hands were occupied holding trumpets and pitchers of candles?

Rather than being given explanations to these quite obvious difficulties, we are instead told that Gideon's army surrounds the camp and at the signal of his trumpet blast, the men blow their trumpets and smash their lamps. Actually, it may be understandable why the enemy flees in fear: Perhaps they thought they were dealing with three hundred insane fanatics.

Chapter 8. When the tribal leaders of Ephraim express their anger at him for not enlisting their help to fight the Midianites, Gideon replies:

> 3. "God hath delivered into your hands the princes of Midian, Oreb and Zeeb: and what was I able to do in comparison to you?"

This of course leads to the conclusion that Gideon endangered his troop of three hundred men by taking so few into battle against "multitudes," and then further by handicapping them with the burden of carrying musical instruments and pitchers of candles, all for the sake of pride. This would be bad enough; the fact that the Lord is said to have condoned the action is beyond comprehension.

The answer appears to sooth the tribal leaders, however, and Gideon continues on his way, still chasing the enemy. Arriving tired in Succoth he asks for food. But the Succoth leaders refuse him, saying that since Gideon has not yet conquered the enemy they are afraid that if they help him the Midianites might return and destroy their city. This reasonable fear so angers Gideon that he threatens to return and destroy their city's tower himself.

In due course, Gideon routs the enemy and returns as promised to Succoth, where he does not content himself with destroying the city tower but also takes captive the seventy-seven political and religious leaders of the city whom a young male hostage has identified. This great leader whom we are supposed to admire then tortures the prisoners to death with wild thorns and briars, allegedly to teach the men of Succoth a lesson (v. 16). Apparently they didn't learn the lesson well enough for Gideon, however, because *he next kills the entire male population.*

Gideon seems to be on a true killing spree at this point, for he then turns to the captured kings and asks them for information on the men they killed at Tabor. From their description he determines the slaughtered must have been his brothers and tells the captured kings:

19. ". . . if ye had saved them alive, I would not slay you."

A not very likely assertion. In any event, Gideon orders Jether, his firstborn, to do the deed. But the youth, apparently having never killed before, is afraid, so Gideon kills the two kings himself and then takes the ornaments that were on their camels' necks, engaging in another behavior that he seems to enjoy—looting. Just a few verses later we read that although Gideon refuses the Israelites when they ask him to be their leader, he does make an interesting request:

24. And Gideon said unto them, "I would desire a request of you, that ye would give me every man the earrings of his prey. (For they had golden earrings, because they were Ishmaelites.) . . .
26. And the weight of the golden earrings that he requested was a thousand and seven hundred shekels of gold; beside ornaments, and collars, and purple raiment that was on the kings of Midian, and besides the chains that were about their camels' necks.

When the Nazis of Hitler's Germany stole the jewelry from their Jewish dead it was accounted a depraved act. Why is there no condemnation mentioned in reporting this similar pillaging by Gideon?

Now comes yet another instance of the incredible forgetfulness of the masses of Old Testament times.

27. And Gideon made an ephod thereof, and put it in his city, even in Ophrah: and all Israel went thither a whoring after it: . . .

One wonders if God took a vacation at this time because despite the idolatry, "the country was in quietness forty years in the days of Gideon" (v. 28).

Oddly, many Old Testament reigns are said to have lasted exactly forty years. Reliable history reports that a certain event took seventeen years to transpire, that another period lasted fifty-two years—in other words, it cites the kind of numbers that are usually found in reality. The habitual use of round numbers—and so many identical ones at that—leads inescapably to strong doubt as to the historical correctness of such biblical reports. (See also HISTORICAL RELEVANCE OF THE BIBLE.)

Gideon apparently spent much of his forty years of peace in bed, since we are told in verse 30 that he married many wives and had no less than seventy sons. It is nowhere explained how Gideon could have seventy children *all of whom were males.* Such a thing is even more preposterous than

205

many other Old Testament stories. It is reasonable to assume that he must have fathered a goodly number of female children as well. They are not mentioned—women being decidedly inferior creatures according to Old Testament mind-set. Christians and sexual Puritans must, of course, make what they can of the Old Testament's many casual references not only to POLYGAMY but also to concubines.

It matters little to anyone alive today if a caste of men who lived three thousand years ago had fifty wives and fifty concubines each. More power to them, if they could afford the expense and stand the no doubt endless clamor in their tents. But the endless indiscriminate, lustful relationships cannot be so casually dismissed by those who have some difficulty in seeing God's wisdom in creating sex at all, except perhaps as suitable for the lower animals.

How are passages such as these explained by those fundamentalist believers who advocate a return to biblical morality? Let us suppose today that it is discovered that our president has, in addition to his wife, four or five concubines living in the White House—four or five attractive young women with whom he has sexual intercourse at any moment the urge prompts him. One can imagine the wave of revulsion that would sweep the land. The president would be considered to have committed a grave moral offense, and those very fundamentalists would cry most loudly for his head. He would be impeached.

Chapter 9. The next fearless leader of Israel of whom we learn is Gideon's son Abimelech. If we believe the biblical account, Abimelech is perhaps history's only mass murderer specializing in fratricide: his first recorded act is to go to his father's house in Ophrah and *slaughter all seventy of his half-brothers.* Only the youngest, Jotham, escapes and hides. Evidently favorably impressed by such savagery, the people do not lynch the monster but rather make him king.

When Abimelech's brother Jotham hears that Abimelech has been appointed king, he stands on top of Mount Gerizim and shouts across to the men of Shechem. How far a distance this is, we have no way of knowing, but, without the benefit of a public address system, he recites an interesting parable about trees, trying to convince the Israelites to recognize Abimelech's abomination. For three years they presumably ponder Jotham's exhortation until finally, stirred up by God—according to the author— the men of Shechem revolt and set up an ambush. These rebels must not have been especially godly, however, since we are told that they robbed all who came along as they waited for Abimelech (v. 25)!

In any event, Abimelech is warned and escapes.

Next, a man named Gaal moves to Shechem and tries to rouse the peoples against Abimelech, but again allies warn Abimelech, who is living in another city, and he routs his opponent. The very next day the men of Shechem go to battle against Abimelech yet another time; the result is that the city is leveled to the ground and all the inhabitants are killed (v. 45). The people of a nearby town—understandably afraid of this madman murderer—take refuge in a fort next to the temple of Baalberith. Their fears are entirely justified when Abimelech storms down on them with his forces, each carrying a bundle of firewood on their shoulders (not trumpets and pitchers as his father had used). The firewood is stacked against the walls of the fort and all the people—about a thousand men and women—are burned to death!

Continuing on his murderous rampage, Abimelech next attacks and captures the city of Thebez. This city has a fort inside its gates, however, and the residents flee to it. This is what befalls Abimelech:

52. And Abimelech came unto the tower, and fought against it, and went hard unto the door of the tower to burn it with fire.

53. And a certain woman cast a piece of a millstone upon Abimelech's head, and all to brake his skull.

54. Then he called hastily unto the young man his armourbearer, and said unto him, "Draw thy sword, and slay me, that men say not of me, 'A woman slew him.' " And his young man thrust him through, and he died.

These details, though not literally impossible, are nevertheless highly improbable. Consider the size of the stone dropped from the top of the tower. One would certainly not throw either a pebble or a walnut-sized rock in such a situation. It must, therefore, have been such as the woman could barely lift—at least approximately the size of, say, a cantaloupe. Such a missile dropped from considerable height would indeed kill anyone whom it struck. The text states reasonably enough that his skull was broken. Such a fatal injury to the head, however, would induce immediate unconsciousness and, in fact, almost certainly immediate death. Therefore the detail that Abimelech retained consciousness and was able to issue lucid instructions to his armorbearer is, while quite typical of scriptural narrative, preposterous.

Chapter 11. The repeated bloodthirstiness on the part of the Israelite leaders and the attributed complicity by God should no longer surprise us. In this chapter we find the story of Jephthah, a great warrior whose mother was a prostitute and who had been driven out of the land by his brothers. They later ask him back to deal with attacking Amorites who

are demanding the return of land the Israelites have taken from them,
Jephthah explains to the Amorites why this is not possible:

> 23. So now the Lord God of Israel hath dispossessed the Amorites
> from before his people Israel, and shouldest thou possess it?
> 24. Wilt not thou possess that which Chemosh thy god giveth thee
> to possess? So *whomsoever the Lord our God shall drive out from before
> us, them will we possess.* (IA)

Jephthah goes on to explain that other kings have not asked for their
lands back and that he can't understand why they are making an issue
of the matter since the Israelites have been in possession of the land for
three hundred years. He tells the Amorite king that "the Lord the Judge"
will decide the case.

The Amorites, of course, don't accept this; they attack. Jephthah leaves
for battle vowing to God that if he will help him win:

> 31. Then it shall be, that whatsoever cometh forth of the doors of
> my house to meet me, when I return in peace from the children of Ammon,
> shall surely be the Lord's, and I will offer it up for a burnt offering.

Jephthah wins the war and returns home—to be met by his only child,
an unnamed daughter. He informs her of his vow unto God.

> 37. And she said unto her father, "Let this thing be done for me:
> let me alone two months, that I may go up and down upon the mountains,
> and bewail my virginity, I and my fellows." . . .
> 39. And it came to pass at the end of two months, that she returned
> unto her father, who did with her according to his vow which he had
> vowed: and she knew no man. And it was custom in Israel.

What should we think of any modern clergyman who committed such
an atrocity? We should think precisely the same of Jephthah and the Old
Testament authors who clearly endorse the crime instead of using it as
a clear-cut example of faith extended to the point of moral idiocy.

Chapters 13–16 are covered under SAMSON in Volume 1.

Chapter 17. This chapter tells an uninteresting little story about a man
named Micah who steals from his mother and then confesses, whereupon
she does not chastise him but rather builds an idol for him, to go with
the many others he has enshrined. These actions are justified by the author
of Judges because

6. In those days there was no king in Israel but every man did that which was right in his own eyes.

"Biblical morality" would appear to leave a great deal to be desired. Apparently Micah considered it right to steal from his mother, to keep a shrine of pagan idols, and to encourage a young priest who was passing through to stay with him as an adopted son, saying:

13. . . . "Now know I that the Lord will do me good, seeing I have a Levite to my priest."

Why the Lord did not punish Micah only He knows.

Chapter 18. We are back into the bloodshed and savagery typical of the Old Testament as we meet the Danite Jews who are seeking a land in which to dwell. Five men go out and explore the possibilities, eventually coming to an area called Laish where the people live "quiet and secure" and far from their protector group, the Zidonians. The scouts report back:

9. And they said, "Arise, that we may go up against them: for we have seen the land, and behold, it is very good: and are ye still? be not slothful to go, and to enter to possess the land.
10. When ye go, ye shall come unto a people secure, and to a large land: for God hath given it into your hands; a place where there is no want of any thing that is in the earth."

Remember the worldwide wave of revulsion that greeted the 1990 Iraqi invasion of Kuwait. Why in so many similar instances in the Old Testament is the believer supposed to condone behavior that he would not tolerate for one moment in his own place and time?

Not only do the Danites take the Laish land, but before going, they pay a visit to Micah and take his idols and ephod and terephim, employing an army of six hundred men to do so. They talk his priest into going with them to the new land as well. Micah naturally follows them, protesting, which seems to surprise them. To their question "What aileth thee?" Micah explains that he is upset because they have taken his idols and priest.

25. And the children of Dan said unto him, "Let not thy voice be heard among us, lest angry fellows run upon thee, and thou lose thy life, with the lives of thy household."

Thus threatened, Micah returns home and the Danites continue to Laish where they "smote them with the edge of the sword, and burnt the city with fire" (v. 27). Why they burnt a perfectly good city in which they proposed to live is not explained. Considering how long it must have taken them to rebuild, given their archaic means of construction, it seems like a remarkably stupid act.

Chapter 19. Again the fact that there was no king in Israel is given as "justification" for acceptance of Old Testament behavior that would in no way be condoned today.

> 1. And it came to pass in those days, when there was no king in Israel, that there was a certain Levite sojourning on the side of mount Ephraim, who took to him a concubine out of Bethlehemjudah.
> 2. And his concubine played the whore against him, and went away from him unto her father's house to Bethlehemjudah, and was there four whole months.

To anyone with the slightest familiarity with either psychology or the art of literature, it will come as no news that there are whores in the world. It does seem odd, however, that a woman who had given herself up to such pursuits would go home to live with her father, and further, that that act would be construed as unfaithfulness to her lover. Stranger things have happened, surely, but one may be forgiven for being skeptical about such reports.

The next few verses are patently absurd. They relate that when the man goes to his "father-in-law's" house to rejoin his concubine, he is welcomed by the old man and resides with him for three days, whereupon he determines to leave.

But the father-in-law invites him to stay longer, which he does. This same peculiar story is twice more repeated, to what morally edifying point is not apparent. Eventually the man and his concubine leave.

After some time on the road they come to the community called Gibeah, where they seek lodging. An old man charitably invites the party to spend the night at his own house.

> 24. Now as they were making their hearts merry, behold, the men of the city, certain sons of Belial, beset the house round about, and beat at the door, and spake to the master of the house, the old man, saying, "Bring forth the man that came into thine house, that we may know him."

There has never been the slightest debate concerning the interpretation of the verb *to know* in such scriptural contexts: the meaning is sexual.

The men wish to commit sodomy and take other sexual liberties with the passing traveler. The old man's response is one of the most horrendous in all literature:

> 23. And the man, the master of the house, went out unto them, and said unto them, "Nay, my brethren, nay, I pray you, do not so wickedly, seeing that this man is come into mine house, do not this folly.
> 24. "Behold, here is my daughter a maiden, and his concubine; them I will bring out now, and humble ye them, and do with them what seemeth good unto you: but unto this man do not so vile a thing."

The old fool knows precisely what he is doing. His use of the phrase *so vile a thing* makes that clear beyond doubt. He is authorizing the sexual abuse and humiliation—the rape—not only of his own flesh and blood, his daughter, but also of a concubine belonging to a perfect stranger, an offer he has no authority even to suggest. Further, the old man is implying by his actions that while one ought not to abuse a man sexually, it is permissible to do what one might wish with a woman, an attitude that has persisted in some regards—again, using such biblical examples as this for support—into the current century.

The next verse is likewise morally horrifying, though all too typical:

> 25. But the men would not hearken to him: so the man took his concubine, and brought her forth unto them; and they knew her, *and abused her all the night until the morning:* and when the day began to spring, they let her go.

In other words, the defenseless woman was gang-raped for long hours.

The story up to now is horrible enough and certainly not to be preached to the tender ears of children, whether Christian, Jewish, pagan, or atheist. What follows is unfit even for adult readers:

> 26. Then came the woman in the dawning of the day, and fell down at the door of the man's house where her lord was, till it was light.
> 27. And her lord rose up in the morning, and opened the doors of the house, and went out to go his way: and, behold, the woman his concubine was fallen down at the door of the house, and her hands were upon the threshold.
> 28. And he said unto her, "Up, and let us be going." But none answered. Then the man took her up upon an ass, and the man rose up, and gat him unto his place.
> 29. And when he was come into his house, he took a knife, and

laid hold on his concubine, and divided her, together with her bones, into twelve pieces, and sent her into all the coasts of Israel.

If one can believe such outrageous tales, this compounds the atrocity. Reconstruct the situation: The woman was the man's concubine. He had just spent many days in pleasant company with her father. Then, when menaced, he, to protect himself, agrees with his aged host that she and perhaps the old man's daughter should be thrown upon the untender mercies of the depraved marauders in the streets. One or both women, we may assume, were sexually abused for a period of several hours, although the Old Testament authors are so inept at their craft that only the concubine's suffering is described.

The poor woman is either dead or else lies pitifully in the doorway of the house—ill, beaten, exhausted, frightened, expecting comfort from her mate. Far from being lifted up, fed, having her wounds bathed, her fears set to rest, she is instead taken back to her lover's home where she is not comforted but, if not already dead, murdered in cold blood! He was the evildoer, not she; yet, being a lordly male, he arrogates to himself the right to punish her. For what crime she is so abused is, of course, never explained.

That such a monstrous murder would occur at all, at whoever's hand, is dismaying enough, but the situation is far worse than that—if a further degree of depravity is even theoretically possible. Not only is he a killer beast in human form, but he also proves to be a criminal sexual psychopath by cutting her corpse up into twelve pieces.

The reader would be advised to deal with this not merely as an abstraction but to envision the ungodly spectacle. The woman's head must have been one of the twelve pieces. Perhaps her legs and arms, cut in twain, added up to another eight, the remaining three being hacked-up portions of her torso. Even with the sharpest of modern knives it would take quite some time to effect such a dismemberment. With the relatively dull blades of thousands of years ago, it must have been quite a long piece of work.

The psychopathic murderer had accomplices in his atrocity for it is said that he "sent her into all the coasts of Israel." How many members of his tribe, each carrying a decaying piece of human meat, were dispatched to various portions of Israel, the Bible does not explain, but if anyone, particularly Christian and Jewish clergy, will share with me whatever defensive commentary they have about this vulgar story, it will be publicized if it is within my power. Please do not waste time by suggesting that the reader is supposed to be shocked and therefore morally instructed by such an account; that is *not* the evident purpose of the unknown author of this disgusting narrative. He tells it merely as a fascinating story, as might the author of a modern tale published in *True Detective* mysteries, the purpose of which is never to edify nor instruct but merely to horrify and divert. Some scholars feel that the story represents a justification for a subsequent war against the Benjaminites. How much factual history there is in this interpretation it is now impossible to say. But no matter how interpreted, the story is vile, disgusting, and certainly dissonant with today's repeated calls for a "return to the morality of the Bible." May God forbid that we should ever return to so violent and depraved a moral standard.

One of the few wise portions of the book of Judges is the statement in verse 30 in which the reader is urged to ponder the story: "Consider of it, take advice, and speak your minds." I speak mine when I say that to classify such an ancient horror story as in any sense spiritual or divine is to make a mockery of the terms.

Chapter 20. Further details of the ugly drama are now given. In any even moderately civilized society, an individual who committed such atrocities would be a moral leper, an outcast, but no such fate met this gentleman. We are told that *four hundred thousand swordsmen* gathered together and asked the man what had happened. Once again, of course, we are not told how the message was able to be heard by such a vast assemblage before the days of public-address systems.

> 4. And the Levite, the husband of the woman that was slain, answered and said, "I came into Gibeah that belongeth to Benjamin, I and my concubine, to lodge.
> 5. And the men of Gibeah rose against me, and beset the house round about upon me by night, and thought to have slain me: and my concubine have they forced, that she is dead.
> 6. And I took my concubine, and cut her in pieces, and sent her throughout all the country of the inheritance of Israel: for they have committed lewdness and folly in Israel.

To employ a Yiddishism, the Levite is guilty of such incredible *chutzpah* that it takes one's breath away. To save his own skin, he sent his unfortunate bedmate out into the streets to be gang-raped, and now he justifies this by blaming it on the carousers and saying that *they* had "committed lewdness and folly in Israel." He actually has the gall to say,

> 7. Behold, ye are all children of Israel; give here your advice and counsel.

Almost any of us could give such a criminal a great deal of advice, but the Israelites take the matter with remarkable aplomb.

> 8. And all the people arose as one man, saying, "We will not any of us go to his tent, neither will we any of us turn into his house."
> 9. But now this shall be the thing which we will do to Gibeah; we will go up by lot against it; . . .

Instead of punishing the offender, the children of Israel decide to go to war against the men of Benjamin to avenge the crime. So a war begins over the incident, a war in which over the next few verses we are told 90,100 men are killed! The fatalities are again reported in round numbers, which lessens the credibility of the figures, but they add up to the inescapable conclusion that anyone who states that all this recounting of blood, gore, murder, and depravity was authored by God and is therefore morally instructive and spiritually uplifting is either a liar or a dunce. No one can read the endless repetitions of the same sickening theme and not eventually be angered that for centuries such violence has been portrayed as the direct, personal word of an all-loving God.

Needless to say, we must be as understanding and fair in our judgments of Middle Eastern tribes of the distant pre-Christian era as possible for we are gazing back down enormous corridors of time. Even lifetime scholars of ancient peoples concede that they can know only rare aspects of the totality of life in such places and times. Certainly little practical effect can come from expressing our scorn for the almost daily barbarism and bloodthirstiness that, according to Scripture, characterized life in Old Testament times. But our contempt need not be withheld from those of the present day who argue that the tragic ills of contemporary society can be productively approached by a return to the morality of biblical times. Every atheist in the world can perceive the obvious fact that the Ten Commandments and other moral and ethical admonitions that can be found in Scripture have merit. However, there is more to biblical morality than that.

These chapters of Judges cannot even boast of the slightest literary beauty—that partial though utterly irrelevant defense given for certain other unedifying portions of the Old Testament. Such faint illusion of beauty as exists is attributable entirely to the reaction, conditioned by several centuries of experience, of modern English-speaking peoples to the resonant beauty of their own language as spoken in an earlier, more formal age. The phraseology has so often been employed in the form of old prayers, solemn oaths, sonorous poetry, and Shakespearean drama, that it creates the illusion of beauty whether the actual content is charming or not. But re-read the chapters of Judges—and others in the Old Testament—with the single purpose of discovering literary eloquence and one will be forced to realize that there is little trace of it. The writing is, in fact, even more pointlessly repetitive than modern midcentury Marxist rhetoric, inept in many details and obscure in others. (See also MORALITY.)

JUSTICE. There is apparently no natural justice in the universe. Some justice reigns in the conduct of our affairs, though not nearly enough, but it is all created by humans. Life, in general, is unfair.

I first felt this in a personal sense when, in beginning this commentary, I looked back on my own life. I have enjoyed far more than my proper share of good fortune—my health has generally been good, my fellow creatures for the most part have treated me kindly, my work has been generously received, and I have been fairly compensated for my efforts. But all about me millions of people enjoy no such luck. Some are doomed physically by genetic accident at the moment of conception. Others are injured while in the womb. Still others are crippled while undergoing the process of birth. Millions more are struck by injury and disease while still young. And always about us are the poor, the aged, the insane. Much of their suffering is caused by no human agency, although human wars and terrors—even ignorance—often exacerbate the burden.

To believe that such tragedies are imposed by a vengeful Deity is an insult to God. If portions of the ancient Scriptures assert that God is bent on bloody revenge and violence, so much the worse for belief in the holiness of such texts.

If it is true that justice is not inherent in the universal order, then every one of us is absolutely required to do what pitifully little we can to set the scales in better balance. It is easy enough to recommend ideals, but some of us, observing that ideals are rarely achieved, proceed to the error of considering them worthless. This attitude is eminently harmful. True North cannot be reached either, since it is an abstraction, but it is of enormous importance, as all the world's travelers can attest. Even though we shall never be completely virtuous, we should still strive to be more commendable. Even though we can never be perfectly courageous, we should nonetheless strive to be braver than we might sometimes feel. Even though we cannot be faultlessly compassionate, we should persevere as far on the road to that ideal as our moral frailties permit.

Moral behavior increases the amount of justice in the world. A common error in thinking about morality concerns the timeless question whether there is an all-knowing, all-loving, all-powerful God. Affirm any one of this inconsistent triad, philosophy holds, and one or the other divine attributes is false or limited. The question itself has never been resolved to the satisfaction of the world jury, nor is it the case that only virtuous people believe in the Deity and only sinful individuals do not. Most of the world's crimes are committed by people who accept the existence of God. But some, the faith of their childhood having been weakened, assume that if there is no personal, conscious God, there is no particular reason for persisting in our efforts to lead moral lives.

Dostoevski's Grand Inquisitor stated that if there is no God then anything is permitted. He was mistaken. The debate need not be continued in the abstract since we have the evidence of two of the largest societies of all time—the former Soviet Union and China—which have long been officially atheistic. Despite their widespread assumption of the nonexistence of a personal God, not only is not *everything* permitted, much *less* is permitted in fact than in societies that are largely democratic and well populated by believers.

If there is a God who holds all power, then he obviously can do a great deal to increase virtue and diminish suffering in the world. But if there is no God, or his power is limited, then the entire task is up to human beings. Actually, even if God exists it should be clear by now that he is quite content to leave the necessary work of improvement to mankind. The Deity has never yet miraculously introduced into the human drama a hospital, orphanage, convent, church, synagogue, temple, cancer-research institute, homeless shelter, or any other helpful social institution. He leaves that to the more compassionate of his creatures. May their tribe increase.

Herber Schneidau, in a perceptive essay "The Bible Under Attack," refers to "Yahweh's (God's) desire for justice and righteousness." The concept is apparently taken as a clearly established tenet of Old Testament morality. Such an assumption also includes something perfectly sensible. If God is in favor of justice and righteousness who in his right mind could be against such ideas?

The classic difficulty arises when we search the Scriptures for unambiguous evidence that God does come down invariably on the side of justice and righteousness. The prophets often assert that he does, but guided by the admonition of Jesus to judge things by their fruits—their actual results rather than promotional advertising—we find countless acts attributed to God that by all normal standards as well as common sense are shockingly unjust and unrighteous. If a man as a matter of reflex accidentally touches the ark of the covenant to keep it from falling and is therefore immediately executed, we are obviously witness to an act that is impossible to attempt to justify. Even children recognize that an earthly ruler who imposed such punishments would be identified as a barbaric tyrant. Were any of his followers to attempt to describe such acts as righteous and just, society's moral stomach would automatically turn.

The Scriptures, obviously, contain descriptions of acts consistent with the idea of God's wisdom and love, but it is garbage reasoning to point only to such passages and totally ignore those that transmit precisely the opposite message. (See also BY THEIR FRUITS YE SHALL KNOW THEM; POVERTY; REVENGE; SOUL, THE.)

L

LAMENTATIONS, or the Lamentations of Jeremiah. The churches have for many centuries taught that the book of Lamentations was written by Jeremiah. No critic alive today has any idea how such an absurd view came to be common in the first place. Says Father John McKenzie in his excellent *Dictionary of the Bible:*

> Modern critics are almost unanimous in agreeing that the language and the conceptions are too different from those of Jeremiah to permit the traditional attribution; the author is unknown.

From my first casual reading of this section of the Bible I concluded that it was highly improbable that all of its contents could have been written by one author. Subsequent research showed that I had formed an opinion now held by all informed Bible scholars.

Though some Christians and Jews consider the book of Lamentations prophetic, it is nothing of the sort. The descriptive passages were written at or shortly after the time of the events they describe, chiefly, the Fall of Jerusalem to the Babylonians in 587 B.C.

Whoever the various authors were no one of them was God, since each of the five chapters are in the form of a poem and of no great distinction to the genre. If God ever did write a poem, it would certainly be better than even the most exalted poetry of human authorship. The most damaging information against divine authorship, however, is that the poem resembles a particular Sumerian lamentation on the fall of the city of Ur, which occurred not long after the year 2000 B.C. Since the Sumerian document was written fourteen centuries earlier, the inescapable conclusion is that plagiarism is involved. God is not a plagiarist.

The book of Lamentations, however, is at least less rambling than many others of the Old Testament, restricting itself chiefly to a consideration of the sufferings of Jerusalem after the capture of that city by Nebuchadnezzar.

Chapter 1. As with most of the book, the first chapter may be most profitably read as poetry. Verses 1, 2, and 6, put into poetry form below, show it is powerful and moving in its imagery, not unlike a poem a Parisian might have written when that city fell to the Nazis in the early days of World War II:

> How lonely sits the city
> that was full of people.
> How like a widow she has become;
> she that was great among the nations,
> she that was a princess among the cities
> has become a vassal.
> She weeps bitterly in the night,
> tears on her cheeks;
> among all her lovers
> she has none to comfort her;
> All her friends have dealt treacherously with her;
> they have become her enemies.
>
> From the daughter of Zion has gone all her splendor.
> Her princes have become like stags that can find no pasture.
> They have gone without strength
> before the one pursuing them.

The lamenting author continues, citing the reason for the sad state of affairs:

> 8. Jerusalem hath grievously sinned; therefore she is removed: all that honoured her despise her, because they have seen her nakedness: yea, she sigheth, and turneth backward.

Doubtless the author ascribes the fall of the city—variously described as Judah, Zion, and Jerusalem—to the direct will of God rather than the military superiority of the opposing force. The reader will by now have become familiar with the general policy of Old Testament writers to blame almost any personal or social disaster on God. This peculiar attribution was usually rationalized—as it is here—by the factor of the sinfulness of the sufferer. How that could account for the afflictions of innocent children or particularly virtuous individuals is never explained, nor can it be. It must not be thought that in Lamentations the author is merely suggesting that the Lord *permitted* disaster to befall his chosen people; it is specifically stated that he was the *instigator* of it. Note also that in verse 10 it clearly states that what the Lord God had commanded and promised would not happen did in fact take place.

In verse 17 the social entity is likened, curiously, to a menstruating woman.

With the exception of the single theological assumption that national or tribal calamities are caused solely by sin—an assumption with which no serious theologian of today agrees—there is nothing of a truly religious or moral nature in the first chapter. (See also POETRY IN THE BIBLE.)

Chapter 2. The second chapter repeats the message of the first except that it places even stronger emphasis on God as the acting, causative agent of the calamities lamented, again in response to the city's wickedness. There is perhaps no depiction of anguish and depression more striking in all literature.

One of the more interesting verses is verse 14:

> Your prophets have seen for you
> false and deceptive visions;
> they have not exposed your iniquity to restore
> your fortunes,
> but have seen for you oracles
> false and misleading.

Religious criers-of-doom frequently blame a populace for not having heeded members of the clergy, but here we see an instance in which not even the prophets are exempt from the general condemnation.

Chapter 3. The writing style of chapter 3 is noticeably different from that of chapter 2. The verses mostly comprise one sentence, the thoughts are more direct. The author seems totally seized by his central idea and describes in even more florid language the degree of God's anger and harsh severity. God is said to have made chains heavy and to have acted "as a bear lying in wait and as a lion in secret places."

It is commonly assumed—and not only by Christians—that Jesus said something startlingly new in his famous New Testament turn-the-other-cheek advice (Matt. 5:39; Luke 6:29). But in verse 30 we read, "Let him offer his cheek to the ones smiting him."

By verse 31—perhaps having wearied of unremitting pessimism—the author writes:

31. For the Lord will not cast off for ever:
32. But though he cause grief, yet will he have compassion according to the multitude of his mercies.
33. For he doth not afflict willingly nor grieve the children of men.

This commonsense observation is logically incompatible with the message conveyed by the earlier portions of the book. Just a few verses farther the author again reverses the idea:

37. Who is he that saith, "And it cometh to pass, when the Lord commandeth it not?"
38. Out of the mouth of the most High proceedeth not evil and good?
39. Wherefore doth a living man complain, a man for the punishment of his sins?

Whereupon the author finishes off the chapter lamenting more misfortunes and calling on God to turn his vengeful actions instead toward those who oppress Jerusalem.

Chapter 4 continues in the same gloomy tone and is perhaps most chiefly of interest for the reference to the mysterious creatures called *Nazarites,* who we are told are colored white, red, and black and are remarkably wrinkled (vv. 7, 8). Then the author returns to the same theme of placing blame, this time again ascribing it to the priests.

13. For the sins of her prophets, and the iniquities of her priests, that have shed the blood of the just in the midst of her,
14. They have wandered as blind men in the streets, they have polluted themselves with blood, so that men could not touch their garments.

Chapter 5. Here the author quite unnecessarily instructs God to remember "what has come to us," and to "observe us and see our reproach." Since God knows all things, why does he require such advice?

The last verse ends the book on a touchingly low note, expressing how the people feel totally alienated from their maker.

22. But thou hast utterly rejected us; thou art very wroth against us.

The reader is advised to contemplate again the fact that he is unlikely—unless aided—to analyze passages of Scripture in the way that he would if he encountered precisely the same words or ideas in any other literary source. The Bible has been spoken of in such complimentary terms for so many centuries that its pages still seem to give off a confusing aura of mystery, glamor, and beauty. Even the mighty power of correctly applied reason has difficulty penetrating the fog of custom, reputation, and prestige.

Part of the analytical problem is that the actual or alleged events described are so ancient that we simply do not regard them in the way we would happenings that occur in modern times and in places with which we are familiar. (See also DISASTERS; EVIL, THE PROBLEM OF; PROPHECY AND PREDICTION.)

LANGUAGE OF THE BIBLE. The ancient language in which so many versions of the English Bible are written has such a beguiling beauty of its own that even the most innocuous thought may seem poetic or profound. Consider any mundane suggestion—say, for instance, my mother's favorite admonition to me as a child, heard almost every time I left the house: "Do you have a clean handkerchief?" Phrased in the Elizabethan manner, the thought—which can hardly be confused with the words of the Almighty— might sound as follows:

> A wise son, when he goeth abroad from his abode, will lend an ear to the words of his mother when she saith, "Son of my home, dost thou go forth into the world provided with no clean cloth with which to mop thy brow, clean thy face, and guard thy health? For he who giveth no thought to the handkerchief in his pocket may heed not other counsel of his mother."

All that is lacking is a rendition of the words in the voice of Sir Laurence Olivier and the heart of almost any Englishman or American would be touched. The point: Be not ye moved by pulchritude of language but seek ye after wisdom within, for that is where it is at.

Note for example the following two verses from the second chapter of Genesis:

> 2. And on the seventh day God ended his work which he had made; and he rested on the seventh day from all his work which he had made.
> 3. And God blessed the seventh day, and sanctified it: because that in it he had rested from all his work which God created and made.

We have only to think about these verses for a brief moment to realize that no matter how noble and flowery they sound (1) an all-powerful God would certainly not require rest; and (2) the verses cannot be divinely inspired—as literalist Christians attest—because certainly an all-wise God would not deliver such a patently absurd message, not profound in any sense of the word.

Ambiguity of Message. Besides the problem of lending seeming depth to sometimes otherwise innocuous texts, the language of the Bible often lends a confusing ambiguity to the content. Some scholars feel that truths are revealed through the Bible only if it is understood as poetry and mythological imagery. Says Fritz Marti, professor emeritus of Southern Illinois University, commenting in his *Religion, Reason and Man* (Green) on the beauty of the metaphors found in Job 38:

> Nowhere is the picture broken by any silly questions about an astronomic or biological timetable. It is neither physics nor a tract for or against evolution. It is sheer poetry and deeply religious. It is a glorious expression of faith. It has nothing to do with quibblings about beliefs. Beliefs concern only the intellect. The fundamentalist believer is mostly a weird intellectual, who often lacks real faith altogether. As a self-appointed attorney for God, who is in no need of attorneys, he very easily turns out to be more godless than the agnostic and the unbeliever. At all events, he seems deaf to poetry.

Still others feel Scripture must be understood in a metaphysical sense, or as an allegory.

Certainly the one way the message should not be interpreted is totally literally. Consider the precept *Thou shalt not kill.* In the literal sense that seems clear enough, but only devout pacifists accept it as such. Most others, while agreeing that killing is essentially wrong and demonstrably evil in most circumstances, nevertheless argue that there are specific situations—such as cases of self-defense or war—in which killing is not only permitted but to be encouraged. Certainly the ancient Israelites accepted this as so, as evidenced by the many instances where not only was killing accepted as right, but also was carried out *at the explicit command* of God. (See also SITUATIONAL ETHICS.)

Thus, there is simply no overall, absolutely clear-cut scriptural message. The interpretations occur in the mind—the brain tissue—of the reader. A dozen receivers of the same word may perceive it in a corresponding number of ways, some of which will be mutually exclusive.

The common terms or jargon of the Bible may create additional ambiguity because of their vagueness. In practice the churches have profited by the very vagueness that troubles the rational reader. If it is impossible to say positively what certain terms mean they may therefore be used with almost anarchic abandon.

Consider for example the phrase *the son of man.* There are so many interpretations of this concept that it has almost no meaning at all except what an individual speaker or writer may wish to convey. Since all male human beings are sons of men there would be little point in singling out Jesus as one, except perhaps on the part of those concerned to deny his divinity. In practice the phrase is used most often by those who wish to *affirm* his divinity.

The same is true of *the son of God.* If we move past the assumption that God exists and is the Supreme Creator, it follows that we are all his sons—or daughters. Confusion, not clarity, is added by using the qualifying phrase the *only-begotten* since the word *begotten* in all common usage has a physical, sexual connotation, and no one has ever asserted that God the Father physically impregnated Mary. The assumption is that the impregnation was effected by not physical but miraculous means, by the Holy Ghost.

There is, of course, no lack of speculative commentary on such questions. Some of it is remarkable for its philosophical creativity, but little of it constitutes a straightforward answer to the questions that trouble us.

Another problem that appears when examining the literary aspects of the Bible results from the use of italics. Since the common reason for the employment of italics is to place *special emphasis* on certain words and messages, the reader not familiar with the Bible should be told that this is not at all the case in scriptural text. Italicized words in the Bible, in fact, are in most cases of *less* importance than nonitalicized words. It was nevertheless a thoughtful gesture on the part of those who introduced the practice because *it indicates that words so printed were not present in the earlier texts from which the later editions were translated.* These passages were inserted into the Bible by scholars who translated the various versions. Their motivation was evident enough; it was merely to further clarify certain passages, many of which, God knows, are obscure and confusing, even with the additions. Since these translators would never have dreamed of claiming that they were personally divinely inspired in adding their clarifications to the text, it therefore follows that *at least those portions cannot in any sense be said to be inspired.* (See VERSIONS OF THE BIBLE.)

Another factor that adds confusion to understanding the original intent of the biblical message is the matter of quotations. As every journalist, psychologist, general semanticist, and public figure knows, the task of accurately quoting a complex statement made by another, in the absence of mechanical aids, is so difficult as to be almost impossible. An attentive listener is generally able to repeat the gist of a remark with reasonable accuracy if very little time has elapsed, but if there is an insistence upon precise wording the results are invariably unsatisfactory.

To this day I much prefer that interviews be tape-recorded because in that way at least there is a greater chance that one will be properly quoted. Even then, however, there is room for error since what the public is finally given is not the entire recording but a few isolated excerpts, and because of the carelessness of the transcriber, the exercise of journalistic license, or faulty audio quality the message is still frequently mangled. So many slips can change the meaning of a quotation—a misplaced comma, the absence of spoken emphasis, the omission of a word or inadvertent substitution of a word with one of opposite meaning, or the inaccurate description of the general context in which the statement was made.

It is important that the reader consider such information when contemplating the accuracy of quotations in the Bible. Since we have concluded that even the best, most experienced, and professional journalists do a considerably less-than-perfect job of quoting statements, even with modern mechanical aids, we are then faced with the choice between two alternatives in regard to scriptural quotes. Either (1) there is the same common degree of human error in quoting Jesus, God, the prophets, and the saints as there is in the quotation of all other public figures, or (2) the quotations are all precise and correct simply because God himself has miraculously seen to the matter, knowing—as he naturally would—how prone his children are to err in even their best-intentioned acts.

To the believer it is naturally comforting to seize upon the second alternative since the first is so alarming as to be unthinkable. But, alas, as soon as we have chosen the apparently more appealing of the two, we are face-to-face with the uncomfortable fact that if we pick up various editions of the Bible, each bearing the imprimatur of one church or another—sometimes even of the same faith—we note that *quotations attributed to Jesus, God, and others are often markedly different from edition to edition.* And what of the many passages of Scripture that flatly contradict other portions?

These problems are inevitable because a language is not at all like a system of mathematical statements. A language consists on the one hand of a strange assortment of noises made by the human mouth, and on the other of an equally peculiar assortment of marks on paper. Not a single one of these noises or marks, or any combination thereof, can be said precisely to equal the physical or abstract reality it hopes to convey. This is readily obvious in terms of abstract words such as *peace, freedom, faith, spirit,* and so forth. But few people perceive that it also applies to words that seem very matter of fact, such as *roller skate, watermelon,* or *loud.*

A language, in other words, is somewhat like a body of liquid. It is a constantly shimmering, shifting mass, once removed from the related reality, its interpretation determined by the individual *perception* of the receiver. It therefore follows that there can conceivably be as many different interpretations of any particular message as there are persons who are exposed to it. (See also COMMUNICATION.)

Languages evolve, not only over long periods of time but also daily. Generally accepted meanings or connotations of words often change. Meanings can be altered based on the cultures involved. How an African jungle resident or Far Easterner defines *pretty*, for example, is clearly different from the American concept of the word. To further complicate the problem, some languages vanish. Jesus, for example, spoke in Aramaic. But no one today speaks pure Aramaic. So no matter along which avenue we approach this aspect of our large study we are confronted with difficulties.

As for those who perceive only sweetness and comfort in the Bible, no matter the meanings of the individual words, this may be the result of a mirror effect. Those who draw warmth and light from the Bible are themselves often warm and light-giving individuals. If the Bible were to be totally removed from their belief-structure, these same people would continue to be dear and decent human beings.

LAST DAYS, THE. Typically, religious belief assumes a great deal while firmly establishing relatively little. So we should not be surprised that there is much unclarity in the ongoing discourse about the Last Days. If we attempt to suspend our biases and predispositions on the topic and approach it analytically, the first question that occurs is, The Last Days of what? We have heard of the last days of Pompeii, the last days of a white sale at Macy's, the last days of any number of things. Let us eliminate all such considerations and narrow our field by suggesting that the subject at hand is the Last Days of the world.

While we have made progress with our definition, we have certainly not resolved the question, for it is common to use the word *world* in at least two ways. The first case we encounter in such sayings as *around the world,* by which it is clear that we are referring only to the planet earth, which bears precisely the same relationship in comparison to the entire physical universe as that between a single grain of sand and the vast reaches of the Sahara Desert. But Christians assert that when we talk about the end of the world we are actually talking about not just our modest planet but indeed all the billions of galaxies with their innumerable stars, most of which have their equally innumerable planets.

Such progress leads to still another question: What happens to all the "ended" matter? According to the laws of physics—which most informed religious believers assert were divinely established so that the universe would run systematically rather than chaotically—there is in fact no place for burned-up matter to go. When objects encountered on the earth are burned up or otherwise extinguished, they do not mysteriously vanish from the universe; they simply take other forms. The answer to our question, therefore, is quite simple: Since no matter has yet "ended" we have no idea what would happen to it if it did.

The next question about the Last Days is, To what purpose would a perfect God extinguish his own massive and beautiful universe? It is a simple enough matter to construct a scenario that might account for his deciding to wipe out Sodom and Gomorrah, Iraq, Kansas City, Las Vegas, or some other specific piece of real estate. Granted, for any such hideous catastrophe to be justified, we would have to assume the sinful depravity of every single inhabitant of such regions, a situation that has never actually been witnessed. Even so, it is theoretically *possible* that everyone in say, Detroit, Michigan, might eventually become so egregiously sinful that capital punishment on a massive scale might be inflicted. But it has never been suggested—nor will it ever be—that everyone on earth, including innocent babes in arms, is so sinful that the entire human population deserves sudden death by one horrible means or another.

These few casually gathered considerations are not particularly perceptive or insightful. Clearly it does not require the mind of an analytical philosopher to conceive them. Almost any moderately sensible and informed person not hopelessly blinded by religious prejudice might think of them or at least agree to their reasonableness if they were suggested to him.

In putting our modest thoughts together in this order, we perceive that any Deity who actually elected to eradicate totally his lovingly created domain simply because he was angry with a tiny percentage of its living inhabitants would be doing something utterly stupid. Surely no believer can seriously argue that the God who in another breath he asserts is perfection itself is also capable of stupid and/or irrational acts.

Fortunately, we can take another approach in seeking to answer our questions about the Last Days. We can look at the relevant record, whether under the rubric of history, theology, or natural science. We shall never know for how many thousands of years men have seriously believed and publicly announced that the end of the world was not only possible, but also literally at hand. Such heralds of doom have usually been quite specific. If we can depend on the record of the Gospels, *even Jesus clearly instructed his followers that the Great End would come while some of them were yet alive.* Since practically all of his followers were adults, it is clear enough, then, that he expected the curtain to ring down on the human drama within seventy-five years or so after his speech of the moment, at the latest. He turned out to be mistaken in that prediction. If we believe that Jesus Christ was, in the most literal sense, either (1) God in human form, or (2) the uniquely chosen son of God, then we are forced to conclude that written reports in the Gospels attributing such groundless predictions to him, and on a matter of such grave importance, were in error. Millions of people will have no trouble accepting this simple hypothesis since we know from personal experience that the public record—our books, magazines, newspapers, radio and television newscasts, and so forth—often turns out to be in error in regard to one specific assertion or another.

But those who believe it is not even possible to speak of error in Scripture will remain in perplexity, unable to extricate themselves from the logical trap they have constructed by their constellation of beliefs and assumptions.

But not only Jesus predicted the end of time. There were rare instances of such prophecies in pre-Christian times, and during the last almost two thousand years of Christian dominance there have been hundreds of instances—perhaps thousands more that never came to public attention—of sincere believers who were so confident that the Last Days were upon them they actually sold their belongings—perhaps gave the proceeds to the poor—moved out of their homes, donned white robes, and awaited what turned out to be only hideous embarrassment when the world continued on its natural enough course.

As regards other sorts of social experiments, we should have little trouble concluding that if a given school of thought had proved wrong—in case after case, in thousands of instances—it would be reasonable to assume that it would very likely be wrong again in future such cases. At least some proportion of the world community is reluctant to apply the lesson to this particular question because it originates in Holy Scripture. (See also IRRATIONALISM; JOEL; PROPHECY AND PREDICTION; SCIENCE AND RELIGION; SOUL, THE; TIME.)

LEVITICUS. This third of the five books of law by which the Israelites were governed covers primarily the areas of worship—RITUALS and offerings—and priest-specific codes.

Chapter 4. The comparative study of religion has proved of enormous scholarly benefit to mankind since the customs of any one of the planet's thousands of separate religions will inevitably be better understood if considered within the larger context in which it exists.

228

The following passages concern certain religious rituals of the African Zambezi tribe, translated by J. G. Tompkins:

> If the witch doctor do a taboo thing he shall catch a young water buffalo, bring it to the altar and kill it.
> And the witch doctor must take handfuls of the water buffalo's blood and sprinkle it seven times before the god Muwalla.
> Then he shall take a knife and cut off from the buffalo the fat from the guts, and the two kidneys, and the skin, and also all the muscle meat, the water buffalo's head and legs, his guts and the filth of his bowels. All of this the witch doctor shall carry outside the village where he will build a fire and burn all the chopped-up parts of the water buffalo.

Not only will the modern white reader perhaps feel a patronizing contempt for the primitive pagan custom described, but educated black Africans will feel some embarrassment at having such jungle customs brought to the attention of readers in parts of the world where better education is available to the masses.

As it happens, the passages come not from an African tribe at all but from commandments said to be given to the ancient Hebrews by the Lord and found in the first few verses of Leviticus chapter 4. If modern man feels disgust at such rituals when he believes they are part of the culture of uneducated residents in an African jungle village, why should he not respond similarly upon learning that the customs were practiced by ancient Hebrews? The Jews themselves, being an eminently civilized and intelligent people, put a stop to such nonsense many centuries ago. Why then the common inability on the part of certain presumably educated people in our own time to call such absurdity and savagery by its right name. Why such continued respect for a book that includes so many hundreds of instances of precisely such foolish detail? Because, believing that the Bible is the divinely inspired word of God, certain human beings are prepared to suspend not only reason but even common sense about any and all passages found within, no matter how vile or bloodthirsty.

Chapter 10. Here we read that two of the sons of Aaron, Abihu and Nadab,

> 1. . . . took either of them his censer, and put fire therein, and put incense thereon, and *offered strange fire before the Lord,* which he commanded them not.

What is meant by *strange fire* no one claims to know. Indeed if one even tries to imagine what could possibly constitute strangeness in the context of the common chemical phenomenon of fire, one can think only of color. But what would it matter to any sensible person if the color of a fire was somehow changed, if it gave off more or less smoke, or if it came from one kind of wood or another? When one considers the truly monstrous crimes of which humans have been guilty over the centuries, and of which there is no shortage in our own day, what might be appropriate punishment for the burning of strange fire. The punishment chosen by the all-loving God is found in the following verse.

> 2. And there went out fire from the Lord, and devoured them, and they died before the Lord.

No such shocking and vengeful fate befell the murderers of the Inquisition, Hitler, Stalin, or the numerous serial killers of our own time and place. So far as we can judge, in fact, the Lord God seems to have taken no particular interest whatever in such moral monsters. What difference does it make, therefore, to insist that he was so infuriated by strange fire that he burned alive two young men who might have been making a discovery that could have advanced the science of chemistry?

Chapter 11. This section, one of the most interesting in all religious literature, has nothing whatever to do with what might reasonably be described as religion. It is not concerned with the practice of any virtues, and it has no connection with admirable behavior. Although its passages convey instructions in truly unmistakable terms and in a book that millions of people insist is the literal word of God, these instructions are nevertheless ignored by even the great majority of the most fervent defenders of the faith. A few of the admonitions are still honored by orthodox Jews, but among Jews generally there is little or no regard for the full message of the chapter.

Chapter 11 concerns itself with dietary taboos. Moses or Aaron or whoever else wrote the chapter asserts that the Lord—one must assume out of displeasure with the eating habits of the human race—troubled himself to hand down a divine menu. Now it might be thought that this is a touching and affectionate gesture by a Deity who, knowing the stupidity and ignorance to which the human race is even today prone, would give advice to his earthly children concerning things they ought and ought not to eat. Most of us would indeed profit by sound counsel from a nutritionist.

Clearly a good many things on the planet earth—some of which are enticing to the eye—ought not to be ingested. This is certainly the case, for example, with those plants that are poisonous. How many poor souls have perished in dreadful agony because they have experimentally nibbled at a colorful berry, root, mushroom, or green blade none but God will ever know. Though he certainly would have such knowledge—by virtue of being by definition all-wise and all knowing—*he has never troubled himself to warn mankind against poisonous plants*. In light of this omission, let us carefully study the bill of fare that he reportedly does recommend.

> 3. Whatsoever parteth the hoof, and is clovenfooted, and cheweth the cud, among the beasts, that shall ye eat.

First, we see that the *reason* given for eating certain foods and avoiding others can only be described as ludicrous: it has to do with the division of hoofs and the characteristic of cud chewing. No biologist or dietician believes that either factor is of the slightest relevance to the nutritional value of food. Because the essential reason underlying the message is ridiculous, one is therefore not surprised to see that it produces equally ridiculous results. For example, this chapter of the Old Testament clearly forbids the eating of rabbits. Mankind knows perfectly well, from countless centuries of experience, that there is nothing scientifically wrong with eating the flesh of rabbits. Vegetarians, of course, would insist that it is wrong to eat the flesh of any living creature. We may leave that matter aside for a moment since chapter 11 clearly stipulates that God believes that there is nothing wrong with eating once-living flesh.

Concerning the warning in verse 7—that the meat of pigs ought not to be eaten—it is sometimes argued that this advice is sound enough because some pork contains the tiny *trichinella* worm that can cause trichinosis if the meat is not sufficiently cooked. But this is a sensible argument for one course of action only, and that is cooking pork very well. Many centuries before Christ even the wisest of men could not have had any awareness whatever of the cause-and-effect relationship between the eating of pork on the one hand and the development of trichinosis on the other. If the symptoms of trichinosis appeared within minutes after the eating of pork, as symptoms do in the case of allergies or the ingestion of poisonous substances, then of course a five-year-old child could perceive the relationship. But trichinosis does not appear until a considerable amount of time has elapsed. A cause-and-effect connection might still have been guessed at if it were assumed that a given individual or tribe ate almost nothing but pork, but there is no evidence that this was the case in Old Testament times. The human race in those days dropped like flies from a tragically long list of serious diseases, although surprisingly little is said about such important matters in the Old Testament. References to trichinosis in the debate about verse 7 therefore are nothing more than a classic instance of post facto rationalization, evident especially since the argument was introduced thousands of years after the communication in Leviticus.

Note also in this connection that God did not say, "Ye shall not eat the flesh of swine because doing so may make you ill." This is a simple enough instruction, certainly not beyond the intelligence of even a dim-witted man, and by all means not beyond the capability of pure intelligence itself; but the Almighty offered no such reasonable explanation. The reason given that the flesh of a pig ought not to be eaten is because "he cheweth not the cud."

Since I do not believe that God can be guilty of absurdities, my assumption is that Moses, Aaron, or other unknown writers are at fault here, not God.

Particularly interesting in pointing out the temperament of the God prescribing these dietary laws are the following verses:

> 9. These shall ye eat of all that are in the waters: whatsoever hath fins and scales in the waters, in the seas, and in the rivers, them shall ye eat.
> 10. And all that have not fins and scales in the seas, and in the rivers, of all that move in the waters, and of any living thing which is in the waters, they shall be an abomination unto you: . . . (IA)

Abomination is a strong and dramatic word; if human authors choose their words carefully we may safely assume that God would exercise even more precision. Are we therefore to conclude that he intended to communicate that the eating of nonfinned and nonscaled sea creatures is *evil,* which is what the word *abomination* inescapably implies? Anyone who has enjoyed a dinner at one of the world's many fine seafood restaurants— many in Christian communities—will no doubt have relished the lobster, clams, oysters, crab, squid, and other delicacies commonly served. Anyone who has enjoyed a meal in Japan will probably have tasted the flesh of eel. Turtle soup is of course a delicacy in several parts of the world. Nevertheless, those who have enjoyed such foods—if we are to believe Leviticus—are committing an evil act, a moral sin.

Although many passages of Scripture can be interpreted in a variety of ways, the same cannot be said of this one. If I say to you, "Thou shalt not eat strawberries," there cannot be the slightest doubt about what I mean. Likewise, there cannot be the slightest doubt in regard to the meaning of this biblical text. Interestingly enough, certain Christian fundamentalists—

the very ones who insist that every word of the Bible is literally the word of God and must be interpreted and obeyed as such—enjoy a good lobster dinner.

We are next told which flying creatures are forbidden and which are acceptable (vv. 13–23). Choices that are okay include locusts, beetles, and grasshoppers. Apparently even chicken is forbidden by these passages. How many fundamentalists—or anyone, for that matter—today adhere to a diet so defined?

The later verses of chapter 11 describe further actions required because of the uncleanliness of certain meats. It is said that any pot that comes in contact with an unclean animal must be considered unclean as well and immediately not just cleaned but destroyed. Even ovens and storage cabinets are to be broken if touched by so-called unclean meat. If water that might have come into passing contact with the body of an unclean creature—say a rabbit or an oyster—subsequently comes into contact with a seed of, say, corn or grain, even that seed and/or the resultant plant is to be considered unclean and therefore inedible.

Chapters 13–14. The references here to leprosy attacking garments (v. 13) and houses (v. 14) are as nonsensical as statements that a man was suffering from termites or a woman from an infestation of moths.

Information on another probable biblical inaccuracy that relates to this chapter come to me in a personal letter sent to me on February 24, 1983, by Charles C. Shepard, M.D., Chief, Leprosy Section of the Respiratory and Special Pathogens Laboratory Branch of the Center for Infectious Diseases, Department of Health and Human Services. Shepard wrote:

> The cases mentioned in the Old Testament were probably not leprosy but more likely were some inaccurately defined skin condition. Many of the skeletons of people who died of leprosy had characteristic body changes, but these changes were not found in skeletons of persons from the present Israel and Egypt who lived before about 600 A.D.

It appears that the all-wise, all-knowing God inspired authors of Leviticus to write commentary about *misdiagnosed diseases*.

Chapter 20. This chapter is one of the more depraved portions of the ancient Scriptures in that its author seems to dwell at unnecessary length on a long list of sexual offenses. Whoever he was he took care, of course, to attribute no commandments to Moses himself; the several clear-cut instructions of the chapter are given as direct quotations from God. The meaning of the commandment given in verse 2 is by no means clear:

> 2. Whosoever he be of the children of Israel, or of the strangers that sojourn in Israel, that giveth any of his seed unto Molech; he shall surely be put to death: the people of the land shall stone him with stones.

The words are clear enough. Everyone knows of the dreadful infliction of death by stoning, and Molech is, of course, a false god or idol. The phrase *giveth any of his seed,* as used in the Bible, invariably seems to mean the physical act of sexual ejaculation. However, the total image called to mind here by the combination of words is so bizarre that it is not easily assimilated. Some translators, apparently having trouble with such an image, have consequently interpreted *his seed* to mean a man's children. This would at least make this verse sensible considering the amount of sacrificing of human babies that went on in biblical times. But why then did he not just say that instead of using a phrase that in other instances in the Bible refers to human sperm?

So insistent is God that the man who gives his seed to Molech shall be executed that even those who avert their eyes from the criminal and thus avoid killing him are themselves threatened:

> 5. Then I will set my face against that man, and against his family, and will cut him off, and all that go a whoring after him, to commit whoredom with Molech, from among their people.

Parenthetically, there is a good deal of this business about going a-whoring in the Old Testament, to the point where the concentration on the subject matter itself seems bizarre and neurotic.

Verse 9 clearly instructs that *everyone* who CURSES his father or mother is to be executed.

Verse 10 commands that death is the absolutely required punishment for those who commit adultery. In a sense, the Christian conservatives who believe that capital punishment is a perfectly appropriate solution for the admittedly serious problem of marital infidelity are absolutely right, if the question is, Does the Bible indeed make such a recommendation? But the overwhelming majority of the world's Christians choose *not* to be guided by any such bloodthirsty order, partly because it would lead to the mass-slaughter of perhaps as many as one hundred million Americans, including, of course, millions of Christians. Perhaps the Christian Reconstructionists could enlist further support for their bizarre recommendation on the ground that it would go very far toward relieving pressures created by the population explosion.

Verse 11 is of special interest:

11. And the man that lieth with his father's wife hath uncovered
his father's nakedness: both of them shall surely be put to death; their
blood shall be upon them.

The wife of a man's father is, of course, that man's mother, unless
the father has two or more wives. Even so the act would be considered
adultery and thereby already punishable by death in verse 10, so why this
particular crime is singled out for specific mention is unclear.

Verse 13 orders the same final punishment for HOMOSEXUALITY, describing such acts as "an abomination." The not-insignificant number of Christian ministers, monks, priests, and laymen who are themselves homosexuals
presumably do not recognize this passage of Scripture as divinely inspired.

For a reason so unclear that it is safe to say no living Christian or
Jew shall ever know of it, verse 14 not only names a crime for which
the punishment is death but actually also insists that the execution be by
fire. Anyone who has ever burned even the tip of one finger for a fraction
of a second knows the burning of human tissue causes the most excruciating
pain imaginable. But here the all-loving Father instructs mankind to perpetrate this torture on other human beings. The reader is undoubtedly curious
to know at once what vile atrocity demands such a fiendishly sadistic form
of capital punishment.

14. And if a man take a wife and her mother, it is wickedness: they
shall be burnt with fire, both he and they, that there be no wickedness
among you.

Verse 15, not surprisingly, requires death as the punishment for any
man who uses an animal sexually. For what reason it is difficult to even
speculate about, the verse adds absurdity to cruelty by stating "and ye
shall slay the beast." Evenhandedly, verse 16 considers the same offense
as committed by the opposite sex:

16. And if a woman approach unto any beast, and lie down thereto,
thou shalt kill the woman, and the beast: they shall surely be put to
death; their blood shall be upon them.

Verse 17 requires capital punishment for any man having sexual intercourse with his sister or half-sister, although—if Genesis can be believed—
Cain and Abel seemed not to have worried about such a prohibition.

Verse 18 is one of the most bizarre statements, within the context
not merely of the Bible, but also of all recorded literature.

LEVITICUS

> 18. And if a man shall lie with a woman having her sickness, and shall uncover her nakedness; he hath discovered her fountain, and she hath uncovered the fountain of her blood: and both of them shall be cut off from among their people.

At least the penalty of death is not required for this offense. Today Bible believers, quite wisely, totally ignore this divine instruction, which they view as pertaining to hygiene, not morality.

It is a fair question why the Christian Reconstructionists, who are so insistent in recommending serious punishment for certain other offenses, pay no attention to this one.

In the present day, many Christians and Jews are distinguished by their involvement in the campaign to abolish capital punishment. It follows that they have turned their backs on the more bloodthirsty passages of ancient Scripture.

As the Bible's defenders over the centuries have conceded more and more ground in terms of the questions of historical truth, they have fallen back on the "value for edification" of one passage, chapter, book, or another. This ground will in time prove even more of a quagmire than former territory that once seemed firm. If there is anything clear about the Old Testament it is that portions of it are not only not morally edifying but are also precisely the opposite—scandalous and shocking. (See also ATONEMENT; MORALITY.)

LIBERALISM. Few concepts more readily infuriate Christian and Jewish Bible-believing conservatives than that of liberalism. Though even a casual study of history reveals that many beliefs and opinions once considered liberal and innovative are now part of the conservative belief system, the fact remains that conservatives generally react with horror to anything described as liberal. The leading conservative periodical *National Review* explicitly stated (at the height of the cold war) that the threat of liberalism far exceeds that of Marxism. What, then, is this idea that fundamentalists so abhor?

Liberalism is not a thing, in the sense that a *watermelon* or *typewriter* are things. It is rather a state of mind, a philosophical attitude, and one that is not precisely the same in any two nations or at any two points of time in history. Nevertheless some instructive observations can be made about it.

The word comes from the same Latin root as does the word *liberty,* a clue that leads us to realize that the essence of liberalism is an insistence on the free development of the individual. Though the liberal spirit, like the conservative, has probably existed since the beginning of human time, it was not until the Renaissance that the idea burst to full flower in Western civilization. After centuries of acceptance, men began to use the tools of REASON and science to question those long-held beliefs whose truth is not self-evident. Today the idea of religious freedom is a fundamental American belief, but when it was first introduced—by liberals—it was regarded as dangerous heresy by Europe's Christians; nor even now is it whole-heartedly endorsed by Christian conservatives.

Other basic Western freedoms, those of speech, assemblage, and press, have followed the same path. The history of Europe during the past four hundred years can be interpreted as a record of man's courageous struggle for freedom against the ancient authority of kings, tsars, emperors, churches, and those traditionalist conservative philosophers who held that freedom would bring only chaos and confusion.

Liberalism in time brought about both constitutional, democratic government based upon the consent of the governed and the climate of economic freedom that gave rise to capitalism. At this point in history a fascinating dilemma emerged. According to theory, if men operate under few or no economic restraints, prosperity should result for many individuals. Unfortunately, such a climate engenders a minority of individuals who are prepared to take unethical advantage of their rivals, customers, or employees, and who accumulate enormous concentrations of wealth and power, which sometimes leads to disastrous results for large numbers of people.

It quickly became evident, then, that the old robber barons and the heartless tycoons who were motivated by nothing more than an inordinate lust for profit had to be discouraged by law from continuing their depredations. Today we take for granted that the American people must have legal protection against those who would sell them poisoned foods or dangerously defective merchandise. Our general ignorance of history means we are surprised to learn that such moral progress was achieved only in the face of the most bitter opposition from an earlier generation of conservatives, to whom the only objective worthy of attention was keeping economic forces totally free, regardless of how many deaths, how much physical suffering or outrageous robbery resulted. But once the people had agreed to protect themselves with the power of the state, they raised a question as yet unanswered: To what extent is it proper for the government to enter into the economic domain? (See CHURCH AND STATE RELATIONS.)

The classic liberal philosophy had obviously failed to anticipate this problem. Our complex industrial society therefore brought about a further evolution of liberalism so that today, though liberals are still staunch defenders of human liberty, they usually hold that the state is entirely justified in doing what it can to promote economic justice for all, including customers and workers.

The conservative defends the status quo, as of one date or another, but the liberal knows that the status quo is an illusion, that in reality nothing is permanent, and that the wise individual does not struggle futilely against the tides of change but rather seeks to control and channel them to productive ends. He no longer holds—if he ever did—that men can be made perfect by education and economic opportunity but does insist that they can be greatly improved by such means.

The conservative—and there is no argument on the point—has historically tried to stifle dissent and punish the dissenter. The liberal knows that freedom to dissent is absolutely basic to the American philosophy of government.

Conservatives generally approve of capital punishment; oppose gun control; think that the poor should depend on either their own resources or else turn to purely private charity; have few practical suggestions for actually helping the Mexican-American, Puerto Rican, African-American, Native American, or any other economically handicapped community; tend to be simplistic and fundamentalist in their philosophical views; and are fiercely nationalistic in terms of foreign policy.

Liberals for the most part oppose capital punishment; favor some degree of gun control; believe that the millions of American poor absolutely require a degree of government assistance; have specific programs to assist minority communities; tend to be more libertarian and relativist in their philosophical views; and realize that in a world still armed with nuclear weapons, old-fashioned bluster and threats toward other nations are dangerous emotional luxuries.

Wise conservatives and liberals agree, of course, on many specifics. A responsible and vigorous conservative force is required to carry on with the liberal camp the kind of constructive debate from which can emerge answers to the problems that perplex us. (See also CONSERVATISM; FANATICISM; FREEDOM.)

M

MAGIC IN THE BIBLE. It has been known for centuries that professional magicians perform their wondrous tricks by completely nonmystical means. The various methods employed are sleight-of-hand, distraction of attention, palming, the use of mirrors, and threads so thin they cannot be detected by observers in a theater, or other aids to illusion. Nothing whatever is the least bit occult, bizarre, unexplainable, or supernatural about such demonstrations. Neither God nor the Devil is involved. It is all pure, wonderful trickery. Everyone over the age of ten generally knows this. The fun of magic, nevertheless, lies in simply permitting oneself to be mystified.

To make the above observations, of course, is to agree that nothing in the realm of magic contradicts the long-established laws of physical nature. When a colored ball seems to be floating in midair we may be quite certain it is not doing so. It is supported by some sort of semi-invisible thread, and the secrecy further protected by the use of dim lights, distracting mysterious music, and a certain amount of unnecessary movement by the magician. All simple enough.

But references to magic in the Bible are never based on such a commonsense understanding. A modern magician could easily contrive to make an audience believe that he had converted his walking stick into a snake and then reversed the process, but when such an event is described in Scripture (Exod. 4:3) it is clear that the authors of such accounts actually *believed* the stick became a snake and vice versa. Which is, of course, just one more awkward instance of biblical error.

If an all-powerful God exists, he can certainly perform any wonder he might wish, and—if we accept certain scriptural assumptions about the devil—he too can perform stunts beyond the capability of mere mortals.

MAGIC IN THE BIBLE

It makes no sense to argue that God would personally participate in the performance of such parlor tricks while in millions of other instances he permits innocent believers to perish in pitiable anguish despite their most fervent prayers to him for deliverance. (See also MIRACLES.)

MALACHI. For centuries churchmen have believed, and hence taught, that this book had one author and that his name was Malachi. As usual they were mistaken. A number of authors contributed to the book, actually titled *Burden of Oracle of the Word of Jehovah to Israel by the hand of Maleakhi. Maleakhi* is the Hebrew word meaning *my messenger.* It will help to understand what sort of error this was to imagine that someone today writes an anonymous book about, say, President Clinton and calls the author "his friend." Five hundred years from today, our successors locate the document and because of unfamiliarity with the present form of our language publish an edition of the document with the title of the author given as *Hisfriend.*

It is not possible to say precisely when any portion of the Bible was written, but there is general agreement now that the first draft of Malachi was prepared some time after the rebuilding of the temple—516 B.C.— and earlier than the reforms of Nehemiah and Ezra, which occurred before 432 B.C.

Chapter 1. Although we don't know for sure who the authors were, we do know that they attributed personal, direct statements to God that intelligent humans cannot accept as coming from an all-knowing, all-wise, all-loving Deity. Take, for example, the following supposed quote from God himself:

> 8. "And if ye offer the blind for sacrifice, is it not evil? And if ye offer the lame and sick, is it not evil? Offer it now unto thy governor; will he be pleased with thee, or accept thy person?

In the absence of previous clarification, my first assumption when reading this verse was to wonder how anyone could be permitted to offer people—blind, lame, ill, or otherwise—on a sacrificial altar. When I read further and discovered that it was animals being sacrificed, I still questioned the instruction as coming from the Almighty. Even granting the unprovable assumption that God would take personal pleasure and gratification at having animals painfully slaughtered and burned in his honor, what could it possibly matter to him if a steer so used happened to have, say, one lame leg?

It would perhaps be understandable if those priests who depended upon the temple offerings of animals for their own sustenance wished to have only totally healthy creatures so presented since if an animal was ill the meat might be contaminated. But even professional meatpackers don't reject animals on the ground that there is something wrong with its sight or that it walks with a limp since they know that feature will in no way harm the quality of the meat.

An odd aspect of the old controversy about animal sacrifice, maimed or whole, is that to the present day we hear occasional reports of the bizarre practice. In every such instance the popular reaction is loathing and revulsion. Religious believers and secularists are now united in condemning the practice as primitive and savage. If that is the common reaction today, why are we supposed to approve of instances of it that took place centuries ago? (See also GIFTS TO GOD.)

Chapter 2. In this chapter we clearly see that unlike the prophets Amos, Isaiah, and Jeremiah, who wisely concentrated on virtuous and charitable behavior on the part of the Israelites rather than strict ceremony, the authors of Malachi stress the ritualism of religion, criticizing the people for being less than generous in their offerings, and demanding that everything be run in an orderly and honest fashion—by the book. (See ATONEMENT; LEVITICUS; RITUAL.)

In verse 3 the anonymous author attributes one of his own vile fantasies to God:

> 3. Behold, I will corrupt your seed, and spread dung upon your faces, even the dung of your solemn feasts; and one shall take you away with it.

After such vulgarity one is relieved to find an edifying idea:

> 10. Have we not all one father? hath not one God created us? why do we deal treacherously every man against his brother, by profaning the covenant of our fathers?

The authors also take a clear-cut position on the question of DIVORCE, although the Bible itself is certainly not consistent in this respect:

> 14. "Yet ye say, 'Wherefore?' Because the Lord hath been witness between thee and the wife of thy youth, against whom thou hast dealt treacherously; yet is she thy companion, and the wife of thy covenant.
> 15. "And did not he make one? Yet had he the residue of the spirit.

And wherefore one? That he might seek a godly seed. Therefore take heed to your spirit, and let none deal treacherously against the wife of his youth.

16. "For the Lord, the God of Israel, saith that he hateth putting away: . . ."

Chapter 3 contains verses that modern televangelists have been fond of quoting:

8. "Will a man rob God? Yet ye have robbed me, But ye say, 'Wherein have we robbed thee?' In tithes and offerings. . . .

10. "Bring ye all the tithes into the storehouse, that there may be meat in mine house, and prove me now herewith," saith the Lord of hosts, "if I will not open you the windows of heaven, and pour you out a blessing, that there shall not be room enough to receive it."

Chapter 4. As we have seen repeatedly, one of the least attractive elements in the Bible is the surly vengefulness manifested in the various authors' readiness to gloat over the actually prayed-for sufferings of the unrighteous.

1. "For, behold, the day cometh, that shall burn as an oven; and all the proud, yea, and all that do wickedly, shall be stubble: and the day that cometh shall burn them up," saith the Lord of hosts, "that it shall leave them neither root nor branch. . . .

3. "And ye shall tread down the wicked; for they shall be ashes under the soles of your feet in the day that I shall do this," saith the Lord of hosts.

With this lust for vengeance and the promise of the coming of the prophet Elijah, we reach the end of the Old Testament. We might have expected that the conclusion of the mighty volume of Jewish Scriptures should end with a flourish. It does not because the unknown author of Malachi chapter 4 had no idea he was writing the end of the Old Testament. The likelihood is that he had no idea he was writing the last portion of this short book itself. Perhaps he even composed a great deal more than what now appears, and that other portion has been lost to the ages. Or he may have put down his writing instrument one day to take his midday meal and just never returned to his task.

I hope that it is therefore instructive that the Old Testament ends, as it began, in mystery, doubt, and confusion. (See also RITUAL.)

MEDICINE. Typically, conservative factions automatically object to a new and sound idea when it is introduced, simply because of its novelty. When over the course of time the wisdom and utility of the idea is eventually so clearly demonstrated that only the insane would continue to reject it, conservatives then switch course, adopt the concept, and hope that the uninformed will remain largely ignorant of the relevant historical record. This is in no way more clear than in the field of medicine.

The churches eventually, to their great credit, accepted scientific medical advances and the equally sound patterns of organization laid down chiefly by the devout Florence Nightingale, but in the beginning the church wanted to hear nothing whatever about medicine. It was considered impious to suggest that diseases were not simply the result of either divine punishment or the machinations of malign spirits. Even the most basic, beneficial discoveries were approached with suspicion and distrust. As late as the last century President Timothy Dwight of Yale College preached a sermon against vaccination! The record of the churches when anesthetics were first introduced is shameful.

In our own day, it is a matter of common knowledge that for the first few years of public semi-panic about AIDS, Protestant fundamentalists and conservative politicians openly referred to the disease as a direct punishment of God for the moral outrage of homosexual behavior, and this belief is still, unfortunately, held by many of that persuasion even though everyone informed about science knows that AIDS has a material, physical cause.

It should not be assumed that religion opposed medicine for so long simply because everyone did and the churches were merely in step with a general social reaction. That was not what took place. Religion itself *was* the opposition to medical advance. (See also DISEASE.)

Blood Transfusions. In August of 1977 the Jehovah's Witnesses church released a sixty-four-page booklet explaining the reasons for the Witnesses' refusal to receive blood transfusions, even when such refusal will lead to certain death. The only reason the Witnesses take this position—one assumed by no other Christian or Jewish sect—is the reference made to the ingestion of blood in three Bible passages: Gen. 9:3–6, Lev. 17:11–14, and Acts 15:28–29. United States citizens are actually dying because of the Bible, though that sort of tragedy is not unprecedented in Christian experience. In reality, there is no sensible reason for a seriously ill or injured individual to refuse a transfusion of human blood. Hundreds of thousands of lives, in many parts of the world, are saved each year by recourse to the procedure. Inevitably, a certain number of people die after having received transfusions, but this is a risk of medical procedures of every kind. No one could seriously argue that all medical treatment ought to be abandoned simply because a small percentage of it leads to unfortunate consequences.

The stupidity of such a position on transfusions is augmented by nothing so much as the statement of a Witnesses official, William L. Barry, that blood taken from criminals and given to other persons *"makes them take on some of the characteristics of the criminal."* (IA)

The other hundreds of millions in the world who believe in the Bible simply disregard the absurd scriptural admonition to abstain from ingesting blood. The last factor establishing the nonsensical, contradictory nature of the Witnesses' position is that they do eat meat, every morsel of which has some blood in its capillaries.

METHUSELAH. As most everyone knows, even if they are not familiar with the Bible, Methuselah, who according to Genesis 5 lived to be 969 years of age, is presumably the oldest person who ever lived and thus the symbol of longevity.

It is perfectly reasonable to be skeptical about reports of the alleged ages of Methuselah and other figures of the Old Testament said to have lived for several centuries. Such allegations are inconsistent with thousands of years of evidence, a great wealth of it existing all around us at the present time. Men or women who live even one century are considered quite unusual.

If miracles can take place, by nature they will be unusual. But because they would make sense only if they dramatized some important moral point, we can properly target for our skepticism any exceedingly unusual report that seems to make no point. Perhaps if a given individual was truly saintly, brilliant, and wise, it might be argued that the extension of his years would have some benefit for humankind. No such suggestions of virtue appear in the few cases to which the Old Testament refers.

Would the reader himself want to live several hundred years knowing what we know about the physical and mental conditions of life for almost everyone of advanced age? Obviously not. The aging process itself, as it applies to all forms of life, is programmed into the physical order of the universe itself. Everything that is born develops, withers, and in time dies. Since stories of men living to an unusually old age are therefore contrary to the natural order of things, which those who believe in a Deity assume to be divinely ordained, not only do all the world's nonbelievers refuse to accept such stories, but even a good many Christians and Jews consider that it is not a matter of dogma to have to embrace them. (See also NATURE; PATRIARCHS, LONGEVITY OF.)

MICAH. The first three chapters of this book of prophecy contain a theme that is found often in the Scriptures, though rarely in lived reality: that sinful, corrupt behavior is followed by a conscious decision on the part of God to punish the guilty. We have only to look at human experience all about us to know that the wicked are as likely to prosper as they are to suffer, and that the virtuous are as likely to suffer and die as anyone else. That there are certain forms of sinfulness—sexual excess, alcoholism, narcotics addiction, sadism, gluttony—that may produce their own unfortunate effects clearly has nothing to do with divine retribution.

Chapter 4. In all probability Micah would be read by no one but bibliographers and scholars were it not for the poetic gifts of one or another of its several authors. Who has not heard and enjoyed:

> 3. . . . they shall beat their swords into plowshares, and their spears into pruninghooks: nation shall not lift up a sword against nation, neither shall they learn war any more.

Concerning this verse two things can be said: (1) its language is beautiful, and (2) its prophecy has failed.

Chapter 5. Many Christians enjoy believing the passages that seem to prophesy the coming of Jesus.

> 2. But thou, Bethlehem Ephratah, though thou be little among the thousands of Judah, yet out of thee shall he come forth unto me that is to be ruler in Israel; whose goings forth have been from of old, from everlasting.

It does indeed sound as if Micah is speaking of the birth of Jesus. But the troubling aspect of the chapter occurs beginning in the next verse, where we find predictions of events that will supposedly occur as soon as the Messiah has been born: (1) all the exiled remnants of the Israelite tribe will be reunited; (2) seven shepherds and eight princes will be appointed to protect the Jews from the Assyrians; (3) all of Israel's enemies will be destroyed; (4) all weapons will be destroyed and the city's defensive walls no longer needed; (5) there will be no more witchcraft practiced.

We have only to realize that none of these events have ever happened to understand why Jews still anticipate the coming of their Messiah. *If the Bible is correct here, then Jesus cannot have been the Messiah.*

Chapter 6. Here we return to the prediction of doom in punishment of the people because they obey the laws of King Omri, who according to 1 Kings 16:25, "wrought evil in the eyes of the Lord, and did worse than all that were before him."

MICAH

Chapter 7. Micah continues with more predictions of doom in the first part of the chapter but ends with promises of glory, assuring Israel that their enemies will "move out of their holes like worms of the earth: they shall be afraid of the Lord our God, and shall fear because of thee" (v. 17). Again—a promise that has not yet been borne out. (See also JOEL; PROPHECY AND PREDICTION.)

MIRACLES. The world jury, after thousands of years of considering evidence, is still out in regard to the question of miracles. Some believe everything about them, others nothing at all. The truth possibly lies somewhere between the two extremes.

It is certainly not the case that the validity of the Christian faith was established by miracles since reports of such wonders are not encountered only within the context of Christian experience but in fact go back to the earliest written records of man. There is no shortage of miracle stories in the Old Testament, nor are they unknown in the literature of ancient Egypt, Abyssinia, or other Middle Eastern kingdoms. One also encounters stories of supernatural events in Mohammedan and Oriental religious tradition.

It is instructive and conducive to humility for Christians and Jews to be made aware that there is no entirely satisfactory definition of the word *miracle*. It can, of course, be used in intelligible conversation since there is a rough general sense in which the term is commonly interpreted, but what one might refer to as a miracle may not be so perceived by another. Christian theologians state that even the most awe-inspiring and unnatural events produced by the power of Satan and other evil spirits are not to be properly spoken of as miracles.

Presumably, over a considerable period of time, additional light will be thrown on the present puzzle by responsible research in the field of parapsychology. It may be that some individuals—many of whom have no connection with religion—have remarkable powers that either are not the property of the rest of us or that we are not aware that we share. The line between the professional art of magic and the areas of sorcery and voodoo is not as clearly defined as the orderly mind might wish. It is established that normal individuals do have remarkable powers that ordinarily go untapped.

On my own television programs over the years, for example, I have seen incredible feats performed while certain subjects were in the state of hypnosis. In one instance Gene Rayburn, the game-show host who was at the time the announcer on my old "Tonight" program, was hypnotized and instructed that his body would turn as rigid as a steel rod. He at once assumed a stiff and erect posture, with hands clenched at his sides. He was then lifted up and placed between two chairs with just the tip of his heels on one and the skull bone at the back of his head on the other. The strongest man in the world—if perhaps by a freakishly concentrated moment of exertion he could even assume such a position—would certainly collapse to the floor after a few seconds. Nevertheless, acting upon the instruction of a professional hypnotist, Gene not only performed this ordinarily impossible task for several minutes, but he also did not budge when Steve Lawrence, Skitch Henderson, and myself sat together on his body!

In other instances I have seen professional performers—in this case self-hypnotized—stick long needles through their tongues, through both cheeks, in one side of their forearm and out the other, and so forth. In none of these cases did the individuals feel the slightest pain, nor was a drop of blood shed. There are thousands of volumes available on the subject, but clearly certain individuals, by whatever means, are able to tap reservoirs of power. As a result, they can perform astounding feats or cause others, who know nothing of the philosophy behind such acts, to perform such wonders also. To the devout who over the centuries might have encountered such demonstrations within social contexts that could be described as religious, the events have no doubt seemed miraculous. (See also FREE WILL; MAGIC IN THE BIBLE.)

Assuming that Jesus was literally God, it would be reasonable to expect that any miracles he might perform would exceed in their wonder and glory any that were performed under religious auspices that were not Christian, since for some three thousand years the Western religious mind has viewed all such other religions as false, if not products of the Devil himself. But alas for such reasonable expectations, the wonders worked by the Egyptian priests who competed with Moses, as well as the miracles said to have been performed by Moses himself, are vastly more dramatic than those attributed to Jesus.

Many other religions take a tolerant view toward their philosophical rivals and do not lay claim to being the one and only true religion, personally authorized by God. Christianity makes precisely such a claim. If it had a monopoly on miraculous happenings, that would be supportive evidence carrying considerable weight. But what are Christians to make of the fact that numerous other groups have claimed to exercise even more impressive miraculous powers?

One obvious response is that all non-Christians who make such claims are either deluded or lying. Such a defense is unacceptable because the

Bible itself provides numerous instances in which staggeringly dramatic events that could not possibly be explained within the context of the laws of physics were occasioned not under Christian auspices but under either Jewish or pagan authority.

Another response is that non-Christian miracles are not truly such but are merely magical wonders worked by the power of Satan. This argument also presents serious difficulties. Before anything can be said to have been done by the power of Satan, it would first have to be established that there is indeed such a personage as Satan and that he has powers second only to those of God himself. This plain-enough assertion has by no means been accepted by the world jury.

If there is a Devil and he is personally responsible for such miracles as are alleged to have occurred under—say—Islamic auspices, what success have Christians had in inducing the hundreds of millions of Mohammedans around the world to accept the idea that their miracles are authorized not by God but by the Devil?

Some rationalists—and all atheists—may be troubled that in developing the present case I have not simply ruled out the possibility of occurrences of a miraculous nature. The reason for this is entirely sound: the evidence does not indicate that the issue itself has been settled, one way or the other.

In analyzing Scripture one should be more concerned with internal contradictions than reports of miracles. We can approach the question of inconsistency easily with nothing more than the tools of logic whereas the same method by no means settles the question of miracles. For all anyone can prove to the contrary, miracles have indeed taken place. Once the existence of an all-powerful Deity is accepted, it follows that such a God can perform any wonder he may wish.

There are, of course, different sorts of purported miracles and it is helpful to distinguish among them. It is obviously one thing if a witness reports having observed a certain man walking upon the surface of water, floating through the air, or drifting unimpeded through a stone wall. It is a report of quite another sort if one states that one's grandmother was miraculously cured of cancer. While such miracle cures may indeed take place, the situation nevertheless remains unclear because of ample medical testimony about spontaneous remission of many diseases, including cancer.

I once asked two renowned cancer specialists whether they had observed cases of spontaneous remission in their own patients; both said they had. I then inquired whether they had the slightest reason to believe that in any of these cases there might have been spiritual or religious components to the equation. "None whatever," one doctor said; the other concurred.

Many—including even some religious believers—assume that stories such as that of Jonah spending three days inside the slippery, mucous-membrane-walled digestive tract of a whale are superstitious nonsense rather than miracles. The skeptical hypothesis does, by commonsense standards, seem far more likely to lead to truth than the traditional literal interpretation. However, it can hardly be denied that an all-powerful God would be able to perform such remarkable feats.

One is still entitled to be skeptical of such reports, simply because if God were determined to work wonders for the evident purpose of impressing mankind with the fact of his existence and power, it does seem that he could do far better than having a man swallowed by an enormous sea mammal. By virtue of the suggested location of the act it would be unlikely to have many witnesses, if any. Nor does the act itself have any inherently appealing or instructive facets. (See also JONAH.)

The miracle of Jesus standing securely on the surface of the water is a far better production, so to speak. It is also both marvelous and admirable that Christ—and other wonder workers—would heal the painfully ill or bring the dead back to life. Such stories, though still unacceptable to the scientifically minded, at least have dramatic validity to them. They are instructive and constructive. Stories of the Jonah-in-the-whale sort lack such appeal and therefore over the centuries have probably created as much doubt as faith.

Many modern Christian scholars think that if a report in the Bible is flatly contradictory to the established facts of science, then there must be something wrong with the report. The facts of science, as regards Jonah, would have led to his being either suffocated, drowned, poisoned by the vast quantities of sea water and gastric chemicals in the whale's stomach, or driven mad by the extreme fear any normal person would inevitably feel in such a hideous predicament. He would be in total darkness, able to breathe little or no oxygen but only gaseous fumes, awash in a bitter liquid to which his own wastes would be added, tossed about as the beast itself turned, dove, or surfaced—all of which adds up to a story that few, however devout, today believe.

Perhaps the most difficult to accept for the true believer who is not a personal witness is the miracle involving actual or alleged interruption of the normal course of planetary or stellar bodies in space. Examples would be Joshua commanding the sun to stand still (Josh. 10:12–14) and the miracle reported at Fatima, Portugal, in 1907 when thousands of witnesses were supposed to have observed erratic movement by the sun. The primary reason such reports are difficult to accept for religious believers with at least some degree of familiarity with science is that there is absolutely no corroborative evidence from elsewhere on the planet. Let us briefly consider this difficulty.

Assume that next Wednesday at 3:45 P.M. American Mountain Standard Time, many residents of Denver, Colorado, perceive that the sun splits into four quarters, each of which has a different color and whirls about separately for three minutes before rejoining the whole, after which the sun resumes its normal course and behavior. If we assume that the residents of Denver who tell of all this are stating what they consider to be truth, then we must naturally be impressed by the fact that absolutely nowhere else on the planet did either average citizens or professional astronomers notice anything the least bit unusual in the behavior of the sun during the time in question. The testimony of several billion witnesses obviously merits more respect than that of a small group of, let us say, two hundred thousand people, however devout. We would therefore conclude that in reality the sun was in no way affected, nor was its natural course in any degree altered, and further, that the testimony of the Denver residents represented some sort of mass illusion in which large numbers of people shared.

As quoted in an article "Who Do Men Say That I Am?" by Kerry Temple (*The Humanist,* May/June 1991), Notre Dame's John Collins contends that "anything involving changes of nature we are more inclined to regard as theological fictions."

Thomas Sheehan, in the book *The First Coming,* says:

> These natural miracles are simply legends which arose among early Christians and which were projected backward, under the impact of faith, into the life of the historical Jesus. The motive may have been to make him appear at least the equal of the numerous miracle workers widely reported in the rabbinical and Hellenistic religious literature of the times.

Even if we totally accept the existence of miracles, on whatever level, there is still something profoundly disturbing about such scant evidence as exists concerning them. Miracles are often said to occur in a context in which there is no particular necessity for them, whereas in hundreds of millions of cases where divine intervention was desperately needed and would have been gratefully received, a miracle was not forthcoming. Why God would turn away from true disasters but concern himself with trying to top the powers of Egyptian magicians by filling the beds of innocent people with frogs has a fascination of its own. Needless to say, no theologian has ever been able to answer the question. (See also JONAH; NATURE; SCIENCE AND RELIGION.)

MORALITY. Most religious believers assert that, in essence, morality is simply a matter of doing what God wants us to do. If we accept the assumptions that (1) there is a God and (2) he is perfectly good, it would then logically follow that by the very perfection of his goodness God could not possibly wish us to do anything evil. All of this reasoning is, in truth, of not the slightest practical value for we have no certain way of knowing precisely what it is that God wishes us to do.

The believer may respond to this perhaps unpalatable fact by directing us to the Ten Commandments, but his suggestion would be of little interest to hundreds of millions of non-Christians and non-Jews among the human population. Even if these "laws" brought down from Mount Sinai by Moses were accepted by everyone on earth, we are still entangled by the difficulty that they are a very confusing guide indeed to human behavior. Not only are they not ten in number, but much blood has been spilled over the centuries as a result of arguments among the various sects of believers concerning the interpretation of one moral precept or another contained therein.

The Bible and Morality. That morality by no means depends on accepting the Bible as the literal word of God is demonstrated by the life of Florence Nightingale, clearly a remarkably God-oriented individual. Her incredible record of self-denial and service to humanity may be unequaled in modern or even ancient times. She reported her firm belief that on four separate occasions God spoke to her. Whether such a thing occurred, we have no way of knowing. *But, though Miss Nightingale was quite convinced of the reality of what she interpreted as a divine message, she nevertheless had serious reservations about the Bible.* In an 1873 reply to a suggestion by Benjamin Jowett that she prepare a selection of Bible stories for publication, she wrote:

> The story of Achilles and his horses is far more suitable for children than that of Balaam and his ass, which is only fit to be told to asses. The stories of Samson and Jephthat are only fit to be told to bulldogs; and the story of Bathsheba to be told to Bathshebas. Yet we give all these stories to children as "Holy Writ."

In referring to the books of Kings and SAMUEL, she wrote, "Witches. Harlots. Talking asses. Asses talking. Young gentlemen caught by the hair. Savage tricks. Priests' tales."

Apparently no one alive accepts literally all of the Bible's moral, ethical, and ritualistic instructions and lives in accordance with them. Most devout Bible believers, to their great credit, have the good sense to be selective.

They place quite proper emphasis on certain teachings that have practical value and totally ignore passages—mostly in the Old Testament—that are now considered embarrassing and irrelevant to the moral and ethical needs of modern Jews and Christians. This is a perfectly admirable process since it is a component of wisdom to select whatever is good and reject whatever is counterproductive. But not many believers are prepared to acknowledge that this very process of selection necessitates that they hold up a self-defined moral standard as being superior to that of the Scriptures they profess to idolize. Precisely, then, what is it that enables believers to accept certain biblical teachings while rejecting others? It is nothing more than a combination of good common sense and ethical sensitivity.

The Bible clearly teaches that the *proper and, in fact divinely author-ized, treatment for habitual juvenile delinquency is immediate capital pun-ishment* (Lev. 20:9). There is no reference, in this context, to particular crimes so extreme that they might deserve the ultimate penalty. The offense that the biblical instruction deals with is simply that of rude, impertinent, unruly, and troublesome behavior. (See LEVITICUS.)

No Christians or Jews anywhere in the world today would promptly deliver their difficult sons and daughters to the nearest executioner. We consider it barbaric that in Muslim Saudi Arabia, for example, if an unmarried young woman becomes pregnant, the law demands that her parents take her into the public square and, with the help of the community, stone her (and the infant, especially if a girl child) to death. Yet that is clearly what the Bible instructs should be done. Believers and nonbelievers alike should be grateful that today's Western religionists have the intelligence and sensitivity in regard to this issue to choose another solution on the grounds that *it is morally superior to that suggested by the Scriptures.*

Why do the churches not deal openly with this question? In over half a century of attending Christian schools and churches and reading an enormous amount of Christian literature, I have never once seen the issue raised, although I have little doubt that it is touched upon in relatively obscure scholarly journals of whose existence, it would seem, the masses of the faithful are kept in ignorance. But since we are talking about morality, what are the *moral* grounds for keeping such questions in shadow?

Belief in God and Morality. For unknown centuries philosophers have debated whether a belief in one or more gods is absolutely essential to a code of moral behavior. For a very long time the argument could be conducted only in theoretical terms because there existed no known society *not* guided by a belief in divine agencies that could be studied to determine whether, so far as human behavior was concerned, it was (1) better than, (2) inferior to, or (3) much the same as societies that acknowledged a Deity.

As of 1917, however, it became possible to remove the discussion from the realm of pure theory; in that year followers of Karl Marx took control of Russia and began to construct an officially atheistic society. The millions of people within the U.S.S.R. borders did not, of course, all become atheists overnight. Nevertheless a long, slow process was begun. As the devout died off and the churches no longer instructed new generations in the faith, masses of young Russians grew up being taught only officially atheistic moral conduct.

This facet of the political reality of the twentieth century afforded us a laboratory in which to study the question of what happens to the behavior of humans who no longer feel religiously inculcated guilts and no longer believe in hellfire and eternal damnation. We find, upon examining such evidence even cursorily, that the gloomy predictions of the defenders of one faith or another have not been borne out.

Ordinary citizens of China and other communist societies take just as dim a view of murder, lying, adultery, thievery, rape, alcoholic excess, physical brutality, and other sins as do Catholics, Protestants, Jews, Muslims, and other believers. It is certainly evident that communist officials—like their right-wing counterparts—are quite prepared to resort to cruel measures to sustain themselves in power, but their actions in this regard are in no way different from those of leaders in Christian cultures over the centuries. European history is filled with accounts of every society's ruling class resorting to the most bloodthirsty and sadistic measures to impose their will on whatever populations came under their power. (See also CRUSADES, THE.)

Therefore, the argument that there is no real morality at all if there is no belief in God is untenable. Our glance about the world has sufficed to produce many instances, some in our own communities, of individuals living essentially virtuous lives although feeling either a reasonable certainty or at least a strong suspicion that there is no God. It is not necessary to turn to material evidence to refute the argument; simple reason will do just as well. Those who believe that if man thought there were no God he would behave even less virtuously speak from a position of grave reservation about the human capacity for virtue itself.

If it could be demonstrated that there were no God, virtuous behavior, far from becoming less important, would in fact be of even greater importance because sinful men, or good men in moments of weakness, would have no expectation that an all-powerful Deity would somehow eventually set things right. They would therefore be thrown more on their own resources, which would set virtue at a premium. (See also VIRTUES, THE.)

Although it is not possible—by definition—for God to change his mind, nevertheless the God portrayed in the pages of the Bible does so constantly.

People who believe in such a God, therefore, have every reason to suppose that from time to time he might take a direct hand in the conduct of human affairs to set aright what men have disposed of so poorly. But if there is no Great Intervenor, virtuous behavior is as necessary to our continued sustenance as air and water.

Perhaps the many acts that are now directed purely to God—singing, walking in processions, lighting candles, burning incense, breast beating, bowing down, and all the rest—could be converted to a purpose more directly beneficial to humanity. The benign impulses out of which we assume such practices grow could result in more aid being given to the ill, the poor, the blind, the crippled, the imprisoned, the orphaned, and the oppressed in every corner of the world. Indeed one of the things that redounds greatly to the credit of a percentage—alas, not all—of the world's Christians and Jews is that they devote a good part of their energies and resources to helping the poor. Such efforts are even more admirable in those parts of the world where local authorities, themselves not the least bit concerned with the welfare of the downtrodden, actually physically attack those who do try to be helpful. We also witness the morally pathetic spectacle of right-wing speakers and journalists who rarely, if ever, express sincere sympathy for the poverty stricken but usually manifest a cruel contempt for such unfortunates. Perhaps the churches will commission an official polling agency to determine which of these two groups is the larger. (See also BY THEIR FRUITS YE SHALL KNOW THEM; CHARITY; POVERTY.)

If there is a God, he cannot but be favorably impressed by the behavior of a well-intentioned individual who not only lives a generally decent life but also devotes his energies to the service of those who sorely need them.

The traditional no-morality-without-belief-in-God argument might at least have a certain pragmatic function if it could be demonstrated that adherence to either the Jewish or Christian faith—or to some other—resulted in a standard of behavior markedly superior to that of humanity generally. Unfortunately the evidence does not support such a hypothesis. Prisons of every land have for the past two centuries been occupied chiefly by those who considered themselves religious believers of one kind or another rather than by atheists or agnostics. The scoundrel cultures of the Mafia or the Medellin Cartel arise in a thoroughly Christian context, specifically Catholic.

Christians sometimes respond to such evidence, of which a great deal more could be introduced, by denying that criminals of various sorts are Christians at all. But to say of such offenders, "Well, they're not really Christians," is no more sensible than to say of criminals residing in the United States, "Well, they're not really Americans," or of criminals who

254

happen to vote Republican, "Well, they're not really Republicans." The reality is simple enough, albeit painfully uncomfortable to face. If a man who has professed for, say, twenty-five years that he is either a Catholic, a Mormon, a Democrat, a Rotarian, or an adherent of any other social group subsequently proves himself a threat to society, the tendency of his former associates to disavow him is perhaps understandable but can hardly be considered grounds for responsible argumentation.

Perhaps Christians more than other groups resort to such ad hoc excommunications because in its highest, finest interpretation, the Christian code has great beauty and charm. There seems little doubt that if any appreciable number of Christians actually behaved, for example, as if they loved their neighbors and enemies, the Western world at least would be a far more attractive and livable place.

But if morality does not depend on a belief in God, the next question the traditionally religious believer may ask is, Does morality depend on the belief in a future life? While some questions on this subject may be classically complex and wrapped in mystery, this one is not. Even if we could become quite certain that there is no God and no conscious afterlife, morality would still be of enormous importance simply because rules for behavior are absolutely necessary for the conduct of all societies' affairs.

This is not a matter for mere discussion among disinterested philosophers. Rather it is as practical and concrete as the rules for, say, building a motorcycle. The clear evidence of this is the existence in *all* cultures of something called law. The legal machinery in a modern society like the United States is so massive that it could not possibly escape our attention. Not only do laws exist but every day we also hear demands for additional legislation. When perceiving the necessity for specific laws and working to enact them, rarely do individuals or their societies think that religious beliefs are relevant. Whether we are atheists or devout believers, we do not want criminals breaking into our homes or the banks where our money is kept. We do not want our daughters, wives, or mothers raped. We do not want strangers to park their automobiles on our front lawns.

No one ever said, "I have recently come to conclude that there cannot possibly be a God nor an afterlife. Consequently you are perfectly at liberty to physically assault me, steal my money, rape my wife, and throw me out of my home." Clearly morality exists because of its admirably practical applications. (See also FREEDOM; FUTURE, THE.)

The Concept of Good and Evil. In wrestling with the ancient philosophical puzzle of how to define the words *evil* and *good* and to apply them reliably, we naturally turn our attention to those physical things required for our survival. By doing so we easily see that the self-same act can be described as good in one case and bad in another, depending on attendant circumstances.

Imagine that a man has languished without water on a scorching desert for several days. If you were to approach that man and pour a bucket of cold water over his head, he would eagerly open his mouth, drink as much of the downpour as he could quickly absorb, and be grateful to you for the comforting shower the rest provides him. He would consider that you have done him a great service and would describe your act as wonderfully good.

But encounter this same man in a situation where he is near drowning in arctic temperature and the identical act will be viewed as a cruel and inhumane crime.

Just so are moral codes. Even those societies that we consider morally corrupt have a certain sense of right and wrong. The problem, so far as society's interests are concerned, is that their individual moral codes are often abrasive to us. The Gypsy culture, for example, is perfectly prepared to justify business methods the rest of us condemn as roundly dishonest. Gypsies view all non-Gypsies as suckers to be plucked, but we would be in serious error were we to conclude from this that Gypsies are morally lax in other respects.

The same point may be made about the Mafia culture that is richly laced with views and practices that society in general properly condemns as criminal and depraved. Members of the Sicilian or Sicilian-American underworld are readily disposed to drug trafficking, murder, thievery, extortion, political corruption, arson, robbery, violence, intimidation, and other criminal offenses as well. But at the same time the Mafia culture is rigidly loyal to the Catholic faith. Mafia leaders are generally given Catholic funerals and buried in hallowed ground, and it would be a very unusual member indeed who thought that anyone else had the right to rape or otherwise abuse his mother, wife, sister, or daughter. (See also CRIME, BIBLICAL IMPETUS TO.)

Hundreds of instances from other geographical contexts could be introduced to underline the point. Some form of moral and ethical code is a natural component of human behavior, even though it is equally as certain that no two individuals have a moral code that is precisely the same in every particular. One may legitimately argue that moral instruction for both individuals and masses is absolutely necessary, but it will hardly be generally agreed that it therefore follows that the entire world population ought to become Mormon, Seventh-Day Adventist, Buddhist, Hare Krishna, or necessarily affiliated with any specific form of religion whatever.

Conceding that to certain groups acts are sinful that to others may be either morally neutral or highly virtuous, there is still a very large body of social behavior recognized by almost all humanity as good. The attraction of it grows chiefly from two sources:

1. Its general social practicability. Communities—from families to nations—function more effectively in the absence of discord, anger, sexual license, thievery, and other forms of troublesome behavior. One is certainly more comfortable and secure if one's neighbors behave peaceably and sensibly.

2. Habits taught in the nursery. We early learn that rudeness, selfishness, and the other slight offenses of our early years are apt to be greeted coldly and angrily. Smiles, displays of affection, and obedience are rewarded by affection and praise. The moral sense is thus strengthened.

Significantly, loving mothers and fathers would never dream of suggesting that Junior ought not to overturn his bowl of oatmeal because doing so would displease God or contradict some scriptural command. Even a two-year-old is capable of learning the practical wisdom of avoiding such acts. In the same simple way, we learn in the early years of childhood that it is better to be truthful than to lie, better to befriend others than physically assault them, better not to take the belongings of others, and better to speak pleasantly rather than angrily. Religious believers have no firmer grasp of such obvious moral points than do atheists.

Some years later we learn that occasionally the norms of society on the one hand conflict with the satisfaction of perfectly natural appetites on the other. By that time our general moral dispositions or biases are developed, and virtuous behavior is recognized as admirable and productive.

Jeremy Bentham was perfectly right in suggesting that morality must in the end be to our advantage. Nor is there anything the least bit wrong with his suggestion that the morality of a society ought to lead it to produce the greatest happiness for the greatest number of its citizens. Unfortunately, philosophers have never reached unanimous agreement on what happiness is, or which specific human acts are likely to produce it. This is so partly because such questions involve matters of opinion, and opinions are as diverse and numerous as the humans who have them.

This is also not to argue—although some have—that pleasure is the only guide man needs to locate virtue. That it is a perfectly valid guide in many instances is clear enough, but it is equally certain that it cannot apply to all cases. A man may, for example, choose to decrease his own pleasure and sacrifice his own satisfactions because of a desire to better the conditions of his loved ones. But even in these cases he is simply setting aside his own physical needs for the underlying reason that he wishes to enhance the pleasure of—or protect the physical security of—those for whose benefit his self-sacrifice is enacted.

The negative aspect of morality, as we have already pointed out, is evil, or what religious believers call sin. Christians never tire of telling the world that man is not only occasionally given to sin but innately depraved, corrupt in all his thoughts and actions, and that this is true not as a result of unfortunate personal experiences but from the moment of conception.

When considering any forms of behavior of which we disapprove it's always instructive to pose the question, "Why not?"
- Why *not* kill anyone we feel deserves to be killed?
- Why *not* restrict freedom to assemble, to speak, to write, publish?
- Why *not* construct concentration camps for individuals or classes of individuals to whom we are negatively disposed?

Asking the question in such terms forces us to search for reasons to justify what we automatically consider virtuous behavior or discourage what we consider evil behavior.

Consider those sins specifically identified in the Christian tradition as the most serious: covetousness, pride, lust, anger, gluttony, envy, and sloth. The pride of one individual may—and often will—cause discomfort in others. Even in those instances in which a glow of pride is perfectly justified— as for example in the case of an athlete or political leader at a particular moment of triumph—it is always far more attractive if the victor is gracious and modest rather than boastful or conceited in his moment of glory. How warmly our hearts respond to the generous gesture of respect for a defeated opponent or of gratitude for those who have helped make the victory possible. How inevitably are we dismayed, even embarrassed, by a victor's arrogance in taking sole credit for his happy achievement.

As for the coveting of money and other material possessions, most individuals who accumulate riches do so at the expense of others. The legions of those who do not have nearly as much as they need to survive in dignity are enormous, whereas the list of those who are very rich is short. The crimes of the rich have been recorded by too many biblical prophets, saints, seers, and theologians to need elucidation here.

Sexual Morality. What sort of social behavior, one wonders, would give rise to the emotion of shame? Where, between the extreme sexual views espoused by—say—Mahatma Gandhi and Larry Flynt, is there a rational and moral middle ground?

Note that I do not say middle *point* because such a term would imply that one narrow formula of sexual behavior is appropriate for everyone, everywhere, at every time. This is simply not the case. Societies in the real world have different codes of sexual conduct, every society does have one; no society has ever opted for sexual anarchy.

Everyone who engages in sex does so because of the component of pleasure—which was programmed by NATURE or God—and it is precisely in regard to this factor that so many difficulties arise.

Why *not* engage in sexual activity with anyone, anytime, anywhere? Almost at once we realize that society's historic prohibitions against certain forms of sexual behavior grow out of well-justified concern for the well-being and preservation of the family. But what is so important about the family that vast cathedrals of legislation have been erected to defend it?

The essential reason societies absolutely must be concerned about the integrity of the family is that it is the context within which human beings are manufactured and brought to maturity. Humans are "grown" in the same sense that crops of grain or other vegetables are grown.

It would be a very peculiar agricultural society in which it was considered perfectly all right to trample upon the grain of others, to destroy their irrigation systems, and to disrupt their planting and harvesting procedures even though doing so would cause starvation. No society has ever permitted such crimes, nor should it.

Nor, for the same reasons, should any society permit anarchy so far as the raising of new "crops" of humans is concerned.

Evolutionary conditioning has pointed us in the right direction. We are innately disposed to have tender concern for little creatures, and not only for those of our own species. Every normal person has a certain attitude toward infant elephants, lions, tigers, horses, dogs, or cats that is markedly distinct from the individual's attitude toward adult members of the same species. We may or may not like a given four-year-old cocker spaniel on sight, but seeing a two-week-old cocker spaniel makes our hearts melt in a quite different way. It is precisely this natural tendency, found in the hearts of all except those who have been cruelly treated in their own early years, that accounts for our tender solicitude about human infants and children.

Moreover, it has been self-evident for countless centuries and was eventually confirmed by Freud and his colleagues, that as the ancient adage phrased it: As the twig is bent, the tree shall grow. Children who are raised in a warm, affectionate environment—one in which the mother and father love each other, make the fact of their love clearly evident to their children, and express that love physically and emotionally to their children as well—almost inevitably grow up normal and well-adjusted. And we also know, to our sympathetic concern and in some cases deep sorrow, that children who are deprived of their natural emotional birthright—those born to alcoholic fathers; prostitute mothers; drug-addicted, insane, or cruelly abusive parents—do not fare well in their later lives.

That is all there is to the admittedly complex and frequently frustrating contradictions concerning standards of sexual conduct and the actual behavior related to them.

Everyone by now is aware of the relative collapse of the American family in the present century. We are all familiar with statistics about DIVORCE—58 percent as of 1991—the sexual and physical abuse of children, juvenile delinquency; we are aware of statistics indicating millions of drop-outs, runaways, even young perpetrators of the most violent crimes. We know now how to produce any number of Charles Mansons: with a sicko for a father and a moral moron for a mother, you can produce unlimited numbers of the kinds of dangerous monsters who are crowding our prisons. Granted, not *all* prison inmates may be so described. But some of them may. And if they murdered, raped, or otherwise brutalized a member of your family, your mind would be remarkably clear about the matter.

Parenthetically, it is certainly not enough to be censorious about depraved and dangerous individuals. Even they are human beings, and if there is any way that they can be rehabilitated—or to use a religious term, *saved*—such assistance ought to be given to them. But surely at a far more important, fundamental level our society must be concerned with the question of what we might do to *diminish* the number of sadistic murderers, rapists, and other thugs.

When you address the subject in those terms, you come very quickly to the question of how the rearing of children in a family context can be conducted more sensibly.

Theologians of earlier centuries—indeed, thoughtful men and women throughout all recorded history—have wrestled with the difficult problems of sexual morality. Sometimes they simply despaired of working out any reasonable program of sexual conduct at all and took the extreme position that sex itself was some sort of evil curse, perhaps occasioned by the alleged disobedience of Adam and Eve, and that the highest possible, most moral course was to turn one's back on sex totally. There have been in various religions—not only in Christianity—those who took vows of chastity simply because they considered that the sexual urge itself was the work of the Devil. Fortunately for the preservation of the human species, such extreme philosophies have never been widely influential.

But a less extreme position, espoused by Mahatma Gandhi among others, has been influential. It holds that sex is indeed inherently evil, but that it is, alas, necessary for the continuation of human life. The logical implication of this view is that there is no justification for sexual activity except in the context of the conscious intent to create new life.

260

We need not debate the merits of such a position, but almost all the religious believers of history and the present moment have simply ignored it, although millions of them have tried to lead moral lives.

This discussion has deliberately gone somewhat far afield here in examining some of the philosophical and historical underpinnings of the present attitudes toward sexuality. It has been necessary to do so to explain the reasons for taking a dim view of attitudes toward sex that are now influential, if not totally dominant, in our society. Some of this can be detected in sexual humor.

The sex joke, or the dirty joke of any kind, has always been with us and will often appear in even the most puritanical of societies or individual groupings.

About thirty-five years ago, the *Reader's Digest,* always a politically conservative and remarkably straightlaced magazine, nevertheless frequently printed "naughty" jokes about brassieres, girdles, breasts, sex, and similar subject matter. The jokes were tame compared to what is common today, but the fact that they appeared in *Reader's Digest* at all did elicit my early interest.

To tell an off-color story is not to commit an evil act, although everything, of course, depends on the context in which the story is told. A vulgar joke is harmless if told to an audience of fifty-year-old men on a camping trip but would be highly objectionable if a fifty-year-old man told it to an audience of seven-year-old children.

But there is a major difference between sexual or scatological humor that erupts now and then, as a sort of a momentary kicking-over of the traces of sexual repression, and the heavy, constant barrage of extreme vulgarity and obscenity that no longer counterpoints popular humor but has become an essential element of it. I submit that there are factors of societal sickness involved, in that many such jokes express a strong disrespect for marriage, sexual responsibility, parental authority, women, motherhood, and moral precepts in general.

Indeed, my thesis does not even require a defense because I have never encountered the argument that the present wave of vulgarity and moral anarchy in American comedy is a sign of a wonderfully healthy society.

The overwhelming majority of both believers and nonbelievers are deeply concerned about the degree of sexual irresponsibility in our society. The chaos has partly flowed out of the Woodstock or hippie mentality of the 1960s. All the nonsense about "Do your own thing" without regard to the question whether that thing was positive or negative; the sudden, explosive growth of strange religions and cults; the ultracasualness of sexual contact; the increased and flaunted use of narcotics were all part of it. During the

1960s, many other threads of the American societal fabric also began to fray. Such relatively unimportant factors as audience behavior, table manners, wearing sensible and tasteful attire, personal neatness, the acquisition of basic factual knowledge, and the ability to speak or write in coherent sentences began to deteriorate.

I do not mean to suggest that general social and sexual irresponsibility was unknown before the 1960s—it has perplexed the human race down through the ages. What was new about the sixties was that the irresponsible behavior now found philosophical defenders. The present situation with its general ugliness—graffiti, heavy-metal "music," street violence, sexual cruelty, hate crimes—is the result.

All major philosophical camps are apparently unanimous in arguing that our society must place greater emphasis on sexual responsibility if it is not soon to be reduced to even worse chaos. Those who claim this means returning to biblical morality, however, may be assuming that the Scriptures say something different than they actually do on the question.

A strict return to biblical morality would mean that the sensible prohibitions against incest would become considerably confused. Almost everyone has given at least passing thought to the problem of the immediate descendants of Adam and Eve, since it obviously would have been impossible for them to multiply their number unless brothers had had sexual intercourse with their sisters, or perhaps even the children with their parents.

But incestuous behavior continued to be reported in a matter-of-fact manner throughout the Old Testament: Abraham married his half-sister Sarah (Gen. 20:12); Lot's daughters had intercourse with him, which they initiated (Gen. 19:30–38); Tamar had sex with her father-in-law Judah (Gen. 38:16), to name just a few examples. (Even when laws began to be written to control the practice [see LEVITICUS 18 and 20], there was still no prohibition against a father sleeping with his daughter.) Only after the passage of many centuries did genetic biologists advise us that the forbidding of incest is perfectly sound since such close breeding among humans can have unfortunate hereditary effects.

Another example of ancient biblical morality applying to sex that would certainly never be accepted by either modern religious or secular Americans concerns prostitution. Over the centuries the Israelites narrowed their view of the practice, but earlier we find it not only tolerated but also incorporated into religious custom, as in the case of the "sacred prostitutes" whose bases of operation were certain houses of worship. Perhaps the prominent fundamentalist clergymen who were implicated in public sex scandals in the late 1980s might perceive certain merits in the revival of such ancient customs. However, since the fundamentalist majority would regard with horror any modern attempt to affiliate prostitution with religion, they ought either to abandon or greatly modify their calls for "a return to biblical morality."

As regards unmarried persons having sexual relations with others—married or unmarried—the laws given in Deuteronomy chapter 22 were strict and severe. Although believers today sometimes accept—or at least don't strongly criticize—betrothed couples engaging in sexual relations before the ceremony, in biblical times the mandated punishment for such behavior was death.

Masturbation. Another point that has confused the minds of the great majority of Christians concerns the question whether the quite natural and common practice of masturbation is either morally neutral or gravely sinful. Considering the almost morbid fascination with sexual themes evident in the writing of some authors of Scripture, it is odd that *there seem to be no references to masturbation as evil in any of the Bible's sixty-six books.*

There has been considerable controversy through the centuries as to whether the story of Onan (Gen. 38:4–10) represents an act of masturbation, but I tend to agree with many clergymen and biblical scholars who feel this was not masturbation, at least not in the generally accepted interpretation of the word, but more likely interrupted coitus. This is yet another case of controversy caused by Scripture being unclear on a point.

Even though the forbidding of masturbation lacks a biblical basis, the Catholic church inculcated a morbid guilt about the act in its youthful adherents through horrifying lectures and sermons. The point was by no means simply to convey the lesson that masturbation was wrong in the sense, say, that rudeness or shoplifting were wrong. No, indeed; the lesson was that to indulge in solitary sexual activity was one of the most horrible sins imaginable, and that millions, moreover, were presently roasting in the literal flames of hell solely because of their habituation to the practice.

The true evil of such teaching, sad to say, is that whereas one can easily learn not to be rude or to appreciate that shoplifting is an antisocial practice and therefore give up such activities, almost no one—statistically speaking—is able to stop masturbating permanently simply by an act of the will. It is of direct relevance that the body itself masturbates regardless of the will or even the conscious interest of the individual in whom such eruptions naturally occur starting around the age of thirteen, sometimes in sleep. It could also easily be argued that the emotional pressure that the thou-shalt-not teaching adds to the equation leads not to less but to more instances of the very act that is forbidden. (See also FREE WILL.)

Because of the total failure of such teaching over the centuries, even the most devout believers develop in their youth habits of compartmentalized thinking and moral deviousness. It is perhaps because of the unnatural and certainly counterproductive combined shame and guilt in which the entire drama of masturbation is played out that many are never able to acquire mature attitudes toward sex itself, with the result that both love and marriage relationships are entered into with an a priori handicap.

Due to the same causes even the mere subject of masturbation may be our society's last taboo. Think of it—there is almost no subject that is now not openly discussed and written about. Even on television, which for its first three decades was circumspect and conservative in regard to its subject matter, it is now common to hear remarkably candid discussions about rape, incest, homosexuality, lesbianism, pornography, prostitution, transvestitism, fetishism, and other modes of sexual behavior, whether normal or perverted. Even the Phil Donahue, Oprah Winfrey, Sally Jessy Raphael, and Geraldo Rivera shows had not—as of 1992—had an open discussion about masturbation, a fact that would be considered strange indeed by the proverbial unbiased visitor from another realm. When compared to rape—which everyone agrees is an enormously serious and heinous crime—masturbation is so much less important as to be hardly worth mentioning. Nevertheless, discussing this much less important form of sexual behavior makes most people ill-at-ease.

Although the Ten Commandments clearly make no mention of auto-eroticism, at one point such behavior does touch on something mentioned in the Decalogue, and that is in the instruction on the evil of coveting one's neighbor's wife. Strictly interpreted, this would of course permit the unlimited sexual coveting of all the unmarried women of the world. When we turn from theory to reality and are aware that almost all acts of masturbation are accompanied by the automatic creation of imaginary images, we realize that that portion of the human psyche that gives rise to sexual fantasies has not the slightest interest in the question whether the object of such a fantasy is married. So however the matter is construed we are merely dealing with one more moral question concerning which the often-demanded "return to biblical morality" is of no practical use whatever. (See also CHRONICLES, THE FIRST BOOK OF THE; CHRONICLES, THE SECOND BOOK OF THE; EUTHANASIA; EZRA; HOMOSEXUALITY; SITUATIONAL ETHICS; SUICIDE.)

N

NAHUM. No one has any idea who Nahum was, or even if such a person ever existed. In the first verse of the book, we find him identified as an Elkoshite, which makes us none the wiser since there is no present knowledge of such a community, although some scholars have placed it in southwestern Judah. It is interesting that the name *Nahum* means *comfort* or *compassion* since, unlike other biblical prophets who decry the sins of the people, this one contents himself with predictions of disaster.

As a predictor of the future Nahum is of little account. As a poet, however, he is a genius. Many think his poetry is the most remarkable in the Hebrew Scriptures. If judged as such, the three short chapters of Nahum are brilliant and colorful.

Consider verses 5 and 6 from chapter 3:

> "I am against you," says the Lord of Hosts.
> "I will uncover your breasts to your disgrace
> And expose your naked body to every nation,
> To every kingdom your shame.
> I will cast loathsome filth over you,
> I will count you obscene,
> to treat you like excrement."

It is easy to recognize the poetic vividness of the text. But it is also both vulgar and morally unappealing as the prophet seems to be gloating over the coming destruction of Nineveh. Few scholars today believe that such loathsome references to human feces are a direct quotation of God.

Because the average Bible reader of the present day finds a peculiar

265

glamour in the names of ancient communities, one must force oneself to perceive that they do indeed represent actual cities resided in by living human beings. Once we have done this, then we can ask ourselves: What would we think today if at a Sunday morning Christian service a clergyman stood up and with eyes agleam recited a poem in which he looked forward with relish to the actual physical destruction of, say, San Francisco or Chicago, using such words as *vengeance, wrath,* and *fury?* Would we think the speaker admirable? (See also LANGUAGE, BIBLICAL; POETRY IN THE BIBLE.)

NATURE. Imagine a particular group of Christians prepared to argue that nature—which as everyone knows is a composite of beautiful, boundless oceans; colorful skies; serene mountain ranges; lovely flowers; the perfumes of spring; and other such delectable wonders—is, in some direct sense the handiwork of God. If we begin by not questioning the assumption that there is a God, then it does seem somehow poetically reasonable to thank that God for the beauties just described.

Let us leave that first warm group of Christians for a moment and travel now, in our imaginations, to a second assembly hall occupied by another party of equally spiritual Christians. Let us take up with this second group the question whether it is not correct to describe such phenomena as earthquakes, lightning bolts, hurricanes, tornadoes, bacterial plagues, viral infections, volcanic explosions, harmful genetic mutations, cancerous growths, and the like as part of the natural order. Again there will be unanimous agreement on the point.

Now let us imagine bringing these two separate communities into a third meeting hall. Envision the dismay the combined groups will feel when they learn that they have been tricked into agreeing with the logically inevitable conclusion that it is Almighty God whom we have to thank for not only the beauty but the violent destructiveness of natural phenomena.

Nature is far from being a nicely balanced system; it is, in fact, constantly at war with itself. Nature on the rampage destroys other aspects of nature. Millions of nature's animals, day and night, devour large numbers of other sensitive creatures alive. Water is a part of nature and so is fire, but one extinguishes the other. Even among nature's supreme children—humans—the way of the world is ceaseless competition often escalating to warfare.

The vast planetary tragedy is further compounded as one *part* of an individual wars with another part of that same creature. Our stomachs, for example, if they are deprived of food and drink, will after a time literally begin to feed on nutrients stored in other parts of our anatomy. Our nervous system frequently attacks our other systems. Every DISEASE is as much a part of nature as every mountain, cloud, or tree.

There is nothing simple in any of this. The very things on which we must depend for life not only can—but also do—daily destroy us, by the millions.

Consider gravity. We cannot live without it. Were it suddenly to be turned off we should all either fly at once off into space or be quickly crushed against the ceilings and roofs under which we might at such moment find ourselves. In every moment of time, nevertheless, gravity plucks thousands from cliffs, window ledges, tree limbs, buildings under construction, flying vehicles, and other posts, and plunges them to their death.

None of us could long live without sunlight, but the sun, too, is a heartless killer that destroys us by inducing cancerous growths on our skins, driving us mad with thirst, or drying up the streams and lakes that sustain us.

Air is obviously a basic requirement for the continuation of life, but it, too, daily causes cruel tortures to underwater divers and, concentrating itself into a moving form—as tornadoes, hurricanes, or other storms—decimates neighborhoods.

So it is for all animal life. For man alone, however, is reserved a further exquisite torture in that even such tenderly beautiful aspects of life as love and sex can lead to the most tragic suffering and death, as we learn to our daily sorrow.

Whether such realities rule out the possibility of a conscious God is a question that can be debated separately. But such penalties do rule out any simplistic, Sunday-school nature-is-God view of the divine power. (See also FREE WILL; MIRACLES; SCIENCE AND RELIGION.)

NUMBERS, THE BOOK OF. The original name that the Jews gave to this book is *Bemidhbar,* which means *in the wilderness.* Its misnomer came about because the Greek translators of the Old Testament, noting the opening references to military censuses, called the book by a word that, translated into English, is *Numbers.*

Whatever its proper name, Numbers is one of the least edifying books of the Bible. The best scholarship now contends that the figures in its census lists are absolutely worthless. Comments John L. McKenzie, S.J.:

> The census lists can hardly represent Israel in the period of the desert sojourn. W. F. Albright has proposed that they come from the period of David, who was probably the first to make a census of Israel (2 S. 24); the numbers, he believes, suit Israel of this period very well.

Although they were allegedly taken forty years apart, each census lists something over 600,000 adult males as able "to go to war." Observes Isaac Azimov:

> If one counts in the women and children, the "mixed multitude" or half-breed hangers-on to whom the Bible occasionally refers, one gets the picture of some two million people wandering about the Sinai Peninsula. This seems *implausibly large,* considering this is more than the number of Israelites in the Davidic Kingdom at its height. One suspects that the numbers represent a *later tradition of questionable accuracy.* (IA)

Chapter 3. We are asked here to believe that God personally dictated a considerable portion of early sections of the book of Numbers since a great many passages begin with the phrase "The Lord spoke to Moses and said. . . ." Assuming the existence of God, it would be fortunate indeed if (1) he spoke to Moses and (2) either Moses or one of his associates had written down the exact words spoken. We may be quite sure that this did not happen since a good many of the statements attributed to God are absurd, illogical, stupid, or otherwise unworthy of a divine source. Consider by way of illustration:

> 11. The Lord spake to Moses and said:
> 12. "I take the Levites for myself. Out of all the Israelites.
> 13. "The Levites shall be mine. *For every eldest child, if a boy, became mine when I destroyed all the eldest sons of Egypt.* So I have consecrated to myself all the firstborn in Israel, both man *and beast.* They shall be mine. I am the Lord." (IA)

The unknown authors of such passages ask us to believe that God personally killed unknown thousands of innocent Egyptian children and young men—certainly one of the worst mass murders in history if it did indeed occur. Further, it is senseless to suggest that *because* of such an atrocity the firstborn male child of every Israelite woman was the Lord's. Apparently it has occurred to only a few scholars, over the past 2,000 years, to inquire into the *meaning* of references to one thing or another as "belonging to the Lord." If God made everything in the universe, as all believers insist, then everything *is* the Lord's.

Inanity is added to absurdity in that the passage suggests that the firstborn of animals are also of some particular interest to God.

The chapter provides a long and uninteresting list of names of the sons of Levi, their descendants, their cultic duties, and so forth. As part of all this the Lord twice more says the same thing about the eldest sons of Egypt and Israel. In one repetition, however, a new puzzlement is introduced:

> 46. "The eldest sons of Israel will outnumber the Levites by two hundred and seventy-three.
> 47. "This remainder must be ransomed, and you shall accept five shekels for each of them, taking the sacred shekel and reckoning twenty gerahs to the shekel;
> 48. "You shall give the money with which they are ransomed to Aaron and his sons."

By this device—perhaps a more effective method than Bingo—Moses raises 1,365 shekels of silver for the religious coffers.

Chapter 5. This portion of the book of Numbers has become infamous among feminists because it purports to quote God on the subject of sexually unfaithful wives while saying nothing about the same sin committed by husbands. A truly nonsensical ritual is prescribed by God in which the woman suspected of infidelity is forced by the priests to drink a vile concoction of water, dust from the floor of the tabernacle, and ink washed from a scroll. The priest calls down upon the unfortunate woman's head a curse, presumably guaranteeing that if she has indeed been guilty of adultery the drinking of the liquid will cause her to have a miscarriage.

Most women who commit adultery do not become pregnant as a result. The prescribed ritual could therefore have no effect in such cases. To the extent that a sensitive pregnant woman might be terrified by the dramatic procedure, however, it is possible that her hysteria could induce a miscarriage even if she were totally innocent and had become pregnant by her husband. Oddly, this chapter of Scripture has not been introduced into the modern debate on the subject of ABORTION, for there is no mistaking that the author's intent here is *to quote God as authorizing abortion.*

The entire passage is nonsense. If it refers to an actual ritual we can at least be grateful that it is no longer practiced. (See also CURSING; RITUAL, WOMEN'S LIBERATION.)

Chapter 6. Most of this chapter deals with the bizarre rules applying to individuals known as *Nazirites* (or *Nazarites,* according to the King James Version). The name comes from the Hebrew word meaning *one set apart or of high rank.* This group sought to isolate themselves from the world for a specific period of time of renunciation in an effort to be holy. In later centuries groups of Christians called monks have done the same and, of course, so have monks of Oriental and other non-Christian religions.

The Nazirite observed a primary abstinence from "wine and strong drink," which is understandable enough since we know drunkenness can cause blurred perception, something that might be detrimental to the state of meditation or sanctity that the Nazirites observed. But no religious sect today—no matter how strict—requires its adherents to refrain from eating grapes or raisins, as does this one (see verse 3), nor do we know of any *reason* that this should be the case.

Other nonsensical instructions given to the Nazirites are (1) he shall not have his hair cut or trimmed during the term of his vow but shall let it grow long enough to plait, and (2) he shall touch no dead body, not even that of his immediate family. This latter command is followed by a description of the cleansing ritual required of the Nazirite who is so unfortunate as to be *accidentally* near a person who dies suddenly: He must shave his head and bring to the priest on the eighth day a sin offering of two turtles (doves), or two young pigeons (verse 10). Then he must begin his period of renunciation all over again, letting his hair regrow and thereafter offering a year-old male lamb as a guilt offering. Guilt for what? We are not morally to blame for accidents.

The chapter next lists other valuable merchandise that the Nazirite must bring as offerings during his period of separation:

> 14. And he shall offer his offering unto the Lord, one he lamb of the first year without blemish for a burnt offering, and one ewe lamb of the first year without blemish for a sin offering, and one ram without blemish for peace offerings,
>
> 15. And a basket of unleavened bread, cakes of fine flour mingled with oil, and wafers of unleavened bread anointed with oil, and their meat offering, and their drink offerings.

Finally, at the end of his period of separation the Nazirite shall again shave his head and put the hair itself on the fire upon which his sacrifices are burned. After all this, the Nazirite may once again partake of wine. So much for principle.

Chapters 7 and 8 consist primarily of an uninteresting and unedifying inventory of gifts and offerings the Israelites presented to the Levites (priests), which included wagons and oxen, bulls, goats, rams, lambs to be used for offerings, grains, silver platters and bowls, gold trays and boxes, and incense.

Also described are the various ceremonies by which the Levites are to be dedicated to the priesthood: the shaving of their entire bodies, washing of all their clothes, and a baptism of sorts. Most of these ceremonies, too, modern believers have had the good sense to ignore.

Chapter 9. An extended miracle is now described in which, when the followers of Moses set up the tabernacle, a cloud covered it "and in the evening a brightness like fire appeared over it till morning" (v. 15).

> 17. Whenever the cloud lifted from the tent, the Israelite struck camp, and at the place where the cloud settled, there they pitched their camp.

Again and again, the chapter repeats this message—simple enough to convey however unlikely as historical fact—each time with slight variations.

Chapter 10. The Lord now tells Moses to make two trumpets of silver to be used for summoning the community and for breaking camp. In the process of instructing the followers of Moses how to use the trumpets to call for attention, the Lord makes a promise that, unfortunately, was frequently not honored.

> 9. When you go into battle against an invader and you are hard pressed by him, you shall raise a cheer when the trumpets sound, and this will serve as a reminder of you before the Lord your God, and *you will be delivered from your enemies.* (IA)

Comments William McCarthy in *Bible, Church and God* (Truth Seeker Company, Inc.):

> This is explicit, positive—God Almighty's sacred promise to protect the Jews. He didn't keep it. In the history of the world no nation, in peace or war, has been so God-forsaken as has Israel. Slaves in Egypt, slaves to the Philistines, slaves in Babylon, slaves to Syria, the Persians, the Greeks, the Turks, ten of the twelve tribes so broken up and scattered in slavery we speak of them as the "lost tribes of Israel." The other two tribes were scattered by the Romans all over the world, persecuted everywhere and robbed in most countries of the past and some of the present.

Chapter 11. God has behaved himself for a rather extended period, according to the chapters just cited, but he now reverts—so we are told— to the sort of savagery that the pentateuchal authors so often attribute to him:

> 1. There came a time when the people complained to the Lord of their hardships. When he heard he became angry and fire from the Lord broke out among them, and was raging in one end of the camp. When the people appealed to Moses he interceded with the Lord and the fire died down.

The next adventurous detail grows out of the Israelites' boredom with having to depend on *manna* as the chief staple of their diet. They remind themselves of how well they ate in Egypt. (It is good to hear that there were positive elements to their experience as slaves in that land.) Now they have an appetite for meat. The prospect of having to provide hundreds of thousands of wilderness travelers with meat understandably worries Moses, who therefore carries out one more of what we are to assume were daily conversations with God. God's solution is peculiar, though typically mean-spirited:

> 16. The Lord answered Moses, "Assemble seventy elders from Israel, men known to you as elders and officers in the community. Bring them to me at the Tent of the Presence and there let them take their stand with you."

Moses is told to say to the people,

> 19. "Ye shall not eat one day, nor two days, nor five days, neither ten days, nor twenty days;
> 20. "But even a whole month, until it come out at your nostrils, and it be loathsome unto you: because that ye have despised the Lord which is among you, and have wept before him, saying, 'Why came we forth out of Egypt?' "

Verse 20 is largely nonsense. Is the Lord telling hundreds of thousands of people that they shall eat absolutely nothing for thirty days? We know that if any appreciable number of people literally ate nothing for a full month, a good many of them would starve to death as a result. How would a loving mother or father explain to their little ones that despite their pangs of hunger and their anguished cries, they nevertheless could not be given so much as a morsel because God had so ordained? Notice, too, the references to "it" coming out of the nostrils of the people. What in God's name is supposed to be represented by the word *it* no one has ever known.

Now Moses has the audacity to question the ability of the Lord to do this, to remind God—as if a Supreme Being would need to be reminded of anything—that there are 600,000 men alone in their party, and undoubtedly a greater number of women and children. God naturally replies, "When did I become weak? Now you shall see whether my words come true or not" (v. 23). The quotation makes the creator sound like a petulant child.

In any event, God's solution is ingenious. He causes a wind to come and it "rains" quails on the camp until they are piled up three-feet deep over the entire area. The people, understandably, immediately rush to consume the gift of meat the Lord has thus provided. By now we should not be surprised to read what happens next:

> 33. But the meat was scarcely between their teeth, and they had not so much as bitten it, when the Lord's anger broke out against the people and he struck them with a deadly plague.
> 34. That place was called Kibrothhattaavah because there *they buried the people who had been greedy for meat.* (IA)

At the present moment people are greedy for meat all over the planet, but we should be very surprised if any Jewish or Christian clergyman suggested that those who longed to eat a juicy hamburger, a well-cooked steak, or perhaps some roast beef not only ought to be punished but in fact should also be made subject to the death penalty. We are not told how many thousands of unfortunate souls were buried during this incident. If we were we should not believe the number because the story is preposterous in all its elements.

Chapter 12. The Israelites now begin to criticize Moses for his interracial marriage; they question why God speaks through such a man and not to them directly.

No scholar of standing today maintains that Moses wrote all the books attributed to him, and many doubt that he wrote any of them. In this chapter we are face-to-face with a passage that was one of the first to plant seeds of doubt in the minds of those theretofore convinced of the Mosaic authorship of Numbers:

> 3. (Now the man Moses was very meek, above all the men which were upon the face of the earth.)

As Thomas Paine rightly observes, "If Moses said this of himself, instead of being the meekest of men, he was one of the most vain and arrogant of coxcombs."

In any event, the story continues in verse 4 where we are told that the Lord summons Moses, Aaron, and Miriam to the tabernacle where he makes an imposing entrance "in a pillar of a cloud." In an angry *poem* God basically tells them that Moses alone is faithful, which is why he communicates with him not in visions or dreams as he has with all the other prophets, but "face-to-face, openly and not in riddles." (Elsewhere, of course, the Bible tells us no one has ever seen God.)

To emphasize the point he strikes Miriam with a hideous skin disease. Although both Miriam and Aaron have been critical of Moses, it is only Miriam—the woman—who is punished. Had the Bible been written by women the story would no doubt have been different.

The sight of the unfortunate woman is so shocking that Moses begs God to heal her. Instead, the Lord refers to another nonsensical custom:

> 14. Suppose her father had spat in her face, would she not have to remain in disgrace for seven days? Let her be kept for seven days in confinement outside the camp and then be brought back.

Let the reader imagine that in his own time and place a father commits an outrageous offense of actually spitting on the face of his daughter. Suppose that witnesses intervene and separate the two. Any unbiased person present would naturally wonder what might be a suitable punishment for the father. Imagine our astonishment at being told that the man was in no danger of punishment, and, moreover, that it was the poor daughter—his victim— who had to "remain in disgrace" for a full week outside the community. Perhaps our fundamentalist friends who make daily appeals for a return to the morality of the Bible might clarify this particular reference for us.

Chapter 13. Concerning the Israelite invasion of Canaan in the thirteenth century B.C., Father Bruce Vawter (in *A Path Through Genesis*) makes what will seem to all but scholars a remarkable observation:

> The Israelites entered Canaan . . . as conquerors, but conquerors so little to the manner born that their success . . . would convince us that *their destiny was wholly of their own devising. . . . In everything that is humane and cultivated they were the inferiors of the peoples who they destroyed or enslaved, painfully, over a period of two centuries.* Archaeologists have learned to detect the signs of the Israelites' conquest in the burnt and broken masonry of skilled workmanship which lies beneath the crude and slavish imitation laid by later hands. Whoever is unduly sensitive to a spectacle of this sort will not regard the Israelite invasion as much different from the pillage of Rome by the barbarians from the North. (IA)

Dr. Vawter nevertheless then proceeds to justify the Israelite conquest by observing that although the Canaanites were culturally superior, they had "a decadent morality and a religion of vain observance." Since there seems little or no record of large-scale virtuous social behavior in any ancient civilizations, this was almost certainly the case. The only serious question concerns the degree, if any, to which the behavior of the Israelites was in any significant sense superior to that of those they conquered and slaughtered.

Chapter 14. The Israelites, understandably apprehensive over reports by certain of their spies of the great stature and strength of the inhabitants of the land they hope to occupy, again begin to doubt the authority of Moses and Aaron. Caleb and Joshua support Moses and Aaron against the doubters, and the Lord apparently jumps into the debate. As usual the human authors of the relevant passages portray him as a bad-tempered bully. In verse 12 he threatens to strike the people with pestilence—at least a decipherable threat—and to disinherit them, a warning the meaning of which is not clear.

Moses, sensibly enough, addresses the Lord as any ruffian ought to be addressed, by attempting, albeit illogically, to show him the error of his ways:

15. "Now if thou dost kill this people as one man, then the nations who have heard thy fame will say,
16. " 'Because the Lord was not able to bring this people into the land which he swore to give to them, therefore he has slain them in the wilderness.'
17. "And now, I pray thee, let the power of the Lord be great as thou has promised, saying,
18. " 'The Lord is slow to anger, and abounding in steadfast love, forgiving iniquity and transgression.' "

Verse 18 seems to be describing a different God from he to whom we have been introduced in most of the rest of the Old Testament. This God—or so we are instructed—after considering the argument of Moses, changes his mind! He does, however, petulantly cling to at least part of his threat by saying,

21. "But truly, as I live, and as all the earth shall be filled with the glory of the Lord.
22. "None of the men who have seen my glory, and my signs which I wrought in Egypt and in the wilderness, and yet have put me to the proof these ten times and have not hearkened to my voice;
23. "Shall see the land which I swore to give to their fathers; and none of those who despise me shall see it."

God not only stipulates that untold thousands of adults—perhaps the majority of those who came out of Egypt—shall in the end die in the wilderness, without ever having seen the Promised Land, but his habitual cruelty flashes forth again when he says:

33. "And your children shall be shepherds in the wilderness forty years and shall suffer for your faithlessness, until the last of your dead bodies lies in the wilderness."

Study this curse that the authors of the chapter have attributed to God. Its harsh, cruel, and vengeful emotional coloration resembles one of Hitler's diatribes in the present century.

In yet one more instance, therefore, we have seen conduct attributed to God—by definition the embodiment of all virtue—that would rightly merit any human king the reputation of an irrational and bloodthirsty tyrant. So inescapably do the given factors of the case lead to this conclusion that one must observe that no actual tyrant known to history has ever been guilty of one-hundredth of the crimes, massacres, and other atrocities attributed to the Deity in the Bible.

No fair-minded student of the biblical record, who makes an earnest effort to let that record speak for itself, can fail to conclude that the Bible is, in the most literal sense, the greatest insult to God ever perpetrated.

Chapter 15. If one encountered the substantive contents of this chapter outside the context of the Bible, one would assume that, to the extent it could be considered religious at all, it might be associated with the superstitious ritual of an ancient, primitive African, South American, or Australian tribe. It chiefly concerns the circumstances under which offerings are to be made to the Lord.

In one sort of situation a young bull is to be burnt. In another case only a male goat is considered suitable. In yet another, only a female goat. Perhaps the most important commentary one could make about such nonsense is that the most orthodox and devout of the Jews themselves abandoned such bloody customs centuries ago. Certainly the most pious rabbi of any temple on the attractive Wilshire Boulevard of my home city would think it an act of criminality if one came into his place of worship and began slaughtering and burning animals.

In addition to this sort of inanity, cruelty and savagery appear throughout the chapter:

32. While the people of Israel were in the wilderness, they found a man gathering sticks on the Sabbath day.
33. And those who found him gathering sticks brought him to Moses and Aaron and to all the congregation.
34. They put him in custody, because it had not been made plain what should be done with him.
35. And the Lord said to Moses, "The man shall be put to death. All the congregation shall stone him with stones outside the camp."

Again, it is instructive—and certainly to a degree edifying—that the pious orthodox Jews of the twentieth century would not dream of ordering the death penalty for one who performed casual labor on the Sabbath and would, in fact, call the police and have arrested any fellow Jew who thought that he should personally murder the individual guilty of such an alleged offense.

If the Jews of today are right about this, then it follows that the Lord God was *wrong* in recommending a morally opposite action.

But since the Almighty—by definition—cannot be the author of any wrong whatsoever, it follows that this story, like hundreds of similar tales, is not only a falsehood but again a tale supremely insulting to God.

Chapter 16. More vile savagery is perpetrated—by God, we are again told—after a group of 250 Jewish leaders announce that in their view Moses and Aaron are taking too much authority upon themselves. Moses, of course, runs to God at once complaining about the insubordination. The Lord, apparently surprised by the news, becomes so angry that he says,

> 21. "Separate yourselves from among this congregation, that I may consume them in a moment."

Moses relays the customary sadistic threat to the congregation, after which—we are asked to believe—God punishes *not only the insubordinate leaders, but also the members of their families, including innocent infants unable to walk.*

> 31. And as he finished speaking all these words, the ground under them split asunder,
> 32. And the earth opened its mouth and swallowed them up, with their households and all the men that belonged to Korah and all their goods.
> 33. So they and all that belonged to them went down alive into Sheol; and the earth closed over them and they perished from the midst of the assembly.
> 34. And all Israel that were around about them fled at their cry; for they said, "Lest the earth swallow us up!"
> 35. And fire came forth from the Lord and consumed the 250 men offering the incense.

I have held a life-long disgust for the casual ease with which writers who consider themselves religious and who spend their lives speculating and writing about religious matters can discuss the burning of human flesh. Anyone who has either seen a human being burned or witnessed the piteous and terrible results of such a tragedy will surely have a more realistic grasp of the subject than the mindless theologians and prophets who actually speak with *approval* about such torture. When anyone tells me that God himself—in this instance and in countless others in biblical text—inflicted such pain on 250 of his chosen people, I respond that the man who relates such a story is either a liar or a dunce. In either case the individual certainly represents a model of insensitivity to human suffering.

If we assume that there is a God, it follows that the tellers of such tales are the worst blasphemers imaginable when they attribute to the Deity a viciousness far beyond the power of most humans to inflict.

The remainder of chapter 16—incredibly enough—tells us that on the very next day *God personally slaughtered 14,700 Jews,* whose capital offense was that of criticizing Moses and Aaron for their hand in the hideous slaughter of the day before! So much for the social ideal of freedom of speech.

Chapter 17. Here we again find Aaron's authority being questioned. This time God supposedly plans a miracle to convince the people that Aaron is the chosen leader so that they will stop their complaining: He has each of the Twelve Tribes deliver a wooden stick with their leader's name on it. Aaron's name is to be put on the stick designated for the tribe of Levites. God then says that only one of the sticks will have buds by morning; and the person whose name appears on that stick is to be considered the Lord's choice to rule the Israelites.

After the deed is done, Aaron's stick not only buds, but the buds also blossom and grow almonds.

Alas, this plan of the all-knowing God apparently fails because the people continue to grumble:

> 12. And the children of Israel spake unto Moses, saying, "Behold, we die, we perish, we all perish.
> 13. "Whosoever cometh any thing near unto the tabernacle of the Lord shall die: shall we be consumed with dying?"

Their lamenting doesn't even make sense in this case; remarkably, in this latest demonstration from God no one has been killed.

Chapter 18. This portion of Numbers, we are asked to believe, consists almost entirely of direct quotations attributed to God as he gives full authority for the care of the sanctuary to Aaron and his sons, alone among the Levites. That the assignment will be profitable is made clear enough:

8. The Lord God said to Aaron, "I, the Lord, commit to your control the contributions made to me, that is all the holy gifts of the Israelites. . . .

9. "Out of the most holy gifts kept back from the altar fire, this part shall belong to you: every offering, whether grain offering, sin offering, or guilt offering . . . belongs to you and your sons. You shall eat it as befits most holy gifts; every male may eat it. . . .

12. "I give you all the choicest of the oil, the choicest of the new wine and the corn, the first fruits which are given to the Lord. . . .

14. "Everything in Israel which has been devoted to God shall be yours."

Since in other portions of Scripture we are told that God requires all sacrifices and gifts to him to be perfect, pure, and unblemished, it remains to question how any can, therefore, be considered the "choicest."

Chapter 19 consists entirely of the most incredible mumbo-jumbo and superstition. It is no more morally edifying, or even illustrative of common sense, than the voodoo jungle ritual that Western civilization otherwise regards with benign contempt. For two thousand years Christian missionaries have sought to induce primitive tribesmen of Africa, Asia, Australia, South America, and remote islands to put aside their rituals. But Christianity itself— as its most devout adherents concede—has no validity unless it grows out of a divinely inspired Old Testament. Alas for Christian consistency, the Old Testament gives numerous examples of the very same religious nonsense so characteristic of primitive and unlettered tribal theology and ritual.

We may take the disinterested or even charitable anthropological approach and appreciate primitive cultures on their own terms. This is precisely what we should do; we never take seriously the jungle, outback, or mountain witch doctors' or priests' claims that their peculiar and often bizarre forms of belief and practice are directly authenticated by God. For precisely the same reasons we should refuse to take seriously a great many of the Old Testament's claims to divine endorsement.

Chapter 20. Perfectly respectable Bible scholars—Christians and Jews— have observed that certain portions of the Scriptures simply make no sense. A relevant instance is the story of the lack of water in Kadish. Once again, we are told, the people have blamed Moses for their predicament. He, as usual, turns to God, who instructs him that he need only tap a nearby rock with his walking stick to produce great quantities of water:

10. And Moses and Aaron gathered the congregation together before the rock and he [Moses] said unto them, "Hear now, ye rebels; must we fetch you water out of this rock?"

11. And Moses lifted up his hand, and with his rod he smote the

rock twice: and the water came out abundantly, and the congregation drank, and their beasts also.

But now note what the Lord says.

12. And the Lord said to Moses and Aaron, "Because you did not believe in me, to sanctify me in the eyes of the people of Israel, therefore you shall not bring this assembly into the land which I have given them."

Whether either man deserved such a punishment is a debatable question; perhaps Aaron did after his calf forging reported in Exodus, but the curse is harsh as regards Moses, who had certainly rendered heroically important service to the Lord. (See also CALF OF GOLD.)

In the latter part of the chapter we are asked to believe that God reminded Moses that Aaron was not to enter the promised land but rather instructs Moses to

25. "Take Aaron and Eleazar his son, and bring them up unto mount Hor:

26. "And strip Aaron of his garments, and put them upon Eleazar his son: and Aaron shall be gathered unto his people, and shall die there."

Moses follows these instructions, leaving the aged Aaron to die, naked, upon the top of the mountain. What moral lesson is to be learned from this peculiar story the reader may decide for himself.

Chapter 21. Sometime thereafter the Israelites again begin to grumble, but notice that there is a discrepancy in their quoted complaint:

5. And the people spake against God, and against Moses, "Wherefore have ye brought us up out of Egypt to die in the wilderness? for *there is no bread,* neither is there any water; and our soul *loatheth this light bread.*

Such contradictions are, of course, consistent with the hypothesis of human authorship, but inconsistent with that of divine authority. In any event, according to the text, the Lord then shows his regard for his Chosen People in what will by now be seen as his customary way:

6. Then the Lord sent fiery serpents among the people, and they bit the people, so that many people of Israel died.

Why serpents? And why did they need to be aflame?

Inasmuch as the tribes themselves at this point numbered hundreds of thousands, it is reasonable to suppose, from the use of the word *many,* that a large number were killed in this horrible fashion, though it would have been a despicable enough punishment had only one person been so victimized.

At this point in the narrative we are asked to believe that the Lord once more repented of what he had done, took pity on the people (at least after Moses entreated him to), and offered what is—if one may believe the book of Numbers—a typically bizarre divine solution to a problem that never would have existed had the Deity not willed it in the first place.

> 8. And the Lord said to Moses, "Make a fiery serpent, and set it on a pole; and everyone who is bitten, when he sees it, shall live."
> 9. And Moses made a serpent of brass, and put it upon a pole, and it came to pass, that if a serpent had bitten any man, when he beheld the serpent of brass, he lived.

It can profit the reader to contemplate this passage. For any remotely reasonable God, it would have sufficed simply to terminate the existence of the horde of flaming snakes he had created. But he chose not to do this. Nor did he elect the alternative of suggesting that the people fall to their knees, confess whatever sin they were supposed to have committed, and affirm their belief in the authority of both God and Moses.

Again, nothing so relatively reasonable is suggested. Instead the reader is asked to accept an Arabian Nights sort of plot-twist according to which Moses is credited with the ability to perform a remarkable feat of crafts-manship. (It requires great proficiency to make anything whatever out of raw metal, which is why the task is always performed by trained specialists.)

Even if one were to accept the implication that Moses had such technical competence, it would be reasonable to expect the Deity to have instructed him to form some object of religious significance to the Israelites, something that could provide edification to the people. Instead we are told that he manufactures a *pagan* symbol—a snake—and sets it atop a tall stick. How he made the brass object burn—well, is comment really necessary?

It is useless, of course—albeit very reasonable given the precedents in the Pentateuch—for a scholar to entertain the thought that looking at a metal snake on a stick would cure anything, except perhaps boredom. If one posits an all-powerful Deity who frequently meddles in the affairs of one particular, obscure tribe, then it can hardly be argued that such a Deity could not offer any instruction whatever or perform any remarkable physical feat however bizarre, incomprehensible, or impossible.

It is easy enough to laugh at such preposterous tales—as Voltaire, Thomas Paine, Mark Twain, H. L. Mencken, and numerous others have done. The modern reader's laughter must cease when he pauses to reflect that scores of millions of American conservatives, staunch political workers on behalf of Barry Goldwater, Ronald Reagan, Pat Robertson, Dan Quayle, Pat Buchanan, and others, absolutely insist that every word of such accounts is not only equally as true as a news item that one might hear this evening on the authority of Peter Jennings or Ted Koppel, but in fact also has a far greater guarantee of its truth in that its inspiration comes from God himself.

Such ignorance and credulity are connected with the political and social dilemmas that plague our nation.

In any event, such a curative as looking at a brass object—the forming of which is clearly a violation of the divine commandment forbidding the making of graven images—could have been effective only for those who happened to enjoy the good fortune of being within perhaps a few hundred yards of the bronze idol when they were bitten by the poisonous reptiles. For those Israelites attacked on the other side of the nearest mountain, or at a considerable distance down the road, the method can have had no effect, to judge purely by the factors given in chapter 21.

Chapter 23. Here we find the people of Moab, including the Midianites, who, upon seeing the vast horde of Israelites tramping toward their land, quite sensibly become afraid. They send a delegation to Balaam to enlist the help of his nation against the invaders. Balaam tells the delegation he will consider their request and give them an answer the following morning.

> 9. And God came unto Balaam, and said, "What men are these with thee?"

Why would an all-knowing God have to ask such a question in the first place? Balaam explains the situation, whereupon God advises Balaam not to help the Moabites and Midianites against the Israelites.

Morning comes and Balaam gives the delegation from Moab his answer. The delegates return to their land and inform Balak, their leader, that Balaam will not fight. Balak is not satisfied with this answer and sends another delegation out. Balaam again consults with the Lord about what to do, and *God changes his mind.* This time he tells Balaam to go with the delegation (v. 20).

Acting on the Lord's new instructions, Balaam rides out with the men the next day. Read what happens:

22. And God's anger was kindled because he went: and the angel of the Lord stood in the way for an adversary against him. . . .

How can it make any sense to say that God was angry with Balaam for going out with the delegation when only a moment earlier, we are told, God instructed Balaam to do so? Even today writers make such mistakes, but professional editors customarily detect them and prevent their publication by making simple corrections. Why cannot the Bible, too, be edited and corrected so as to avoid the embarrassment its present form occasions? Simply because its most vociferous defenders insist it is already perfect and nothing perfect ought to be subject to any sort of revision.

The following verses tell how the angel (which apparently only the frightened donkey can see) continues to block the path. Balaam tries to keep the animal on course, but it keeps balking away from the spirit being. Finally the travelers come to a narrow place where it is no longer possible for the mule to step around the invisible messenger.

27. And when the ass saw the angel of the Lord, she fell down under Balaam: and Balaam's anger was kindled, and he smote the ass with a staff.
28. And the Lord opened the mouth of the ass, and she said unto Balaam, "What have I done unto thee, that thou hast smitten me these three times?"
29. And Balaam said unto the ass, "Because thou hast mocked me: I would there were a sword in mine hand, for now would I kill thee."
30. And the ass said unto Balaam, "Am not I thine ass, upon which thou hast ridden ever since I was thine unto this day? was I ever wont to do so unto thee?" And he said, "Nay."

If an animal spoke to most human beings, they would be absolutely flabbergasted. And yet the author of this chapter of Numbers asks us to believe that Balaam doesn't blink an eye but converses with the beast as if it were the most natural thing in the world.

Many readers will remember the television comedy series of the 1960s called "Mr. Ed." It was a clever little show, but not for one minute did anyone watching believe the horse really talked. That the author here asks us to believe precisely that—and that millions of adult fundamentalists firmly believe him—is yet one more example of absurdity.

In any event, Balaam is now suddenly able to see the Lord's angel and repents, although it is not clear for what the poor man is repenting since he was only doing what the Lord had instructed him to do in the first place. But he does nevertheless offer at this point to return home.

283

But does God say, "Good. Do that"? No. Instead he repeats his earlier instruction, which Balaam was already following. So what was the point of the entire talking-ass story?

Chapter 23 follows Balaam to his meeting with the Moab king Balak where, upon the direction of the Lord, he recites a blessing on the Israelites rather than a curse as Balak has expected. Balak takes him to another spot and points out another group of Israelites in the desert below and asks Balaam to curse at least that portion of the invaders.

Notice what Balaam says:

> 19. "God is not a man, that he should lie; neither the son of man, that he should repent: hath he said, and shall he not do it? or hath he spoken, and shall he not make it good? . . ."

Balaam must be talking about a God different from the one most of the Old Testament authors are writing about when they report on numerous occasions that God has done precisely that.

Chapter 25. In the present day there is an enormous amount of both conversion and falling away. People switch their religious allegiances by the millions. If God has any interest in this large, seething process—which would be reasonable to expect—there would appear to be no visible evidence of his displeasure. This is in striking contrast to the way he reacted only a few thousands years ago, if we believe Old Testament accounts.

> 3. And Israel joined himself unto Baalpeor: and the anger of the Lord was kindled against Israel.
> 4. And the Lord said unto Moses, "Take all the heads of the people, and hang them up before the Lord against the sun, that the fierce anger of the Lord may be turned away from Israel."

Moses communicates this message to the judges of his community. As a result all those who worshipped the Moabites' gods were immediately put to death and, even more horrible, their heads publicly displayed. This allegedly divine decree leads to two possible conclusions: (1) God never said anything so savage, or (2) if he did, then we live in a truly cursed universe presided over by a homicidal maniac. Obviously it is the former of the two possibilities that is the more reasonable to accept, even though that acceptance means that either Moses was a liar, or—as seems more likely—the unknown authors of such passages told one more untruth about him.

Another outrage is referred to beginning in verse 6, when we are told the story of the Israelite Zimri and his Midianite wife Cozbi, whom Zimri brings to the tabernacle, perhaps wishing to convert her to the Jewish religion. The priest Phinehas, however, does not greet the woman as a soul to be welcomed to the fold. Instead he:

> 7. . . . took a javelin in his hand;
> 8. And he went after the man of Israel into the tent, and thrust both of them through, the man of Israel, and the woman through her belly.

Supposedly this was to keep a plague from killing the Israelites, although in verse 9 we read that 24,000 died anyway.

As if this were not a hideous enough assertion, Moses says—supposedly on the authority of God—that because of what Phinehas has done he will be *rewarded,* and in a most dramatic way:

> 12. Wherefore say, "Behold, I give unto him my covenant of peace:
> 13. And he shall have it, and his seed after him, even the covenant of an everlasting priesthood; . . ."

In the present day, practically the entire civilized world is shocked by outrages and terrorist atrocities committed by Muslim fanatics who feel not the slightest guilt in killing innocent bystanders because they are secure in their belief that they are doing God's work. If we are right to be angered and dismayed by such dangerous irrationality today, then how can we possibly approve even worse crimes said to be committed by God and his Chosen People only a few thousands years ago?

Chapter 31. Although there are more than enough mass atrocities recorded in both ancient and modern history, there are *none* that exceed in villainy the massacre of the Midianites.

The reader must, at this point, open his own copy of the Scriptures and refer to the text; otherwise what I am about to say will appear preposterous. Here we are faced with not one of those almost casual references to a criminal atrocity, with which the Bible sadly abounds, but with a detailed account of a particular military engagement. The reader of such details is faced with a choice. He must conclude that either Moses was in the most literal sense a far worse monster than any totalitarian despot known to history or that the thirty-first chapter of Numbers is an outrageous fantasy.

Midian was by no means an area regarded as a natural enemy of Israel for centuries. It was the home of the father of one of Moses' wives and the land where Moses himself had lived as a fugitive after committing his first murder.

Second, the Midian area was hundreds of miles away from the Israelite encampment at the time the reported incidents are alleged to have taken place and therefore offered no threat to God's Chosen People. Even so:

1. The Lord spake unto Moses, saying,
2. "Avenge the children of Israel of the Midianites: afterward shalt thou be gathered unto thy people."

Moses immediately assembles a fighting force of precisely 12,000 soldiers and instructs them to travel hundreds of miles to do battle with the unsuspecting Midianites. Among those reportedly slain in the resulting massacre, as Joseph Wheless observes in *Is It God's Word?* is "poor old Balaam, him of the talking ass—though he lived hundreds of miles away at Pethor in Mesopotamia." Balaam—the same one who just a few chapters previous we have read blessed the Israelite people three times, turning down great riches and incurring the wrath of King Balak in so doing.

After perpetrating wholesale slaughter on the men of Midian and burning all the towns and villages thereof, the followers of Moses took "all the women of Midian captives, and their little ones, and took the spoil of all their cattle, and all their flocks, and all their goods."

Because—as we've seen earlier—there is something about the archaic phraseology of the various scriptural styles that tends to put something of an impenetrable glaze on the mind of the casual reader, it is necessary to sift out and state in the simplest possible terms the inventory of the pillage taken by the Israelites: about 200,000 women and children captives and some 808,000 animals, including 675,000 sheep, over 72,000 cattle, over 61,000 asses. (See also LANGUAGE OF THE BIBLE.)

Anyone having the slightest familiarity with farming or ranching knows that it would be exceedingly difficult, if not impossible, to herd such a vast horde of animals several hundred miles through arid desert land. But the soldiers manage to accomplish the task and eventually return to camp with their captives and booty. Moses comes out to meet them and is *immediately furious that they have brought prisoners.*

15. And Moses said unto them, "Have ye saved all the women alive?
16. Behold, these caused the children of Israel, through the counsel of Balaam, to commit trespass against the Lord in the matter of Peio, and there was a plague among the congregation of the Lord.
17. Now therefore *kill every male among the little ones, and kill every woman that hath known man by lying with him. . . .*"

Moses has just commanded the heinous murder of *approximately 100,000 young lads,* no doubt already more than sufficiently terrorized at seeing their older brothers, uncles, fathers, and grandfathers bloodily hacked to pieces before their eyes. While they cannot have eagerly looked forward to a life of SLAVERY at the hands of Moses and his bloodthirsty followers, most no doubt would at least prefer such a fate to the only immediate alternative—painful death.

Such sadistic treatment was now inflicted upon these little ones—at the express instruction of a man even non-Jews of the present day are asked to respect as great and holy. If the slaughter of the innocent male children were not enough to convince us that Moses has not the slightest claim to such respect, let us concentrate on the second part of the instructions, which is to plunge a length of pointed metal into the warm, tender bodies of roughly *68,000 weeping, trembling, helpless women.*

To respond to such realities in any remotely humane way, we must set aside the rounded numbers of the statistics and witness the drama with a cast of specific individuals. Consider the women of your own family— your wife, sisters, aunts, daughters, nieces, grandmothers, and granddaughters. These relatives so precious to us have not any more claim to life and liberty than did the Midian women who were brutalized and hacked to pieces at the personal instruction of Moses, and—we are absurdly asked to believe—at the personal insistence of God.

There is even more to the vile evil of the incident:

18. "But all the women children, that have not known a man by lying with him, *keep alive for yourselves. . . .*"

The reader must not mistakenly suppose that Moses is here evidencing the slightest tenderness of heart, the minutest compassion. In instructing that the approximately 32,000 captured young women—children and teenagers—are not to be killed, he is not dreaming of granting them their freedom but clearly has in mind that his lusty soldiers may use such *sweet, innocent virgins for their own sexual pleasure.* If the reader has a daughter, let him consider for a moment what his natural and inevitably morally sound judgment would be if he heard that, say, Saddam Hussein had advised his soldiers that not only need they feel no guilt about capturing and sexually using the reader's female children, but that they were also in fact to consider it a direct order from God to do so.

Is there any fair-minded reader who can possibly avoid concluding that in issuing such orders Moses is no more worthy of our respect than Attila the Hun? Indeed Attila would be Moses' clear moral superior in that we have no evidence that he was ever guilty of hypocrisy or ever sought to cast the mantle of religious sanction over his orders to commit atrocities.

In the context of what we have just considered, the rest of chapter 31 turns the stomach even more. It deals with instructions for "purifying" both captured materials and the military slaughterers, not in terms that make the slightest intelligible moral sense but on the rankest nonsense about "work of goat's hair" and "all things made of wood." There is, as is so often the case in the Old Testament, reference to acts that are or are not to be performed on the Seventh Day. Heavy emphasis on "the Seventh Day" is usually—perhaps even invariably—an indication that we have left the area of morality and love of God and entered that of primitive, tribal mumbo-jumbo.

Since these individuals lived in primitive times, it is possible at least to add a charitable component to one's judgment of their doings and writings, in the sense that Christ, as we are told, said of his torturers, "Forgive them, Father, for they know not what they do." But what excuse do modern fundamentalists who agree with such nonsense offer for continuing to indulge in such destructive fantasies?

Chapter 32. This chapter returns to the by now tiresome theme of a not just but furious God. This time he is angry at the tribes of Reuben and Gad because they, quite sensibly, finding the land of Jazar and Gilead ideal for raising their sheep, petition Moses to allow them to stay there. Moses attacks them for not wanting to continue to war against those tribes at the time inhabiting the Promised Land. The result of their action, Moses warns, will be forty more years roaming the wilderness, an essentially inane prediction. The two tribes finally agree to continue slaughtering unsuspecting men, women, and children rather than settling down in areas that common sense told them were perfectly adapted for normal, peaceful pursuits.

Chapter 33 is a tiresome recapitulation of the alleged journeys and military ventures of the children of Israel. Perhaps the most significant thing one may say about the chapter is that there is not so much as a syllable of moral instruction in it. Indeed quite the reverse is the case; it is filled with bad examples.

Chapter 34. In this chapter we are told that, in one of the longest of his alleged statements to Moses (who must have had either an incredible memory or been the fastest stenographer known to history), the Lord gives specific instructions on which tribe and subtribe ought to take which subdivisions of Canaanite real estate.

Chapter 35 is somewhat more interesting. Although the first verses of it continue the foregoing inanity, the Lord eventually instructs Moses:

11. "Then ye shall appoint you cities to be cities of refuge for you; that the slayer may flee thither, which killeth any person at unawares. . . ."

Forgetting whether it is just and moral to let murderers go scot-free—a prospect that certainly horrifies today's conservatives, among others—such verses at least raise our hopes; perhaps we are to encounter one of those rare instances in the early books of the Bible in which rational and civilized observers of the modern age would perceive a certain sensibility and fairness. Alas, such hopes are doomed to frustration; the rules by which the business of the six cities of refuge are to be conducted are bizarre.

Verses 16 through 21 explain the criteria by which a man will be deemed guilty or innocent of murder. If the murder is found to be accidental according to the standards involved, the slayer is proclaimed innocent, although he must still remain in the city of refuge (vv. 22, 23) until "the death of the high priest, which was anointed with the holy oil" (v. 25). Further, if the acquitted person ventures out of the city and happens to run into one of the victim's relatives seeking revenge, that person may then slay him without incurring guilt for the deed.

Christian and Jewish conservatives absolutely insist that such absurd passages are every bit as much the word of God as are the more sensible and uplifting portions of Scripture. Perhaps our friends of the Christian Reconstructionist persuasion, who want to rebuild American society according to scriptural standards and practices, will now recommend this specific formula as a wise part of the solution to the present wave of criminal violence.

In any event, the original individual judged innocent is nonetheless a prisoner in the city for an indeterminate amount of time.

Not surprisingly, this chapter, with its inherent nonsense, is now frequently utilized by those who favor capital punishment. There is not the slightest question about it; if every passage of the Bible is literally the word of God, then it inescapably follows that, except in the context of war, murder is an offense punishable by death.

Chapter 36. This chapter takes us back again to such edifying moral advice as the division of real estate spoils among the invading tribes of Israel. It primarily concerns the instruction that all women are required to marry within their own tribe so the land they inherit will not leave that tribe and thereby change the allotment ordained by God as permanently fixed. (See also AUTHENTICITY OF THE BIBLE; CONSERVATISM; CRIME, BIBLICAL IMPETUS TO; GIFTS TO GOD.)

O

OBADIAH. This book, consisting of one chapter of twenty-one verses, is the shortest in the Bible. It is commonly described as too narrow, vengeful, and unworthy to be considered divinely inspired. Since theologians and church scholars must resist such a characterization, they understandably contrive to discover subtle elements in the text that, one can only assume, would greatly surprise the original authors, whoever they were. As usual, nothing is known of the identity or the number of the writers who contributed to the book. Even the best scholarship has no idea of the identity of the Obadiah whose vision the book purports to describe. Some authorities say there are nine other Obadiahs mentioned in the Bible, others twelve. Knowing the correct number would help us little.

The first two verses of the book contain a structural absurdity:

1. The vision of Obadiah. Thus saith the Lord God concerning Edom; "We have heard a rumour from the Lord, and an ambassador is sent among the heathen, Arise ye, and let us rise up against her in battle.

2. "Behold, I have made thee small among the heathen: thou art greatly despised. . . ."

The first speaker is the unknown author who announces that he will deliver a statement of God himself. That statement—a quotation—is unintelligible, however, in that it refers to the Lord in the third person rather than in the first, as one would reasonably expect.

Verse 20 includes something that no living scholar can understand.

20. And the captivity of this host of the children of Israel shall possess that of the Canaanites, even unto Zarephath; and the captivity of Jerusalem, which is in Sepharad, shall possess the cities of the south.

Whatever this means, It has no relationship to anything subsequently known as history, nor does anyone today—or for that matter, anyone for many centuries past—have any idea where the community of Sepharad was supposed to be. It is not mentioned elsewhere in the Bible and is not known to ancient history. According to *The Interpreter's One-Volume Commentary on the Bible,* certain ancient rabbis identified Sepharad with Spain. As a result of this mistake, Spanish Jews have since that time been referred to as Sephardim. (See also DREAMS; PROPHECY AND PREDICTION.)

ORIGINS OF MONOTHEISTIC RELIGIOUS PRACTICES. As Adam Smith observed in *Wealth of Nations,*

> The great phenomena of nature—the revolutions of the heavenly bodies, eclipses, comets; thunder, lightning, and other extraordinary meteors; the generation, the life, growth, and dissolution of plants and animals—are objects which, as they necessarily excite the wonder, so they naturally call forth the curiosity of mankind to inquire into their causes. Superstition first attempted to satisfy this curiosity by referring all those wonderful appearances to the immediate agency of the gods. Philosophy afterwards endeavored to account for them from more familiar causes, or from such as mankind were better acquainted with, than the agency of the gods.

That the early Israelites practiced POLYTHEISM is implied in the fact that the first of the Ten Commandments addresses the issue of worshipping other gods: "Thou shalt have no other gods *before* me" (Exod. 20:3). Although the Bible contains scattered references to a few monotheists, such as Amos and Hosea, the most complete biblical profession of monotheism does not appear until the time of Isaiah (chapters 40–55).

Historically, philosophical monotheism was taught by many Greek philosophers, but it was Judaism that separated itself from the Hellenistic world with its belief in only one supreme Deity.

The Importance of the Bible. The fall of the Jerusalem Temple to the Babylonians and the resulting dispersal of thousands of Israelites imparted to the sacred writings paramount religious importance. That they had been important even before the time of the exile goes without saying. Now that the worshipers were scattered and no longer had access to the temple and its physical leadership, the written word had to assume a new kind of value.

Observance of Religious Ceremonies. The ensuing suggested relationship between two sets of phenomena may at first seem totally unjustified. May the reader only suspend judgment until he has heard the argument in full. The hypothesis offered for his consideration is that there is a definite connection between the beginnings of organized religion and certain instances of mass hysteria that occur in our own time.

I do not refer here to Bible meetings, charismatic public functions, and other similar types of religious group psychology, although these, too, may well offer up valuable clues leading to the solution of the mystery. Rather I have in mind those peculiarities of group conduct observable during the past few decades at public performances of Elvis Presley, the Beatles, and other rock-music idols.

Let us use the example of Presley to explore the point. Judged by traditional artistic standards, Elvis was a relatively inferior practitioner of his art. That his voice had a strange, hollow tone, that he did not play the guitar very well, that he boasted no special musical ability, and that he exercised generally poor judgment in selecting material add up to a rather mediocre output compared with that of many artists of the rock world, not to mention entertainers such as Frank Sinatra and Bing Crosby. Presley's initial appeal lay in his personality and physical appearance. Like James Dean he had a shy, socially unstructured manner with which millions of teenagers of the 1950s could identify. The fact that he was good-looking added to his popularity.

But we have only to watch five minutes of any of Presley's produced television specials to observe on the faces of the impressionable young women in his audience a heightened emotion approaching—and in some cases actually becoming—hysteria.

Had these same young women chanced upon Elvis in a grocery store or gas station, they would certainly have been bowled over by the experience, but *if they were alone* they would not have fainted, wept, cried aloud, jumped about, or behaved in any other irrational manner. Accompanied by even one friend, however, they might have done so. Accompanied by a dozen friends, they most certainly would have.

From this example we can understand that what we are considering is a *social response,* an instance of *mob* psychology. In the case of Elvis, for the most part these emotions were positive. In instances of group violence—such as we have seen at certain concerts given by the rock group Guns N' Roses or at some recently released "gang" movies—these responses unfortunately turn negative.

An important factor in such cases of group fixation is the relatively early death of the person perceived as being of heroic stature. In the case of the deaths of Presley and Dean, their particular admirers were so shocked that some of them simply could not accept the evident reality. As a result, to the present day one hears the most absurd rumors that either Presley or Dean is still alive. There is no shortage of witnesses who report having seen them, just as there is no shortage of witnesses who are apparently convinced that strange creatures from God-knows-where in outer space have personally communicated with them, touched them, or taken them into their space vehicles. On the one hand, no responsible, rational person believes such reports, but those who tell them apparently do not intend to deceive. What connection such modern-day realities have with the foundations of many ancient religions—by no means only Christianity— remains to be explored.

I consider it highly probable that, in the same way, religious ceremonies originated in situations in which large numbers of people came together— for wars, planting or reaping celebrations, burials of leaders—in other words, in contexts where *mass suggestibility* would inevitably be a factor. Although these social procedures initially had *nonreligious* purposes, secondary considerations—public expressions of fear, thanksgiving, propitiation, or conciliation to actual or alleged unknown superior powers—gradually came to dominate.

There is nothing either antireligious or proreligious in these observations. If there is a God who chooses to guide the conduct of his human creatures into certain behavioral channels, it is perfectly reasonable to assume that he would utilize natural human propensities to effect his will.

Such theories are, however, flatly irreconcilable with the biblical sketch of religious history. That they are far more reasonable than certain accounts in Genesis will hardly be viewed as persuasive by those whose minds are already closed to any but literalist, fundamentalist interpretations of Scripture.

Honoring the Sabbath. The Israelites did not create their own religion and customs as a result of either divine revelation or rational speculation. Their society—like that of every other in history—was in a constant process of evolution, during which time it was powerfully influenced by cultures near to it and those that preceded it in time. Babylonian-Assyrian influence, for example, helped give the Israelites their conception of the calendar year, as did Canaanite custom. The idea of the SABBATH, however, appears to have originated with the Israelites, although no scholar has been able to reach an authoritative and decisive conclusion concerning the full meaning and importance of the Sabbath during that early period of history.

Grace before Meals. Only those who have gone so long without sustenance that they desperately need it can fully understand the remarkably sensitive food-seeking mechanism with which all creatures—including man—are endowed. For a person or animal in this predicament, all other interests are subordinated. The environment is keenly examined. All available objects are inspected in terms of their possible edibility.

The individual in such straits who finally finds and devours food is immediately seized by two powerful, simultaneously experienced sensations: (1) the physical satisfaction of the act of eating or drinking, and (2) a profound and moving sense of gratitude. If the individual is religiously affiliated, or even casually so conditioned, he may express the attendant emotion by either muttering "Thank God" to himself as he gulps down his food or by uttering a more formal prayer.

Traveling in the wilderness for so many years, the ancient Israelites undoubtedly found many occasions to be in this type of situation. The practice of saying grace before meals grows out of such primitive experience. Whether the individual simply finds food in the natural world or is able to eat something he has personally planted, tended, and grown, he is in either case dependent upon and therefore grateful to NATURE for what he eats. Both primitive cultures and those that are philosophically sophisticated perceive a connection between nature and God. (See also BELIEFS AND MYTHS; HISTORICAL RELEVANCE OF THE BIBLE; JEWS AND JUDAISM; RELIGION.)

P

PATRIARCHS, LONGEVITY OF. That there are numerous instances of mutually contradictory assertions in the Bible is not only self-evident but has also been irrefutably documented by armies of scholars. Yet one more such case concerns the remarkable ages to which certain characters of the Old Testament are said to have lived.

Every schoolchild knows that humans do not live to be hundreds of years old. Fortunately, either Moses, or those who wrote the books attributed to him, said something quite sensible on the subject in stating that "The days of our years are three-score and ten" (Ps. 90:10).

Whoever originally translated this verse into English or other European languages may have been guilty of carelessness because if interpreted literally the statement attests that what are numbered to three-score and ten are *days,* not years. Since seventy days is obviously not a normal human life span, the original author presumably intended to refer to annual increments of time. It is clear that whenever this observation was originally written, the maximum human life span was then what it is now. Indeed the subbranch of genetics in modern science has discovered the natural cellular mechanisms by means of which the bodies of all living things eventually cease to grow and hence begin the long, slow process of disintegration ending in death.

So we are witness to one more example of the Scriptures saying two mutually contradictory things on the same subject.

That the unknown authors of these first portions of the Old Testament would attribute such impossibly long life spans to some of the patriarchs is perhaps understandable; what is more difficult to explain is why anyone today would accept such preposterous assertions as fact.

In regard to this subject, as well as many others, the anonymous Israelite scribes undoubtedly borrowed a literary device from the Sumerian civilization, which was much older than theirs. About this Sumerian practice, which appears in their listing of their kings, Jacquette Hawkes, in *The First Great Civilizations,* says:

> Unfortunately it [the list] is quite useless for chronological purposes because not only are the earlier reigns quite fantastically long, but also the scribes have adopted the convention that the dynasties succeeded one another, whereas in fact many of them were contemporary. . . . These dynasties last for well over 250,000 years and it is likely that most of the kings are as legendary as their years. (IA)

(See also CONTRADICTIONS, BIBLICAL; HISTORICAL RELEVANCE OF THE BIBLE; METHUSELAH.)

PETER, THE FIRST EPISTLE OF. This is the first of two short books that apparently communicated an open address, a public letter, directed to a group of new Christians in a certain part of the world—namely, Pontus, Galatia, Cappadocia, West Asia, and Bithynia.

Chapter 1. As is common in the Bible, despite the first verse of the first chapter, there is evidence that this book may not have been written by its alleged author, in this case the apostle Peter. Supporting this belief is the fact that most of the quotes referred to by Peter relate to the Old Testament, although surely someone who knew Jesus Christ intimately would be more apt to quote *that* source of information than prophets of hundreds of years before.

Regardless of the identity of the author, however, he was apparently a man of virtue, courage, and faith, although at times mistaken. In chapter 1 we see that he, like most Christians in those early days, was convinced that he would personally witness the end of the physical world. Referring to Christ he says,

> 20. Who verily was foreordained before the foundation of the world, but was manifest in these last times for you.

Chapter 2. Here we find the interesting passage that runs counter to the traditional view of the Jews as God's Chosen People, if the letters were indeed written to converts in foreign countries as stated in 1 Peter 1:1.

9. But *you are a chosen race*, a royal priesthood, an holy nation. . . .
(IA)

Also emphasized in the second chapter is the importance of submission in the early Christian code:

13. Submit yourselves to every ordinance of man for the Lord's sake: whether it be to the king, as supreme;
14. Or unto governors, as unto them that are sent by him for the punishment of evildoers, and for the praise of them that do well.
17. Honour all men. Love the brotherhood. Fear God. Honour the king.
18. Servants, be subject to your masters with all fear; not only to the good and gentle, but also the froward.

Apparently no Christian presently on earth pays the slightest attention to such advice, despite the fact that the same faithful refer to the New Testament as the literal word of God.

Chapter 3. Peter—or whoever the author was—speaks with the beauty of Christ himself when he writes:

9. Nor rendering evil for evil, or railing for railing: but contrariwise, blessing; knowing that ye are thereunto called, that ye should inherit a blessing.

This admonition, like so many others, has been disregarded by Christians for the past two thousand years as readily as the clear instructions from Jesus himself to return love for evil, to forgive those who offend us, and to turn the other cheek if struck.

In this chapter, too, we find reference to the story of Noah in terms that make it clear that the unknown author accepted the literal validity of the Genesis account.

20. When sometime were disobedient, when once the longsuffering of God waited in the days of Noah, while the ark was a preparing, wherein few, that is, eight souls were saved by water.

Even if we take the story of Noah literally it is simply not the case that the souls in question were "saved by water." Quite to the contrary, they were endangered by water, which, we are told, wiped out all the rest of the human race.

Chapter 4 brings a return to the theme of the last days:

7. But the end of all things is at hand: be ye therefore sober, and watch unto prayer. . . .

17. For the time is come that judgment must begin at the house of God; and if it first begin at us, what shall the end be of them that obey not the gospel of God?

(See also BELIEFS AND MYTHS; LAST DAYS, THE.)

PETER, THE SECOND EPISTLE OF. Most scholars now agree that the second epistle attributed to Peter was not only not written by the apostle, but it was also not written by the same author who wrote the first epistle. Comments Robert Paul Roth in the Holman Study Bible:

> The authorship, date and destination of the second letter of Peter are extremely uncertain. No New Testament writing had a more difficult time establishing itself in the canon. Scholars, both ancient and modern, have seriously doubted its petrine composition; . . . in the 3rd Century Eusebius says, "As for the current second Epistle, it has not come down to us as Canonical. . . ." Following the observation of Jerome, many modern scholars find the Greek style significantly different from I Peter; . . . *we have other writings under the name of Peter and the other apostles which are known to be spurious.* (IA)

The reader should reflect upon the meaning of this last concession. It is, of course, that not only Second Peter but other early Christian writings as well were out-and-out false documents—pious frauds—however good the intentions of their authors and revisers may have been. Roth goes on to observe:

> *In spite of these scholarly judgments, the church has traditionally regarded this Epistle as of genuine Petrine authorship.* (IA)

Although Walter M. Abbott, S.J., in his series of reviews titled "Updating Bible Lore" (*America,* April 27, 1963), says that "Peter's authorship of the second epistle was doubted by Catholic scholars as far back as the Third Century," he goes on to say that the official *Catholic Biblical Encyclopedia* (1956) nevertheless asserted that "internal evidence makes it clear that Peter was the author" (IA).

In *The Bible: Word of God in Words of Men,* Father Jean Levie concedes:

There are grave difficulties of the authenticity of the Second Epistle of St. Peter. The letter is part of the canon of inspired Scripture. If Peter did not write it, it must be the work of an author who clearly wanted the letter written by him to be considered as St. Peter's . . . and the advice he gives to be accepted also on the authority of Peter. Father Chaine . . . suggests as a solution . . . that the author, who may have been a disciple of Peter, had a position of authority in the church or else had been delegated by some such authority, hence he was aware that he was transmitting apostolic teaching.

This is a clever, though of course unconvincing, argument. One can be quite sincerely sympathetic to such distinguished scholars as Fathers Chaine and Levie because their predicament on such points is essentially hopeless. Naturally they cannot concede as much publicly.

Chapter 1. Despite the now-established virtual impossibility of Peter's having written the book, the author nonetheless attempts to authenticate his authority:

> 16. For we have not followed cunningly devised fables, when we made known unto you the power and coming of our Lord Jesus Christ, but were eyewitnesses of his majesty.
> 17. For he received from God the Father honour and glory, when there came such a voice to him for the excellent glory, "This is my beloved Son, in whom I am well pleased."
> 18. And this voice which came from heaven *we heard, when we were with him in the holy mount.* (IA)

What the author seems to be, in addition to a liar, is a plagiarist. Says *The Interpreter's Dictionary of the Bible* (Abingdon):

> All of the Letter of Jude is virtually incorporated in II Peter 2. Since Jude is most certainly a post-apostolic writing, the apostolic origin of II Peter can be defended only on the basis that Jude borrowed from II Peter. However, that II Peter is the borrower is evident from the fact that Jude is intelligible without II Peter, while certain sentences of II Peter require a knowledge of Jude in order to be understood. . . .

Chapter 2. Since the actual author of 2 Peter is guilty of a falsehood in attributing his writing to someone else, there is unconscious irony where we read:

1. But there were false prophets also among the people, even as there shall be false teachers among you, who privily shall bring in damnable heresies, even denying the Lord that bought them, and bring upon themselves swift destruction.

The second letter is extremely short, running to two and a half pages in the average Bible. It is a remarkably angry message, attacking false prophets and those guilty of dissipation, carousing, adultery, and other sins of the flesh. One of the more interesting aspects of the letter is that its unknown author was well familiar with the Old Testament. This, of course, was true of all the writers of the New Testament, but the emphasis on Genesis in Second Peter is particularly noteworthy. The letter refers to Noah as the "preacher of righteousness" (v. 5) and again in verse 6, "Whereby the world that then was, being overflowed with water, perished." He also speaks of the destruction of Sodom and Gomorrah and the subsequent deliverance of Lot.

Chapter 3. When fundamentalists and others are questioned about the oft-predicted but as yet unseen LAST DAYS, they generally quote a verse from the third chapter of Peter to "explain" the contradiction and argue their case:

8. But, beloved, be not ignorant of this one thing, that *one day is with the Lord as a thousand years, and a thousand years as one day.*

This verse is very close to meaningless. The reader presumably has no difficulty recognizing the concept of one day. Let us suppose that some spiritual advisor informs him, at midday today, that since noontime of the preceding day, not twenty-four hours but 1,000 years have passed; the individual would be unlikely thereafter to trust the sanity of his advisor fully. There is a loose, poetic sense in which, if we grant that God is timeless and eternal, a thousand-year slice of time as perceived by humans might seem no more than the blink of an eye to the Almighty, but such considerations have nothing whatever to do with the assertion attributed to Jesus that the end of time, the Last Days, would come while many hearing him were still alive.

Verse 8 has also been used to "explain" the discrepancy in the Genesis creation story with the clear evidence of science. Isaac Asimov has pointed out, in his *Guide to the Bible: New Testament,* that the verse in fact refers to a quotation from Psalms 90:

4. For a thousand years in thy sight are but as yesterday when it is past, and as a watch in the night.

So again the unknown author of 2 Peter uses someone else's writings to answer ingeniously the Christians who, as Asimov states "must have grown impatient while waiting for the second coming that seemed endlessly delayed." (See also AUTHENTICITY OF THE BIBLE; BELIEFS AND MYTHS.)

PIOUS FRAUD. That outright deception has frequently been resorted to by translators and copyists of the Bible over the centuries is undeniable. Since it naturally makes Christian authorities uncomfortable to concede as much, they sometimes obscure the bald realities in graceful or scholarly language that tends to hide the truth that lies behind it. An instance at hand is a comment by Eugene H. Maly, president of the Catholic Biblical Association of America, official theologian of the Second Vatican Council, professor of Sacred Scripture at Mt. St. Mary's of the West Seminary in Norwood, Ohio, and chairman of the editorial board of *The Bible Today:*

> The biblical text has not come down to us completely unscathed. Throughout the ages, copyists whose task it was to preserve the original Hebrew, Aramaic or Greek text have introduced literally hundreds of variant readings. At times this was done consciously to make more intelligible an obscure reading, or *to make the text conform to the personal theological convictions of the copyists themselves.* Much more frequently it was due simply to human error. The translators of the original texts added to the confusion through an incomplete knowledge of the original languages or through a too-free translation. (IA)

Maly's speculation about the reasons for the deception almost succeeds in obscuring the fact that it is indeed deception that has occurred. Ponder the variety of ways in which Maly contends errors have been introduced into the Bible: (1) well-intentioned attempts to make a passage more intelligible; (2) deliberate altering of text to accommodate personal beliefs; (3) simple clerical error; (4) ignorance of the language from which a translation is made; and (5) "too-free" a translation.

What Father Maly cannot bring himself to refer to are such additional sources of error as the addition to text by later scribes to give greater authority to one theological view or another; errors committed by the earlier Hebrew, Aramaic, or Greek copyists; and errors and deceptions possibly created by the original authors themselves. With so many gateways open to falsehood it is hardly surprising that scholars now concede the existence of thousands of mistakes. (See also ERROR; VERSIONS OF THE BIBLE.)

Among biblical trade–lingo is the word *pseudepigrapha.* Its meaning is "false writings." The falsity emerges from the essential dishonesty of certain Old Testament authors who attributed their writings to various prophets and kings. For example, whoever first suggested that Genesis was written by Moses was either a liar or self-deluded.

As regards the *New* Testament, Swiss theologian Oscar Cullmann, in a lecture delivered at New York's Union Theological Seminary in March of 1959, refers to the fact that the New Testament consists of text selected from a considerably larger body of early Christian literature. As Cullmann explained:

> *Our four canonical Gospels are the only ones on which we can rely.* Again and again we must marvel at the fact that from the large number of primitive Christian writings only those were accepted as canonical which really came from the oldest time and which were free from heretical tendencies. (IA)

If we accept this reasonable scholarly statement, it would follow that most of the early Christian writers were either guilty of serious error or deliberate falsehood in attempting to add to the book that has so greatly affected millions over long centuries. Neither case reflects credit upon their scholarly or spiritual integrity.

Concerning the willingness of the early "fathers" to lie, Marjorie Strachey, in *The Fathers Without Theology,* says,

> Most of them saw no harm in a "pious fraud." And this kind of untruthfulness was freely imputed to the Apostles, to Jesus Christ, and to God the Father. They were fond of literary forgeries, Rufinus thought nothing of altering his author's words in his translations of Origen, Cyril of Jerusalem complains that his letters were tampered with in his own lifetime, reports of synods were frequently falsified, so much so that Harnack says the so-called official documents are "a swamp of mendacity." . . . We are helpless . . . in the face of the systematically corrupted tradition.

One area in which it is *not* necessary to accuse the biblical authors of a conscious intent to deceive is in those narratives that are patently nonsensical. There is a perfectly natural human tendency to surround widely admired public figures with preposterous beliefs, sometimes while they are still living, more frequently after they have died.

As mentioned previously, when the young actor James Dean was killed in an automobile in the mid-1950s, for example, almost at once strange stories began to be heard. One such suggested that Dean was not dead at all but living in retirement because he had been horribly disfigured; another story said the accident itself was a fabrication designed to cover up Dean's suicide. There were other equally outlandish tales.

We have also seen the remarkable stories and theories—a good many of them mutually exclusive—that emerged following the tragic assassinations of Martin Luther King, Robert Kennedy, and John Kennedy, and the untimely passing of Elvis Presley, Jim Morrison, and Marilyn Monroe.

After the death of Abraham Lincoln, published stories appeared that gave descriptions of conversations and events that had never taken place. There is still debate whether it was Lincoln's assassin John Wilkes Booth who was really killed at the tobacco barn in Virginia.

This process of enlarging on the facts, then, is common even in our own times, when printing presses, radio, television, tape recordings, and motion picture films can so widely disseminate an accurate report of events. It is only natural that such instant mushrooming of legend, myth, deliberate falsification, wishful thinking, innocent distortion, and other forms of error would be prevalent in centuries when populations were generally illiterate and it was frequently impossible to separate rumor from reliable information.

One problem scholars encounter when trying to decipher which biblical texts have been deliberately falsified is that the scriptural and historical documents against which these narratives can be compared and verified are now themselves conceded to be spurious beyond the slightest doubt. Eusebius, for example, quotes what is falsely represented as an actual correspondence between a certain Prince Abgar of Edessa and Jesus. Another totally false document is the alleged report by Pontius Pilate to the Emperor Tiberius concerning the death and resurrection of Jesus. A third is a letter— attributed to Lentunus, the *imagined* predecessor of Pilate to the Roman Senate—in which appears a physical description of Jesus.

There are also five fragments of a Russian translation of *The Jewish Wars* (written by Flavius Josephus in either the eleventh or twelfth century) that contain accounts of the life and sufferings of Jesus. Present Christian scholarship is unanimous in condemning them as spurious. Many other examples could be given. The point is that just as Christians have on numerous occasions felt it perfectly permissible to burn, mutilate, hang, stab, and shoot their opponents in what they imagined was a defense of spiritual values, so too they have shown no reluctance to lie like troupers. In such instances ancient scholars, monks, and scribes were perfectly aware that they were defending the source of all truth by the method of untruth. One can only hope that all their impostures have been detected. It is a sobering thought that some of these holy liars might have succeeded and that to this day one portion of Scripture or another might unknowingly owe its inspiration not to God but to the human weakness for prevarication. (See also CRIMES, BIBLICAL IMPETUS TO.)

Obviously, there is an element of unfairness in judging the behavior of past ages by the moral standards of the present, but to grant as much is by no means to argue that modern man therefore has no right whatever to be critical of ancient practices. Indeed, the slight traces of the truth of history that filter down to us contain an admixture of far too much patriotic puffery and far too little sound criticism. Imagine a society of, say, a thousand years ago in which it was considered perfectly permissible to beat naughty children about the head and shoulders with a stout stick. Today one would naturally have to take the general acceptance of the custom at the time into account when judging instances of such past acts. Again this is not to say that one is obliged either to approve of or to apologize for such barbaric behavior. (See also CORPORAL PUNISHMENT.)

Just so, we must naturally consider the *reasons* the authors of Scripture and would-be Scripture so often engaged in deception. They must have occasionally despaired of inducing their followers to behave morally and, since the authority of God is greater than that of man, the idea must have early occurred—in practically all cultures—that to invoke divine endorsement of a moral pronouncement was to stand a better chance of its being carefully attended to. But deception is still deception; to perceive reasons for it does not require us to approve of it.

Father Bruce Vawter does make a valid point, however, when he argues in *A Path Through Genesis:*

> For some curious reason unpleasant beliefs like purgatory and hellfire and a personal devil and unpleasant practices like auricular confession are said to have been the inventions of priestcraft to command more surely the simple faithfuls' fear and obedience. One wonders at the naivete that could imagine such a change in human nature, since the charlatans whose business it is to know human nature have always borne down rather heavily on the themes of sweetness and light and the certainty of salvation, rather than enticed a following by offering them a chance at damnation. Anyone who has sat in a confessional box the size of a coffin during the long hours of a hot summer afternoon knows that, whoever invented the sacrament of Penance, it was not a parish priest.

But regardless where the canonical error and falsehoods have originated, they are there. Since God by definition cannot have authored or endorsed a lie, it follows that it is absurd to consider Scripture as divinely inspired in its entirety.

The Honest Missionary. Consider the almost universal moral judgment of the philosophy of caveat emptor—let the buyer beware. While there is often blindness to the ethicality of particular sales on the part of sellers, even such offenders have no trouble perceiving where justice lies when they are the purchasers. The man who charges more for something than it is actually worth or who disguises a flaw in the object sold is obviously breaking the moral law. Since this is so as regards material goods, why is it not so when the object being dispensed is a book that contains the very philosophy of Christianity? Is there a single case in the last two thousand years in which a Christian missionary made substantially the following argument to a would-be convert?

> Brother, I am pleased that you have found my arguments reasonable and are considering joining our fold. I believe that by doing so you will be acting in harmony with the will of God and his only son, Jesus Christ. But since I personally have as much respect for honesty and truthfulness as I have for all the other virtues, I therefore must make it clear to you that the Christianity I am dispensing is a product far from perfection. We Christians have, sadly, been responsible for slaughtering millions of our enemies. The Inquisition, for example, was a totally Christian crime. The slaughters of the Huguenots, the massacre at Drogheda, the practice of slavery in Europe and its colonies, these and countless other atrocities have been committed by Christians acting in their formal capacity as Christians.
>
> I must also confess that this Bible upon which my entire case has been based is itself by no means the fully consistent and morally edifying document that as a Christian I wish had been vouchsafed to us by our God. Frankly I have no real explanation to offer you as to how Matthew may say one thing of Christ while John issues a contradictory report on the same subject. Nor can I explain why there are so many instances of precisely this sort of discrepancy in both the Old and New Testaments.
>
> Now, although I have personal confidence that God himself will eventually explain such mysteries to us, I did want to explain to you the deficiencies of our faith—and the book upon which that faith is based—before you make your final decision to become a Christian. If I had not told you this I surely would have been guilty of precisely the same sin we so strongly condemn in those who sell us a horse that is lame, an automobile with hidden defects, a foodstuff that is decayed, or indeed any other faulty merchandise.

Although we cannot know if such recourse to the ideal of truth has ever occurred in the two thousand years of Christian history, we certainly should not hold our breaths until such a combination of proselytization

and honesty occurs. (See also AUTHENTICITY OF THE BIBLE; CONTRA-
DICTIONS, BIBLICAL.)

POETRY IN THE BIBLE. We are forced to concede one more problem
when we consider those portions of Scripture that all knowledgeable scholars
and a good many lay people recognize as poetry. We are not raising the
question here whether a given passage of poetry in the Bible might also
incorporate other factors such as the historical, but merely considering the
poetry as such. If the fundamentalists are right, the author of the poetry
of the Bible is God.

Another point on which all observers would agree is that no human
being, not even Shakespeare, could write poems of such excellence as could
the creator of the universe. The awkward fact is that those passages of
Scripture that are clearly poetic are, by and large, not nearly as good as
the work of the best human poets.

We are therefore forced, by logic, to make a choice. Either God is
not quite as good a poet as Shakespeare, among others, which we've already
conceded would be absurd to say, or the relatively inferior poetic components of the Bible were not, after all, either written or directly inspired—
dictated—by the Almighty. There is nothing the least bit absurd about
the latter conclusion.

It is no reasonable defense against this argument to suggest that we
cannot properly judge biblical poetry because we are dealing only with
translations of it rather than the original versions. That is true, but it by
no means resolves the difficulty for if, in all the world's present languages
(most of which also present Shakespeare and other major poets in languages
other than English) human poetry is better than divine, it follows that
the Lord God has been inattentive. He has not kept his eye on the process
of translation. In this assumption, of course, we again return to absurdity.

POLYGAMY. Consider the case of a wealthy society woman who, finding
herself unable to be faithful to her first husband, decided to take another
but without the customary procedure of divorce separating the two weddings.

When her case was finally brought to public attention, it was discovered
that over the course of several years she had acquired three additional
husbands in the same way. The men themselves, it would appear, made
no complaint. Each felt that so long as he was permitted the woman's
sexual favors, he would not deprive the four other gentlemen of the same
privilege. For her part the woman provided for each man handsomely and

the *menage a cinq* lived in at least the same degree of peace and amicability that characterizes most ordinary marriages.

Despite the fact that the participants in this odd arrangement did not object, it is easy to imagine the wave of public revulsion and outrage that greeted the news of their situation.

This purely imaginary story may enable the reader to have a clearer perception of the practice of having multiple mates than what ordinarily comes to mind at contemplation of either the word *polygamy* or some specific instance of it. The point is certainly not to recommend the practice; I would be as disapproving and scandalized as anyone else at finding that such a case actually existed. But why? On what grounds? According to what principles?

Whatever the reader's reaction, he should understand that precisely such a living arrangement has in fact occurred in hundreds of millions of cases over very long periods of time, the only difference being that it was men rather than women who considered themselves rightly entitled to be sexually active with as many wives as they could financially support.

Mohammed is considered to be one of the most intensely dedicated religious believers of all time, and yet it is his religion, Islam, that permits multiple marriage partners to the present day. In our own country, in parts of Utah, there are still polygamous Mormon families who refuse to accept the fact that God could change his mind. They therefore refuse to believe that their church—The Latter Day Saints—has issued a new dispensation on the issue, after being subjected to verbal and physical abuse from those outside the Mormon faith who consider the practice of polygamy disgraceful.

The problem for fundamentalist Christians on this issue, of course, comes from the fact that the Old Testament—every word of which they believe to be the inspired word of God—clearly condones the taking of many wives. Solomon himself is said to have had hundreds. Christianity, therefore, faces precisely the same intellectual predicament that troubled Mormonism: that God is said to have changed his mind on a moral question of enormous importance.

Parenthetically, the same would appear to be true as regards prostitution. We learn from the Bible that in the early days not only was prostitution common, but it was also directly connected to religion, whereas today the selling of sexual favors is considered not only immoral but illegal.

If the reader is not already sufficiently shocked, he might pause to consider that even incest—now considered child molestation or, if the participants are adults, a particularly depraved offense—is nevertheless condoned by God himself, if we believe the clear evidence of Scripture.

Only those who evaluate such questions on their individual merits find no problem with the subject matter. (See also CRIMES, BIBLICAL IMPETUS TO; MORALITY; RELIGIOUS THEORIES, DEVIANT.)

POLYTHEISM. It is wrong to suggest that the ancient Jews were always monotheists. The books of the Old Testament contain numerous references to the worshipping of false gods. Concerning this T. W. Doane says:

> In the first place we know that they revered and worshipped a bull, called *Apis,* just as the ancient Egyptians did. They worshipped the sun, the moon, the stars, and all the hosts of heaven.
> They worshipped fire, and kept it burning on an altar, just as the Persians and other nations. They worshipped stones, revered an oak tree, and bowed down to images. They worshipped a Queen of Heaven, called the Goddess *Astarte* or *Mylitta,* and burned incense to her. They worshipped *Baal, Moloch,* and *Chemosh* and offered up human sacrifices to them after which, in some instances, they ate the victim.

While such behavior is barbaric by modern standards, it is unfair to judge the ancient Jews by the moral requirements of the present. The worship of both natural and man-made objects, human sacrifice, and cannibalism are commonly encountered among the religious rituals of primitive societies. (See also JEWS AND JUDAISM; ORIGINS OF RELIGIOUS PRACTICES.)

We base many of our judgments largely on not only the immediate information available to us but also on the social conditioning of our entire lifetime. It would be surprising, therefore, if many modern Christians and Jews did not make the error of assuming that the attitudes of the ancient Jews concerning the gods of other tribes were the ones now common. In the present day, for example, if we are shown a wooden statue and told that it is regarded as a god by a primitive South Pacific tribe, we may smile tolerantly or be dismayed at such inane superstition. The one thing we would never do is assume that the wooden object before us was in any sense a real god. We would be quite certain that it was merely a carved image that primitive, ignorant people believed to be divine. That, as I say, represents the modern mind at work.

But the modern mind is a product of the thousand-and-one influences that created the world as we now know it. Few of those influences existed in Old Testament times. That the Jews detested gods other than Yahweh is clear enough, but for centuries they regarded those gods as *beings possessed of actual power.* Only very gradually did the Jews of whom we read in the early books of the Old Testament come to perceive that the various worshipped representations of wood, metal, and stone were merely material objects and not in any sense possessed of a consciousness.

From this it inescapably follows that the Jews of early Israelite history were equally as superstitious as the other Semitic or pagan tribes with which they came into contact. (See also RELIGIOUS THEORIES, DEVIANT.)

POVERTY. Poverty, like all other social problems, poses moral questions. Although in our own cities we daily see more and more examples of homelessness and poverty, the overwhelming wretchedness of poverty in Bombay, that fabulous Asian city on the west coast of India, struck me most forcefully.

Entering the harbor from open sea, one first espies Bombay's surprisingly massive high-rise office and apartment buildings. My initial impression, therefore, was that this was a city of progress, prosperity, and technological sophistication.

Later, afoot in the "New York of India," one gets more sharply focused impressions. There are indications enough of prosperity, but it is enjoyed by only a small percentage of the total population.

In Bombay poverty lurks visibly and invisibly around every street corner, behind almost every door. Thousands live permanently on the sidewalks. When one's cab stops in a traffic jam or at a busy intersection beggars appear from nowhere—women with children in arms, cripples—hands outstretched, pitiful voices pleading. Coins or paper money are often given by Western visitors, but one has the impression of offering a cup of water to a man whose house is burning; the gesture seems so pitifully inadequate in terms of the overall need. And these are the professional beggars. Millions of others are too defeated even to plead for money.

Our group, like most curious foreign visitors who have been told about "the cages," naturally travels to this incredible red-light district of the city. Viewed from behind locked cab doors, the overpowering reality of the cages turns out to be very different from what one has imagined: a street or two of a few dozen individual houses of prostitution. Driving slowly through street after street, one sees crowded rows of narrow houses with young women displayed in open "shop windows," most fronted by iron bars. Each "cage" displays three, sometimes as many as five, young whores— mostly teenagers, some younger—who stare blankly, not seductively, into the night. The women are born into such a life. It is all they know, and all they have known from infancy.

On our second day in this enormous teeming metropolis, Jayne and

POVERTY

I visit Asha Dan, Mother Teresa's famed refuge for the destitute that is operated by the Missionaries of Charity. In contrast to the neighborhood sidewalks that are inhabited by thousands of the homeless, the mission is a comfortable, clean compound guarded by a uniformed attendant who opens the gate to admit our cab.

Inside we find ourselves beside a large dormitory. It holds about a hundred metal cots, each topped by a thin mattress pad covered with an attractive, lavender Indian-print material. About half the beds are occupied by old men.

"Are these people ill?" Jayne asks a nun who greets us.

"They are dying," the young Indian woman replies, her face serene and oddly cheerful. We nod and smile to some of the men, who have been brought in off the street so that they can die with at least some measure of comfort and dignity.

In an adjacent area, all the beds are covered with dark blue material. Each patient has a red-and-white checked blanket. Most are in the forty-to-seventy age bracket, though one teenage boy smiles pitifully at us as we pass.

In an orphan's dormitory across the way, we meet another nun who explains, quite matter-of-factly, "These are the mentally handicapped children." We look at the little ones who sit vegetable-like in straw-and-bamboo chairs, the seats of which slant backward to cradle them gently. Only with the greatest of difficulty do we avoid weeping.

As we walk, two small children—a boy and a girl perhaps three years old—attach themselves to Jayne and follow us, chattering aimlessly. An eight-year-old boy, severely retarded, lurches forward but an older youth smiles helpfully and steers us out of the way.

We chat for a few minutes with four attractive teenage girls from a nearby Catholic school, who identify themselves as social workers. We offer them a woefully inadequate gift for the compound: a shopping bag full of fruit, jams, jellies, candies, and crackers we've brought from our cabin aboard the S.S. *Rotterdam.* Later we present them with travelers' checks.

We next visit a large barracks where a woman sits at a sewing machine and a dozen children at two nearby tables are busy with school books. A bright orange wall is decorated with cheerful decals of Charlie Brown, Donald Duck, Mickey Mouse, and other American comic-strip characters.

Before saying goodbye to our hosts, we visit a small chapel. Behind the altar—only a small, raised table covered with a white cloth—a traditional crucifix hangs on the wall. In front of the altar a young nun, looking like a picture of the Virgin Mary in her white gown and pale blue head covering, leads a dozen young women wearing the traditional colorful saris in a soft chant: "Father, we adore you, lay our lives before you. Father, we love you."

A few minutes later, we are back on the streets. As our cab stops for a red light we are approached by a beggar who can only crawl. In the few seconds we have, we hand him whatever loose money we have. A leper, he has no fingers on either hand.

As our ship sails back out to sea, I stare across the vast expanse of water, realizing anew—as must all Americans—that most of humankind lives in poverty, hunger, and squalor. Once we fully understand that truth, that distressing reality, we must react: We must examine the immorality and injustice of the social conditions responsible for such a tragic state of affairs and take our place among those who actively work to correct those conditions. Simply referring to Scripture does not seem an adequate solution to the problem. (See also ALTRUISM; CHARITY; JUSTICE.)

PROPHECY AND PREDICTION. It is difficult, perhaps impossible, to speak with any precision about prophecy. In numerous instances prophets who risked short-term predictions have been shown to be mistaken. For example, those who predicted that Richard Nixon would be assassinated while president of the United States did not have to wait long to find out whether their prophecy was valid or invalid. As a logical construct, the problem is that in contrast to other abstract theory all that can be scientifically established about prophecy is its frequent error, never its validity.

Since this runs counter to what the average person supposes, a word of explanation is required. The fact that Richard Nixon was not killed while president conclusively establishes that all predictions to the contrary were erroneous. But if he had been assassinated, that unhappy fact would *not,* in any sense whatever, have established the validity of such a prediction. All that the facts could show was that (1) certain individuals had made statements predicting the assassination, and (2) Nixon subsequently was in fact killed. But the fact that the second event followed the first in no way establishes a connection between the two.

It is a matter of public record that a number of individuals predicted the assassination of President John Kennedy. In today's troubled world such predictions seem to be made for every president and, no doubt, for the leaders of other nations as well. From time to time, sad to say, such leaders will be killed. But—again—there is not the slightest reason to believe that these tragic instances have any connection with the predictions of them.

The numerous actual or alleged prophecies of the Old Testament are, for the most part, even less precise than an assertion that at some point in the future a given American president will be assassinated. Obviously, predictions relating to the killing of presidents have a maximum period of eight years during which their invalidity can be demonstrated. The predictions of the Old Testament take practically all of eternity as their time target. Therefore, given the incredibly wide range of diversity of human experience, there is a good mathematical probability that over the course of many centuries all sorts of events might come to pass that could seem to be in some degree of harmony with one ancient prophecy or another.

The reader may create a prophecy at this very moment. Let us experiment with constructing one together, which the reader is naturally free to revise to his or her own satisfaction. Let us say that the eyes of the faithful will one day be lifted up and their hearts gladdened because it will come to pass that a righteous, long-haired man will come out of the East to remind humans of their subservience to God. It might well be that during the next, say, ten thousand years dozens of individuals may so conduct their lives as to merit being designated the great leader referred to in the prophecy we have just created in the total absence of divine inspiration. Naturally additional specifics may be added that can limit the range of possibilities, but that range will still be statistically enormous. It might be specified, for example, that the leader will be of the white race, will be a woman, or be able to work wonders by the power of Christ.

If the reader and I could stand apart from and above time for the next ten thousand years, we might not be surprised that at some point far in the future it might be said that we have predicted the appearance of some remarkable person who by the combination of spirituality, intelligence, sensitivity, charm, etc., indeed attracts an enormous following and serves admirably as a moral teacher.

Our prediction, of course, is unlikely to be taken seriously if it is encountered in the context of these pages, but if precisely the same prophecy were incorporated into a purely religious document, it might well in time come to be spoken of very respectfully indeed. (See also JOEL; LAST DAYS, THE; MALACHI; NAHUM; OBADIAH; PETER, THE SECOND EPISTLE OF; REVELATION, THE [OF ST. JOHN THE DIVINE].)

PSYCHOLOGY AND RELIGION. Another specific area in which the Bible has done actual harm is in the scriptural "explanation" of mental illness as being caused by demonic possession or personally ordained by God as punishment for sin. The Bible is once more in factual error.

It is by no means necessary to introduce the debate over the demonic possession theory into this question. Even among the small minority who cling to what is commonly regarded as a superstitious belief there is no longer anyone who argues that *all* mental illness is caused by demonic possession. Informed Catholic clergymen, who are not theologically at liberty to dismiss totally the concept of possession of innocent souls by evil spirits, concede that such cases are extremely rare. Clearly, such instances account for a small fraction of one percent of the millions of cases of mental illness of which we have knowledge in our own time.

So long as in ages past Christians believed that practically all mental and emotional seizures were caused by Satan and his minions, practically nothing in the way of intelligent treatment could be offered the many tragically afflicted souls. On the contrary, the practices to which they were subjected were horrible. The mentally ill endured the terrifying ritual of exorcism, were chained and shackled, brutally beaten, imprisoned, and generally treated like animals.

When Freud and other modern psychologists began to take a more reasonable, charitable view of such phenomena, they were subjected to the bitter abuse that the churches have historically reserved for those who presumed to question traditional beliefs and customs, however irrational. In due course, naturally, the churches came around to adopt a good many of the very views they had long attacked. Since this has generally been the case in the conflict between SCIENCE AND RELIGION, we should not be surprised to encounter it in the area of psychology and psychiatry.

Multiple Personality Disorders. Perhaps the most intriguing and perplexing problems known to modern psychology are the cases of individuals with not one but several personalities, each clearly defined by different views on important questions, different blood pressures, different emotional attitudes, and different pleasures.

The classic fictional instance described by Robert Louis Stevenson in *The Strange Case of Dr. Jekyll and Mr. Hyde* was bizarre enough, but only two separate selves were involved. Since Stevenson's time, medical science has documented numerous instances of the phenomenon. Those who know nothing of such a disorder may assume that the unfortunate patients suffering from it are merely imagining that they have various names, and that the seemingly separate selves to which those names are given simply vary somewhat in general personality in the sense that one might be cheerful, another pessimistic, a third aggressive, or a fourth amusing.

Multiple personalities would be mysterious enough if their disorder was that simple, but the realities are far more complex. Not only do the separate selves in one individual have their own names, but they usually report separate ages as well. Far from sharing a common memory bank, certain recollected details are accessible only to one or some of the per-

313

sonalities. Handwritings may be different, even the familiarity with other languages.

Nor would it be safe to assume that the differences are purely psychological. Striking physical differences are common as well. One of a given group of individual selves may suffer from a particular medical disorder, such as an allergy. If that self is, say, allergic to strawberries he will naturally stay away from them and may break out in hives if he eats them. When the individual is not that particular self, however, he can eat as many strawberries as he wants without suffering negative allergic reactions. Scott Miller, a University of Utah psychologist, has measured actual differences in eye shape among various personalities in one individual.

While most such patients suffered serious abuse in childhood, that fact in itself leaves unanswered the question why only a small percentage of badly abused children respond by splitting into what are apparently separate minds.

One aspect of this remarkable phenomenon that has received no attention, so far as I know, concerns the profoundly perplexing philosophical and theological questions that arise out of multiple personality disorders. It has always been difficult to define or apprehend the human self. Words such as *brain, mind,* or *soul* are used but they certainly do not add up to the totality of the human being.

The basic moral assumptions of the Judeo-Christian code are difficult—perhaps impossible—to harmonize with what is now clearly established about multiple personality disorders. All moral codes, obviously, are premised on a belief in freedom of the will, but that implies the will of a given individual. If that individual has separate selves, it would appear that he has separate wills, not all of which will agree on one moral/ethical question or another. (See also FREE WILL.)

What of instances in which one self is at least in part evil whereas another is virtuous? One thinks, in this connection, of the old short story about Siamese twins who cannot be imprisoned if one commits a serious crime because the other one is totally innocent.

A considerably more common variation of the ailment concerns cases in which an apparently normal individual firmly believes in separate philosophies, which are at least in part mutually exclusive. An example would be a person who is absolutely convinced that he is both a pure capitalist and a good Christian. (See also CRIMES, BIBLICAL IMPETUS TO; DISEASE; MEDICINE.)

R

REASON. I am not deluded that those problems generally described by the words *emotional* or *psychological* can be satisfactorily dealt with by nothing more than a good dose of reason. If that were so the psychiatric process could take place in perhaps half an hour rather than the years sometimes required. There is no sense whatever in reasoning with a hypochondriac, a kleptomaniac, a sexual fetishist, a homicidal maniac, a compulsive gambler, an alcoholic, a heroin addict, a Don Juan, a nymphomaniac, or any of the other emotional cripples who now constitute a depressingly large percentage of the population of the planet. Reason can be one of the ingredients of the therapeutic process but it alone does not suffice.

Yet it seems highly probable that if, starting at the earliest possible point in our childhoods, we had all been taught a respect for reason, we would subsequently be protected against at least a good many of the slings and arrows that presently cause so much suffering. If our society should now publicly cherish reason, we would be doing a dazzlingly important thing to establish a set of public standards against which social conduct might be measured and against which dangerous misbehavior might be called to account. (See also EDUCATIVE PROCESS, THE.)

It has long been obvious that society cannot function unless moral and ethical standards are clearly acknowledged and publicly encouraged. The true horror of Nazi dominance in Germany was not the individual atrocities, monstrous as they were. The essence, the nucleus, of the horror was that in that time and place *practically every sort of brutality was permitted, if it was performed for a "good cause."* Traditional personal standards had simply become irrelevant. The history of religion, too, is full of similar examples. (See also CRUSADES, THE; RELIGIOUS THEORIES, DEVIANT.)

No individual is born for all time immune from the commission of destructive, antisocial acts. Every beautiful, innocent infant in the crib could quite readily be turned into a vicious murderer. Nor would the task be in the least difficult. We would only have to abuse the child verbally and physically and deny it love—nothing more would be required. Anyone who has looked into the childhoods of Charles Manson, the Son-of-Sam killer, and the serial murderers of our society will have no difficulty in accepting this assertion.

Happily, we also know how to train children to be decent, affectionate, and constructive adults. One way to do this is to begin teaching the reasoning process at the kindergarten level. At the same early stage we must also provide preliminary training for the eventual roles of wife, husband, mother, and father. No training is needed for the physical act that results in conception and the birth of a new individual. Indeed, what we require in that sphere is training in how to *prevent* births, whether by virtuous abstinence or the use of contraceptives. The physical elements, in any event, are instinctual. There are inherent components to mothering as well, although this instinct, compared to the sexual, is relatively feeble and all too easily blocked.

There must also be a moral component to the recommended course of instruction. The specific virtue inculcated must be that of *honesty,* with particular emphasis on intellectual honesty. An ethical climate must be encouraged that will make the individual uncomfortable in the face of falsehood. The perfect realization of such an ideal is impossible, but indoctrination in the methods of logical reasoning and argument in the total absence of a moral component will lead—as it already demonstratably does—to an employment of the rules and devices of reason in the interest of unedifying purposes and causes: sophistry and casuistry are ancient arts. Their imagined justification—for only in extremely rare cases can there be any true justification—is that the all-important factor is the victory of the "True Faith." There would be a bad moral odor to all of this even if there were only one "True Faith." When there are ten thousand and their number grows daily, evil unites with madness to create something very much like the present world condition. (See EVIL, THE PROBLEM OF.)

Reason can approach the achievement of its noblest goals only if it is guided by ethical and moral considerations.

I am not trying to bring about a world—nor even a personal lifestyle—in which reason is totally dominant. Any such outcome is impossible. Even if it were achievable, it would not be totally desirable. I am concerned merely to give reason its rightful place, which it certainly does not occupy at present.

Reason and morality do not have an adversary but a complementary relationship. Reason enables us to evaluate such moral strictures as are suggested to us. Reason tells us that moral codes designed to discourage murder, thievery, rape, marital infidelity, and cruelty are wise and practical, whereas moral rules of a narrowly sectarian or even bizarre nature are decidedly less worthy of respect.

Reason and Religion. There have always been two schools of thought concerning the relationship between reason and religion: (1) those who would prefer that the masses be left in undisturbed tranquillity so far as difficult theological questions are concerned, and (2) those who deny that only the ignorant can be true believers and therefore employ philosophy and reason to defend a faith. In the Catholic context, Augustine and Aquinas were the two leading philosophical spokesmen for the proposition that reason and religion are by no means mutually exclusive.

Nevertheless, in one sense reason and religion are not only opposed but are also mortal enemies, and that is when specific aspects of belief are nonsensical, absurd, morally dangerous, or otherwise an insult to even minimal intelligence. Although religion often regards reason with some suspicion, such fears are themselves sensible only to the extent that reason does tend to corrode the structures of certain religious stories or beliefs that are, in terms of common sense, either highly unlikely or impossible. (See BELIEFS AND MYTHS.)

To deal with a specific instance: no non-Mormon has any faith in the assertions of a man named Joseph Smith that he was in personal communication with God and found a buried treasure of old plates containing writings about an ancient civilization. To the extent that we apply the rigorous standards of rationality to such unlikely allegations, it is clear that the great majority of the world's jury will perceive many reasons to doubt or discard the mystic's assertion and little or no reason to accept it.

Another example of unreasoned faith is the fundamentalist's belief in the every-word-the-literal-voice-of-God theory about the Bible. Understandably, poorly educated Christians would be unfamiliar with the past three hundred years of Bible scholarship on the part of various distinguished and frequently devout theologians, lexicographers, historians, priests, ministers, rabbis, and others sincerely concerned with solving the great mystery of the Scriptures. But surely fundamentalist Bible teachers cannot be totally unfamiliar with such an impressive and extensive accumulation of scholarship.

Why then—in the face of veritable mountains of evidence that would cause any intelligent and unprejudiced student to at least consider revising his previous conceptions—do such leaders cling to their long-outmoded views? They do so not as a result of having fairly considered the evidence of scholarship but rather because of having early drawn back from it in horror simply because *they were emotionally and psychologically unable to accommodate the possibility that their lives to date may have been lived under the influence of an enormous shadow of error.* Such individuals are intellectually blinded by their prejudice. They must make some public pretense at having considered the evidence that contradicts them, but in fact many have not done so.

Once the untrained mind has made a formal commitment to a philosophy—and it is irrelevant whether that philosophy is generally reasonable and high-minded or utterly bizarre and irrational—the powers of reason are surprisingly ineffective in changing the believer's mind.

Science, reason, and the factual record, all taken together, are inconsistent with a great part of religious belief. If we examine the details of every argument that pitted the church against science over, say, the last five hundred years, we find that, by and large, science has represented the more reasonable and factually correct side of the debate. (See also SCIENCE AND RELIGION.)

But even in personal terms, most of us who have tried to "talk sense" to a philosophical opponent have seen that no matter how reasonable and accurate our statements may be, they do not seem to penetrate the other's consciousness. I recall some years ago having a good-natured argument with a friend—a radio newsman who was a Christian Scientist. I was defending the Catholic position. At one point during our conversation the fellow said, "I'm firmly convinced that if my faith were strong enough I could drive my car for the rest of my life without ever putting gasoline in it."

I recognized at once that there was no hope of dealing logically, or even by means of common sense, with such an assertion. I went over the ground once or twice to make sure that I had correctly interpreted what my friend had said, although there was nothing inherently complex in his profession of faith. Indeed, he had meant the statement to be taken at face value. The fact that no Christian Scientist in the world has even been able to drive an internal combustion automobile without fuel did not seem to him to have any relevance whatever.

The man was—at least in all other respects—not a fanatic. He was bright enough to work in a profession that requires a certain degree of intelligence. He was articulate, cheerful, personable. I liked him. But he nevertheless was able to express this and a number of other opinions that at least 99 percent of the human race would consider nonsensical.

Aristotle said that the proper function of man is an activity of soul in accordance with reason, or at least not independent of reason. The entire history of philosophical speculation shows that there will often be difficulty in applying rational standards to religious concepts. This does not mean that it is hopeless to make such an attempt. Even such masters of logic as Augustine and Aquinas employed their powers to the greatest possible limits and only then acknowledged a small area of religious truth that was to be described as *mystery,* precisely because reason could not enter into its domain.

But the essence of the modern evangelical, charismatic movement is inherently unreasonable and, in the case of certain individuals, even contemptuous of reason. To those who finally seek within the sacred grove of mystery a small refuge from the bright light of reason, one may say that one wishes them well, or that they are at least in part deluded, or that insofar as such belief increases the practice of virtue it can perhaps, on that ground alone, be defended.

But those who disdain reason must be vigorously opposed. The only way they could possibly justify their position in terms intelligible to those who approach the large question impartially would be to argue that faith is a gift of God and reason a gift of the Devil. Of course they have never so argued since they are unfree to counter the dogmatic belief that God made all things. They do not have the freedom of such ancients as Plato, who erroneously argued that a demi-urge was responsible for the ugly physical realities. So long then as they are both logically and theologically obliged to assume that reason, too, is a gift of God, they are therefore bound to respect it.

Because their essential impulses are unreasonable, some religious opinions are to a remarkable extent impervious to reason. Very few reason their way into a faith. The keys of entrance are usually emotional, sometimes virtuous, at other times fanatical and dangerous.

It is not by the process of thinking—not by any act of systematic analysis—that children come to accept the hundreds of different forms of religion into which they are drawn in large numbers. They are generally enrolled in parochial schools, Sunday School classes, and other young people's church organizations by parents, with entirely admirable intentions at the one extreme and usually nothing more harmful than social habit and conformity on the other. The popular mind—quite rightly—shares the impression that the inculcation of certain moral lessons in the young is a societal necessity. Since there are few means of bringing about such training, parents by the millions therefore enlist their children in the ranks of their own spiritual armies. Our religious beliefs and biases are almost invariably originally developed through channels other than those on which our rational powers resonate.

One reason that religious views have a remarkably strong hold on us is that at a very early stage in our personal development they come to seem part of our inner selves, part of the ego, of that center so mysterious that we cannot in fact precisely locate it. Consequently any aspersions upon our *views*—as Jews, Catholics, Protestants, etc.—are inevitably perceived as attacks upon *us*. Defensive responses, perhaps inculcated by millions of years of evolutionary animal and human social conditioning, are immediately brought into play so that it seems important that (1) our views be buttressed, and (2) the critic be dealt with severely.

Our spiritual advisors may attempt to demonstrate that our religious opinions can be reasonably defended. A good many of them *can* be so construed in that they concern either questions of historical fact or moral views consistent with those perceived as sound even by unbelievers.

But certain other of our religious opinions cannot be defended by reason. As explained above, most churches acknowledge this and refer to such beliefs as *mysteries,* a word that carries with it the frank concession that such views are incompatible with pure reason or science. When it is asserted that the views must be firmly held despite their inadmissibility on rational grounds, the effect is to place an even lower premium on the powers of reason than we are individually disposed to anyway. In the cases of millions of us, reason never recovers from these early assaults and therefore cannot be depended upon as an aid to social sanity at future moments of stress, not only in regard to religious questions but also in the context of social and political matters.

All sizable religious denominations—Christian or otherwise—have their intellectual adherents. If the overwhelming majority of superior minds were found in one particular corner, that fact would merit careful attention and could perhaps even be persuasive. The confusing reality is that almost every camp can boast its resident philosophers and scholars who adhere to certain ideas while challenging those of other religious groups. For example, for centuries in the West—Europe and North America—Christianity has been considered by its adherents vastly superior, especially intellectually, to any philosophy practiced in Africa or Asia. It has taken until the twentieth century for Judaism to be generally acknowledged by Christians to be on a par with Christianity, despite the fact that Christianity has always in-directly acknowledged Judaism by including the Old Testament in the Christian Bible.

But Muslims, Buddhists, Hindus, and others were considered to be practicing inferior, if not "idolatrous" religions. Christian theologians consider themselves more intellectual than their Muslim equivalents and sometimes even deny that there *is* such a thing as Muslim theology. A long tradition of learning is closely related to the Muslim religion, Islam, but since much of it has never been translated from Arabic, and since most Westerners do not trouble to learn that language, this intellectual scholarship has gone unrecognized or been denigrated in the West.

We should all rethink our religions. This is not to suggest that religion itself is irrational. It is simply not very intelligent to accept everything your personal religion, if you have one, delivers to you. Nor would it make sense to reject everything your religion proposed. To be intelligent in this context involves considering the separate components of your faith one by one.

As a result of that process you may become a more committed believer than ever before, or you may leave your church altogether. You may leave the Jewish faith and become a Christian, or vice versa. You may leave the so-called Church of Scientology and become a Catholic.

In this context, it doesn't matter whether you make a move or remain where you are. The important thing is to think—to *reason*—about your beliefs. If we arbitrarily assume that there is a God, it may be argued that reason can take us only so far in speculating about religion. Ultimately we must make the leap of faith, in the absence of conclusive evidence, to maintain one specific belief or another. But if reason has limits then let us go to those limits.

All religions are not equal. Some religions are far more reasonable than others. Some people have such a sweet, benign reaction to the word *religion* itself that they somehow feel it is rather marvelous if another individual is "religious," in the absence of any consideration of what his religious views are or what he actually does as a result of holding such views.

Some religious opinions are beautiful, moral, enlightening, uplifting; others are bizarre, crazy, socially dangerous, vengeful, personally destructive. There are millions of religious fanatics in the world. Some of them act crazy. You wouldn't want them in your house. You wouldn't want your daughter to marry one of them. In addition to all the fine, admirable things done for religious reasons throughout the centuries, countless evil acts have also been perpetrated by religious individuals *for religious reasons.* (See also FANATICISM; IRRATIONALISM.)

Refer to any neighborhood library for the specifics of the murders, pogroms, persecutions, purges, slaughters, beheadings, burnings at the stake, boilings in oil, human sacrifices, instances of genocide, crusades, wars— all supposedly "justified" by their churchly perpetrators. Face this fact: get it into the sharpest, clearest possible focus as you apply your emerging intelligence to religion in the same way you would apply it to any other subject matter.

*　　*　　*

How can you tell if one religion is dumber than another? One way is to ask: What does a given church say about the age of the physical universe? A number of them answer forthrightly enough—the earth is anywhere from five to ten thousand years old.

You may be quite sure that a church that formally teaches any such thing is, at least on this point, guilty of serious "dumbth." Modern scientists—including many distinguished Christian and Jewish scholars—know that the physical universe is *billions* of years old.

Another way to separate the dumbbells from the wiser believers is in regard to the question of "the end of the world." For unknown centuries individuals have been predicting that the end was not only possible but very near. In many cases they gave specific dates when this was to occur, *all of which have passed.* Yet millions of American Christians are not simply fearful but even absolutely convinced that the world is going to end in the next twenty or thirty years.

Even if the world ends next Tuesday, these people are still guilty of an error-in-reasoning in their arguments because they have developed them irrationally. They have failed to distinguish between conclusive evidence and consistent evidence. Conclusive evidence really settles the question or proves the point. There is simply no getting away from the fact when evidence is conclusive.

Consistent evidence is of another sort altogether. If certain evidence is consistent, it simply means that so far as this particular bit of data is concerned, it does not render the hypothesis invalid.

Assume that in the Bible it is said that in "the Last Days" purple sunsets will be seen. Let us then assume that in 1993 scientists begin to notice a number of strangely purplish skies during the hours in which the sun is setting. Given the history of religious experience, thousands of people would close up their business affairs, fall to their knees, or rush to their churches because they had become absolutely confident that the world was indeed approaching its end. You and I can perceive that they would be guilty of the consistent/conclusive evidence mistake.

We must take reason to its boundaries in our analysis of matters religious. On the other hand, reason, too, will concede it has only limited application to questions concerning beauty, painting, music, sex, poetry, dreams, and certain other areas of human conjecture. It is not that reason is totally irrelevant in the consideration of such phenomena but rather that it ought not to be expected to resolve all possible questions. (See also MORALITY.)

RELIGION. The average person—including even countless thousands of the devout—passes his entire life either without adequately grasping the multiplicity of religious forms, or greatly underestimating their extent. He may, for example, imagine he is considering only five or six—certainly fewer than a dozen—varieties of faith. In reality the forms are so numerous that even scholars go to their graves without having personally encountered all of them.

Not only is the list of religions lengthy but many of the faiths on the list are themselves also markedly altered according to factors of location. A Lutheran in the German town of Ulm is noticeably different in his Lutheranism from his brother in the faith living in Gallup, New Mexico. The Sicilian Catholic differs in his Catholicism from his fellow believers living in Ireland.

Precisely the same is true when we consider factors of time rather than space.

Humankind, despite the protestations of many that they most highly value religious ideas and practices, really holds the bulk of religious activity and thought in utter contempt. True, each man has reverence for his own theological opinions, but there is almost a direct ratio between that personal reverence and the disdain we feel for religious views that differ from our own.

Since each believer is a member of only one religion, it follows that each has respect for only a minority of religious ideas and is prepared to laugh off as unthinkable the views of the majority.

The Buddhist, for example, smiles at the Jew's belief that Jews are God's Chosen People. The Baptist reacts to the doctrines of Christian Science with a snort of intellectual contempt; the Methodist is privately convinced that the Mormon is theologically deranged; the Muslim is aghast at Christian belief and behavior in general; the Catholic regards the Protestant as a deluded soul; and the Protestant may look upon Catholicism as some sort of worldwide conspiracy. It may safely be said, then, that not only is the bulk of religious thought regarded lightly by the irreligious but by the religious as well.

If we assume that it is possible for one of the world's hundreds of religions to be better than all the others, then the question is: according to what standards? Judged by what results? Surely there can be no serious suggestion that churches should be evaluated in terms of the beauty of their music or architecture, the success of their football teams, or the amount of money they raise through televised or other public appeals. Obviously these and other such factors are totally irrelevant.

One sensible basis on which a religion *can* be evaluated is its ability to affect the lives of its adherents beneficially. If we observe a religion the members of which are habitually spiteful, vindictive, murderous, or otherwise aggressive, and another faith whose followers lead lives of sweet peace and reason, lives characterized by charity, compassion, and loving kindness, we would not suffer a moment's hesitation in judging which is superior. Following the advice of Jesus, we would make such a judgment by concentrating on the fruits, the *results* of the various forms of religious indoctrination. In the context of centuries of analysis, very few of today's religions have a great deal to be proud of on such a basis, and much for which they should be painfully ashamed. (See also BY THEIR FRUITS YE SHALL KNOW THEM.)

We know from the clear record of history that religion has done much harm. Because of this, many have raised the question: Does religion, in fact, do any good?

Yes, the religions of the world—despite their inherent structural faults and the human weakness of their adherents—have indeed done not just a little but a great deal of beneficial work.

Some religious people do admirable and socially productive good deeds, as they have for centuries. Hardworking ministers, rabbis, priests, nuns, as well as lay persons better the world in a thousand-and-one ways by their work in schools, hospitals, charitable organizations, and in personal contacts.

An editorial in the March 1978 edition of the Catholic periodical *St. Anthony's Messenger* called for repudiation of a proposed march by uniformed members of the Nazi party in Skokie, Illinois, and encouraged Christians to protest peaceably by wearing the Star of David that European Jews were forced to wear during the period of Hitler's dominance in Germany. This is merely one of millions of individual acts that might be cited to support the theory of religious benefits to humanity.

One encouraging aspect of the centuries-old story of the Christian and Jewish religions is that today's representatives of those esteemed faiths are, in the moral sense, superior to their ancestors. This is a statistical truth and therefore not meant to apply to all individual cases, since it is as obvious that there are morally despicable Jews and Gentiles in the present day as that there were admirable members of the two religions in earlier times. But even a casual examination of the two groups' histories and published literature shows that today's believers are not nearly as intolerant and vindictive as their forefathers.

Defenders of religion ask the question how, if Christianity has less merit than its hundreds of subsidiary churches have claimed, certain pious figures have nevertheless lived exemplary lives guided by its standards. Granted, there is a tragic scarcity of individuals of heroic virtue in whatever philosophical camp they may be encountered. But one high-minded, superior person is worth a thousand sermons so far as influencing others is concerned. The quality of inspirational leadership is so rare and has such remarkable power that conversions can be brought about simply by the authority of such examples. Just so, one hideous example of religious hatred—such as the Ayatollah Khomeini's formal call for the assassination of author Salman Rushdie—can do more harm to the image of a religion, in this case Islam, than a thousand published critiques.

Our world is in a specially troubled period today, and it is refreshing to encounter so many well-intentioned Christians—for the most part very decent people—who wish not only to retain their own sense of HOPE in the present darkness but also to encourage others to live morally sane lives. I would encourage my Christian friends to ponder the question as to how they came to be so socially civilized when their ancestors so often produced violent, spiteful, and vengeful polemic literature.

Part of the solution, I suggest, lies in the civilizing effect of humanist, progressive, reformist elements in modern society. Another part involves the factors of public relations and image consciousness. In a day when communication is instantaneous and widespread, the kinds of obscure things that used to happen in local communities or other limited areas are now a matter of immediate worldwide interest. Far more observant critics have access to public attention than in former times. Today's religious spokesmen, therefore, cannot get away with the kind of vindictive preaching and threatening that used to characterize much of their public utterance. These major factors, mutually influencing each other, account for the admirable improvement in the public conduct of representatives of most of our modern religions.

Not all present-day religious rhetoric is sweetness and light. Right-wing fundamentalist elements of Protestantism and Catholicism—sometimes more strongly political than spiritual—continue to employ more than a little of the old brimstone and sulphur.

But to look at the central question—Is religion good or bad?—my own view is that it is morally neutral and that the question can only be meaningfully applied to specific aspects of the various theologies. For example, one might intelligently inquire about such factors as

- The Catholic belief in the infallibility of the pope.
- The Mormon belief in the literal existence of Golden Plates delivered to Joseph Smith by an angel.

- The Christian belief in original sin.
- The belief in a literal, material, eternal hell.
- The Jewish belief in Moses' personal authorship of the first five books of the Scriptures.
- The Crusades or the Spanish Inquisition.
- The Christian practice of burning heretics alive at the stake.
- The Christian Science insistence on the essential unreality of matter.

Concerning these and thousands of other specific assertions one might raise questions of wisdom or absurdity, fanaticism or tyranny, virtue or sin, accuracy or error. For religion as a separate abstract entity, however, the question is meaningless.

Science versus Religion. There is absolutely no way to be certain of what "the laws of God" are. We can, on the other hand, know and measure the laws of nature. If we assume—as believers do—that God is the creator of nature, it is logically inescapable that in studying nature we are studying the laws of God.

Second, it must be observed that the means of studying nature is what men call *science*. It is therefore absurd for any religious believer to perceive himself as defending God by attacking science. This obviously does not preclude opposing specific errors of individual scientists, which are generally well opposed in any event by an army of their peers. But it does argue that we must respect the rules of evidence that our own physical nature enables us to perceive since these, by the logic of basic religious assumptions, derive from that physical nature for which none of us individually is in the slightest degree responsible.

No reputable scholar in the world today denies that the Bible was, in large and direct measure, responsible for the painstakingly slow development of the sciences in general and of astronomic physics in particular. It was five years after Columbus's first voyage to the new world that Copernicus, then a young student at the University of Bologna, made the first astronomical observations that confirmed his apparently already growing doubts concerning the firmly held belief that the earth was motionless.

If an astronomer today makes a remarkable and dramatic discovery he may immediately publish it without the slightest fear and may, in fact, be honored for his perception and competence. The situation was quite different in the Christian Europe of five hundred years ago. Common beliefs about the nature of the physical universe were either directly based on the nonsensical account given in Genesis or at least had to conform to that account. To announce any surprising scientific discovery to the contrary—however valid and wise—was to lay oneself open to a charge of not just error but heresy. (See also CRIME, BIBLICAL IMPETUS TO.)

If scholars will forgive the digression, it must be stressed, for those who do not know, that heresy does not necessarily involve the teaching of false views. Many heretics have been essentially right in their teachings while their critics have been essentially wrong. Heresy is simply a word that any dominant religious authority uses to convey the judgment that one idea or another is contrary to the doctrine of its authority.

The situation would have been atrocious enough if certain religious leaders, with their combined arrogance and ignorance, had only contradicted the valid observations of courageous scientists, burned their books, hindered their freedom to teach, or attacked their integrity. Practically, the church authorities went a great deal further than that. They were quite prepared to arrest the offenders, to brutalize and torture them, even to put them to death in the most hideous way possible: by applying flames to exquisitely sensitive human flesh. (See also CRUSADES, THE; RELIGIOUS THEORIES, DEVIANT.)

Every informed person is perfectly aware that this was indeed the case, but even now millions do not wish such truths to be stated, though they profess to adore the one who said: "The truth shall make you free." What a pity that his followers have often been at least as concerned to suppress one truth as to preach another.

Although the search for truth ought to be the special province of religion, it clearly is not. The disinterested seeking of truth is the special province of scholarship. If one is formally committed to a religious philosophy, however virtuous or admirable, it can no longer be rightfully asserted that one is perfectly free to seek out the material and philosophical realities of his universe. To the extent that he *is* free to do so, then precisely to the same extent he is judged to be less than totally committed to his formally professed faith.

On purely rational grounds there is no reason why either God or man cannot produce an actual religion every belief of which is true. But that such a thing is possible has not led to its ever having actually occurred.

In surveying their long and imposing list of victories, scientifically minded people may make the error of assuming that, except for a few fanatics in rural communities, the general philosophical controversy about religion has essentially been settled.

For example, the preface to *Critiques of God,* edited by Peter Angeles (Prometheus Books), announces:

> The concept of a God as a casual agent has been taken less and less seriously during the past few hundred years . . . as our knowledge of the universe increases, we recognize that all forms of phenomena can be explained in terms of the interrelatedness of natural processes, without reference to God.
>
> Beliefs in supernatural beings have vanished from our culture . . . [there is] the realization that *there is no God left to which to relate.* (IA)

While the inability to believe in God as traditionally defined has indeed become increasingly common in the intellectual and scientific community during the past two centuries, it may be that because these individuals in these fields largely associate with each other they are blinded to social information that clearly contradicts the God-is-dead hypothesis. What is observable is that church affiliation has not declined but been on the rise. Where some years back religion was thought to be chiefly the province of children, old women, the poorly educated, and men of conservative bias, now a true revival of religious faith, in a wide variety of forms, is taking place among even the youth of Western nations.

There are peaks and valleys in all aspects of human development, of course; one therefore properly concentrates on general trends. But rationalists must further support their own claim to rationality by perceiving what is, in fact, going on in the streets about them. (See also SCIENCE AND RELIGION.)

RELIGIOUS THEORIES, DEVIANT. Of all the fields of human knowledge, only religion gives rise to a seemingly infinite variety of theories. Although most Christians view a unified faith as an appealing ideal, the reality is at the other extreme.

Because some diverse theories and practices are bizarrely preposterous, even to poorly informed believers, churches readily concede the existence of a lunatic fringe of religious theorizers. Consequently, when a hypothesis is presented that comes as a sharp surprise to the majority of conventional believers, there is an understandable tendency to relegate it to the loony-bin category and thus give it no further consideration. But not all startling theories deserve such a fate. If there is a God who made all things, then he made the human mind. It can hardly be argued that he created the intellect of men but would prefer that they not use it for any purposes except those necessary for physical survival. Intellectual camps at odds over religious issues would be wise to attend to their more responsible critics with exquisite care. Even when the issues are not neatly two-sided, much can still be learned. The refusal to hear arguments that are contrary to current beliefs is not only unreasonable, it is idiotic.

It is conceivable that the word *criticism* itself has misled at least some traditionalists not of the scholarly persuasion. The common connotation of the word is negative, and therefore the possibility that religious criticism may actually result in an endorsement of that which is analyzed will literally not occur to those who know only the unacademic use of the term.

Defenders of scriptural tradition also erroneously assume that all those who correctly point to the logical inconsistencies and factual inaccuracies of Scripture attack divine revelation itself. This objection is poorly reasoned. No blanket defense can possibly address all such critics. Atheistic rationalists obviously deny the possibility of communication from what they consider a nonexistent being. Theistic critics of Scripture not only concede either the reality or the theoretical possibility of divine revelation but may also in fact long for it. They simply have the good sense to realize that whoever would encourage respect for a patent absurdity by claiming that it was authored by God deserves to be opposed. They are therefore in truth defending the idea of divine revelation against the insults and embarrassments to which certain fundamentalist superstition and unreason would subject it.

Even if a man preaches the error, say, that two and two add up to five, it is not helpful to respond to that assertion—as Christians throughout history have done—by cracking the man's skull, or imprisoning or ostracizing him. It is better to point out the error in his reasoning and to provide him with the right answer. That prophets are, as the old saying has it, generally without honor in their home communities is not due to that contempt supposed to be bred by familiarity but simply because a prophet is a critic. He criticizes, in fact, far more than he prophesies.

Prophets and other social critics get into trouble not so much because they are wrong—or for that matter right. They are regarded warily because *they alarm us by threatening the status quo, by threatening to make us think.* Their new ideas are disturbing not so much on their own merits but rather because they are new. This applies to doers as well as thinkers. We shrink from the novel prescription even before we have analyzed it.

It is irrelevant that the new proposal might be described by all disinterested parties as a decided improvement. It is still very likely to be resisted purely on the grounds of its unfamiliarity. It is difficult enough to keep track of things in this troublesome world as they stand. Not surprisingly, therefore, significant change in our way of perceiving our world is almost invariably viewed as at the least troublesome and at the extreme a threat. This understandable human propensity toward stasis fuels the more vocal and sometimes violent resistance to reformation. And it is partly this resistance that has created the often bloody history of Christianity.

One of the fascinating aspects of biblical criticism is the violent response that has been occasioned by nothing more radical than the rendering of the Bible into plain, modern English—which certainly makes it far more intelligible to millions of people than the beautiful but archaic King James version. One would think that a true lover of the Bible would applaud any steps that would make it more accessible to the average reader. This clearly does not occur in many cases, which is a classic demonstration of how staunch Christian conservatism seeks to overpower reason.

The world's libraries are full of hundreds of scholarly works documenting the bloody massacres perpetrated by the highest Christian authorities upon those who had made the tactical mistake of consulting their own reason rather than blindly submitting to authority on theological or biblical questions. If we take as valid the observation of Jesus that a tree may be known by its fruits, then the many savage fruits of religious belief—including those reported in the Bible—must certainly be taken into account.

That the heretics were sometimes as irrational in their views as were their murderers is also due—in the most direct and inescapable sense—to the combined influence of the Bible and those savage, persecutorial tendencies of the human mind that have so often broken out both within and outside the ranks of Christendom down through the centuries.

Almost all criticism of Western religious belief and practice centers either directly or inferentially on the Bible. The Bible is therefore of enormous interest and importance not only to atheists and agnostics but to Jews, Protestants, Catholics, and Muslims as well. Even those who may assume that to them personally the Bible is of no more importance than any other collection of ancient religious documents reside in a culture whose popular attitudes and customs are directly affected by beliefs drawn from the Judeo-Christian Scriptures.

Anyone who presumes to challenge the authority of such religious literature runs the risk of being branded not only a heretic—often a justified accusation—but also an enemy of society, a charge usually unjustified. Most of the world's progress has been achieved by heretics. Without them we would presently find ourselves mired in forms of primitive superstitious beliefs so ancient that their origin cannot be identified.

Catholics, generally speaking, have long imagined that Christendom was at peace in regard to biblical interpretation until the time of such troublemakers as Wycliffe, Huss, Calvin, and Luther; this was not the case.

Father Levie's *The Bible, Word of God in Words of Men* provides a useful and informative summary of the various thematic approaches to biblical criticism of the past century. In it he criticizes the liberal Protestant work of the period as being "purely historical rather than religiously orthodox." To most informed and unbiased observers of the present day the comment will sound more complimentary than critical. Levie observes:

> It was the history rather than the religious understanding of the doctrine, and of Jewish and Christian thought, which preoccupied many of these university professors. A great number of these Protestant commentaries of the pre-1914 period were imbued with an atmosphere of philosophical and theological skepticism, especially in Germany, though less in England, combined very often with remarkable technical, philosophical, exegetical and historical skill.

What Father Levie fundamentally objects to here is the work of a veritable army of renowned scholars who were prepared to permit the evidence their research unearthed to tell its own story impartially. Father Levie and many other Christian and Jewish commentators are absolutely correct, of course, in fearing that such research might lead to theological conclusions clearly outside the boundaries of orthodoxy. But surely to state as much is to criticize the orthodox view, not that of free-minded Christian scholars.

Father Levie properly draws our attention to the social background out of which such relatively unprejudiced scholarship emerged.

> We must also go back to the past, to the end of the 18th and the beginning of the 19th Centuries, to discover the historical reasons for the liberal character of German critical exegesis. In the 18th Century the intellectual movement in France was influenced by Voltaire and in Germany was dominated by the *Aufklarung*. German literature of the 18th Century with Lessing, Goethe, and even Schiller, was more pagan than Christian; . . . Schleiermacher's theology, for example, was . . . sharply divorced from the fundamental tenets of Christian Christology . . . with its constant Positivist emphasis on historical or scientific research, and its growing suspicion of all metaphysics, the Christianity of the German universities between 1870 and 1914 clearly showed its liberal character.

The unbiased reader will conclude that it is strange to criticize high-minded scholarship by saying that it is eminently respectful of historical rather than theological considerations, for history is a matter of fact and interpretation whereas theology is far more speculative, perhaps even totally so. The very word *theology* pertains to the knowledge of God, the supreme unknowable. We can perhaps achieve near-perfect certainty about a great

331

many facts of history, but anyone who can state that he has absolute knowledge about the Almighty is remarkably presumptuous. Many do not hesitate in making such an assertion, but in the context of the planetary population they have always been in a minority, even if we consider only the world of scholarship.

Father Levie, among his many reasonable and insightful comments on the drama to which he directs our attention, enables us to understand the psychological dynamics of the ongoing debate by observing:

> As often happens in all human controversies, the first objection to a traditional view is absolute, ruthless, going straight to the precise contrary; the conservative reaction is sweeping, aggressive, equally obstinate on secondary points as on the fundamental assertion. Time is required to see matters in perspective, together with the intervention on both sides of keen, perspicacious minds capable of freeing themselves both from the restrictions of their background and habits of thought and from the attraction of novelty and scientific allurements, so that light may be produced by the conflict of ideas.

Levie deserves our applause here but is on less firm ground when, concerning Catholic exegesis, he states:

> . . . it has come to understand that, rather than make God conform to our methods of teaching Christianity, we must adapt our teaching methods *to God's plan.* (IA)

The problem here is that we can deal rationally and responsibly with our own scholarly methods but must humbly concede that we are in a position of very modest ability in regard to acquiring certain knowledge of "God's plan." It is modern man's tragic and painful inability to perceive a divine, conscious plan in not only the blood-spattered record of history extending to the present moment, but also in the observably chaotic and confused biblical record itself that is the essence of the problem. Father Levie must inevitably *assume* the existence of something perceptible as God's design and only thereafter pick and choose among the biblical wreckage, so to speak, to locate evidence conformable to the church's version of that plan. While that version may or may not be correct, it is certainly not identical to the divine plan as seen through Protestant, Jewish, Buddhist, Islamic, or other non-Catholic eyes.

Father Levie's study does provide an excellent summary of the dramatic discoveries of the past century in the Near East, a great many of which threw new light on Old Testament passages in that they provided information about the history, languages, customs, literature, and religion of the several civilizations with which the Israelites were in contact over a period of many centuries. Although his outline gives the general impression of a partly accidental, partly chaotic or haphazard historical process, Father Levie is again constrained by the boundaries of his permitted theological assumptions to perceive such order as he can among the chaos. He therefore observes, "Study of this kind helps us to plumb the depths and complexity of the divine plan of Revelation." That the procedure has been deep and complex is enough to inspire sympathy for Father Levie's attempts to perceive both true divinity and rational plan in the melange.

Nevertheless, while Christian scholars have sacrificed a remarkable expanse of ground in regard to certain passages of the Old Testament, they have been considerably more reluctant to do so within the context of the New Testament. This is presumably on the sound realization that as the factual, historical validity of Christian accounts is slowly chipped away the authority of modern day churches is correspondingly weakened and could in time be totally destroyed. Observes Father Vawter in *A Path Through Genesis:*

> We need to return to our origins often that we may be mindful of what manner of men we are. "If Christ has not risen, vain is your faith, for you are still in your sins." *The resurrection is the historical fact, the thing which God has done, that underlies Christianity. If the resurrection is not true, then Christianity is a sham and Christian morality is an idle and vain pursuit.* (IA)

But the more scholarly of modern Christian exegetes perceive that there is little ultimate profit in erecting sturdy defenses around the New Testament while at the same time permitting an endless series of concessions about the Old. Says Father Vawter,

> *If God did not covenant with Israel, neither did the God of Abraham and Isaac and Jacob raise Jesus from the dead, for there is no fulfillment without a promise.* The Old Testament is the Witness to the Covenant, and Genesis is its beginning. (IA)

The Catholic's doctrinal justification for concessions made due to biblical inconsistences and error is that tradition as well as Scripture is a source of truth. Most Catholics who are aware of this doctrine believe that it dates from the time of Christ. They are mistaken. *Up to the time of the*

Middle Ages the Church asserted that the Bible was the only source of revelation. Only as it was confronted with more and more dissent that it was obliged to condemn as heresy did the church finally concede that certain of its canons could not in fact be attributed to the biblical record.

As we now consider some of the deviant theories that have historically caused consternation and reprisal from the dominant religious authorities, it may perhaps enhance the drama if the reader realizes that the book he holds in his hands would have been at one time—and may still be by some—considered heretical. If the reader had, only a few centuries ago, read this volume and subsequently repeated to friends that he thought its arguments generally reasonable, he would literally have put himself in danger of arrest, imprisonment, hideous torture, and death. (See also CRIME, BIBLICAL IMPETUS TO; CRUSADES, THE.)

Idolatry. Perhaps the earliest deviance from the faith was idolatry. Although it is often overlooked as such, idolatry is a form of religion. In the Old Testament idolatry was described as the worship of alien gods represented by man-made images or idols, although those idols were sometimes also used symbolically in the worship of Israel's God.

Since New Testament times the practice has been perceived not so much as a worship of other gods but as an obsessive fixation on anything less than God—money, power, a child or spouse, sex, vanilla ice cream, anything at all—over the adoration and worship of the biblical God.

Repeatedly throughout Scripture we see that the divine response to such practices is death. This precedent has been cited down through the ages to justify incredible atrocities against anyone who dared even question the reigning religion.

Paulicians of Armenia. Rising in the seventh century and taking their name from Saint Paul, the Paulicians preached a return to his views as contrasted with what they regarded as the introduction of pagan elements into Christian belief and practice. They were opposed, specifically, to the worship of images, statues, relics, and even to undue adoration of the sacraments and the Virgin Mary. They accused fellow Catholics of worshiping saints and angels, and they felt that the Old Testament was by no means of equal importance with the New. The Paulicians condemned the belief that study of Scripture was the rightful activity only of priests and monks and argued that every believer had a perfect right to explore the Bible for himself.

The Paulician controversy was no brief or minor episode of religious dissent; by the ninth century Paul's followers had become powerful and militant and the original debate had escalated—as it so often has in the history of Christendom—to organized military conflict. *Perhaps as many as a hundred thousand Paulicians were slaughtered in Armenia alone at the instruction of the Empress Theodora.* By the tenth century a colony of the sect had been imported into Bulgaria, where it reinforced an earlier party already established there. Explains J. M. Robertson in *A Short History of Free Thought* (Russell):

> Thus it came about that from Bulgaria there passed into western Europe, partly through the Slavonic sect called Bogomilians, partly by more general influences, a contagion of democratic and anti-ecclesiastical heresy; so that the very name *Bulgar* became the French *bougre*—heretic—and worse. It specified the most obvious source of the new anti-Romanist heresies of the Albigenses, if not of the Waldenses.

Subsequent evidence of the Paulician sect is noted about the year 1000 when it is reported that a villager of Chalons destroyed a crucifix and a religious picture because in his view they were clearly being worshipped. The same hardy soul attested to the general Paulician lack of confidence in the Old Testament by arguing that the prophets were by no means entirely to be believed.

The year 1000 was itself a time when, in the opinion of many, the world was to come to an end and the Day of Judgment would come to pass. Perhaps because of the evident fact that widespread predictions of disaster turned out to be invalid, men began to think more freely about religious matters generally or at least to speak more openly about the doubts and reservations they entertained.

The Inquisition. The limited scope of my study does not allow for adequate treatment of those savage dramas involving such heretics as the Cathari, Petrobrussions, followers of Arnold Brescia, the Caputiati Apostolici, the Brethren of the Free Spirit, the Waldenses and Albigenses, or the Goliards. It suffices here to make but two points: (1) that the Bible played an important role in the larger argument, and (2) that the most incredible savagery and cruelty were perpetrated upon the doubters. A typical instance would be the Inquisition and attack upon the Christian heretics of the French Province of Languedoc ordered by Pope Innocent III around the beginning of the thirteenth century. Comments J. M. Robertson:

> The Crusade was planned exactly on the conditions of those against the Saracens—the heretics at home being declared far worse than they. The Crusaders were freed from payment of interest on their debts, exempted from the jurisdiction of all courts, and absolved from all their sins, past

or future. To earn this reward they were to give only 40 days' service—a trifle in comparison with the hardships of the crusades to Palestine. "Never therefore had the cross been taken up with a more unanimous consent" (Sismondi, *Crusades*). Bishops and nobles in Burgundy and France, the English Simon de Montfort, the Abbott of Citeaux, and the Bernardine monks throughout Europe combined in the cause. *The result was such a campaign of crime and massacre as European history cannot match.*

Despite the object of mission of the Count of Toulouse, and the efforts of his nephew, the Count of Albi, to make terms, village after village was fired, all heretics caught were burned, and on the capture of the city and castle of Carcassone, *every man, woman and child within the walls was slaughtered, many of them in the churches, whither they had run for refuge.* The legate, Arnold, Abbott of Citeaux, being asked at an early stage how the heretics were to be distinguished from the faithful, gave the never-to-be-forgotten answer, "Kill all. God will know His own." (IA)

Richard Simon. Richard Simon (1638–1712) was one of the great seventeenth-century scholars of Scripture; his historical critique of the New Testament may still be read with considerable profit. Comments Georges Auzou, professor at the Grand Seminaire in Rouen, in *The Word of God,* about Simon's report:

> Its modern reader is impressed and astonished by the perspicacity, exactness, and discernment of this scholar from Dieppe, two centuries in advance of his time in the Biblical movement, and for that reason inevitably opposed in a lively manner.

Simon himself would certainly have thought of adjectives more pejorative than *lively* to describe the bitter attacks to which he was subjected. He was concerned in part to discourage that easy recourse to allegorical explanations when the literal is considered difficult or impossible to swallow. He was, then, a literalist, but very far indeed from the know-nothing sort common in American Protestant sects of the last century. Simon was one of the first to explain the absurdity of attributing the entire Pentateuch to Moses. He also developed a theory concerning prior oral or written sources used either by Moses or later scribes who recorded the patriarch's experiences.

Father Auzou stands at Simon's side in reporting:

The perceptions of Richard Simon, which would have led to a sound knowledge of the Bible, met with a conspiracy of opposition and of silence. The results of this attitude were soon manifest; the end of the 17th and the whole of the 18th Century manifested an appalling superficiality and lack of vitality in intellectual matters. For Biblical studies, these were barren years.

It would not have been difficult to predict Simon's fate. As Barrows Dunham observes in his wise and witty *Heroes and Heretics: A Social History of Dissent* (Knopf),

> Bossuet read the book on Holy Thursday, seized the edition, had all but two copies destroyed, and went on to crush Simon beneath a weight of genuine, if calamitous, eloquence. The result was that the science of Biblical criticism did not rise again in France until the 19th Century.

Jean Astruc. Jean Astruc, personal physician to Louis XV, was a distinguished eighteenth-century student of Scripture to whom all churches now owe a debt: he was the first to observe a difference between those portions of Genesis in which God is addressed by the name *Yahweh* and those in which he is referred to as *Elohim.* A number of scholars, many of them German, followed Astruc's lead and thus made historically important contributions to Bible scholarship. Astruc naturally met the same fate as Simon. Indeed there seems to have been a direct correlation between the degree of the individual scholars' brilliance and freshness-of-thought and the ferocity with which they were attacked.

For a period roughly extending from our Revolutionary War and the presidency of George Washington to our Civil War and the presidency of Abraham Lincoln, the European world was the scene of an incredible and dramatic debate about the Bible, conducted for the most part by distinguished scholars and taking the primary form of literary and historical criticism. Concerning this Auzou observes:

> It is painful indeed to remember that this great labor was accomplished almost exclusively in non-Catholic circles, very often by those without any faith. Of course by intervening late in the debates, the Catholics detached themselves from an ideology unacceptable to them and in the end were preserved from a number of hazardous solutions. But it is not glorious to run to the help of the victorious. As the Catholic scholars were not ready, the great battle took place without them, especially among the liberal Protestants.

337

Julius Wellhausen was one of the dominant figures in the nineteenth-century debate on the Scriptures. Though he was a popularizer, he was nevertheless gifted at critical analysis and therefore well-suited to the important work that in time became his primary concern—developing a critical theory about the drawn-out process by which the Pentateuch was constructed. So perceptive was Wellhausen that his hypothesis is still dominant. In brief outline he argues that Jean Astruc had been on the right track and that the various portions of the Pentateuch, in fact, may be divided into *four* categories, not just two: (1) the *Yahwist,* apparently composed during the tenth and ninth centuries; (2) the *Elohist,* from the ninth and eighth centuries; (3) the *Deuteronomist,* from the seventh century; and (4) the *Priestly,* from the fifth century, although it does contain some ancient materials.

Wellhausen's most controversial contribution was his reconstruction of the evolution of the religion of Israel, which joined documentary hypothesis with his theory of the religious and cultural evolution of Israel. Because he did not distinguish between the literary and the historical hypotheses, his study was seen as an attack upon religion and Wellhausen was labeled a heretic; in 1906 the Pontifical Biblical Commission formally rejected his theories and announced that the official view of the church was that Moses *was* the author of the Pentateuch, either directly or by means of writers approved by him. It is recognized today, of course, that these two alternatives simply do not cover the case since Moses can hardly have personally approved of authors who wrote long after he was dead.

The Papal Response. By 1893 Bible scholarship had affected the Catholic church seriously enough for Pope Leo XIII to issue the papal encyclical *Providentissimus* that laid down guidelines for all subsequent Catholic research and speculation on the Scriptures. The document makes the point that no one—not even the most esteemed scholars—can begin study of the sacred books without a guide, by which the pope meant, of course, the Catholic church. Says Father Levie:

> Leo XIII protests against the biased tendency he frequently finds in rationalist criticism, which unhesitatingly trusts ancient books and documents of profane history but evinces instinctive mistrust towards Scripture.

One would have thought that the pope would have recognized that spokesmen for both camps—including himself—were biased. He can naturally be forgiven for not having perceived that the mistrust to which he refers was manifested by scholars whose very expertise had led them to raise perfectly fair questions concerning the validity of certain passages of Scripture. If His Holiness actually believed that scholars simply rise from their breakfast tables in the morning determined from the start to distrust Scripture then he knew less about human nature than one would expect from a leader in so exalted a position of trust. Millions have indeed learned to distrust Scripture, but in practically every case their skepticism has grown out of nothing more diabolical than the act of *reading* the Good Book.

Nor was Leo XIII much more helpful in advising Catholic scholars how to approach difficulties posed by the biblical text. The pope suggested that the scholar must make certain of the real meaning of the text, thus, as Father Levie puts it, "freeing it from more-or-less traditional but inaccurate interpretations" that have often been preached by Catholic—as well as Protestant and Jewish—churchmen. Why has the church, over long centuries, not instructed its hundreds of millions of faithful that these traditional interpretations were inaccurate?

Unfortunately, His Holiness states an untruth when he writes that "this most wise decree by no means . . . restrains the pursuit of Biblical science but rather protects it from error and greatly assists its real progress." The encyclical does restrain the pursuit of biblical science in that it poses formidable boundaries beyond which no Catholic scholar is permitted to step. It is true that within those boundaries there is quite enough to keep any exegete busy for more time than mortals are allotted, but to place a priori boundaries around a field of research is unquestionably to limit and restrain. An individual churchman may, of course, leap past those boundaries at any time he wishes, but doing so may render him liable to a charge of heresy and, as innumerable examples have demonstrated, will frequently lead to the scholar's finding himself no longer a member of his original church.

The encyclical carries another error in that it suggests that there can be no real discrepancy between theologians and scientists as long as each camp confines itself to its own province. This steps away from the very difficulty with which scholars wrestle. There are indeed real discrepancies— hundreds of them—between the traditional theological view of the Scriptures and the clear evidence of science and literary analysis. It is literally impossible for anyone—theologian, scientist, butcher, baker, or candlestick maker— to "confine himself to his own province."

A scientist, speaking as such, may advise us that the physical universe is not a mere six thousand years old, as ignorant people once supposed, but billions of years old, if not indeed eternal. In offering us such instruction, the scientist may be giving no thought whatever to the Bible. But anyone who listens to a theologian on Sunday and a scientist on Monday will immediately perceive the discrepancy between their two pronouncements on the age of the physical world. Therefore, it is nonsense to talk about theology and science as disciplines that have nothing to say to each other.

It is very well to quote Saint Augustine to the effect that "the Holy Ghost . . . did not intend to teach men these things, that is to say the essential nature of the things of the physical universe." If churchmen were really guided by the good saint's admonition, they would have been far more humble and circumspect than they observably have been in their preachings on the Old Testament down through the centuries. Would that from the beginning they had meekly confessed that *Scriptures were no guide whatever concerning scientific questions.* Alas, they did nothing of the sort. They ignorantly insisted that the Scriptures were not only a source of sound scientific information but were also the highest source of all concerning such knowledge. That this arrogance was ultimately responsible for hundreds of thousands—perhaps millions—of intelligent believers deciding to leave the church is something that the popes must have eventually perceived, to their deep sorrow.

Leo XIII teaches other error in the encyclical in apologizing for the scientifically erroneous portions of Genesis because the sacred writers simply "went by what sensibly appeared." In some cases they did; in a great many other cases they did nothing of the sort. Whoever wrote the nonsense about the creation of the physical universe in six days had absolutely no recourse to sensible appearances but was indulging in speculation without the slightest admixture of evidential fact.

Father Levie sums up *Providentissimus* by observing:

> In 1893 Catholic exegesis still lacked valid solutions to the historical problems and objections raised by contemporary criticism. . . . In the time of *Providentissimus, dictation* of the Scriptures by God was commonly spoken of, an expression that is nowadays carefully avoided. (IA)

It may well be avoided if it is assumed that the word *dictation* applies to every portion of Scripture. But it cannot be avoided at all in regard to the many hundreds of scriptural passages that are given as *direct word-for-word quotations from the mouth of God,* in precisely the same sense that an author or journalist today might offer a direct quotation from President Clinton, Billy Graham, or any other personage.

The obvious scientific and historical errors, contradictions, internal inconsistencies, and out-and-out nonsense found in the Old Testament are by no means limited to the prose text. *They are also encountered in what are clearly intended to be accepted as direct quotations of the spoken words of God.* This last offense of the authors or redactors of Scripture is by far the most serious. If a man calls a mountain or city by the wrong name, if he says there are unicorns and dragons or states any other absurdity, that is noteworthy although not terribly unusual in religious experience. But if that same author attributes to God himself statements that are either criminal, undecipherable, sadistic, factually erroneous, or questionable in any other important regard, then one absolutely must choose between the two alternatives that present themselves: either (1) the man himself is totally mistaken in imagining that he has directly quoted the Almighty, or (2) he has in fact directly quoted God, but God is therefore by no means the all-knowing, all-loving, all-wise spirit that we have heretofore been taught that he is. (See also CONTRADICTIONS, BIBLICAL; ERROR.)

In defense of the encyclical, Leo XIII—as did Pius XII after him—occasionally sought to avoid an obvious implication of a statement by the device of denying it. For example, in regard to the recommended return to the original texts the encyclical states that this does not at all conflict with the ancient decree of the Council of Trent concerning the official character of the Latin Vulgate. This is not true. A return to the original text is quite certain to cast doubt on a good many passages of the Latin Vulgate. This cannot be denied; it has happened.

It is not surprising, then, that the French scholar Alfred Loisy courageously referred to the encyclical as "an unacceptable programme for men of learning." Serious students of the history of Bible scholarship should consult the commentaries of Loisy, a teacher of Scripture at the Catholic Institute, whose studies led him ultimately to a number of sharp divergences from traditional Christian theology.

Around the turn of the century the general increase in the sophistication of scholarly expertise was so troubling to the traditional faith of many that a Father Lebreton used the word *panic* to describe the general state of affairs among some French and Italian Catholic clergy. Observes Levie:

> As it developed after 1900, Modernism constituted for the church a very great danger, which could only be warded off by radical action, generally and speedily applied. The decree *Lamentabili Sane Exitue* and the Encyclical *Pascendi Dominici Gregis* were necessary . . . measures which cut down the evil at its roots.

Father Levie goes on to comment at length about "a narrow and short-sighted" campaign that he says was

> . . . organized by narrow-minded reactionaries. . . . It was at work for some years . . . and thus cast suspicion on certain persons in high places or those engaged in various work who were regarded as insufficiently conservative or tainted with Modernism.

Pope Benedict, of course, was concerned to repress Modernism itself, an ambition he handily achieved, at least for the short term, but he did recognize the need for responsible, analytic study of the Scriptures.

Father Dolindo Ruotolo. A dramatic chapter in the history of modern biblical exegesis was initiated in 1939 by this Italian priest, who published under a pseudonym a pamphlet in which he heatedly criticized such modern methods as the application of scientific, critical, and historical techniques to the study of Scripture. The Holy Office itself judged Ruotolo so far out of touch with the achievements of the latest religious scholarship that on November 20, 1940, they placed his pamphlet, as well as the priest's earlier conservative writings, on the Index of prohibited reading.

A particular object of Father Ruotolo's wrath was the Papal Biblical Institute itself. Stunned by the priest's criticism, the commission replied in a letter coauthored by its president, Cardinal Tisserant and its secretary, Father Voste, O.P., which said of Ruotolo's pamphlet: "primarily a virulent attack on the scientific study of Holy Scripture . . . it scorns all learning and any knowledge of Oriental languages and auxiliary sciences."

These arguments led quite naturally to the next important official Catholic announcement concerning biblical research: the *Divino Afflante Spirito* of 1943.

Hugh J. Schonfield. Another dissenting view of religion is held by this widely respected English scholar of Scripture who is either remarkably imaginative or extremely perceptive. In *The Passover Plot* (1965), Schonfield argued that Jesus plotted and directed his own crucifixion and then staged a false "resurrection" to convince Jews that he was their long-awaited Messiah. In 1974 Schonfield published *The Jesus Party,* a study of the thirty years immediately following the death of Jesus. He suggests that the first Christians were a small political party consisting of devout Jews who wished to free Palestine from the authority of Rome. The author calls these first Christians *Nazoreans,* from the Hebrew word for "keepers" of the Jewish tradition.

Like Jesus himself, the Nazoreans were convinced that the kingdom of God was at hand, in a very practical sense, and that the Almighty's first act in aid of his chosen would be the overthrow of Roman rulers. Their confidence was undermined, however, when a Jewish rebellion against the Romans failed totally (A.D. 66). Fearful of Roman counteraction, according to Schonfield, the authors of the Gospels disguised the Nazoreans' *political* ambitions by placing greater emphasis on purely religious, moral, and ethical teaching. Through the passage of some time, according to the theory (and in a day when illiteracy was common), new Christians were born and converted who were totally unaware of the original political interests of the first disciples.

The thought may occur to some readers that Schonfield is merely one of the many well-intentioned amateurs who have over the past two thousand years developed peculiar biblical interpretations, but the fact is that for half a century he has been a scholar widely known in intellectual circles for his familiarity with both Scripture specifically and Near Eastern history generally.

Dom Aelred. In 1972 this courageous Catholic Benedictine priest, in his book *The End of Religion,* said of the Bible:

> [It is] the world's most overrated book. . . . It is regarded conventionally by many as the *fons et origo* (source and origin) of true religion, yet it carries no simple and self-evident message directly and powerfully relevant to our everyday lives. It is made up, for the most part, of historical documents, extravagant enunciations, and exclusivist devotions, requiring long and deep research before they can be properly understood.
>
> Parts of the Old Testament, the Gospels, and the Epistles abound in memorable, heart-touching sayings; most of them call for careful elucidation before they can be correctly grasped and appropriately applied.

Aelred, like millions of decent Christians before him, admits to being horrified by passages such as Num. 15:32–36, in which God urges Moses to order his followers to stone to death a man whose only offense was picking up sticks on the Sabbath.

Parenthetically, it should be of contemporary American interest that a high percentage of those in the pro–death penalty ranks are conservative fundamentalist Christians who justify their support of capital punishment by observing—entirely accurately—that it is frequently resorted to in the Old Testament, often by God himself. Such references, however, point up nothing so much as the inconsistency of those who unearth them. If they truly based their attitudes toward the death penalty on the Old Testament, the American population might shortly be decimated, since an extremely long list of offenses is referred to in the Scriptures as being properly punishable by painful execution. How many millions of poor wretches have been burned alive or otherwise killed over the centuries because the Bible clearly instructs that witches should be killed (Lev. 20:27), only God knows—and he keeps such statistics to himself.

343

REVELATION, THE (OF ST. JOHN THE DIVINE). The book of Revelation is the most singularly misnamed portion of the Scriptures: it is clearly the least revelatory. Whether one agrees or disagrees with other portions of the Bible, it is generally not difficult to perceive the general meaning of such books. The same cannot be said of the Revelation. It is bizarre, lurid, obscure, and susceptible to a thousand-and-one interpretations, many of which are mutually contradictory. Symbolism and poetic imagery have their place in religious as in other literature. The fables of Aesop are moral stories in which animals are clearly meant to represent humans, and one is no more hard put to interpret the symbolism of such stories than to perceive the political lessons George Orwell intended to convey in *Animal Farm.* In contrast, Revelation conceals rather than reveals.

The serious student of the Bible can more effectively see beneath the surface of biblical accounts if he entertains the assumption that a given portion is not necessarily inspired by the creator but is merely a fascinating document he has found by chance, perhaps in an old monastery or bookshop, and to which he therefore brings no preconceived prejudices. This method of analysis will be particularly instructive if it is applied to Revelation. Any rational individual who comes upon the book with no foreknowledge of it might assume that its author was highly imaginative. In one sort of literature the imagination is so free: pure fantasy, some of which is called science fiction in the modern age. Considering this final book of the New Testament as a text of science fiction with a moral prediction tacked on, one could rightly judge it as a fascinating example of the genre.

Another possible explanation for the book is that it represents the telling of a dream. It is clearly similar to the sort of human mental experience characterized by dream states in which the sleeper's mind, no longer constrained by reason or sensory information, may roam at random in the total absence of control by physical laws, moral considerations, or the constraints of logic. In such a freely creative state the dreamer may imagine himself flying, walking on water, swimming beneath the surface of the sea, converted into an animal or a plant. He may, in fact, dream anything at all since there are no bounds on his imaginative powers. (See also DREAMS.)

A third possible explanation of the bizarre imagery encountered in Revelation is that the entire book represents either the ravings of a madman or a series of creative impressions transcribed while under the influence of a hallucinogenic drug. We are not surprised when institutionalized mental patients describe what is patently obscure or impossible as crystal clear. We would not be surprised if they perceived the mysterious as the simple, the hallucinatory as the real, or for that matter if they stated the opposite of what has been considered physical reality down through the ages. We would be sympathetically disposed to such misguided souls and attempt to help them out of their metaphysical confusion.

Any one of the aforementioned possibilities might be entertained in regard to this final book of the Bible. One thing the intelligent reader may be sure of, however, is that it does not represent any sort of concrete physical reality, past, present, or future. The evil of such a work comes from the attribution of its authorship or inspiration to God. It is an insult to the Deity—by definition the perfection of all truth, knowledge, and wisdom—to assert that this particular nightmarish fantasy is to be taken literally as God's personal message to his human creatures. Men with overheated imaginations may write such documents. At least one such has done so in this case. But there is no reason to assume that *God* would be the victim of delusions and phantasmagoric visions. Yet, certain fundamentalist Christians see these bizarre opium-visions of the unknown seer called John as not merely a puzzle to be deciphered but as an *inevitable* conclusion, a *logical* outcome of the previous biblical books, an actual consummation—*revelation*—in which the entire biblical text is somehow at last made clear.

Perfectly respectable scholars have dealt with this book in which it is difficult to separate reason from madness, sense from nonsense, practicality from absurdity, and lucidity from incoherence. Alas, their works are apparently of little interest to the millions of souls who worship the idol of unreason and seem uncomfortable when confronted with the actual laws of God's nature.

A very serviceable outline of the Catholic interpretation of Revelation—the Catholic title is *Apocalypse*—is available through the Catholic Information Service of the Knights Of Columbus, P.O. Box 1971, New Haven, CT 06521. Although it was written by the noted Bible scholar, Father Bruce Vawter, his name is not given in the pamphlet. One of Vawter's first points is that *the common assumption that Revelation is literally a prediction of the future is quite mistaken.* He says,

> This is an unfortunate misunderstanding of the meaning of the word *apocalypse.* . . . In itself, perhaps, it would not be so tragic, but what is extremely bad is the multitude of utterly unfounded and absolutely erroneous interpretations to which this misunderstanding has given rise.

Father Vawter's commonsense concession for Revelation directs us to one of the classic difficulties of the New Testament, one so formidable, in fact, that it would appear never to have been satisfactorily resolved.

The author of Revelation refers to "what must *soon* take place" (1:1, IA). There's nothing the least bit ambiguous about this and, to nail the point down, the text says that in regard to the foreseen events, "the time is near." Jesus himself, in other parts of Scripture, is quoted as having been absolutely clear in suggesting that certain cataclysmic events would take place not just "soon"—a term subject to assorted applications—but within the lifetime of some who saw and heard Jesus. (See also LAST DAYS, THE.)

Chapter 1. In some books of the Bible difficulties do not become apparent at the outset. This is not so with Revelation; its opening words give immediate rise to puzzlement.

> 1. The Revelation of Jesus Christ which God gave him to show to his servants what must soon take place; and he made it known by sending his angel to his servant John.

The following questions present themselves:

1. By what authority is the alleged revelation that "of Jesus Christ"?

2. "Which God gave him." These words draw a clear distinction between Jesus and God, thus throwing us back to the doctrine of the Trinity that the church has long upheld, even though it has been conceded that such a concept cannot be rationally explained. Can God the father know something of which God the son is ignorant?

3. "To show to his servants what must *soon* take place" (IA). But the predicted events have *not* taken place despite the passage of twenty centuries. We have therefore long passed the time that could be considered "soon" after the writing of the original document.

4. "And he made it known by sending his angel." What angel? And why an angel at all?

5. "To his servant John." For long centuries the church taught—and many Christians still believe—that it was John the Apostle who authored the book of Revelation. The best scholars today agree that the disciple was not the author and concede that his identity is, in fact, unknown. They suggest that the imaginative writer was either (1) John the Elder, pastor of the seven churches to which the first three chapters of the book are addressed, (2) an unknown person named John, or (3) a pseudonymous writer attaching the apostle's name in order to elicit prestige for the lurid and depressing visions portrayed therein, and therefore a liar.

Not only is the church unable to identify the author of Apocalypse but many devout Christian scholars have also argued that the book is a compilation rather than the literary product of one writer. There is additional confusion in the fact that the best scholarship, despite centuries of the most painstaking effort, has not even been able to determine when the book was written.

Anyone not already hopelessly biased on the question who gives careful thought to the Apocalypse will have no difficulty in agreeing with the third-century Christian saint Dionysius of Alexandria, who argued that most scholars took a very dim view of the book on the ground that it was an affront to reason. The true author, Dionysius felt, was Cerinthus (one of the first writers of science fiction or perhaps simply demented) who, presumably to put a better light on his preposterous tale, dishonestly attributed it to an esteemed saint.

In the year 360, a solemn high council of the Christian church convened at Laodicea chose *not* to include the Apocalypse as part of the canon.

In time, however, the church changed its mind about this matter—as it occasionally has about important questions over the centuries—so that now to question the authority of the Apocalypse is considered a grave insult to the faith. There are many good Christians, nevertheless, to whom the book still rightly seems nonsensical at least in part.

Chapter 4. In the first two verses of this chapter John (or whoever the author was) sets up the wild fantasy that will continue through the next eighteen chapters by saying, "A door was opened in heaven . . . and immediately I was in the Spirit." He then goes on to relate the incredible images that more closely resemble the ravings of a madman, drug-induced delusions, dream symbolism, or fantastic fiction from an overly creative imagination than a message from the very source of clarity, Almighty God. Consider:

> 6. And before the throne there was a sea of glass like unto crystal: and in the midst of the throne, and round about the throne, were four beasts full of eyes before and behind.
>
> 7. And the first beast was like a lion, and the second beast like a calf, and the third beast had a face as a man, and the fourth beast was like a flying eagle.
>
> 8. And the four beasts had each of them six wings about him; and they were full of eyes within: and they rest not day and night, . . .

That certain simple-minded believers accept that those of us who reach heaven shall one day see such incredible creatures is perhaps even more bizarre than the fantasy itself.

Chapter 5. In verse 6 we read:

6. And I beheld, and, lo, in the midst of the throne and of the four beasts, and in the midst of the elders, stood a Lamb *as it had been slain,* having seven horns and seven eyes, which are the seven Spirits of God sent forth into all the earth. (IA)

Scholars are in agreement that "a Lamb" refers to the crucified Christ. The confusion comes from "as it had been slain"—nowhere in the New Testament description of the crucifixion is Jesus described as having seven horns and seven eyes. And who do the literalists say are the "seven Spirits of God" sent forth into all the earth?

Chapter 6 describes horrendous calamities that will befall planet earth— supposedly at the personal, vengeful command of an all-loving God—as each of seven seals on heaven's book are opened:

- A white horse will bring wars;
- A red horse will bring anarchy;
- A black horse will herald incredible increases in costs of food and other consumer products;
- A pale horse will summon death and hell to "control" one-fourth of the world by war, famine, disease, and wild animals;
- Martyrs will plead for final justice but will be told to wait for others to join them in martyrdom;
- Earthquakes will shake the earth, the sun will darken, the moon will turn red, and stars will fall from the skies.

Attribution of such feverish imagery to God is an insult that on a more rational planet would be blamed on the crankiest of atheists. The very idea that such macabre events, even if merely symbolic, could possibly emanate from the source of all truth, wisdom, love, and reason is patently absurd. That some Christians nevertheless cling to these promises of revenge leads one to wonder if the practices of turning-the-other-cheek and forgive-and-forget are sweet thoughts merely given lip-service by those same believers.

Chapter 7. If we are to believe John's fantastic predictions of destruction, we must now accept that one of God's angels calls a halt to the destruction, which presumably will have already caused millions of deaths on planet earth. The purpose of the reprieve? *To put a protective mark on the foreheads of 144,000 Jews who will reportedly then be delivered from further tribulation!* We are not told, of course, how those lucky individuals are selected or why they number precisely 144,000, when other biblical texts assure us that *all* Jews—numbering many more than this paltry number—are God's Chosen People.

348

Chapters 8 and 9 continue John's visions of doom that will burn one-third of the earth, destroy one-third of the seas and their creatures and ships, poison one-third of the rivers and springs, and make the entire planet a dreary place indeed by dimming the light provided by the sun, moon, and stars. Naturally thousands more will die from all these cataclysmic events.

This is apparently not enough viciousness and violence, again presumably brought about by the direct command of our all-kind, all-loving creator, for in chapter 9 we read:

3. And there came out of the smoke locusts upon the earth: and unto them was given power, as the scorpions of the earth have power.

4. And it was commanded them that they should not hurt the grass of the earth, neither any green thing, neither any tree; but only those men which have not the seal of God in their foreheads.

In other words, 99+ percent of the human race, including—oddly—all Christians!

5. And to them it was given that they should not kill them, but that they should be tormented five months: and their torment was as the torment of a scorpion, when he striketh a man.

6. And in those days shall men seek death, and shall not find it; and shall desire to die, and death shall flee from them.

7. And the shapes of the locusts were like unto horses prepared unto battle; and on their heads were as it were crowns like gold, and their faces were as the faces of men.

8. And they had hair as the hair of women, and their teeth were as the teeth of lions.

9. And they had breastplates, as it were breastplates of iron; and the sound of their wings was as the sound of chariots of many horses running to battle.

10. And they had tails like unto scorpions, and there were stings in their tails: and their power was to hurt men five months.

These verses describe small grasshopper-like creatures—locusts—who look like horses except that they have the faces of men and are wearing tiny gold crowns on their little heads. We are also told that the hair of these creatures is like that of a woman, although in a day when both women and men wore long hair it is not easy to perceive what distinction is intended. Moreover these tiny creatures have metal breast plates, to defend them against what, of course, is never specified.

From approximately 4,000 to 2,500 B.C., the Sumerian city-states of

Mesopotamia built a high and powerful culture, one accomplishment of which was the creation of cuneiform writing. They also developed the art of sculpture. We have seen photographs of these enormous figures with the bodies of bulls, heads of men, and wings of birds. Only the insane would suppose that such figures represented anything physically real. But some fundamentalist Christians tell us that believers must accept such remarkable imagery as literal truth of things to come.

Chapter 10. In the first few verses of this chapter it appears that John might finally reveal the answer to some of our questions as he describes an angel who opens a "little book" and begins to speak in a thunderous voice. It is not to be:

> 4. . . . I was about to write: and I heard a voice from heaven saying unto me, "Seal up those things which the seven thunders uttered, and write them not."

In verse 7 we at least receive a partial explanation:

> 7. But in the days of the voice of the seventh angel, when he shall begin to sound, the mystery of God should be finished, as he hath declared to his servants the prophets.

Are we surprised that in such a farfetched story as this, the author will tell us he supposedly has heard the entire sensible plan that God has for mankind and is unable to reveal it until some future time when we will have survived almost insurmountable catastrophes?

Chapter 10 concludes with another bit of nonsense, the point of which is never explained:

> 9. And I went unto the angel, and said unto him, "Give me the little book." And he said unto me, "Take it, and eat it up; and it shall make thy belly bitter, but it shall be in thy mouth sweet as honey."
>
> 10. And I took the little book out of the angel's hand, and ate it up; and it was in my mouth sweet as honey: and as soon as I had eaten it, my belly was bitter.

If we accept the literal interpretation of this text, we must now assume that the book that contains the answers to all the secrets of the universe, the explanation of all God's mysteries, has been destroyed by the digestive system of a human being. This might be the author's exalted excuse for a stomachache caused from overeating before going to sleep, the trauma of a nightmare, or the physical suffering caused by ingestion of a drug.

Chapter 11. The author now reportedly becomes an active participant in the events taking place when an angel instructs him to measure the temple and count the worshipers. Again no reason is given for this apparently pointless command, nor does the information seem to have any relevance in the remainder of the drama.

Then it is back to the ridiculous "revelations" of coming events where we learn of two missionaries who will preach repentance for three and one-half years and be given the power to kill anyone who opposes them by means of fire shooting from their mouths. They will also supposedly be able to cause droughts and call down plagues. The author of Revelation would have us believe that after the stated period:

> 7. And when they shall have finished their testimony, the beast that ascendeth out of the bottomless pit shall make war against them, and shall overcome them, and kill them.

Why?

The dead prophets' bodies will then, according to "John," be put on display and *everyone on earth* will celebrate their demise. Perhaps suddenly realizing that this "reward" for faithfully preaching God's word would not be accepted by fair-minded believers, John now tells us that God will, after three and one-half days, bring the dead men back to life and take them to heaven in a cloud, even while he sends an earthquake that destroys one-tenth the city of Jerusalem and kills precisely seven thousand men.

After such a display of petulance on the part of their divine ruler, twenty-four elders—whose names or roles are, incidentally, never identified—do not lament but praise the fear and destruction wreaked on mortal man by the all-kind, all-wise creator.

Chapter 12. Although early portions of Christian Scripture admonish the faithful to "be subject for the Lord's sake, to every human institution," few Christians in the present day consider such advice wise or sensible when the institutions are evil or are administered by evil leaders. Still it is possible to make a philosophical case in defense of the proposition. We might, for example, argue that justice will be properly meted out in an afterlife and therefore we ought not to risk violent revolution to oppose even the most tyrannical or depraved earthly governments. Unfortunately for scriptural consistency, however, the book of Revelation flatly contradicts this peaceable advice and adopts a stance of open hostility to the Roman state.

REVELATION, THE (OF ST. JOHN THE DIVINE)

In any event, Revelation is in clear error as regards its prediction of the literal destruction of the city of Rome and the empire over which it ruled. We know that Rome—like all the world's major cities—has seen its share of war, fire, vandalism, and other forms of suffering. But the city survived, and far from its empire being destroyed it lived long enough to accept Christianity, to make it the official religion of the Roman state, and therefore to facilitate its spread over a good part of the known world.

To the extent that John intended his predictions about the city to be taken seriously we can say with total confidence that all the details about "that ancient serpent, who is called the devil in state, the deceiver of the whole world" (v. 9) who, upon being defeated militarily, would be left in a pit for a thousand years, let loose for a short time, and then defeated again have never come to pass. It is sometimes argued that things that have admittedly never yet occurred might still take place in the infinity of the future, but no such argument can possibly be advanced here since the authors were referring to events connected with one specific empire— the Roman—which has not existed for many centuries.

Chapter 13-16. In these passages we find one of the most speculated about ideas from the Apocalypse as regards a powerful beast that Satan will call up from the sea and to whom will be given ultimate power and authority.

> 16. And he causeth all, both small and great, rich and poor, free and bond, to receive a mark in their right hand, or in their foreheads:
> 17. And that no man might buy or sell, save he that had the mark, or the name of the beast, or the number of his name.
> 18. Here is wisdom. Let him that hath understanding count the number of the beast: for it is the number of a man; and his number is Six hundred threescore and six.

Says the *Interpreter's Dictionary of the Bible* (Abingdon Press, 1962):

> Most of the tyrants of history, from Nero to Kaiser Wilhelm and Hitler, as well as the pope of the Roman Catholic Church, have at one time and another been said both to answer to the description of the beast and to furnish in the numerical values attaching to their names in Hebrew or Greek the amount of the sum indicated [666].

Some present-day fundamentalists believe that the modern use of number-based computer networks allowing for electronic funds access and instant credit approval represent the beast!

As the book of Revelation drones on in absurdity, remember that there are actually large numbers of human beings on earth today who accept such irrational fiction as a *road map of inevitable reality.* In light of this, consider such presumably God-inspired tragedies as

- torment by sulphur flames,
- malignant sores,
- death of everything in and on the ocean,
- more poisoning of rivers and streams,
- scorching of mankind by the intense heat of the sun,
- darkness over the kingdom ruled by the beast, and
- the much-talked about Battle of Armageddon between the forces of good and evil (which, parenthetically, many fundamentalists conceived the brief 1991 war in the Persian Gulf to be).

Chapters 17 and 18. The section that concerns Babylon is the one portion of John's manuscript that is not incredibly obscure. It is possible, in fact, that when the author wrote the word *Babylon*—he meant precisely what he said: the city of Babylon. In the modern age, for example, if an author were to write a phantasmagoric, psychedelic description, the purpose of which was to dramatize the sinfulness and corruption of, say, Las Vegas, San Francisco, Paris, or Rio de Janeiro, it would be reasonable to assume, barring clear evidence to the contrary, that while the author might purposely deal in vague generalizations regarding various sorts of immorality, he clearly intended his comments about the city in question to apply to that city and its inhabitants and to no other.

However, Protestant polemics has a tradition according to which the author of Revelation, in writing about the city of Babylon, did not intend his readers to understand Babylon at all but desired that they interpret that he was referring to the city of Rome, the seat of the Roman Catholic Church centuries later. The fact that Rome—like all metropolises on earth—has been the seat of more than enough corruption, depravity, and sinfulness of all kinds is clear enough, but no intelligent person could refer to this as proving that the original author could not possibly have been expressing his opinions about Babylon itself.

Chapter 20. When writing this book John was faced with a number of problems, at least one of which was incapable of solution. The plot line about events of the Final War must naturally lead to the defeat of Satan. How he, being gifted with not only physical but incredible spiritual and psychic powers, can be defeated is one troublesome question. But it would be possible to develop an argument that if at the ending of hostilities, one party's predicament is less advantageous than that of the other, he may be said to have lost a war. But combatants do not merely lose wars; they are customarily punished for having done so, and here is the more knotty difficulty.

If an author of a science fiction or fantasy story wanted to illustrate the nature of a given evil person's defeat he would not be in the least troubled. The loser could be imprisoned, physically assaulted, tortured, verbally abused, or killed. The Apocalypse holds out as Satan's fate that he be cast into a lake of fire.

Since Christian tradition has for centuries taught that the devil's *natural* habitat is fire, this is the logical equivalent of saying that an evildoer whose natural residence is, say, Palm Springs, California, would be subjected, upon the event of his defeat, to reside in Palm Springs, California.

Chapter 21. One more exceedingly serious problem for Christian defenders of Revelation grows out of the fact that in the book's twenty-first chapter the author cites an approximate quotation from the book of Tobit. But Tobit, unfortunately for consistency of argument, is apocryphal, which means it is a deception and as such not accepted by the church.

Tobit 13:16-17	Revelation 21:18-21
Jerusalem will be built with sapphires and emeralds, and her walls with precious stones, and her towers and battlements with pure gold. The streets of Jerusalem will be paved with beryl and ruby and stone of ophir.	And the building of the wall of it was of jasper: and the city was pure gold, like unto clear glass. And the foundations of the wall of the city were garnished with all manner of precious stones. The first foundation was jasper; the second, sapphire; the third, a chalcedony; the fourth, an emerald; The fifth, sardonyx; the sixth, sardius; the seventh, chrysolyte; the eighth, beryl; the ninth, a topaz; the tenth, a chrysoprasus; the eleventh, a jacinth; the twelfth, an amethyst. And the twelve gates were twelve pearls: every several gate was of one pearl: and the street of the city was pure gold, as it were transparent glass.

REVELATION, THE (OF ST. JOHN THE DIVINE)

Chapter 22. Christians are perfectly free to believe that Christ will physically return to earth. He may indeed. If he wished to do any such remarkable thing, it is no matter whether he comes in clouds of glory, on a Boeing 707, out of a thunderclap, or indeed by any means at all. The really dramatic thing would be that he has returned. No intelligent person has ever suggested that he personally knows when and where such a divine appearance will be made, although in every generation a few poor souls so delude themselves, in each case shortly to be embarrassed by the sweep of the river of time past the island on which they have planted their absurd hopes.

But again, if God wished to communicate so remarkably simple a message to man as that Jesus Christ would one day come back to earth, he could have done so in ways far superior to the meandering, disturbed chapters of the Apocalypse.

The book of Revelation begins a summation of the Word of God with a final admonition:

18. "For I testify unto every man that heareth the words of the prophecy of this book, 'If any man shall add unto these things, God shall add unto him the plagues that are written in this book:

19. " 'And if any man shall take away from the words of the book of this prophecy, God shall take away his part out of the book of life, and out of the holy city, and from the things which are written in this book. . . .'"

Certain fundamentalist believers interpret these instructions to apply not just to the book of Revelation but to the entire Bible and use them in their arguments defending the divine inspiration and literal interpretation theories. Nevertheless, believers *have* added and subtracted from the scriptural record repeatedly, despite which we have been told that the canonical decisions have through the centuries been directly inspired by God.

The point bears repeating—many of the most esteemed Christian Bible scholars believe that Revelation is the work of several authors, not one.

Verse 20 repeats the Last Days theme of the New Testament:

20. "He which testifieth these things saith, 'Surely I come quickly.' Amen. Even so, come, Lord Jesus." . . .

A fitting conclusion indeed to a testament of error, contradiction, and mystery. (See also AUTHENTICITY OF THE BIBLE; PIOUS FRAUD; SOUL, THE.)

REVENGE. If anything is clear about the Old Testament, it is that revenge is not to be discouraged—as most religious believers now assume—but that it is so often encouraged as to be regarded as an absolute obligation. The classic instance of this, of course, concerns the infamous divine advice of "an eye for an eye." There is a clever Jewish defense for this savage instruction: They argue that bloodthirsty as the instruction is, it is at least better than the death-penalty-executed-by-a-community revenge common in ancient times.

In time, however, the civilized and compassionate Jews felt they were taking a bum rap from non-Christian Gentiles who referred to the eye-for-an-eye guideline. Rabbi Philip S. Bernstein in "What the Jews Believe" (*Life,* September 11, 1950) summed up:

> The sages were not content to let this law stand. They said that the intent of the law was to compel the offender to pay in damages the accepted equivalent for the loss of an eye. *Thus the written law was not repudiated* but became the basis of a sensible adaptation to the realities of human society.

Both the ancient sages and Rabbi Bernstein deserve to be complimented on such assertions, with the exception of the contention that "the written law was not repudiated." The law was indeed repudiated since today there is not a Jew on earth who demands an eye for an eye. What happened was the same happy process we have seen at work over the centuries: a sometimes painfully slow but nevertheless ongoing tendency to reduce savagery largely by throwing overboard certain scriptural impedimenta.

In any event, in repeated instances the Old Testament not only permits but also recommends revenge. This leads to yet one more instance in which the Bible is at odds with itself since in the New Testament Jesus quite clearly rejected the Old Testament justification for revenge with his touching turn-the-other-cheek philosophy.

Though modern Jews and Christians tend to perceive the Christian position as morally preferable, statistically speaking it is very rare that such lofty and compassionate ideas affect those same believers' actual conduct.

Few are more adamant than Christians in insisting that capital punishment be not only retained but also much more widely applied. There are Christians on the more civilized and humane side of the debate, but they are relatively few in number. The great majority of pro-gun promoters are Protestant Christians. Such people are, needless to say, viscerally Old Testament in their absolute insistence on revenge of wrongs committed against them. (See also CONTRADICTIONS, BIBLICAL; CRIME, BIBLICAL IMPETUS TO; REVELATION, THE [OF ST. JOHN THE DIVINE].)

RITUAL. Every intelligent person knows that it could not possibly be of the slightest moral importance to God how men cooked goat meat, so long as they did not somehow contrive to injure each other or themselves in doing so. If we were to read in early social documents of, say, Eskimo, Maori, or Aztec culture that God preferred that meat be stewed in soy sauce rather than natural gravy, or in water rather than milk from the mother of a dead animal, we would feel tolerant of such ignorance or perhaps amused by the superstition. Just such an absurdity is supposed to command the intellectual respect of a graduate of a modern university for no other reason than that the teaching is encountered in scriptural text.

Ritual versus Morality. It is not necessary to make an either-or choice between ritual and moral behavior. If such a choice were necessary, even the most tradition-oriented individuals would today certainly opt for morality. But the debate is not conducted in such simplistic terms. Those on one side of the question argue merely that ritual has such distracting allurements that one can easily be deluded that he is behaving in a religious or moral manner when in fact he is merely concerning himself with the bric-a-brac of religion, not its essence, which concerns person-to-person behavior.

But the counterargument is that ritual is nevertheless justified—not for the primitive, superstitious reasons that occasioned the introduction of certain now-quaint practices in Old Testament times—but rather because the performance of certain duties, the involvement with traditional customs, creates an interior atmosphere of respect for God, religion, and man and that this in turn makes ethical behavior more likely.

Clearly both arguments carry some practical truth. (See also GIFTS TO GOD; MAGIC IN THE BIBLE; ORIGINS OF RELIGIOUS PRACTICES.)

ROMANS. For once scholars generally agree that the author of this biblical book is Paul and the place and time of its origin is A.D. 58, Corinth. Although the *purpose* of the letter is more obscure, it does touch on most of the theological themes of the New Testament. But, of course, the book gives rise to problems.

Chapter 1. Paul begins this letter with a ringing pronouncement of the case against atheism. He argues first that there is a certain naturalness to belief in God, that we do so instinctively. The astonishing wonders of the natural universe itself, he suggests, are testimony to God's power. I do not suggest that the particulars of Paul's argument are persuasive. We know, in fact, that they are not, for the obvious reason that men do not incline to atheism because of a lack of appreciation of the mighty glory of universal nature. When we look into the lives and thinking of actual individuals who have addressed this eternally knotty question we find, in fact, just the reverse of what believers suggest—that the *more* men know of science and nature, the more likely they are to question, at least innocently, belief forms suggested to them when they were children. To this point in Romans the problem is merely set out, not resolved. But Paul is on solid ground when he criticizes those who on the one hand doubt God as traditionally perceived and instead make absurd idols of wood and stone and pay holy respect to such man-made artifacts.

In complimenting the Roman readers of his letters, Paul makes a simple error of fact when he says that their faith in God "is becoming known around the world" (v. 8).

Paul knew so little about the planet earth that, like almost everyone of his time, he assumed it was a flat disc, and not a very large one at that. One would hardly criticize writers of his day for being ignorant of facts that could not possibly have been brought to their attention. The reason such criticism is required in the present context is simply the long-held insistence that every word of Scripture is *the word of God*. It does not demand the bias of a fanatical atheist to perceive that a God, defined as the very embodiment of perfection, could not possibly deliberately teach error.

Paul is hard on the Jews. Although during the past two thousand years there have been many Christians and Jews of good will, albeit a minority, who have attempted to relate to each other with a combination of reason, compassion, and fairness, their heart-warming efforts will forever be doomed to frustration and defeat. Some philosophical and social questions are notoriously difficult to understand properly, much less resolve. This is not one of them. No ultimate mutually satisfactory resolution of the Jewish/Christian problem is possible because the essential claims of the two faiths are in flat contradiction, beyond the slightest hope of compromise or conciliatory amelioration. Jews are as convinced today as they were in pre-Christian times that they have not just that same sort of relationship to God that hundreds of the world's tribes have believed they enjoyed, but that there is something unique about their situation in that God, in a very clear-cut way, singled them out from among the innumerable peoples and cultures of earth as the sole means by which his personal wishes would in time be made known to humanity in general. So convinced are the Jews of the legitimacy of this belief that they argue that God has guaranteed their prosperity and survival by granting them the right to certain territories that previously belonged to other nearby tribes.

Any earthly ruler who issued such orders would obviously be branded a criminal by both disinterested observers and those whose lands were unjustly taken away. The unfairness and injustice of such a bequeathment has made it impossible for millions of both casual observers and concerned scholars over long centuries to perceive anything in the least divine or holy in the matter.

The plot line, nevertheless, does represent firm and traditional Jewish conviction. Religious Jews find it literally impossible to imagine, much less perceive, that having once showed them such special attention, God could later change his mind and pass his special favor along to a group of heretics following a troublesome mystic named Jesus.

Christians, for their part, believe not only that Jesus was in some unique way the son of God but literally Almighty God himself in human form. Not only has the non-Christian world never been able to make the slightest sense out of the claim that a given individual can be (1) God and (2) God's son at one and the same time, but the original Christian church also concedes that the subject is a mystery that cannot be rationally explained. The truth of it can hardly be called self-evident.

It certainly is not self-evident to Jews, which brings us back to our starting point. Although Jews and Christians are obliged—by that simple morality that existed long before religion and that does not depend upon any one faith—to treat each other civilly and fairly, there will never be any way in which two such clearly exclusive philosophies can be blended harmoniously. A choice must always be made.

Paul is on perfectly solid ground in referring to the sinfulness of individual Jews, though the point would carry more historic weight had it been the case that Christians were remarkably less sinful than non-Christians, a state of affairs that has yet to be demonstrated.

But there is something dangerous in Paul's argument here because he suggests that the *reason* Jews have—as William Neil put it in his *Harper's Bible Commentary*—"cut themselves out of the divine plan" is their sinfulness. We know that Christians are also a remarkably sinful people. Why does it not follow, according to Paul's logic, that Christians, too, have cut themselves out of God's scheme? It was Jesus himself, we are told, who said, "By their fruits you shall know them."

Look about the Christian world today. Consider the morally nauseating degree of corruption and crime in those portions of the planet inhabited by chiefly Christian populations. Is Christian Latin America a gleaming example of the results of Christian indoctrination? Is Christian Sicily such an example? Was the Christian Germany that voted Hitler into power and started a world war in which ultimately some forty million were killed? Or the Christian Spain that welcomed the dictator Franco? Has the American South during the last three hundred years, given that its population has been almost totally Christian, morally distinguished itself in regard to the treatment of blacks?

Paul does not contest but accepts the description of Abraham as "father of many nations." Is there anything the least bit unfair in asking for the names of those nations, many or few, of which Abraham is the literal father? None of us would have the slightest difficulty in listing scores of tribes and peoples that clearly do *not* consist of the sons and daughters of Abraham. An anthropologist could extend the list to include hundreds.

In the long history of Protestant-Catholic confrontation the reformers have depended much on Paul and his idea of "justification by faith." If we simply accept that there is a conscious God and that at least some form of Christianity is his preferred religion, then it is not an affront to reason that by the simple act of faith in Christ individuals could be said to merit some special moral favor. Precisely what the word *justification* has meant, in this context, is by no means clear. Christians themselves never tire of reminding us of the utter depravity of man, and we know from both personal experience and local observation the names of countless Christians who, despite their best intentions, lead incredibly sinful and corrupt lives. What then, in the context of such undeniable realities, does the word *justification* mean?

It certainly cannot mean that sinful behavior itself is justified, because such behavior can never be justified. It is disgusting, reprehensible; even the secular law recognizes much of it as criminal, which is to say unjust. It is vastly more reasonable to talk, then, about the forgiveness of sins, assuming the attempt to acquire such forgiveness is accompanied by true remorse, a concession of guilt, and a desire for personal reform. But what has it to do with justification? The answer is nothing whatever.

Chapter 5. It has for centuries been part of Catholic dogma that physical death—which we know comes in time to every blade of grass and every living creature, including man—nevertheless *would never have occurred but for the sin of Adam,* interpreted as a literal individual precisely in the sense that President Clinton or actor Jack Nicholson are actual individuals.

12. Wherefore, as by one man sin entered the world, and death by sin; and so death passed upon all men, for that all have sinned:

Chapter 13. The famous passage that begins this chapter has caused no end of difficulty for both Christian scholars and common believers.

1. Let every soul be subject unto the higher powers. For there is no power but of God: the powers that be are ordained of God.
2. Whosoever therefore resisteth the power, resisteth the ordinance of God: and they that resist shall receive to themselves damnation.
3. For rulers are not a terror to good works, but to the evil. Wilt thou then not be afraid of the power? do that which is good, and thou shalt have praise of the same:
4. For he is the minister of God to thee for good. But if thou do that which is evil, be afraid; for he beareth not the sword in vain: for he is the minister of God, a revenger to execute wrath upon him that doeth evil.
5. Wherefore ye must needs be subject not only for wrath, but also for conscience sake.
6. For this cause pay ye tribute also: for they are God's ministers, attending continually upon this very thing.
7. Render therefore to all their dues: tribute to whom tribute is due; custom to whom custom; fear to whom fear; honour to whom honour.

If we consider this text in an abstract way, it sounds reasonable enough. When we lift our eyes from the scholar's page and observe the actual governments of the world, we at once conclude, however painfully, that whoever wrote these passages was sadly mistaken.

Millions of decent men and women in our own century, a large number of them Christians, did not accept the legitimacy of such tyrants as Hitler, Stalin, Mussolini, Franco, or Saddam Hussein. (Alas, millions of other Christians did support some of these same leaders.) But to suggest that it is divine law that all citizens must be subject to such authorities is to speak both moral and political nonsense. Granted there are times and places where it is the better part of wisdom to be circumspect. One does not rush blindly into the fire of the oppressor's cannon when nothing can result except one's own destruction. One of the most moving, fact-based films of the 1980s was *Romero,* which depicted the disgustingly immoral acts of the government of El Salvador, including the eventual murder of the heroic Roman Catholic priest Romero because he vocally advocated resistance by the people.

But such persecution has no relevance at all to the clear instruction in Romans that we should all be meekly subject to the kinds of political monsters who have ruled down through history and will, it seems reasonable to assume, continue to trouble us in the future.

To think our way through this actually quite simple problem is to perceive that there cannot possibly be any legitimacy to a once-common view: that kings and other rulers serve by divine right. We must conclude that since it is the height of absurdity to impute such faulty advice to an all-wise, all-knowing Deity, God cannot possibly have written or inspired such passages. (See also DIVINE RIGHT OF KINGS, CHURCH AND STATE RELATIONS; HOMOSEXUALITY; FREEDOM.)

S

SABBATH. The Catholic scholar Reverend Dr. Rumble, M.S.C., in one of his instructive pamphlets, *The Adventist,* makes what will seem to both theologians and laymen a striking comment on not only the debate about the Sabbath specifically but, more importantly, the larger question of to what extent Christians are obliged to conform to behavioral standards said to have been given to Moses by God on Mount Sinai.

> The Book of Exodus makes it clear that the *observance of the Sabbath was a special prescription for the Jews only,* and that it was inseparably connected with the Old Covenant. But Christians live under the New Testament or New Covenant, which insists that *those who have accepted the full and perfect revelation and grace of Christ are no longer bound by the laws and customs of the Jews.* Thus St. Paul, speaking of the higher ideals of the Christian religion as compared with the Law 'graven with letters upon stones,' declares, 'if that which is done away was glorious, much more that which remaineth is in glory' (II Cor. 3:7–11). (IA)

Let us suppose that we encounter a religion the followers of which are largely decent people, quite conscientious about their roles as marriage partners and parents, who attempt to live in peace and harmony with all others, whether members of their church or not. Surely even the most fervent atheist would willingly acknowledge that such individuals are in tragically short supply on our troubled planet and that they deserve praise for the civilized sweetness of their behavior.

Now let us add one more factor: that the adherents of this particular religion not only feel under no obligation to demonstrate a special reverence for that one-seventh part of the week known as Sunday but in fact also believe—simply because their founder so instructed them—that Wednesday is a more appropriate period during which to attend their churches and perform their unique rituals. Surely only a very cold-hearted curmudgeon would think less of the members of this faith solely because of this factor. Our general perception would inevitably incorporate the understanding that, while matters of ritual may serve a social function, only a madman would argue that they are equally as important as living a moral and constructive life.

All of this is so self-evident that the reader might fairly argue that it is a waste of valuable time to apply the rhetoric of persuasion to any proposition so obvious. But not even that obviousness is full protection against those who would say, "Well, while it is good to observe that the members of this faith are behaving themselves socially they are nevertheless headed straight for hell because they differ with the Bible as regards the Sabbath." (See also BELIEFS AND MYTHS; BY THEIR FRUITS YE SHALL KNOW THEM.)

SAINTLINESS. Historically there are more inspiring figures within the Catholic church than in the Protestant denominations, but this may be due to the fifteen-hundred-year headstart the parent church had in furnishing its pantheon. Significantly, with each passing century saints become fewer in number.

A theory first occurred to me some thirty years ago concerning the similarity between the attributes of saintliness and those of creative talent, whether expressed in the dramatic degree identified as genius or in the more common forms. Fortuitously I myself was gifted with a number of creative abilities, yet I am perfectly aware that I am no more responsible for having them than for having brown eyes or five toes on each foot. In using the word *gifts,* we imply a giver. Indeed the term *God-given* is often employed to describe such capabilities. The average person understands this to involve some special intervention by the Almighty in the early physical development of certain individuals whereby the potential is implanted in them for the composition of music, for dazzling proficiency in putting words to paper or paint to canvas, for mathematical or engineering genius, or some other activity. But the implication is invalid: it is unlikely that this is how the drama is actually played out. These gifts appear through the same process as that which accounts for every one of the thousands of separate abilities of which humanity is capable.

The concept of *thousands* must be emphasized. Most of us use ourselves as a standard of measurement. When we observe that our own talents are limited in number, we will project this self-assessment onto the rest of humanity. In reality, however, the number of particular abilities humans possess is so large that there is no way to set limits to it. In fact, it is daily being added to as advances of science and technology bring new acts within the scope of human application. The biblical observation that "There is nothing new under the sun" (ECCLESIASTES 1:9) simply does not conform to reality if interpreted literally. (See also FREE WILL.)

We need not consider here only the dramatic achievements of da Vinci, Michelangelo, Shakespeare, Einstein, Freud, Galileo, Newton, Bach, Aristotle, or other geniuses but also the impressive gifts of the young man at the corner garage who apparently can repair anything mechanical; the doctor who can successfully operate on human brain tissue; the exceptional specialists in the field of athletics, the jugglers, high-wire walkers; the scientists, chemists, physicists, astronomers. I once playfully posited the philosophical assumption that if the abilities of all humans past, present, and future could be united they would be equal to the divine power itself. (Years later I learned that this harmonized with the ancient philosophical concept of *pantheism:* that God is the sum total of all natural existence.)

It is true that almost any of us, by a combination of formal study and hard work, can develop some degree of proficiency in practically any field of human endeavor. But no one has ever seriously argued that all of us are equally capable of all acts. Assign any randomly chosen thousand of us to a six-month course in the study of, say, the piano, and it is self-evident that even if every individual in the test group studies and practices for an equal amount of time, at the end of the process no two will be equally proficient. It is a combination of inherent potential and/ or limitation-of-potential that predetermines such differences. No genius ever decided to become such. Their gifts are no more understood by them than they can be understood by us.

My hypothesis concerning saints and near-saints is basically the same. It involves nothing more than the assumption that moral gifts are implanted in precisely the same way as, at the moment of our physical conception, we are provided with the genetic potential that may later blossom into the genius of an artistic, scientific, philosophical, or other nature.

Saints, then, are those inherently capable of a heroic degree of self-denial, the ability to sacrifice worldly pleasures or honors in favor of service to God and/or their fellow man. It is not that the saint does not *feel* the pangs of hunger, the pain of physical exhaustion, the scorn of his enemies, or other distressing aspects of his existence. Rather he is simply provided with a counterstrength that enables him to override such obstacles in the interest of what he perceives to be a more important consideration.

If it be objected that there are different kinds of saints and that therefore we cannot be talking about only one sort of genetic gift, the answer is that there are also many different kinds of musical abilities; yet we apply the word genius to performance on an instrument, to the composition of symphonies, to the conducting of orchestras, and so forth.

It may be instructive to recall the once-common belief that creative expression came from sources outside the individual—muses, gods, demons, or other creatures. Such theories correspond to nothing real but do point to a sense that creative people themselves have: that a good many of their most original ideas seem to appear with little or no conscious effort of the will but simply float into the mind unbidden. (See also DREAMS.)

From personal experience I can report that among the thousands of melodies I have conceived there has rarely been the slightest sense of work or difficulty connected with the creation of them. They usually appear in more-or-less full form, almost as if I am hearing them on an invisible radio in my head. After this primary stage of creation, of course, one enters upon a more laborious phase of development—playing the newly created melody on the piano, transcribing it into written form so that others may read it, arranging it for an orchestra, revising it. Almost everything after the first stage is mechanical and developmental. But the original act is spontaneous, free, and hence far more mysterious.

Is, then, spiritual genius neither more nor less difficult to explain than the genius of any other sort? For the flowering of any innate abilities, the genius will, of course, have to live in a place and time where the soil is right. To illustrate this, consider the possibility that Bach might have been born, say, three thousand years before he was. At that time the technology of music in most parts of the world had not even begun to develop: Bach would have lived and died in obscurity instead of gaining the eternal fame that will be his lot. There may live among us today a number of geniuses who will die unsung because the physical objects or social conditions required for the expression of their abilities will not themselves be created until ten thousand years into the future.

It may not be that one particular Christian church itself produces saints, but rather that the truth is precisely the opposite: that spiritually gifted individuals create the church and sustain it through time.

In everything I have said about geniuses of virtue to the present, however, there has been a partly simplistic approach to the phenomenon. In reality Beethoven was a great deal more than the music he created; just so there is a great deal more to saints than the statistically rare expression of their gifts.

Consider by way of illustration the total life experiences of those designated as *heroes*. A given hero may live on earth for seventy years, but the daily record of his activities during that span of time reveals that the extent of his truly heroic behavior occupied, say, only three hours and twenty minutes of the total time. To say as much is not to make light of heroic achievement. We must be thankful for even such scant evidence of epic courage in our society since it is almost totally lacking in the lives of most of us.

Just so is the case of saints. When we place them in sharper focus than their glamour usually permits, we find that they are, like the rest of us, remarkably complex individuals. Indeed a number of them—as the Vatican has informed us in recent years—did not exist at all. But even those whose existence is never in doubt did not behave in a saintly fashion twenty-four hours a day for their entire lives. Some—such as Augustine— for years lived sinful lives by Christian standards before being converted to more edifying patterns of behavior.

Indeed, were certain of the saints to be called before the bar of history they would be hard put to defend some of their acts and opinions. The great Thomas Aquinas, for example, explained to us, when he appeared on our PBS television series "Meeting of Minds," why he thought it was not only perfectly permissible but often advisable to burn heretics alive. (It will perhaps aid in judging Aquinas in this limited context if the reader keeps in mind that the learned doctor himself was a heretic in the opinion of some of his opponents in the church.)

But practically all modern believers would consider it atrocious if anyone today even suggested that the punishment for people who preach unpopular religious opinions is to arrest them, fiendishly torture them to make them confess their actual or alleged guilt, and thereafter take them to a public square, tie them to some post, pile combustibles around their feet, light a fire, and then stand about and watch the excruciating burning of human flesh and listen to the shrieks and pleas of the poor souls so assaulted. Perhaps the custom of loud choral singing at public executions became common in earlier centuries to drown out such screams of panic.

Modern man views such spectacles with horror and detestation, largely as a result of secular, modernist, humanist pressure. Most of today's Catholics hold that Aquinas was not in the least saintly in regard to such attitudes. This establishes clearly enough that the achievement of sanctity is a matter of peak experiences rather than lifelong consistency.

As for the question of the source of the ability to achieve even such rare moments of moral glory, the mystery is as yet unresolved. (See also BY THEIR FRUITS YE SHALL KNOW THEM; GRACE; MORALITY.)

SAMUEL, THE FIRST BOOK OF. This book is subtitled "The First Book of the Kings" and relates the account of Samuel. For centuries the churches have taught that it was written by Samuel; now most biblical scholars concede that it is rather a compilation of history and myth about the spiritual leader Samuel, written by others. Since this book reveals, in embarrassing detail, the man's immoralities, there has always been some absurdity in assuming that Samuel himself wrote it.

Chapter 1. The opening passages of the first chapter tell a familiar Old Testament story: that of a man with two wives, one of whom could have no children but who, after various entreaties to the Lord, eventually becomes fertile. Such a story is here introduced as background for the birth of Samuel. Hannah, for years saddened by her barrenness and the fact that her husband Elkanah's other wife Peninnah had borne several children, eventually went to the temple, prayed to the Lord, and made a vow. Subsequently she had a son.

Given that Samuel was a moral monster, his sinfulness presents us with a dilemma. The Lord—since he troubled himself to answer the woman's prayer—was in a specific way to blame for the subsequent crimes committed by Samuel, not to mention the dreadful moral example his conduct has displayed to generations since his time.

It may be observed, in the Bible's defense, that even the most uplifting sagas can hardly be peopled solely by heroic and saintly individuals, that some evil characters must be introduced, if only for the purposes of providing dramatic tension and serving as horrible examples. It is therefore interesting that in today's exhortatory religious literature the churches *do* limit themselves largely to emphasis on the behavior of admirable personages and—except in the case of Satan and his allies—make scant reference to villains. In the case of the Old Testament, however, great percentages of its passages are devoted to descriptions of such unedifying behavior.

If one is determined to interpret the Bible as the word of God then that fact presents a troubling problem. If, however, the Bible is perceived as what it almost certainly is—merely a fascinating account of the combined histories, myths, legends, and fables of a particular ancient people—then the problem evaporates. We know that history, even if largely inaccurately recorded, will present us with far more instances of weakness, sinfulness, and crime than of heroism or saintliness, the human predicament being what it is.

In any event, in gratitude and fulfillment of her vow, Hannah turns Samuel over to Eli, a priest in a community called Shiloh, who already had two sons, neither of whom was very well-behaved.

Chapter 2. It is difficult to accept the first ten verses here as factual. They are represented as a prayer by Hannah, and her prayer is, in the literal sense, a poem and is so printed in most available versions of the Old Testament. Anyone who is competent to write even second-rate poetry knows it is a painstaking exercise and can in no event be extemporized at length. It is therefore virtually impossible that Hannah actually gave voice to what this chapter asserts she said. (See also POETRY IN THE BIBLE.)

The prayer reveals the primitive and patently absurd belief that God is personally responsible not only for the world's blessings but also for its millions of calamities—a point that no longer seems to be held by any educated Christian or Jew. Nevertheless Hannah is quoted as saying:

> 6. The Lord killeth, and maketh alive: he bringeth down to the grave, and bringeth up.
> 7. The Lord maketh poor, and maketh rich: he bringeth low, and lifteth up.
> 8. He raiseth up the poor out of the dust, and lifteth up the beggar from the dunghill, to set them among princes, and to make them inherit the throne of glory: for the pillars of the earth are the Lord's and he hath set the world upon them.

In observing the actual human experience about us we can see that the Lord did not do the things Hannah believed he did. What blessings and glories the Lord may have in mind for the suffering faithful in the future world no man is competent to describe but, so far as we can actually observe, the Lord seems to pay little practical mind to the tribulations of the billions of unfortunates on this planet.

The reader may recall the earlier suggestion that one of the reasons for the popularity of submitting burnt offerings to the Lord was to supply groceries for the temple priests. The following verses speak to the point:

> 13. And the priests' custom with the people was, that, when any man offered sacrifice, the priest's servant came, while the flesh was in seething, with a fleshhook of three teeth in his hand;
> 14. And he struck it into the pan, or kettle, or caldron, or pot; all that the fleshhook brought up the priest took for himself. So they did in Shiloh, unto all the Israelites that came thither.

> 15. Also before they burnt the fat, the priest's servant came, and said to the man that sacrificed, "Give flesh to roast for the priest; for he will not have sodden flesh of thee, but raw."
>
> 16. And if any man said unto him, "Let them not fail to burn the fat presently, and then take as much as thy soul desireth;" then he would answer him, "Nay; but thou shalt give it me now: and if not, I will take it by force."

That is certainly forthright enough. (See also LEVITICUS.)

There is no doubt that Eli's two sons disgraced their father for we are told in verse 22:

> 22. Now Eli was very old, and heard all that his sons did unto all Israel; and how they lay with the women that assembled at the door of the tabernacle of the congregation.

This, of course, means that the two men had sexual intercourse with the women. Whether the woman's service at the door of the temple was of a purely religious nature or whether these women were common temple prostitutes is not clear. But whether Eli's sons were consorting with whores or enticing or raping innocent women, their father describes their deeds as "evil dealings."

In verse 27 we are told that "there came a man of God to Eli." The phrase *a man of God* is of course susceptible to various interpretations. Apparently the author intended to suggest that the visitor in this case was an ANGEL. Among various threats and predictions, the angel tells Eli:

> 30. Wherefore the Lord God of Israel saith, "I said indeed that thy house, and the house of thy father, should walk before me for ever: but now the Lord saith, 'Be it far from me; for them that honour me I will honour, and they that despise me shall be lightly esteemed.' "

The passage states that on the one hand God made a specific promise that he would grant a particular blessing *forever* and then in the next sentence flatly withdrew that promise. Since an all-knowing God would have no delusions about human weakness, it is perhaps not surprising that he might from time to time respond harshly to particular instances of human sinfulness. The mystery here is why he made a promise forever binding that—since he is by definition able to foresee the future—he knew perfectly well could not be kept. Since all of this is a hopeless tangle of contradictions, the simple way to deal with the problem is to sweep it off the table, as we have had to do in so many earlier similar instances, and refuse to believe that the Lord God could be guilty of the sort of muddled thinking that we know, to our sorrow, is all too common among our own kind.

The chapter concludes the bad news with the prediction that Eli's sons, Hophni and Phinehas, will both die on the same day, and then the "good" news that the Lord will raise up a faithful priest to whom the members of Eli's family will one day be able to crawl, to beg for "a piece of silver and a morsel of bread."

Chapter 3. We are now told that God spoke to Samuel one night while he was living in Eli's house as a boy. God calls several times, in fact, and Samuel, thinking it is Eli, scampers back and forth between their two beds to answer the summons. Finally Eli, no doubt in an effort to get some sleep, suggests that the lad respond to the voice: "Speak, Lord, for thy servant heareth."

Samuel dutifully answers the next calling of his name in this manner and the Lord—we are told—proceeds to reiterate all the terrible things that will come to pass because of the wickedness of Eli's sons and the fact that Eli has not controlled his two wayward heirs, thus putting the young lad in the position to remind the aged priest of the bad tidings he has already heard.

> 19. And Samuel grew and the Lord was with him, and did let none of his words fall to the ground.

Although it may be construed as pleasant news that the boy Samuel grew with the Lord with Eli, chapter 3 gives no satisfactory details about how he went from the obscurity of youth and simple service at the temple to the high station of leadership he has achieved at the start of the next chapter.

Chapter 4. Here we find Samuel suddenly fully grown and calling Israel to battle—for what must be the thousandth time. The usual vast panorama of slaughter is repeated, with the Israelites losing thirty thousand men (was the word *approximately* unknown to the Bible's authors?) in one confrontation alone, among them Eli's two sons. They also lose possession of the ark of God to the enemy. Old Eli, hearing the news of the ark's loss, drops dead.

The loss of the ark raises a simple but profoundly important question. We have already been told—and today's fundamentalists absolutely require us to believe—that even to touch the ark was a sin, a criminal offense so grievous that the offender was not only subject to capital punishment but that such punishment was also imposed on the spot. Now any bright ten-year-old, told that the ark of the covenant had been stolen by enemy troops, would immediately ask how this could possibly be the case if anyone who touches the holy object is at once struck dead. A slightly more imaginative child might suggest that because of its dangerous untouchability the ark could actually serve as one of the most effective weapons in military history: if it could be made to fall into enemy hands Israel's forces would not have to kill their enemies but could simply stand at a distance and watch them die.

Chapter 5. In a little game of cat-and-mouse, the Lord—rather than immediately striking dead the Philistines as he did the Israelite who, to protect the ark from falling when an oxen stumbled, touched the ark to steady it—now permits the ark to be not only captured by the enemy but also placed in their temple beside their pagan god, Dagon. For two nights, like a mischievous little boy, God—we are told—tips over the idol Dagon.

The Philistines, however, are frightened by the shenanigans and immediately discuss how to rid themselves of the ark. While they are trying to decide, God strikes.

> 9. And it was so that after they had carried it about, the hand of the Lord was against the city with a very great destruction: and he smote the men of the city, both small and great, *and they had hemorrhoids, or tumors, in their secret parts.* (IA)

Chapter 6. Despite the "curse," the ark of the Lord—a small, portable box regarded by the Jews as extremely holy—remained in the country of the Philistines for seven months while they tried to figure out what to do with it. Eventually they consulted their own priests about the matter.

> 3. And they said, "If ye send away the ark of the God of Israel, send it not empty; but in any wise return him a trespass offering: then ye shall be heralded, and it shall be known to you why his hand is not removed from you."

In other words, if the plague is not removed, then they will know that it was not Israel's God who caused it to befall them.

The Philistines ask, understandably enough, what sort of a gift might be meaningful to a God. A good many people in the modern day, even many who are not religious, believe it is absurd to speak of presenting material GIFTS TO GOD. That God would be happy to receive the gift of improved human behavior is self-evident, but it is by no means clear why he would have any interest in dead goats, burnt grain, and sizzling fat. But the answer of the Philistine priests is even more incredible. In fact, unless the verse is quoted here many unfamiliar with the Bible may refuse to believe what it says:

> 4. Then said they, "What shall be the trespass offering which we shall return to him?" They answered, "Five golden hemorrhoids [or tumors], and five golden mice, according to the number of the lords of the Philistines: for one plague was on you all, and on your lords.
> 5. Wherefore ye shall make images of your hemorrhoids, and images of your mice that mar the land; and ye shall give glory unto the God of Israel: peradventure he will lighten his hand from off you, and from off your gods, and from off your land."

The Jews of the modern world, among other noble distinctions, are noted for their remarkable gift for humor in its various forms. The great majority of the world's leading comedians are Jewish and the same is true of many humorists, playwrights, and journalists. One might be forgiven, therefore, for at least fleetingly entertaining the thought that such passages of the Old Testament are a matter of the authors actually putting the world on. Certainly Woody Allen or Mel Brooks could write nothing more inherently silly than a story about little golden statues of painful hemorrhoids and mice. But no, one must resist such a hypothesis, for if there is anything that distinguishes the Old Testament it is its incredible seriousness.

Yet the Philistine priests now proceed to offer even more absurd advice.

> 7. "Now therefore make a new cart, and take two milk cows on which there hath come no yoke, and tie the cows to the cart, and bring their calves home from them:
> 8. "And take the ark of the Lord, and lay it upon the cart, and put the jewels of gold [the golden mice and hemorrhoids] which ye return him for a trespass offering, in a coffer by the side thereof; and send it away, that it may go.

Apparently, it was literally impossible for an Old Testament priest to say anything so nonsensical as to stimulate the faintest of suspicions in his hearers that he was, at least at the given moment, out of his senses. Readers of this priestly edict know farmers or dairymen do not impress untrained milk cows to serve as oxen in pulling a cart.

Obviously it is possible to yoke a milk cow to a cart for its first time— or for that matter to do the same to a grasshopper or kangaroo—but the cow will be very apt to simply stand in its place and will not be inclined to move until it goes in search of water, feed, or the company of its kind. In the unlikely event that the two cows in this instance would move at all, there would be little chance that they would remain on a path. It would be more normal behavior for them to wander into the nearest field, as is their accustomed habit.

Yet the priests specifically instruct that the cows be permitted to wander at will and by that very means reveal to the Philistines if Israel's God had indeed caused their problems and if the cart should therefore be returned to them.

> 12. And the cows took the straight way to Bethshemesh, and went along the highway, lowing as they went, and turned not aside to the right hand or to the left; and the lords of the Philistines went after them unto the border of Bethshemesh.

At that community the ark is removed from the cart and set down upon a large stone located in the fields belonging to Joshua, a Bethshemite. The Israelite people of the area, according to the story, "rejoiced to see" the ark when it was brought into their neighborhood, as peasants might be fascinated by any unusual object brought to their village with great pomp and a ceremonial procession. If we imagine a gathering of several hundred—or perhaps a few thousand—local villagers standing about, in a mixture of curiosity, wonder, and respect on their faces, no one will be surprised that a certain number of the villagers approached the object, opened its doors, and looked into it. This would be normal behavior even if there were only one bystander; if there were hundreds, the act would be almost inevitable.

Therefore, carefully consider the following verse:

> 19. And he smote the men of Bethshemesh, *because they had looked into the ark of the Lord, even he smote of the people fifty thousand and threescore and ten men:* and the people lamented, because the Lord had smitten many of the people with a great slaughter.

If this were the only troublesome verse in the entire Bible it would be enough by itself to force a choice between the following conclusions: (1) God is a mass murderer, a sadistic killer far worse than any Jack the Ripper, Adolph Hitler, or Attila the Hun; or (2) God is, as defined, all-good and all-loving and therefore the vicious, depraved violence and murder here attributed to him is authored by a liar and blasphemer. Since it is an insult to one's intelligence not to choose between the two alternatives, my own view, arrived at without a moment's hesitation, is that whoever wrote this particular story is one of the supreme liars of history.

If one were to proffer the argument that the act was necessary to impress upon bystanders that the ark of the covenant was a holy object and not to be idly touched, the intelligent response is that God could have made this point adequately enough by striking dead the first poor peasant whose entirely respectful curiosity moved him to touch the wooden box. It was certainly not necessary to kill 50,070 men, a diabolical act that would have, among its other effects, the result of dramatically increasing the number of widows and fatherless children in the area for years to come. So much for the biblical insistence on the integrity of the family.

The Philistines who had originally taken the ark by force and set it in a heathen temple, a much more despicable act by any standards than touching it out of idle inquisitiveness, only suffered a loss of thirty thousand men.

When coming up against such absurd stories, believers tend to concede, "Well, perhaps this one isolated tale is too preposterous to be believed so let it be stricken from the record." That simply will not do. The true believer has no freedom whatever to make such piecemeal concessions. Either the Bible is the word of God or it is not. Once one starts hacking off portions from the main body, one has automatically abandoned absolute confidence in the concept of divine inspiration. Nor can this story possibly be defended as an allegorical illustration as is sometimes resorted to for other passages. This nonsense tale about hemorrhoids and mice and the ruthless murder of over fifty thousand innocent bystanders is clearly intended to be taken as fact. (See also AUTHENTICITY OF THE BIBLE.)

Chapter 7. There seems to be some confusion in 1 Samuel that relates to the community known as Ebenezer. In this chapter we read:

> 12. Then Samuel took a stone, and set it between Mizpeh and Shen, and called the name of it Ebenezer, saying, "Hitherto hath the Lord helped us."

That seems simple enough, until you remember that earlier, in chapter 5, verse 1 we have been told that "the Philistines took the ark of God, and brought it from Ebenezer unto Ashdod."

These two conflicting reports very probably cannot be reconciled. (See also CONTRADICTIONS, BIBLICAL.)

In any event, the important lesson of chapter 7 is summed up in verse 13:

13. So the Philistines were subdued, and they came no more into the coast of Israel: and *the hand of the Lord was against the Philistines all the days of Samuel.* (IA)

Chapter 8. In chapter 8 we are told that Samuel, by now an old man, "made his sons judges over Israel" (v. 1). Nepotism was presumably not then a matter of public concern. His sons were Joel and Abiah, the first of whom was greatly interested in money and took bribes to effect his decisions in court cases. The Israelites, understandably unhappy about this, came to Samuel

5. And said unto him, "Behold, thou art old, and thy sons walk not in thy ways: now make us a king to judge us like all the nations."

Even though Samuel, upon the Lord's instruction, paints a dismal picture of what they might expect from a king,

19. Nevertheless the people refused to obey the voice of Samuel; and they said, "Nay; but we will have a king over us;
20. "That we also may be like all the nations; and that our king may judge us, and go out before us, and fight our battles."

Humans of the twentieth century, who have had a long history of wars, want for nothing so much as peace. Even in times of relative peace the ancient Israelites—at least so far as we can judge them by their sacred Scriptures—were never so happy as when they were at war or preparing for war. It is reasonable to assume that they were no more pleased at the prospect of being themselves killed or wounded than any other people, but that they literally gloried in war is clear beyond question. Most intelligent military specialists agree with the American general Sherman that war is hell. One would have to search the Old Testament carefully to locate any such realistic and intelligent assessment of combat.

Chapter 9. We are now introduced to the son of Kish, a Benjaminite:

2. And he had a son, whose name was Saul, a choice young man, and a goodly: and there was not among the children of Israel a goodlier person than he: from his shoulders and upward he was higher than any of the people.

Since Saul is to be king of Israel, his name in time made famous throughout the world by the ancient Jewish scribes, one might expect that he would be about important business early. Starting in verse 3, however, we are told that he wandered about looking for asses—donkeys, burros —belonging to his father.

For the next several verses we are told that Saul searches for the asses through Mount Ephraim, past the land of Shalisha, the land of Shalim, the Benjaminites, and into the land of Zuph where he finally seeks the counsel of the seer (prophet) Samuel. But we are told:

15. Now the Lord had told Samuel in his ear a day before Saul came, saying,

16. "To morrow about this time I will send thee a man out of the land of Benjamin, and thou shalt anoint him to be captain over my people Israel, that he may save my people out of the hand of the Philistines: for I have looked upon my people, because their cry is come unto me."

17. And when Samuel saw Saul, the Lord said unto him, "Behold the man whom I spake to thee of! this same shall reign over my people."

When Saul asks Samuel where he might find the seer he seeks, Samuel says that it is he. He then tells him:

20. "And as for thine asses *that were lost three days ago,* set not thy mind on them; for they are found. . . ." (IA)

Perhaps geographers can settle the question whether Saul's previously described trip could possibly have taken place in such a short span of time.

Chapter 10. Here we find that Samuel predicts a series of events that will occur as Saul journeys back to his homeland—to prove to him that he is chosen of God. The events all happen as foretold and yet when Saul finally returns home he does not even mention the news about his upcoming kingship to his father.

Meanwhile Samuel has called the Israelites together and told them that he is now ready to appoint the king they have been requesting. He then goes through a process of selection (in some biblical versions it is said that this was by the drawing of lots) that begins with choosing a tribe (the Benjaminites), then a family (the Matris), then a household (Kish), and finally the narrowing down to his final selection of Saul. Since God had already selected Saul as the leader, it is not clear why this drawn-out process was necessary, unless it was to heighten the drama of the moment. In any event, Saul is nowhere to be found.

22. Therefore they enquired of the Lord further, if the man should yet come thither. And the Lord answered, "Behold, he hath hid himself among the stuff."

That phrase has remained in my mind since my first reading of it. When my wife complains that she is unable to locate me immediately in our home or elsewhere, I sometimes explain to her that I was hidden among the stuff. If the language was good enough for the Lord—or King James—it's good enough for me.

In any event, Saul is located and at once pronounced king, whereupon the people shout, in good English fashion, "God save the king!"

Now let us study how the great King Saul conducts himself in office.

Chapter 11. A military man named Nahash, an Ammonite, comes into the area to make war against the city of Jabesh. The men of the city, fearing him, offer to sign a peace treaty that will make them the Ammonite's servants.

2. And Nahash the Ammonite answered them, "on this condition will I make a covenant with you, *that I may thrust out all your right eyes,* and lay it for a reproach upon all Israel." (IA)

In response to this peculiar and bloodthirsty proposition the men of Jabesh ask only for a week's grace, reportedly telling Nahash that they will spend that time seeing if they can scare up military assistance to resist the impending invasion. If they cannot, they say, they will accept the terms of the offer.

Two things make this story inherently unbelievable: (1) that an invading army would allow a "time out" in which to enlist support to war against them; and (2) that the men of the community are all quite willing to have their right eyes put out if they are unable to find any Israelite leader who will come to their defense.

But, the chapter reports that the messengers go out and eventually approach Saul for his assistance. Saul responds:

6. And the Spirit of God came upon Saul when he heard those tidings, and his anger was kindled greatly.

7. And he *took a yoke of oxen, and hewed them in pieces, and sent them throughout all the coasts of Israel* by the hands of messengers, saying, "Whosoever cometh not forth after Saul and after Samuel, so shall it be done unto his oxen." And the fear of the Lord fell on the people, and they came out with one consent. (IA)

The thousands active today in the ANIMAL RIGHTS movement will no doubt find such passages of special interest. We are not told the identities of the poor messengers who had to walk about in the hot climate of the Near East carrying what must have been quickly decaying pieces of dead meat to be used as visual aids in the transmission of Saul's threatening message to the Israelites who, Saul obviously felt, might otherwise remain unconvinced.

This story, as are others we've previously discussed, is reminiscent of *The Godfather* scene in which the Mafia leader sends a horse's head to a man he wanted to intimidate. Why are such things considered admirable when Saul does them and despicable when Mafia chieftains resort to them?

Saul's tactic is successful, however, in raising 330,000 soldiers to help the people of Jabesh wipe out the Ammonites.

Isaac Azimov, in *Azimov's Guide to the Bible* (Avon), says:

> The numbers given . . . represent a late tradition and are impossibly high . . . and anachronistically assume a divided kingdom, something that lay a century into the future.

Chapter 14. The story now takes an interesting turn as Saul's son Jonathan, apparently unaware that Saul has ordered no food be eaten until the evening of a particular day, dips his walking stick into a honeycomb he happens to find and tastes a bit of the sweet liquid.

> 43. Then Saul said to Jonathan, "Tell me what thou hast done." And Jonathan told him, and said, "I did but taste a little honey with the end of the rod that was in mine hand, and, lo, I must die."
> 44. And Saul answered, "God do so and more also: for thou shalt surely die, Jonathan."

Any intelligent father, upon learning that his son had done something in ignorance of the father's orders, would feel only annoyance, if that, since it is absurd to blame a man for an inadvertent offense. But common sense is of little value in analyzing the acts and policies of most of the characters in the Old Testament. Fortunately the people overrule Saul in this instance and prevent what would have been a murder characterized chiefly by its stupidity.

Chapter 15, in a book infamous for its bloodthirstiness, is one of the most savage chapters in the Scriptures. We are told almost immediately that God personally ordered an atrocious slaughter:

2. Thus saith the Lord of hosts, "I remember that which Amalek did to Israel, how he laid wait for him in the way, when he came up from Egypt.

3. "Now go and smite Amalek and utterly destroy all that they have, and spare them not; but *slay both man and woman, infant and suckling, ox and sheep, camel and ass.*" (IA)

That the ancient Israelites would have been happy to engage in such slaughter, even without divine advice, is by now evident enough, but the personal endorsement of God does resolve the problem of potential guilt. Saul, however, does not follow the order precisely, which is to say that he disobeys a direct command from God.

9. But Saul and the people spared Agag, and the best of the sheep, and of the oxen, and of the fatlings, and the lambs, and all that was good, and would not utterly destroy them: but every thing that was vile and refuse, that they destroyed utterly.

This deviation from the plan—however sensible—angers the Lord, who communicates with Samuel again.

10. Then came the word of the Lord unto Samuel, saying,

11. "It repenteth me that I have set up Saul to be king: for he is turned back from following me, and hath not performed my commandments." And it grieved Samuel; and he cried unto the Lord all night.

But the next day, as instructed by God, the prophet goes to find Saul. Hearing the sheep bleating and the oxen lowing, Samuel asks for an explanation. Saul explains that the people have taken the best animals for the purpose of sacrificing them to God in appreciation of the victory. Considering the list of offenses for which either man generally or the ancient Israelites specifically have to this point been guilty, this will not seem a noteworthy offense or indeed an offense at all. Nevertheless Samuel responds:

18. "And the Lord sent thee on a journey and said, 'Go and utterly destroy the sinners the Amalekites, and fight against them until they be consumed.'

19. "Wherefore then didst thou not obey the voice of the Lord, but didst fly upon the spoil, and didst evil in the sight of the Lord?"

Saul, after a brief exchange, agrees with Samuel that he has been guilty of serious sin in not slaughtering every one of the animals belonging to the Amalekites. Those who select their fiction, film, and TV fare because of its high content of sadism and violence will no doubt be gratified by the following passages.

> 32. Then said Samuel, "Bring ye hither to me Agag the king of the Amalekites." And Agag came unto him delicately. And Agag said, "Surely the bitterness of death is past."
> 33. And Samuel said, "As thy sword hath made women childless, so shall thy mother be childless among women." And *Samuel hewed Agag in pieces before the Lord in Gilgal.* (IA)

Understand that this was no killing in hot blood, no murder justified by a sudden violent and uncontrollable outburst of temper of the sort described in legal terms as *temporary insanity* and therefore sometimes deemed a justifiable defense. No, Agag had already been taken prisoner. His attitude was, we are told, in no way obstreperous or argumentative; he came unto Samuel "delicately." Agag, the captured king, addressed Samuel sadly, philosophically. Nevertheless Samuel commits a crime as bad as any Japanese militarists, Nazi Germans, or Stalinist communists have perpetrated: the personal killing of their high counterparts in the enemy camp.

And not only does Samuel kill Agag, a shameful enough crime, but he then spends what must have been quite a few minutes in slicing the poor man's body into separate pieces. Does the reader find the conduct of such men admirable or despicable? If the latter, then why are such sadists held up as worthy of our religious respect?

Chapter 19. In verse 9 we are told a remarkably strange thing:

> 9. *And the evil spirit from the Lord* was upon Saul, as he sat in his house with his javelin in his hand: and David played with his hand. (IA)

In yet one more instance the Bible is at odds with itself. It is hardly part of any modern Jewish or Christian belief that evil spirits come from the Lord. We are told that they are disobedient to the Lord and by no means his servants. Nevertheless, the italicized phrase in the verse states precisely the contrary. One assertion or the other must be mistaken, which once again establishes that it is not only theoretically possible for the Bible to include a certain amount of ERROR but that it obviously does so in repeated instances.

Although modern fundamentalists thunder against SITUATIONAL ETHICS, the Bible contains frequent instances in which a clear enough moral law is broken for no reason more dramatic than simple common sense. An instance is encountered when Michal, David's wife, having learned that the messengers of King Saul wished to kill her husband, advises him to escape:

> 13. And Michal took an image, and laid it in the bed, and put a pillow of goats' hair for his bolster, and covered it with a cloth.
> 14. And when Saul sent messengers to take David, she said, "He is sick."

In this instance Michal lies twice, once by propping up a dummy figure in David's bed, which is clearly intended to make Saul's messengers believe that David lies asleep; second when she tells the messengers that David is ill rather than absent.

Do not assume that Michal had simply put a couple of pillows under a blanket to make it look like a sleeping body. This is not what the text asserts. It is clear that the object was a graven image, and was precisely the sort of object that had been said to horrify the Lord in many earlier texts.

A few lines later we find another case of poor thinking and consequently poor writing.

> 17. And Saul said unto Michal, "Why hast thou deceived me so, and sent away mine enemy, that he is escaped?" And Michal answered Saul, "He said unto me, 'Let me go; why should I kill thee?' "

I have read and re-read this verse and shown it to a few others. It is inexcusably unclear what the quotation attributed to Michal means. She seems to be quoting David as asking why he should kill her, Michal, but since that makes no sense whatever, we must look for some other explanation.

Chapter 31. Here we find a description of the circumstances of Saul's death that is admirably clear and unambiguous. Philistine archers wound him seriously, at which he asks his armor-bearer to kill him lest he be captured and tortured.

> 4. But his armor-bearer was afraid to, so Saul took his own sword and fell upon the pointed blade and it pierced him through.
> 5. When his armor-bearer saw that he was dead he also fell upon his sword and died with him.

Note that there is no possibility of a variety of interpretations. Would that all the other portions of Scripture were so clear. But when we continue reading into 2 Samuel, we find a different story altogether. In the very first chapter a young Amalekite tells David that he found Saul wounded, in terrible pain, and about to be captured, and that Saul pleaded with the man to put him out of his misery, which he did (2 Sam. 1:6–10). Far from thanking the young stranger for his act of compassion, David has him killed on the spot.

Although both accounts provide an interesting narrative, it is impossible that both are true. There is no guarantee that either of them is correct, but we are concerned here only with the factor of mutual exclusivity, which forces us to the realization that at least one of the narratives cannot possibly be described as "the word of God" since it is false, a lie, fiction. In yet one more instance, therefore, we have seen demonstrated the untenability of the every-word-the-word-of-God thesis. (For additional commentary on 1 Samuel, see DAVID in Volume 1.)

SAMUEL, THE SECOND BOOK OF. The second book of Samuel continues the story of David.

Chapter 1. The "how the mighty are fallen" song of lament that closes this chapter may well have been composed by David himself, but there is little comfort in that fact for those who argue that the Bible contains literally no error whatever. Some of the ablest Christian and Jewish scholars express a good deal of doubt and disagreement over whether numerous other poems and songs traditionally credited to David, were, in fact, written by him.

Chapter 6. An odd aspect of David's social behavior is next referred to which might have led to his being considered a sort of patron saint of dancers.

14. And David danced before the Lord with all his might; and David was girded with a linen ephod.

15. So David and all the house of Israel brought up the ark of the Lord with shouting, and with the sound of the trumpet.

16. And as the ark of the Lord came into the city of David, Michal Saul's daughter looked through a window and saw king David leaping and dancing before the Lord; and she despised him in her heart. . . .

20. Then David returned to bless his household. And Michal the daughter of Saul came out to meet David, and said, "How glorious was the king of Israel to day, who uncovered himself to day in the eyes of

the handmaids of his servants, as one of the vain fellows shamelessly uncovereth himself!"

The woman was saying—in plain, modern language—to her husband and king, "Well, you certainly made an ass of yourself at the temple today leaping and dancing about like an idiot." An ephod was a robe, like a woman's dress of the present day. Part of Michal's displeasure grew out of the fact that David had "uncovered himself" before his fellow dancers and bystanders by his uninhibited dancing. Whether such a thing ever happened we have not the slightest way of knowing, but the unknown author at least provides a somehow touchingly human and therefore relatively believable detail in the story of the public dance in the temple.

In David's time it was apparently the custom among the Jews to do public dancing as part of their religious observances, as today singing is commonly a part of the religious service. One shudders to think of the response that would greet modern religious authorities were they to argue that this Old Testament text meant that the Lord required the wildest and most uninhibited dancing in our churches and synagogues. There have been modern instances of dancers performing in churches, but the dancing in such instances is of a dignified and pure style. For David to have so incurred Michal's displeasure he must have been turning himself about in a manner associated with disco or rock dancing of the present day.

Chapter 12. Perhaps the most remarkable thing about this chapter is that verse 11 alleges that God, the embodiment of moral perfection, not only condones adultery but literally causes it to happen. The chapter first asserts that "The Lord sent Nathan unto David" to chastise him for the evil he has done in not only adulterously taking the wife of Uriah but also, in effect, murdering Uriah by deliberately sending him into dangerous battle.

In verse 11, although it is not clear whether Nathan is presuming to dictate words as coming from God or whether God is speaking to David directly, we are told:

> 11. Thus saith the Lord, "Behold, I will raise up evil against thee out of thine own house, and *I will take thy wives before thine eyes, and give them unto thy neighbor, and he shall lie with thy wives* in the sight of this sun.
> 12. "For thou didst it secretly: but I will do this thing before all Israel, and before the sun." (IA)

Apparently the Lord quoted here believes that two wrongs *do* make a right, although for centuries the churches have taught us differently.

Much of the story of David and his adultery is a simple enough moral parable suggesting yet again that the price of sin is death. We certainly ought not to commit adultery and the story tells us of the tragic consequences of David's breaking the moral law. At this early time in history, however, MORALITY seems to have concentrated chiefly on either sex or worship, as we may conclude from the fate that befell the Ammonite city of Rabbah. As you read the following verse, bear in mind that Christians and Jews are taught that such stories are literally true historical accounts.

> 31. And he brought forth the people that were therein, and *put them under saws, and under harrows of iron, and under axes of iron, and made them pass through the brick kiln:* and thus did he unto all the cities of the children of Ammon. So David and all the people returned unto Jerusalem. (IA)

We are told, in other words, not only that the great, moral King David committed a savage atrocity in killing the occupants of the captured city, but that he did so in particularly fiendish ways. Moreover, we are told— on the authority of the sacred Scriptures—that he did this unto *all* the cities of the Ammonites.

It is small wonder that the modern world has difficulty in convincing the citizens of all nations that war is a vicious atrocity when the Bible not only describes countless such bloodthirsty crimes but refers to them as edifying, noble, and pleasing to God. (See CRIMES, BIBLICAL IMPETUS TO.)

If there were a God who took pleasure in inciting his creatures to crimes of unspeakable savagery against the men, women, and children of innumerable cities, no morally sensible person would have anything but loathing for such a God. But since believers argue that God is moral perfection itself, they are therefore faced with a dilemma. If God is indeed all-perfect and loving, then our spiritual forefathers made an abysmal mistake in concluding that the recitations of ancient mass murderers were personally endorsed by such a perfect God.

Chapter 23. This chapter begins by arousing the skepticism of the thoughtful reader: it represents the bulk of the first seven verses as "the last words of David." The phrase *last words* is generally applied to death-bed statements. If this is the valid interpretation, then it is a remarkable thing that David's last words were uttered in the form of poetry, for even professional poets do not *speak* in poetry.

Inasmuch as the passage quoted is represented as being from either the tongue or pen of the greatest ruler Israel ever had, and inasmuch as the statements quoted are reportedly portions of that mighty leader's last earthly comments, it is therefore disconcerting to note that David's closing remarks are not spiritual or edifying but bitter and spiteful, and senseless.

> 6. But godless men are all like thorns that are thrown away; for they cannot be taken with the hands.
> 7. But the man who touches them arms himself with iron and the shaft of a spear and they are utterly consumed with fire.

The very next verse seems to have been written by another hand, at another time; it is merely one more military memo of the sort in which the Old Testament abounds.

> 8. These be the names of the mighty men whom David had: The Tachmonite that sat in the seat, chief among the captains; the same was Adino the Eznite: he lift up his spear against eight hundred, whom he slew at one time.

Let the reader ask himself if he honestly believes that a man named Adino, armed only with a spear, killed precisely eight hundred enemy soldiers on a single occasion. One hopes that if this story is true, those slaughtered were at least soldiers; God forbid that some of the victims were innocent women and children of the sort fighting men of the Old Testament were in the habit of massacring with full abandon. The use of a smoothly rounded figure inevitably gives rise to doubt about such reports.

An equally unlikely story is related starting with verse 13.

> 13. And three of the thirty chief went down, and came to David in the harvest time unto the cave of Adullam: and the troop of the Philistines pitched in the valley of Rephaim.
> 14. And David was then in an hold, and the garrison of the Philistines was then in Bethlehem.
> 15. And David longed, and said, "Oh that one would give me drink of the water of the well of Bethlehem, which is by the gate!"
> 16. And the three mighty men brake through the host of the Philistines, and drew water out of the well of Bethlehem, that was by the gate, and took it, and brought it to David: nevertheless he would not drink thereof, but poured it out unto the Lord.
> 17. And he said, "Be it far from me, O Lord, that I should do this: is not this the blood of the men that went in jeopardy of their lives?" therefore he would not drink it. These things did these three mighty men.

Although the size of the "garrison of the Philistines" is not specified, it would be reasonable to assume that it consisted of at least fifty to one hundred men. Yet, the reader of Scripture is here asked to believe that three Israelites broke through the detachment purely for the purpose of bringing David a drink of water from a particular well. Does the chief rabbi of Jerusalem or the pope believe the story is true in every detail? David then supposedly poured the water on the ground; such a thoughtless action as this by now seems par for the course in Old Testament stories.

What moral lesson is to be learned from the following verse?

18. And Abishai, the brother of Joab, the son of Zeruish, was chief among three. And he lifted up his spear against three hundred, and slew them, and had the name among three.

Again it must be noted that the number of kills claimed is not 293, not 307, but precisely 300 men. Second, it is implied that no one was only wounded, as would be the case in even the most heated military engagements, but that all were killed.

Third, it is alleged that this killing, like others discussed previously, was done with one weapon only—a spear. Think about the physical actuality of these reports. Let the reader imagine for a moment that he has been authorized by God to kill a dozen or so professional fighting men with a spear. An instant's reflection will lead to the realization that the act cannot be done even if the spear-wielder is possessed of remarkable strength and has had the benefit of much experience. It would be quite difficult in fact to kill three hundred of the enemy if one were armed with a revolver or pistol. But a spear sticks in human tissue and bone. If successfully inserted into the unfortunate carcass of one opponent, that very attack would give the victim's fellows the opportunity to set upon the spearman before he could withdraw his weapon. For my own part, I do not believe there is a word of truth in such stories.

The rest of the chapter consists chiefly of more unedifying details. Verses 24 through 39 comprise one more of those lengthy genealogies that must be of slight interest even to the most conscientious of scholars.

Chapter 24. This portion of 2 Samuel is one of the most puzzling in a book that is itself the most confusing in literary and religious history:

1. And again the anger of the Lord was kindled against Israel, and he moved David against them to say, "Go, number Israel and Judah."

We are told nothing about the reason God was—for what seems the hundredth time—angry with his Chosen People. But even assuming that divine wrath was justified in this instance, why should a Deity, by definition pure intelligence, decide to punish his sinful children by "inciting" David to—what? Chastise them? Put a curse on them? Bring a plague upon them? No, merely to take a census of them!

Since it is absurd to attribute such nonsensical instructions to an all-good and all-wise God, one faces the question—certainly of literary interest—why, in the opinion of the all-too-human author of these passages the taking of a census was considered a hateful, despicable thing. Censuses had been taken twice before, once by Moses, with no guilt attendant on the act. Generally when men belong to or are associated with an entity they do not wish to have counted, it is because they have some reason to hide the relevant truth.

A few years ago the publishers of the entertainment trade publication *Variety* refused to honor a combined rule and/or custom of the publishing trade of revealing the size of the periodical's readership. No one has ever doubted that the reason for such reluctance was that very few people, statistically speaking, then read *Variety;* the publishers were therefore afraid that if such a small figure became public knowledge, advertisers would be less willing to buy space in the periodical or, if they bought it, would be unwilling to pay the going rates.

But why did the Israelites alive at the time that 2 Samuel was written not wish to have their numbers known? Some scholars make guesses about the avoidance of taxes or military service. Is this admirable? Either an extremely large number of Israelites and other Hebrews have by this time invaded and occupied the land that belonged to the Canaanites and were therefore reluctant to have the arithmetic become public knowledge, or there were relatively few invaders and it was feared that if details of the smallness of the Israelite camp became commonly known this could be information encouraging to their enemies—who comprised practically every non-Jewish tribe in that area of the Middle East. Of the two alternatives neither reflects particular credit upon those who wished to disguise the truth.

The census, it is reported, took nine months and twenty days to complete:

> 9. And Joab gave the sum of the numbering of the people to the king; and in Israel there were 800,000 valiant men who drew the sword, and the men of Judah were 500,000.

Why only military men were counted is not explained, although it can hardly have been to the disadvantage of either King David or his followers to know precisely the number of the fighting men on whom they could depend in future military engagements. One is, however, suspicious of the round numbers given. One might assume that the ancient Israelites had simply not developed such words and concepts as *approximately* or *more or less,* but this is not the case, since in other instances in the Scriptures the word *about* is used in connection with numbers and countings.

Since the figures suggest a total population of four million, they are not now believed by any scholar, providing yet one more instance of ERROR in the Bible.

There are time-honored, intricate, creative, and intellectually respectable arguments for the existence of God. While it is clear that they have not convinced all disinterested scholars, they nevertheless have seemed persuasive to many. Debate on the question will continue among both laymen and philosophers, as indeed it should. But none of the arguments —all of which have been devised by history's most able spokesmen for Christianity and Judaism, among other religious forms—has ever suggested that humans ought to believe in a Deity simply because the Bible suggests such a course.

Millions firmly believe in the existence of an all-powerful, all-loving, all-knowing power but know little or nothing of the Bible and quite properly consider it totally irrelevant so far as the question of God's existence is concerned. A careful, unbiased reading of the Scriptures is as likely to lead to agnosticism or atheism as to unquestioning belief. There is no purely logical reason why this should be the case but it happens nevertheless because of the unremitting indoctrination, usually by Christian fundamentalism, that the Bible is the source of all necessary knowledge about God, including the fact of his existence. Before anything can be proved from the Bible, the Bible itself must first be established as what its literalist defenders assert it to be: the absolute, inerrant word of God, without even the possibility of exception.

Many passages in the Scriptures are related to factual reality but that proves nothing, any more than a letter from one's grandmother that mentions the city of Chicago in and of itself proves the reliability of the grandma's account.

Clearly feelings of reverence can go beyond the point of justification. The same process holds true in the popular attitude toward figures of heroic proportions. An individual may merit admiration for his or her achievements which may be formidable and have long-lasting effect, but societies will often not stop at that point. They go beyond the boundaries of reason to inflate the heroic figure to godlike portions, sometimes quite literally. This is a grave danger; eventually the honored figure's imperfections will come to light. At that point, because of the earlier insistence that he was without fault, the discovery of those weaknesses to which all humans are prone may destroy popular respect.

It is just so with the Scriptures. By exaggerating its virtues and denying its obvious faults, our literalist brethren make a wager that they are bound to lose. Sadly, they have placed millions at moral risk by being so careless.

It certainly does not follow that even though the Bible contains numerous errors, it is totally without merit. In fact, it is a profoundly important document, a mighty influence on Western culture, and well worth the scholarly study of every thoughtful person.(See also AUTHENTICITY OF THE BIBLE; HISTORICAL RELEVANCE OF THE BIBLE.)

SCIENCE AND RELIGION. The uneasiness in the relationship between science and religion goes back thousands of years. However, there has never been an all-out war pitting one against the other. Instead, the two fields were involved in an endless series of skirmishes, for the most part about narrowly defined specifics. In this long-continued confrontation, religion has enjoyed enormous advantages, the first of which was that for thousands of years it had the field entirely to itself. Science, by way of comparison, is a relatively modern innovation.

To religion's disadvantage, however, long before practically anything whatever had been scientifically established, religion felt obliged to provide lucid explanations for what was sensately perceived about the physical universe. Given that even the brightest, most creatively speculative individuals had so little to work with, it is not surprising that no commonly accepted image of the world emerged. How many pictures purporting to reflect accurately the universe of puzzling but concrete phenomena have been proposed we shall never know, but every culture had its own hypothesis. Had there been any true scientists on earth in ancient days, those representing different tribes, upon making accidental contact, might have combined their efforts by exchanging theories and observations in the way that is common to modern scholarship. But all such thinking was left to astrologers and priests, an isolated and discrete process that had the tragically unfortunate effect of sanctifying the often erroneous views of the scribes and leaders of hundreds of rival faiths.

This might be interpreted as one of the gloomiest of all historical periods, given that it is notoriously dangerous to contradict religious beliefs whereas there is almost no physical danger involved in contradicting any prevailing set of scientific assumptions and facts. Fortunately, specific religions in particular geographic settings have given ground in the face of the gradual accumulation of well-established scientific information. True, the glacial process involved was maddening, and we shall never learn how many individuals paid for their personal brilliance by being subjected to social ostracism, verbal and physical abuse, arrest, imprisonment, TORTURE, and death.

It is sobering and humbling to reflect on which of the two participants in the debate has been historically guilty of the most sadistically cruel crimes and atrocities. Is it still possible to be religious in the light of such knowledge? Certainly. Though nothing more complex than intellectual honesty compels us to improve and refine our religions, precisely such a civilizing process has observably occurred. Religion today is clearly not the bloodthirsty ogre that it certainly was for a very long time.

The Bible is at its best when it encourages respect for the classic virtues, none of which, by the way, were uniquely identified by the Old Testament authors. When the scriptural authors enter the areas of science, they command no special respect whatever. (See also RELIGION.)

SITUATIONAL ETHICS. We wish to believe, because it may be comforting to do so, that moral codes are absolutely binding and always easy to apply in concrete situations. In reality no one does *not* have a "situational" code of ethics and morals so far as actual behavior is concerned. Most of us are perfectly aware that our conduct is dictated by factors other than the bare ethical code we profess. But some—chiefly religious fundamentalists—are perhaps unaware that in practice they do permit mitigating circumstances to affect both their judgment and behavior, despite their assertions to the contrary.

Since the range of human behavior is very wide indeed, there may be a few souls either so saintly and virtuous—or so priggish—that they will indeed tell blunt truths rather than the polite lies that are the conventional social alternative. But it is doubtless that thousands currently criticizing situational ethics nevertheless behave in as situational a way as possible whenever it is convenient for them to do so.

When our nation was involved in such tragic military confrontations as the two World Wars, the Korean, Vietnam, and Persian Gulf wars, when did the denouncers of situational ethics instruct us that we must never lie or in any way mislead the enemy?

And where today are the critics of situational ethics who will insist that the blunt truth be told to innocent children or frightened old people who suffer from fatal diseases? For centuries physicians have prescribed placebos to hypochondriacs and other patients, even though such administration involves the telling of a lie. The practice, however, often produced the desired effect because of the patient's confidence and belief. To insist on absolute truth-telling in the practice of medicine would deny millions of patients such benefits and would, in fact, wreak general havoc throughout the profession.

Another area where situational ethics seems appropriate is in the obeying of the commandment "Honor thy father and thy mother." So far as moral common sense is concerned, the key verb might better have been translated *respect* than *honor,* but even here it requires only a moment's reflection to see that while respect for parents is a perfectly sound principle, individual evaluations are still required. If the reader's father were Charles Manson or Adolf Hitler would honor be called for?

It might be argued that if the actual parent is clearly not deserving of admiration, at least a measure of respect is called for by virtue of his office, so to speak, in the same way that, while a given occupant of the White House may be ignorant, inattentive, unmindful of the poor, or otherwise partly evil and therefore hardly praiseworthy as a person, we ought still to respect him for the office he holds. The suggestion may be reasonable as regards a president, but the analogy is inappropriate where parents are concerned. If a given mother or father is rightly despised by the world, the law, and the church, why should that person's unfortunate children be obliged to feel or feign respect simply because of an ancient commandment?

But it is unnecessary to produce an endless list of instances to prove a point so obvious. (See also ABORTION; DIVORCE; EUTHANASIA; MORALITY; SUICIDE.)

SLAVERY. The Bible is infamous for not identifying involuntary servitude as the great evil it is. The justification of slavery found in the Old Testament is sometimes "defended" on the grounds that the priestly and other authors of the laws referring to slavery simply reflected acceptance of a prevailing custom but that such acceptance by no means implied their approval of the practice. Defenders cite the present-day example that the existence of certain laws referring to capital punishment does not necessarily establish that the majority of the American people—including many lawmakers—personally approve of the practice.

The argument, unfortunately, cannot be used within the context of apologetic criticism of the Book of the Covenant section of Exodus. It is clear that the Israelites and Judeans themselves refer, in innumerable scriptural instances, to slavery in *non*critical terms—except, naturally, when bondage of their own is concerned. But who is not opposed to slavery for himself?

Charles Bradlaugh has written:

I am unaware of any religion in the world which in the past forbade slavery. The professors of Christianity for ages supported it; the Old Testament repeatedly sanctioned it by special laws; the New Testament has no repealing declaration . . . and it is impossible for any uninformed Christian to deny that *the abolition movement in North America was most steadily and bitterly opposed by the religious bodies in the various states* . . . the Bible and pulpit, the church and its great influence, were used against abolition and in favor of the slaveowner. (IA)

To the less-than-honest claim that Christianity—despite its long proslavery record—nevertheless deserves part of the credit for abolition, on the grounds that some individual abolitionists were either nominal or sincere Christians, Bradlaugh returns to the historical record:

The heretic Condorcet pleaded powerfully for freedom whilst Christian France was still slave-holding. For many centuries Christian Spain and Christian Portugal held slaves. Puerto Rican freedom is not of long date: and Cuban emancipation is ever yet newer. It was a Christian King, Charles V, and a Christian friar who founded in Spanish America the slave trade between the Old World and the New. For some 1800 years Christians kept slaves, bought slaves, sold slaves, bred slaves, stole slaves. Pious Bristol and godly Liverpool less than 100 years ago openly grew rich on the traffic. During the ninth century Greek Christians sold slaves to the Saracens. In the eleventh century prostitutes were publicly sold as slaves in Rome, and the profit went to the Church.

Such is the shameful record of the churches in regard to this matter. In America it took common sense and simple human decency, along with force of arms, for the abolitionists to prevail over the biblical mind-set toward slavery. The slavetraders, owners, and overseers were Bible thumpers through and through. There should be no mistake about the attitude of American churches toward slavery during the period before the Civil War. The Bible, needless to say, supported proslavery arguments, but it would no doubt have been twisted to do so had the relevant passages on the subject been only ambiguous. Countless clergymen—chiefly in the South—took the position that down through long centuries the church had specifically sanctioned slavery, in part as a method of converting the heathen to Christian civilizations!

Dr. B. M. Palmer, Bishop Stephen Elliott, and the Reverend James Hanley Thornwell were three among a great many Southern religious leaders who felt not the slightest guilt in defending slavery from the Bible-oriented and traditional position. Neither Baptists, Methodists, or Presbyterians, among others, have anything to be proud of in regard to their church's conduct in the South. Nor should it be thought that Southern Christians at least limited themselves to civilized debate. Proslavery leaders were determined to perpetuate slavery not only by censoring but frequently also by destroying every expression of antislavery sentiment they could get their hands on. They consequently burned books and newspapers, sent spies into the abolitionist camp, and killed both Negroes and whites with little concern for the moral law. Needless to say, every one of the murderers claimed respect for the Bible.

If the Bible had been forthrightly *anti*slavery, if it had expressed in clear terms the vicious evil of the practice, two cataclysmic social dramas could have been avoided. One was slavery itself, for most of its Christian perpetrators would have been dissuaded from acting on the sole grounds of economic self-interest. And without slavery it follows there would have been no Civil War, with its bloody slaughter of millions and its ugly scars that are not completely healed to this day. We have therefore the Bible, among other causes, to thank for both slavery and the Civil War.

Lest we think of all this as some best-forgotten drama that was perhaps important a century ago but no longer has a legitimate claim upon our moral attention, even today, far too many residents of the South—including many who call themselves Christians—have in their hearts the firm conviction that the black man is naturally inferior. Even as we draw close to the end of the twentieth century, many still cling to the belief that the Negro ought to "keep his place," that blacks should not receive wages equal to what whites receive for the same work, and various other attitudes that are as un-American as they are un-Christian. Precisely such problems deeply trouble some sincere and well-intentioned Southern Christians; certain believers have rendered truly heroic service in the cause of social justice. But those persons who dared to challenge the status quo have uniformly been made to pay dearly for their moral sensitivity and social independence. (See also CRIME, BIBLICAL IMPETUS TO; EVIL, THE PROBLEM OF.)

SONG OF SOLOMON. Although Jewish and Christian tradition describes this section of Scripture as the Song of Solomon, the inscription is simply one more error. Not only is there not the slightest proof that Solomon wrote the book, but there is no good reason to believe that he did.

One hypothesis even suggests that the text consists of entirely separate love songs eventually gathered together. Hence it is often also called the Song of Songs. This theory seems reasonable in that it would account for the fact that there is little coherence overall to the book.

Whoever created the various separate poems that have been brought together was exquisitely gifted at the art of poetry. Nothing in the largely sordid record of Solomon's doings—actual or alleged—would suggest that he was a poet, much less one of sublime ability, thus strengthening the case against his being the author.

Nor does anyone have the slightest idea of when work on the collection of poems or songs started or when it was completed. It appears to have grown by accretion over a period of several centuries.

Among the many, not widely shared nuggets of information is the discovery, familiar to the scholarly community, that there are older documents in Egyptian love literature that are quite similar to the Song. Says Roland E. Murphy of the Duke Divinity School, in an informative dissertation in the *Catholic Biblical Quarterly* (October 1977):

> The Song and the Egyptian counterparts breathe the same atmosphere.
> There are common themes: the use of *sister* for the woman, the mutuality
> and uniqueness of the love, emphasis on the senses (seeing, hearing,
> touching, smelling), lovesickness, obstacles to love, frequent references to
> animals and plants, the descriptions of the other's physical charms . . ."

If the Egyptian love poems were written first, as they clearly were, and second, if we assert that God personally inspired every line of the Song of Solomon, we must inevitably conclude that God is guilty of plagiarism. Since such a conclusion is preposterous, it follows that we must revise our thinking on the matter. But in no meaningful sense can the claim be made that the Song of Solomon was personally written, dictated, or inspired by God.

If, therefore, every other book of Scripture were to seem valid but this one, the fact of its inadmissibility would alone demolish the argument of the every-wordists. Ancient Jewish and later Christian attempts to justify the inclusion of this touchingly sensual material as part of the sacred text represent classic instances of rationalization. Anyone with the slightest sensitivity to beautiful poetry must be grateful that the Jewish culture preserved such a priceless example of the art, but that is a long way indeed from claiming that the text is truly sacred.

Christians who, borrowing from the rabbis, suggest that the Song refers to the love between Christ and his church do not convince many scholars. The Walk-Through Bible authors wisely comment, "Only a marital relationship as pure as that portrayed in the Song can serve this purpose," leaving unanswered the question of how many such marriages there are.

A remarkable thing about the Song, however, is that it includes no reference to God. Nor is there any reference to MORALITY, RITUAL, or any other aspect of RELIGION. Consequently, early Jewish scholars heatedly debated whether the lyrics should be included in the canon at all. To this day it is unclear why the decision in favor of canonicity was made, but the matter was, in any event, settled by the council of rabbis in Jamnia in A.D. 90.

Although we use such words as *lyrics, songs, poems,* or *dramatic scenes,* no one has the slightest idea as to which of these terms, if any, is correct in regard to this biblical book. Perhaps the intention of the unknown original writer was merely to create a titillating and erotic playlet. Another theory proposes that the document in its present form represents a collection of love songs sung as part of wedding ceremonies. Yet another theory dates the material back to very early fertility cult liturgy.

The poem is too long to quote here in its entirety, though the reader should refer to his own copy of the Scriptures to savor its delights. The following sections should put an end to assertions that there is something totally pure and unerotic about the poem:

WOMAN

(1:1)   May he kiss me with the kisses of his mouth.

MAN

(1:9–10)   To me, my darling, you are like
My mare among the chariots of Pharaoh.
Your cheeks are lovely with ornaments,
Your neck with strings of beads . . .

WOMAN

(1:13)   My beloved is to me a pouch of myrrh
Which lies all night between my breasts . . .

MAN

(1:15)   How beautiful you are, my darling,
How beautiful you are!
Your eyes are like doves . . .

WOMAN

(2:1–6, 9) How handsome you are, my beloved
And so pleasant!
Indeed our couch is luxuriant . . .
Like an apple tree among the trees of the forest
So is my beloved among the young men.
In his shade I took great delight and sat down
And his fruit was sweet to my taste . . .
Sustain me with raisin cakes,
Refresh me with apples,
Because I am sick from love.
Let his left hand be under my head
And his right hand embrace me . . .
My beloved is like a gazelle or a young stag . . .

MAN

(2:10, 14) Arise, my darling, my beautiful one, and come along
Oh my dove, in the clefts of the rock,
In the secret place of the steep pathway
Let me see your form, let me hear your voice;
For your voice is sweet
And your form is lovely . . .

WOMAN

(3:1, 4) On my bed night after night I sought him
. . . I found him whom my soul loves
I held on to him, and would not let him go
Until I had brought him to my mother's house
And into the room of her who conceived me . . .

MAN

(4:3, 5) Your lips are like a scarlet thread
(7) And your mouth is lovely.
Your temples are like a slice of a pomegranate
Behind your veil . . .
Your two breasts are like two fawns
Twins of a gazelle . . .
You are altogether beautiful, my darling . . .
(9) You have made my heart beat faster, my sister, my bride;
You have made my heart beat faster
With a single glance of your eyes . . .

397

(10)   How much better is your love than wine
          And the fragrance of your oils
          Than all kinds of spices

(11)   Your lips, my bride, drip honey;
          Honey and milk are under your tongue
          And the fragrance of your garments is
          Like the fragrance of Lebanon . . .

WOMAN

(4:16)   Awake, oh North wind
          And come, come the wind of the South;
          Make my garden breathe out fragrance,
          Let its spices be wafted abroad
          May my beloved come into his garden
          And eat its choice fruits . . .

MAN

(5:2)   I was asleep, but my heart was awake
          A voice! My beloved was knocking.
          Open to me, my sister, my darling . . .

WOMAN

(5:3)   I have taken off my dress,
          How can I put it on again? . . .
          My beloved extended his hand through the opening
          And my feelings were aroused for him.

Considering the Tertullian-like, puritanical horror with which many Christian fathers, including not a few of the present day, have approached the entire subject of sex and romantic eroticism, it is an eminently fair question how many impressionable young Christians, formally celibate or not, have found in the Song of Solomon—with its shimmering descriptions of breasts, mouths, hips, stomachs, necks, and eyes—an incitement to what Christian moral philosophy has for centuries regarded as "impure thoughts." An unprejudiced but rational visitor from another planet would regard it as exceedingly strange that a religious document supposed to arouse spiritual sentiments in its readers should instead give rise to lustful emotions.

The only way in which Jews and Christians can remotely justify the inclusion of such clearly erotic verse in religious Scripture is by ignoring the plain meaning and beauty of its words and phrases and concentrating solely on its allegorical possibilities. This view is expressed by Jakob J. Petuchowski, assistant professor of Rabbinics at Hebrew College, writing in *Commentary* (Feb. 1959):

> . . . there is one book in the Hebrew Bible where the only interpretation the Rabbis would consider legitimate was the allegorical and this was The Song of Songs. Instead of taking literally the references in that book to the young lover and his beloved, the rabbis maintained that the whole book was an allegory of the love between God and Israel. Though the *allegorical interpretation of the Song of Songs may have little to commend itself to the modern mind,* it will still have to be conceded that we owe the canonization, and hence the very preservation, of this delightful book solely to this interpretation. (IA)

Chapter 6. Even after centuries of painstaking study, there is no possibility of unanimity of opinion on what the document means, above and beyond the obvious literal interpretation of many of the lines and brief passages. Consider the following:

> 12. Or ever I was aware, my soul made me like the chariots of Amminadib.

Roland Murphy, in his dissertation, refers to this as "the most obscure verse in the song . . . which has resisted all attempts at translation." There are many moments of such admirable frankness in the writings of the most respectable authorities. Unfortunately they are almost invariably addressed to other scholars and not to the masses of the faithful, apparently in the fear that if they were told the full truth about the Scriptures they would not be able to withstand the shock.

The possibility of pagan—or at least polytheistic origin—is consistent with the fact that the long-confusing term *Shulamite,* which is found in this chapter and applies to the young woman of the drama, is similar to the name *Shulamanitu,* a pagan goddess of love and war.

Not even the ablest modern scholars have any idea what the name Baalhamon means.

Chapter 8. Here we find another section of the love poem, the full meaning of which has yet eluded scholars and laymen:

> 8. We have a little sister too young for breasts. What shall we do if someone asks to marry her?
> 9. If she has not breasts we will build upon her a battlement of silver, and if she is adorned, we shall enclose her with Cedar boards.

This has the ring of certain twentieth century poetry in which, while the words are strikingly beautiful, it's every man for himself so far as interpretation is concerned.

SOUL, THE. The debate has raged for a very long time concerning the structurally simple question whether there is, in fact, such a thing as a soul. Even a moment's reflection suffices to suggest that the argument, for both participant schools, is somewhat difficult, in part because when we use the word *thing* there is the implication that we are talking about a physical object. Perhaps, then, our first difficulty is merely semantic, since all participants agree that whatever the soul is, it is certainly not material.

Since Christianity received the Old Testament from the Jews, Christians would be poorly advised to turn their back on Jewish biblical scholarship; the best-informed scholars, of course, do nothing so foolish. But as successive renderings of the Jewish Scriptures are examined, they clearly reveal that the word of God as perceived by Jews has undergone the same kind of evolution over the centuries as have Christian scriptural documents. A new translation of the Torah (Genesis, Exodus, Leviticus, Numbers, and Deuteronomy) was published in 1963 by the Jewish Publication Society of America, the highest authority in its field. As has been the case with all other renderings of the Scriptures over the ages, this version—which naturally incorporated the latest discoveries of eminent scholarship—required a revision of certain points of belief on the part of the faithful.

One revision is that the new edition does not include the word *soul*. As Professor Harry M. Orlinsky of Hebrew Union College explains about previous translations of the Hebrew word *nefesh* as *soul*:

> [The translations are] completely inaccurate. The Bible does not say we have a soul; . . . *nefesh* is the person himself—his need for food—the very blood in his veins.

Christians among others believe that souls are automatically created as a result of even sinful sexual intercourse between two individuals by means of a chemical-biological reaction that occurs when a male's fluid and a female's egg combine and immediately begin the profoundly mysterious process of cell division.

Consider this in the context of the basic Christian distrust and unease with sexuality itself, though the church is as clearly divided on this as it is on other important questions. Sex within a duly consecrated marriage is, of course, permitted. This can hardly be accounted to the church's credit since the alternative would be absurd. This is certainly not to argue that the church is wrong to be wary of the explosive power of sex that, like all power, not only can be but *is* daily abused. The church is right, specifically, in condemning adultery, although the practice was no doubt disapproved of before there ever was any such thing as a church. Nevertheless, in the church's view new souls are created as part of this same sweaty, animalistic process by which new bodies are.

If this is so, as it well may be, then it turns out that God and/or nature are as wasteful in this regard as they clearly are in all other instances of the creation of animal or vegetable life, since failure is more common than success in such a wondrous process. Certain animal species, as a result of their sexual function, produce dozens, scores, even hundreds of new living creatures, although at all times the great majority will die and only a minute portion will reach adult life. Only a small percentage, in fact, will survive infancy. The process of death starts a split second after the first flickering stirrings of life. Millions of tiny creatures all over the surface of our planet, and beneath the surface as well, know only a few moments of life and then succumb to a thousand-and-one agents that terminate their brief existence.

The reproductive process for the human animal is not nearly as wasteful, but wasteful it nevertheless is. Whatever the loving ministrations of God might be for his human creatures, that part of divine intelligence that is represented by physical nature clearly has no "intention" that one individual or another will live while others are dying. How many spontaneous abortions—miscarriages—occur daily among the human population around the globe no one knows, but the arithmetic is that of millions, and the process continues from the moment of conception to that of the emergence into the light that is called birth.

Nor, for that matter, does the process stop there. Among those humans who survive their birth, death begins to intrude into the larger drama from the very first moment. At the initial casual philosophical contemplation of death we tend, however, to think that it is something that strikes the very old and infirm. But anyone who has spent time at a children's hospital (as I did years ago when my oldest son at seventeen became one of the first patients in the United States to benefit from the then developing art of open-heart surgery) becomes aware that a great many of the little ones taken to such houses of tender care do not survive the experience. (See also DISEASE.)

But we are speaking of souls. Since, as we have agreed, millions of freshly minted souls can be said to have lived only a few seconds, minutes, hours, days, or weeks, is there not some enormously puzzling mystery in all this? The soul of a fully adult Thomas Aquinas, let us say, would presumably be as wise as was the physical body of that great gentleman. But the soul of a creature that consists of only sixteen almost invisible, moist cells can hardly be spoken of in such complimentary terms. That individual—if such a word has meaning here—does not have a brain nor any sensory organs capable of absorbing impressions from the surrounding universe. Indeed, it has no name, personality, character, mind, sex, or any other identity.

We cease to be surprised at the profligate wastefulness of physical nature shortly after we become aware of it, but then we know that animal nature is bloody, cruel, savage, instinctive. Indeed the existence of certain species themselves seems strangely pointless. Can a God that is, by definition, the epitome of wisdom and intelligence have had a conscious intention in creating some of the weird creatures that the wonders of modern science now enable us to locate and identify? The answer can be only *yes* or *no*; either gives rise to philosophically difficult questions concerning which we need not here digress. But if God in his infinite wisdom simply sets NATURE in motion and leaves her to govern billions of physical acts and processes that occur at every moment in her vast realm, theologians are unlikely to argue that he also takes such a disinterested view in regard to the creation of souls since, whatever else a soul may be thought to be, it is clearly not of a material nature. What, then, are we to make of a process in which billions of souls have been created only to have their connection with a living body terminated after a few quivering moments?

It is also difficult to see how one can possibly speak of the ideal of justice in all of this. Clearly the factors that result in the continued life of certain individual organisms and the early death of others have absolutely nothing to do with morality or with any form of consciousness at all. We must conclude, therefore, that the enormous process we are considering does not just permit but is characterized by both wastefulness and injustice. That such factors are common enough in human experience we know, to our daily sorrow, but how they fit into a divine plan is yet one more addition to the disturbingly lengthy list of philosophical questions that are of great difficulty for religious believers. They do not present themselves as a problem at all to those who do not consider themselves formally religious.

In the early stages of life a new individual does not resemble a human being in any respect whatever but does bear a remarkable resemblance to a tiny glob of tapioca pudding; and yet even if an individual breathes his last breath at the age of ninety, by which time his soul will have been involved in millions of separate aspects of experience, some of which will involve moral factors, does the question of the eventual fate of souls become any less mysterious?

Christian fundamentalists advise us that souls and bodies both are doomed to the most hideous state possible if they are not either baptized or, in one sense or another, "born again." If the former assertion is valid, then it is dangerously late to begin making baptism available to us as adults, or even, as is the practice in the Catholic and in some Protestant churches, in infancy. Rather, to increase the statistical probability of salvation for countless millions, a method should be devised for introducing baptismal waters into the wombs of all believers who are having sexual intercourse, for at least additional armies of souls would thereby theoretically be granted the opportunity of eternal bliss in the hereafter.

Admittedly, a complication arises even in regard to this happy proposal, for the same Christians who advise us of the one doctrine also absolutely assure us that all the bodies that have ever lived will eventually be reunited with their separate souls. There is a pleasing aspect to this belief in that it is comforting to think that at least the small minority who will reach heaven will eventually have the opportunity again to see departed loved ones, if only a few. It is also a pleasant enough prospect that in the future one might have the opportunity to rub shoulders with the saints, with Aristotle, Plato, Socrates, Dolly Parton, or anyone else whose company we might have enjoyed on earth had our social circumstances permitted such pleasures.

But wait—let us again contemplate those millions of individuals who never developed beyond the tapioca or tadpole stage. It is logically inescapable that the religious belief just referred to will also oblige us to mingle socially in the hereafter with millions of tiny blobs of tissue, or those which, if slightly further developed, are almost indistinguishable from the embryos of gilled water creatures, sheep, or primates of the same age. If all such creatures have souls, as conventional belief assumes, and all souls are eventually reunited with their bodies, well—the difficulty is clear and we have been little enlightened by our speculations.

The Church, by insisting on the immortality of the soul, made a profoundly important contribution to political theory, though it had no such end in mind. Indeed, in later centuries, Christian powers-of-state would often behave with a ruthlessness that belied confidence in the worth of the individual. But if it is true that each soul will live forever, then physical death is not complete extinction and rewards accrue in heaven.

For if the soul may live apart from the body then there is a nonmaterial order of existence. Others, of course, had long believed this or assumed that it might be the case. The Greeks, in fact, had gone so far as to theorize that not only did the soul continue after the body, but that it had existed before the body. This belief—that the soul is eternal—makes the body even more important than does the Christian assumption of just "half" of the process.

Alas, there never has been any way to determine the fact of the matter one way or the other.

It is no proper response to refer to the testimony of individuals who are apparently honestly convinced that they have seen one GHOST or another. First of all, it is not established that the word *soul* and *ghost* are synonymous. Second, science—including that branch of it that operates under religious auspices—is extremely skeptical about reports of disembodied spirits.

Third, if there are ghosts, they seem to behave in a remarkably inane way. The churches tell us that at death the soul goes either to (1) God in heaven, (2) hell, or (3) for some religions, an intermediate stage called purgatory.

All the ghosts we have ever heard about appear to do no such thing. They simply remain on earth frightening passersby on the Queen Mary, in an old castle in Scotland, or in an abandoned bowling alley in Cleveland. If there is any sensible purpose in their visitation it never seems to be communicated.

Even if science were somehow able to trap a particular soul and ascertain that it had formerly been connected to a specific material body, this could settle the issue only in terms of one individual, though it would establish the possibility of such a thing. We must not be beguiled by fantasy. The belief in the soul is as effective as its reality and can have important social results even if totally groundless.

SUICIDE. Are there ever situations in which suicide is justified? The fundamentalists say no.

The great majority of the human race, however, readily recognizes that, in certain, fortunately rare and extreme circumstances, suicide is a perfectly reasonable course. In responding to such questions, one must immediately assess available alternatives to the act. In almost all real-life experiences other choices of varying degrees of palatability exist. Consequently, suicide is almost always wrong. But the point in question is whether there are *any* circumstances in which it is right.

There are, of course. The United States—which our fundamentalist advisors tell us is a basically Christian nation—in its official capacity provides certain of its secret agents and military representatives with suicide pills that, under specified circumstances, they are urged to take, as a means of quickly ending their lives. If, for example, an intelligence operative, who has a great deal of highly classified information the revelation of which could do serious harm to his nation's interests, is captured and knows he is about to be tortured, he might reasonably elect to sacrifice his own life to save the lives of countless others. In so doing, he is not regarded by his fellow Americans as a moral leper but as a hero. The pilots of the U-2 airplanes were provided with such life-ending drugs.

The ongoing debate over EUTHANASIA is obviously related to the question of the morality of suicide. Both debates are sometimes further confused, rather than clarified, by language problems. On the one hand there is a given act—let us say the conscious ending of one's life. Although this is suicide, there are those who, troubled by the term rather than the reality the term represents, simply choose to use phrases such as *heroic self-sacrifice.* But whatever words one uses, the material reality involved is the same.

Clearly not all suicides provoke precisely the same moral questions. We do not regard a despondent teenage boy who kills himself after having been rejected by a young woman in the same light as a self-killing by a terminally ill cancer patient in agonizing pain who elects to hasten his inevitable demise since he feels under no moral obligation to submit to months of such unnecessary suffering.

Despite the harshness with which fundamentalist moralists express their judgments, it is comforting to assume that a compassionate God, who must be fully aware of all relevant and therefore mitigating circumstances, will be fairer in his judgments than his human creatures customarily are. In a day when it would have been legally permissible to stone to death Mary Magdalene, Jesus—we are told—saved her life by suggesting that any man present who could say that he was without sin might cast the first stone. He also remarked that Mary's sins were forgiven her because she had loved much.

Those who deny that there can ever be the slightest grounds for suicide have perhaps never considered the thousands of cases of criminals so violent and depraved that they have been sentenced to death. No doubt many of those convicted, knowing that their execution is certain and that it will be hideously painful, would, if given a choice, elect to bring about their own destruction. The societies involved clearly wish that the lives of such individuals be terminated. Therefore, in regard to such cases, societies cannot advance the ancient argument that suicide is a crime against society: the decision has already been made that the death of the convicted individuals has been imposed precisely to *protect* society. Those who argue that such a practice cannot be countenanced are guilty of inconsistency. (See also SITUATIONAL ETHICS.)

T

TIME. Modern men do not properly understand the perception of time that prevailed during the periods in which the assorted portions of the Bible were written. Bruce Malina, in an insightful commentary on Oscar Cullman's *Christ and Time* (*Catholic Biblical Quarterly* [January 1989]), draws our attention to the observation of Joseph Needham that the custom of denominating years in our now-familiar A.D. sequence was not even dreamed of until A.D. 525 when Dionysius Exiguus proposed the system of situating Jesus at the midpoint between the old and new ways of reckoning chronology. Needham is quoted as saying:

> It is less well known that the Mayan series of B.C. years, extending backwards from the birth of Christ, was introduced as late as the 17th century A.D. and Bossuet, in 1681, may have been the first to use it.

It is difficult enough for well-crafted watches and clocks to keep perfect time and far more difficult for man unaided to gauge accurately the passing seconds, minutes, hours, days, weeks, months, years, and centuries. From our point at about 2,000 years on the time scale, a great many events thought of as "of the early church" seem to be clumped together in one short period. But it was not until A.D. 350 that the church combined the various ancient scrolls of the Hebrew scriptures and the newer manuscripts of the New Testament to form the one Bible as we more or less know it today.

Because the year A.D. 350 is so very long ago, we mistakenly think of it as quite close to the time of Christ. We might have a clearer concept of the time span, if we consider it in terms of our present date. If we think back over the two hundred years of our own nation's history—to the time of Washington, Jefferson, Benjamin Franklin—those days seem far back indeed. If we next imagine a date 150 years into the future, it too seems incredibly distant. It would require this period—as long as all of U.S. history to date, plus another century and a half into the future—to equal the 350 years of Christian history before the Bible as we know it was compiled.

We must somehow in our minds stretch out those pre–New Testament time factors to get a proper perspective on the sequence of events that led to the creation of the various forms of the Bible. (See also HISTORICAL RELEVANCE OF THE BIBLE; LAST DAYS, THE; PATRIARCHS, LONGEVITY OF; PETER, THE SECOND EPISTLE OF.)

TORTURE. One of the most admirable organizations on earth today is Amnesty International. If any current members of the group had done their heroic work only two or three centuries ago, however, they would have been branded as heretics, infidels, aides to the devil, and immediately subjected to torture or public death—usually by the religious factions of the time. Courageous Christian clergymen and laymen of the present day who morally distinguish themselves by criticizing torture, atrocity, and political cruelty on principle are taking a radical departure from the religious practice of thousands of years. Far from assuming the forefront of the movement protesting against torture, the churches not only failed to encourage the early reformers but also did precisely the opposite.

The humanistic force in history has had to civilize the churches in this regard. Fortunately, they are making notable progress in this century, but in the past the churches were so busy perpetrating torture that they quite readily included reformers among their victims. The churches must not be permitted to excuse themselves by saying that it was actually their secular arm that wielded the axes, racks, pincers, swords, daggers, pots of boiling oil, and all the other monstrous devices; that laymen were simply performing the role in much the same way as today's executioners, hired by the state to gas, hang, inject, shoot, or electrocute victims of capital punishment, do. Those opposed to the death penalty would never direct their protest to these men since they are simply employees of the state.

Just so, we cannot direct our reformist arguments to those who actually lighted the matchwood of the thousands of stakes that illuminated too many skies across the face of the earth. The monks, the priests, the bishops, the cardinals—not excluding the great and still-revered philosophers of the church—authorized such horrible practices; they therefore bear the true moral responsibility.

The United Nations' Universal Declaration of Human Rights specifies that "No one shall be subjected to torture, or to cruel, inhuman, or degrading treatment or punishment." The reality, however, is that great numbers of people *are* being tortured in our time. Amnesty International believes that in recent years torture has been practiced by governments in sixty nations: the former Soviet Union, Spain, Iran, Guinea, Uruguay, Paraguay, Argentina, Brazil, and Chile, to name a few. Torture victims are rarely foreign enemies or prisoners of the states involved—the nations are torturing their own citizens.

In the United States today one needs little courage to criticize those who physically abuse their fellow human beings; making the same statements in Iran, China, Chile, or the other fifty-seven offending nations would take considerable bravery. Just so, it required enormous courage to dissent in eighteenth-century Europe. During the several centuries of glorious European achievement—centuries that gave us the plays of Shakespeare, the music of Bach and Beethoven, the sculptures and paintings of Michelangelo, the works of Leonardo da Vinci—yes, during the periods of the Renaissance, the Reformation, and the Enlightenment, when Europe was at the height of its cultural glory, *torture was common.*

Cesare Beccaria (1738–1794), an obscure Italian scholar, is quoted even today as an authority on the subject. He wrote that he wished only to raise certain fundamental questions about the method of determining who had—or had not—committed a crime and the methods of punishing those deemed guilty.

The governor of Milan at that time was a Count Firmian. Under his administration a number of beneficial reforms were established in the area of Lombardy. Agriculture was encouraged, libraries and museums were built and enlarged, public works expanded, and the church was shorn of her undue privileges. In his first ten years in office Firmian eliminated ecclesiastical immunity for crimes. The right of church asylum for evildoers was abolished, and the proceedings of the Holy Office of the Inquisition were stopped. This general progressive and humanistic climate made it possible for Beccaria to envision his own reforms.

But in spite of the new climate of enlightenment, torture was still considered a perfectly permissible method to achieve supposed justice. If a man or woman were merely suspected of a crime they would be arrested and, in the total absence of conclusive evidence of their guilt, tortured to force them to confess. A prisoner would admit to anything if his suffering became great enough. If an innocent man later retracted his confession, he was tortured again.

Torture was also a means to discover criminals and their accomplices, actual or alleged. There was also the extraordinary or special torture that preceded the execution of a sentence of death. Such were the customs in Christian Europe. Although torture was permitted only for crimes legally punishable by death, scarcely an act in the whole criminal code merited a lesser penalty.

Capital punishment was mandated for such crimes as sending someone a threatening letter, shoplifting, wounding cattle, destroying trees, breaking down the bank of rivers. If you were a Gypsy you could be executed for remaining in England more than one year. At least forty different kinds of forgery alone were capital offenses. The death sentence was also imposed for committing sodomy with a woman with her consent, for stealing a sheep or a letter, or for committing a sacrilege.

All twentieth-century arguments given in support of capital punishment for such crimes as treason or violent murder were also advanced in those days when the offense was stealing a handkerchief from a man's pocket or some other now-trivial transgression.

In writing about Beccaria's remarkable achievements, James Anson Farrer has said:

> It was this system that Beccaria's little work destroyed, and had that been its only result, it would still deserve to live in men's memories for its historical interest alone. For upon the legislation of that time—and especially upon that of Italy—this pamphlet on criminal law broke like a ray of sunlight on a dungeon floor, making even blacker that which was black before, by the very brilliancy which it shed upon it.
>
> To Beccaria primarily—though not, of course, solely—belongs the glory of having expelled the use of torture from every legal tribunal throughout Christendom.

(See also CRIME, BIBLICAL IMPETUS TO; CRUSADES, THE; EVIL, THE PROBLEM OF; RELIGIOUS THEORIES, DEVIANT.)

TRINITY, THE. There is something profoundly sad about the argumentation concerning the concept of the Trinity. The dynamics of repentance and salvation would not be significantly altered if God were suddenly to communicate that the man Jesus Christ was not identical with the Father but nevertheless was his only physically begotten son, indeed born of a virgin—the greatest, most moral creature ever born and therefore worthy of the ultimate in human devotion, respect, and love. Would any Christian church in the world close its doors at receiving such intelligence? Of course not. Humans would be no more nor less inclined to virtue or to sin than they already are. Nevertheless, unknown numbers of Christians have been mutilated and slaughtered by fellow Christians who happened to differ with them on this question.

Old Testament intimations of the Trinity. In Genesis, chapter 18, the Trinity may be curiously foreshadowed.

> 2. And he lift up his eyes and looked, and lo, three men stood by him: and when he saw them, he ran to meet them from the tent door, and bowed himself toward the ground,
> 3. And said, "My Lord, if now I have found favour in thy sight, pass not away, I pray thee, from thy servant: . . ."

Notice that three men appear but Abraham addresses them all together as "my Lord." Reading farther we find:

> 9. And *they* said unto him, "Where is Sarah thy wife?" And he said, "Behold, in the tent."
> 10. And *he* said, "I will certainly return unto thee according to the time of life; . . ."

Were the New Testament followers of Jesus and the early church fathers influenced in their development of Christian motifs by these passages, and perhaps others like them that did *not* enter the canon of the Old Testament? We know that various texts used by the Hebrews and early Christians have been lost. We also have no way of knowing what stories and themes other than those that now appear in the Bible may have been handed down orally over several thousand years. Since even the Dead Sea Scrolls have not yet been collected in one place and fully translated by objective scholars who do not have a Christian or Judaic bias, we have no way to follow the development of the Trinity idea from the mists of prehistory to the Council of Nicaea in A.D. 325.

These same verses can, of course, be interpreted altogether differently. The three men may represent a vestige of POLYTHEISM, which was practiced by the Semitic tribes at some point in antiquity. According to the biblical report, the Israelites engaged in frequent struggles against idolatry. These are very strong themes in the books of Joshua and JUDGES; indeed much of the Old Testament deals with the Jews' continual turning away from the purity of worship prescribed in the Torah. (See also RELIGIOUS THEORIES, DEVIANT.)

It is therefore possible to argue that the Trinity is a return to the three men of Genesis or, at the very least, a partial acceptance of the polytheism that surrounded the early Christian church. The church had developed within the polytheistic Roman Empire and in lands in Asia Minor that had been strongly influenced by Greek and other Near Eastern cultures that worshipped numerous gods. Further, monotheism (which the Jews have scrupulously retained all during the Christian era) was restored to its pre-Christian rigor by Mohammed, when he introduced Allah to the Arabs in the early seventh century A.D.—but not before a titanic struggle against the polytheism then practiced at Mecca. The Muslims uphold monotheism with a far stricter rigor than Catholicism emphasizes the Trinity and veneration of the saints (a practice many critics say verges on polytheism). Protestants, although they say the Apostles' Creed and thereby witness to faith in the Trinity, in actual practice spend most of their time talking about Jesus Christ and would not elevate even Mary to any level near her son's rank.

The furor over Salman Rushdie's *The Satanic Verses* exploded in February 1989 when the Ayatollah Khomeini of Iran issued a death warrant for the Muslim-born author. One of the book's ideas that angered Muslims was a disputed notion that Mohammed may once have considered permitting the faithful to worship three goddesses whom he is said to have briefly considered introducing as Allah's consorts. Whatever the truth of this legend, the Koran in many places inveighs against even a hint that God had wives or a son. This is why the followers of Mohammed treat Jesus as only a major prophet and neither as God nor the son of God.

A devout Catholic was once overheard to say, "These Muslims never could understand the idea of the Trinity." Neither, of course, can Unitarians, some Protestants, skeptics, agnostics, or atheists be persuaded that the Trinity is a valid belief.

TRUTH. Since the Christian definition of God implies a belief in the divine origin of truth itself, the ideal has rarely been pursued for its own sake in the history of religion. In fact, to announce that one intends to pursue an unbiased search for truth is unlikely to increase one's popularity. One is more likely to be marked as eccentric and will certainly run the risk of not only condemnation but censorship and also, in certain cases, martyrdom.

Many religious believers strongly oppose the view that all truth is relative. They concede only that relativity is a characteristic of many truths but by no means all. Certain truths—or beliefs—they argue, are absolute. This is nowhere more clear than in the case of those statements that come directly from the mouth of God. This argument has a certain reasonableness and internal consistency—if it is confined only to these few factors. When we delve into specifics, absurdities occur.

For example, when we ask *how* imperfect humans can have certain knowledge concerning the opinions of God on moral questions, we are inevitably referred to the Scriptures. There the entire debate falls apart; when we carefully examine the pages of Scripture we encounter numerous instances of bizarre and savage statements about morality that are more of an insult to God than an example of his wisdom.

Every religious believer in the world will insist that those who belong to sects other than his own are very much in error on a number of fundamentally important questions; yet the beliefs of these others are generally supported by their interpretation of one portion of Scripture or another, and their adherence to their truth may exceed one's own in rigidity.

Truth and Science. A good many ideas about scientific matters that have occurred to both professional scientists and laymen over the centuries have eventually been shown to be erroneous. This is not to say that the bulk of what we now accept as established science is in error: it is well-established indeed. But the body of knowledge now so honored represents merely the skimming of the cream from the top of an enormous cauldron of speculation, experimentation, and the construction and destruction of countless thousands of hypotheses.

If some of what scientists have in the past at first imagined is now conceded to be erroneous, we are nevertheless not justified in assuming that the energy expended upon their hypotheses was totally wasted. In science—as in ordinary life—discovering what is *not* the case is a definite aid in the search for truth. Even today, with all our dazzling technological and scientific achievements, people in general are firmly convinced of the truth of many erroneous opinions. Therefore, anyone who can deflate an error does humankind a great service. He will not always be honored for having so served the cause of truth, for while some errors are patently harmful and destructive, others may bring considerable comfort. Anything that threatens that comfort is therefore likely to be rejected and its introducer ridiculed or persecuted. (See also RELIGION; SCIENCE AND RELIGION.)

One of the major churches from time to time runs advertisements in popular magazines promoting its specific form of religious belief. One of these is headlined: "Does Science Prove the Bible Wrong?"

Now there is not the slightest doubt, even among the most devout theologians, that over the past several centuries scientific and other scholarship *has* shown the Bible to be wrong—in a thousand-and-one specific instances. If the authors of such magazine advertisements had a serious respect for truth they would acknowledge this. Their refusal to do so is probably ultimately as responsible for as many believers leaving their church as are drawn into the fold by their promotional campaigns. Nevertheless they continue to state a lie: "The fact remains that science has yet to produce any evidence that discredits the basic truths of Holy Scripture."

One perceives in this statement the church's withdrawal to the small territory of "the basic truths." The specialists who produce such campaigns are surrounded by vast stores of factual evidence from which they cannot escape except by further abandoning the rules of evidence and REASON; for the Bible itself, beyond question, advances its basic truths *on the evidence of certain assertions of a scientific, factual, and historical nature.*

For example, no basic truth of Christianity is more fundamental than that of the doctrine of original sin. That doctrine in turn stands or falls on one and only one set of assertions: that there was an actual, specific human named Adam; his actual mate named Eve; a speaking snake; an actual tree with forbidden fruit; an actual garden; and certain events involving these individuals in that particular place and time. It is apparent, therefore, that it is an absolute affront to reason to concede on the one hand that the entire creation myth in the early passages of Genesis—whatever its other merits—cannot possibly be factual and yet to continue to insist that the doctrine of original sin is valid. (See also AUTHENTICITY OF THE BIBLE; BELIEFS AND MYTHS; CONTRADICTIONS, BIBLICAL; HISTORICAL RELEVANCE OF THE BIBLE; PIOUS FRAUD.)

V

VERSIONS OF THE BIBLE. Most Christians and Jews simply assume that the "right" version of the Scriptures is the one with which they personally are most familiar. The psychological basis for this assumption requires no lengthy explanation. Habit and custom are vastly more powerful than is commonly perceived. From among the enormous volume of sensory data available to us at any moment, we select what to "see" on the basis of previous conditioning. This common process applies at all times and places except when we examine the ancient religious literature of our specific cultures.

Whenever a new edition or version of the Testaments is introduced, therefore, it will be heatedly criticized. It might be thought that this would be less the case where religious scholars of impeccable credentials have labored long on the necessary research and editing, but qualifications of scholarship or spirituality have little correlation with the intensity of the usually angry responses. Although such attacks would perhaps seem most unedifying behavior to a disinterested observer from another galaxy, the animosity is largely merely the acting out of the traditional response to the introduction of anything new.

Because of its psychological usefulness and survival value, a conservative tendency exists in all of us. It would be impossible to engage daily in fresh interpretations of the sense data around us in our many activities. Each of us, therefore, develops working assumptions that enable us to function in a habitual manner and thus accomplish most daily tasks.

Another reason for popular defense of traditional verities is that an *opinion*—which in reality is separate from *self*—nevertheless gradually comes to seem part of the self. That mysterious ego from which much of our energy springs has a remarkable capacity for self-defense. We daily add opinions, guesses, assumptions, as well as factually supported knowledge to our inner selves so that in time it seems to us that whoever attacks one of our opinions is, in fact, attacking us personally. The more civilized individual is able to perceive the distinction between his *views* on the one hand and *himself* on the other.

It is axiomatic that one ought to approach every complex question with as open a mind as possible. This is often as difficult to do as it is easy to say. Despite the difficulty, the attempt is obligatory if one is to educate one's self and communicate rationally with others. It is troublesome enough to be open-minded on political questions; the difficulty is compounded in theological disputes.

As most Bible scholars are aware, and as most Christians and Jews are not, the Old and New Testaments have undergone a constant and endless process of loss, revision, translation, addition, and subtraction from the first renderings of the various books, chapters, and verses thereof. While the conservative tendency distrusts the new and derives comfort from the old, we ought not to be deluded that if we could just go back far enough in time we would find some identifiably "true" version of the Scriptures. The fact is *there has never been any such version,* at any time, in any language. Most—if not all—languages spoken and written in the twentieth century are strikingly different from what they were only four hundred years ago. By the twenty-fifth century languages will probably be largely unintelligible to any twentieth-century visitor if he could somehow advance himself to that future time.

Wise historical scholarship begins with original sources and first manuscripts; it simply cannot be done with the Christian and Jewish Scriptures because no original manuscript of any book of the Bible is known to exist, nor is there a single scholar who expects to find one. *For those who believe that God in one sense or another personally inspired the Scriptures, the fact that none of the actual documents he inspired now exist means that the Almighty did not concern himself to preserve his Word in its pristine form.* Since it can hardly be argued that he was unable to do this had he so wished, the alternative is that, while the Almighty had the power to so preserve his Word in its original rendering, he simply did not exercise it. From this it follows that *in the unlikely event that some chance combination of scholarship and accident—even inspiration— should ever produce a version of the Bible correct in every word, no one living would have the slightest way to distinguish it from any of the scores of other versions that have a claim on our attention.*

The Problem with Translation. Every professional translator is well

416

aware that there is no such thing as a simple, word-for-word translation from language to language. Most people assume that there is nothing more to translation than taking one word—let us say the English *bread*—and replacing it with, say, the Spanish word for *bread,* or *pan.* That seemingly sensible process would render a translation that was close to gibberish if we were dealing with any extensive text. The world's various tribes have constructed their individual languages not by any purely logical or scientific process but in a quite haphazard way in which, except for recent times, there were no authorities to serve as police. Anyone who wishes to coin a word may do so, although it is a separate question how much currency others will give his creation.

This leads to odd, sometimes amusing ways of expressing certain ideas. To consider one example, a common American expression that may stem from the 1920s is, "How do you like *them* apples?" A foreigner, even if he were a scholar, would be likely to assume that the question has something to do with apples. Americans know this is not the case. The word *apples* in this context is an abstraction that simply means the things under discussion at the moment.

In a physical contest, for another example, one American might beat another to the ground, tower over him, and shout angrily, "How do you like *them* apples?" Since we are familiar with the idiom we have no difficulty interpreting the question as what it is—a cruel, angry taunt. In taking a thought originally expressed in one language and attempting to clarify it for those who speak or read a different language, it would be totally confusing to translate literally common examples of idioms and slang.

This problem would not be especially serious, perhaps, if languages were only lightly sprinkled with odd and unfactual ways of saying things. The reality is quite the opposite. Our languages are crammed full of such locutions.

When we realize that the various languages in which the first drafts of the Scriptures were written—Hebrew, Greek, Aramaic—had their own idioms and none of those first drafts survives, it is impossible for us to know if the early translators and the thousands who followed them dealt correctly with the numerous idioms they encountered.

Another way to approach the question is to forget for the moment about early religious documentation and refer to translations of, say, the last two hundred years. Various important works originally written in German, Russian, Spanish, Italian, Latin, Greek, or French have been translated into English so that they might be enjoyed by additional millions not familiar with the original languages. In such instances it is common for scholarly or popular reviewers to comment not only on the original work itself but on the quality of its rendering. One translator may have done a superb job, while another's work left a great deal to be desired. The ideal of perfection never comes up for the reason that it is impossible to achieve.

The Bible also consists in part of poetry, and no translation is more difficult than one involving that literary form. Poetry is a strongly nuanced form of human communication, so much so in fact that even specialists and scholars dealing with one language alone will heatedly differ as to the meaning or implications of a particular word, line, sentence, or extended thought.

All these factors suffice to demonstrate that it is only poorly informed laymen who speak of translating the Bible "perfectly" or "with total accuracy." (See also AUTHENTICITY OF THE BIBLE; CONSERVATISM; COMMUNICATION; ERROR; PIOUS FRAUD; RELIGIOUS THEORIES, DEVIANT; WISDOM LITERATURE.)

The Septuagint. The name itself comes from the Latin *septuaginta,* or seventy. This pre-Christian Jewish-Greek version of the Old Testament is so named because of a spurious account of its origin: that Ptolemy II Philadelphus, around 250 B.C., shut up seventy-two translators in seventy-two individual cubicles on the Alexandrian island of Pharos for a period of seventy-two days, after which the separate translations were compared and found to be identical. The only details of this account that historians still accept is that the version was made in Alexandria around the 250 B.C. period. Most scholars today agree that the text is a collection of several versions of the various books, each completed by many different translators.

The primary reason for the creation of the Septuagint was that the early Gentile converts, who in a fairly short time came to outnumber the Jews, could not read Hebrew. It therefore became necessary to make available a copy of the Scriptures that the new believers could understand. Since Greek was the most common tongue of that day—even spoken by a good many Jews—the choice was obvious.

The churches' difficulty in arriving at a clear, simple agreement concerning the contents of the Bible is something that has plagued them in all stages of biblical development. Since the Septuagint was written many centuries before our English, German, or other European versions, it is significant that the order in which the scriptural books appear in the Septuagint is quite different from that of the Jewish Bible from which the translation was made. For example, the common divisions into The Law, The Prophets, and The Writings were not followed. Rather, the Septuagint produced a sequence in which the legal and historical books came first, the didactic and poetic second, and the prophetic at the end.

Another difference, however, is far more perplexing to the faithful. Explains Bruce Metzger in *An Introduction to the Apocrypha:*

The copies of the Septuagint contain a dozen or more other books interspersed among the books of the Hebrew canon. Most of these are identical with the traditional Apocrypha, but with certain differences. The apocalyptic book of II Esdras is not found in any Greek codex of the Old Testament. The Prayer of Manasseh is not in all copies of the Septuagint, and when it is present it is found among the odes or hymns which in some manuscripts are appended to the Psalms. On the other hand, some Septuagint manuscripts include III and IV Maccabees and Psalm 151, which are not reckoned among the traditional books or parts of the Apocrypha.

The best scholarship now assumes that the fact that the Jewish canon did *not* include the disputed books demonstrates either that there was no fixed canon at Alexandria, or that if there was, the Jews at that time were perfectly aware that the disputed books were not properly canonical.

It is not acceptable to look upon this as merely a matter for literary debate in the sense that one might dispute whether a particular play was truly written by Shakespeare. The Septuagint is not only the first translation of the Scriptures, but it is also the first *interpretation* of them. What is at question, then, is *divine inspiration.* When one group of scholars rejects certain scriptural books while another group accepts them, the first is denying that the books are divinely inspired, and if they are correct, then the latter are deluded in their opinion to the contrary. Either case weakens the theory of divine inspiration of every word. (See also APOCRYPHAL, THE.)

Targum. Around the time of Christ, the Aramaic language began to replace Hebrew as the language of the Jews. As a result the Old Testament was no longer understood by many of the devout. At first simple verbal translations were made during temple services, but that soon became too cumbersome. The decision was made to translate the Scriptures into the language spoken in Palestine, Syria, and Mesopotamia.

Beginning with the Targum version of Job in the first century A.D., many unique translations have been made into the Aramaic language. A complete copy of a Palestinian Targum on the Pentateuch was discovered in the Vatican Library in 1956. Of all the Targum books, some have been extremely literal, some sweeping paraphrasings. In one translation—of Isaiah 53—the meaning has been totally overturned as the translators changed the wails of suffering to descriptions of the glorious and triumphant Messiah.

Because of such "freedoms" with the original text, the Targums have value in the cautious criticism of text but are virtually worthless in any other regard.

The Latin Vulgate. Commissioned by Saint Jerome in the third century, the Latin Vulgate was the last in a series of Old Latin versions. The Council of Trent later decreed this version as "authentic"—that is, essentially free of error in issues of faith and morals and therefore considered a "safe" source of Catholic doctrine.

Among the odds and ends of nonsense for which the Bible and its translators have been responsible is the presence of horns on various representations of Moses and other Jews since Renaissance times. Michelangelo's famous statue of the Old Testament leader, created for the tomb of Pope Julius II, provides the classic instance. While a child would observe that men do not have horns, the great genius Michelangelo nevertheless gave them to Moses. Why? The compilers of the Vulgate Bible mistranslated the Hebrew word meaning *ray of light* as *horns*. Eventually what was at first ludicrous became sinister in that the image of the Jew-with-horns was absorbed into the vicious stream of European Christian anti-Semitism.

A word is required in response to the defense that it is not the fault of the Bible if its translators have occasionally made fools of themselves. Note that this argument implies a clear separation between the Bible on the one hand and translators and copyists of it on the other. In reality, however, there is no such separation for there is no single, observable object identifiable as *The Bible* in the sense that there are unique material realities identifiable as the Grand Canyon, the Eiffel Tower, or the Constitution of the United States. At no time in its confused history has the Bible, in any sense, been a unit. What we refer to by the term *The Bible* is merely a collection of the work of various thousands of original authors, redactors, revisers, liars, deceivers, prophets, poets, copyists, scribes, printers, and clerks who have created the thousand-and-one versions of the Scriptures.

The Bible is not responsible for what men may write about it in the form of commentary but the argument does not hold up when what men have written, translated, or revised is the Bible itself as we know it.

John Wycliffe Version. Two versions of translated Scripture are attributed to reformer Wycliffe and his followers. The first was completed primarily by Nicholas of Hereford around 1382 and the second (completed by John Purvey to overcome the academic style of the first) came out about the year 1400. Wycliffe's intention was to combat the corrupt papal authority of the time by making the Bible comprehensible to the ordinary man. The result, of course, was that Wycliffe was branded a heretic, his translators were imprisoned, many of his followers (the Lollards) were burned at the stake, and the others forced underground.

Wycliffe's versions, both drawn from the Latin, are important as the first English translations and because the vernacular language incorporated affected all subsequent biblical renditions.

Rheims-Douai (or Douay) Bible. Around the mid-sixteenth century, English-speaking Catholics became concerned about the proliferation of what they considered heretical Protestant versions of the Bible. They decided to do their own. Translated from Jerome's Latin Vulgate, the New Testament portion was published in 1582 at Rheims, the Old Testament in 1609-1610 (after the college where the work was being completed had returned to using the name Douai, hence the double name).

Wanting to be as accurate as possible in their interpretation of the various scriptures, the Douay translators frequently resorted to anglicized Latin words, thereby introducing a great many of them into the English language. The Council of Trent, which had commissioned the work, forced the translators to rely heavily on the Latin Vulgate, which caused many of the passages to be hopelessly obscure and often corrupted.

The Douay version contains seven books not regarded genuine by Protestants: Baruch, Ecclesiasticus, Judith, 1 and 2 Maccabees, Tobias (or Tobit), and Wisdom. Catholics also accept parts of the books of Daniel and Esther, of which Protestant authority is suspicious. This version has undergone numerous, extensive revisions over the years, including the incorporation of many phrases from the later-issued King James Version. In 1810, the papal council authorized the Douay, as it then stood, for use in America.

The King James Version. Undoubtedly the most famous rendition of the Holy Bible is the Authorized, or King James, version, published in 1611. Defenders of the Bible frequently assume that King James I was a heroic and spiritual figure without whose courage and devotion the English Bible might somehow have been lost or successfully suppressed. In truth James I was something of an ass and could make no claims whatever to intellectual, political, or moral greatness. His objections to the Calvinistic notes in the at-that-time-popular Geneva Bible and his personal vanity that sought to guarantee his contemporary fame and future reputation by sponsoring an English-language version of the Bible inspired him to commission some 150 scholars connected with Oxford, Cambridge, and Westminster Universities to produce the remarkable literary and scholarly work we know.

James I so continually interfered with the project that modern scholarship doubts that he ever finally authorized the version that bears his name. Surely no one can seriously suggest that the hand of God was at work in such a muddled process. To make such an assertion is at once to raise the question of how the divine hand could permit the publication and vast dissemination of the thousands of errors made by the well-intentioned English scholars who did at least perpetuate the fame of the otherwise historically uninteresting James.

VERSIONS OF THE BIBLE

Despite its inaccuracies the more conservative Christians of the modern age have a respect for the King James Version that they have not developed for other renditions. H.G.G. Herklots observes in *How Our Bible Came To Us* (1957):

> Despite . . . the praise which has been accorded to the version, by many generations of literary critics, it was not universally welcomed at its first appearance. It seemed modern and newfangled. Some people even thought it dangerous that the Scriptures should be available to ordinary people at all and preferred that they should remain buried in the decent obscurity of Latin. What was good enough for their fathers was good enough for them.

The translators of the Authorized Version themselves sought to deflect the criticism they fully expected by making the following observations in that edition's introduction, and Herklots quotes them:

> Zeal to promote the common good, whether it be by devising any new thing ourselves, or revising that which hath been labored by others, deserveth certainly much respect and esteem, but yet findeth but cold entertainment in the world. It is welcomed with suspicion instead of love, and with emulation instead of thanks: and if there be any hole left for cavil to enter (and cavil, if it do not find an hole, will make one), it is sure to be misconstrued and endangered to be condemned.

The King James Version has had the strongest influence on the minds of modern Christians. It is written in a language that itself has the ring of ancient poetry, legend, and drama that we derive from Shakespeare, Marlowe, old prayers, and other sources of the Anglo-Saxon past. One must make a strenuous effort indeed to distinguish between a response to such verbal music on the one hand and the message it conveys on the other. (See also LANGUAGE OF THE BIBLE.)

Its more familiar phrases echo in our minds, like the memory of long-forgotten bells in small country towns. Consider 1 Corinthians chapter 13:

> 4. Charity suffereth long, and is kind: charity envieth not; charity vaunteth not itself, is not puffed up,
> 5. Doth not behave itself unseemly, seeketh not her own, is not easily provoked, thinketh no evil;

Such passages, by a combination of their beauty and familiarity, lead us to the rarely questioned assumption that the same beauty must have been available to believers for as long as the Scriptures have been read aloud to devout congregations. But the language of the King James Bible is not only incomprehensible to the vast majority of Christians and other inhabitants of the earth, few of whom speak English, but it is also a relatively modern translation from an earlier Greek version, in which the same phrases are not nearly as musically appealing. Observes Herklots:

> The Authorized Version is the Bible which we take for granted; we are disturbed when translators in our own age render it differently. "What are they doing to our Bible?" we ask.

For a very long period of time the phrase *Authorized Version of the Bible* has been used by millions without any noteworthy attention to its implications. If only a certain version of the Scriptures is designated as authorized, it follows that *all other versions are unauthorized.* But since the actual edition so described is read by only a small percentage of those who read the Bible at all, it would be a peculiar state of affairs if only that minority portion of the world's Bible-lovers were possessed of the one, true, properly authorized version, and the great majority were reading editions that had not been so sanctioned.

Who is, or was, the authorizer?

Revised Standard Version. Commissioned by the International Council of Religious Education that represented most of the major U.S. and Canadian Protestant denominations, the complete Revised Standard Version of the Bible was finally published in 1952. While incorporating much newly discovered biblical material and proven criticisms and modernizing the format to include such things as quotation marks, and poetry printed in verse format, the version also retained some of the beauty of the King James language.

Although conservatives have criticized certain changes as blasphemous, atheistic, and communistic and publicly burned copies of the rendition, the popularity of the version continues to grow and it may perhaps yet be the most enduring of all twentieth-century translations.

Scofield Bible. The 1967 edition of the Scofield Bible contains many errors. It does not hold an honored place among the ranks of serious Bible scholarship, but the average reader should nevertheless have some defense against its misstatements and half-truths. As an example of the latter, consider the observation in the introduction to the Scofield Bible:

> . . . recent archeological discoveries in Egypt, Mesopotamia, Palestine and other Bible lands have provided a mass of material illustrative of biblical statements and *corroborative of Biblical accuracy.*

This is an incredible assertion. Among the many archeological discoveries of just the last century some have indeed been corroborative of biblical narratives while others have been just the opposite. It is just as dishonest for a Christian author to refer only to discoveries corroborative of biblical accuracy as it would be for, say, an atheist to refer only to discoveries that contradict biblical assertions. Neither would seem interested in whole truths.

Another error, by Scofield himself, is encountered in one of the introductory passages titled "A Panoramic View of the Bible" in which the Bible is referred to as "the most . . . ancient of books." While the earliest written portions of Scripture are ancient indeed, they're not the most ancient books at all.

While this brief survey can scarcely do justice to the history of Bible revision, it should at least be helpful in indicating that the Bible exists in numerous versions rather than one, and that today, as before, serious divergences of opinion exist among even the ablest, most devout scholars in regard to (1) whether certain books and portions are properly part of the Bible at all, and (2) what their meaning is.

Inevitably, future generations of Christians and Jews will produce their own revisions. Each, when it is introduced, will be vigorously attacked by the conservatives of the time and with equal energy—it is enough to move God to laughter—defended by the conservatives of a later period.

VIRTUES, THE. The earnest seeker after truth who on the basis of long study of the Scriptures concludes that their authors were in no sense divine is by logic forced to hold that all churches that depend on the Scriptures for their authenticity are therefore merely human creations, however well intentioned. This realization in turn leads to a thousand-and-one considerations that derive from it. One of these is that many sincerely virtuous people have invested the hope of their lives in the validity and integrity of their individual faiths, some of which are mutually exclusive. It would be convenient if there were only one religion; in fact, however, there are thousands of different religious forms, almost every one credited as the source of virtue for the individuals who adhere to it. The assumption, however tentative, that religions dependent on the Bible are only as valid as the Bible itself leaves one faced with the question of how even invalid faiths can produce—as they do—many decent and dedicated individuals.

The explanation to this puzzling question is that the churches have not hallowed the people but precisely the opposite: that is, that certain individuals with natural propensities for virtue, with dispositions inclining them to charity, tolerance, sexual decency, fairness in business dealings, and personal warmth, reflect credit upon any larger social entity with which they might affiliate simply because of the inherent beauty of their personal characters. Such an individual, therefore, might reflect credit not only on his church but also upon his nation, university, profession, political party, or even his bowling team.

Religious people might find it difficult to believe, even for purposes of speculation, that personal virtue can flourish outside the framework of religion. But everyone knows admirable individuals whose integrity is not derived from a religious background. There might be an innate, specialized, genetic gift for virtue, just as there clearly are specialized gifts for music, art, mathematics, philosophy, or athletic prowess. Those who become saints—and almost every faith has its holy ones—may in fact be nothing more than geniuses of virtue, just as others are geniuses in the arts or sciences.

This speculation here is not about a matter of what might be called spiritual endowment but rather something quite physical—located, in fact, in the province of genetic biology. Indeed in the late 1980s studies revealed an actual gene for shyness. Earlier researchers had discovered a genetic connection with certain forms of aggressive or pugnacious behavior. It does not ravage reason to wonder if some beneficent modification of the gene for aggression might be connected with the tendency to be courageous. Courage has, in all times and places, been considered a virtue, not a moral failing. Some of the most striking discoveries of modern science will be those that give rise to such questions and, one hopes, their resolutions. (See also FREE WILL; SAINTLINESS.)

The three main virtues specified in the Bible are faith, hope, and love. Of the three, only love can deal with objective reality since faith and hope refer to realms of experience beyond our control.

The unbeliever may have as many experiences of love as the believer. He may also be as readily given to hope, though there are naturally certain things he cannot permit himself to hope for—such as heaven—simply because he does not believe in their existence. (See also BY THEIR FRUITS YE SHALL KNOW THEM; FAITH; HOPE; MORALITY.)

W

WAR. At the approach of war, in any and all societies, the first military draftee is God. Even in those extremely few officially atheistic states— China and the former Soviet Union, for example—religion nevertheless exists and believers outnumber atheists. Therefore, billions call upon God for military assistance, in precisely the same way in which they might appeal to a neighboring nation or people to serve as an ally.

In World War II, American fighting men—the overwhelming majority of whom were Christians and therefore must have assumed that their faith was supreme—had less confidence than their non-Christian Japanese opponents, some of whom—the kamikaze pilots—deliberately committed suicide, not simply as a heroic personal gesture but because of their serene belief that to die so would assure them immediate access to God's personal presence.

Fortunately, some Christians and Jews—as well as others—accurately perceive that war itself is the supreme atrocity, given that it willingly employs all available vices, and very few virtues, to produce its hideous effects.

May I be presumptuous enough to suggest a rough draft of a prayer more appropriate in wartime than some we have heard?

> Dear God, please forgive us for what we are about to do. For a period of time, perhaps years, we will be engaged in the maiming, shooting, stabbing, burning, and general slaughter of vast numbers of your human creatures, all of whom, both common sense and faith require us to concede, are surely as precious in your sight as we are.
>
> We will, at least, not do you the grievous insult of pretending that you endorse our aims, and certainly there can be no suggestion that you

approve of our methods. That these are evil and destructive, O Lord, is clear even to our children—perhaps more so to them than to those of us who are hardened adults.

We acknowledge that what we are now prepared to do runs counter to the essence of your advice, since it can have nothing whatever to do with either love or the much-vaunted respect for human life.

We hope soon to return to your ways, dear Lord, and perhaps you will grant us a small measure of praise for being honest enough to concede that until the cessation of hostilities we are prepared to set those ways aside and to be guided by the gods of horror and destruction, if there are such.

To the boundless number of sins we are now about to commit, at least we will not add that of hypocrisy. We will not ask you to bless our tanks and bombers, as our fellow believers have done in times past. We concede that absolutely nothing we are about to do can properly be advanced under the banner of a decent religion.

Amen.

Such prayers will probably never be countenanced, at least among Christians and Jews, for the painfully embarrassing reason that such an approach to God is flatly opposed to that savage and bloody alternative so often endorsed by the Holy Bible. (See also CRIME, BIBLICAL IMPETUS TO; EVIL, THE PROBLEM OF; GIDEON; MORALITY; SITUATIONAL ETHICS.)

WILL TO BELIEVE. It would perhaps be comforting if what occasioned the present wave of conversion and conviction was the inherent beauty of one religious philosophy or another, but no such conformity or pattern can be discerned. What appears to appeal to most new converts is the sense of conviction on the part of those who convert them.

Given the complexity of life's physical and psychological manifestations, confusion is common and islands of certainty few and far between. Certainty itself—quite aside from the questions of content—is therefore appealing. Perhaps this factor accounts for the feeling on the part of many who are converted of having come at last to a safe, secure harbor. Their former doubts and confusion are put to rest in an instant. Unfortunately, the most bizarre religious forms seem as capable of producing this appealing sensation as the more reasonable and social kinds of belief. In other words, the simple fact of firm conviction itself establishes nothing whatever about the wisdom or validity of that about which one is convinced. (See also FANATICISM; RELIGION; FREE WILL.)

WISDOM LITERATURE. Just as we have earlier seen the lack of originality that characterizes many portions of the Old Testament, we now note that the same is true of the Wisdom sections. Notes Georges Auzou, in an explanation of the religious literature of Egypt approximately two thousand years before Christ in *The Formation of the Bible:*

> What was most remarkable, however, and what we must especially take note of from the point of view of the Bible, was a form of literature called "Teaching" *which is the distant forerunner of the "Wisdom" literature of Israel.* We know this from certain writings of the Third Millennium. (IA)

Auzou refers to the wisdom of *Kagemni* (2000 B.C.), the wisdom of *Ani* (2500 B.C.), and the wisdom of *Merikara* (2300 B.C.). Nor is the content of such writings mere pagan superstition and fantasy. Father Auzou explains:

> A high standard of morality which teaches submission to the Divine Will . . . can be found in the documents. . . . The "teachings" are full of a delicate psychology; they have a great sense of human relations and of one's duties toward one's neighbor.

(See also AUTHENTICITY OF THE BIBLE.)

WOMEN'S LIBERATION. If men had sex with trees, there would be a great deal of pathology, fear, hatred, and mistrust directed against that form of plant life. But the biologically proper object of the sexual appetite of men is women—and that is why the founding fathers of the church were so monstrous in the denunciations of one-half of the human race. There is no shortage of anti-feminist teaching in the Hebrew Scripture, and the continuing poor treatment of women over the long centuries was not opposed by the Christian Bible but, instead, encouraged by it. In fact, the Bible must bear a large part of the responsibility for the degradation and subjugation of the "fairer" sex. While there are more than enough areas of ambiguity and obscurity in the Scriptures, they are very forthright on the question of female inferiority. Early prophets and biblical teachers had an attitude toward women that today would have them summarily invited out of any civilized gathering on grounds of general boorishness.

It is quite possible that nothing so morally objectional was intended by the original authors; they simply were part of a culture that never dreamed of questioning the common assumption that women were inferior to men and that it was therefore only reasonable that they should be subject to them. A few verses might be cited that run counter to this observation, but for every such verse, dozens speak even more forcefully of women's natural inferiority.

Many of Paul's statements—especially those found in the second chapter of his first letter to Timothy—are used even today as ammunition for the conservative argument against the equality of women.

Paul was not announcing anything the least bit radical or even new in his statements but merely supporting the status quo of his day, and indeed for many a day thereafter. Obviously a culture that permitted a husband to have sex with his wife's maid, with other wives, with concubines, and even with prostitutes, and that permitted a husband to divorce his wife "if she finds no favor in his eyes because he has found some indecency in her" (Deut. 24:1)—and the rabbis interpreted the word *indecency* in a remarkably broad sense—that culture was one in which there could be no suggestion of feminine equality. That such unjust attitudes can still prevail is sad indeed.

Consider the following letter from Edward Symanski of Buffalo, New York, published in the *Buffalo News* (April 1991):

> In response to Janet Dipasquale's letter on women's ordination, a woman simply can't ever take the place of Christ at the altar because she's a female and that at most would make her a priestess, something totally alien in the Old and New Testaments and the Catholic Church's 2,000-year-old history.
>
> It is plainly written that Christ selected only men as his apostles, on whom he conferred the priestly powers of the Last Supper. The dignity of the priesthood is so great that no one takes it on himself, but only he who is called by God—and women were not, for reasons we are all too small to question.
>
> Since this exclusion is of divine origin, today's church practice is a continuation of this divine law. It is irreversible Catholic doctrine. Those who continue to add fuel for further agitation, knowingly or otherwise, seem to forget the "high dignity" they profess to serve or should serve. . . .

It has only been relatively recently that woman's position in even the so-called civilized societies of the West has risen at all above that of a decidedly second-rate citizen. Except at rare times and places throughout history, a woman was not permitted to do anything of importance except by the sufferance of her lord and master, whether that husband was in fact a lordly and masterly personage or merely an opinionated or sadistic ass with no inherent superiority to the poor woman being tyrannized.

Such treatment, in fact, continued on the American scene into the nineteenth century, when the first wave of feminists became organized and vocal in demanding justice. Without the efforts of such women as Susan B. Anthony, Elizabeth Cady Stanton, Lucretia Mott, Lucy Stone, Belva Ann Lockwood, and Victoria Woodhull, American women might never have been permitted to participate in elections. It took over a half a century of concentrated effort for women at last in 1920 to be accorded the right to vote. Most of the early reformists by then were long since dead.

The struggle for enfranchisement was actually a means to effect changes in laws that were even more oppressive of the female sex. Until Anthony and the others finally brought change in the late 1800s, American women were considered completely subordinate to their spouses. Legally they could not own property. In numerous cases women lost their own family's homes or farms because their husbands sold the property or lost it from drinking or gambling. Women in that day had no right to sign a contract or instigate a lawsuit over property rights or monies due.

At home women had no legal custody over their own children! If a husband wanted their daughter to contribute to the family income by prostitution, or their son by working long, hard hours in a sweatshop, the wife could not protest. In the unlikely event that a woman had a job, the employer was required by law to turn her wages over to her husband. A husband was permitted by law to beat his wife for various "transgressions"—as long as the weapon he used was not over an inch in diameter.

Women were not allowed to enter restaurants unescorted after six P.M. or to speak at public meetings. Only the Quakers allowed women to speak in their meetings or to be ministers. Only one American college at the time admitted women: Mount Holyoke. In most areas women were not even permitted to attend high school, and some completed only a few early grades of primary school.

As a result there were few professional women. There were midwives but no female doctors. Although Belva Ann Lockwood eventually succeeded in getting admitted to law school and completed the course of study with honors, she was refused a degree, and could not practice her craft. Even after a petition to the president years later got her the well-earned and necessary degree, it took another long struggle before she could practice law before the Supreme Court and thereby provide her clients with full recourse under the law.

Needless to say, no one thought women should be paid at the same scale as men, even when they did precisely the same work or did it better. Anthony herself, in one of her first jobs as teacher, replaced a man whose salary was $10 a week. She was paid exactly one-fourth of that wage.

Those who were determined to "keep women in their place" often had the Bible on their side. Elizabeth Cady Stanton correctly said that "the Bible and the church have been the greatest stumbling blocks in the way of woman's emancipation." Mrs. Stanton, of course, had been moved by her own scriptural studies to take a dim view of the traditional interpretation.

> The only point in which I differ from all ecclesiastical teaching is that I do not believe that any man ever saw or talked with God, I do not believe that God inspired the Mosaic code, or told the historians what they say he did about women, for all the religions on the face of the earth degrade her, and so long as woman accepts the position that they assign her, her emancipation is impossible. Whatever the Bible may be made to do in Hebrew or Greek, in plain English it does not exalt and dignify woman. My standpoint for criticism is the revised edition of 1888. I will so far honor the revising committee of nine men who have given us the best exegesis they can according to their ability, although Disraeli said the last one before he died contained 150,000 blunders in Hebrew and 7,000 in the Greek.

Mrs. Stanton therefore set about the task of translating the Bible into a nonsexist edition. In her introduction to *The Woman's Bible,* she says:

> The canon and civil law; church and state; priests and legislators; all political parties and religious denominations have alike taught that woman was made after man, of man, and for man, an inferior being, subject to man. Creeds, codes, Scriptures and statutes are all based on this idea. The fashions, forms, ceremonies and customs of society, church ordinances, and discipline all grow out of this idea. . . .
>
> The Bible teaches that woman brought sin and death into the world, that she precipitated the fall of the race, that she was arraigned before the judgment seat of Heaven, tried, condemned and sentenced. Marriage for her was to be a condition of bondage, maternity a period of suffering and anguish, and in silence and subjection she was to play the role of a dependent on man's bounty for all her material wants, and for all the information she might desire on the vital questions of the hour, she was commanded to ask her husband at home. Here is the Bible position of woman briefly summed up.

There are few modern intellectuals and scholars—including those of Christian persuasion—who defend the traditional attitude toward women. But even to the present day, when such foolish assumptions have been widely abandoned, there are still Christian laymen—primarily although not solely fundamentalists—who vociferously insist that the entire movement to do nothing more than bring women to the level of equality with men is not only misguided but also, in the most literal sense, the work of the devil!

It is no proper response to refer to one excess or other committed by modern participants in the feminist cause. When there are millions working on a given campaign, it is inevitable that a certain amount of foolishness will result. Occasional excesses cannot possibly be used as excuses to deny justice. About such abominations one can only say that it is not in the least remarkable that the Woman's Liberation movement should now be so vigorous. What is odd is that it is so relatively peaceful and restrained. (See also CRIME, BIBLICAL IMPETUS TO.)

Paul's View on Wives' Subjection to Husbands. A troublesome question that has never been satisfactorily resolved down through the centuries is that concerning the primacy of authority in marriages. The Scriptures can certainly not be accused of ambiguity on this issue, as they can on so many others. The Bible says that wives are properly subject to their husbands and that is that.

I would have no particular objection if indeed Almighty God communicated to humankind a simple message that (1) wives should be subject to husbands, (2) husbands should be subject to wives, or (3) both husbands and wives should consult the patterns formed by the discarded entrails of dead kangaroos in regard to decision-making when there is a difference of opinion.

If the Almighty did indeed issue any such arrangement it would be reasonable to assume that the course he recommended was the wisest possible. If, in examining that course, we should discover that its fruits were decidedly less than satisfactory, we would then be perfectly entitled to entertain a doubt whether, in fact, the original proposal had proceeded from God or merely from some well-intentioned human arrogating to himself the right to speak for the Deity.

If, then, Paul and Christians of the present day were considering the question of supremacy within marriage in a purely ideal context, and second placing it in the experience of unknown hundreds of thousands of years in which, largely for physical reasons, men have had to be the hunters, breadwinners, and general providers, their prescription for peace in marriage does not ravage reason. But two contradictory considerations immediately present themselves. If our decision in this regard is motivated by the clear superiority of a given husband, there will very likely be an equal number of cases in which the superior individual is the wife. Indeed none of us will have difficulty in identifying couples from our own social circles in which intelligent and attractive women seem to have made very poor choices in selecting their mates. Second, we do not live in ideal cir-cumstances but must daily slog through a life characterized by innumer-able instances of imperfection.

Dear Christian women among my readers, many of you have found yourselves married to social incompetents—alcoholics, drug abusers, wife beaters, child molesters, petty and major criminals of all sorts, not to mention men inept, weak, ignorant, uncaring, or sexually confused. Had you arrived here from another part of the universe and therefore been encumbered with no biases whatever related to life on planet earth, would it seem sensible to you that now, simply because you are a female, you must be subject to whatever pathetic goofola you might find yourself married to, simply because you were initially impressed by his good looks, financial security, family position, or other such factors?

Of course not. The suggestion itself is immediately dismissed as laugh-able. Why, then, does such an absurdity suddenly become sensible and sanctified simply because it conforms to thousands of years of male dominance and therefore inevitably became drawn into the religious codification of various ancient cultures, of which the Jewish and Christian are only two? (See also DIVORCE.)

Conclusion

Well, I have as of now—the Fall of 1992—completed two weighty volumes of commentary on sacred Scripture. Critical response to the first volume, I'm pleased to report, was largely supportive; even those reviewers who, because of their religious affiliations, were obliged to differ with some of my views and conclusions did so in a tone that clearly indicated they respected my intentions.

As I have stated earlier, my primary purpose for publishing the results of my ruminations on the Bible is to encourage the reader to undertake his or her own odyssey through its thousands of pages. Whatever the results of such studies—and they will, inevitably, vary widely—there is one striking fact that I believe all earnest students of Scripture will find: that the Bible is dramatically different from what the average believer imagines it to be.

First of all, the relatively small percentage of Christians who give thought at all to the question of the origin of the Old Testament books seems to entertain the hazy assumption that for unknown thousands of years before the time of Christ the Jews had collected a body of scriptural documents that are now known as the Old Testament. This is simply not the case.

Modern scholarship knows of no manuscript of the Old Testament written in Hebrew that can be dated earlier than the ninth century B.C. What we now perceive as the Old Testament, or the Jewish Bible, far from being agreed-upon many centuries before Christ, was actually arrived at after considerable argumentation by a group of rabbis convened at Jamnia, Palestine, around A.D. 100. Their opinions were not unanimous, but they did at least specify what they thought might rightly be included in the Jewish Canon.

CONCLUSION

Millions of Christians believe the Bible to be the literal word of God as clearly as the American Declaration of Independence is the word of the founding fathers who contributed to it. It is not.

The combination of Old and New Testament material loosely identifiable as the Christian Bible simply did not exist as such, in any authoritative sense, until late in the fourth century when a Catholic council convened at Carthage to discuss the matter. There was much consternation among the devout when they learned that several books that had long been read and respected in the churches—such as the Gospel of St. Thomas and the Shepherd of Hermas—were now excluded. Comments Alan Watts:

> The point is that the books translated in the King James Bible were declared canonical and divinely inspired by the authority (a) of the Synod of Jamnia, and (b) of the Catholic Church, meeting in Carthage more than 300 years after the time of Jesus. It is thus that *fundamentalist Protestants get the authority of their Bible from Jews who had rejected Jesus and from Catholics who they have abominated as The Scarlet Woman mentioned in Revelation.* (IA)

It is also commonly assumed by the faithful that most biblical reports of events are generally eyewitness descriptions in the sense that today's edition of the *New York Times* is directly related to the events that it describes. This view turns out to be one more of the endless parade of errors that Christians and Jews have made about the Scriptures. It is no longer a question whether all the books of the Bible were written in the times with which they are concerned. The better question now is: Were *any* of them so written? Christian and Jewish scholars, particularly during the last century, have given up the argument one by one in regard to separate books of the Bible. It is now generally conceded, for example, that the Books of Kings were written long after the times they describe.

Millions of believers assume that—perhaps granting a few minor exceptions—the Bible is reliable as history. It is not. It is even considered a viable defense of the traditionalist position that the books in question are said to be founded on earlier documents or oral traditions. As for particular books this may well be the case. It must be immediately clarified, however, that even when this is so, the fact in itself has no relevance whatever to the question as to whether the "final" versions of the books are totally true, totally false, or a mixture of both. If this afternoon I write a fantasy about the present day, and if another author five hundred years in the future uses my document as the basis for a supposedly nonfiction story of his own, the fact that he has consulted my materials obviously adds

436

no truth to his report. The consultation of ancient documents supports the truthful reliability of later versions only within the context of reliable history, and even then the degree of accuracy is always properly under question. But religious writings are of a genre quite distinct from history. They may from time to time incorporate certain details of credible information but only to the extent that they do so can they be described as historical.

The great majority of church members believe that each book of the Bible had one author. They are surprised to discover this is not true. They are further surprised to learn that even those books attributed to the various prophets, kings, and saints were for the most part not authored by those persons whose names are printed in large type atop the various scriptural divisions.

We are conditioned to accepting such phrases as *by Ernest Hemingway, by Thomas Mann,* or *by Franz Kafka* as evidence that the persons so named indeed created the works attributed to them. It might be thought that within the narrower context of religious literature we could be even more certain that when the name of such giants of spiritual history as, say, Moses or Peter were affixed to certain documents that they had indeed been the authors. Unfortunately we have been given false information about much of this.

It is commonly assumed that the books of the Bible were written in the order in which they are now published. We know that this is not so, although at this point we have no way of knowing the original sequence of the various verses, chapters, and books. Not only is there no way of acquiring certain information about the time, place, and authorship of the various sections of Scripture, but despite the informed and concentrated efforts of thousands of dedicated scholars, it is also not even possible now to issue a verdict by means of which the world could say that it at least knows what the Bible originally was. There is still mutually exclusive disagreement among reputable authorities on which portions ought rightly to be included or thrown out.

Some, becoming aware of these "problems," retreat to the Bible-as-literature position. The comment of Gerald Larue *(Old Testament Life and Literature)* is relevant in this regard:

> Often hailed as a "literary classic," the Bible has been approached as great literature, and there have been those who have read with deep appreciation, particularly in the King James Version, the magnificent prose and poetry appearing in many passages. Biblical themes have been compared with those of other literary masterpieces. The impact of the Bible upon the

literature of the Western world has been traced and recognition given to the permeation of our culture by this great document. Such an approach may ignore the intention of the authors of the Bible and the relevance of what they said to their own time, or, in stressing literary characteristics, may slight the religious convictions of the writers.

The Bible as a Book. One of the oddities of the publishing industry is the category of books purchased in large numbers but rarely read. Certain works—called coffee-table books—are expensive, in large part pictorial, and because of their tasteful design, make attractive decorative artifacts just as do vases or other objects of art.

Another category of books that sell well but are seldom read are thick, best-selling novels that are purchased in large numbers as gifts by people who think, usually erroneously, that their friends will appreciate receiving them. Most people, especially in our time, are so constituted that the mere sight of any book numbering more than four hundred pages congeals their minds. The Bible has such an effect on millions who nevertheless have at least one edition or another in their homes.

In the homes of at least a great many of its purchasers the Bible is analogous, so far as its use is concerned, to a dictionary or encyclopedia, recipe collection, atlas, or phone book—used on such rare occasions when the reader may find himself with an idle moment or a personal problem concerning which he is seeking guidance. The sales figures of Bibles, therefore, do not necessarily provide a reliable picture of how much thoughtful, analytical reading of Scripture takes place. It would seem, rather, that although the Bible is the best-selling book of all time, only a small percentage of those who own one seem truly familiar with it.

Indeed I would not be at all surprised to learn that a higher percentage of secular humanists have studied the Bible carefully than Christians or Jews.

The Bible as a Reliable Record. Strangely enough, some fundamentalist Christians seem unaware of the retreat of organized religion before the advance of science and scholarship in regard to certain quite specific questions, some of which relate to the biblical record. They know there has been controversy, but they turn their backs on the details, assuming that if the critics are rationalists they are therefore merely evil and "anti-God."

Concerning those who entertain such attitudes, I can say only that I wish them well but could not possibly join their number. Whatever my mind is, I did not create it and am therefore no more to blame for the hypotheses it develops when awake than for the dreams that emerge from it in the sleeping state. If one starts with the assumption that God created

438

all things, it inescapably follows that the mind of man is also his product. And what perfect Deity would any more blame man for the free exercise of his God-given intellect than for the exercise of such other divine gifts as hearing, sight, smell, touch, or taste?

Religious believers are certainly not immune to philosophical error. Among their recent mistakes is the absurd argument that since secular rationalists have dispensed with the idea of God it therefore follows that they must "worship" man. Anyone past the age of twelve must be convinced of the human potential for depravity. Both Christian and Marxist societies — to name only two—have shown themselves more than ready to resort to violence for the achievement of their ends. Any modern generation that has seen Hitler, Stalin, Mussolini, Dachau, Hiroshima, Nagasaki, My Lai, the Gulag Archipelago, the Chinese political prisons, Saddam Hussein's treatment of the Kurds, and all the sickening rest can scarcely be of the opinion that man is in some fundamental sense a stranger to evil. Religious believers therefore ought not to divert their energies attacking the straw man of a rationalist worship of humanity.

Probably less than one percent of the human race lives according to a scientific, rationalist approach to life. It is hardly fair, therefore, to blame the same one percent—by no means all of whom control the levers of power in any society—for the assorted disasters, atrocities, follies, and errors of which societies are capable. If ever the affairs of a single society are actually conducted according to the principles of reason and justice and that noble program should fail, that would finally be the proper time to blame those who had conducted such an experiment.

But such a thing has clearly not as yet come to pass on our planet. What *has* taken place is almost two thousand years of Christian dominance in Europe. If there is anything that does not redound to the credit of the Christian philosophy it is the aggregate of human acts in Western culture over the centuries in question. Since we understandably prefer to think about the pleasant things in life and close our minds, to the extent possible, to its many tragedies, there is an understandable tendency to focus on the glories and achievements of European history.

But impressive as they are, they are few and far between. The individual heroes could all be gathered together in one banquet room of modest dimensions. The general record of European history—not to mention that of other times and places—has been far more an account of man's shame and ignorance than of his glory. The way affairs have generally been conducted in Christian Europe for long centuries is, as the old phrase puts it, a hell of a way to run a railroad. It is therefore understandable why it would eventually occur to reasonable men that there might be more preferable systems.

CONCLUSION

One may consider such observations in the long view, on a broader philosophical level, but one must also move past that stage of analysis to the level of concrete, specific applications. We might hear a rationalist say, "I honestly believe that it is more important to give a small child daily affectionate attention than to sprinkle water on his head as part of a ritual called baptism." An infinite variety of responses can be made to this.

One could point out, for example, that the two are not mutually exclusive. My point is that, given the undeniable horror of much European conduct during the centuries of Christian dominance, religious believers must perceive that there *is a connection between that horror and the rationalists' skepticism concerning religious claims to a monopoly of truth, beauty, and wisdom.*

It is nonsense for believers to assume that those who raise questions about the Bible, who perceive undeniable inconsistencies and contradictions in Scripture, are motivated by a perverse determination to disbelieve in God or the divinity of Jesus. A good many of the eminently qualified scholars who have troubled themselves to subject the Bible to study have themselves been believers. But whether they were or not is beside the point. Defenders of the faith have no right to judge the inner heart of anyone who confesses to being perplexed by a given passage of Scripture.

There is an enormous variety of opinion even among the devout. Those who profess a belief in either the divinity or at least the special holiness of Jesus Christ are naturally impressed by his famous saying: The truth shall make you free. If this is so, then why would any Christian willingly close his eyes to the truth about the Bible?

All analysts newly come to the task of understanding the Bible must necessarily be classed as naive simply because of the enormous complexity of the large *terra incognita* into which they have perhaps casually wandered. It was, therefore, never my intention to deliver a commentary on the massive library referred to as the Scriptures that could serve, once and for all, as a document that settled numerous knotty questions, some still impenetrable after three thousand years of study and debate. But I do hope that careful attention to the details of my argument will convince the reader that the Bible is by no means the simple, transparent text that some well-intentioned expositors have claimed but is rather a collection of texts that originated in mystery, that speak mystery on almost every page, and that have never come even remotely close to having a universally accepted version.

This is certainly not to suggest that study of the Bible is therefore a waste of time. On the contrary any series of documents that openly makes the boldest claims possible—that they represent messages from none other than the creator of the universe—obviously must be taken seriously.

As for determining the validity of the two extreme positions, that every word of such documents (1) literally originates on the level of the supernatural and divine, or (2) represents only a grand and passionate illusion, the world jury has never yet decided on the matter.

A good part of my argument is based on the perfectly fair question: Assuming that a conscious, all-powerful, and perfect God exists, what sort of a written message would it be reasonable to expect from him? Could it possibly be one riddled with factual errors—regardless of whether those errors are attributable to the largely unknown original human authors or to the editors and translators—or one exhibiting frequent internal contradictions and including numerous instances of moral advice that today's faithful have long abandoned for the eminently sensible reason that it is a shocking affront to the moral sense that flickers in almost all human hearts?

I have obviously not simply left all such questions up in the air. I have answered at least some of them to my personal satisfaction and now wish fervently to encourage further study and contemplation of the Scriptures so that others may clear their own minds on the matter. It is my hope that the reader will consult not only his own heart and mind but the views of numerous others in contemplating the many moral and logical questions that a study of scriptural documents forces upon the consciousness. Can truth be defended by error and deceit? Most unfortunately it can. Is it morally proper that it be so defended? That is a question so shattering that it deserves not just attention, which is obvious, but the most sensitive daily consideration for the reason that the dilemma presents itself, in painfully practical form, at every turn of our separate paths through life.

I close by repeating a point made earlier in this volume and in the one that preceded it. There are millions of decent Christians and Jews who, though they may be startled by the compliment, are themselves morally superior to their distant ancestors and, more importantly, to the scriptures they consider sacred. I assume that what is true today has always been so and that it is not so much the churches that make men and women virtuous but rather that admirable believers reflect credit upon the churches in which they happen to find themselves.

Some of the finest people I have ever known have been religious believers. Ours would certainly be a simpler world if all those lovely people had been encountered in only one church. But it has not been so, nor will it ever be.

My own original title for this study was "The Mystery of the Bible." I hope that my modest analysis has cleared up some of the mystery, but not even the ablest scholarship over long centuries could possibly resolve it all.

CONCLUSION

Whatever effect my observations have on readers' attitudes toward Scripture it is still the case that the most important aspect of religion is the moral essence. Questions of right and wrong, of justice and injustice, have always been—as they will always be—fundamental. All the rest of the world's animals know nothing of right or wrong. For humans the awareness is both our blessing and our curse. We have, even if only in the mythical sense, tasted the fruit of the tree of good and evil. Our chief work in this world will always be to do the one and avoid the other. I know of no secular humanist who is not perfectly aware of this.

Selected Bibliography

Adler, Mortimer. 1987. *Ten Philosophical Mistakes.* New York: Macmillan.

Aelred, Dom. 1972. *The End of Religion.* n.p.

Allegro, John M. *The Dead Sea Scrolls and the Origins of Christianity.* New York: Criterion Books.

———. 1984. *The Dead Sea Scrolls and the Christian Myth.* Buffalo, N.Y.: Prometheus Books.

Alexander, Pat, ed. 1978. *Eerdmans' Family Encyclopedia of the Bible.* Grand Rapids, Mich.: Wm. B. Eerdmans Publishing Company.

Angeles, Peter, ed. 1976. *Critiques of God.* Buffalo, N.Y.: Prometheus Books.

Arnheim, Michael. 1984. *Is Christianity True?* Buffalo, N.Y.: Prometheus Books.

Asimov, Isaac. 1968. *Asimov's Guide to the Bible: The Old Testament.* Garden City, N.Y.: Doubleday.

———. 1969. *Asimov's Guide to the Bible: The New Testament.* Garden City, N.Y.: Doubleday.

———. 1971. *The Land of Canaan.* Boston: Houghton, Mifflin.

Augstein, Rudolf. 1977. *Jesus, Son of Man.* Translated by Hugh Young. New York: Urizen Books.

Auzou, Georges. 1963. *The Formation of the Bible.* St. Louis: B. Herder.

———. n.d. *The Word of God.* n.p.

Barnhart, Joe E. 1986. *The Southern Baptist Holy War.* Austin: Texas Monthly Press.

Barth, Karl. 1957. *Christ and Adam.* New York: Harper and Brothers.

Bates, Ernest Sutherland, ed. 1936. *The Bible.* New York: Simon and Schuster.

Baumer, Franklin L. 1960. *Religion and the Rise of Skepticism.* New York: Harcourt Brace.

Beardslee, William A. 1970. "Literary Criticism of the New Testament." In *Guides to Biblical Scholarship.* New Testament Series. Philadelphia: Fortress Press.

SELECTED BIBLIOGRAPHY

Bedau, Hugo Adam, ed. 1982. *The Death Penalty in America.* 3rd ed. New York: Oxford University Press.

Beebe, H. Keith. 1970. *The Old Testament.* Belmont, Calif.: Dickenson.

Benson, Dennis C. 1988. *The Visible Church.* Nashville: Abington Press.

Bihlmeyer, Karl. 1966–68. *Church History.* 3 vols. Revised ed. by Hermann Tuchle. Westminster, Md.: Newman Press.

Boa, Kenneth. 1981. *Talk Thru The New Testament.* Wheaton, Ill.: Tyndale House.

Boorstin, Daniel. 1985. *The Discoverers: A History of Man's Search to Know His World and Himself.* New York: Random House.

Bouyer, Louis. 1958. *The Meaning of Sacred Scripture.* Notre Dame, Ind.: University of Notre Dame Press.

Bratton, Fred Gladstone. 1959. *A History of the Bible.* Beacon Press.

Bright, John. 1981. *A History of Israel.* 3rd ed. Louisville, Ky.: Westminster Press.

Brown, James. 1956. "The New Old Testament: Ancient Israel in Its Near Eastern Setting." In *Commentary,* April.

Brown, Raymond E. 1977. *The Birth of The Messiah.* Garden City, N.Y.: Doubleday.

———. 1990. *Responses to 101 Questions on the Bible.* Mahwah, N.J.: Paulist Press.

Browne, Lewis. 1934. *How Odd of God.* New York: Macmillan Company.

Bultmann, Rudolf. 1971. *The Gospel of John: A Commentary.* Louisville, Ky.: Westminister Press.

Buff, William Henry. 1987. *Self-Contradictions of the Bible.* Buffalo, N.Y.: Prometheus Books.

Burtchaell, James T. 1989. *The Giving and the Taking of Life: Essays Ethical.* South Bend, Ind.: University of Notre Dame Press.

Butterworth, Eric. 1977. *How to Break the Ten Commandments and Discover a Formula for Contemporary Living.* New York: Harper & Row.

Buttrick, George A., and Keith R. Crim, eds. 1976. *The Interpreter's Dictionary of the Bible.* 7 vols. Nashville: Abingdon Press.

Carmichael, Joel. 1963. *The Death of Jesus.* New York: Macmillan.

Chamberland & Feldman. 1961. *The Dartmouth Bible.* Boston: Houghton Mifflin Co.

Charlier, Dom Celestin. 1958. *The Christian Approach to the Bible.* Westminster, Md.: Newman Press.

Chase, Mary Ellen. *Life and Language in the Old Testament.* New York: Gramercy Publishing Company.

Clemens, Thomas, and Michael Wyschogrod. 1987. *Understanding Scripture: Explorations of Jewish and Christian Traditions of Interpretation.* New York: Paulist Press.

Coats, George W., and Burke O. Long, eds. 1977. *Canon and Authority.* Philadelphia: Fortress Press.

Coe, Michael D. 1984. *Mexico.* London: Thames and Hudson.

Cohen, Edmund D. 1986. *The Mind of the Bible-Believer.* Buffalo, N.Y.: Prometheus Books.

Cole, William Graham. 1959. *Sex and Love in the Bible.* New York: Association Press.

Collins, Raymond. 1988. *Letters That Paul Did Not Write.* Wilmington, Del.: Michael Glazier.

Comay, Joan, and Ronald Brownrigg. 1980. *Who's Who in the Bible: The Old Testament and the Apocrypha.* New York: Bonanza Books.

Coughlin, Robert. 1964. "Who Was the Man Jesus?" In *Life,* December.

Cross, Frank L., and Elizabeth A. Livingston, eds. 1974. *The Oxford Dictionary of the Christian Church.* New York: Oxford University Press.

Culpepper, R. Alan. 1983. *Anatomy of the Fourth Gospel: A Study in Literary Design.* Philadelphia: Fortress Press.

Cushing, Cardinal Richard. n.d. *Questions and Answers on Communism.* n.p.

Cuthbert, Father. n.d. *God and the Supernatural: A Catholic Statement of the Christian Faith.* New York: Sheed and Ward.

Dart, John. 1988. *The Jesus of Heresy and History: The Discovery and Meaning of the Nag Hammadi Gnostic Library.* Revised and expanded edition of *The Laughing Savior* (1976). San Francisco: Harper and Row.

Davies, A. Powell. 1957. *The First Christian.* New York: Farrar, Straus, & Cudahy.

Dean, Wally F. 1988. *Honest to God.* New York: Carlton Press, Inc.

De Vaux, R., and J. T. Milik. 1955–85. *Discoveries in the Judean Desert.* 7 vols. New York: Oxford University Press.

Diamond, Allen. 1979. *The Holiest Bible.* New York: Vantage Press.

Dibelius, Martin. 1985. "The Synoptic Problem." In *The Origins of Christianity.* Edited by R. Joseph Hoffmann. Buffalo, N.Y.: Prometheus Books.

Dilthey, Wilhelm. n.d. *The 18th Century and the Historical World.* n.p.

Dimont, Max I. 1964. *Jews, God and History.* New York: New American Library.

Doane, T. W. 1882. *Bible Myths and Their Parallels in Other Religions.* San Diego, Calif.: Truth Seeker Co.

Doherty, J. E. n.d. *The Dead Sea Scrolls and the Bible.* n.p.

Douglas, Mary, and Steven Tipton, eds. 1982. *Religion and America.* Boston: Beacon Press.

Dunham, Barrows. 1964. *Heroes and Heretics: A Social History of Dissent.* New York: Alfred A. Knopf.

Durand, Alfred, Joseph Huby, and John J. Heenan. 1957. *The Word of Salvation.* Milwaukee, Wis.: Bruce Publishing Company.

Encyclopedia Britannica, The New. 1974–86. "Biblical Literature," "Judaism." 15th ed. Chicago: Encyclopedia Britannica Company.

Engel, Frederic André. 1976. *An Ancient World Preserved: Relics and Records of Prehistory in the Andes.* New York: Crown.

Field, A. N. 1971. *The Evolution Hoax Exposed.* Rockford, Ill.: Tan Books & Publishers, Inc.

Finley, Merrill L. 1956. *Christ and the Colonel.* Girard, Kans.: Haldeman-Julius Publications.

SELECTED BIBLIOGRAPHY

Finegan, Jack. 1959. *Light from the Ancient Past*. Princeton, N.J.: Princeton University Press.
Fleming, Partee. 1988. *Is God's Bible The Greatest Murder Mystery Ever Written?* Memphis, Tenn.: A-M Press.
Foot, G. W., and W. P. Ball, eds. n.d. *The Bible Handbook for Free-Thinkers and Inquiring Christians*. London: Pioneer Press.
Frainc, Jean de. 1967. *The Bible and the Origin of Man*. 2nd ed. Staten Island, N.Y.: Alba House.
Friedell, Egon. 1953–54. *A Cultural History of the Modern Age*. New York: Alfred A. Knopf.
Funk, Robert W., Brandon Scott, and James R. Butts. 1988. *The Parables of Jesus*. Sonoma, Calif.: Polebridge Press.
Gaebelein, A. C. 1987. *What the Bible Says About Angels*. Grand Rapids, Mich.: Baker Books.
Gaylor, Annie Laurie. 1981. *Woe to the Women—The Bible Tells Me So*. Madison, Wis.: Freedom From Religion Foundation.
Goldberg, M. Hirsh. 1977. *The Jewish Connection*. New York: Bantam Books.
Graham, Billy. 1962. *Billy Graham Answers Your Questions*. Minneapolis: Worldwide Publications.
Graham, Henry G. 1977. *Where We Got the Bible*. Rockford, Ill.: Tan Books & Publishers, Inc.
Graves, Robert, and Joshua Podro. 1954. *The Nazarene Gospel Restored*. Garden City, N.Y.: Doubleday.
Grier, William H., and Price M. Cobbs. 1971. *The Jesus Bag*. New York: McGraw-Hill Book Company.
Hamblin, Dora Jane. 1973. *The First Cities*. Emergence of Man Series. New York: Time-Life Books.
Harrelson, Walter. n.d. *From Fertility Cult to Worship*. n.p.
Harrington, Daniel J. 1979. *Interpreting the New Testament*. Wilmington, Del.: Michael Glazier.
Hartshorne, Charles, and William L. Reese. 1976. *Philosophers Speak of God*. Chicago: University of Chicago Press.
Havener, Ivan. 1987. *Q: The Sayings of Jesus*. Wilmington, Del.: Michael Glazier.
Hawkes, Jacquetta. 1973. *The First Great Civilizations*. New York: Knopf.
Hawton, Hector. 1971. *Controversy: The Humanist/Christian Encounter*. London: Pemberton Books.
Helms, Randel. 1988. *Gospel Fictions*. Buffalo, N.Y.: Prometheus Books.
Henderson, John S. 1981. *The World of the Ancient Maya*. Ithaca, N.Y.: Cornell University Press.
Herklots, H.G.G. 1957. *How Our Bible Came to Us*. New York: Galaxy Books/ Oxford University Press.
Herschel, Abraham J. 1962. *The Prophets*. New York: Harper and Row.
Higgins, Godfrey. 1965. *Anacalypsis*. New Hyde Park, N.Y.: University Books.
Hinton, Richard W., ed. 1961. *Arsenal for Skeptics*. New York: A. S. Barnes & Co.

Hirsch, E. D., Jr. 1988. *Cultural Literacy—What Every American Needs to Know.* New York: Random.

Hoffmann, R. Joseph, ed. 1985. *The Origins of Christianity: A Critical Introduction.* Buffalo, N.Y.: Prometheus Books.

Hoffmann, R. Joseph, and Gerald A. Larue, eds. 1988a. *Biblical vs. Secular Ethics.* Buffalo, N.Y.: Prometheus Books.

———. 1988b. *Jesus in History and Myth.* Buffalo, N.Y.: Prometheus Books.

Hopkins, Father Martin. 1964. *God's Kingdom in the Old Testament.* Chicago: Henry Regnery Company.

Hoskyns, Edwyn, and Bart and Noel Davey. 1931. *The Riddle of the New Testament.* London: Faber and Faber.

Hunt, George. 1989. "American Catholic Intellectual Life." In *America,* May 6.

Hutchinson, Paul. 1955. "The Onward March of Progress." In *Life,* December 26.

Ingersoll, Robert G. "The Truth About the Holy Bible." From *Great Freethought Reprint Series.* Ridgefield, N.J.: Independent Publication.

Intrater, Aaron, and Leon H. Spotts. 1965. *The Voice of Wisdom.* Cleveland: Bureau of Jewish Education.

Isorini, Jacques. 1967. *The True Trial of Jesus.* n.p.

Isser, Stanley. 1990. "Two Traditions: The Law of Exodus 21:22–23 Revisited." In *Catholic Biblical Quarterly,* January.

Jastrow, Morris, Jr. 1919. *A Gentle Cynic.* Philadelphia: J. B. Lippincott Company.

Jomier, Jacques. 1967. *The Bible and the Koran.* Chicago: Henry Regnery Company.

Josephus, Flavius. 1984. *The Jewish War.* New York: Viking Penguin.

Kaiser, Walter C., Jr. 1988. *Hard Sayings of the Old Testament.* Inter Varsity.

Kang, C. H., and Ethel R. Nelson. 1979. *The Discovery of Genesis.* St. Louis, Mo.: Concordia Publishing House.

Kaufmann, Yehezkel. 1960. *The Religion of Israel from Its Beginnings to the Babylonian Exile.* Chicago: University of Chicago Press.

———. 1970. *The Babylonian Captivity and Deutero-Isaiah.* New York: Union of American Hebrew Congregations.

Keller, Werner. 1956. *The Bible As History.* New York: William Morrow & Co.

Knecht, F. J. 1973. *Child's Bible History.* Rockford, Ill.: Tan Books & Publishers, Inc.

Knuth, Donald E. 1991. *Bible Texts Illuminated.* Madison, Wis.: A-R Editions, Inc.

Landis, Benson Y. 1963. *An Outline of the Bible Book by Book.* New York: Barnes & Noble.

Larue, Gerald. 1968. *Old Testament Life and Literature.* Boston: Allyn and Bacon.

Launderville, Dale. 1989. Review of John I. Durham, *Exodus* (Waco, Tex.: Word Books, 1987). In *Catholic Biblical Quarterly,* April.

Laws, Sophie. 1988. *In the Light of the Lamb: Imagery, Parody and Theology in the Apocalypse of John.* Wilmington, Del.: Michael Glazier.

SELECTED BIBLIOGRAPHY

Laymon, Charles M., ed. 1971. *The Interpreter's One-Volume Commentary on the Bible.* Nashville: Abingdon Press.

Leach, Maria. 1956. *The Beginning.* New York: Funk and Wagnalls Company.

Leaney, A.R.C. 1958. *Harper's New Testament Commentaries: The Gospel According to St. Luke.* New York: Harper.

Levie, Jean. 1962. *The Bible; Word of God in Words of Men.* New York: P. J. Kennedy.

Lewis, Joseph. 1946. *The Ten Commandments.* New York: Freethought Press Association.

Lindsell, Harold. 1976. *The Battle for the Bible.* Philadelphia: Zondervan Publishing House.

Lingle, Roy Petran. 1956. *At This the Rock.* Philadelphia: Rationalist Press.

Lloyd, Seton. 1984. *The Archaeology of Mesopotamia.* Rev. ed. London: Thames and Hudson.

Lyttleton, Lord George. 1797. *Dialogues of the Dead.* Worcester, Mass.: Thomas, Son & Thomas.

McCabe, Herbert, 1986. *The Teaching of the Catholic Church.* Wilmington, Del.: Michael Glazier.

McCabe, Joseph. 1929. *The Story of Religious Controversy.* Boston: The Stratford Company.

———. 1946. *The Testament of Christian Civilization.* London: Watts & Co.

McCarthy, William. 1946. *Bible, Church and God.* New York: Truth Seeker Company.

McDowell, Josh, and Don Stewart. 1980. *Answers to Tough Questions.* San Bernardino, Calif.: Here's Life Publishers, Inc.

MacKensie, R. A. 1963. *Faith and History in the Old Testament.* St. Paul, Minn.: University of Minnesota Press.

McKenzie, John L. *The Dictionary of the Bible.* New York: Macmillan.

———. 1966. *The World of the Judges.* Englewood Cliffs, N.J.: Prentice-Hall.

Magnusson, Magnus. 1977. *B.C.: The Archaeology of the Bible Lands.* London: The Bodley Head.

Malina, Bruce. 1989. "Commentary on Oscar Cullman's *Christ and Time.*" In *Catholic Biblical Quarterly,* January.

Mangan, Celine. 1983. *1-2 Chronicles, Ezra, Nehemiah.* Wilmington, Del.: Michael Glazier.

Mangasarian, M. M. 1926. *The Neglected Book, Or the Bible Unveiled.* New York: Truth Seeker Company.

Marti, Fritz. 1974. *Religion, Reason and Man.* London: Green.

Martin, Ralph P. 1975. *The New Testament Foundations,* 2 vols. Grand Rapids, Mich.: Wm. B. Eerdmans Publishing Company.

Marty, Martin. 1989. "You're Going to Have to Be Institutionalized." In *The Critic,* Summer.

Matheson, Sylvia A. 1972. *Persia: An Archaeological Guide.* London: Faber and Faber.

Mattill, A. J., Jr. 1987. *Ingersoll Attacks the Bible.* Gordo, Ala.: Flatwoods Free Press.

Mead, Frank S. 1980. *Who's Who in the Bible.* New York: Galahad Books.

Merton, Thomas. 1985. *Disputed Questions.* New York: Harcourt Brace Jovanovich.

Mesters, Carlos. 1972. *God, Where Are You?* Maryknoll, N.Y.: Orbis Books.

Metzger, Bruce M. 1957. *An Introduction to Apocrypha.* New York: Oxford University Press.

Miranda, Jose Porfirio. 1973. *Being and the Messiah.* Maryknoll, N.Y.: Orbis Books.

Morris, Henry M. 1984. *The Biblical Basis for Modern Science.* Grand Rapids, Mich.: Baker Book House.

Morton, Andrew Queen. 1966. *Paul, The Man and the Myth: A Study in the Authorship of Greek Prose.* London: Hodder and Staughton.

Murphy, Roland E. 1977. "?" In *Catholic Biblical Quarterly,* October.

Nash, Jay Robert. 1976. *Darkest Hours.* Nelson-Hall.

Neil, William. 1962. *Harper's Bible Commentary.* New York: Harper and Row.

Newton, R. Heber. 1884. *Book of the Beginnings.* New York: G. P. Putnam's Sons.

Nielsen, Kai. 1973, 1990. *Ethics Without God.* London: Pemberton Books, and Buffalo, N.Y.: Prometheus Books.

———. 1976. "Morality and the Will of God." In *Critiques of God.* Edited by Peter A. Angeles. Buffalo, N.Y.: Prometheus Books.

Noble, John, and Glenn D. Everette. n.d. *I Found God in Soviet Russia.* n.p.

O'Malley, William J. 1989. "Scripture from Scratch." In *America,* February 4.

Osborne, Charles, ed. 1975. *The Israelites.* Emergence of Man Series. New York: Time-Life Books.

Orwell, George (Eric Blair). 1931, 1968. "A Hanging." In *The Collected Essays, Journalism, and Letters.* Vol. 1. New York: Harcourt, Brace.

Parrinder, Geoffrey. 1980. *Sex in the World's Religions.* London: Redwood Burn Limited.

Patai, Raphael. 1959. *Sex and Family and the Bible.* Garden City, N.Y.: Doubleday.

Penter, John. 1981. *Circumstantial Evidence.* San Francisco: Faraday Press.

Perrin, Norman. 1974. *The New Testament: An Introduction.* New York: Harcourt Brace Jovanovich, Inc.

Petuchowski, Jakob J. 1959. In *Commentary,* February.

Pfeiffer, Charles F. 1952. Introduction to the Revised Standard Version of the Bible. Philadelphia: A. J. Holman.

Pike, E. Royston. 1958. *Encyclopedia of Religion and Religions.* New York: Meridian Books, Inc.

Potter, Charles Francis. 1965. *Did Jesus Write This Book?* New Hyde Park, N.Y.: University Books.

Prager, Dennis, and Joseph Telushkin. 1983. *Why the Jews?* New York: Touchstone Books/Simon and Schuster.

Richardson, Alan. 1959. *The Gospel According to St. John: Introduction and Commentary.* London: SCM Press.

Robertson, Archibald. n.d. *The Bible and Its Background.* London: Watts & Co.
———. 1949. *Jesus: Myth or History?* London: Watts & Co.
Robertson, J. M. 1957. *A Short History of Free Thought.* New York: Russell.
Robinson, John A. T. 1977. *Can We Trust the New Testament?* Grand Rapids, Mich.: Wm. B. Eerdmans Publishing Company.
Rowley, H. H. 1961. "Authority and Scripture: I." In *Christian Century,* March 1.
Rowley, H. H., ed. 1957. *Eleven Years of Bible Bibliography.* Indian Hills, Colo.: Falcon's Wing Press.
Rumble, Rev. n.d. *The Adventist* (a pamphlet).
Russell, Bertrand. 1967. *Why I Am Not a Christian and Other Essays on Religion and Related Subjects.* New York: Simon and Schuster.
Sandars, Nancy K. 1985. *The Sea Peoples: Warriors of the Ancient Mediterranean.* Rev. ed. London: Thames and Hudson.
Sanders, Jack. 1982. "The Salvation of the Jews in Luke-Acts." In *Seminar Papers: Society of Biblical Literature.* Atlanta: Scholars Press.
Schepps, Samuel J. 1979. *The Lost Books of the Bible.* New York: Bell Publishing Company.
Schievella, Pasqual. 1985. *Hey! Is That You, God?* New York: Port Jefferson Station.
Schonfield, Hugh J. 1974. *The Jesus Party.* n.p.
———. 1965. *The Passover Plot.* Tempest Brookline.
Schultz, Samuel J. 1960. *The Old Testament Speaks.* New York: Harper & Row.
Schuster, Ignatius. 1959. *Bible History.* Rockford, Ill.: Tan Books & Publishers, Inc.
Schweitzer, Albert. 1968. *The Quest of the Historical Jews.* New York: Macmillan Publishing Co, Inc.
Sheehan, Thomas. 1990. *The First Coming.* New York: Marlboro Books.
Shneour, Elie. 1986. "Occam's Razor." In *Skeptical Inquirer,* Summer.
Simon, Arthur. 1987. *Christian Faith and Public Policy: No Grounds for Divorce.* Grand Rapids, Mich.: Wm. B. Eerdmans Publishing Company.
Sims, Albert E., and George Dent. 1960. *Who's Who in the Bible.* Secaucus, N.J.: Citadel Press.
Smart, Ninian, and Richard B. Hecht, eds. 1982. *Sacred Texts of the World.* New York: Sacred Crossroad Publishing Company.
Smith, Adam. n.d. *Wealth of Nations.* n.p.
Smith, George. 1876. *Chaldean Account of Genesis.* Out of print.
Smith, George Adams. *The Expositors' Bible, Volume II: The Book of the Twelve Prophets.* New York: George H. Doran Company.
Smith, Homer William. 1955. *Man and His Gods.* Boston: Little, Brown.
Smith, Morton. 1974. *The Secret Gospel.* New York: Harper and Row.
———. n.d. *The Secret Gospel of Mark and Clement of Alexandria.* Cambridge, Mass.: Harvard University Press.
Smith, Morton, and R. Joseph Hoffmann, eds. 1989. *What the Bible Really Says.* Buffalo, N.Y.: Prometheus Books.

Stanton, Elizabeth Cady. 1895, 1972. *The Woman's Bible.* Reprint of 1st ed. Salem, N.H.: Ayer Company.

Stiebing, William H., Jr. 1989. *Out of the Desert?: Archaeology and the Exodus/ Conquest Narratives.* Buffalo, N.Y.: Prometheus Books.

Strachey, Marjorie. 1957. *The Fathers Without Theology.* London: W. Kimber.

Stuhlmueller, Carroll. 1970. *Creative Redemption in Deutero-Isaiah.* Rome: Biblical Institute Press.

Sunderland, Jabez Thomas. 1893. *The Bible: Its Origin, Growth, and Character.* New York: G. P. Putnam's Sons.

Symanski, Edward. 1991. Letter published in *Buffalo News,* April.

Taylor, Kenneth N. 1962. *The Paraphrased Epistles.* Minneapolis: Tyndale House.

Taylor, William Carey. 1955. *The New Bible Pro and Con.* New York: Vantage Press.

Thomas, Norman. n.d. *The Conscientious Objector in America.* Ozer.

Throckmorton, Burton H., ed. 1979. *Gospel Parallels: A Synopsis of the First Three Gospels.* Nashville/New York: Thomas Nelson.

Trible, Phyllis. 1978. *God and the Rhetoric of Sexuality.* Philadelphia: Fortress Press.

———. 1984. *Texts of Terror: Literary-Feminist Readings of Biblical Narratives.* Philadelphia: Fortress Press.

Tyson, Joseph B. 1984. *The New Testament and Early Christianity.* New York: Macmillan.

Van Der Woude, A. S., ed. 1986. *The World of the Bible.* Grand Rapids, Mich.: Wm. B. Eerdmans Publishing Company.

Vawter, Bruce. 1956. *A Path Through Genesis.* New York: Sheed and Ward.

Voltaire, François-Marie Arouet de. 1962. *Philosophical Dictionary.* Vols. 1 and 2. New York: Basic Books.

Wach, Joachim. 1958. *The Comparative Study of Religions.* New York: Columbia University Press.

Ward, Maisie. 1956. *The Authenticity of the Gospels.* New York: Sheed and Ward.

Warner, Marina. 1983. *Alone of All Her Sex: The Myth and Cult of the Virgin Mary.* New York: Knopf.

Watchtower Society. 1961. *New World Translation of the Holy Scriptures.* New York: Watchtower Bible & Tract Society, Inc.

———. 1967. *Did Man Get Here By Evolution Or Creation?* New York: Watchtower & Bible Tract Society, Inc.

———. 1969. *Is The Bible Really The Word of God?* New York: Watchtower & Bible Tract Society, Inc.

———. 1973. *God's Kingdom of a Thousand Years Has Approached.* New York: Watchtower Bible & Tract Society, Inc.

Wells, G. A. 1975. *Did Jesus Exist?* Buffalo, N.Y.: Prometheus Books.

Westermann, Claus. 1969. *Isaiah 40 to 66: A Commentary.* Louisville, Ky.: Westminster Press.

Wheless, Joseph. 1926. *Is It God's Word?* New York: Alfred A. Knopf.

SELECTED BIBLIOGRAPHY

White, Andrew Dickson. 1896, 1965. *A History of the Warfare of Science with Theology in Christendom*. Abridged ed. New York: Free Press.

White, E. G. 1957. *The Triumph of God's Love*. Washington, D.C.: Review and Herald Publishing Association.

Winchell, Paul. 1982. *God 2000: Religion Without the Bible*. Sylmar, Calif.: April Enterprises.

Yadin, Yigael. 1971. *Bar-Kokhba*. Jerusalem: Steimatzky's Agency Ltd.

Yearsley, Macleod. 1933. *The Story of the Bible*. London: Watts & Co.

Young, Davis A. 1982. *Christianity and the Age of the Earth*. Grand Rapids, Mich.: Zondervan Publishing House.

Zahn, Gordon. 1962. *German Catholics and Hitler's Wars*. New York: Sheed and Ward.